KT-508-912

Ancona

Pescara

L'Aquila

ROMA

ROME AND LAZIO

Campobasso

Foggia

Bari

SOUTHERN ITALY

Napoli

Salerno

Potenza

Taranto

Catanzaro

Messina

Reggio di Calabria

Palermo

Catania

Agrigento

ITALY

EYEWITNESS TRAVEL GUIDES

ITALY

DK

LONDON, NEW YORK,
MELBOURNE, MUNICH AND DELHI
www.dk.com

PROJECT EDITOR Fiona Wild
ART EDITORS Vanessa Courtier, Annette Jacobs
EDITORS Francesca Machiavelli, Sophie Martin,
Helen Townsend, Nicky Tyrrell
DESIGNERS Jo Doran, Anthea Forlee,
Paul Jackson, Marisa Renzullo

MAIN CONTRIBUTORS
Ros Belford, Susie Boulton, Christopher Catling,
Sam Cole, Paul Duncan, Olivia Ercoli, Andrew Gumbel,
Tim Jepson, Ferdie McDonald, Jane Shaw

MAPS
Lovell Johns Ltd, Dorling Kindersley Cartography

PHOTOGRAPHER
John Heseltine

ILLUSTRATORS
Stephen Conlin, Donati Giudici Associati srl, Stephen Gyapay,
Roger Hutchins, Maltings Partnership, Simon Roulstone,
Paul Weston, John Woodcock

Reproduced by Colourscan (Singapore)
Printed and bound by South China Printing Co. Ltd., China

First published in Great Britain in 1996
by Dorling Kindersley Limited
80 Strand, London WC2R 0RL
**Reprinted with revisions 1997, 1999, 2000,
2001, 2002, 2003, 2004, 2005**

Copyright 1996, 2005 © Dorling Kindersley Limited, London
A Penguin Company

A CIP CATALOGUE RECORD IS AVAILABLE FROM THE BRITISH LIBRARY.
ISBN 1 4053 0781 1

Floors are referred to throughout in accordance with European
usage; ie the "first floor" is the floor above ground level.

**The information in this Dorling Kindersley Travel Guide
is checked annually.**

Every effort has been made to ensure that this book is as up-to-date
as possible at the time of going to press. Some details, however,
such as telephone numbers, opening hours, prices, gallery hanging
arrangements and travel information are liable to change. The
publishers cannot accept responsibility for any consequences
arising from the use of this book, nor for any material on third
party websites, and cannot guarantee that any website address
in this book will be a suitable source of travel information.

We value the views and suggestions of our readers very highly.
Please write to: Publisher, DK Eyewitness Travel Guides,
Dorling Kindersley, 80 Strand, London WC2R 0RL, Great Britain.

◁ **Fertile wine-growing region around Panzano in Chianti, Tuscany**

CONTENTS

David **by Bernini, Rome**

INTRODUCING ITALY

NORTHEAST ITALY

NORTHWEST ITALY

Gondolas weaving through the maze of canals in Venice

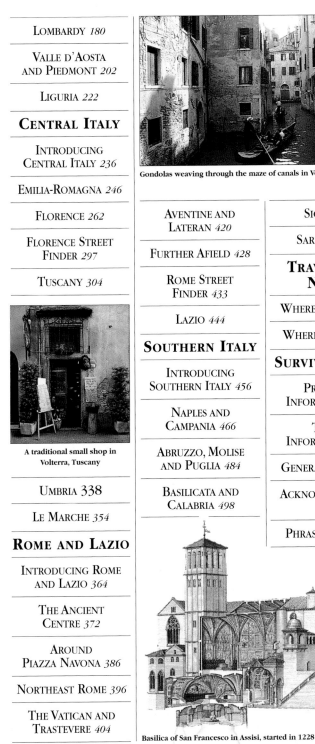

A traditional small shop in
Volterra, Tuscany

Basilica of San Francesco in Assisi, started in 1228

HOW TO USE THIS GUIDE

THIS GUIDE helps you get the most from your visit to Italy, providing expert recommendations as well as detailed practical information. *Introducing Italy* maps the whole country and sets it in its historical and cultural context. The 15 regional chapters, plus *Rome*, *Florence* and *Venice*, describe important sights with the help of maps and images. Each section is introduced with features on regional architecture and food specialities. *Travellers' Needs* gives details of hotels and restaurants and the *Survival Guide* contains practical information on everything from transport to personal safety.

ROME

The centre of Rome has been divided into five sightseeing areas. Each area has its own chapter, which opens with a list of the sights described. All the sights are numbered and plotted on an *Area Map*. The detailed information for each sight is presented in numerical order, making it easy to locate within the chapter.

Sights at a Glance lists the chapter's sights by category: Churches, Museums and Galleries, Historic Buildings, Streets and Piazzas.

All pages relating to Rome have red thumb tabs.

A locator map shows where you are in relation to other areas of the city centre.

1 Area Map
For easy reference, the sights are numbered and located on a map. The sights are also shown on the Street Finder *on pages 433–41.*

2 Street-by-Street Map
This gives a bird's-eye view of the heart of each sightseeing area.

A suggested route for a walk is shown in red.

Stars indicate the sights that no visitor should miss.

3 Detailed information
All the sights in Rome are described individually. Addresses and practical information are provided. The key to the symbols used in the information block is shown on the back flap.

1 Introduction
The landscape, history and character of each region is described here, showing how the area has developed over the centuries and what it offers to the visitor today.

ITALY AREA BY AREA
Apart from Rome, Florence and Venice, Italy has been divided into 15 areas, each of which has a separate chapter. The most interesting towns and places to visit have been numbered on a *Pictorial Map*.

Each area of Italy can be identified quickly by its colour coding, shown on the inside front cover.

2 Pictorial Map
This shows the main road network and gives an illustrated overview of the whole region. All entries are numbered and there are also useful tips on getting around the region by car and train.

3 Detailed information
All the important towns and other places to visit are described individually. They are listed in order, following the numbering given on the Pictorial Map. Within each entry, information is given on the most important sights. The name of the provincial capital is given for smaller towns at the top of each entry.

Story boxes explore specific subjects further.

For all the top sights, a Visitors' Checklist provides the practical information you need to plan your visit.

4 Italy's top sights
These are given two or more full pages. Historic buildings are dissected to reveal their interiors; museums and galleries have colour-coded floorplans to help you locate the most interesting exhibits.

INTRODUCING ITALY

Putting Italy on the Map

ITALY SITS AT THE HEART of the Mediterranean, shielded from the rest of Europe by the vast sweep of the Alps. The Po, its longest river, arcs across the industrial north, while the Apennine mountains split the boot-shaped peninsula down its length. Italy, with a population of 57.5 million governed from Rome, covers 301,268 sq km (116,320 sq miles) and includes Sicily and Sardinia.

SWITZERLAND

Bolzano

Lago di Como

Tren

Lago Maggiore

Bergamo

Brescia

Vicen

Milan

Mantova

Veron

Turin

Po

Parma

Ferra

Tanaro

Bologna

Rhône

Durance

FRANCE

Genoa

La Spezia

Avignon

Nice

San Remo

Lucca

FLORENCE

MONACO

Livorno

Pisa

Ligurian Sea

Siena

Marseille

Piombino

Elba

Bastia

CORSICA

Tyrrhenia

Ajaccio

Sea

EUROPE

NORWAY   FINLAND

SWEDEN

Porto Torres

Olbia

ESTONIA

RUSSIAN FED

Sassari

LATVIA

DENMARK

LITHUANIA

Alghero

REPUBLIC OF IRELAND

UNITED KINGDOM

BELORUSSIA

NETHERLANDS

GERMANY

POLAND

SARDINIA

BELGIUM

LUXEMBOURG

CZECH REPUBLIC

UKRAINE

SLOVAKIA

FRANCE

SWITZERLAND

AUSTRIA

HUNGARY

ITALY

ROMANIA

Cagliari

SPAIN

Roma

BULGARIA

PORTUGAL

ALBANIA

GREECE

ALGERIA   TUNISIA

MEDITERRANEAN

Aerial view of Venice, showing the Grand Canal

TUNISIA   TUNIS

◁ **View over Florence of the richly decorated 15th-century Duomo and Campanile**

Satellite photograph of southern Europe and the Mediterranean

KEY

Motorway

Major road

Ferry service

International boundary

0 kilometres 200

0 miles 100

Northern Italy

AIRLINE CONNECTIONS link the rest of Europe with Milan, Turin, Bologna, Pisa, Florence, Verona and Venice. Major roads and railways also provide excellent links to cities all over Europe. Transport services are very efficient, with motorways and railways along both coasts, and across the area's main east-to-west axis at the foot of the Alps. Milan, Verona and Bologna are the key transport hubs, while Florence forms the focus of links to the south.

SWITZERLAND

FRANCE

Florence by Road
Good fast roads link Florence to Pisa to the west, Rome and Siena to the south, and Bologna to the north.

FLORENCE AND ENVIRONS

Nord

Amerigo Vespucci

FS Rifredi

FS Santa Maria Novella

FS Campo di Marte

VIA PISTOIESE
VIA BOLOGNESE
VIALE EUROPA
VIA SENESE
VIA DELLE BAGNESE
AUTOSTRADA DEL SOLE MILANO-ROMA
VIA ROMA
Signa
Certosa
Chianti

0 kilometres 4
0 miles 2

KEY

Ferry port

Airport

FS Main railway station

- - - International boundary

- - - Regional boundary

Motorway

Main road

Railway line

VENICE

Marco Polo

Mestre

FS

Canale Osellino

Laguna Veneta

S14

S11

Turkey-Egypt-
Greece-Ancona

FS Santa Lucia

San Marco

0 kilometres   4

0 miles   2

Venice by Road
*Venice is joined to
the mainland by a
causeway. This pro-
vides easy access to
motorway links with
Verona and Padua.*

AUSTRIA

Cortina d'Ampezzo
Tolmezzo

Cividale del Friuli
Udine

Pordenone
Gorizia

Aquileia
Grado   Trieste
Treviso

SLOVENIA

Mestre
VENICE

Greece
Turkey
Egypt

Po
Delta

Valli di
macchia

Ravenna

Rimini
Pèsaro

SAN MARINO   Fano
San Leo
Urbino
Urbania   Ancona
sepolcro   Jesi   Conero
Arezzo   Grotte di   Peninsula
Frasassi   Loreto
Cortona   Gubbio

Perugia   Assisi
Lago   Spello
Trasimeno
Montefalco   Norcia
Todi   Spoleto
Orvieto

Greece
Ionian Islands
Cyprus
Turkey

KEY TO COLOUR-CODING

Northeast Italy

Venice

The Veneto and Friuli

Trentino-Alto Adige

Northwest Italy

Lombardy

Valle d'Aosta and Piedmont

Liguria

Central Italy

Emilia-Romagna

Florence

Tuscany

Umbria

Le Marche

Ascoli Piceno

Pescara

Isole Tremiti

terbo   L'Aquila
Lanciano

Sulmona
Scanno   San Severo

ROME
VATICAN CITY   Lucera   Foggia
Troia   **Brindisi**

Sermoneta
Sperlonga   0 kilometres   100
Terracina   Formia
Gaeta   Benevento   0 miles   50   **Taranto**
Caserta

**Reggio di
Calabria**

NAPLES   Monte
Vesuvio

Southern Italy

INTERNATIONAL AIRLINE services operate to Rome, Naples and Palermo in southern Italy. Transport links within the region are generally slower than in the north, particularly inland and on the islands of Sicily and Sardinia. Coastal road and rail links are good, however, especially those linking Rome and Naples, the region's main transport hubs. Two trans-Apennine motorways offer the quickest cross-country routes.

Sicily and Sardinia

Ferries operate to Sicily from Naples, Villa San Giovanni and Reggio di Calabria. Onward connections include boats to Malta and Tunisia. Ferries run to Sardinia from several mainland ports, notably Civitavecchia, Genoa and Livorno.

KEY

⚓	Ferry port
✈	Airport
▪▪	International boundary
▪▪	Regional boundary
▬	Motorway
▬	Main road
—	Railway line

ROME AND ENVIRONS

0 kilometres 10

0 miles 5

VIA CASSIA
VIA FLAMINIA
VIA SALARIA
A1
VIA NOMENTANA
GRANDE RACCORDO ANULARE (GRA)
VATICAN CITY
VIA AURELIA
FS
VIA TIBURTINA
A24
VIA CASILINA
VIA APPIA NUOVA
A12
VIA CRISTOFORO COLOMBO
Leonardo da Vinci (Fiumicino)
Tevere (Tiber)
A1
Ciampino

Rome by Road

*Motorway links approach
Rome from Naples,
Pescara and Florence.
All feed into the city's
ring road, the Grande
Raccordo Anulare.*

Vasto
Termoli
Isole Tremiti
Rodi Garganico
Vieste
Gargano Peninsula
San Severo
Manfredonia
Lucera
Foggia
Troia
Benevento
Trani
Bari
Albania
Greece
Egypt
Castel del Monte
Ruvo di Puglia
Caserta
Melfi
Venosa
Lagopesole
Alberobello
Brindisi
Greece
Monte Vesuvio
Matera
mpei
Salerno
Taranto
Lecce
ri
Amalfi
Sorrento
Metaponto
Galatina
Otranto
Paestum
Greece
Cilento
Maratea
Rossano
Cosenza
Sant'Eufemia Lamezia
Isole Eolie
Naples
Tropea
Stilo
Messina
Gerace
Milazzo
Villa San Giovanni
Tindari
Reggio di Calabria
Naples
Malta
Taormina
nna
A20
Catania
iazza
rmerina
Naples
Malta
Pantalica
Siracusa
Noto

0 kilometres 100

0 miles 50

KEY TO COLOUR-CODING

Rome and Lazio

Rome

Lazio

Southern Italy

Naples and Campania

Abruzzo, Molise and Puglia

Basilicata and Calabria

Sicily

Sardinia

A PORTRAIT OF ITALY

ITALY HAS DRAWN PEOPLE *in search of culture and romance for many centuries. Few countries can compete with its Classical origins, its art, architecture, musical and literary traditions, its scenery or food and wine. The ambiguity of its modern image is also fascinating: since World War II Italy has climbed into the top ten world economies, yet at its heart it retains many of the customs, traditions and regional allegiances of its agricultural heritage.*

Italy has no single cultural identity. From the northern snow-capped peaks of the Alps, to the rugged southern shores of

Wedding Ferrari in typical Italian style

Sicily, lies a plethora of distinctive regions and peoples. Politically, Italy is a young country: it did not exist as a unified nation state until 1861, and its 21 regions have maintained their cultural individuality. Visitors to Italy are often pleasantly surprised by the diversity of its dialects, cuisines and architecture. There is also a larger regional division. People speak of two distinct Italies: the rich industrial north and the poorer agricultural south, known as *Il Mezzogiorno* or Land of the Midday Sun. The frontier separating the two is indeterminate, lying somewhere between Rome and Naples.

The north is directly responsible for Italy's place among the world's top industrial nations. It has been the powerhouse behind the Italian economic miracle, its success achieved by internationally renowned names such as Fiat, Prada, Ferragamo, Pirelli, Olivetti, Zanussi, Alessi and Armani. In contrast, the south, once a cradle of high culture and civilization, has been dogged by unemployment and

A secluded villa surrounded by cypress trees on a Tuscan hilltop

◁ Three sundials covering the façade of Palazzo del Governatore, on Piazza Garibaldi, Parma organized crime. Some of its areas rank among the most depressed in Europe, although many southern towns did benefit from an injection of Millennium funds.

The historic divide between north and south is a powerful factor in contemporary politics. The federalist party, the Northern League, owes its popularity to this split.

A conversation in the open air

Those in favour of separation complain that the south is a drain on resources: Milan is seen as efficient and rich, while Naples is viewed as chaotic, dirty and corrupt.

History and geography have both contributed to the division. The north is closer in both location and spirit to Germany and France while the south has suffered a succession of invasions from foreign powers: Carthaginians and Greeks in ancient times, Saracens and Normans in the Middle Ages and until the middle of the 19th century, the Bourbons from Spain held sway.

TRADITION

Distinctive variations in Italy's regions have much to do with the mountainous landscape and inaccessible valleys. Tuscan and Ligurian hill-towns, for instance, have quite different silhou-

ettes, and the farmhouses in Puglia, the famous *trulli*, are unlike those found in the landscape of Emilia-Romagna.

In southern Italy the landscape, architecture, dialects, food, and even the appearance of the people, have closer affinities with the Eastern Mediterranean and North Africa than with Europe. In the far south, study of the local dialects has revealed traces of ancient Greek and old Albanian, preserved in tightly knit communities isolated by the rugged geography. Christianity and pagan ritual are closely linked; sometimes the Virgin is portrayed as a thinly disguised Demeter, the Earth goddess.

Throughout Italy, ancient techniques of husbandry endure and many livelihoods are closely connected to the land and the seasons. Main crops include sugar beet, maize, wheat, olives and grapes; colourful Easter celebrations *(see p62)* pay tribute to the bounty of the soil. Although some of the north's postwar economic prosperity can be attributed to industry (especially car production in and around Turin), much of it has grown from the expansion of family-owned artisan businesses and the export of hand-made goods abroad. This is recognized as a distinct sector of the economy. The internationally successful retail clothes chain Prada is a recent example. The "Made in Italy" label,

Café-goers relaxing in Marina di Pisa, Tuscany

Medieval skyscrapers emerging from the Tuscan landscape of San Gimignano

found on goods such as clothes, shoes and leather bags, guarantees a high standard.

CULTURE AND ARTS

Sophia Loren

The arts in Italy have had a long and glorious history and Italians are very proud of this. Given the fact that Italy has more than 100,000 monuments (archaeological sites, cathedrals, churches, houses and statues), all of which have major historical significance, it is not surprising that there is a shortage of funds to keep them in good repair. Many museums in Italy, particularly those in the south, are closed, or partially closed. You may find churches in Venice hidden behind permanent scaffolding or those in Naples shut due to recent earthquake damage. However, with tourism now accounting for around 3 per cent of Italy's Gross Domestic Product, efforts are being made to put as many buildings and collections on show as possible. The Jubilee 2000 helped matters by allocating large amounts of money for the restoration of buildings and sites belonging to the Catholic Church.

The performing arts are also underfunded, yet there are some spectacular cultural festivals. Almost every town of any size has its own opera house and La Scala opera house in Milan stages world-class productions.

Cinema is another flourishing art form in Italy and has been so since its invention. The sets at Cinecittà, on the

Bernini's 17th-century Fontana del Tritone, Rome

Roadside stall near Positano, Campania

outskirts of Rome, have been used by many famous directors such as Fellini, Pasolini, de Sica, Visconti and many others. Italian films such as *La Vita è Bella* and *The Son's Room* have found critical acclaim and box-office success both in Italy and abroad. In Italy the arts belong to everyone: opera is attended by people from all backgrounds, regardless of social status, as are cinemas and galleries.

Social Customs and Politics

Italian society is still highly traditional, and Italians can be very formal. Between the generations degrees of familiarity exist: reserve *ciao* (hello or goodbye) for friends your age or younger, and greet older people with *piacere* (pleased to meet you), *buon giorno* (good day) or *buona sera* (good evening) and on parting, say *arrivederci* (goodbye). Strangers are met with a handshake, but family and friends receive a kiss.

Italian chic, Armani style

Italian chic decrees that the clothes you wear should give the impression of wealth. If Italians wear similar outfits, it is because they are conformists in fashion as in other aspects of daily life.

Italian politics, in contrast, are not so well regulated. Governments in the postwar era were characterized by short-lived coalitions, dominated by the Christian Democrats. In 1993 Italy experienced a political crisis when an organized network of corruption was exposed, disgracing a huge number of politicians and businessmen. Although the investigations failed to eradicate corruption, they led to the formation of two large coalitions, centre-left and centre-right. Silvio Berlusconi, leader of the Forza Italia party, became prime minister in 1994 but lasted only a short while as he, too, was accused of corruption. In 1998 Massimo D'Alema became Italy's first left-wing Prime Minister. In 2001 the centre-left coalition, led by Francesco Rutelli, the former mayor of Rome, lost the election to Berlusconi's centre-right coalition.

Modern Life

Food and football are the great constants; Italians live for both. Much time is spent on preparing food and eating.

Statue of Emperor Domitian in the Vatican Gardens

The solution to heavy traffic in Rome: motorbikes and scooters

The Italian diet, particularly in the south, is among the healthiest in the world. Football is a national passion and inspires massive public interest and media attention, not least as a way of expressing regional loyalties.

As far as religion is concerned, the number of practising Catholics has been in decline for some years. Although Rome lies at the centre of world Catholicism, today many Italians are uninterested in religion, but still attend mass in number on saints' days or feast days. As a consequence of immigration, other religions are now on the increase.

The emphasis on conformity and a commitment to the institution of the family remain key factors in Italian society despite the country's low, and falling, birth rate. Grandparents, children and grandchildren still live in family units, although this is becoming less common. All children are pampered but the most cherished ones are, usually, male. Women's Liberation fought a powerful campaign in the 1970s and did much to change attitudes to women in the workplace, particularly in metropolitan areas. However, the idea that men should help with housework and the care of the children is still a fairly foreign notion among the older generation.

Strolling through one of Bologna's many porticoes

With the miracle of its postwar economic recovery, where industry and technology were united with design, Italy has become a success story. Although the economy was dented by the worldwide recession of the early 1990s, the exposure of corruption in many walks of public life and political upheaval, Italy appears unchanged to foreign visitors. Its ability to keep its regional identities and traditional values allows it to ride out any changes virtually unscathed.

Medieval and Early Renaissance Art

Tʜᴇ sᴛᴏʀʏ ᴏғ early Italian art, from the 13th century until the late 15th century, illuminates one of the richest periods in European art history. For the first time since Classical antiquity, painters and sculptors created a convincing pictorial space in which figures, modelled "in the round", were given life. Ethereal buildings were replaced by those firmly rooted in the real world, reproducing what artists actually saw. This revolution in art included the reintroduction of the fresco technique, giving artists huge surfaces for telling pictorial stories.

c.1305 Giotto di Bondone, *The Meeting at the Golden Gate* (Cappella degli Scrovegni, Padua) Giotto broke away from the ornate Byzantine style to visualize naturalness and human emotions. His way of working would later be dubbed the Florentine style.

1235 Bonaventura Berlinghieri, *St Francis Altarpiece* (San Francesco, Pescia)

1285 Duccio di Buoninsegna, *Rucellai Madonna*, panel (Uffizi, Florence). Duccio dominated the Sienese painting style which combined bold linear movements with a new human intimacy.

1339 Ambrogio Lorenzetti, *Good Government Enthroned* (Sala dei Nove, Palazzo Pubblico, Siena)

1220	1240	1260	1280	1300	1320

MIDDLE AGES　　　　　　　　　　　　　**FORERUNNERS TO RENAISSANCE**

1220	1240	1260	1280	1300	1320

c.1259 Nicola Pisano, Pulpit (Baptistry, Pisa cathedral)

c.1316–18 Simone Martini, *Vision of St Martin* (Lower Church of San Francesco, Assisi)

c.1265 Coppo di Marcovaldo, *Madonna and Child* (Santa Monica dei Servi, Orvieto)

c.1297 Giovanni Pisano, Pulpit (Sant'Andrea, Pistoia)

c.1280 Cimabue, *Madonna Enthroned with Angels and Prophets*, also known as *Santa Trinità Madonna* (Uffizi, Florence)

c.1336 Andrea Pisano, *Baptism of St John the Baptist*, panel on the South Doors (Baptistry, Florence cathedral)

c.1291 Pietro Cavallini, *Last Judgment*, detail (Santa Cecilia, Trastevere, Rome)

c.1425–52 Lorenzo Ghiberti, *Gates of Paradise*, panel on the East Doors. (Baptistry, Florence cathedral). These elaborate doors mark a transition from the Gothic style to the Early Renaissance style, in Florence.

1357 Andrea Orcagna, *Enthroned Christ with Madonna and Saints* (Strozzi Altarpiece, Santa Maria Novella, Florence)

c.1410 Nanni di Banco, *Four Crowned Martyrs* (Orsanmichele, Florence)

c.1435 Donatello, *David* (Museo del Bargello, Florence)

c.1452–65 Piero della Francesca, detail of *The Dream of Constantine* (San Francesco, Arezzo)

c.1456 Paolo Uccello, *Battle of San Romano* (Uffizi, Florence)

1360	1380	1400	1420	1440	1460

EARLY RENAISSANCE

1360	1380	1400	1420	1440	1460

1423 Gentile da Fabriano, *Adoration of the Magi* (Uffizi, Florence)

c.1350 Francesco Traini, *Triumph of Death* (Campo Santo, Pisa)

c.1425–8 Masaccio, *The Tribute Money* (Cappella Brancacci, Florence)

c.1440 Fra Angelico, *Annunciation* (San Marco, Florence)

c.1463 Piero della Francesca, *Resurrection* (Pinacoteca, Sansepolcro)

c.1465 Fra Filippo Lippi, *Madonna with Child and Angels* (Uffizi, Florence)

c.1465–74 Andrea Mantegna, *Arrival of Cardinal Francesco Gonzaga* (Palazzo Ducale, Mantova)

c.1470 Andrea del Verrocchio, *David* (Bargello, Florence)

FRESCO TECHNIQUE

Fresco, meaning "fresh", refers to the technique of painting onto a thin layer of damp, freshly laid plaster. Pigments are drawn into the plaster by surface tension and the colour becomes fixed as the plaster dries. The pigments react with the lime in the plaster to produce strong, rich colours, such as those in Masaccio's *The Tribute Money*.

The Tribute Money by Masaccio (Cappella Brancacci, Florence)

High Renaissance Art

THE HIGH RENAISSANCE in the late 15th century was marked by an increasing sense of realism in many religious works and the technical mastery of such renowned artists as Michelangelo, Leonardo da Vinci and Raphael. The different schools of Renaissance painting, while drawing on Classical models, produced varying styles: Florentine painting was noted for its cool clarity, while sensuous colour and warm light characterized many Venetian works. By the mid-16th century, however, these styles shifted to the fanciful, contorted imagery of Mannerism.

c.1480 Andrea Mantegna, *Dead Christ* (Brera, Milan)

1481–2 Sistine Chapel wall frescoes painted by various artists.

c.1481–2 Pietro Perugino, *Christ Delivering the Keys of the Kingdom to St Peter,* wall fresco (Sistine Chapel, Rome)

c.1483–88 Andrea del Verrocchio, completed by Alessandro Leopardi, *Equestrian Monument of Bartolomeo Colleoni* (Campo dei Santi Giovanni e Paolo, Venice)

c.1487 Giovanni Bellini, *San Giobbe Altarpiece* (Accademia, Venice)

c.1495 Leonardo da Vinci, *Last Supper* (Santa Maria delle Grazie, Milan)

c.1503–1505 Leonardo da Vinci, *Mona Lisa* (Louvre, Paris)

1505 Raphael, *Madonna of the Goldfinch* (Uffizi, Florence)

1519–26 Titian, *Madonna of the Pesaro Family* (Santa Maria Gloriosa dei Frari, Venice)

1508–12 Michelangelo, *Sistine Chapel ceiling* (The Vatican, Rome). Over 200 preliminary drawings were made for this incredible vision of God's power and humanity's spiritual awakening.

1480 | **1500** | **152**

HIGH RENAISSANCE

1480 | **1500** | **152**

1485 Leonardo da Vinci, *Virgin of the Rocks* (Louvre, Paris)

c.1485 Sandro Botticelli, *Birth of Venus* (Uffizi, Florence)

c.1486 Leonardo da Vinci, *Uomo Vitruviano* (Accademia, Venice)

1499–1504 Luca Signorelli, *Damned Consigned to Hell* (Cappella Nuova, Orvieto cathedral)

1501–1504 Michelangelo, *David* (Galleria dell'Accademia, Florence)

1505 Giovanni Bellini, *Madonna and Child with Four Saints* (San Zaccaria altarpiece, Accademia, Venice)

c.1508 Giorgione, *Tempesta* (Accademia, Venice)

1509 Raphael, *School of Athens* (Stanza della Segnatura, The Vatican, Rome). The scale, magnificence and harmony of this fresco represent the ideals of the High Renaissance. These ideals sought to express superhuman rather than human values.

1517 Sodoma, *Marriage of Alexander and Roxana* (Villa Farnesina, R...)

1516 Michelangelo, *Dying Slave* (Louvre, Paris)

1512–14 Raphael, *Angel Delivering St Peter from Prison,* detail from the *Liberation of St Peter from Prison* (Stanza di Eliodoro, The Vatican, Rome)

1523 Rosso Fiorentino, *Moses Defends the Daughters of Jethro* (Uffizi, Florence)

1530–32 Giulio Romano, *Ceiling and wall frescoes* (Sala dei Giganti, Palazzo del Tè, Mantova)

c.1532 Michelangelo, *"Blockhead" Captive* (Galleria dell' Accademia, Florence)

1534–5 Paris Bordone, *Fisherman Delivering the Ring* (Accademia, Venice)

c.1540–42 Titian, *David and Goliath* (Santa Maria della Salute, Venice)

c.1562–6 Jacopo Tintoretto, *Finding of the Body of St Mark* (Brera, Milan)

c.1550 Moretto, *Ecce Homo with Angel* (Pinacoteca Tosio Martinengo, Brescia)

1540	1560

MANNERISM

1540	1560

1534–41 Michelangelo, *Last Judgment*, wall fresco (Sistine Chapel, Rome)

c.1546 Titian, *Portrait of Pope Paul III Farnese with his Nephews*, (Museo di Capodimonte, Naples)

c.1534–40 Parmigianino, *Madonna and Angels* or *Madonna with the Long Neck* (Uffizi, Florence). Attenuated proportions and contrasting colours make this a fine example of the Mannerist style.

1538 Titian, *Venus of Urbino* (Uffizi, Florence)

c.1540 Agnolo Bronzino, *Portrait of Lucrezia Panciatichi* (Uffizi, Florence). Elongated features, such as Lucrezia's fingers, are typical of the exaggerated Mannerist style.

1556 Veronese, *Triumph of Mordecai* (San Sebastiano, Venice)

c.1526–30 Correggio, *Assumption of the Virgin* (Dome of Parma cathedral). Neither a Mannerist nor a High Renaissance painter, Correggio was a master of illusion, skilled at making ascending figures float convincingly, as seen in the fresco above.

Italian Architecture

Corinthian capital

THE BUILDINGS OF ITALY span almost 3,000 years, drawing influences from a wide variety of sources. Etruscan and Roman buildings borrowed heavily from ancient Greece, while in later centuries Norman, Arabic and Byzantine styles coloured Italy's Romanesque and Gothic architecture. Classical ideals infused the country's Renaissance buildings, later giving way to the inspired innovations of the Baroque period.

The Basilica di San Marco

Orvieto's Duomo *displays the ornate and intricate decoration, notably sculpture, common to many Gothic cathedrals. Building stretched from the 13th to the early 17th centuries.*

The Basilica di San Marco *(AD 832–1094) in Venice combines Classical, Romanesque and Gothic architecture, but its key inspiration was Byzantine (see pp106–9).*

200	400	600	800	1000
CLASSICAL		**BYZANTINE**		**ROMANESQU**
200	400	600	800	1000

Triumphal arches *such as Rome's Arch of Constantine (AD 313) were a uniquely Roman invention. Built to celebrate military victories, they were adorned with reliefs depicting episodes from successful campaigns (see p370).*

The round-arched Romanesque style emerged from the Dark Ages in structures such as the Duomo in Modena. The churches usually had simple interiors that derived from Roman basilicas.

The building of domes over square or rectangular spaces was a major development of the Byzantine era.

ETRUSCAN ARCHITECTURE

Virtually the only architectural memorials to the Etruscans are their necropolises (c.6th century BC), found primarily in Tuscany, Lazio and Umbria. Little else survives, probably because most day-to-day buildings were made from wood. The Etruscans' close cultural and trading ties with Greece, however, suggest their architecture would have borrowed heavily from Greek models. Rome, in turn, looked to Etruscan architecture for inspiration, and most early Roman public buildings were probably Etruscan in style.

Model of Etruscan temple with Classical Greek portico

The cathedral of Monreale *in Sicily, built in the 12th century, contains Norman elements blended with exotic Arabic and Byzantine decoration (see pp514–15).*

Bramante's Tempietto at San Pietro in Montorio, Rome (built 1502–10) was a Renaissance tribute to the precise, Classical temples of ancient Rome (see p370).

Baroque façades, such as this one added to Syracuse's Duomo between 1728 and 1754, were often grafted onto older churches.

Industrial innovations in glass and metal were applied in new buildings, like Mengoni's imposing Galleria Vittorio Emanuele II (1865) in Milan (see p188).

The Classical ideals of Rome and ancient Greece were reintroduced into Italian architecture during the Renaissance.

Papal patronage and the vigour of the Counter-Reformation fuelled the Baroque, a period of architectural splendour, invention and exuberance.

The Mole Antonelliana (1863–89), in Turin, topped by a soaring granite spire, was for a time the tallest building in the world (p216).

Torre Velasca's 26-floor tower in Milan (1950s) pioneered the use of reinforced concrete.

1400	1600	1800	2000
RENAISSANCE	BAROQUE	19th CENTURY	20th CENTURY
1400	1600	1800	2000

Siena's Duomo (1136–1382), an imposing Romanesque-Gothic cathedral, went through 200 years of architectural transformation (see pp332–3).

Santa Maria Novella in Florence has a Renaissance façade (1456–70) by Alberti and a Gothic interior.

Gian Lorenzo Bernini (1598–1680), architect of St Peter's Square, was a dominant figure in Roman Baroque.

Andrea Palladio (1508–80) built Neo-Classical villas and palazzi. His style was imitated in Europe for over two centuries (see p76).

Lantern / Inner shell / Outer skin of dome, supported by 24 ribs

Brunelleschi's dome for the Duomo in Florence, completed in 1436, was a masterpiece of Renaissance design and ingenious engineering (see p245).

The Gesù in Rome was designed for the Jesuits by Vignola in 1568. With its powerful façade and lavish decoration it was the prototype for countless other Baroque churches (see p371).

The Pirelli building in Milan, designed by Ponti and Nervi (late 1950s), is a great example of modern Italian architecture (see p179).

Saints and Symbols in Italian Art

SAINTS AND SYMBOLS are especially important in Italian art. They form part of an established visual language used by artists to narrate stories of the Bible and the Catholic church to church-goers. Paintings of the saints were the focus for prayer and each offered assistance in a particular aspect of daily life. Patron saints protected specific cities, or trades, and individuals who bore their name. Saints' days and religious festivals still play an important part in Italian life.

St John carries a book of the Gospel bearing his name.

St Thomas Aquinas is usually shown with a star, barely visible in this painting on his Dominican habit.

St Dominic is usually portrayed wearing the habit of his order. The lily is another of his attributes.

St Cosmas and St Damian are always shown together, dressed in physicians' clothing.

St Mark the Evangelist often holds his book of the Gospels.

St Lawrence carries a palm leaf as well as the gridiron on which he was roasted.

Virgin Enthroned with the Child and Saints (c.1450) was painted on dry plaster by the Dominican friar, Fra Angelico. It is on display at the Museo di San Marco, Florence (see p268).

The Virgin, usually shown in blue robes, is depicted as Mater Amabilis – the "Mother Worthy of Love".

St Peter Martyr, here with a palm leaf, is sometimes depicted with a head wound, carrying a sword.

SYMBOLS

In order to identify different saints or martyrs they were given "attributes" or symbols – particular objects to carry, or clothing to wear. These were items that played a particular role in their life story. Martyrs were known by their instruments of torture or death. Symbolism also appears in the sky, animals, flowers, colours and numbers.

The lamb symbolizes Christ, the Lamb of God, or in early Christian art, the sinner.

The skull is a "memento mori" to remind us of death and impermanence.

**Winged man
(St Matthew)**

**Winged lion
(St Mark)**

**Winged ox
(St Luke)**

St Peter the Apostle, the "rock" on which the Christian church was founded, carries the keys to heaven.

The Madonna, with the Christ Child, is an emblem of perfect motherly love.

Giovanni Bellini's painting of *Madonna and Child with Four Saints* (see p115)

St Catherine of Alexandria is shown here with a piece of the wheel on which she was martyred.

St Jerome is always portrayed as an old man, often a hermit, whose life was devoted to scholarship.

***Detail from* Madonna and Child with Four Saints**, *by Giovanni Bellini. The painting was produced for an altarpiece at San Zaccaria, Venice in 1505, where it is still on display.*

The angel, a messenger of God to man, is portrayed in this scene as a musician of Heaven.

St Lucy is depicted here holding her own eyes in a dish. She became the patron saint of the blind and symbolizes light.

The lily*, flower of the Virgin, is the symbol of purity, resurrection, peace and chastity.*

The cockle shell *most often represents pilgrimage. It is a particular attribute of St Roch.*

The palm *represents, in Christian art, a martyr's triumph over death.*

Writers, Poets and Dramatists

ITALY HAS PRODUCED many writers (in Latin and Italian) who have won worldwide acclaim. Each of them provides an illuminating insight into the country's turbulent past: the classical poets Virgil, Horace and Ovid give vivid accounts of the concerns and values of ancient Rome; medieval Florence and Tuscany are brought to life in the poetry of Dante and Petrarch and the salacious tales of Boccaccio. In less than a century these three great writers created a new literary language to rank with any in Europe. Italy's modern literature still commands international attention – Umberto Eco has to his credit one of the most widely read books of the 20th century.

Primo Levi *(1919–87) gave an astonishing account of his survival of the Jewish Holocaust and World War II's aftermath in* The Truce *and* If This Is A Man.

Trentino- Alto Adige

Valle d'Aosta and Piedmont

Lombardy

Liguria

Emilia-Romagna

Dario Fo (born 1926) won the Nobel prize for Literature in 1997.

Tuscany

Umberto Eco *(born 1932), a professor at the University of Bologna, wrote the novel* The Name Of The Rose, *which explored his passion for the Middle Ages. The book was made into a film (above) in 1986.*

Giovanni Boccaccio *(1313–75) is notable for providing a fascinating social record of his era.* The Decameron, *his captivating collection of 100 short stories, is set in the plague-stricken Florence of 1348.*

Pinocchio, *written by Carlo Collodi (1826–90) in 1883, is one of the world's best known children's stories. "Collodi" was Carlo Lorenzini's pseudonym, taken after his mother's birthplace in Tuscany.*

Dante's *(1265–1321)* Divine Comedy *(c.1321), is a journey through Hell, Purgatory and Paradise. It includes horrific accounts of the torments suffered by the damned.*

CLASSICAL ROMAN WRITERS

Texts in Latin by Classical Roman philosophers, poets, dramatists and politicians are part of the bedrock of Western culture. Today the names Virgil *(The Aeneid)*, Ovid *(Metamorphoses)* and Pliny *(Historia Naturalis)* are literary legends. Fascinating histories such as Livy's *Early History of Rome*, Caesar's *Gallic Wars*, Tacitus's *Annals* and Suetonius's *The Twelve Caesars*, give us an invaluable window on the distant Roman past, as do the caustic *Satires* of Juvenal. Many Latin works owe their survival to the teams of medieval monks who diligently copied and illustrated them. In the Renaissance the stories of Ovid's *Metamorphoses* were plundered by many writers and the works of Cicero had a profound influence on prose style; Seneca was seen as a master of tragedy and Plautus's *Pot of Gold* served as a model for comedies.

Detail from medieval copy of Pliny's *Historia Naturalis*

Venetian author Carlo Goldoni (1707–93) reacted against the satirical tradition of La Commedia dell'Arte, preferring to write more forgiving plays on contemporary Venice society.

e Veneto
d Friuli

Le Marche

abria

Petrarch (1304–74), one of the earliest and greatest lyric poets, produced works which showed the first indications of Humanism.

Lazio

***St Francis of Assisi** (1182–1226) was the first author to write in Italian instead of formal Latin. As well as letters and sermons, he wrote poems and songs, including the popular* Canticle of the Sun.

Abruzzo, Molise and Puglia

Campania

Basilicata and Calabria

Roman writer Alberto Moravia (1907–90) is usually labelled a "Neo-Realist". His novels and short stories focus on the corrupt values of contemporary society. Among his best known works are *Gli Indifferenti* and *Agostino*.

***The Sicilian** Nobel Prize-winner Luigi Pirandello (1867–1936) was preoccupied with themes of illusion and reality.* Six Characters In Search Of An Author *is his most famous work.*

Sicily

0 kilometres		200
0 miles	100	

Music and Opera in Italy

Stradivarius violin

BEFORE ITALY'S UNIFICATION, particularly during the 17th and 18th centuries, each major city had its own traditions of music-making. Rome, as the papal city, had musical traditions less hedonistic than elsewhere, and avoided opera. Florence had its day at the turn of the 16th century, with its celebrated *camerata* (groups set on reviving the traditions of Ancient Greek spectacle). Venice fostered church music on a grand scale, and Naples, during the 18th century, was renowned for comic opera. In the 19th century, Milan became the undisputed centre of Italian opera, centred on La Scala.

THE MEDIEVAL AND RENAISSANCE PERIODS

THROUGH BOCCACCIO *(see p30)*, among others, it is known that singing, dancing and poetry often went hand in hand in medieval and Renaissance Italy. Italy concentrated on music as part of a pure art form.

Important contributors to the music of these periods include Guido d'Arezzo (c.995–1050), a monk who perfected musical notation, and Francesco Landini (1325–97), one of the first known composers whose songs displayed a distinct concern for lyricism. The next 150 years were to be characterized by the *Ars Perfecta* style, culminating with composer Giovanni Palestrina (1525–94). His vocal style subjected dissonance to strict control, and it was employed for most church music. Madrigals (vocal settings of poems by Petrarch and other poets) were also popular.

The early 17th century saw Italian composers such as Carlo Gesualdo (c.1561–1613) and Claudio Monteverdi challenge these traditions by introducing more declamation and more of the unexpected.

La Pietà, Venice, where Vivaldi performed

THE BAROQUE ERA

CLAUDIO MONTEVERDI'S music straddled the transition from the Renaissance period to 17th-century Baroque. The word "baroque" means highly ornamented, even bizarre, and embellishment was rife. Monteverdi's madrigals began as standard pieces for four voices but ended up as mini-operas. This was due to the popularity of an individual instrumental style and the development of the *basso continuo* (a supporting organ, harpsichord or lute that unleashed the possibility for solos and duets). At this point, the beginnings of the string orchestra were in place.

A new fashion for declamation meant that various emotional states were being represented with sighs and sobs rather than just description. Monteverdi's *Vespers* followed others' in exploiting the stereophonic possibilities of San Marco in Venice by contrasting different forces

MAJOR ITALIAN COMPOSERS THROUGH THE AGES

Claudio Monteverdi *(1567–1643) was best known for his* Vespers *of 1610. Both his madrigals and operas are considered major landmarks in the development of music.*

Antonio Vivaldi *(1678–1741) wrote over 600 concertos, many of which are for the violin. The* Four Seasons, *a set of concertos, is among the best-selling classical music of all time.*

Gioachino Rossini *(1792–1868) was most famous for his comic operas, like* The Barber of Seville. *The romantic, expressive side of his more serious works was often overlooked.*

Luciano Pavarotti performing in the most modern surroundings

in different parts of the building. In the 1680s, Arcangelo Corelli (1653–1713) turned to classicism. Corelli was famous for the *Concerto Grosso*, a style that contrasted the solo string group with the full ensemble. He was followed by Antonio Vivaldi (1678–1741), who concentrated his efforts on developing the solo form of the *Concerto Grosso*. He used wind and plucked instruments as well as violins.

THE EMERGENCE OF OPERA

OPERA FIRST emerged during the wedding celebrations of Italy's wealthy 16th-century families. Monteverdi was the first composer to establish his work firmly in the opera repertoire. During the 17th century, Alessandro Scarlatti (1660–1725) formulated a model which consisted of an orchestral overture followed by a sequence of narrative, set as *recitative*, and interrupted by *da capo* (three-part) arias. Themes for the weightier *opera seria* were largely drawn from mythology, while the lighter *opera buffa* had stock scenes that sometimes owed a large debt to the traditions of Commedia dell'Arte. Famous for his comic operas, such as *The Barber of Seville*, was the composer Gioachino Rossini. Among other contributors, Vincenzo Bellini (1801–35) and Gaetano Donizetti (1797–1848) developed *bel canto* singing, a style stressing fine tone and ornamentation.

The two most prominent opera composers of the latter half of the 19th century were Giuseppe Verdi and Giacomo Puccini (1858–1924). Verdi often turned to the works of Shakespeare as well as to more recent subjects in order to form a basis for his work, while many composers, like Puccini, turned to the new trend of *verismo* (slices of contemporary realism) – *La Bohème* is one of the most refined examples of this style.

Puccini's *Tosca*, first staged in 1900

Giuseppe Verdi (1813–1901), whose first works were for La Scala, was the most important opera composer of the 19th century. His most celebrated works include Rigoletto and Aida.

THE 20TH CENTURY

IN THE EARLY 20th century, Puccini's *La Fanciulla del West* (The Girl of the West) brought cowboys into opera, *Turandot* looked towards the Orient and *Tosca* brought torture and murder. Some composers have attempted to emulate French and German music, and only a few Italian pieces, such as those by Ottorino Respighi (1879–1936), have been regularly performed. The most important name in Italian music today is Luciano Berio (born 1925), who developed Music Theatre, a relatively new art form lying somewhere between drama and opera. Recently, however, Berio has continued the tradition of Grand Opera with his elaborate production of *Un Re in Ascolto*. But it is perhaps Luciano Pavarotti who must be credited with renewing an international interest in opera. In the 1990s, his often televised performances with "Three Tenors" stars José Carreras and Placido Domingo secured a massive world audience for opera. Another star of opera and classical music is internationally renowned conductor Riccardo Muti, director of La Scala.

The illuminated interior of Rome's Teatro dell'Opera

Italian Design

ITALY HAS HAD PHENOMENAL success evolving stylish, desirable forms for everyday objects. Its 20th-century achievements can be credited to a handful of forward-thinking industrial giants, such as Olivetti, willing to entrust important product decisions to a group of inspired designers, like Ettore Sottsass. The design genius was to rethink the function of consumer objects, apply new technology, and then make the result look seductive.

The streamlined aesthetic of Italian design extends even to pasta; this Marille version was created by car designer Giorgio Giugiaro for Voiello in 1983.

Sleek, sculptural Alessi cutlery (1988), designed by Ettore Sottsass, combines maximum utility with elegance and aesthetic integrity.

The Alessi kettle (1985), designed by Michael Graves, achieved such popularity in its first year of production that over 100,000 were sold.

One of the best known coffeemakers is Bialetti's Moka Express. Although designed in 1930, it is still enormously popular today.

Christophe Pilet's chair, designed for Giulio Cappellini's collection of contemporary furniture, expresses the idea of the living style of the 1990s.

The folding Cumano table, designed by Achille Castiglione for Zanotta in 1979, is still revered as a "designer object".

The Patty Difusa chair, with unusual wooden arms that curve into legs, was designed by William Sawaya for Sawaya & Moroni in Milan.

Pininfarina's streamlined form for the Ferrari Testarossa (1986) pushes car design almost into the realms of sculpture.

Light in weight, and compact in shape, Olivetti's Valentine typewriter revolutionized the role of the desk typewriter. Designed by Ettore Sottsass in 1969, its portability allowed the user to work anywhere.

*B**abc***

Italian printer Giambattista Bodoni (1740–1813) designed the sophisticated typeface that bears his name and is still popular 200 years after its creation.

Milan's Giorgio Armani is best known for his updating of classic items such as the jacket, creating a flattering, smart and comfortable, "deconstructed" look.

Prada, the Milan-based fashion house headed by Miuccia Prada, features minimalist, cutting-edge designs and the use of innovative fabrics.

Florence has a long reputation as a producer of high quality crafts, particularly fashion accessories such as handbags, shoes, belts, jewellery and briefcases.

Gucci's classic items, including bags and shoes, are a revered totem for the fashion-conscious.

The Artemide company is renowned for combining metal and glass in many of their designs, especially lamps and lighting fixtures.

Piaggio's innovative Vespa scooter (1946), by Corradino d'Ascanio, provided cheap, fast and reliable transport at a time when few could afford the expense of a car. Hugely successful, the Vespa is still a common sight on Italy's streets.

The Fiat 500 (1957), like the Vespa, became a symbol of mobility and democratization, an expression of Italy's rapid postwar recovery.

Scientists, Inventors and Explorers

ITALY HAS fostered a long tradition of important scientific thought and discovery, fuelled in the Renaissance by such men as Galileo, who searched for a new understanding of the universe. Meanwhile, explorers such as Columbus had set off to find new worlds, a move heralded in the 13th century by Marco Polo. The spirit of scientific enquiry continued up to the 20th century, with the invention of radio and pioneering work in the field of nuclear physics.

Guglielmo Marconi invented the first practical system for sending radio signals. In 1901, he succeeded in picking up a signal that had been sent to England from Newfoundland.

Trentino
Alto Adige

Lombardy

Valle d'Aosta and Piedmont

The Ve
and F

After deducing that an electric current made frogs' legs move, Alessandro Volta invented the electric battery, a "pile" of metal discs in contact with acid. He demonstrated it to Napoleon in 1801.

Liguria

Tuscany

Genoese-born Christopher Columbus sailed west from Spain in 1492. He reached the Indies in three months, navigating with such aids as an astrolabe.

The explorer Amerigo Vespucci established that the New World was a separate land mass. A pamphlet wrongly described him as its discoverer, and so, in 1507, America acquired its name.

Leonardo da Vinci was the ultimate Renaissance man, accomplished in both arts and sciences. He conceived his first design for a flying machine in c.1488, more than 400 years before the first aeroplane took off. This model is based on one of his technical drawings.

The telescope enabled astronomers to produce accurate lunar maps. Domenico Cassini, astronomy professor at Bologna University, refined the instrument. In 1665 he traced the meridian line in the church of San Petronio.

| 0 kilometres | | 200 |
| 0 miles | | 100 |

Padua University, founded in 1222, was a centre of scientific learning in the Renaissance. Galileo, inventor of the telescope, taught physics here, and the lectern he used is still on view.

The Venetian Marco Polo set off for the east as a youth in 1271. He stayed at the court of the Mongol emperor, Kublai Khan, for nearly two decades before returning home. He is seen here arriving at Hormuz in the Persian Gulf from India.

Galileo Galilei proved that the earth revolved around the sun, overturning Church doctrine. He was convicted of heresy in 1633. Here he shows the rings of Saturn to Venetian senators.

Emilia-Romagna

Le Marche

Umbria

Lazio

Abruzzo, Molise and Puglia

Winner of the Nobel Prize for Physics in 1938, Enrico Fermi directed the first controlled nuclear chain reaction. He built the world's first nuclear reactor for producing power at the University of Chicago, US.

Pliny the Elder wrote his catalogue of human knowledge, *Natural History*, in AD 77. He died when Vesuvius erupted two years later, but his book retained its authority for 1,500 years.

Campania

Basilicata and Calabria

Spectacles were invented in Italy in the 13th century. They are first recorded in Venice, still an important centre for glasswork today.

Sicily

The mathematician Archimedes was born in c.287 BC in Syracuse, Sicily, then a Greek colony. Legend has it that he discovered the principle of specific gravity while in the bath.

TEMPLA DOMVM EXPOSITIS·VICOS·FORA·MOENIA·PONTES:
  VIRGINEAM TRIVII·QVOD·REPARARIS·AQVAM.
PRISCA·LICET·NAVTIS·DARE·COMMODA·PORTVS:
  ET·VATICANVM·CINGERE·SIXTE·IVGVM:
PLVS·TAMEN·VRBS·DEBET·NAM·QVAE·SQVALORE·LATEBAT:
  CERNITVR·IN·CELEBRI·BIBLIOTHECA·LOCO·

THE HISTORY OF ITALY

THE CONCEPT of Italy as a geographic entity goes back to the time of the Etruscans, but Italy's history is one of discord and division. Prior to the 19th century, the only time the peninsula was united was under the Romans, who by the 2nd century BC had subdued the other Italian tribes. Rome became the capital of a huge empire, introducing its language, laws and calendar to most of Europe before succumbing to Germanic invaders in the 5th century AD.

Julius Caesar

Another important legacy of the Roman empire was Christianity and the position of the pope as head of the Catholic church. The medieval papacy summoned the Franks to drive out the Lombards and, in AD 800, crowned the Frankish king Charlemagne Holy Roman Emperor. Unfortunately, what seemed to be the dawn of a new age turned out to be anything but. For five centuries popes and emperors fought to decide which of them should be in charge of their nebulous empire.

Meanwhile, a succession of foreign invaders – Normans, Angevins and Aragonese – took advantage of the situation to conquer Sicily and the south.

The north, in contrast, saw a growth of independent city states, the most powerful being Venice, fabulously wealthy through trade with the East. Other cities, such as Genoa, Florence, Milan, Pisa and Siena, also had their days of glory. Northern Italy became the most prosperous and cultured region in western Europe and it was the artists and scholars of 15th-century Florence who inspired the Renaissance. Small, fragmented states, however, could not compete with great powers. In the 16th century Italy's petty kingdoms fell prey to a foreign invader, this time to Spain, and the north subsequently came under the control of Austria.

One small kingdom that remained independent was Piedmont, but during a war between Austria and France it fell to Napoleon in 1796. In the 19th century, however, it was Piedmont that became the focus for a movement towards a united Italy, a goal that was achieved in 1870, thanks largely to the heroic military exploits of Garibaldi. In the 1920s, the Fascists seized power and, in 1946, the monarchy was abandoned for today's republic.

16th-century map of Italy, of the kind used by Venetian and Genoese sailors

◁ **Fresco by Melozzo da Forlì of the court of Sixtus IV (1471–84), a powerful and worldly Renaissance pope**

The Age of the Etruscans

THE ETRUSCANS were Italy's first major civilization. The frescoes, jewellery and pottery found in their tombs are evidence of a highly artistic, cultured people. Their origin is a mystery, as is their language, but from the 9th century BC they spread through central Italy, their chief rivals being the Greeks in the south. Etruria was never a unified state, just a loose confederation of cities. In the 6th century Etruscan kings ruled Rome, the city that would ultimately eclipse them.

ITALY IN 650 BC

▊ *Etruscan kingdoms*

☐ *Greek colonies*

The double flute was a speciality of the Etruscans. The instrument was played at festivals and funerals alike.

Terracotta Winged Horses
This beautiful relief of yoked horses (4th century BC) decorated the façade of the Ara della Regina temple at Tarquinia.

Bronze Sheep's Liver
The inscriptions served as a guide for telling the future from animals' entrails.

Terracotta Cremation Urn
The lid of the urn shows the deceased holding a writing tablet. The Etruscans introduced the alphabet to Italy.

TOMB OF THE LEOPARDS
Feasts and revelry are common themes in the frescoes that decorate Etruscan tombs. These musicians are from a tomb fresco (c.500 BC) at Tarquinia (*see p450*).

TIMELINE

9th century BC Pre-urban communities established along river valleys in Etruria		**c.700 BC** Growth of cities in Etruria; earliest Etruscan inscriptions	**616 BC** Etruscans become rulers of Rome under Tarquino the Olde
	753 BC Legendary date of foundation of Rome by Romulus		
900 BC	**800 BC**	**700 BC**	
c.900 BC First traces of Iron Age in Italy; Villanovan period			
	c.800 BC Greeks settle in Sicily and south of Italy	**715–673 BC** Reign of the wise Numa Pompilius, second king of Rome	*Etruscan gold earrings*

A Boxing Match
Athletic competitions were held at funerals. This vase, which dates from about 500 BC, was made in Etruria, but imitates the Greek black-figure style of pottery.

The musicians and the dancer in the tomb painting are painted with a realism that indicates the influence of Greek art.

The lyre was made from a tortoise shell and played with a plectrum.

Apollo of Veii
This magnificent statue of Apollo (c.500 BC) shows the stylized facial features characteristic of Etruscan art.

Bronze Mirror
Wealthy Etruscans lived in great luxury. The women used polished bronze mirrors with engraved backs. This one shows Helen of Troy and the goddess Aphrodite.

WHERE TO SEE ETRUSCAN ITALY

Rock tombs *like these at Sovana (p336) are common in the volcanic tufa of central Italy.*

Tuscany, Lazio and Umbria are rich in Etruscan remains, especially tombs. There are huge necropolises in Lazio at Cerveteri and Tarquinia (*p450*). The latter also has an important museum. Other museums with major collections of Etruscan art and artifacts include Villa Giulia (*p430*) and the Vatican's Museo Gregoriano (*p412*) in Rome, the Museo Archeologico in Florence (*p269*), the Museo Nazionale in Chiusi (*p322*) and the Museo Guarnacci in Volterra (*p324*).

Temple of Neptune
This fine temple at Paestum (5th century BC) is a legacy of Greek colonization of the south.

Mixing bowl, imported from Greece

509 BC Last Etruscan king, Tarquinius Superbus, expelled from Rome; establishment of Roman Republic

450 BC Roman law codified in the Twelve Tables

390 BC Gauls sack Rome; Capitol saved thanks to alarm sounded by cackling geese

0 BC   500 BC   400 BC

499 BC Battle of Lake Regillus; Romans defeat alliance of Latins and Etruscans

474 BC Etruscan fleet defeated by Greeks off Cumae; blow to Etruscan naval power

c.400 BC Gauls start to settle along valley of the Po

396 BC Veii, a major Etruscan city in present-day Lazio, falls to Rome

Relief of Capitoline geese, found in the Roman Forum

From Republic to Empire

**Roman mask
and helmet
(1st century BC)**

From the scores of tribes inhabiting ancient Italy, one people, the Romans, emerged to conquer the peninsula and impose their language, customs and laws on the rest. Rome's success was due to superb skill in military and civil organization. The state was a republic ruled by two consuls, elected each year, but as the extent of Rome's conquests grew, power passed to generals such as Julius Caesar. The Republic became unworkable and Caesar's heirs became the first Roman emperors.

Cisalpine Gaul was annexed in 202–191 BC.

Etruria was in Roman hands by 265 BC.

Julius Caesar
The great general, conqueror of Gaul, returned to Italy in 49 BC to defeat Pompey. His rise to absolute power marked the end of the Republic.

Oscan Inscription
The languages of the peoples conquered by Rome lived on for centuries before being replaced by Latin. The Oscans lived in what is now Campania.

War Elephant
In 218 BC the great Carthaginian general Hannibal brought 37 elephants across the Alps – to spread alarm in the Roman ranks.

Roman Aqueduct
The Romans' talent for engineering found its most spectacular expression in huge aqueducts. These could be up to 80 km (50 miles) long, though for most of that distance the water ran underground.

High ground

Cleaning vent

Reservoir

Underground water channel

Arches carrying water across low ground

TIMELINE

Via Appia

300 BC		250 BC		200 BC

312 BC Building of Via Appia and Aqua Appia aqueduct

308 BC Etruscan city of Tarquinii falls to Rome

287–212 BC Life of Archimedes, the great Greek mathematician of Syracuse

265 BC Romans capture last Etruscan city

275 BC Greek King Pyrrhus defeated by Romans at Beneventum

264–241 BC First Punic War (between Rome and Carthage)

237 BC Romans occupy Corsica and Sardinia

Hannibal, Carthaginian leader in the Second Punic War

218 BC Second Punic War; Hannibal crosses the Alps

216 BC Roman defeat at Battle of Cannae

191 BC Gaulish territory south of the Alps falls to Rome

Cicero Addresses the Senate
*State business was debated in the
Senate. The great orator Cicero
(106–43 BC) argued for the
Republic and against tyranny.*

Roman Legionary
*This bronze shows a
legionary in standard kit
of helmet, breastplate,
leather kilt with iron
plates, greaves on his
shins, and sandals.*

The Via Appia
was extended
from Capua to
Brindisi in 190 BC.

FINIUM
ERIA

CAPUA

VIA APPIA

BRUNDISIUM
Brindisi

TARENTUM
Taranto

Sicily
became the
first Roman
province in
241 BC.

RHEGIUM
Reggio di Calabria

WHERE TO SEE ITALY FROM THE REPUBLICAN ERA

Republican structures are very rare, most
having been rebuilt under the Empire.
In Rome itself, two notable exceptions
are the 2nd-century BC Temples of the
Forum Boarium (*p423*). However, the
legacy of the age to modern Italy is not
hard to appreciate. Countless roads, such
as the Via Appia Antica (*p431*), and
towns were planned originally by Roman
engineers. Two striking examples of
towns with original Roman street plans
are Lucca (*pp310–11*) and Como (*p185*).

***These huge basalt blocks** at Tharros in
Sardinia (p535) were part of a Roman road.*

ROMAN ROADS

After conquering other tribes, the Romans
imposed their authority by building roads
along which legions could march rapidly
to deal with any trouble. They also built
towns. Many, such as Ariminum (Rimini),
were "colonies", settlements for Roman
citizens – often veteran legionaries.

**Aerial View of
Bologna**
*Roman street plans
are still visible in
city centres today.
The route of the old
Via Aemilia cuts
straight through the
centre of Bologna.*

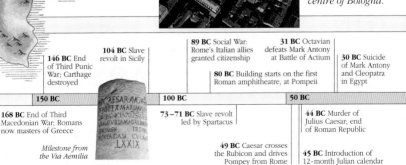

146 BC End of Third Punic War; Carthage destroyed	**104 BC** Slave revolt in Sicily	**89 BC** Social War: Rome's Italian allies granted citizenship	**31 BC** Octavian defeats Mark Antony at Battle of Actium	**30 BC** Suicide of Mark Antony and Cleopatra in Egypt
		80 BC Building starts on the first Roman amphitheatre, at Pompeii	

150 BC   **100 BC**   **50 BC**

168 BC End of Third Macedonian War; Romans now masters of Greece	**73–71 BC** Slave revolt led by Spartacus	**44 BC** Murder of Julius Caesar; end of Roman Republic
Milestone from the Via Aemilia	**49 BC** Caesar crosses the Rubicon and drives Pompey from Rome	**45 BC** Introduction of 12-month Julian calendar

CAESAR·AVG
IMPERAMAXIM
PONTMAXIM
VIA·FLAMIN·IAM·ABAR
NVMEN TRIVM
REFECDAM·CVRA
LXXIX

The Golden Age of Rome

FROM THE AGE of Augustus to the reign of Trajan, Rome's power grew until her empire stretched from Britain to the Red Sea. Despite the extravagance of emperors such as Nero, taxes and booty from military campaigns continually refilled the Imperial coffers. Under the wiser rule of Trajan, Hadrian and Marcus Aurelius in the 2nd century AD, Roman citizens enjoyed wealth and comfort, with most of the work performed by slaves. Entertainment included visits to the baths, the theatre and the games. The town of Pompeii, buried when Vesuvius erupted in AD 79, preserves many fascinating details of everyday life.

ROMAN EMPIRE IN AD 117

▢ *Maximum extent of the Empire*

Mosaic of Gladiators
Bloodthirsty gladiatorial combats were very popular. The gladiators were mostly slaves captured in war.

Frescoes of festoons and medallions

Trajan's Column
The carvings record Trajan's successful campaigns in Dacia (present-day Romania) in the first decade of the 2nd century AD.

The triclinium (main dining room) had a beautiful frieze of cupids.

Roman Shops
Buildings in towns were lined with small shops open to the street, like this pharmacy. The front was closed with wooden panels and locked at night.

HOUSE OF THE VETTII

This reconstruction shows one of Pompeii's finest houses *(see pp478–9)*. The Vettii were not aristocrats, but freedmen, former slaves, who had made a fortune through trade. The rooms were richly decorated with frescoes and sculptures.

TIMELINE

Bronze cooking pots from kitchen at Pompeii

9 BC Dedication of Ara Pacis *(see p400)* in Rome to celebrate peace after wars in Gaul and Spain	**AD 17** Tiberius fixes boundary of Empire along the Rhine and Danube	**AD 79** Eruption of Vesuvius destroys Pompeii and Herculaneum
50 BC	**AD 1**	**AD 50**
27 BC Augustus takes title Princeps, in effect becoming the first Roman emperor	**AD 37–41** Reign of Caligula	**AD 67** Traditional date for martyrdom of St Peter and St Paul in Rome
	AD 43 Roman conquest of Britain in reign of Claudius	**AD 80** Inaugural games in Colosseum
	AD 68 Deposition and suicide of Nero	

Augustus
The adopted son of Julius Caesar became the first emperor, reducing the Roman Senate to impotence and ruling by decree.

The atrium had a skylight in the roof with a pool that collected rainwater below.

Front entrance

WHERE TO SEE IMPERIAL ROME

The best places to discover how people lived are Pompeii *(pp478–9)* and Herculaneum. Artifacts and works of art from these sites are held at the Museo Archeologico in Naples *(pp474–5)*, while local museums all over Italy contain statues and other remains. Famous sights in Rome include the Pantheon *(p394)* and the Colosseum *(p383)*. Hadrian's Villa, at Tivoli *(p452)*, and Ostia *(p451)* are also fascinating to visit, but the whole country preserves traces of Rome's glory – from the Arch of Augustus in Aosta *(p207)* to Villa del Casale *(p521)* in Sicily.

The Forum (pp380–81), *with its temples and law courts, was the centre of daily life in ancient Rome.*

Reception room

Mosaic of a Banquet
The Romans ate reclining on low couches. A popular accompaniment for many dishes was garum, *a salty sauce made of dried fish.*

Peristyle or colonnade

The internal garden was a feature borrowed by the Romans from the Greeks.

Household Shrine
Religious rites were practised both in public and in private. This shrine from the House of the Vettii was dedicated to the lares, *the household gods.*

AD 97 Roman Empire reaches largest extent in reign of Trajan

AD 161–180 Reign of Marcus Aurelius

AD 193–211 Reign of Septimius Severus

AD 212 Roman citizenship extended to include people from all parts of the Empire

AD 100	AD 150	AD 200

late 1st century Amphitheatre Verona built

AD 134 Hadrian's Villa at Tivoli completed

AD 216 Baths of Caracalla completed in Rome

AD 125 Pantheon rebuilt by Hadrian

Emperor Septimius Severus

The Splitting of the Empire

Glass flask with Christian symbol (4th century AD)

A DECISIVE TURNING POINT in the history of the Roman Empire came with Emperor Constantine's conversion to Christianity in AD 312 and his decision to build a new capital at Constantinople (Byzantium). By the 5th century the Empire was split into two. Rome and the Western Empire could not stem the tide of Germanic invaders migrating southwards and Italy fell first to the Goths and later to the Lombards. The Eastern Empire retained nominal control over parts of Italy from its stronghold at Ravenna, which became the richest, most powerful city of the age, while the great palaces and arenas of Rome were reduced to ruins.

ITALY IN AD 600

Byzantine territories

Lombard territories

The Donation of Constantine
A medieval legend, encouraged by the papacy, tells how Constantine granted Pope Sylvester temporal power over Rome.

Belisarius (500–565) was a general who won much of Italy back from the Goths.

Theodolinda of the Lombards
The 6th-century queen converted her people to orthodox Catholicism. Here, gold is melted for the church she built at Monza (see p193).

Justinian reigned from 527 to 565. He was a great lawgiver and one of the most powerful Byzantine emperors.

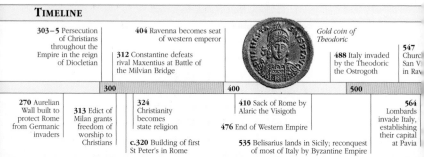

TIMELINE

303–5 Persecution of Christians throughout the Empire in the reign of Diocletian

404 Ravenna becomes seat of western emperor

312 Constantine defeats rival Maxentius at Battle of the Milvian Bridge

Gold coin of Theodoric

488 Italy invaded by the Theodoric the Ostrogoth

547 Churc San V in Rav

300 · **400** · **500**

270 Aurelian Wall built to protect Rome from Germanic invaders

313 Edict of Milan grants freedom of worship to Christians

324 Christianity becomes state religion

c.320 Building of first St Peter's in Rome

410 Sack of Rome by Alaric the Visigoth

476 End of Western Empire

535 Belisarius lands in Sicily; reconquest of most of Italy by Byzantine Empire

564 Lombards invade Italy, establishing their capital at Pavia

Charlemagne
The King of the Franks was invited by the pope to crush the Lombards. In return, he was crowned Holy Roman Emperor in AD 800.

Saracens Besieging Messina *(843)*
In the 9th century Sicily was conquered by Muslims from Africa. Saracen raiders even reached Rome, where Pope Leo IV built a new wall to defend the Vatican.

The emperor holds a large gold paten, the dish in which the bread is placed for Mass.

Maximian, Archbishop of Ravenna

WHERE TO SEE EARLY CHRISTIAN AND BYZANTINE ITALY

Though the fall of the Roman Empire led to war, famine and depopulation, the continuity of the Christian religion has preserved many monuments of the late Empire and Byzantine period. Rome has the catacombs *(p432)* and great basilicas, such as Santa Maria Maggiore *(p403)*. In Ravenna, the administrative capital of the Byzantine Empire, are the churches of San Vitale and Sant'Apollinare *(pp260–61)* with their magnificent mosaics. Sicily and the south also preserve many Byzantine churches, while the finest example of late Byzantine architecture is San Marco in Venice *(pp106–9)*.

Stilo *in Calabria has a beautiful Byzantine church, the Cattolica* (p504)*, dating from the 10th century.*

Priests

THE COURT OF JUSTINIAN
Byzantine churches were decorated with glorious mosaics of coloured glass and gold leaf. This one from the apse of the church of San Vitale in Ravenna *(see p260)*, completed in 547, depicts members of the Imperial court.

Santa Costanza *in Rome* (p431) *was built in the 4th century as the mausoleum of Constantine's daughter. Late Roman mosaics decorate the vaults.*

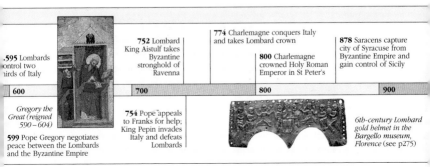

.595 Lombards control two thirds of Italy

Gregory the Great (reigned 590–604)

599 Pope Gregory negotiates peace between the Lombards and the Byzantine Empire

752 Lombard King Aistulf takes Byzantine stronghold of Ravenna

754 Pope appeals to Franks for help; King Pepin invades Italy and defeats Lombards

774 Charlemagne conquers Italy and takes Lombard crown

800 Charlemagne crowned Holy Roman Emperor in St Peter's

878 Saracens capture city of Syracuse from Byzantine Empire and gain control of Sicily

600	700	800	900

6th-century Lombard gold helmet in the Bargello museum, Florence (see p275)

The Rise of Venice

MEDIEVAL ITALY saw waves of foreign invaders joining in the struggle for power between popes and emperors. In the confusion, many northern cities asserted their independence from feudal overlords. The most powerful was Venice, governed by its doge and Great Council, which grew rich through trade with the East and by shipping Crusaders to fight the Saracens in the Holy Land. Its maritime rivals on the west coast were Genoa and Pisa.

Enrico Dandolo, Doge of Venice (c.1120–1205)

THE MEDITERRANEAN (1250)

— *Genoese trade routes*
— *Venetian trade routes*

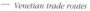

Matilda of Tuscany

Matilda, Countess of Tuscany (1046–1115) supported the radical Pope Gregory VII against the Emperor Henry IV. When she died, she left her lands to the church.

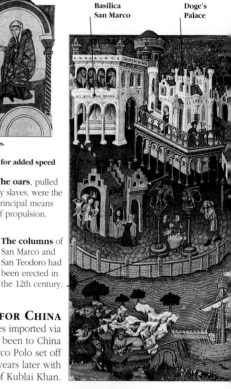

Basilica San Marco

Doge's Palace

Canopy over the half-deck

Sails – for added speed

The oars, pulled by slaves, were the principal means of propulsion.

The columns of San Marco and San Teodoro had been erected in the 12th century.

Venetian Galley

The galleys used by Venice, both as warships and for carrying cargo, were similar to ancient Greek vessels.

MARCO POLO'S DEPARTURE FOR CHINA

Venice traded in Chinese silks and spices imported via the Middle East, but no Venetian had been to China before Marco Polo's father Nicolò. Marco Polo set off with his father in 1271, returning 25 years later with fantastic tales of his time at the court of Kublai Khan.

TIMELINE

1000 Doge of Venice, Pietro Orseolo II, defeats Dalmatian pirates in Adriatic

11th century School of Law at Bologna develops into Europe's first university

Medieval students

1139 Naples incorporated into Kingdom of Sicily

1000	1050	1100

1030 Norman knight Rainulf granted county of Aversa by Duke of Naples

1061 Normans Robert Guiscard and Roger de Hauteville capture Messina from the Arabs

1063 San Marco in Venice rebuilt

1084 Normans sack Rome

1076 Salerno, last Lombard city, falls to Normans

1073–85 Pope Gregory VII reforms church and papacy

1130 Ro II crown king of Sicily

1115 Death of Countess Matilda

St Francis of Assisi
(1181–1226)
In The Dream of
Pope Innocent III
*by Giotto, painted
around 1290–1295,
St Francis holds up
the tottering edifice
of the Roman church.
The Franciscans' rule
of poverty brought
about a religious
revival in reaction
to the wealth of
the church.*

WHERE TO SEE EARLY MEDIEVAL ITALY

Of the many
churches built
in this period,
especially fine
examples are
Venice's San
Marco (p106),
Sant'Antonio
(p152) in Padua
and the Duomo
in Pisa (p314).
The Leaning
Tower (p316)
also dates back to the 12th century.
Medieval castles include Frederick II's
Castel del Monte in Puglia (p493)
and Castello dell'Imperatore in Prato.

*Castello dell'
Imperatore, Prato,
was built about 1240.*

**Monastery of
Sant'Apollonia**

**Today's Riva degli
Schiavoni**

Nicolò Polo, his brother Maffeo and
son Marco prepare to embark. They
sailed first to Acre in the Levant.

Fourth Crusade
*Discord between
the leaders of the
crusade and
Pope Innocent III
culminated in
the sacking of
Constantinople
in 1204.*

Frederick II
(1194–1250)
*The emperor kept a
court of poets and
scholars in Sicily. He
won Jerusalem from
the Arabs by diplomacy,
but was constantly at
war with the pope and
the cities of Lombardy.*

1198 Frederick II
becomes king of Sicily

1155 Frederick Barbarossa
crowned Holy Roman Emperor

1204 Sacking of Constantinople

1209 Franciscan Order founded

1216 Dominican
Order founded

1250 Death of Frederick II

1260 Urban IV invites Charles of
Anjou to rule Naples and Sicily

1265 Birth of Dante

50	1200	1250

*Frederick
Barbarossa dressed
as a Crusader*

1220 Frederick II
crowned Holy
Roman Emperor

1237 Lombard League defeat
Frederick at Battle of Cortenuova

1228 Gregory IX excommunicates
Frederick II; struggle between Guelphs
(the papal party) and Ghibellines
(supporters of the emperor)

1271 Marco
Polo sets off
on journey
to China

The Late Middle Ages

OLD FEUDS BETWEEN pope and emperor thrived throughout the 14th century, kept alive by two warring factions – the Guelphs, who backed the papacy, and the Ghibellines, who favoured Imperial power. The cities of Lombardy and Tuscany used the political confusion to grow in strength. It was against this turbulent backdrop that a great new age in painting was inspired by artists such as Duccio and Giotto. Also at this time the Florentine poets Dante and Petrarch laid the foundations of Italian literature.

Sienese bishop's staff

ITALY IN 1350

- ▨ *Papal States*
- ☐ *Holy Roman Empire*
- ▨ *Angevin Kingdom of Naples*

MEDIEVAL TOWN SQUARE

The campanile or bell tower

Throughout central Italy, the town square was an expression of civic pride and independence. Towns, such as Perugia (*see pp342–3*), tried to overshadow their rivals in the splendour of their town halls. The centre of Perugia has changed little since the 14th century when the town's main rival was Siena.

A griffin, symbol of Perugia

Condottieri

Cities paid condottieri, *leaders of bands of mercenaries, to fight their wars. Siena hired Guidoriccio da Fogliano, seen here in a fresco by Simone Martini (1330).*

The main chamber of the town hall, the Sala dei Notari, is decorated with the coats of arms of Perugia's mayors.

The Fontana Maggiore was begun in 1275 and includes panels by Nicola Pisano. Prominently placed, it is an emblem of the town's wealth.

Dante's Inferno

One of the harshest punishments in Dante's vision of hell is reserved for corrupt popes, such as Boniface VIII (reigned 1294–1303), who are placed upside down in fiery pits.

TIMELINE

1282 Sicilian Vespers; uprising against French rule in Palermo; 2,000 French soldiers killed

1296 Work begins on the Duomo in Florence

1298 Marco Polo returns from China to Venice

1309–43 Reign of Robert the Wise of Naples

1310 Work begins on Palazzo Ducale in Venice

1313 Birth of Boccaccio

1275   **1300**   **1325**

1282 Peter of Aragon lands at Trapani, conquers Sicily and is crowned king in Palermo

The poet and scholar Petrarch

1304 Birth of Petrarch

1309 Clement V moves papacy to Avignon

1321 Dante completes *La Divina Commedia* and dies the same year

1337 Death of Giotto

The Black Death
Bubonic plague reached Italy in 1347, carried on Genoese ships from the Black Sea. It killed over a third of the population, reducing the remainder to a state of superstitious terror.

WHERE TO SEE LATE MEDIEVAL ITALY

Many central Italian cities and towns have public buildings from the 13th and 14th centuries; among the most impressive are Palazzo Vecchio (*p283*) in Florence and Siena's Palazzo Pubblico (*p330*). Smaller towns that preserve much of their medieval character include Volterra (*p324*) and the walled Monteriggioni (*p324*) in Tuscany, Gubbio (*p342*) and Todi (*p349*) in Umbria and Viterbo (*pp448–9*) in Lazio. The Duomo in Orvieto (*pp348–9*) is a fine example of a late 13th-century Gothic cathedral.

Piazza dei Priori in Volterra (p324) *is one of the most beautiful medieval squares in Italy.*

The cathedral was started in 1350 and used to include an outside pulpit in the square.

Construction of Alessandria
Almost all towns were ringed with strong walls. This fresco (1407) by Spinello Aretino is a valuable record of medieval building techniques.

Return of Pope Gregory XI to Rome (1378)
For 70 years the popes had lived in Avignon, protected by the French kings, while nobles and republicans fought for control of Rome.

1339 Simon Boccanegra becomes first doge of Genoa; Giovanna I Queen of Naples

Medieval doctor

1378–1415 Period of Schism, with rival popes and antipopes in Rome and Avignon

1347–9 Black Death

1380 Genoese fleet surrenders to Venetians at Chioggia

1350

1375

1400

1354 Cola di Rienzo killed in Rome

1385 Gian Galeazzo Visconti becomes ruler of Milan

1406 Pisa annexed by Florence

1347 Cola di Rienzo tries to re-establish Roman Republic

1378 Gregory XI returns from Avignon to Rome

The Renaissance

Leonardo da Vinci (1452 – 1519)

Fifteenth-century Italy saw a flowering of the arts and scholarship unmatched in Europe since the days of Greece and Rome. Architects turned from the Gothic to Classical models for inspiration, while painting, with its new understanding of perspective and anatomy, produced a generation of artists that included such giants as Leonardo da Vinci, Raphael and Michelangelo. The patronage for this cultural "rebirth" came from the wealthy families that ruled the city states of the north, led by the Medici of Florence. In spite of intense rivalry, they oversaw a period of uneasy stability out of which the Renaissance grew.

ITALY IN 1492

▨	*Republic of Florence*
☐	*Papal States*
▨	*Aragonese possessions*

Galeazzo Maria Sforza was the son of Milan's ruler.

Piero de' Medici, Lorenzo's father, was given the nickname "the Gouty".

Handing over the Keys of St Peter
Perugino's fresco in the Sistine Chapel (see p416) links the authority of the pope to the New Testament and, through the Classical buildings in the background, to ancient Rome.

Self-portrait of the artist

Execution of Savonarola *(1498)*
Having assumed the leadership of Florence in 1494, the fanatical monk was hanged, then burned for heresy in Piazza della Signoria.

TIMELINE

1420 Martin V re-establishes papacy in Rome	**1435** Publication of *On Painting* by Alberti, which contains the first system for the use of linear perspective	**1436** Brunelleschi completes dome of Florence cathedral

1458–64 War between Houses of Aragon and Anjou over Kingdom of Naples

1469 Lorenzo the Magnificent becomes ruler of Florence

1425

1450

1434 Cosimo de' Medici comes to power in Florence

1442 Naples captured by Alfonso of Aragon

1452 Birth of Leonardo da Vinci

Cosimo de' Medici

1444 Federico da Montefeltro becomes Duke of Urbino

1453 Fall of Constantinople

Filippo Brunelleschi

The Battle of Pavia (1525)
The French King Francis I was captured at this battle against the army of the Habsburg Emperor Charles V, who won control of Italy.

THE PROCESSION OF THE MAGI

Benozzo Gozzoli's fresco (1459) in the Palazzo Medici-Riccardi, Florence, depicts members of the Medici family and other contemporary notables. It contains many references to a great church council held in Florence in 1439.

WHERE TO SEE RENAISSANCE ITALY

Many cities were flourishing centres of the arts in the 15th century. None can rival Florence *(pp262–303)* with its great palazzi and the Uffizi gallery *(pp278–81)*, but Venice *(pp80–131)*, Urbino *(pp360–61)* and Mantova *(p199)* all preserve great treasures. In Rome, do not miss the Vatican's Sistine Chapel and Raphael Rooms *(pp414–17)*.

*The **Spedale degli Innocenti** by Brunelleschi in Florence (p269) shows the Classical symmetry and restraint of Renaissance architecture.*

Humanism
Carpaccio's painting of St Augustine is thought to show Cardinal Bessarion (c.1395–1472), one of the scholars who revived interest in Classical philosophy, especially Plato.

Lorenzo de' Medici (the Magnificent) was depicted as one of the three kings travelling to Bethlehem.

Pope Julius II
During his reign (1503–13), the worldly Julius made the papacy a major power in European politics. Raphael's portrait shows him as a shrewd old statesman.

1483 Sixtus IV consecrates Sistine Chapel

1487 Birth of Titian

1494 Italy invaded by Charles VIII of France

1503 Giuliano della Rovere elected Pope Julius II; he proves the most powerful of the Renaissance popes

Niccolò Machiavelli

1527 Rome sacked by Imperial troops

1475

1500

1475 Birth of Michelangelo

Raphael

1483 Birth of Raphael

1498 Savonarola executed; Machiavelli secretary to ruling Council in Florence

1512 Michelangelo completes Sistine Chapel ceiling

1513 Giovanni de' Medici crowned Pope Leo X

1525 Francis I of France captured at Battle of Pavia

1532 Machiavelli's book *The Prince* is published, five years after his death

The Counter-Reformation

Gian Lorenzo Bernini

AFTER THE SACK OF ROME in 1527, Italy was at the mercy of Charles V, Holy Roman Emperor and King of Spain. Pope Clement VII, who had opposed Charles, crowned him emperor in Bologna. In response to the growing threat from Protestantism, a series of reforms, known as the Counter-Reformation and backed by the Inquisition, imposed rigid orthodoxy. New religious orders, such as the Jesuits, were set up to take the battle for men's souls far overseas. The missionary spirit of the age inspired the dramatic forms of the Baroque.

ITALY IN 1550

▨ Spanish possessions
☐ States allied with Spain

Emperor Charles V and Pope Clement VII
The two former enemies settled their differences and the future destiny of Italy in the Treaty of Barcelona (1529).

The Virgin Mary intervenes on the side of the Christians.

BAROQUE STUCCO DECORATION

This stucco relief by Giacomo Serpotta (c.1690) in the Oratory of Santa Zita in Palermo is a magnificent example of Late Baroque exuberance. The subject is a favourite of the period, the Battle of Lepanto, a great naval triumph for the combined forces of Christendom against the Turks (1571).

The centre of the ingenious creation is, in effect, a framed painting in perspective.

Baroque Architecture
Guarino Guarini's decoration of the dome of the Chapel of the Holy Shroud in Turin (see p213) was completed in 1694.

The young boy rests his hand on a helmet, symbol of the victorious Christians.

TIMELINE

1530–37 Alessandro de' Medici ruler of Florence	**1542** Inquisition established in Rome	*Andrea Palladio*	**1580** Death of architect Palladio
	1545–63 Council of Trent sets out agenda of Counter-Reformation		**1589** Palestrina publishes setting of the Latin Hymnal
			1600 Philosopher Giordano Bruno burne for heresy in Rome

1550	**1575**

1540 Founding of Jesuit Order	**1541** Michelangelo completes *Last Judgment* in Sistine Chapel	**1571** Victory over Turkish fleet at Battle of Lepanto	
		1564 Birth of Galileo	
1529 Charles V crowned Holy Roman Emperor in San Petronio, Bologna	**1560** San Carlo Borromeo appointed Bishop of Milan		*Giovanni Pierluigi da Palestrina*

Trial of Galileo
The great astronomer was often in trouble with the Inquisition. He was summoned to Rome in 1633 and forced to deny that the Earth and planets moved round the sun.

Lepanto was the last major sea battle in which Venetian galleys played an important role.

Cherubs, a favourite motif in Baroque decoration

St Ignatius Loyola
The Spanish saint was the founder of the Jesuits – sanctioned by the pope in Rome in 1540.

The turban, symbol of the defeated Turks

Revolt of Masaniello *(1647) High taxes made Spanish rule in Naples unpopular. A proposed tax on fruit sparked off this failed revolt.*

WHERE TO SEE BAROQUE ITALY

The Ecstasy of St Teresa *by Bernini (p402) has the dynamic theatricality characteristic of the best Baroque sculpture.*

The Baroque is strongly associated with Rome and in particular with its great public spaces such as Piazza Navona *(pp388–9)* and the many churches by Borromini and Bernini. Other cities and towns with striking Baroque architecture include Lecce *(pp496–7)* in Puglia, Palermo *(pp510–13)*, Noto *(p527)* and Syracuse *(pp526–7)* in Sicily, and Turin *(pp212–17)*.

1626 New St Peter's consecrated in Rome

1631 Duchy of Urbino absorbed by Papal States

1669 Venice loses island of Crete to the Turks

1694 Andrea Pozzo completes ceiling fresco for the church of Sant'Ignazio in Rome

1678 Birth of Vivaldi

1625	1650	1675

1633 Galileo condemned by papal authorities

1642 *L'Incoronazione di Poppea* by Monteverdi

1647 Revolt in Naples in response to tax on fruit

1669 Major eruption of Mount Etna

1693 Eastern Sicily ruined by earthquake that kills 5 per cent of the island's population

1674 Revolt against Spanish rule in Messina

The Grand Tour

The Romantic poet Shelley, visitor to Italy

THE TREATY of Aix-la-Chapelle in 1748 marked the start of 50 years of peace. It was about this time that Italy, with its great art treasures and Classical ruins, including the newly excavated Pompeii, became Europe's first great tourist destination. Young English "milords" visited Rome, Florence and Venice as part of a new type of pilgrimage, the Grand Tour; while artists and poets sought inspiration in Rome's glorious past. In 1800, Napoleon, who conquered and briefly united Italy, threatened to destroy the old order, but in 1815 the status quo was restored.

Charles III's Fleet at Naples *(1753)*
Ruler of Naples from 1734 to 1759, when he became King of Spain, Charles attempted genuine political reforms.

Goethe in the Roman Campagna
Goethe toured Italy in the 1780s. Great poets who followed his example included the Romantics Keats, Shelley and Byron.

Farnese Hercules
(see p475)

Venetian Carnival
The colourful folklore of Carnival attracted many tourists, but Venice's days of greatness were over. In 1797, the proud maritime republic was ceded to Austria by Napoleon.

The Dying Galatian
(see p376)

GALLERY OF VIEWS OF ANCIENT ROME BY PANNINI

Giovanni Pannini (1691–1765) painted views of Roman ruins for foreigners. This painting is a capriccio, an imaginary scene incorporating many well-known views and Classical statues.

TIMELINE

1713 Treaty of Utrecht gives Naples and Sardinia to Austria and Sicily to Piedmont

Medici coat of arms

1725 *The Four Seasons* by Vivaldi

1735 Peace of Vienna confirms Charles III as King of the Two Sicilies (Naples and Sicily)

1748 First excavations at Pompeii

1700	1720	1740

1707 Birth of playwright Carlo Goldoni

1718 Piedmont and Sardinia united under House of Savoy; Sicily passes to Austria

1737 End of Medici dynasty in Florence; Grand Duchy of Tuscany passes to Austrian House of Lorraine

Antonio Vivaldi, great Venetian composer

View of the Roman Forum by Piranesi
The popular series of etchings Vedute di
Roma *(Views of Rome) by Giovanni Battista
Piranesi (1720–78) inspired a new interest
in excavating the ruins of ancient Rome.*

The Colosseum was as popular
a subject in the 18th century as
it is on today's picture
postcards.

The Laocoön
(see p407)

View of the Pantheon
(see p394)

WHERE TO SEE 18TH-CENTURY ITALY

The 18th century produced two of Rome's
best-loved tourist attractions: the Spanish
Steps *(p399)* and the Trevi Fountain *(p400)*.
It was also the age of the first purpose-built
museums, including the Vatican's Museo
Pio-Clementino *(p411)*. The Neo-Classical
sculpture of Antonio Canova (1757–1822)
was immensely popular during this period.
His tomb is in Santa Maria Gloriosa dei Frari
in Venice *(pp94–5)*. Of Neo-
Classical buildings, the most
imposing is a vast monument
to enlightened despotism:
the Palazzo Reale at
Caserta *(p480)*.

Pauline Borghese, *Napoleon's sister, was the
model for Antonio Canova's* Venus *(1805) in
the Villa Borghese collection in Rome (p429).*

Napoleon
*When Napoleon
conquered Italy
in 1800, he was seen
by many as a
liberator. The
enchantment
wore off as he
took priceless
works of art
back to Paris.*

Congress of Vienna *(1815)*
*The conference decided that Austria should
keep Lombardy and Venice, thereby sowing
the seeds of the Italian unification movement.*

	La Scala Opera House, Milan (see p187)	**1797** Venice given to Austria by Treaty of Campo Formio; France controls rest of northern Italy	**1800–1801** Napoleon conquers Italy	
			1808 Murat becomes King of Naples	**1809** Pope Pius VII exiled from Rome
	1778 La Scala opened in Milan			

1760	**1780**		**1800**	
	1773 Pope dissolves Jesuit Order	**1780** Joseph II succeeds to Austrian throne; minor reforms in Lombardy	**1806** Joseph Bonaparte King of Naples	
1768 Corsica sold by Genoa to France		**1796–7** Napoleon's first campaign in northern Italy	**1815** Congress of Vienna restores status quo in Italy, though Austria keeps Venice	
1765–90 Reign of Leopold Grand Duke of Tuscany, who introduces enlightened reforms				

The Risorgimento

THE WORD "RISORGIMENTO" (resurgence) describes the five decades of struggle for liberation from foreign rule, culminating in the unification of Italy in 1870. In 1848, patriots rose up against the Austrians in Milan and Venice, the Bourbons in Sicily and the pope in Rome, where a republic was declared. Garibaldi valiantly defended the republic, but all the uprisings were too localized. By 1859, the movement was better organized with Vittorio Emanuele II at its head. Two years saw the conquest of all but Venice and Rome, both of which fell within a decade.

Vittorio Emanuele

ITALY IN 1861

▨ *Kingdom of Italy*

The guns were rusty, old converted flintlocks.

Giuseppe Mazzini
(1805–72)
An exile for much of his life, Mazzini fought alongside Garibaldi to unite Italy as a republic, rather than a kingdom.

The red shirt was the badge of the Garibaldini.

Italian Railways
The short railway line from Naples to Portici was opened in 1839. Politically fragmented, Italy was slow to create an effective rail network.

Revolt of Messina
When, in 1848, Messina revolted, Ferdinand II subjected the town to a savage bombardment, earning himself the nickname King Bomba.

TIMELINE

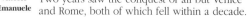

1831 Insurrection in Romagna and Le Marche against papal rule

1840 First major railway links established

1849 Accession of Vittorio Emanuele II as ruler of Piedmont

| 1820 | 1830 | 1840 | 1850 |

1820s Carbonari secret society active in Papal States

1831 Mazzini founds *Giovine Italia* (Young Italy) movement

Daniele Manin, hero of the Venetian uprising of 1848

1847 Economic crisis

1848 Revolutions throughout Italy

1849 Republic of Rome crushed by French troo[...]

1852 Cavour becomes pri[...] minister of Piedmont

Battle of Solferino *(1859)*
With the help of a French army led by Napoleon III, the Piedmontese won Milan and Lombardy from the Austrians.

WHERE TO SEE RISORGIMENTO ITALY

Almost every town in Italy honours the heroes of the Risorgimento with a Via Garibaldi, a Via Cavour, a Piazza Vittorio, a Via Mazzini and a Via XX Settembre (the date of the fall of Rome in 1870). Many cities also have Risorgimento museums. One of the best is in Turin *(p215)*.

The Victor Emmanuel Monument (p374) *is a prominent, but largely unloved, Roman landmark.*

Two old paddle steamers brought the Thousand from Quarto near Genoa.

Count Camillo di Cavour *(1810 – 61)*
Cavour's diplomacy as prime minister of Piedmont ensured that the House of Savoy became rulers of the new Italy. He also coined the word "Risorgimento".

The skiffs were lent by other ships moored in Marsala harbour.

Giuseppe Verdi
(1813–1901)
Composers such as Verdi, Donizetti and Rossini made the 19th century the great era of Italian opera. Verdi's early operas inspired the Risorgimento.

GARIBALDI AND THE THOUSAND

Giuseppe Garibaldi (1807–82) was a leader of courage and genius. In 1860, he landed at Marsala with 1,000 volunteers. The garrison at Palermo surrendered, Sicily fell and he went on to conquer Naples, thus presenting Vittorio Emanuele with half a kingdom.

1859 Battles of Magenta and Solferino; Piedmont acquires Lombardy from Austria and duchies of Parma, Modena and Tuscany

1861 Kingdom of Italy proclaimed with capital at Turin

Pope Pius IX, who remained a virtual prisoner in the Vatican when Rome became capital of Italy

1882 Deaths of Garibaldi and Pope Pius IX

1893 Troops sent to suppress insurrection in Sicily

1860	**1870**	**1880**	**1890**

1866 Italy wins Venice from Austria

1878 Death of Vittorio Emanuele; accession of King Umberto I

1870 Rome falls to royalist troops and is made capital of new kingdom; Vatican announces doctrine of papal infallibility

1890 Italian colony of Eritrea established by royal decree

1860 Garibaldi and the Thousand capture Kingdom of the Two Sicilies

Modern Italy

Fascism under Mussolini (1922–43) promised the Italians greatness, but delivered only humiliation. In spite of this, Italy has become one of Europe's leading economies with a standard of living undreamt of at the turn of the century. This has been achieved in the face of great obstacles. Since 1946, the Republic has passed through many crises: a series of unstable coalitions, the terrorist outrages in the 1970s and, in the 1990s, corruption scandals involving numerous government ministers and officials.

1936 Fiat produces first "Topolino" car

1922 Fascists march on Rome; Mussolini invited to form government

1918 Austrian advance halted at the river Piave, just north of Venice

1940 Italy enters World War II

1943 Allies land in Sicily; Italy signs armistice and new Badoglio government declares war on Germany

1900 Assassination of King Umberto I

1915 Italy enters World War I

1911–12 Italy conquers Libya

| 1900 | 1920 | 1940 |

| 1900 | 1920 | 1940 |

1908 Earthquake destroys many towns and villages in Calabria and eastern Sicily; Messina almost completely razed to the ground; over 150,000 die

1936 Italy conquers Abyssinia; pact with Germany, forming anti-Communist "Axis"

1920s Postwar years see continued emigration to the United States. Here, emigrants cheer as they reach New York aboard the *Giulio Cesare*

1943 Mussolini imprisoned, then freed by Germans

1946 Referendum in which Italy votes to become a republic; Christian Democrat party forms first of a long series of coalition governments

1917 Defeat at Caporetto on Italy's northeastern border; Italian troops, such as these Alpini, retreat to defensive positions

1909 In his *Futurist Manifesto*, Filippo Marinetti condemns all traditional art as too static. His idea of a new dynamic art is expressed in works such as Umberto Boccioni's bronze *Unique Forms of Continuity in Space*

1978 Prime Minister Aldo Moro kidnapped and assassinated by the Red Brigades

1996 Fire destroys La Fenice theatre in Venice

1994 TV magnate Silvio Berlusconi becomes prime minister after forming political party "Forza Italia". Alleged financial irregularities force him to resign later that year

1996 Earthquake in Assisi seriously damages the Basilica di San Francesco, destroying Giotto's frescoes

2000 Rome enters the 21st century with millions of pilgrims celebrating the Holy Year known as the Jubilee

1960 *La Dolce Vita*, Federico Fellini's film satire on Rome's decadent café society, is released

1992 Judge Giovanni Falcone killed by Mafia in Sicily

1992 Scandals expose widespread corruption in the postwar political system

2002 Goodbye to the lira as the euro is adopted

1966 River Arno bursts its banks, flooding Florence and damaging many priceless works of art

1990 World Cup staged in Italy

| 1960 | 1980 | 2000 |

| 1960 | 1980 | 2000 |

1960 Olympic Games held in Rome

1978 Election of Pope John Paul II

1983 Bettino Craxi, Italy's first Socialist prime minister, forms government

1969 Bomb outrage in Milan at Piazza Fontana; 13 killed and many injured

1982 Italian football team wins World Cup in Spain

2001 Silvio Berlusconi is voted back into power

1997 Dario Fo wins the Nobel prize for literature

1999 Roberto Benigni wins 3 Oscars for his film *La Vita è Bella*, including best actor and best foreign language film

1957 Treaty of Rome; Italy one of the six founder members of the European Economic Community

ITALIAN CINEMA SINCE WORLD WAR II

The social problems of late 1940s Italy inspired a wave of cinema known as Neo-Realism. Leading exponents included Roberto Rossellini, who made *Roma Città Aperta* (1945), Vittorio de Sica, the director of *Bicycle Thieves* (1948), Pier Paolo Pasolini and Luchino Visconti. Since that time, the major Italian directors have cultivated their own personal styles.

Vittorio de Sica (1901–74)

Visconti's later films, such as *Death in Venice* (1971), show formal beauty and decadence, while Federico Fellini's *La Dolce Vita* (1960) and *Roma* (1972) depict life as a grotesque carnival. Italy has also produced some commercially successful films, such as Sergio Leone's late 1960s westerns and the Oscar-winning *Cinema Paradiso* and *La Vita è Bella*.

ITALY THROUGH THE YEAR

HROUGHOUT ITALY, the variety of local character and colour is astonishing. This is mainly due to the survival of regionalism, particularly in the southern parts of the country. Old traditions, customs and lifestyles are still greatly respected and there is a deep attachment to the land, which is reflected in a healthy interest in the food and produce, as well as a perseverance of seasonal religious and secular events. Annual festivals, whether in rural or urban areas, range from wine-tasting and gastronomic celebrations to elaborate commemorations of every patron saint imaginable.

SPRING

THE ITALIAN SPRING begins early, particularly in the south. City streets and main sights are rarely overcrowded (except at Easter in Rome). The weather, however, can be unpredictable and wet in the central and northern parts of the country. Spring specialities, such as asparagus, spinach and artichokes, begin to feature on restaurant menus. This is a season of great celebration; festivals and fairs abound, especially in Sicily, and the Easter papal address always draws massive crowds to St Peter's.

Tuscan asparagus

MARCH

Mostra Vini Spumanti, *(mid-Mar)*, Madonna di Campiglio, Trentino-Alto Adige. Fair celebrating sparkling wine.
Sa Sartiglia, Oristano, Sardinia. Three-day carnival ending on Shrove Tuesday.

Procession of the Grieving Madonna on the isle of Procida

Su e zo per i ponti *(Sun, varies)*, Venice. A lively race through the city's streets, up and down the bridges.

APRIL

Procession of the Grieving Madonna *(Good Friday)*, Procida, Campania. A colourful religious procession throughout the island.
Holy Week *(Easter Week)*. Numerous Easter celebrations from Palm Sunday to Easter Sunday, throughout the country.
Papal Address *(Easter Sunday)*, Rome. The pope makes his Easter address from the Vatican.
Dance of the Devils and Death *(Easter Sunday)*, Prizzi, Sicily. Dance recital symbolizing the attempts of evil to vanquish the forces of God.
Scoppio del Carro *(Easter Sunday)*, Florence. Firework display is lit by a mechanical dove in front of the Duomo.
Festa della Madonna che Scappa in Piazza *(Easter Sunday)*, Sulmona, Abruzzo. Re-enactment of a meeting between the Virgin and the Risen Christ.
Festa degli Aquiloni *(first Sun after Easter)*, San Miniato, Tuscany. Kite lovers perform aerial acrobatics at this festival.
Festa di San Marco *(25 Apr)*, Venice. St Mark, the patron saint of Venice, is commemorated by a gondola race across St Mark's Basin.
Mostra Mercato Internazionale dell'Artigianato *(last week)*, Florence. An important European exhibition of arts and crafts.

Scoppio del Carro (Explosion of the Carriage) festival in Florence

Sagra Musicale Lucchese *(Apr–Jul)*, Lucca, Tuscany. Festival of sacred music held in Romanesque churches.

MAY

Festa di Sant'Efisio *(1 May)*, Cagliari, Sardinia. Paraders in traditional Sardinian costume.
Festa di San Nicola *(7–9 May)*, Bari, Puglia. A statue of St Nicholas is taken to the sea.
Festa dei Ceri *(15 May)*, Gubbio, Umbria. Festival, including a race with four teams carrying large candles.
Festa di San Domenico Abate *(first Thu)*, Cocullo, Abruzzo. Includes a procession with a statue of St Dominic covered with live snakes.

Spring strawberries

Festa della Mela *(late May)*, Ora (Auer), Trentino-Alto Adige. An annual "Festival of the Apple".
Greek Drama in Theatre *(May–Jun)*, Syracuse, Sicily. Festival of Greek drama.
Maggio Musicale *(May–Jun)*, Florence. This is the city's biggest arts festival, including music, drama and dance.

Street carpeted with flowers for the Infiorata in Genzano

SUMMER

SUMMER brings the crowds to Italy, particularly the cities. Italians, however, flee and head for the coast, usually in August. The queues for tourist attractions can be long and hotels are often fully booked. Festivals vary; religious events are interspersed with those of the arts and local folklore.

JUNE

Festa della Fragola *(1 Jun)*, Borgo San Martino, Piedmont. Musical and folkloric performances in celebration of the strawberry.
Biennale *(Jun – Sep)*, Venice. The world's biggest exhibition of contemporary art takes place during odd-numbered years only.
Infiorata *(Corpus Christi day)*, Genzano, Lazio. A procession through streets carpeted with flowers.
Festa di San Giovanni *(mid-Jun – mid-Jul)*, Turin, Piedmont. Festival in honour of the city's patron saint, John.
Calcio Storico *(24 Jun and two other days in Jun)*, Florence. Football in 16th-century costumes; fireworks.
Festa di Sant'Andrea *(27 Jun)*, Amalfi, Campania.

Fireworks and processions.
Festival dei Due Mondi *(late Jun – early Jul)*, Spoleto, Umbria. International festival of drama, music and dance.
Gioco del Ponte *(last Sun)*, Pisa. "The Bridge Parade" of marchers in antique armour.
Estate Romana *(late Jun – mid-Sep)*, Rome. Open-air cinema, performances, ballet and concerts.

JULY

Corsa del Palio *(2 Jul)*, Siena. Tuscany's most famous event *(see p331)* presents a medieval flag-waving exhibition and horse race.
Festa della Madonna della Bruna *(first Sun)*, Matera, Basilicata. A lively procession of clergymen and knights in costume.

Musician from Florence's Calcio

Festa dei Noiantri *(last two weeks of Jul)*, Rome. A colourful festival in the streets of Trastevere.
Festa della Santa Maria del Carmine *(16 Jul)*, Naples. Featuring the illumination of the city's bell tower.
Umbria Jazz *(Jul)*, Perugia. World-famous jazz artists perform.
International Film Festival *(Jul – Aug)*, Taormina, Sicily.

The Sienese Palio in action

Opera Festival *(Jul – Aug)*, Verona, Veneto. Renowned opera festival *(see p137)* overlapping with the **Shakespeare Festival**, providing music, drama, opera and dance.

AUGUST

Medieval Palio *(first weekend Aug)* Feltre, Veneto. Parades and archery competitions, medieval-style.
Festa del Mare *(15 Aug)*, Diano Marina, Liguria. This "Festival of the Sea" boasts a spectacular firework display.
Festa dei Candelieri *(14 Aug)*, Sassari, Sardinia. "Festival of the Candle", dating from the 16th century.
Corsa del Palio *(16 Aug)*, Siena, Tuscany. See July entry.
Venice Film Festival *(late Aug – early Sep)*. International festival on the Lido.
Rossini Festival *(Aug – Sep)*, Pesaro, Le Marche. A celebration of the composer's work, in his birthplace.
Settimane Musicali di Stresa *(late Aug – end Sep)*, Stresa, Lombardy. Four weeks of concerts and recitals.

Sun, sand and sea – essential ingredients of a Tuscan beach holiday

AUTUMN

AUTUMN IS A SLOW, gentle season in Italy but that doesn't mean there are fewer festivals and fairs. In addition to the various religious events at this time of year, gastronomic festivals are especially popular, commemorating such delectables as chestnuts, local cheeses, sausages and mushrooms. Autumn is the season of the *vendemmia*, the grape harvest, which is often used as an excuse for village festivities at which the latest local wines flow freely.

The climate *(see pp68–9)* in late autumn is often cold and wet in the north. The south, however, can be quite warm right through October.

Advertisement for the September Palio in Asti, Piedmont

SEPTEMBER

Sagra dell'Uva *(early Sep)*, Rome. Harvest festival with grapes at bargain prices and lots of folk entertainment.
Neapolitan Song Contest *(7 Sep)*, Piazza di Piedigrotta, Naples. Usually entered by couples; the singer often plays a mandolin, while their partner plays the castanets.
Festa di San Sebastiano e Santa Lucia *(1–3 Sep)*, Sassari, Sardinia. Includes a contest where competitors improvise short poems.
Procession of the Macchina di Santa Rosa *(3 Sep)*, Viterbo, Lazio. Commemoration of the saint's body being transported to the Church of Santa Rosa in 1258.

The widely cultivated olive tree

Giostra del Saracino *(first Sun)*, Arezzo, Umbria. Joust of the Saracen and knights, dating from the 13th century.
Regata Storica *(first Sun)*, Venice. A procession of historic boats followed by a colourful gondola race.
Human chess game *(second week)*, Marostica, near Vicenza. A popular costumed game held in the main square every even year.
Rassegna del Chianti Classico *(second week)*, Chianti, Tuscany. Celebration of the local wines.
The Miracle of San Gennaro *(19 Sep)*, Naples. Re-enactment of the liquefaction of the saint's blood, in a lively mass at the Duomo.
Palio *(third Sun)*, Asti, Piedmont. Includes a costumed medieval procession and bareback horse racing.

OCTOBER

Amici della Musica *(Oct–Apr)*, Florence, Tuscany. The "Friends of Music" concert season begins.
Fiera del Tartufo *(first Sun)*, Alba, Piedmont. A variety of

events centred around the locally grown white truffle.
Festa di San Francesco *(4 Oct)*, Assisi, Umbria. Feast in honour of the saint.
Wine festivals *(first week)*, Castelli Romani, Lazio.
Sagra del Tordo *(last Sun)* Montalcino, Tuscany. Celebration of the thrush; costumed archery contests.
Festa dell'Uva *(dates vary)*, Bolzano, Trentino-Alto Adige. Grape festival with live music and a costumed procession featuring allegoric carts.

A roast chestnut stall in autumn

NOVEMBER

Festa dei Popoli *(Nov–Dec)*, Florence, Tuscany. Film festival showing films in their original languages with Italian sub-titles.
Festa della Salute *(21 Nov)*, Venice. Cherished by Venetian locals, this feast gives thanks to the Virgin Mary in memory of a 1630 plague.

The human chess game in the town square of Marostica

WINTER

THERE ARE FAIRS, markets and religious events up and down the country at this time of year. Neapolitan Christmas cribs are famous and nearly every church has one. The Christmas holiday itself is low key; more is made of other religious events such as the liquefaction of San Gennaro's blood in Naples and the Carnevale in Venice.

DECEMBER

Festa di Sant'Ambrogio *(early Dec)*, Milan. The official opening of La Scala Opera season *(see p187)*.
Festa della Madonna di Loreto *(10 Dec)*, Loreto, Le Marche. Celebration of the Virgin's Holy House.
Mercato della Befana *(mid-Dec – 6 Jan)*, Rome. Well-known Christmas fair held in Piazza Navona.
The Miracle of San Gennaro *(19 Dec)*, Naples. See September.
Christmas fair *(mid-Dec)*, Naples. Fair selling crib figures and decorations.
Fiaccole di Natale *(Christmas Eve)*, Abbadia di San Salvatore, Tuscany. Features carols and processions in memory of the first shepherds.
Midnight Mass *(24 Dec)*, at churches all over the country.
Christmas Day *(25 Dec)*, St Peter's Square, Rome. Public blessing by the pope.

Carnevale, Viareggio

Rome during one of its rare snowfalls

and volleys from hunters firing into the air to scare off ghosts and spirits of the old year and welcome in the new.
La Befana *(6 Jan)*, throughout Italy. Children's holiday with presents and sweets.
Pitti Immagine Uomo, Pitti Immagine Donna, Pitti Immagine Bimbo, Fortezza da Basso, Florence. Month of international fashion shows for women, men and children.
Festa di San Sebastiano *(20 Jan)*, Dolceacqua, Liguria. A laurel tree covered with colourful communion hosts is carried through town.
Festa d'o' Cippo di Sant'-Antonio *(17 Jan)*, Naples. A procession for St Anthony, protector of animals.
Carnevale *(a month-long event finishing Shrove Tue)*, Viareggio, Tuscany. A carnival famous for its lively, topically themed floats.
Fair of St Orsa *(30 – 31 Jan)*, Aosta, Valle d'Aosta. Exhibition of traditional arts and crafts.

FEBRUARY

Carnevale *(last ten days before Lent, finishing Shrove Tuesday)*, Venice. Pre-Lent festival meaning "farewell to meat". Events are

La Befana at Piazza Navona, Rome

JANUARY

Capodanno *(1 Jan)*, all over the country. New Year's Day is celebrated with fireworks

PUBLIC HOLIDAYS

New Year's Day (1 Jan)
Epiphany (6 Jan)
Easter Sunday and Monday
Liberation Day (25 Apr)
Labour Day (1 May)
Ferragosto (15 Aug)
All Saints' Day (1 Nov)
Immaculate Conception (8 Dec)
Christmas Day (25 Dec)
Santo Stefano (26 Dec)

organized, but anyone can buy a mask and watch the array of gorgeous costumes on show.
Sagra delle Mandorle in Fiore *(first or second week)*, Agrigento, Sicily. Annual almond blossom celebration.
Bacanal del Gnoco *(11 Feb)*, Verona. Traditional masked procession with both international and local allegorical floats. Masked balls are held in the town's squares.
Carnevale *(dates vary)*, Mamoiada, Sardinia. Processions include *mamuthones* wearing sinister black masks.

Carnevale revellers in Venice

The Sporting Year

Football is by far the most important sport in Italy, uniting the country when the national team *(Azzurri)* plays. Other sports throughout the year also attract a large following, so fans are never at a loss for varied activities. For most big sporting events, tickets can be obtained for cash at club outlets such as the venue itself. Agencies provide hard-to-get tickets at often higher prices. Beware of the inevitable touts at popular events as their expensive tickets may not be valid.

World Cup mania

Calcio Fiorentino, one of Italy's few indigenous sports, is said to be the medieval precursor of modern football.

The professional water polo season takes place from March through to July. The Canottieri Napoli team play consistently well through the championship.

Coppa Italia football final

Memorial d'Aloia rowing competition, held in Umbria

Italian Tennis Open, Rome

The Giro d'Italia cycling race takes place over many stages. Mario Cipollini has won a record number of stages.

January	February	March	April	May	June

Indoor Athletics Championships

Rome Marathon

Rugby is becoming increasingly popular. Italy takes part in the Six Nations Championship in February and March, along with England, Scotland, Wales, Ireland and France.

International Showjumping, Rome

The Italian leg of the Circuito Mondiale in Mugello. Luca Cadalora was champion in 1991.

Although the San Marino Grand Prix is not technically an Italian motor race, it is held each May at Imola, near the home of Ferrari (see p252).

The Italian Outdoor Swimming Championships
are held each year in July. Top swimmer Giorgio
Amberti and his team mates, pictured above,
celebrate a relay team victory.

Italy has some of the best ski resorts
in Europe, and in 2006 Turin will host
the Winter Olympics. Above is Alberto
Tomba, winner of the 94–95 Cup.

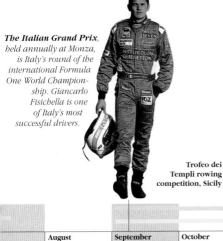

The Italian Grand Prix,
held annually at Monza,
is Italy's round of the
international Formula
One World Champion-
ship. Giancarlo
Fisichella is one
of Italy's most
successful drivers.

Trofeo dei
Templi rowing
competition, Sicily

The San Remo Car Rally, held
each year in October, was made
famous by driver Micky Biason
and the Lancia Delta Integrale.

August	September	October	November	December

Roberto Baggio, below right, in
action at the 1994 World Cup

ena Palio
(see p331),
eld on 2
ly and 16
ugust

The Italian football season
runs from September through to
June. It culminates with the Coppa
Italia final, which is equivalent to
the British FA Cup. Italy's football
obsession, however, reaches fever
pitch when the World Cup takes
place every four years.

KEY TO SPORTING SEASONS

	Football
	Water polo
	Rugby
	Basketball
	Volleyball
	Skiing

The Outdoor Athletics
Championship has become very
popular in recent years, especially
the steeplechase, where Francesco
Panetta made his name.

The Climate of Italy

THE ITALIAN PENINSULA has a varied climate falling into three distinct geographical regions. Cold Alpine winters and warm, wet summers characterize the northern regions. In the extensive Po Valley, arid summers contrast with freezing, damp winters. The rest of Italy has a pleasant climate with long, hot summers and mild winters. Cooler weather along the backbone of the Apennines can bring snow during the winter months.

TRENTINO-ALTO ADIGE

°C				
		28		
	16	17	17	
	4		5	5
				-5
☀	6 hrs	8 hrs	4 hrs	2 hrs
☂	67 mm	100 mm	83 mm	20 mm
month	Apr	Jul	Oct	Jan

Average monthly maximum temperature

Average monthly minimum temperature

Average daily hours of sunshine

Average monthly rainfall

LOMBARDY

°C				
		28		
	18	18	17	
	8		10	6
				-1
☀	5 hrs	9 hrs	5 hrs	3 hrs
☂	74 mm	78 mm	89 mm	64 mm
month	Apr	Jul	Oct	Jan

LIGURIA

°C				
		28		
	18	20	21	
	11.5		14	12
				6.5
☀	7 hrs	9 hrs	8 hrs	4 hrs
☂	66 mm	30 mm	74 mm	69 mm
month	Apr	Jul	Oct	Jan

VALLE D'AOSTA AND PIEDMONT

°C				
		26		
	17	15	17	
	6		7	7
				-2.5
☀	5 hrs	9 hrs	4 hrs	3 hrs
☂	95 mm	87 mm	85 mm	45 mm
month	Apr	Jul	Oct	Jan

TUSCANY

°C				
		29		
	17	16	20	
	8		15	10
				2
☀	8 hrs	11 hrs	6 hrs	5 hrs
☂	72 mm	30 mm	90 mm	65 mm
month	Apr	Jul	Oct	Jan

SARDINIA

°C				
		29		
	19	20	22	
	10		14	14
				7
☀	8 hrs	11 hrs	6 hrs	4 hrs
☂	31 mm	7 mm	48 mm	50 mm
month	Apr	Jul	Oct	Jan

EMILIA-ROMAGNA

°C				
		30		
	17	19	16	
	8.5		10	4
				-1
☀	6 hrs	11 hrs	5 hrs	3 hrs
☂	58 mm	39 mm	81 mm	46 mm
month	Apr	Jul	Oct	Jan

Trento
Aosta • Milano • Brescia • Verona • Pa
Torino •
Parma • Modena • Bol
Genova •
Fl
Livorno •
Olbia •
Sassari •
Cagliari •

NORTHEAST
ITALY

Northeast Italy at a Glance

T HE SHEER VARIETY TO BE FOUND in northeast Italy makes it a fascinating area to explore. The majestic Dolomites dominate the north, straddling Trentino-Alto Adige and the Veneto, and are dotted with medieval castles and modern skiing resorts. On the plain, the cities of Verona, Vicenza and Padua are all noted for outstanding architecture and museums, while the rural hinterland boasts beautiful villas. The incomparable and spectacular city of Venice, with its magnificent monuments, rises from the lagoon. Further east, in Friuli, there are important Roman remains. This map pinpoints some of the highlights.

Castel Tirolo,
Merano

TRENTINO-ALTO ADIGE
(See pp160–69)

Palazzo Pretorio,
Trento

Alto Adige *is a dramatic region of snow-covered mountain valleys scattered with forbidding castles and onion-domed churches in the Tyrolean style (see pp164–5).*

The Veneto

The Dolomites *(see pp78–9) form the spectacular back-drop to many towns in northeast Italy, among them Trento, the region's capital (see pp168–9).*

La Rotonda,
Vicenza

Ponte Scaligero,
Verona

0 kilometres   40

0 miles   20

Verona *is one of the loveliest cities in the Veneto, boasting the Castelvecchio and a Roman arena now used for performances of opera (see pp136–41).*

Vicenza, *a model Renaissance city, is dominated by the buildings of Palladio, such as the Palazzo della Ragione and La Rotonda (see pp144–7).*

◁ **Dusk over the atmospheric city of Verona**

Udine in Friuli is an interesting city which centres on the elegant Piazza della Libertà. The piazza contains imposing statues, such as this colossal Hercules, and the Porticato di San Giovanni (see pp156–7).

Friuli-Venezia Giulia

Porticato di San Giovanni, Udine

THE VENETO AND FRIULI *(See pp132–59)*

VENICE *(See inset)*

Basilica mosaic

Aquileia, once a splendid Roman city, is filled with ancient remains, such as this Mausoleum. Its Basilica houses early Christian mosaics (see p158).

Padua boasts several major sights, among them the Basilica di Sant'Antonio and the Cappella degli Scrovegni with its frescoes by Giotto (see pp148–53).

Basilica di Sant'Antonio, Padua

VENICE *(See pp80–131)*

The Palazzo Ducale is a masterpiece of Venetian Gothic architecture *(see pp110–12).*

Basilica di San Marco in Venice is one of Europe's finest Byzantine buildings, with a magnificent gilded interior (see pp106–9).

Basilica di San Marco

Palazzo Ducale

0 kilometres 1

0 miles 0.5

Regional Food: Northeast Italy

Gelati

MANY TRADITIONAL SPECIALITIES of the Veneto are dominated, not surprisingly, by fresh fish and seafood from Lake Garda and the Adriatic. This is complemented by seasonal produce – peas, courgettes, asparagus from Bassano del Grappa, radicchio from Treviso – and meat and cheese from the mainland. Pasta is eaten throughout the northeast, but more typical is polenta, made from maize flour, and also the many types of risotto. The influences from neighbouring countries and trading partners may be tasted in the sweet and sour, spicy or pickled dishes found throughout the region, from the mountains in the north to the beaches of the south.

Radicchio alla Griglia is a dish of slightly bitter red endive leaves from Treviso which are grilled lightly over a hot fire.

Mussels **Bream**

Crab

Squid

Prawns

Scallops

Antipasto di Frutti di Mare is a mixed seafood platter, dressed with a little olive oil and lemon juice. It is a particular favourite in Venice, where the seafood comes fresh from the Adriatic.

Red mullet

Fiori di Zucchini, a seasonal delight, are courgette flowers stuffed with delicate fish mousse then fried in a light batter.

Brodo di Pesce, or fish soup, is typically Venetian and served all along the coast. It usually contains a mixture of fish, and is sometimes flavoured with saffron from Friuli.

Risotto alle Seppie contains cuttlefish ink, which colours the rice a dramatic black in this traditional risotto.

Risi e Bisi, a soft and liquid risotto – almost a thick soup – is made of rice with fresh peas and small pieces of bacon.

Carpaccio, wafer-thin slices of raw beef sprinkled with oil, is here served with rocket leaves and slivers of Parmesan cheese.

Zuppa di Cozze is a classic way of cooking mussels, with a delicious sauce of white wine, garlic and parsley.

Spaghetti alle Vongole *often appears on coastal menus: it is spaghetti with fresh clams in a piquant chilli-pepper sauce.*

Polenta, *like pasta, is a filling staple of the Italian diet. Made from maize, it is often grilled and served with a tasty sauce.*

Sarde in Saor *is a traditional Venetian dish of fried fresh sardines marinated in a sweet and sour sauce.*

Anguille in Umido *are eels, gently stewed in an aromatic tomato sauce flavoured with white wine and garlic.*

Fegato alla Veneziana *is a traditional Venetian speciality of tender calf's liver, lightly cooked on a bed of onions.*

Tiramisù, *Italy's most famous dessert, is a wonderfully rich blend of coffee-soaked sponge cake and mascarpone cheese.*

THE WINES OF THE NORTHEAST

The Veneto produces large quantities of everyday wines – red, white and rosé *(chiaretto)*. When choosing an unknown white, you might select a Bianco di Custoza rather than an anonymous Soave. But do not rule out Soave; there are some fine examples, notably by Pieropan and Anselmi. The best whites from the northeast come from Friuli, where winemakers Puiatti, Schiopetto, Jermann and Gravner excel in their craft. Trentino-Alto Adige, too, produces some crisp whites. Much light and fruity red wine is produced near Bardolino and Valpolicella, with some outstanding bottles coming from Allegrini and Masi. Recioto della Valpolicella is a rich, sweet dessert wine, while Recioto Amarone is less sweet, but stronger still.

Recioto Amarone *is a rich and full-bodied red wine, full of fruit and very high in alcohol.*

Bianco di Custoza *is a dry white "super Soave" from the eastern shores of Lake Garda. Good white wine producers in the Veneto region include Pieropan, Anselmi, Maculan, Tedeschi, Allegrini and Cavalchina.*

Pieropan *produces some of Soave's finest quality wine. The single-vineyard wines from this renowned estate are excellent.*

Prosecco *is the Veneto's own sparkling wine, and a delightful aperitivo. It may be* secco *(dry)* or amabile *(medium-sweet).*

Bianco di Custoza

Collio Pinot Bianco

Collio Pinot Bianco *is a superb, fragrant white wine made in the Collio hills next to the Slovenian border. Puiatti is a top producer.*

Understanding Architecture in Venice and the Veneto

TRADE CONTACT WITH THE EAST led medieval Venice to develop its own exotic style – known as Venetian Gothic – blending Byzantine domes and Islamic minarets with European Gothic pointed arches and quatrefoils. In the 16th century, Palladio introduced his interpretations of Classical architecture through a series of churches, public buildings and rural villas in Venice and the Veneto. The 17th century brought the Baroque style, though its exuberance was tempered by Palladio-influenced restraint.

Andrea Palladio (1508–80)

THE ARCHITECTURE OF VENICE: BYZANTINE TO BAROQUE

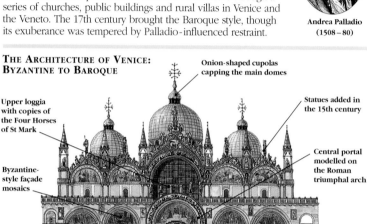

Onion-shaped cupolas capping the main domes

Upper loggia with copies of the Four Horses of St Mark

Statues added in the 15th century

Byzantine-style façade mosaics

Central portal modelled on the Roman triumphal arch

The Basilica di San Marco, western Europe's finest Byzantine church (completed 11th century), was given lavish treatment to make it a dazzling shrine for the relics of St Mark, the Evangelist, and a fitting symbol of Venetian aspirations (see pp106–9).

THE GENIUS OF PALLADIO

Doric columns supporting the ground floor, Ionic above

Shaded loggias for escaping the heat

Palazzo Chiericati is a huge mansion of 1550, its simple style borrowed from the ancient Roman[...] It was once surrounded by water t[...] reflect the statues of Classical deitie[...] along its roof (see p146).

Symmetrical façade

Arcades linking the wings to the central block

Villa Barbaro at Masèr was one of the villas designed by Palladio from the 1550s when it became fashionable for rich Venetians to acquire rural estates. This villa is typical, combining a working farm, housed in the side wings, with the elegant buildings of a country house (see p143).

WHERE TO SEE THE ARCHITECTURE

A vaporetto trip along the Grand Canal in Venice *(see pp84–7)* is a splendid way of getting an overview of Venetian architecture. Ca' d'Oro, Ca' Rezzonico and Ca' Pesaro may also be visited as they contain museums and a visit to the Basilica di San Marco

Typical Venetian Gothic window

and the Palazzo Ducale is a must. There are numerous examples of Palladio's architecture in the Veneto, but the star is the Villa Barbaro *(see p143)*. Several of his villas line the Brenta Canal *(see p154)*, and the town of Vicenza *(see pp144–7)* is full of his buildings, including La Rotonda, his famous villa.

Arcading influenced by the Palazzo Ducale

Florid tracery inlaid with azure

Finials once covered in gold leaf

Ca d'Oro, *the 15th-century "House of Gold", reveals Moorish influence in its roof finials and sinuous pointed arches (see p90).*

Keystones carved as helmeted heads

Deep recesses creating play of light and shade

Swags of fruit, ribbons and flowers

The 17th-century Ca' Pesaro *typifies the Venetian Baroque style – Classical columns and rich, but subtle ornamentation (see p85).*

Giant composite columns

Istrian marble, chosen to catch the changing light of the lagoon

Statues and memorials to patrons of the church

San Giorgio Maggiore, *built in 1559–80, is marvellously sited at the entrance to the Venetian inner harbour. It broke from the prevailing Gothic style, introducing the clean simplicity and harmonious proportions of Classical architecture to Venice, and more resembles an ancient Roman temple than a Christian church (see pp116–17).*

Pediment with coat of arms

Sundials at each end

The Dolomites

THE DOLOMITES ARE THE MOST DISTINCTIVE and beautiful mountains in Italy. They were formed of mineralized coral which was laid down beneath the sea during the Triassic era, and uplifted when the European and African continental plates dramatically collided 60 million years ago. Unlike the glacier-eroded saddles and ridges of the main body of the Alps, the pale rocks here have been carved by the corrosive effects of ice, sun and rain, sculpting the cliffs, spires and "organ pipes" that we see today. The eastern and western ranges of the Dolomites have slightly different characteristics; the eastern section is the more awe-inspiring, especially the Catinaccio (or Rosengarten) range which is particularly beautiful, turning rose pink at sunset.

Onion dome, a common local feature

STRADA DELLE DOLOMITI
One of the most spectacular routes through the Dolomites links Bolzano *(see p166)* with Cortina d'Ampezzo *(see p155)*. It follows the lie of the land, passing some of the greatest peaks, and the most majestic landscape.

S49
Dobbiaco
Rienza
S51
TRE CIME DI LAVAREDO
Lago di Misurina
Cortina d'Ampezzo
SASSO LUNGO
S48
TORRI DEL VAIOLET
Canazei
MARMODADA
CINQUE TORRI
S51
Pieve di Cadore
Bolzano
Adige
S241
S12
S51

0 kilometres   10
0 miles   5

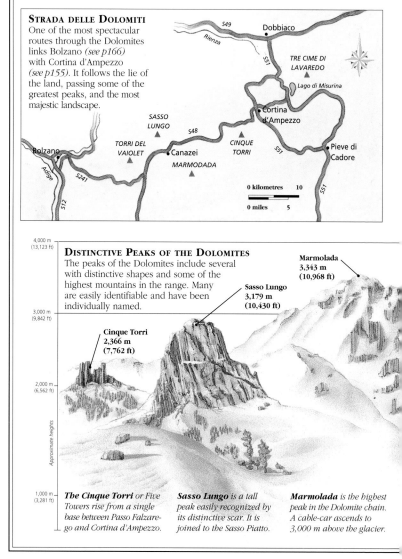

DISTINCTIVE PEAKS OF THE DOLOMITES
The peaks of the Dolomites include several with distinctive shapes and some of the highest mountains in the range. Many are easily identifiable and have been individually named.

4,000 m (13,123 ft)
3,000 m (9,842 ft)
2,000 m (6,562 ft)
1,000 m (3,281 ft)

Approximate heights

Marmolada 3,343 m (10,968 ft)

Sasso Lungo 3,179 m (10,430 ft)

Cinque Torri 2,366 m (7,762 ft)

The Cinque Torri or Five Towers rise from a single base between Passo Falzarego and Cortina d'Ampezzo.

Sasso Lungo is a tall peak easily recognized by its distinctive scar. It is joined to the Sasso Piatto.

Marmolada is the highest peak in the Dolomite chain. A cable-car ascends to 3,000 m above the glacier.

Lago di Misurina *is a large and beautiful lake lying beside the resort of Misurina. The crystal clear waters reflect the surrounding mountains, mirroring various peaks such as the distinctive and dramatic Sorapiss, in shimmering colours.*

Outdoor activities *in this area of dramatic landscapes include skiing in winter, and walking and rambling along the footpaths, and to picnic sites, in summer. Chair-lifts from the main resorts provide easy access up into the mountains themselves, transporting you into some breathtaking scenery.*

Torri del Vaiolet
2,243 m
(7,375 ft)

Tre Cime di Lavaredo
2,999 m
(9,839 ft)

The Torri del Vaiolet *is part of the beautiful Catinaccio range, known for its colour.*

Tre Cime di Lavaredo *or Drei Zinnen dominate the valleys north of the Lago di Misurina.*

NATURE IN THE DOLOMITES

Forests and meadows support a breath-taking richness of wildlife in the region. Alpine plants, which flower between June and September, have evolved their miniature form to survive the harsh winds.

The Flora

Gentian roots *are used to make a bitter local liqueur.*

The orange mountain lily *thrives on sun-baked slopes.*

The pretty *burser's saxifrage grows in clusters on rocks.*

Devil's claw *has distinctive pink flower heads.*

The Fauna

The ptarmigan *changes its plumage from mottled brown in summer to snow white in winter for effective camouflage. It feeds on mountain berries and young plant shoots.*

The chamois, *a shy mountain antelope prized for its soft skin, is protected in the national parks, where hunting is forbidden.*

Roe deer *are very common as their natural predators – wolves and lynx – are decreasing in number. An appetite for tree saplings causes problems for foresters.*

VENICE

················

LYING IN THE *extreme northeast of Italy, Venice, gateway to the Orient, became an independent Byzantine province in the 10th century. Exclusive trading links with the East and victory in the Crusade of 1204 brought wealth and power, which were only gradually eroded by European and Turkish rivals. Today, Venice's ties are with the local Veneto region which stretches from the flat river plains to the Dolomites.*

Venice is one of the few cities in the world that can be truly described as unique. It survives against all the odds, built on a series of low mud banks amid the tidal waters of the Adriatic, and regularly subject to floods. During the Middle Ages, under the leadership of successive doges, Venice expanded its power and influence throughout the Mediterranean to Constantinople (modern Istanbul). The immense wealth of the city was celebrated in art and architecture throughout the city.

The riches of St Mark's alone bear witness to Venice's position as a world power from the 12th to 14th centuries. After slowly losing ground to the new states of Europe, however, it fell to Napoleon in 1797. Finally, Venice joined the Kingdom of Italy in 1866, so bringing unity to the country for the first time in its history. Today, Venice has found a new role. Her palazzi have become museums, shops, hotels and apartments and her convents have been turned into centres for art restoration. Yet little of the essential fabric of Venice has altered in 200 years. The city's sounds are still those of footsteps and the cries of boatmen. The only engines are those of barges delivering supplies or waterbuses ferrying passengers between stops. The same well-worn streets are still trodden. More than 12 million visitors a year succumb to the magic of this improbable place whose "streets are full of water" and where the glories of the past are evident at every turn.

A busy street on the island of Burano, with its distinctive, brightly painted houses

◁ Gondola prows, with their characteristic *ferri*, and Santa Maria della Salute in the background

Exploring Venice

Venice is divided into six ancient administrative districts or *sestieri*: Cannaregio, Castello, San Marco, Dorsoduro, San Polo and Santa Croce. You can walk to most places in Venice itself, and take a ride on a waterbus to any of the islands. A combined museum ticket (Museum Card) gives you lower admission fees in many museums, such as Ca' Rezzonico, the Palazzo Ducale and Museo Correr.

SIGHTS AT A GLANCE

Churches

Basilica di San Marco pp106–9 **18**
Madonna dell'Orto **1**
San Giacomo dell'Orio **6**
San Giorgio Maggiore **31**
San Giovanni Grisostomo **3**
San Giovanni in Bragora **29**
Santi Giovanni e Paolo **24**
Santa Maria Gloriosa dei Frari pp94–5 **8**
Santa Maria dei Miracoli **4**
Santa Maria della Salute **17**
San Nicolò dei Mendicoli **13**
San Pantalon **11**
San Polo **7**
San Rocco **10**
San Sebastiano **14**
Santo Stefano **23**
San Zaccaria **27**

Buildings and Monuments

Arsenale **30**
Campanile **21**

Palazzo Ducale *pp110–12* **19**
Rialto **5**
Scuola di San Giorgio degli Schiavoni **28**
Statue of Colleoni **25**
Torre dell'Orologio **20**

Museums and Galleries

Accademia pp102–3 **15**
Ca' d'Oro **2**
Ca' Rezzonico **12**
Museo Correr **22**
Peggy Guggenheim Collection **16**
Scuola Grande di San Rocco pp96–7 **9**

Lagoon

Burano **33**
Murano **32**
Torcello pp118–9 **34**

KEY

Street-by-Street: San Polo *pp92–3*

Street-by-Street: Dorsoduro *pp98–9*

Street-by-Street: Piazza San Marco *pp104–5*

✈ International airport

FS Railway station

⛴ Ferry boarding point

🚤 *Vaporetto* boarding point

🚣 *Traghetto* crossing *(see p636)*

🛶 Gondola mooring

ℹ Tourist information

Santa Maria della Salute, at the mouth of the Grand Canal

SEE ALSO
- *Street Finder* pp120–29
- *Where to Stay* pp542–4
- *Where to Eat* pp578–9

LOCATOR MAP

Verona   **VENICE**
Padua

CAMPO D.
S ALVISE

CAMPIELLO
PIAVE

CAMPIELLO DELL'
SAN ANCONETA
DO
CAMPO SAN
MARCUOLA

CAMPO
SANT'ANTONIO   CAMPO DEI
GESUITI

de

CAMPIELLO
D. PIETA

CAMPO
S FELICE

Canal

CAMPO SAN
GIACOMO
DELL'ORIO

Grande

CAMPIELLO
DEL
CASON   CAMPIELLO
WIDMAN

CAMPO DEI
SANTI
APOSTOLI

CAMPO S
MARIA NOVA

CAMPO D.
SANT'AGOSTIN

CAMPIELLO SANTA
MARIA NOVA

CORTE
2A D.
MILION   CAMPO
SAN
MARINA

CAMPO SAN
BARTOLOMEO

CAMPO S
GIUSTINA   CAMPO DELLA
CONFRATERNITA

CAMPO D.
CELESTIA

CAMPO
SAN
POLO

CAMPO S
SILVESTRO

Ponte
di Rialto

CAMPO
SAN
SILVESTRO

CAMPO
SAN LIO

CAMPO S
MARIA
FORMOSA

CAMPO
SAN
LORENZO

CAMPO
S TERNITA

Canale delle
Galeazze

FRARI

Canal   Grande

CORTE
TEATRO

CAMPO
D. FAVA

CAMPIELLO
DO POZZI

CAMPO SAN

CAMPO
SAN
BENETO

CAMPO
SAN LUCA

CAMPO
MANIN

CAMPO
D. GUERRA

CORTE
VENIER

Arsenale
Vecchio

Darsena
Grande

CAMPIELLO
DEL TEATRO

CLLO
NUOVO

CAMPIELLO
CALEGHERI

CAMPO
SAN MOISE

PIAZZA
SAN
MARCO

CAMPO SAN
PROVOLO

CAMPO
BANDIERA
E MORO

CAMPO
ARSENALE

CAMPO S
SAMUELE   CAMPO
SANTO
STEFANO   CAMPO
SAN
MAURIZIO

CAMPO SAN
ZACCARIA

CAMPIELLO
D. PIOVAN

CAMPO
SAN VIDAL

CAMPO DEL
TRAGHETTO

Ponte
dell'Accademia

PO D'
RITA

CAMPO S
SAN VIO

CAMPO
ANT'AGNESE

CAMPO SAN
BIAGIO

CAMPO
NANI E
BARBARO

Canale
della
Grazia

Canale   della   Giudecca

CAMPO DEL
REDENTORE

CAMPIELLO
CAMPALTO

CAMPIELLO
OSPIZIO

THE LAGOON

Marco Polo

Mestre
FS

Canale Osellino

Veneta

S11

Laguna

FS

VENEZIA

GETTING AROUND

The only road into Venice is the S11 from Mestre, which carries you over the causeway to the Tronchetto and Piazzale Roma where there are car parks and bus stops. Rail travellers arrive at Santa Lucia station on the Grand Canal. In the city, public transport is by *vaporetto*, or waterbus – the No.1 is best for sightseeing as it travels the length of the Grand Canal *(see pp130–31)*.

The Grand Canal: Santa Lucia to the Rialto

THE BEST WAY to view the Grand Canal as it winds through the heart of the city is from a *vaporetto*, or waterbus. Several lines travel the length of the canal *(see p636)*. The palaces lining the waterway were built over a span of five centuries and present a panoramic survey of the city's history, almost all bearing the name of some once-great Venetian family.

San Marcuola
The church was rebuilt in the 18th century, but the planned new façade overlooking the canal was never completed.

San Geremia houses the relics of St Lucy, once kept in the church of Santa Lucia where the railway station now stands.

Palazzo Labia
Between 1745–50, Giambattista Tiepolo decorated the ballroom with scenes from the life of Cleopatra.

Canale di Cannaregio

Palazzo Corner-Contarini

San Marcuo

Riva di Biasio

Ferrovia

FS

Ponte degli Scalzi

Fondaco dei Turchi
A warehouse for Turkish traders in the 17th–19th centuries, this is now the Natural History Museum.

San Simeone Piccolo
This 18th-century domed church is based on the Pantheon in Rome.

THE GONDOLAS OF VENICE

The gondola has been a part of Venice since the 11th century. With its slim hull and flat underside, the craft is perfectly adapted to negotiating narrow, shallow canals. There is a slight leftward curve to the prow, which counteracts the force of the oar, preventing the gondola from going round in circles.

In 1562 it was decreed that all gondolas should be black to stop people making an ostentatious show of their wealth. For special occasions they are decorated with flowers. Today, gondola rides are expensive and usually taken by tourists *(see p637)*. However, *traghetti* (gondola ferries) are a cheap, convenient way of crossing the Grand Canal.

Gondolas tied up by steps

Ca' d'Oro

The delicate Gothic tracery of the façade makes this a striking landmark. Its art collection (see p90) includes Bernini's model for a fountain (c.1648).

Palazzo Vendramin Calergi

This is one of the finest early Renaissance palaces in Venice. The German composer Richard Wagner (left) died here in 1883.

The Pescheria has been the site of a busy fish market for six centuries.

Palazzo Sagredo

Graceful Veneto-Byzantine and Gothic arches are both featured on the waterfront façade.

Palazzo Michiel dalle Colonne takes its name from its distinctive colonnade.

The Rialto Bridge *(see p93)* spans the canal in the commercial heart of the city.

San Stae

San Stae

The façade of this Baroque church is richly adorned with statues. It is a popular concert venue.

Ca' d'Oro

Ca' Pesaro

The huge, stately Baroque palace today houses a gallery of modern art and the Oriental Museum.

Rialto

The Grand Canal: the Rialto to San Marco

AFTER PASSING the Rialto, the canal doubles back on itself along a stretch known as La Volta (the bend). It then widens out and the views become more spectacular approaching San Marco. Façades may have faded and foundations frayed with the tides, yet the canal remains, in the words of the French ambassador in 1495, "the most beautiful street in the world".

Palazzo Mocenigo
Lord Byron stayed in this huge 18th-century palace in 1818.

Sant' Angelo

San Tomà

Palazzo Garzoni
is a renovated Gothic palace, now part of the university.

Ca' Rezzonico
Now a museum of 18th-century Venice (see p99), the palace was the last home of the poet Robert Browning, seen here with his son Pen.

San Samuele

Ca' Rezzonico

Palazzo Grassi
The elegant palazzo dates from the 1730s. Bought by Fiat in 1984, it is now used for art exhibitions.

Ponte dell'Accademia

Palazzo Capello Malipiero
The palace was rebuilt in 1622. Beside it stands the 12th-century campanile of San Samuele.

Accademia

Accademia
The world's greatest collection of Venetian paintings is housed here in the former Scuola della Carità (see pp102–3), which has a Baroque façade by Giorgio Massari.

Palazzo Barbaro
Novelist Henry James wrote The Aspern Papers *here in 1888.*

The Riva del Vin is the quay where wine *(vin)* used to be unloaded. It is one of the few spots where you can sit and relax on the banks of the Grand Canal.

LOCATOR MAP

■ *See Venice Street Finder maps 6, 7*

Palazzo Barzizza, rebuilt in the 17th century, preserves its early 13th-century façade.

Peggy Guggenheim Collection
A one-storey palazzo houses Guggenheim's great modern art collection (see pp100–1).

Santa Maria della Salute
The vast weight of this Baroque church is supported by over one million timber piles (see p101).

Palazzo Gritti-Pisani
The former home of the Gritti family is now the luxury Gritti Palace Hotel (see p544).

San Marco Vallaresso

Santa Maria del Giglio

Salute

Harry's Bar, founded in 1931 by Giuseppe Cipriani, is famous for its cocktails.

Palazzo Dario
Beautiful coloured marbles give the 1487 palace a highly individual façade. Legend has it the building is cursed.

The Dogana di Mare (customs house), built in the 17th century, is crowned by two bronze Atlases supporting a golden globe topped by a weathervane.

Travelling slowly along the Grand Canal by gondola ▷

Madonna dell'Orto, with 15th-century façade statues of St Christopher and the Apostles

Madonna dell'Orto ❶

Campo Madonna dell'Orto.
Map 2 F2. 041 275 04 62.
Madonna dell'Orto. ◻ 10am–5pm Mon–Sat, 1–5pm Sun. Sun (Jul & Aug), 1 Jan, 25 Dec.

T HIS LOVELY Gothic church, founded in the mid-14th century, was dedicated to St Christopher, patron saint of travellers, to protect the boatmen who ferried passengers to the islands in the northern lagoon. A 15th-century statue of the saint, recently restored by the Venice in Peril fund, stands above the main portal. The dedication was changed and the church reconstructed in the early 15th century, after the discovery, in a nearby vegetable garden (orto), of a statue of the Virgin Mary said to have miraculous powers.

The interior, faced almost entirely in brick, is large and uncluttered. On the right is a magnificent painting by Cima da Conegliano, *St John the Baptist and Other Saints* (c.1493). The vacant space in the chapel opposite belongs to Giovanni Bellini's *Madonna with Child* (c.1478), stolen in 1993 for the third time.

The church's greatest remaining treasures are the works of art by Tintoretto, who was a parishioner of the church. His tomb, which is marked with a plaque, lies with that of his children, in the chapel to the right of the chancel. The most

dramatic of his works are the towering masterpieces that decorate the chancel (1562–4). On the right wall is the *Last Judgment*, whose turbulent content caused John Ruskin's wife, Effie, to flee the church in horror. In *The Adoration of the Golden Calf* on the left wall, the figure carrying the calf, fourth from the left, is believed to be a portrait of the artist. Inside the chapel of San Mauro, off the end of the right nave, stands a statue of the Madonna by Giovanni de' Santi. It was restored by the Venice in Peril fund, and inspired the rededication of the church.

Ca' d'Oro ❷

Calle Ca' d'Oro. **Map** 3 A4.
041 523 87 90. Ca' d'Oro. ◻ 8:15am–7:15pm daily (2pm Mon).

I N 1420 Marino Contarini, a wealthy patrician, commissioned the construction of what he hoped would be the city's most magnificent palace (see p77). The building's intricate carving was entrusted to a team of Venetian and Lombard craftsmen, while the façade was beautifully adorned with the most elaborate and expensive decorative finishes of the day, including gold leaf, vermilion and ultramarine.

Tullio Lombardo's Double Portrait

Over the years the palace was extensively remodelled, and by the 18th century was in a state of semi-dereliction. In 1846 it was bought by the Russian Prince Troubetzkoy for the famous ballerina Maria Taglioni. Under her direction the palace suffered barbaric restoration, losing, among other things, its staircase and much of its original stonework. It was finally rescued by Baron Giorgio Franchetti, a wealthy patron of the arts, who bequeathed both the building and his private art collection to the state in 1915.

Pride of place on the first of the gallery's two floors goes to Andrea Mantegna's *St Sebastian* (1506), the artist's last work, which occupies a special alcove of its own. Elsewhere, the floor's main exhibits are ranged around the *portego* (gallery). This is largely dominated by the vivid 15th-century *Double Portrait* (c.1493) by the sculptor Tullio Lombardo; Sansovino's lunette of the *Madonna and Child* (c.1530); and several bronze reliefs by the Paduan Andrea Briosco, "Il Riccio" (1470–1532). Rooms leading off the *portego* to the right contain numerous bronzes and medallions, with some examples by Pisanello and Gentile Bellini. Paintings here also include the famous *Madonna of the Beautiful Eyes*, attributed to Giovanni Bellini, a *Madonna and Child*, attributed to Alvise Vivarini (both late 15th century), and Carpaccio's *Annunciation* and *Death of the Virgin* (both c.1504). A room to the left of the *portego* contains non-Venetian paintings, notably a *Flagellation* by Luca Signorelli (c.1480). A lovely staircase leads to the second floor, which opens with a room hung with tapestries. It has bronzes by Alessandro Vittoria and paintings by

The magnificent Gothic façade of the Ca' d'Oro, or House of Gold

Titian and Van Dyck. The *portego* displays frescoes (c.1532) by Pordenone from the cloister of Santo Stefano, while an anteroom contains damaged frescoes by Titian taken from the Fondaco dei Tedeschi.

Giovanni Bellini's 1513 altarpiece in San Giovanni Grisostomo

San Giovanni Grisostomo ❸

Campo San Giovanni Grisostomo. **Map** 3 B5. 041 522 71 55. Rialto. 10:30am–noon, 3:30–6pm daily.

THIS PRETTY little terracotta-coloured church lies in a bustling quarter close to the Rialto. Built between 1479 and 1504, it is a lovely Renaissance design, the last work of Mauro Coducci.

The interior is built on a Greek-cross plan. The light meter illuminates Giovanni Bellini's *St Jerome with Saints Christopher and Augustine* (1513) above the first altar on the right. This was most probably Bellini's last painting, executed when he was in his eighties.

Over the high altar hangs Sebastiano del Piombo's *St John Chrysostom and Six Saints* (1509–11).

Santa Maria dei Miracoli ❹

Campo dei Miracoli. **Map** 3 B5. 041 275 04 62. Rialto, Fondamente Nuove. 10am–5pm Mon–Sat, 1–5pm Sun & public hols. Sun (Jul & Aug), 1 Jan, 25 Dec.

A N EXQUISITE masterpiece of early Renaissance architecture, the Miracoli is the church where many Venetians like to get married. Tucked away in a maze of alleys and waterways in eastern Cannaregio, it is small and somewhat elusive.

Santa Maria dei Miracoli is decorated in various shades of marble, with some fine bas reliefs and sculpture. It was built in 1481–9 by the architect Pietro Lombardo and his sons to enshrine *The Virgin and Child* (1408), a painting believed to have miraculous powers. The picture, by Nicolò di Pietro, can still be seen above the altar.

The interior of the church is embellished by pink, white and grey marble, at its best when lit up by rays of pale sunshine. It is crowned by

Decorative column from inside Santa Maria dei Miracoli

a barrel-vaulted ceiling (1528) which has 50 portraits of saints and prophets. The balustrade, between the nave and the chancel, is decorated by Tullio Lombardo's carved figures of St Francis, Archangel Gabriel, the Virgin and St Clare.

The screen around the high altar and the medallions of the Evangelists in the cupola spandrels are also Lombardo's work. Above the main door, the choir gallery was used by the nuns from the neighbouring convent, who entered the church through an overhead gallery. Santa Maria dei Miracoli has recently undergone a major restoration programme, which was funded by the American Save Venice organization.

SANTA MARIA DEI MIRACOLI
This beautifully proportioned façade is composed of decorated panels and multicoloured polished marble.

Carving of saint

The semi-circular crowning lunette emphasizes the church's jewel-box appearance.

A false loggia is formed of Ionic arches, inset with windows. The marble used was reportedly left over from the building of San Marco.

Virgin and Child by Giorgio Lascaris

The marble panels are fixed to the bricks by metal hooks. This method prevents the build-up of damp and salt water behind the panels, and dates from the Renaissance.

Street-by-Street: San Polo

THE RIALTO BRIDGE and markets make this area a magnet for visitors. Traditionally the city's commercial quarter, it was here that bankers, brokers and merchants conducted their affairs. Streets are no longer lined with stalls selling spices and fine fabrics, but the food markets and pasta shops are unmissable. Away from the bridge, streets quickly become less crowded, leading to tiny squares and quiet churches.

The Rialto Markets have existed for centuries, and are renowned for their produce. The Pescheria sells fresh fish and seafood.

The 17th-century church of San Cassiano houses a carved altar (1696) and a *Crucifixion* by Tintoretto (1568).

Sant'Aponal has a façade decorated with worn Gothic reliefs. The church was founded in the 11th century, but is now deconsecrated.

The Frari

San Silvestro

San Giovanni Elemosinario is an inconspicuous church that was rebuilt in the early 16th century, although its campanile dates from the end of the 14th century. Inside it are interesting frescoes by Pordenone.

KEY

- – – – Suggested route

0 metres   75

0 yards   75

STAR SIGHT

★ **Rialto**

LOCATOR MAP
*See Venice Street Finder
maps 2, 3, 6, 7*

The lively Erberia, selling fresh fruit and vegetables

Rialto ❺

Ponte di Rialto. **Map** 7 A1. 🚤 *Rialto.*

THE RIALTO takes its name from *rivo alto* (high bank) and was one of the first areas of Venice to be inhabited. A banking and then market district, it remains one of the city's busiest and most bustling areas. Locals and visitors alike jostle among the colourful stalls of the Erberia (fruit and vegetable market) and Pescheria (fish market).

Stone bridges were built in Venice as early as the 12th century, but it was not until 1588, after the collapse, decay or sabotage of earlier wooden structures, that a solid stone bridge was designed for the Rialto. Completed in 1591, the new bridge remained the only means of crossing the Grand Canal until 1854, when the Accademia bridge was built.

Few visitors leave Venice without crossing the famous bridge. It is a wonderful place to watch and photograph the constant activity of boats on the Grand Canal below.

San Giacomo dell'Orio ❻

Campo San Giacomo dell'Orio.
Map 2 E5. 📞 041 275 04 62.
🚤 Riva di Biasio or San Stae.
🕐 10am–5pm Mon–Sat, 1–5pm Sun & public hols. ● Sun (Jul & Aug), 1 Jan, 25 Dec. 🚫 🎫 🚷

THIS CHURCH is a focal point of a quiet quarter of Santa Croce. The name "dell'Orio" may derive from a laurel tree *(alloro)* that once stood near the church. San Giacomo was founded

in the 9th century, rebuilt in 1225 and thereafter repeatedly modified, resulting in a mixture of styles. The campanile, basilica ground plan and Byzantine columns survive from the 13th century. The ship's keel roof and the columns are Gothic, and the apses are Renaissance.

The new sacristy contains a beautiful ceiling by Veronese and some interesting altar paintings.

San Polo ❼

Campo San Polo. **Map** 6 F1.
📞 041 275 04 62. 🚤 San Silvestro.
🕐 10am–5pm Mon–Sat, 1–5pm Sun & public hols. ● Sun (Jul & Aug), 1 Jan, 25 Dec. 🚫 🎫 🏛 🚷

FOUNDED IN THE 9th century, rebuilt in the 15th and revamped in the early 19th in Neo-Classical style, this church is worth visiting for the lovely Gothic portal and the Romanesque lions at the foot of the 14th-century campanile – one holds a serpent between its paws, the other a human head.

Inside, follow the signs for the *Via Crucis del Tiepolo* – 14 pictures of the Stations of the Cross (1749) by the painter Giandomenico Tiepolo: many include vivid portraits of Venetian life. The church also has paintings by Veronese, Palma il Giovane (the Younger) and a dramatic *Last Supper* by Tintoretto.

San Giacomo di Rialto's
clock face (1410), which has sadly been a poor time-keeper over the years, adorns one of Venice's oldest churches.

DEGLI OREFICI

Market entrance

★ **Rialto**
One of Venice's most famous sights, the bridge offers fine views of the Grand Canal, and marks the heart of the city ❺

A Romanesque lion at the base of San Polo's 14th-century campanile

Santa Maria Gloriosa dei Frari ⑧

Mᴏʀᴇ ᴄᴏᴍᴍᴏɴʟʏ ᴋɴᴏᴡɴ as the Frari (a corruption of Frati, meaning brothers), this vast Gothic church dwarfs the eastern area of San Polo. The first church on the site was built by Franciscan friars in 1250–1338, but was replaced by a larger building completed in the mid-15th century. The airy interior is striking for its sheer size and for the quality of its works of art, including masterpieces by Titian and Giovanni Bellini, a statue by Donatello and several grandiose tombs.

The campanile
is 83 m (262 ft) high, the tallest in the city after that of San Marco.

Foscari Monument
Doge Foscari died in 1457, after a long and eventful 34-year reign.

★ Assumption of the Virgin
Titian's glowing and spectacular work (1518) draws the eye through the monk's choir, to the altar, and heavenwards.

Rood Screen
*(1475)
Pietro Lombardo and Bartolomeo Bon carved the rood screen and its decorative marble figures.*

The *Madonna di Ca' Pesaro* (1526) shows Titian's mastery of light and colour.

★ Monks' Choir
This consists of three-tiered stalls (1468), carved with bas-reliefs of saints and Venetian city scenes.

FLOORPLAN

The Frari's imposing cruciform interior, which is 90 m (295 ft) long, holds 12 sights that should not be missed.

KEY TO FLOORPLAN

1 Tomb of Canova
2 Monument to Titian
3 *Madonna di Ca' Pesaro* by Titian
4 Choir stalls
5 Corner Chapel
6 Tomb of Monteverdi
7 Tomb of Doge Nicolò Tron
8 High altar with *Assumption of the Virgin* (1518) by Titian
9 Tomb of Doge Francesco Foscari
10 *John the Baptist* (c.1450) by Donatello
11 B Vivarini's altar painting (1474), Bernardo Chapel
12 *Madonna and Child with Saints* (1488) by Bellini

VISITORS' CHECKLIST

Campo dei Frari. Map 6 D1. [041 275 04 62. San Tomà. 10am–6pm Mon–Sat, 1–6pm Sun & religious hols. 1 Jan, 25 Dec. except for those attending mass. frequent.

★ Madonna and Child

The sacristy's altarpiece (1488) by Bellini, with its sublime use of colour, is one of Venice's most beautiful Renaissance paintings.

The former monastery, which houses the State Archives, has two cloisters, one in the style of Sansovino, another designed by Palladio.

Entrance

Tomb of Canova

Canova designed, but never constructed, a Neo-Classical marble pyramid like this as a monument for Titian. After Canova's death in 1822, the sculptor's pupils used a similar design for their master's tomb.

STAR FEATURES

★ **Assumption of the Virgin by Titian**

★ **Madonna and Child by Bellini**

★ **Monks' Choir**

Scuola Grande di San Rocco ❾

Restored main entrance to the Scuola di San Rocco

FOUNDED IN HONOUR of San Rocco (St Roch), a saint who dedicated his life to helping the sick, the Scuola started out as a charitable confraternity. Construction began in 1515 under Bartolomeo Bon and was continued by Scarpagnino until his death in 1549. The work was financed by donations from Venetians keen to invoke San Rocco's protection and the Scuola quickly became one of the wealthiest in Venice. In 1564 its members decided to commission Tintoretto to decorate its walls and ceilings. His earliest paintings, the first of over 50 works he eventually left in the Scuola, fill the small Sala dell'Albergo off the Upper Hall. His later paintings occupy the Ground Floor Hall, immediately within the entrance.

Tintoretto's magnificent *Crucifixion*, painted in 1565 for the Sala dell'Albergo in the Scuola di San Rocco

GROUND FLOOR HALL

THE GROUND FLOOR cycle was executed in 1583–7, when Tintoretto was in his sixties, and consists of eight paintings illustrating the life of Mary. The series starts with an *Annunciation* and ends with an *Assumption*, which was restored some years ago.

The tranquil scenes of *The Flight into Egypt*, *St Mary Magdalene* and *St Mary of Egypt* are remarkable for their serenity. This is portrayed most

Detail from *The Flight into Egypt* (1582–7) by Tintoretto

lucidly by the Virgin's isolated spiritual contemplation in the *St Mary of Egypt*. In all three paintings, the landscapes are rendered with rapid strokes, and are an important part of the composition.

UPPER HALL AND SALA DELL'ALBERGO

SCARPAGNINO'S great staircase (1544–6), with its upper flight decorated with two vast paintings commemorating the plague of 1630, leads to the Upper Hall. Here, biblical subjects decorate the ceiling and walls, painted by Tintoretto from 1575–81.

The ceiling paintings portray scenes from the Old Testament. The three large and dynamic square paintings in the centre show episodes from the Book of Exodus: *Moses Strikes Water from the Rock*, *The Miracle of the Bronze Serpent* and *The Fall of Manna in the Desert*. These all allude to the charitable

aims of the Scuola in alleviating thirst, sickness and hunger respectively. All three paintings are crowded compositions displaying much violent movement.

The vast wall paintings in the hall feature episodes from the New Testament, linking with the ceiling paintings. Two of the most striking paintings are *The Temptation of Christ*, which shows a handsome young Satan offering Christ two loaves of bread, and *The Adoration of the Shepherds*. Like *The Temptation of Christ*, *The Adoration* is composed in two halves, with a female figure, shepherds and ox below, and the Holy Family and onlookers above.

The beautiful carvings below the paintings were added in the 17th century by sculptor Francesco Pianta. The figures are allegorical and include (near the altar) a caricature of Tintoretto with his palette and brushes, representing Painting.

The easel painting *Christ Carrying the Cross*, also in the

Detail from *The Temptation of Christ* (1578–81) by Tintoretto

Upper Hall, was once attributed to Giorgione, though many believe it to be by Titian.

Near the entrance to the Sala dell'Albergo, you can see the *Annunciation* by Titian. The Sala dell'Albergo itself holds the most breathtaking of his works – the *Crucifixion*

(1565). Henry James remarked of this painting: "no single picture contains more of human life; there is everything in it, including the most exquisite beauty." Tintoretto began the cycle of paintings in this room in 1564, when he won the commission with the ceiling painting *San Rocco in Glory*. On the wall opposite the *Crucifixion* are paintings of episodes from the Passion: *Christ before Pilate, The Crowning with Thorns* and *The Ascent to Calvary*.

San Rocco ⑩

Campo San Rocco. **Map** 6 D1.
041 523 48 64. San Tomà.
Apr–Oct: 8am–12:30pm, 3–5pm daily; Nov–Mar: 8am–12:30pm Mon–Fri; 2–4pm Sat, Sun, public hols.

O N THE SAME square as the celebrated Scuola Grande di San Rocco is the church of the same name. Designed by Bartolomeo Bon in 1489 and largely rebuilt in 1725, the exterior suffers from a mixture of styles. The façade was added in 1765–71. Inside, the chancel is decorated with a series of paintings by Tintoretto depicting scenes from the life of San Rocco.

San Pantalon ⑪

Campo San Pantalon. **Map** 6 D2.
041 523 58 93. San Tomà, Piazzale Roma. 4–6pm Mon–Sat.

Fumiani's epic ceiling painting (1680–1740) in San Pantalon

T HE OVERWHELMING feature of this late 17th-century church is its vast painted ceiling, dark, awe-inspiring and remarkable for its illusionistic effect of height. The ceiling comprises a total of 40 scenes, and admirers claim that this is the world's largest work of art on canvas.

The scenes show the martyrdom and apotheosis of the physician St Pantalon. The artist, Gian Antonio Fumiani, took 24 years (1680–1704) to achieve the masterpiece, before allegedly falling to his death from the scaffolding.

KEY TO PAINTINGS

☐ **GROUND FLOOR HALL 1** The Annunciation; **2** The Adoration of the Three Kings; **3** The Flight into Egypt; **4** The Massacre of the Innocents; **5** St Mary Magdalene; **6** St Mary of Egypt; **7** The Presentation in the Temple; **8** The Assumption.

☐ **UPPER HALL WALLS 9** San Rocco; **10** St Sebastian; **11** The Adoration of the Shepherds; **12** The Baptism of Christ; **13** The Resurrection; **14** The Agony in the Garden; **15** The Last Supper; **16** The Vision of San Rocco; **17** The Miracle of the Loaves and Fishes; **18** The Resurrection of Lazarus; **19** The Ascension; **20** Christ Heals the Paralytic; **21** The Temptation of Christ.

☐ **UPPER HALL CEILING 22** Moses Saved from the Waters; **23** The Pillar of Fire; **24** Samuel and Saul; **25** Jacob's Ladder; **26** Elijah on a Chariot of Fire; **27** Elijah Fed by the Angels; **28** Daniel Saved by the Angels; **29** The Passover; **30** The Fall of Manna; **31** The Sacrifice of Isaac; **32** The Miracle of the Bronze Serpent; **33** Jonah Emerges from the Whale; **34** Moses Strikes Water from the Rock; **35** Adam and Eve; **36** Three Children in the Furnace; **37** God Appears to Moses; **38** Samson Brings out Water from the Jawbone of an Ass; **39** The Vision of the Prophet Ezekiel; **40** The Vision of Jeremiah; **41** Elisha Distributes Bread; **42** Abraham and Melchizedeck.

Ground Floor Hall

Upper Hall

Street-by-Street: Dorsoduro

BUILT UP ON A STRATA of solid subsoil is the *sestiere* of Dorsoduro – the name means "hard backbone". It has as its focal point the lively Campo Santa Margherita, the largest open space in this part of Venice. The square bustles with activity, particularly in the morning when the market stalls are open, and in the evening when it is the haunt of students from nearby Ca' Foscari, now part of Venice university. The surrounding streets contain some architectural stunners, notably Ca' Rezzonico and the Scuola Grande dei Carmini, which has decorations by Tiepolo. Of the area's waterways, the delightful Rio San Barnaba is best appreciated from the Ponte dei Pugni, near the barge selling fruit and vegetables – itself a time-honoured Venetian sight. Alongside the Rio Terrà Canal there are some lively cafés and a fascinating shop selling masks for Carnevale.

Santa Margherita

Campo Santa Margherita is an ideal place for relaxing in a café.

Palazzo Zenobio, built at the end of the 17th century, has been an Armenian college since 1850. With permission, visitors can see the fine 18th-century ballroom.

Scuola Grande dei Carmini contains nine ceiling panels (1739–44) in the hall on the upper floor, painted by Tiepolo for the Carmelite confraternity.

Santa Maria dei Carmini has a Gothic side porch carved with Byzantine reliefs.

KEY

– – – Suggested route

0 metres	50
0 yards	50

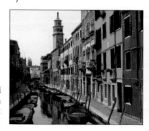

Fondamenta Gherardini runs beside the Rio San Barnaba, one of the prettiest canals in the *sestiere*.

LOCATOR MAP
*See Venice Street Finder
maps 5, 6*

Tiepolo's *New World* fresco, part
of a series in Ca' Rezzonico

★ **Ca' Rezzonico**
*The ballroom covers the width
of the palazzo once owned
by Browning* ⑫

Palazzo Giustinian
was home to
Wagner in 1858.

Ca' Foscari
was completed in
1437 for Doge
Francesco Foscari.

RIO DI CA' FOSCARI

C D ASEO

C S AONERI

C FOSCARI

C DELLA VIDA

C D BOTTEGHE

CALLE BERNARDO

CANAL GRANDE

CAMPO
SAN
BARNABA

CALLE DEL TRAGHETTO

Ponte dei Pugni was
a traditional scene of
fist fights between rival
factions. They were
finally banned in 1705
for being too violent.

STAR SIGHT
★ Ca' Rezzonico

San Barnaba is a thriving
community, with its own
floating barge stall crammed
with fresh fruit and
vegetables. It is a focal point
for tourists and locals alike.

Ca' Rezzonico ⑫

Fondamenta Rezzonico 3136. **Map**
6 E3. 📞 *041 241 01 00.* 🚤 *Ca'
Rezzonico.* ⏰ *10am–6pm Wed–
Mon (Nov–Mar: to 5pm).* ⏰ *1 Jan,
1 May, 25 Dec.* 🎫 🔒 🎧 🔊 ♿ 🚫

THIS PALAZZO HOUSES the
museum of 18th-century
Venice, its rooms furnished
with frescoes, paintings and
period pieces taken from
other palaces or museums.
Building began with Longhena
(architect of La Salute,
see p101) in 1667, but the
funds of the Bon family,
who commissioned it, ran dry
before the second floor was
started. In 1712 the unfinished
palace was bought by the
Rezzonico family of Genoa.
A large portion of their
fortune was spent on the
completion of the palace.

The Rezzonico family sold
it on, in 1888, to the famous
poet Robert Browning and
his son, Pen. The outstanding
attraction in the palace today
is Giorgio Massari's ballroom,
which occupies the entire
breadth of the building. It
is adorned with gilded
chandeliers, carved
furniture by Andrea
Brustolon and a ceiling
with *trompe l'oeil* frescoes.
Other rooms have frescoes
by Giambattista Tiepolo,
including his lively
Nuptial Allegory (1758),
and one by his son, Gian-
domenico, originally in
his villa at Zianigo. There
are paintings by Longhi,
Guardi, and – rare in Venice –
Canaletto. On the top floor is
a reconstructed 18th-century
apothecary's shop and the
Pinacoteca Martini.

Nave of San Nicolò dei Mendicoli, one of the oldest churches in Venice

San Nicolò dei Mendicoli ⓭

Campo San Nicolò. **Map** 5 A3. 041 275 03 82. San Basilio. 10am–noon, 4–6pm Mon–Sat.

CONTRASTING WITH the remote and rundown area which surrounds it, this church still remains one of the most charming in Venice. Founded in the 7th century, it has been rebuilt extensively over the years. The little porch on the north flank is 15th century and once sheltered the beggars, or *mendicanti*, who gave the church its name.

Thanks to the Venice in Peril fund, in the 1970s the church underwent one of the most comprehensive restoration programmes since the floods of 1966. Flooding had become such a problem that the priest often ferried himself around the church in a small wicker boat. The floor, which was 30 cm (1 ft) below the level of the canals, was rebuilt and raised slightly to prevent further flood damage. The roofs and lower walls were reconstructed, and paintings and statues restored.

The interior is delightfully embellished, particularly the nave with its 16th-century gilded wooden statues. These include the figure of San Nicolò himself. On the upper walls is a series of paintings of the life of Christ (c.1553) by Alvise dal Friso and other pupils of Veronese.

Outside, a small column supports a stone lion, in a humbler echo of the Column of San Marco in the Piazzetta.

San Sebastiano ⓮

Campo San Sebastiano. **Map** 5 C3. 041 275 04 62. San Basilio. 10am–5pm Mon–Sat, 1–5pm Sun. Sun (Jul & Aug) & public hols.

THIS CHURCH HAS one of the most homogeneous interiors in the whole of Venice. The splendour was created by Veronese who, from 1555 to 1560 and again in the 1570s, was commissioned to decorate the sacristy ceiling, the nave ceiling, the frieze, the east end of the choir, the high altar, the doors of the organ panels and the chancel.

The paintings feature radiant colours and rich costumes. Those on the sacristy ceiling depict the *Coronation of the Virgin* and the *Four Evangelists*.

Of the other paintings, the finest are the three that tell the story of Esther, Queen of Xerxes I of Persia, famous for securing the deliverance of the Jewish people.

Veronese is buried here. His tomb is situated in front of the beautifully paved chapel to the left of the chancel.

Accademia ⓯

See pp102–3.

Peggy Guggenheim Collection ⓰

Palazzo Venier dei Leoni. **Map** 6 F4. 041 240 54 11. Accademia. 10am–6pm Wed–Mon. 25 Dec.

INTENDED AS A four-storey palace, the 18th-century Palazzo Venier dei Leoni in fact never rose beyond the ground floor – hence its nickname,

The truncated palazzo housing the Peggy Guggenheim Collection

Il Palazzo Nonfinito (The Unfinished Palace). In 1949 the building was bought as a home by the American millionairess Peggy Guggenheim (1898–1979), a collector, dealer and patron of the arts.

A perspicacious and high-spirited woman, she initially befriended, and then furthered the careers of, many innovative abstract and Surrealist artists. One was Max Ernst, who became her second husband. The collection consists of 200 fine paintings and sculptures, each representing the 20th century's most influential modern art movements. The dining room has notable Cubist works of art, including *The Poet* by Pablo Picasso, and an entire room is devoted to Jackson Pollock, who was "discovered" by Guggenheim.

Maiastra by Constantin Brancusi

Other artists represented are Braque, Chagall, de Chirico, Dalí, Duchamp, Léger, Kandinsky, Klee, Mondrian, Miró, Malevich, Rothko, Bacon and Magritte, whose Surreal *Empire of Light* (1953–4) shows a night scene of a darkened house in a wooded setting with a bright day sky above. The sculpture collection, which includes Constantin Brancusi's elegant *Maiastra* (1912), is laid out in the house and garden.

Perhaps the most provocative piece is Marino Marini's *Angelo della Città* (Angel of the Citadel, 1948), located on the terrace overlooking the Grand Canal. This shows a prominently displayed man sitting on a horse, erect in all respects. Embarrassed onlookers avert their gaze to enjoy views of the Grand Canal.

The Guggenheim, one of the most visited sights in Venice, is the best place in the city to see modern art. Light-filled rooms and the large modern canvases provide a striking contrast to the Renaissance paintings that usually form the highlights in most Venetian churches and museums. A bonus for English speakers is the team of assistants, who are often visiting arts graduates from English-speaking countries.

The garden has been paved and features an array of sculptures. Peggy Guggenheim's ashes are also preserved here, near the place where her pet dogs were buried. A shop and restaurant are housed in buildings off the garden. Call for information on temporary exhibits.

The Baroque church of Santa Maria della Salute, at the mouth of the Grand Canal

Santa Maria della Salute ⑰

Campo della Salute. **Map** 7 A4.
📞 *041 523 79 51.* 🚊 *Salute.*
🕐 *9am–noon, 3–5:30pm daily.*
♿ *to sacristy.* 🚫

THE GREAT BAROQUE church of Santa Maria della Salute, standing at the entrance of the Grand Canal, is one of the most imposing architectural landmarks of Venice. Henry James likened it to "some great lady on the threshold of her salon".

Interior of the Salute with the octagonal space at its core

The church was built in thanksgiving for the city's deliverance from the plague epidemic of 1630, hence the name *Salute*, which means health and salvation.

Each November, in celebration, worshippers light candles and approach across a bridge of boats spanning the mouth of the Grand Canal for the occasion.

Baldassare Longhena started the church in 1630 at the age of 32, and worked on it for the rest of his life. It was not completed until 1687, five years after his death.

The interior is comparatively sober. It consists of a large octagonal space below the cupola and six chapels radiating from the ambulatory. The large domed chancel and grandiose high altar dominate the view from the main door.

The altar's sculptural group by Giusto Le Corte represents the Virgin and Child giving protection to Venice from the plague. The best of the paintings are in the sacristy to the left of the altar: Titian's early altarpiece of *St Mark Enthroned with Saints Cosmas, Damian, Roch and Sebastian* (1511–12) and his dramatic ceiling paintings of *Cain and Abel, The Sacrifice of Abraham and Isaac* and *David and Goliath* (1540–9). *The Wedding at Cana* (1551) on the wall opposite the entrance is a major work by Jacopo Tintoretto.

Accademia ⑮

Spanning five centuries, the matchless collection of paintings in the Accademia provides a complete spectrum of the Venetian school, from the medieval Byzantine period through the Renaissance to the Baroque and later. The basis of the collection was the Accademia di Belle Arti founded in 1750 by the painter Giovanni Battista Piazzetta. In 1807 Napoleon moved the collection to these premises, and enriched it with works of art removed from churches and monasteries.

KEY TO FLOORPLAN

- ☐ Byzantine and International Gothic
- ▨ Renaissance
- ☐ Baroque, Genre and Landscape
- ☐ Ceremonial Painting
- ▨ Temporary exhibitions
- ☐ Non-exhibition space

The former church of Santa Maria della Carità

The courtyard (1561) designed by Palladio

The Tempest
In this enigmatic landscape (c.1507), Giorgione was probably creating a fantasy rather than portraying any specific subject.

Feast in the House of Levi (1573) by Paolo Veronese

Madonna and Child between St John the Baptist and a Saint
In this beautiful painting (c.1504), Giovanni Bellini places the figures in a spacious landscape, so marking a new phase in his development.

Coronation of the Virgin
Paolo Veneziano's polyptych (1325) has a central image of the Virgin surrounded by a panoply of religious scenes. This detail shows episodes from the Life of St Francis.

Entrance

Healing of the Madman (c.1496) by Vittore Carpaccio

BYZANTINE AND INTERNATIONAL GOTHIC

ROOM 1 SHOWS the influence of Byzantine art on the early Venetian painters. In Paolo Veneziano's glowing *Coronation of the Virgin* (1325), the linear rhythms are unmistakably Gothic, but the gold background and central panel are distinctly Byzantine.

In contrast, *The Coronation of the Virgin* (1448) by Michele Giambono reveals a delicate naturalism, typical of the International Gothic style.

RENAISSANCE

THE RENAISSANCE came late to Venice, but by the second quarter of the 15th century it had transformed the city into a thriving art centre rivalling Florence and Rome. Central to Venetian art in the 15th century was the *Sacra Conversazione*, in which the Madonna is portrayed with various saints in a harmonious composition. Giovanni Bellini's altarpiece for San Giobbe (c.1487) in room 2 is one of the finest examples of this subject.

In contrast, the High Renaissance exuberance of Paolo Veronese is exemplified in the monumental *Feast in the House of Levi* (1573). The painting occupies a whole wall in room 10. Tintoretto's huge masterpiece *The Miracle of St Mark Freeing a Slave* (1548) is also on display here.

BAROQUE, GENRE AND LANDSCAPE

VENICE LACKED native Baroque painters, but a few non-Venetians kept the Venetian school alive in the 17th century. The most notable was the Genoese Bernardo Strozzi (1581–1644). The artist was a great admirer of the work of Veronese, as can be seen in his *Feast at the House of Simon* (1629) in

room 11. Also represented in this room is Giambattista Tiepolo, the greatest Venetian painter of the 18th century.

The long corridor (12) and the rooms that lead from it are largely devoted to light-hearted landscape and genre paintings from the 18th century. Among them are pastoral scenes by Francesco Zuccarelli, works by Marco Ricci, scenes of Venetian society by Pietro Longhi and a view of Venice by Canaletto (1763). This is a fine example of his sense of perspective.

CEREMONIAL PAINTING

ROOMS 20 and 21 return to the Renaissance, featuring two great cycles of paintings from the late 16th century. The detail in these large-scale anecdotal canvases provides a fascinating glimpse of the life, customs and appearance of Venice at the time.

Room 20 houses *The Stories of the Cross* by Venice's leading artists. In room 21, minutely detailed *Scenes from the Legend of St Ursula* (1490s) by Carpaccio mix reality and imagination by linking episodes from the life of the saint to the settings and costumes of 15th-century Venice.

Feast in the House of Levi (1573) by Paolo Veronese

Street-by-Street: Piazza San Marco

THROUGHOUT ITS LONG history Piazza San Marco has witnessed pageants, processions, political activities and countless Carnival festivities. Visitors flock here in their thousands for two of the city's most important historic sights – the Basilica and the Palazzo Ducale. These magnificent buildings complement lesser sights, such as the Campanile, Museo Correr and Torre dell'Orologio, not to mention the gardens of the Giardinetti Reali, open-air orchestras, elegant cafés – notably Quadri and Florian's – and numerous smart shops.

Lion of St Mark

Torre dell'Orologio
The clock tower, with hidden clockwork figures, dates from the Renaissance 20

Gondolas are moored in the Bacino Orseolo, named after Doge Pietro Orseolo who established a hospice for pilgrims here in 977.

The Piazza was described by Napoleon as the "most elegant drawing room in Europe".

MERCERIE

PROCURATIE VECCHIE

PIAZZA SAN MARCO

PROCURATIE NUOVE

Museo Correr
Giovanni Bellini's Pietà *(1455–60) is one of many masterpieces hanging in the galleries of the Correr* 22

Harry's Bar has attracted American visitors since Giuseppe Cipriani and his friend Harry set it up in 1931. Shown here is Ernest Hemingway, one of the bar's many famous patrons.

San Marco Vallaresso

★ **Basilica
di San Marco**
*This 13th-century
façade mosaic shows
the body of St Mark being
carried into the basilica* ⓲

LOCATOR MAP
See Venice Street Finder map 7

The Campanile
*The present Campanile replaced
one that collapsed in 1902* ㉑

**The Bridge of
Sighs** (1600) was
built as a passage-
way between the
Palazzo Ducale
and the prison. It
reputedly took its
name from the
sighs of prisoners
being led to trial.

LARGA SAN MARCO

RIO DEL

PALAZZO

**Ponte
della Paglia**

PIAZZETTA

MOLO SAN MARCO

★ **Palazzo Ducale**
*Once home to Venice's rulers,
and to the offices of State, the
Doges' Palace is a triumph of
Gothic architecture* ⓳

The vaulting of
the stairway in the
magnificent Libreria
Sansoviniana (1588)
is decorated with
frescoes and gilded
stucco. The national
library of St Mark
is housed here.

**San Marco
Giardinetti**

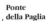

0 metres	75
0 yards	75

The Zecca, designed by Sansovino
and started in 1537, was the city
mint until 1870, and gave its name
to the *zecchino* or Venetian ducat.

STAR SIGHTS

★ **Basilica di San
Marco**

★ **Palazzo Ducale**

Basilica di San Marco ⑱

Venice's famous basilica blends the architectural and decorative styles of East and West to create one of the greatest buildings in Europe. The exterior owes its almost Oriental splendour to countless treasures from the Republic's overseas empire. Among these are copies of the famous bronze horses, brought from Constantinople in 1204, and a wealth of columns, bas-reliefs and coloured marbles studded across the main façade. Mosaics from different epochs adorn the five doorways, while the main portal is framed by some of Italy's loveliest Romanesque carving (1240–65).

The Pentecost Dome, showing the Descent of the Holy Ghost as a dove, was probably the first dome to be decorated with mosaics.

St Mark and Angels
The statues crowning the central arch are additions from the early 15th century.

The elegant arches echo those of the lower floor, forming a repeat pattern.

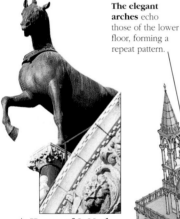

★ Horses of St Mark
The four horses are replicas of the gilded bronze originals, now protected inside the Basilica's museum.

Star Features

★ Façade Mosaics

★ Horses of St Mark

Romanesque carvings adorn the arches of the main portal.

Entrance

★ Façade Mosaics
A 17th-century mosaic shows the body of St Mark being taken from Alexandria, reputedly smuggled past Muslim guards under slices of pork.

Ciborium
The fine alabaster columns of the altar canopy, or baldacchino, are adorned with scenes from the New Testament.

The Ascension Dome
features a magnificent 13th-century mosaic of Christ surrounded by angels, the 12 Apostles and the Virgin Mary.

St Mark's body, believed lost in the fire of AD 976, supposedly reappeared when the new church was consecrated in 1094. The remains are housed in the altar.

The Mosaic Pavement shows beautiful pictures of birds and beasts, some of which are allegorical.

St Mark's Treasury

The Tetrarchs
This charming sculptured group in porphyry (4th-century Egyptian) is thought to represent Diocletian, Maximian, Valerian and Constantine. Collectively they were the Tetrarchs, appointed by Diocletian to help rule the Roman Empire.

VISITORS' CHECKLIST

Piazza San Marco. **Map** 7 B2. [phone] 041 522 52 05. 🚤 San Marco. **Basilica** ⬭ Apr–Sep: 9:30am–5pm Mon–Sat, 2–5pm Sun; Oct–Mar: 10am–4pm Mon–Sat, 2–4pm Sun. ⬆ sightseeing limited during services. **Museum, Treasury & Pala d'Oro** ⬭ as above. 🎟️ 📷 ⬭ Treasury only. ♿ 📷 🚫

THE BUILDING OF ST MARK'S

Built on a Greek cross plan and crowned with five huge domes, this is the third church to stand on the site. The first, which enshrined the body of St Mark in the 9th century, was destroyed by fire. The second was pulled down in favour of a church reflecting Venice's growing power. The present design was inspired by the Church of the Apostles in Constantinople and was completed and decorated over the centuries. From 1075, all ships returning from abroad had, by law, to bring back a precious gift to adorn "the House of St Mark". The mosaics inside are mostly 12th–13th century and cover 4,240 sq m (45,622 sq ft). Some were later replaced by such artists as Titian and Tintoretto. Until 1807 St Mark's was the doge's private chapel, used for ceremonies of State, after which it succeeded San Pietro di Castello as the cathedral of Venice.

13th-century carving of a grape harvester on the main portal

Exploring the Basilica

S⊤ MARK'S MAGNIFICENT INTERIOR is clad with dazzling mosaics, which begin in the *narthex*, or atrium of the Basilica, and culminate in the glittering panels of the Pentecost and Ascension domes. The Genesis Cupola in the atrium has a stunning Creation of the World described in concentric circles. The *pavimento* or floor is also patterned with mosaics in marble and glass. Steps from the atrium lead to the Museo Marciano, home to the Basilica's famous horses. Other treasures include the jewel-encrusted Pala d'Oro, behind the high altar, the Nicopeia icon and the precious hoards of silver, gold and glassware in the Treasury.

Madonna di Nicopeia
This Byzantine icon, looted in 1204, is one of Venice's most revered images.

The Porta dei Fiori or Gate of Flowers is decorated with 13th-century reliefs.

Cappella dei Mascoli

North side aisle

★ **Pentecost Dome**
Showing the Apostles touched by tongues of flame, the Pentecost Dome was lavishly decorated in the 12th century.

Atrium

Steps to Museo Marciano

Cappella Zen

Baptistry

★ **Ascension Dome**
A mosaic of Christ in Glory decorates the enormous central dome. This masterpiece was created by 13th-century Venetian craftsmen, who were strongly influenced by the art and architecture of Byzantium.

★ **Treasury**
A repository for precious artifacts from both Italy and Constantinople, the treasury houses objects such as this 11th-century silver-gilt coffer.

MOSAICS

CLOTHING THE DOMES, walls and floor of the Basilica are over 4,000 sq m (43,000 sq ft) of gleaming golden mosaics. The earliest, dating from the 12th century, were the work of mosaicists from the East. Their delicate techniques were soon adopted by Venetian craftsmen, who gradually took over the Basilica's decoration, combining Byzantine inspiration with Western influences. During the 16th century, many sketches by Tintoretto, Titian, Veronese, and other leading artists were reproduced in mosaic.

Among the most dazzling mosaics – many of which have been heavily restored – are those in the 13th-century central Ascension Dome and the 12th-century Pentecost Dome over the nave.

PALA D'ORO

BEYOND THE CAPPELLA di San Clemente lies the entrance to the most valuable treasure of San Marco: the Pala d'Oro. This jewel-spangled altarpiece, situated behind the high altar, consists of 250 enamel paintings on gold foil, enclosed within a gilded silver Gothic frame. Originally commissioned in Byzantium in AD 976, the altarpiece was further embellished over the centuries. Napoleon stole some of the precious stones in 1797, but the screen still gleams with pearls, rubies, sapphires and amethysts.

MUSEO MARCIANO

STEPS FROM the atrium, signposted Loggia dei Cavalli, take you up to the church museum, where the gallery offers a splendid view into the basilica. The gilded bronze horses, housed in a room at the far end of the museum, were stolen from the top of the Hippodrome (ancient racecourse) in Constantinople (modern Istanbul) in 1204 but their origin, either Roman or Hellenistic, remains a mystery. Also on show are mosaics, medieval manuscripts and antique tapestries.

BAPTISTRY AND CHAPELS

THE BAPTISTRY (closed to the public) was added by Doge Andrea Dandolo (1343–54), who is buried here, with Sansovino, who designed the font. The adjoining Cappella Zen (also closed to the public) became a funeral chapel for Cardinal Zen in 1504 in return for a bequest to the State. The left transept of the Cappella dei Mascoli is decorated with scenes from the life of Mary, while the third chapel in the same transept houses the icon of the Madonna di Nicopeia. Looted in 1204, it was once carried into battle at the head of the Byzantine army.

★ Pala d'Oro
The altarpiece, created in the 10th century by medieval goldsmiths, is made up of 250 panels such as this one.

The sacristy door has fine bronze panels by Sansovino which include portraits of himself with Titian and Aretino.

The Altar of the Sacrament is decorated with mosaics of the parables and miracles of Christ dating from the late 12th or early 13th century.

The columns of the inner façade are thought to be fragments of the first basilica.

South side aisle

STAR FEATURES

★ Pala d'Oro

★ Treasury

★ Ascension and Pentecost Domes

Noah and the Flood, atrium mosaics from the 13th century

Palazzo Ducale ⑲

THE PALAZZO DUCALE (Doges' Palace) was the official residence of each Venetian ruler (doge) and was founded in the 9th century. The present palace owes its external appearance to the building work of the 14th and early 15th centuries. To create their airy Gothic masterpiece, the Venetians broke with tradition by perching the bulk of the palace (built in pink Veronese marble) on top of an apparent fretwork of loggias and arcades (built from white Istrian stone).

Mars by Sansovino

★ **Giants' Staircase**
This 15th-century staircase is crowned by Sansovino's statues of Mars and Neptune, symbols of Venice's power.

Sala del Senato

Sala del Collegio

Anticollegio

The Arco Foscari has copies of Antonio Rizzo's 15th-century Adam and Eve.

Exit

★ **Porta della Carta**
This 15th-century Gothic gate was once the main entrance to the palace. From it, a vaulted passageway leads to the Arco Foscari and the internal courtyard.

Courtyard

★ **Sala del Maggior Consiglio**
This vast hall was used as a meeting place for members of Venice's Great Council. Tintoretto's huge Paradise (1590) fills the end wall.

Sala dello Scudo
The walls of this room, once part of the doge's private apartments, are covered with maps of the world. In the centre of the room are two giant 18th-century globes.

VISITORS' CHECKLIST

Piazzetta. **Map** 7 C2. 🕿 *041 520 90 70.* 🚖 *San Marco.* ⬭ *Apr–Oct: 9am–7pm daily; Nov–Mar: 9am–5pm daily (last adm: 90 mins before closing).* ⬤ *1 Jan, 25 Dec.* 🔲 🔲 🔲 *partial.* 🔲 🔲 🚫

Sala delle
Quattro Porte

Sala del Consiglio
dei Dieci

Torture Chamber
Interrogations took place in the Torture Chamber. Suspects were hung by their wrists from a cord in the centre of the room.

Sala della Bussola

The Bridge of Sighs

Drunkenness of Noah
This early 15th-century sculpture, symbolic of the frailty of man, is set on the corner of the palace.

Main
entrance

The Ponte della Paglia, built of Istrian stone, has a pretty balustrade of columns and sculpted pine cones.

The Loggia
Each arch of the ground level portico supports two arches of the loggia, which commands fine views of the lagoon.

STAR FEATURES

★ **Giants' Staircase**

★ **Porta della Carta**

★ **Sala del Maggior Consiglio**

Exploring the Palazzo Ducale

A TOUR OF THE PALAZZO DUCALE takes you through a succession of richly decorated chambers and halls, arranged over three floors, culminating with the Bridge of Sighs which links the palace to the prisons. Casanova was once imprisoned here and made a daring escape from the Palazzo through a hole in the roof.

Jacopo and Domenico Tintoretto's *Paradise*, one of the world's largest paintings, in the Sala del Maggior Consiglio

SCALA D'ORO AND COURTYARD

A PASSAGE from the Porta del Frumento opens into the palace courtyard. The ticket office and palace entrance are to the left. At the top of Antonio Rizzo's 15th-century Giants' Staircase, the new doge would be crowned with the *zogia* or dogal cap. The Scala d'Oro (golden staircase), designed by Jacopo Sansovino, leads to the palace's upper floors. It takes its name, however, from the elaborate gilt stucco vault created by Alessandro Vittoria (1554–8).

SALA DELLE QUATTRO PORTE TO THE SALA DEL SENATO

THE SECOND FLIGHT of the Scala d'Oro leads to the Sala delle Quattro Porte, with a ceiling designed by Palladio and frescoed by Tintoretto. The end walls of the next room, the Anticollegio, are decorated with mythological scenes by Tintoretto, while Veronese's masterly *Rape of Europa* (1580), opposite the window, is one of the palace's most dramatic works. The adjoining Sala del Collegio was where the doge and his counsellors met to receive ambassadors and discuss matters of State. Embellishing the magnificent ceiling are 11 paintings by Veronese. In the next room, the Sala del Senato, the doge and some 200 senators discussed foreign affairs. The paintings are by Tintoretto and pupils.

SALA DEL CONSIGLIO DEI DIECI TO THE ARMERIA

THE Sala del Consiglio dei Dieci was the meeting room of the powerful Council of Ten, founded in 1310 to protect State security. Two fine works by Veronese adorn the ceiling: *Age and Youth* and *Juno Offering the Ducal Crown to Venice* (both

Dialectic (c.1577) by Veronese in the Palazzo Ducale's Sala del Collegio

1553–4). In the Sala della Bussola, offenders awaited their fate in front of the Council of Ten. The room's *bocca di leone* (lion's mouth), was used to post secret denunciations and was just one of several in the palace. The wooden door here leads to the State Inquisitors' Room and thence to the torture chamber and prisons. The Armoury – one of the finest such collections anywhere in Europe – occupies the following rooms.

SALA DEL MAGGIOR CONSIGLIO

THE SCALA DEI CENSORI takes you to the second floor and past the Sala del Guariento and Antonio Rizzo's statues of Adam and Eve (1480s) to the magnificent Sala del Maggior Consiglio. A vast chamber, it was used as a meeting place for the Great Council and for grand State banquets. By the mid-16th century the Great Council had around 2,000 members. Any Venetian of high birth over 25 was entitled to a seat unless he married a commoner.
Tintoretto's huge *Paradise* (1587–90) occupies the eastern wall. Measuring 7.45 by 24.65 m (25 by 81 ft), it is one of the largest paintings in the world. The itinerary then continues in more sombre vein, crossing the Bridge of Sighs to enter the dank world of the prisons.

A bocca di leone for denunciations

Torre dell'Orologio 🄛

Piazza San Marco. **Map** 7 B2. 🚉 San
Marco. ⬤ for restoration.

THIS RICHLY decorated clock
tower on the north
side of the piazza
was built in the
late 15th century.
Mauro Coducci
is thought to
have worked
on the design.
With its display
of the phases of
the moon and the
signs of the zodiac,
the gilt-and-blue
enamel clock face
was designed with
seafarers in mind.
According to legend, once
the clock was completed,
the two inventors of the
complex mechanism had
their eyes gouged out to
prevent them from ever
creating a replica.

**The clock face of the
Torre dell'Orologio**

On the upper level, the
winged lion of St Mark stands
against a star-spangled blue
backdrop. At the very top
the two huge bronze figures,
known as the *Mori*, or Moors,
because of their dark patina,
strike the bell on the hour.

Campanile 🄜

Piazza San Marco. **Map** 7 B2. 🕾 041
522 40 64. 🚉 San Marco. ◯ Oct–
Dec, Feb–Easter: 9:30am–5pm daily;
Easter–Sep: 9am–9pm. ⬤ Jan. 🖾

FROM THE TOP of St Mark's
campanile, high above the
piazza, visitors can enjoy views
of the city, the lagoon and, vis-
ibility permitting, the peaks of
the Alps. It was from this viewpoint that Galileo demonstrated
his telescope to Doge Leonardo Donà in 1609. To do so he
would have climbed the internal ramp. These days access is
achieved via a lift.

The first tower, completed
in 1173, was built as a lighthouse to assist navigators in
the lagoon. It took on a less
benevolent role in the Middle
Ages, when offenders were
imprisoned – and in some
cases left to die – in a cage

hung near its summit. With
the exception of several 16th-
century renovations, the
tower survived unharmed
until 14 July 1902 when, with
little warning, its foundations
gave way and it suddenly
collapsed. The only casualties
were the Loggetta at the
foot of the tower and
the custodian's cat.
Donations for
reconstruction
came flooding
in and the
following year
the foundation
stone was laid for
a campanile *"dov'
era e com'era"*
("where it was and
as it was"). The
new tower was
finally opened on 25 April
(the Feast of St Mark) 1912.

Museo Correr 🄞

Procuratie Nuove. Entrance in Ala
Napoleonica. **Map** 7 B2. 🕾 041
240 52 11. 🚉 San Marco. ◯ Apr–
Oct: 9am–7pm; Nov–Mar: 9am–5pm
(last adm: 1hr before closing). ⬤ 1
Jan, 25 Dec. 🖾 🛉 🖵 🚫

TEODORO CORRER bequeathed
his extensive collection
of works of art to Venice in
1830, thus forming the core of
the city's fine civic museum.

Its first rooms form a suitably
Neo-Classical backdrop for
early statues by Antonio
Canova (1757–1822). The rest
of the floor covers the history
of the Venetian Republic, with
maps, coins, armour and a

host of doge-related exhibits.
The second floor contains the
picture gallery, whose collection is second only to that
of the Accademia.

The paintings, hung chrono-
logically, trace the evolution
of Venetian painting, and show
the influence that Ferrarese,
Paduan and Flemish artists
had on the Venetian school.

The gallery's most famous
works are by Carpaccio:
*Portrait of a Young Man in a
Red Hat* (c.1490), and *Two
Venetian Ladies* (c.1507). The
latter is traditionally, but
probably incorrectly, known
as *The Courtesans* because of
the ladies' low-cut dresses.
The Museo del Risorgimento
on the same floor looks at the
history of Venice until
unification with Italy in 1866.

**The ceiling of Santo Stefano, built
in the form of a ship's keel**

Santo Stefano 🄟

Campo Santo Stefano. **Map** 6 F2.
🕾 041 275 04 62. 🚉 Accademia
or Sant'Angelo. ◯ 10am–5pm
Mon–Sat, 1–5pm Sun. ⬤ Sun (Jul &
Aug), 1 Jan, 25 Dec. 🖾 🛉 🖵 🚫

DECONSECRATED six times
on account of the blood
spilled within its walls, Santo
Stefano – one of Venice's most
beautiful churches – is now
remarkably serene. Built in
the 14th century, and altered
in the 15th, the church has a
carved portal by Bartolomeo
Bon, and a campanile with a
typical Venetian tilt. The
interior has a splendid ship's
keel ceiling, carved tie-beams,
and the sacristy crammed
with valuable paintings.

**Young Man in a Red Hat (c.1490)
by Carpaccio in the Museo Correr**

Santi Giovanni e Paolo ㉔

KNOWN MORE COLLOQUIALLY AS San Zanipolo, Santi Giovanni e Paolo vies with the Frari *(see pp94–5)* as the city's greatest Gothic church. Built by the Dominicans in the 14th century, it is striking for its vast scale and architectural austerity. Known as the Pantheon of Venice, it houses monuments to no fewer than 25 doges. Among these are several fine works of art, executed by the Lombardi family and other leading sculptors.

The bronze statue is a monument to Doge Sebastiano Venier, who was Commander of the Fleet at Lepanto.

The Nave
The cross-vaulted interior is tied by wooden beams and supported by stone columns.

★ Tomb of Nicolò Marcello
This magnificent Renaissance monument to Doge Nicolò Marcello (died 1474) was sculpted by Pietro Lombardo.

The doorway, which is decorated with Byzantine reliefs and carvings by Bartolomeo Bon, is one of Venice's earliest Renaissance architectural works.

Entrance

★ Tomb of Pietro Mocenigo
Pietro Lombardo's superb tomb (1481) commemorates the doge's military pursuits when he was Grand Captain of the Venetian forces.

★ Polyptych by Bellini
This painting (c.1465) shows St Vincent Ferrer, a Spanish cleric, flanked by St Sebastian and St Christopher.

**The Baroque high
altar**, begun in
1619, is attributed
to Baldassare
Longhena.

**16th-century
altar statues
by Vittoria**

**16th-century
frescoes
attributed to
Palma il Giovane**

**★ Tomb of Andrea
Vendramin**
*Lombardo's masterpiece
(1476–8) takes the form of
a Roman triumphal arch.*

STAR FEATURES

★ Doges' Tombs

★ Polyptych by Bellini

Statue of Colleoni ㉕

Campo Santi Giovanni e Paolo.
Map 3 C5. 🚑 *Ospedale Civile.*

BARTOLOMEO COLLEONI, the
famous *condottiere* or
commander of mercenaries,
left his fortune to the
Republic on condition that
his statue was placed in front
of San Marco. A prominent
statue in the piazza would
have broken with precedent,
so the Senate cunningly had
Colleoni raised before the
Scuola di San Marco instead of
the basilica. A touchstone of
early Renaissance sculpture,
the equestrian statue of the
proud warrior (1481–8) is
by the Florentine Andrea
Verrocchio, but was cast in
bronze after his death by
Alessandro Leopardi. The
statue has a strong sense of
power and movement which
arguably ranks it alongside
the works of Donatello.

Santa Maria Formosa ㉖

Campo Santa Maria Formosa.
Map 7 C1. [041 275 04 62.
🚤 *Rialto.* ⬤ *10am–5pm Mon–Sat,
1–5pm Sun.* ⬤ *Sun (Jul & Aug),
1 Jan, 25 Dec.* ⬤ ⬤ ⬤

DESIGNED BY Mauro Coducci
in 1492, this church is
most unusual in having two
main façades – one overlooks
the *campo*, the other the
canal. The bell tower or
campanile, added in 1688,
is noted for the grotesque
face at its base. Two paintings
stand out in the interior: a
triptych (1473) by Bartolomeo
Vivarini and Palma il
Vecchio's *St Barbara* (c.1510).

San Zaccaria ㉗

Campo San Zaccaria. **Map** 8 D2.
[041 522 12 57. 🚤 *San Zaccaria.*
⬤ *10am–noon, 4–6pm Mon–Sat,
4–6pm Sun & public hols.*
⬤ *chapels and crypt.* ⬤

SET IN A QUIET square just a
stone's throw from the Riva
degli Schiavoni, the church of
San Zaccaria is a successful

**Palma il Vecchio's *St Barbara*
(c.1510) in Santa Maria Formosa**

blend of flamboyant Gothic
and Classical Renaissance
styles. Founded in the 9th
century, its façade was later
rebuilt by Antonio Gambello
in Gothic style. When
Gambello died in 1481,
Mauro Coducci completed the
upper section, adding many
of its Renaissance panels.

The interior's artistic
highlight is Giovanni Bellini's
serene and sumptuously
coloured *Madonna and Child
with Saints* (1505) in the north
aisle. A door off the right
nave leads to the Chapel of St
Athanasius, which in turn leads
to the Chapel of San Tarasio.
The chapel contains vault
frescoes (1442) by Andrea del
Castagno, and polyptychs
(1443–4) by Antonio Vivarini
and Giovanni d'Alemagna.

**A Renaissance panel by Coducci
on the façade of San Zaccaria**

Scuola di San Giorgio degli Schiavoni ㉘

Calle Furlani. **Map** 8 E1. 041 522 88 28. San Zaccaria. Apr–Oct: 9:30am–12:30pm, 3:30–6:30pm Tue–Sat (Sun am only); Nov–Mar: 10am–12:30pm, 3–6pm Tue–Sat (Sun am only). 1 Jan, 1 May, 25 Dec and other religious hols.

W**ITHIN THIS** small gem are some of the finest paintings of Vittore Carpaccio. They were commissioned by the Schiavoni, or Dalmatian Slav community in Venice.

The Scuola was established in 1451 and rebuilt in 1551. It has changed very little since. The exquisite frieze, executed between 1502 and 1508, shows scenes from the lives of patron saints: St George, St Tryphone and St Jerome. Each episode of the narrative cycle is remarkable for its vivid colouring, minute detail and historic record of Venetian life. Outstanding among them are *St George Slaying the Dragon* and *St Jerome Leading the Tamed Lion to the Monastery*.

San Giovanni in Bragora ㉙

Campo Bandiera e Moro. **Map** 8 E2. 041 270 24 64. Arsenale. 9–11am, 3:30–5:30pm Mon–Sat.

T**HE EXISTING** church is essentially Gothic (1475–9) and the interior contains major works of art that demonstrate the transition from Gothic to early Renaissance. Bartolomeo

Lagoon entrance   Arsenale Novissimo, 15th–16th century

Old sail factory

Arsenale Vecchio, 12th–13th century   Corderia   Arsenale Nove, 14th century

18th-century engraving of the Arsenale

Vivarini's altarpiece *Madonna and Child with Saints* (1478) is unmistakably Gothic. Contrasting with this is Cima da Conegliano's large-scale *Baptism of Christ* (1492–5), which adorns the main altar.

Arsenale ㉚

Map 8 F1. Arsenale. **Museo Storico Navale** Campo San Biagio. **Map** 8 F3. 041 520 02 76. 8:45am–1:30pm Mon–Fri; 8:45am–1pm Sat. public hols.

T**HE ARSENALE** was founded in the 12th century and by the 16th had become the greatest naval shipyard in the world, capable of constructing a whole galley in 24 hours, using an assembly-line system. Surrounded by crenellated walls, it was like a city within a city. Today the site is largely disused. Its impressive 15th-century gateway, twin towers and guardian lions can be

viewed from the *campo* or bridge outside. The gateway was built by Antonio Gambello and is often cited as Venice's first Renaissance construction.

Around the corner, in Campo San Biagio, the **Museo Storico Navale** charts Venetian naval history from the heyday of the Arsenale to the present. Exhibits include friezes from famous galleys of the past and a replica of the *Bucintoro*, the Doge's ceremonial barge.

San Giorgio Maggiore ㉛

Map 8 D4. 041 522 78 27. San Giorgio. **Church & Campanile** 9:30am–12:30pm, 2:30–5pm daily (May–Sep: to 7pm). (Campanile). **Fondazione Cini** 041 524 01 19. Mon–Fri by appt; 10am–4pm Sat & Sun (guided tours every hour).

A**PPEARING LIKE** a stage set across the water from the Piazzetta is the little island of

St George Slaying the Dragon (1502–8) by Carpaccio, in the Scuola di San Giorgio degli Schiavoni

San Giorgio Maggiore. The church and monastery, constructed between 1559–80, are among Andrea Palladio's greatest architectural achievements. The church's temple front and the spacious interior with its perfect proportions and cool beauty are typically Palladian *(see pp76–7)*. These qualities are echoed by the church of Il Redentore on the nearby island of Giudecca, built by Palladio in 1577–92.

On the chancel walls of San Giorgio Maggiore, are two fine paintings by Tintoretto: *The Last Supper* and *Gathering of the Manna* (both 1594). In the Chapel of the Dead is his last work, *The Deposition* (1592–4), finished by his son Domenico.

The top of the campanile affords superb views of the city and lagoon. You can see the monastery cloisters below, now part of the **Fondazione Cini**, a cultural centre that is used to host international exhibitions.

Palladio's San Giorgio Maggiore

Murano ㉜

📛 *LN, 41 and 42 from Fondamente Nuove; DM from Ferrovia and Piazzale Roma.*

MUCH LIKE Venice, Murano comprises a cluster of small islands, connected by bridges. It has been the centre of the glassmaking industry since 1291, when the furnaces were moved here from the city because of the risk of fire and the disagreeable effects of smoke. Some of the houses on the water date from this period.

The colonnaded exterior of Murano's Basilica dei Santi Maria e Donato

🏛 Museo Vetrario
Palazzo Giustinian, Fondamenta Giustinian. 📞 041 73 95 86. ⏱ 10am–5pm (Nov–Mar: 4pm) Thu–Tue. ⬛ 1 Jan, 1 May, 25 Dec. 🏷 ♿

In the 15th and 16th centuries Murano was the principal glass-producing centre in Europe and today, most tourists visit for glass alone. The Museo Vetrario in the Palazzo Giustinian houses a fine collection of antique pieces. The prize exhibit is the dark blue Barovier wedding cup (1470–80), with enamel work by Angelo Barovier.

🔒 Basilica dei Santi Maria e Donato
Fondamenta Giustinian. 📞 041 73 90 56. ⏱ 9am–noon, 4–7pm daily (winter: to 6pm). ⬛ Sun am. ✗

With its lovely colonnaded apse, this basilica is the architectural highlight of the island. Despite some heavy-handed restoration undertaken in the 19th century, this 12th-century church still retains much of its original beauty. Visitors should note the Gothic ship's keel roof, the apse with its mosaic Madonna and the beautiful medieval mosaic floor, which dates from 1140.

Burano ㉝

📛 *LN from Fondamente Nuove; LN from San Zaccaria via Lido and Punta Sabbioni.*

BURANO IS THE MOST colourful of the lagoon islands and can be distinguished from a distance by the tilting tower of its church. In contrast with the haunting Torcello, the island is densely populated, its waterways fringed with brightly painted houses, such as the Casa Bepi.

The main thoroughfare is Via Baldassare Galuppi, named after the Burano-born composer. It features traditional lace and linen stalls and open-air trattorias serving fresh fish.

🏛 Scuola dei Merletti
Piazza Baldassare Galuppi. 📞 041 73 00 34. ⏱ Apr–Oct: 10am–5pm Wed–Mon; Nov–Mar: 10am–4pm. 🏷

The people of Burano are fishermen and lacemakers by tradition. You can still see fishermen scraping their boats or mending nets, but today lacemakers are rare. In the 16th century the local lace was the most sought-after in Europe – it was so delicate it became known as *punto in aria* ("points in the air"). After a slump in the 18th century, the industry revived and a lace-making school, or Scuola dei Merletti, was set up in 1872. Although authentic Burano lace is hard to find today, you can watch it being made at the school. A museum displays fine examples of antique lace.

Venetian glass goblet

Brightly painted street in Burano

Torcello ⓞ

ESTABLISHED BETWEEN the 5th and 6th centuries, the island of Torcello boasts the oldest building in the lagoon – the cathedral of Santa Maria dell'Assunta. Founded in AD 639, it contains some splendid ancient mosaics. The adjoining church of Santa Fosca, of pure Byzantine design, is another mark of Torcello's former glory – before being eclipsed by Venice it had a population of 20,000.

★ **Apse Mosaic**
The 13th-century Madonna, set against a gold background, is one of the most beautiful mosaics in Venice.

★ **Doomsday Mosaics**
The highly decorative 12th-century mosaic of the Last Judgment covers the west wall.

Pulpit
The present basilica dates from 1008, but includes earlier features. The pulpit contains 7th-century fragments.

The Roman sarcophagus below the altar is said to contain the relics of St Heliodorus.

★ **Iconostasis**
The exquisite Byzantine marble panels of the rood screen are carved with peacocks, lions and flowers.

Nave Columns
Two rows of slender marble columns, 18 in all, separate the three naves. Their finely carved capitals date from the 11th century.

Torcello's Last Canals
Silted canals and malaria hastened Torcello's decline. One of the remaining waterways runs from the vaporetto *stop to the basilica.*

VISITORS' CHECKLIST

LN from Fondamente Nuove then T from Burano. **Santa Maria & Campanile** 041 270 24 64. Mar–Oct: 10:30am–5:30pm daily; Nov–Feb: 10am–5pm daily. cathedral only. campanile only. **Santa Fosca** for masses only. **Museo dell'Estuario** 041 73 07 61. Mar–Oct: 10:30am–5:30pm Tue–Sun; Nov–Feb: 10am–5pm Tue–Sun. public hols.

The altar
was rebuilt in 1939 and stands below a 15th-century wood relief of *Santa Fosca Sleeping*.

The central dome
and cross sections are supported by columns of Greek marble with Corinthian capitals.

Santa Fosca
Built in the 11th and 12th centuries on a Greek-cross plan, the church has a serene Byzantine interior with a central pentagonal apse.

The Portico of Santa Fosca, with its elegant stilted arches, is built on three sides of the church, and probably dates from the 12th century.

Vaporetto **boarding point →**

The Museo dell'Estuario houses many old church treasures.

STAR FEATURES

★ **Apse Mosaic**

★ **Doomsday Mosaics**

★ **Iconostasis**

Attila's Throne
It was said that the 5th-century king of the Huns used this marble seat as his throne.

VENICE STREET FINDER

ALL THE MAP REFERENCES given for sights, hotels and restaurants in Venice refer to this section of the book. The key map below shows which areas of the city are covered by the Street Finder. The first figure of the map reference indicates which map to turn to, and the letter and number which follow are for the grid reference. Standard Italian spelling has been used on all the maps in this book,

but when exploring Venice you will find that the names on many street signs are written in Venetian dialect. Mostly this means only a slight variation in spelling (as in the word Sotoportico/Sotoportego below), but some names look totally different. For example, the church of Santi Giovanni e Paolo *(see map 3)*, is frequently signposted as "San Zanipolo". A further map showing the vaporetto routes follows the street maps.

RECOGNIZING STREET NAMES

The signs for street *(calle)*, canal *(rio)* and square *(campo)* will soon become familiar, but the Venetians have a colourful vocabulary for the maze of alleys which makes up the city. When exploring, the following may help.

FONDAMENTA S.SEVERO

Fondamenta is a street that runs alongside a canal, often named after the canal it follows.

RIO TERRA GESUATI

Rio Terrà is a filled-in canal. Similar to a *rio terrà* is a *piscina*, which often forms a square.

SOTOPORTEGO E PONTE S.CRISTOFORO

Sotoportico or Sotoportego means a covered passageway.

SALIZADA PIO X

Salizzada is a main street (formerly a paved street).

RIVA DEI PARTIGIANI

Riva is a wide *fondamenta*, often facing the lagoon.

RUGAGIUFFA

Ruga is a street lined with shops.

CORTE DEI DO POZZI

Corte means a courtyard.

RIO MENUO O DE LA VERONA

Many streets and canals in Venice often have more than one name: *o* means "or".

| 0 metres | 500 |
| 0 yards | 500 |

MURANO
(Inset on maps 3–4)

KEY TO STREET FINDER

▢	Major sight
▢	Place of interest
▢	Railway station
⛴	Ferry boarding point
⛴	*Vaporetto* boarding point
⛴	*Traghetto* crossing
⛴	Gondola mooring
🚌	Bus terminus
ℹ	Tourist information
✚	Hospital with casualty unit
P	Parking
👮	Police station
✝	Church
✡	Synagogue
⊠	Post office
=	Railway line

SCALE OF MAP PAGES

0 metres	200
0 yards	200

SCALE OF MURANO INSET

0 metres	500
0 yards	500

Canale del

FONDAMENTA DI SACCA SAN GIROLAMO
SACCA DI
SAN GIROLAMO

CALLE LARGA DEI PENITENTI

FONDAMENTA CASE NUOVE

FONDAMENT
Rio di
FONDAM

Canale Colombola

Canale di Cannaregio
FONDAMENTA DI SAN

CALLE TERAU
CALLE DEL FORNER

CPLO DELLE
COOPERATIVE

Ponte dei
Tre Archi

CALLE TINTORIA

FONDAMENTA Ri

CALLE D. PORTER

CALLE DELLE BECCARIE

CP.D.
BECCARIE
CP.D.
SCARLATTO

C.D. MAGAZEN

Ponte dei
Tre Archi

CALLE D. MADONNA

CALLE

CALLE D. TINTOR
CP.D. COLORI

CALLE D. CANNE

GIOBBE

FONDAMENTA

San
Giobbe

FMTA SAVO

CALLE BUSELLO

CALLE BISCOTELLA

CALLE DELLA CERERIA

Rio di San Giobbe

CAMPO
SAN GIOBBE

CALLE CENDON

CALLE SECON

PONTE DELLA LIBERTA

Rio della Crea

Rio della Crea

CALLE PRIULI DETTA DEI CAVALLETTI

CALLE PEAM

CALLE DELLA

CALLE CARMELITANI

Scalzi

FMTA D. SCALZI

Ponte
degli Sc

Stazione Ferrovie
dello Stato
Santa Lucia

FONDAMENTA S. LUCIA

Ferrovia

FONDAMENTA SAN SIMEON P

CALLE TRAGHE
DI SANTA LUCIA

S S
Pi

CALLE BERGAMASCHI

Can d. Santa Chiara

FONDAMENTA DI SANTA CHIARA

C. VOLTO DI SANTA CHIARA

Piazzale
Roma

FONDAMENTA SAN

CORTE CASE NUOV

FONDAMENTA
DEI TOLENTINI

GIARDINO
EX PAPADOPOLI

CAMPO D

1

MURANO

CAMPO
SPORTIVO

FONDAMENTA STRADA COM.D CIMITERO

Canale

Venier degli

Calle

Angeli

RAMO
DA MULA

FMTA DA MULA

Ponte
Vivarini

Palazzo
da Mula

San Pietro
Martire

FMTA ANTONIO COLLEONI

CPO. STO
STEFANO

CPLO
TURELLA

CPLO
BIGAGLIA

VIA BRIATI

FMTA PLAVE

Faro

Faro

Canale   Serenella

CALLE VIVARINI

erenella

STRADA VICINALE ORTI

CALLE SAN CIPRIANO

C.BERTOLINI

FONDAMENTA
SERENELLA

Colonna

CALLE BERTOLINI

FONDAMENTA

VETRAI

FONDAMENTA

Venier

DEI

VIALE GARIBALDI

CALLE DELL'OLIO

CALLE MIOTTI

CALLE SAN BERNARDO

Calle

DEL CRISTO

CALLE SAN BERNARDO

CALLE DELL'ARTIGIANO

Canale

FMTA SAN LORENZO

CAMPO SAN BERNARDO

CALLE DEL MISTRO

CAMPO SAN SALVADOR

FONDAMENTA CAVOUR

CALLE CONTERIE

SEBASTIANO SANTI

di San Donato

SS Maria
e Donato

Museo dell'Arte
Vetraria

Canal Grande di Murano

Museo

FMTA SAN GIOVANNI DEI BATTUTI

Navagero

CALLE DEL CONVENTO

CALLE VOLPI

FONDAMENTA LORENZO RADI

FONDAMENTA

Ponte
San Donato

FONDAMENTA ANDREA NAVAGERO

GIUSTINIAN

CALLE S.GIACMO

C PARADISO

Canale   Ondello

Canale   dei   Marani

2

3

4

Canale   delle   Fondamente   Nuove

spedale
Civile

AMENTE NUOVE

Rio di Santa Giustina

FONDAMENTA DI SANTA GIUSTINA

CALLE DELLE CAPPUCCINE

CALLE D.MOSCHETTE

CALLE SAN FRANCESCO

Celestia

FMTA CASE NUOVE

CALLE DEGLI ORTI

C.SAGREDO

San Francesco
della Vigna

etto

LLE TOLE

C.D. CAFFETTIER

5

Venice Vaporetto Routes

ROUTES AROUND THE LAGOON

See main map

Torcello
Mazzorbo
Burano
Treporti
Sant' Erasmo
Punta Sabbioni
Vignole
Laguna Veneta

Santa Maria Elisabetta (Lido)
Casino
MARE ADRIATICO

The Vaporetto Routes

The ACTV network runs regular servic[e] around the city and out to most of the islands. Some services are circular; ot[hers] extend their routes during the high sea[son.] There are also additional lines during t[he] summer months. More details of the different types of vaporetti *and how to use them are given on pages 636–7.*

Mestre
Canale delle S[...]

Sant'Alvise

Ponte dei Tre Archi

CANNAREGI[O]

Ponte delle Gu[...]
San M[...]

Ferrovia
FS
Riva di Biasio

SANTA CROCE

Tronchetto B

Piazzale Roma
P

SAN POLO

San Tomà

A[...]
San San[...]

Ca' Rezzonico

Accademia

Bacino della Stazione Marittima

Santa Marta

San Basilio

Zattere

Fusina

Sacca Fisola

Canale della Giude[cca]

Canale di Fusina

GIUDECCA
Palanc[a]

0 metres 500
0 yards 500

Venier 41 DM

MURANO

Da Mula 41 42

Museo 41 42 A

Navagero 41 42 DM

Serenella 42 DM

Burano Sant'Erasmo →

Faro 13 41 42 DM

13

San Zaccaria ↓

Colonna 41 42 DM A

A

13, 41, 42, DM

13, 41, 42, DM

Canale degli Angeli

A

A

Canale dei Marani

DM

Canale dei Marani

41, 42, DM, A

Cimitero 41 42

13, 41, 42, LN, A

SAN MICHELE

24, 41, 42, 51, 52

Canale delle Fondamente Nuove

41 42 51 52 N A

Fondamente Nuove

41, 42, 51, 52, A

Ca' d'Oro 1 N

41 42 51 52

Ospedale

San Giustina

41 42 51 52 N

Celestia

Grande

Rialto 1 24 82 N

CASTELLO

San Zaccaria/Pietá 1 20 41 42 51

52 82 N N A

Arsenale 1 41 A

SAN MARCO 1, 20, 41, 42, 51

laresso 82 N **San Marco** 4 A 1, 82, N

52, 61, 62, N

1, 82, N

1 **Salute**

Canale di San Marco

20

San Giorgio 82 N

51, 52, 61, 62, A

SAN GIORGIO MAGGIORE

41 42 82 N **Zitelle**

41, 42, 82, N

42 82 N ntore

1, 17, 41, 42, 51, 52, 61, 62, N LN, A

20

San Servolo San Lazzaro ↘

Giardini/Biennale 1 41 42 51 61

62 N

Sant'Elena 1 41 42 51

52 61 62

See inset map →

KEY

72	*Vaporetto* route
	Ferry boarding point
	Vaporetto boarding point
FS	Railway station
✈	Airport
P	Parking

ROUTES

1	P. Roma – Lido
6	S. Zaccaria – Lido
13	F. Nuove – Sant'Erasmo – Treporti
17	Lido – Tronchetto
20	S. Zaccaria – S. Lazzaro
24	Rialto – Mestre
41	Circular (via Murano) – anticlockwise
42	Circular (via Murano) – clockwise
51	Circular (via Lido) – anticlockwise
52	Circular (via Lido) – clockwise
61	P. Roma – S. Marta – S. Basilio – Lido
62	Lido – S. Basilio – S. Marta – P. Roma
82	S. Zaccaria – P. Roma – Vallaresso
A	Alilaguna airport service
DM	Piazzale Roma – Ferrovia – Murano
LN	S. Zaccaria – Lido – P. Sabbioni – Burano – F. Nuove
N	Lido – Tronchetto – S. Zaccaria (night service)

THE VENETO AND FRIULI

THE VENETO IS A REGION OF TREMENDOUS CONTRASTS, *encompassing the breathtaking natural beauty of the Dolomites, Lake Garda (Italy's largest lake) and the rolling Euganean Hills, and the man-made delights of magnificent ancient cities such as Verona, Vicenza and Padua. Neighbouring Friuli-Venezia Giulia lines the border with Slovenia to the east, taking in the Carnic Hills in the north, the Roman town of Aquileia and the bustling Adriatic port of Trieste.*

The Romans built frontier posts on this fertile land of silt deposits, and these survive today as the cities of Vicenza, Padua, Verona and Treviso. Strategically placed at the hub of the empire's road network, the cities prospered under Roman rule, but suffered in the wave of Germanic invasions of the 5th century AD.

The region's fortunes revived under the benign rule of the Venetian empire. The medieval cities of the Veneto lay on important trade routes such as the Serenissima, the road connecting the flourishing port cities of Venice and Genoa, and the Brenner Pass, used by commercial travellers crossing the Alps from northern Europe. Wealth from agriculture, commerce and the spoils of war paid for the beautification of these cities through the building of Renaissance palaces and public buildings, many designed by the Veneto's great architect, Andrea Palladio. His palazzi and villas are telling symbols of the leisured existence once enjoyed by the area's aristocrats.

Today the Veneto is a thriving wine exporter, textile producer and agricultural centre, and Friuli is a focus for new technology, while remaining largely agricultural. Both regions are popular tourist destinations, despite lying a little in the shadow of Venice, and boast an abundant and enchanting variety of attractions.

A leisurely *passeggiata* in one of Verona's ancient streets

◁ **The Renaissance bridge by Palladio at Bassano del Grappa in the Veneto**

Exploring the Veneto and Friuli

THE FLAT LANDSCAPE of the Veneto plain is dramatically off-set by the spectacular Dolomite mountains which form the northwestern border to the Veneto. Friuli, Italy's most northeasterly region, lies tucked up against Austria to the north and Slovenia to the east. Both the Veneto and Friuli are bordered to the south by the Adriatic, with its beaches and ports, which provide a contrast with the area's gently rolling countryside, the vast stretch of Lake Garda and the many attractive resorts and ancient towns.

View of Verona from the Teatro Romano

KEY

▬▬	Motorway
▬▬	Major road
▬▬	Minor road
▬▬	Scenic route
≈	River
☀	Viewpoint

0 kilometres 25

0 miles 20

SEE ALSO

- *Where to Stay* pp544–7

- *Where to Eat* pp580–82

GETTING AROUND

An extensive rail network and good bus services make this region easy to explore by public transport, though only buses operate around Lake Garda. Motorways and main roads provide good links between the main cities. The Venice Simplon-Orient-Express train, which operates from London to Venice, offers a novel approach to the area.

The bridge at Cividale del Friuli

A mountain chalet in Cortina d'Ampezzo

Verona ●

Verona is a vibrant trading centre, the second biggest city in the Veneto region (after Venice) and one of the most prosperous in northern Italy. Its ancient centre boasts many magnificent Roman ruins, second only to those of Rome itself, and fine palazzi built of *rosso di Verona*, the local pink-tinged limestone, by the city's medieval rulers. Verona has two main focal points: the massive 1st-century AD Arena, which is still the setting for major events, and Piazza Erbe with its colourful market. One of the main attractions, however, is the church of San Zeno Maggiore *(see pp140–41)*, which boasts unusual medieval bronze door panels: they are carved with extraordinary scenes, some biblical, others on the life of San Zeno.

Scaligeri statue in Castelvecchio

View of Verona from the Museo Archeologico

Verona's Rulers

In 1263 the Scaligeri began their 124-year rule of Verona. They used ruthless tactics in their rise to power, but once established, the Scaligeri family brought peace to a city racked by civil strife and inter-family rivalry. They proved to be relatively just and cultured rulers – the poet Dante was welcomed to their court in 1301, and dedicated the final part of his epic *Divine Comedy* to the ruling Cangrande I. Today their legacy remains in their ornate tombs and in Castelvecchio.

In 1387 Verona fell to the Visconti of Milan, and a succession of outsiders – Venice, France and Austria – then ruled the city until the Veneto was united with Italy in 1866.

Verona's enormous Roman Arena seen from Piazza Brà

Key

FS	Railway station
🚌	Bus terminus
P	Parking
ℹ	Tourist information
✝	Church

Ponte Scaligero, part of the old defence system of Castelvecchio

VISITORS' CHECKLIST

261,000. Villafranca 14 km (9 miles) SW. Porta Nuova. Via degli Alpini 9 (045 806 86 80). daily. combined churches ticket. Apr: VinItaly wine fair; Jun–Aug: Estate Teatrale Veronese; Nov: International Horse Fair.

Castelvecchio

Corso Castelvecchio 2. 045 59 47 34. daily (Mon: pm only). 1 Jan, 25–26 Dec.

This impressive castle, built by Cangrande II between 1355 and 1375, houses one of the finest art galleries in the Veneto outside Venice. It is arranged to give striking views of the castle as well as the exhibits within.

The first section contains a wealth of late Roman and early Christian material – silver plate, 5th-century brooches, glass painted with a portrait of Christ the Shepherd in gold, and the carved marble sarcophagus of Saints Sergius and Bacchus (1179).

The section on medieval and early Renaissance art vividly demonstrates the influence of northern art on local painters: the emphasis is on brutal realism as opposed to serene idealism. The late Renaissance works include a fine collection of 15th-century Madonnas.

Jewellery, suits of armour, swords and shield bosses, Veronese's *Deposition* (1565) and a portrait painting attributed to either Titian or Lorenzo Lotto are displayed in other sections.

Outside, a walkway offers views of the river Adige and the medieval **Ponte Scaligero** crossing it, and of the 14th-century equestrian statue of Cangrande I which once graced his tomb (see p138).

Arena

Piazza Brà. 045 800 32 04. daily (Mon: pm only). 1 Jan, 25 & 26 Dec; Jun–Aug: from mid-afternoon on performance days.

Verona's Roman amphitheatre, completed in AD 30, is the third largest in the world, after Rome's Colosseum and the amphitheatre at Santa Maria Capua Vetere, near Naples. The interior, still virtually intact, could hold almost the entire population of Roman Verona, and visitors came from across the Veneto to watch gladiatorial combats. Since then, the Arena has seen executions, fairs, bullfights, and theatre and opera productions.

San Fermo Maggiore

Stradone San Fermo. 045 59 28 13. daily (Nov–Feb: Tue–Sun).

San Fermo Maggiore is not one but two churches: this is most clearly seen from the outside, where the apse has pointed Gothic elements rising above a sturdy Romanesque base. The lower church, begun in 1065 by Benedictine monks on the site of an earlier sanctuary, has frescoes on the simple arcades.

The more impressive upper church dates from 1313 and is covered with a splendid ship's keel roof. The interior also boasts much medieval fresco work including a 14th-century section by Stefano da Zevio depicting Musician Angels. Nearby is the Brenzoni mausoleum (c.1440) by Giovanni di Bartolo, and above it a 1426 fresco of the *Annunciation* by Pisanello (1377–1455).

BOSCO CHIESANUOVA

S. SEPOLCRO

VIA ROSA MORANDO

NAZARO

PIAZZALE PORTA VECCHIO

CORSO VENEZIA

VICENZA PADOVA VENEZIA

LEO GALILEI

| 0 metres | 500 |
| 0 yards | 500 |

SIGHTS AT A GLANCE

The 11th-century apse of the lower church of San Fermo Maggiore

Exploring Verona

Since the days of the Roman empire, Piazza Erbe – built on the site of the ancient Roman forum – has been the centre of Verona. Many of the city's fine palazzi, churches and monuments are nearly as ancient, several dating from the medieval period.

The fountain, erected in the 14th century at the centre of Piazza Erbe

🏛 Piazza Erbe

Piazza Erbe is named after the city's old herb market. Today's stalls, shaded by umbrellas, sell everything from herb-flavoured roast suckling pig in bread rolls to succulent fresh-picked fruit and delicious wild mushrooms.

At the northern end of the square is the Baroque **Palazzo Maffei** (1668), surmounted by statues. In front of it rises a column supporting the **Venetian lion** marking Verona's absorption into the Venetian empire (1405). On the west side is the **Casa dei Mercanti**, a largely 17th-century building that dates originally from 1301. Opposite, wall frescoes are still visible above the cafés.

The **fountain** in the middle of the piazza is often over-shadowed by the market stalls, though the statue at its centre dates from Roman times. It serves as a reminder that this piazza has been used as a market-place for 2,000 years.

🏛 Piazza dei Signori

Torre dei Lamberti

☎ 045 803 27 26. ◻ daily (Mon: pm only). ● public hols. 🏛

In the centre of the square stands an elegant 19th-century **statue of Dante**, whose gaze seems fixed on the forbidding **Palazzo del Capitano**, once the home of Verona's military commanders. Beside it is the

equally intimidating **Palazzo della Ragione**, the palace of Reason, or law court; both were built in the 14th century. The courtyard of the law court has a handsome external stone staircase, added in 1446–50. Stunning views of the Alps can be enjoyed by those prepared to climb the 84-m (275-ft) **Torre dei Lamberti**, which rises from the western side of the courtyard.

Behind the statue of Dante is the **Loggia del Consiglio** (1493), the council chamber topped by statues of Roman worthies born in Verona: they include Pliny the Elder, the natural historian, and Vitruvius, the architectural theorist.

The square is linked to Piazza Erbe by the Arco della Costa, or the Arch of the Rib, named after the whale rib long ago hung beneath it.

The frescoed Renaissance façade of the Loggia del Consiglio on Piazza dei Signori

⚔ Tombs of the Scaligeri

Via Arche Scaligeri.

Beside the entrance to the tiny Romanesque church of **Santa Maria Antica**, once the parish church of the powerful Scaligeri family, lie a profusion of bizarre tombs of the one-time rulers of Verona.

Over the entrance to the church is the impressive tomb of Cangrande I (died 1329), surmounted by an equestrian statue of the ruler, a copy of the original which is now in Castelvecchio *(see p137).*

The other Scaligeri tombs are next to the church, behind a wrought-iron fence which incorporates the ladder emblem of the family's original name (*della Scala*, meaning "of the steps"). Towering above the fence are the tombs of Mastino II (died 1351) and Cansignorio (died 1375), splendidly decorated with a profusion of tiny Gothic spires. Other members of the Scaligeri family lie within a series of plainer tombs which stand nearer the church wall.

14th-century Scaligeri tomb

⛪ Sant'Anastasia

Piazza Sant'Anastasia. ☎ 045 59 28 13. ◻ daily. ● Nov–Feb: Mon. 🏛

The huge and lofty church of Sant'Anastasia was begun in 1290. Faded 15th-century frescoes and carved scenes from the life of St Peter Martyr adorn its Gothic portal.

Inside, there are two notable holy water stoups, supported on figures of beggars, known locally as *i gobbi* (the hunch-backs). These figures were carved a century apart: the earlier one (on the left) dates from 1495.

The sacristy, off the north aisle, is home to the fine but unfortunately damaged fresco of *St George and the Princess* (1433–8) by Pisanello.

The so-called Casa di Giulietta

ROMEO AND JULIET

The tragic story of Romeo and Juliet, two young lovers from rival families, was written by Luigi da Porto of Vicenza in the 1520s and has inspired countless dramas, films and ballets.

At the **Casa di Giulietta** (Juliet's house), No. 27 Via Cappello, Romeo is said to have climbed to Juliet's balcony; in reality this is a restored 13th-century inn. Crowds throng to see the simple façade, and stand on the small marble balcony. The run-down **Casa di Romeo** is a few streets away, in Via Arche Scaligeri.

The so-called **Tomba di Giulietta** is displayed in a crypt below the cloister of San Francesco al Corso on Via del Pontiere. The stone sarcophagus lies in an extremely atmospheric setting.

Both the Casa and the Tomba di Giulietta are open daily (on Mondays in the afternoon only). There is an admission charge.

⌂ Duomo

Piazza Duomo. 045 59 28 13. daily. Nov–Feb: Mon.

Verona's cathedral was begun in 1139 and is fronted by a magnificent Romanesque portal carved by Nicolò, one of the two master masons responsible for the façade of San Zeno *(see pp140–41)*. Here he sculpted the sword-bearing figures of Oliver and Roland, two of Charlemagne's knights, whose exploits were much celebrated in medieval poetry. Alongside them stand evangelists and saints with wide eyes and flowing beards. To the south there is a second Romanesque portal carved with Jonah and the Whale and with comically grotesque caryatids.

The highlight of the interior is Titian's lovely *Assumption* (1535–40), and outside there is a Romanesque cloister in which the excavated ruins of earlier churches are visible. The 8th-century baptistry, or San Giovanni in Fonte (St John of the Spring), was built from Roman masonry; the marble font was carved in 1200.

⌂ Teatro Romano
🏛 Museo Archeologico

Rigaste Redentore 2. 045 800 03 60. 8:30am–7:30pm Tue–Sun, 1:30–7:30pm Mon. 1 Jan, 25 & 26 Dec.

This Roman theatre was built in the 1st century BC; little survives of the stage area, but the semicircular seating area is largely intact. It offers great views over Verona: in the foreground is the only one of three Roman bridges to have survived, though it was rebuilt after World War II.

A lift carries visitors from the Teatro Romano up the cliffs to the monastery above, now an interesting archaeological museum.

The exhibits around the tiny cloister and in the old monks' cells include mosaics, pottery, glass and tombstones. There is also a fine bronze bust of the first Roman emperor, Augustus (63 BC–AD 14), who in 31 BC overcame his opponents, including Mark Antony and Cleopatra, to become the sole ruler of the Roman world.

Statuary and formal hedges in the Renaissance Giardino Giusti

❀ Giardino Giusti

Via Giardino Giusti 2. 045 803 40 29. daily. 25 Dec.

This is one of Italy's finest Renaissance gardens. It was laid out in 1580 and, as with other gardens of the period, there is a deliberate juxtaposition of nature and artifice: the formal lower garden of clipped box hedges, gravel walks and potted plants contrasts with wilder, natural woods above.

John Evelyn, an English author and diarist who visited Verona in 1661, thought this the finest garden in Europe.

⌂ San Giorgio in Braida

Lungadige San Giorgio. 045 834 02 32. daily. during mass.

This lovely domed Renaissance church was begun in about 1530 by Michele Sanmicheli. The altar includes the famous *Martyrdom of St George* (1566) by Veronese, and above the west door is the *Baptism of Christ*, usually attributed to Tintoretto (1518–94).

The imposing façade of Verona's Duomo, Santa Maria Matricolare

Verona: San Zeno Maggiore

Detail from San Zeno's façade

S AN ZENO, built in 1120–38 to house the shrine of Verona's patron saint, is the most ornate Romanesque church in northern Italy. The façade is adorned with an impressive rose window, marble reliefs, and a graceful porch canopy. The highlight, however, is the fascinating 11th- and 12th-century bronze door panels. A squat tower just north of San Zeno is said to cover the tomb of King Pepin of Italy (777–810).

Nave Ceiling
The nave has a magnificent example of a ship's keel ceiling, so called because it resembles the inside of an upturned boat. This ceiling was constructed in 1386 when the apse was rebuilt.

The bell tower, started in 1045, reached its present height of 72 m (236 ft) in 1173.

Altarpiece by Mantegna
The Madonna's halo in Andrea Mantegna's altarpiece of the Virgin and Child with saints (1457–59) echoes the shape of the church's rose window.

★ Cloister (1293–1313)
The arches are rounded Romanesque on one side, pointed Gothic on another.

Former washroom

Crypt
The vaulted crypt contains the tomb of San Zeno, appointed eighth bishop of Verona in AD 362, who died in AD 380.

Nave and Main Altar
The plan of the church is modelled on an ancient Roman basilica, the Hall of Justice. The main altar is situated in the raised sanctuary where the judge's throne would have stood.

VISITORS' CHECKLIST

Piazza San Zeno. **045 59 28 13.** Mar–Oct: 8:30am–6pm Mon–Sat, 1–6pm Sun; Nov–Feb: 10am–4pm Tue–Sat, 1–5pm Sun. for mass. times vary.

BRONZE DOOR PANELS

The 48 bronze panels of the west doors are primitive but forceful in their depiction of biblical stories and scenes from the life of San Zeno. Those on the left date from 1030 and survive from an earlier church on the site; those on the right were made after the earthquake in 1137. The panels are the work of three separate craftsmen, and are linked with masks. Huge staring eyes and Ottoman-style hats, armour and architecture feature prominently. Among the scenes, some of which are unclear, are Adam and Eve, Salome dancing for the head of John the Baptist, and a startling Descent into Limbo.

Striped brickwork is typical of Romanesque buildings in Verona. Courses of local pink brick are alternated with ivory-coloured tufa.

The rose window, dating from the early 12th century, symbolizes the Wheel of Fortune: figures on the rim show the rise and fall of human luck.

Descent into limbo   **Christ in Glory**   **Human head**

The Romanesque porch is one of the finest examples of the style in northern Italy. Since 1138 it has shielded biblical bas-reliefs, above the west doors, from the elements.

Marble side panels, which were carved in 1140, depict events from the Life of Christ (to the left of the doors) and scenes from the Book of Genesis (to the right).

STAR FEATURES

★ **West Doors**

★ **Cloister**

★ West Doors
Each of the wooden doors has 24 bronze plates nailed on to make the doors look like solid metal. A multi-coloured bas-relief above them depicts San Zeno, flanked by the people of Verona, vanquishing the devil.

Lake Garda ●

GARDA, THE LARGEST AND EASTERNMOST of the Italian lakes, borders three regions: Trentino to the north, Lombardy to the west and south, and the Veneto to the south and east. The low-lying countryside around the southern stretches becomes increasingly dramatic further north, until impressive rocky cliffs, sometimes swathed in pines, hug the shoreline of the northern tip. The numerous sporting facilities, many sights, and splendid scenery of snow-capped mountains help make the lake a favourite summer playground.

VISITORS' CHECKLIST

Brescia, Verona & Trento. ℹ️ Via Repubblica 8, Gardone Riviera (0365 203 47). **FS** Peschiera del Garda, Desenzano del Garda. 🚌 to all towns. **Villa il Vittoriale** Via Vittoriale 12, Gardone. 📞 0365 29 65 11. 🕐 Tue–Sun. 🏛️ **Rocca Scaligera** Sirmione. 📞 030 91 64 68. 🕐 Tue–Sun. 🏛️

Eastern tip of Sirmione Peninsula
Beyond the town is a path which follows the rim of the peninsula, passing boiling sulphur springs.

Gardone is noted for its exotically planted park and for the Villa il Vittoriale, the Art Deco home of the poet Gabriele d'Annunzio, which is filled with curiosities.

The Republic of Salò was established here by Mussolini in 1943. The cathedral in this elegant and attractive town of pastel-painted houses contains an altarpiece by Veneziano.

The hydrofoils,
catamarans and steamers which ply the lake offer glimpses of villas and gardens which cannot be seen from the coastal road.

Riva's waterfront is dominated by an old fortress of the Scaligeri. Windsurfers favour this resort because of the consistent offshore winds.

The streets of Malcesine cluster below an imposing medieval castle. A cable car climbs to the summit of Monte Baldo (1,745 m/5,725 ft), offering far-reaching views.

The lake is named after this long-established town.

Bardolino gave its name to the well-known red wine.

Peschiera's attractive enclosed harbour and fortress were built by the Austrians in the 1860s, during the Italian Wars of Independence.

Riva del Garda
Torbole
Limone sul Garda
Tremosine
Malcesine
Campione del Garda
Assenza
Tignale
Brenzone
Gargnano
Castelletto
Bogliaco
Maderno
Gardone Riviera
Torri del Benaco
Portese
Garda
San Felice del Bonaco
Manerba
Moniga
Bardolino
Padenghe sul Garda
Sirmione
Lazise
Desenzano
Peschiera

0 kilometres   5
0 miles   5

KEY

●●● Steamer route

○○○ Car ferry

🔺 Sailing club or centre

ℹ️ Tourist information

🌿 Viewpoint

Sirmione
A fascinating medieval castle, the Rocca Scaligera, dominates the town of Sirmione. At the tip of the peninsula lie Roman ruins.

The 16th-century wooden bridge by Palladio at Bassano del Grappa

Bassano del Grappa ❸

Vicenza. 🏠 39,000. 🚈 🚌
🛈 Largo Corona d'Italia 35 (0424 52 43 51). 🛒 Thu & Sat am.

THIS PEACEFUL TOWN lies at the foot of Monte Grappa. The river Brenta is straddled by the graceful Ponte degli Alpini, which was designed in 1569 by Palladio. It is built of timber to allow it to flex when hit by the spring meltwaters. Bassano is well known for its majolica products (decorated and glazed earthenware), some of which are on display in the **Palazzo Sturm**. The town is also synonymous with the popular Italian after-dinner drink, the clear spirit known as *grappa*. It is produced from the lees (*graspa*) left over from wine production; information about the process is given in the **Museo degli Alpini**.

🏛 **Palazzo Sturm**
Via Ferracina. 📞 0424 52 49 33.
◻ Apr–Oct: Tue–Sun; Nov–Mar: Fri–Sun. 🗒
🏛 **Museo degli Alpini**
Via Anagarano 2. 📞 0424 50 36 50.
◻ Tue–Sun.

Asolo ❹

Treviso. 🏠 2,000. 🚌 🛈 Piazza Garibaldi 73 (0423 52 90 46). 🛒 Sun.

ASOLO IS beautifully sited among the cypress-clad foothills of the Dolomites. This tiny walled town was once ruled by Queen Caterina Cornaro (1454–1510), the Venetian wife of the King of Cyprus, who poisoned her husband so that Venice would gain Cyprus. Cardinal Pietro Bembo, a poet, coined the verb *asolare* to describe the bittersweet life of enforced idleness she endured in exile here. Among others who have fallen in love with the narrow streets and grand houses was poet Robert Browning, who named a volume of poems *Asolanda* (1889) after Asolo.

ENVIRONS: At Masèr, 10 km (6 miles) east of the town, stands the magnificent **Villa Barbaro** (*see pp76–7*). It was designed by Palladio in about 1555, in conjunction with the artist Veronese, and perfectly blends symmetry and light, airy rooms with sumptuous *trompe l'oeil* frescoes.

🏛 **Villa Barbaro**
Masèr. 📞 0423 92 30 03.
◻ Mar–Oct: Tue, Sat, Sun & hols; Nov–Feb: Sat, Sun & hols.
● 24 Dec–6 Jan, Easter Sun. 🗒

Castelfranco Veneto ❺

Treviso. 🏠 30,000. 🚈 🚌
🛈 Via Francesco M Preti 66 (0423 49 14 16). 🛒 Tue am & Fri am.

FORTIFIED IN 1199 by rulers of Treviso as a defence against the neighbouring Paduans, the historic core of this town lies within well-preserved walls. In the **Casa di Giorgione**, said to be the birthplace of the painter Giorgione (1478–1511), about whom little is known, there is a museum devoted to his life. Giorgione innovatively used landscape to create mood, adding figures to intensify the atmosphere – for instance in his broodingly mysterious but evocative most famous work, *The Tempest* (*see p102*). Another of his few directly attributable works hangs here in the **Duomo**: the *Madonna and Child with Saints Liberal and Francis* (1504).

ENVIRONS: About 8 km (5 miles) northeast of the town, at the village of Fanzolo, lies the **Villa Emo** (c.1555). Designed by Palladio, it is a typical example of his work: a cube flanked by two symmetrical wings. Inside there are lavish frescoes by Zelotti.

🏛 **Casa di Giorgione**
Piazzetta del Duomo. 📞 0423 72 50 22. ◻ Tue–Sun. ● pub hols. 🗒
🏛 **Villa Emo**
Fanzolo di Vedelago. 📞 0423 47 63 34. ◻ Apr–Oct: Mon–Sat pm, Sun & pub hols; Nov–Mar: Sat, Sun & pub hols pm. ● 15 Dec–15 Jan. 🗒 🛈

Fresco (c.1561) by Veronese adorning the Villa Barbaro near Asolo

Street-by-Street: Vicenza ❻

Face at No. 21 Contrà Porti

VICENZA IS KNOWN as the adoptive city of Andrea Palladio (1508–80), who started out as a stonemason and became the most influential architect of his time. The evolution of his distinctive style is visible all around the city. In the centre is the monumental basilica he adapted to serve as the town hall, nearby is the Teatro Olimpico, and all around are the palaces he built for Vicenza's wealthy citizens.

Contrà Porti
is bordered by some of the most elegant palazzi in Vicenza.

Loggia del Capitaniato
This covered arcade was designed by Palladio in 1571.

Palazzo Valmarana Braga
Palladio's impressive building of 1566 is decorated with giant pilasters and sculpted scenes. It was not completed until 1680, 100 years after the architect's death.

San Lorenzo

Piazza Stazione

Duomo
Vicenza's cathedral was rebuilt after bomb damage during World War II left only the façade and choir entirely intact.

Andrea Palladio
This memorial to Vicenza's most famous citizen is usually surrounded by market stalls.

CORSO ANDREA PALLADIO

CONTRÀ CAVOUR

VIA BATTISTI

CONTRÀ P LAMPERTICO

C MUSCHERIA

CONTRÀ GARIBALDI

CONTRÀ PESCHE VEC

CONTRÀ SAN ANTONIO

PIAZZA DEI DUOMO

0 kilometres 2

0 miles 1

KEY

– – – Suggested route

STAR SIGHT

★ **Piazza dei Signori**

A large hall is all that
remains of the 15th-century
Palazzo della Ragione.

Torre di Piazza,
built in the 12th
century, is an
impressive 82 m
(269 ft) high.

Santa
Corona

Teatro
Olimpico
Museo
Civico

The lion of St Mark gazing down
on Piazza dei Signori

★ **Piazza dei Signori**
*Palladio's elegant buildings
flank the Piazza dei Signori,
including the majestic two-tier
colonnades of the 16th-century
"Basilica", built around the
old Palazzo della Ragione.*

The Quartiere delle Barche
contains numerous attractive
palaces built in the 14th-
century Venetian Gothic style.

Ponte San Michele
*This elegant stone
bridge, built in 1620,
provides lovely views of
the surrounding town.*

CONTRÀ S BARBARA
PIAZZA DELLE BIADE
CONTRÀ CATENA
CONTRÀ GAZZOLLE
CONTRÀ PIANCOLI
CONTRÀ SAN PAOLO
CONTRÀ PONTE SAN MICHELE
CONTRÀ PESCARIA
RETRONE

La Rotonda
Monte Berico
Villa Valmarana
ai Nani

**Piazza
delle Erbe**,
the city's market square,
is overlooked by a 13th-
century prison tower.

Casa Pigafetta
*This striking 15th-
century house was
the birthplace of
Antonio Pigafetta,
who in 1519 set sail
round the world
with Magellan.*

🏛 Piazza dei Signori
Basilica 0444 32 36 81.
10:30am–1pm, 3–7pm daily.
This square at the heart of
Vicenza is dominated by the
Palazzo della Ragione, often
referred to as the **Basilica**. Its
green, copper-clad roof is
shaped like an upturned boat
with a balustrade bristling
with the statues of Greek and
Roman gods. The colonnades
were designed by Palladio in
1549 as a facing to support the
city's 15th-century town hall,
which had begun to subside.
This was Palladio's first public
commission, and a great
success. Beside it stands the
12th-century Torre di Piazza.

The **Loggia del Capitaniato**,
to the northwest, was built by
Palladio in 1571: the Loggia's
upper rooms contain the city's
council chamber.

🏛 Contrà Porti
Contrà (an abbreviation of
contrada, or district) is the
Vicenza dialect word for street.
On one side of the Contrà is a
series of pretty Gothic buildings with painted windows
and ornate balconies, reminiscent of Venice and a reminder
that Vicenza was once part of
the Venetian empire.

Several elegant Palladian
palazzi stand on this street.
Palazzo Porto Barbarano (No.
11), Palazzo Thiene (No. 12)
and Palazzo Iseppo da Porto
(No. 21) illustrate the sheer
variety of Palladio's style – all
share Classical elements but
each is unique. An intriguing
detail is that Palazzo Thiene
appears to be of stone, though
it is in fact built of cheap, light-
weight brick, cleverly rendered
to look like masonry.

Exploring Vicenza

VICENZA, THE GREAT PALLADIAN CITY and one of the wealthiest cities in the Veneto, is celebrated the world over for its splendid and varied architecture; it also offers the visitor elegant shops and cafés to visit.

Brusazorzi's ceiling fresco in the large entrance hall of the Museo Civico

🏛 Museo Civico

Piazza Matteotti. 📞 0444 32 13 48.
🕐 Tue–Sun. ● 1 Jan, 25 Dec. 🈳 &

The excellent Museo Civico is housed in **Palazzo Chiericati** (*see p76*) by Palladio, built in 1550. Inside is a fresco by Domenico Brusazorzi of a naked charioteer, representing the Sun, who appears to fly over the entrance hall. The upstairs rooms hold many excellent pictures. Among the Gothic altarpieces from churches in Vicenza is Hans Memling's *Crucifixion* (1468–70), the central panel from a triptych whose side panels are now located in New York.

Other rooms contain works by the local artist Bartolomeo Montagna (c.1450–1523).

🔒 Santa Corona

Contrà Santa Corona. 📞 0444 32 19 24. 🕐 daily. ● Mon.

This great Gothic church was built in 1261 to house a thorn donated by Louis IX of France and said to be from Christ's Crown of Thorns. The Cappella Porto houses the tomb of Luigi da Porto (died 1529), author of the novel *Giulietta e Romeo*, on which Shakespeare based his famous play. Notable paintings include Giovanni Bellini's *Baptism of Christ* (c.1500) and the *Adoration of the Magi* (1573) by Paolo Veronese.

🎭 TEATRO OLIMPICO

Piazza Matteotti. 📞 0444 22 28 00. 🕐 9am–5pm Tue–Sun (last adm: 4:30pm). ● during performances, 1 Jan, 25 Dec. 🈳 & 🚻

Europe's oldest surviving indoor theatre is a remarkable structure, largely made of wood and plaster, and painted to look like marble. Palladio began work on the design in 1579, but he died the year after. His pupil Vincenzo Scamozzi took over the project, completing the theatre in time for its opening performance of Sophocles' tragic drama *Oedipus Rex* on 3 March 1585.

Odeon Frescoes
The gods of Mount Olympus, after which the theatre is named, decorate the Odeon, a room used for music recitals.

The Anteodeon contains frescoes depicting the theatre's opening performance, and oil lamps from the original stage set.

Main ticket office

Stage Set
Scamozzi's scenery represents the Greek city of Thebes. The streets are cleverly painted in perspective and rise at a steep angle to give the illusion of great length.

The Auditorium
was designed by Palladio to resemble the outdoor theatres of ancient Greece and Rome, such as the Arena at Verona (*see p137*), with a semi-circle of "stone" benches and a ceiling painted to portray the sky.

San Lorenzo

Piazza San Lorenzo. ○ *daily.*

The portal of this church is a magnificent example of Gothic stone carving, richly decorated with the figures of the Virgin and Child, and St Francis and St Clare. Inside there are fine tombs, and damaged frescoes. The lovely cloister, north of the church, is an attractive, flower-filled haven of calm.

Monte Berico

Basilica di Monte Berico. **C** *0444 32 09 99.* ○ *daily.*

Monte Berico is the green, cypress-clad hill to the south of Vicenza to which wealthy residents once escaped, in the heat of summer, to enjoy the cooler air and pastoral charms of their country estates. Today, shady *portici*, or colonnades, adorned with shrines, line the wide avenue linking central Vicenza to the basilica on top of the hill. The domed basili-

La Rotonda (1550–52), most famous of all Palladio's works

ca itself, built in the 15th century and enlarged in the 18th, is dedicated to the Virgin who appeared here during the 1426–8 plague to announce that Vicenza would be spared.

The ornate interior contains a moving *Pietà* fresco (1500) by Bartolomeo Montagna, a fossil collection in the cloister, and Veronese's fine painting, *The Supper of St Gregory the Great* (1572), in the refectory.

In the separate Foresteria (guest house), the 18th-century frescoes depicting peasant life and the seasons, painted by Tiepolo's son Giandomenico, are equally decorative but are imbued with an earthy realism.

The villa can be reached by an enjoyable, ten-minute walk from the basilica on Monte Berico. Head downhill along Via Massimo d'Azeglio to the high-walled convent on the right where the road ends, then take Via San Bastiano.

La Rotonda

Via Rotonda 25. **C** *0444 32 17 93.*
Villa ○ *mid-Mar–4 Nov: Wed.* 🌀
Garden ○ *Tue–Sun.* 🌀

With its perfectly regular, symmetrical forms, this villa, also known as the Villa Capra Valmarana, is the epitome of Palladio's architecture (*see pp76–7*) of which there are several fine examples throughout the Veneto. The design, consisting of a dome rising above a cube, received immediate acclaim for the way it blends perfectly with its surroundings. A pleasant contrast exists between the terracotta roof tiles, the white walls and the green lawns.

The villa, built in 1550–52, has inspired many copies in cities as far away as London, St Petersburg and Delhi. Fans of *Don Giovanni* will enjoy spotting locations used in Joseph Losey's 1979 film.

La Rotonda can be reached by bus from town, or on foot, following the path alongside the Villa Valmarana ai Nani.

The façade statues of stately toga-clad figures are portraits of sponsors who paid for the theatre's construction.

The courtyard giving access to the Teatro is decorated with ancient sculptures. These were donated by members of the Olympic Academy, the learned body that built the theatre.

Main entrance

The Baroque hilltop church, the Basilica di Monte Berico

Villa Valmarana ai Nani

Via dei Nani 12. **C** *0444 54 39 76.*
○ *mid-Mar–5 Nov: Tue–Sun (Tue & Fri: pm only).* 🌀

The wall alongside the Villa Valmarana, built in 1688 by Antonio Muttoni, is topped by figures of dwarfs (*nani*) which give the building its name.

Inside, the walls are covered with frescoes by Tiepolo, in which the gods of Mount Olympus float about on clouds watching scenes from the epics of Homer and Virgil.

Street-by-Street: Padua **⑦**

Padua (Padova) is an old university town with an illustrious academic history. Rich in art and architecture, it has two particularly outstanding sights. The magnificent Cappella degli Scrovegni (*see pp150–51*), north of the city centre, is famous for Giotto's lyrical frescoes. Close to the railway station, it forms part of the complex incorporating the Eremitani church and museums. The Basilica di Sant'Antonio, which forms the focal point in the southern part of the city, is one of the most popular pilgrimage destinations in Italy.

Palazzo del Capitanio
Built between 1599 and 1605 for the head of the city's militia, the tower incorporates an astronomical clock made in 1344.

Piazza dei Signori is bordered by attractive arcades which house small speciality shops, cafés and old-fashioned wine bars.

Corte Capitaniato, a 14th-century arts faculty (open for concerts), contains frescoes which include a rare portrait of the poet Petrarch.

Ufficio di Turismo

Loggia della Gran Guardia
This fine Renaissance build-ing dating from 1523 once housed the Council of Nobles. It is now used as a conference centre.

PIAZZA CAPITANIATO

VIA SAN CLEMENTE

PIAZZA DEI SIGNORI

VIA MONTE DI PIETA

VIA MANIN

PIAZZA DEL DUOMO

VIA VANDELLI

VIA GRITTI

VIA SONCI

★ Duomo and Baptistry
The 12th-century baptistry of the Duomo contains one of the most complete medieval fresco cycles to survive in Italy, painted by Giusto de' Menabuoi in 1378.

The Palazzo del Monte di Pietà has 16th-century arcades and statues enclosing a medieval building.

KEY

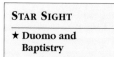

– – – Suggested route

0 metres   75

0 yards   75

STAR SIGHT

★ **Duomo and Baptistry**

Caffè Pedrocchi

*Built like a Classical temple,
the Caffè Pedrocchi has
been a famous meeting
place for students and
intellectuals since it
opened in 1831.*

A bronze statue
of a woman
(1973) by Emilio
Greco stands at
the centre of
this largely
pedestrianized
square.

Stazione
Chiesa degli Eremitani
Cappella degli Scrovegni
Museo Civico

VIA GORIZIA

VIA OBERDAN

PIAZZA
DELLA
FRUTTA

PIAZZA
CAVOUR

PTTA GARZERIA

PIAZZA
DELLE
ERBE

VIA VIII FEBBRAIO

V SAN CANZIANO

Basilica di Sant'Antonio
Orto Botanico

**Padua
University**
*Founded in 1222, this
is Italy's second oldest
university. Elena Piscopia
was the first woman
graduate, in 1678.*

**Palazzo
della Ragione,**
*the medieval court of justice,
contains magnificent frescoes.*

**Piazza
delle Erbe**
*There are some
excellent views to be
had over the market
place from the 15th-
century loggia which
runs alongside the
13th-century Palazzo
della Ragione.*

VISITORS' CHECKLIST

220,000. 📍 🚉 ℹ️ *Piazzale
della Stazione (049 875 20 77).*
🚌 *Piazza Boschetti.* 🏪 *Mon–
Sat at Piazza delle Erbe.*
🎭 *Jun–Sep: Cultural Festival.*

🔒 Duomo and Baptistry

Piazza Duomo. **Baptistry** 📞 049
65 69 14. ⏰ 10am–6pm daily.
⬤ Easter, 25 Dec. 🎫 Ø

The Duomo was built in 1552
to plans partly by Michelangelo, on the site of an earlier,
14th-century cathedral. Beside
it stands a domed baptistry
(c.1200). The interior is entirely decorated with vibrant
frescoes painted by Giusto
de' Menabuoi, dating from
around 1378. The frescoes
depict episodes from the
Bible, including scenes of
the Creation, the Miracles, the
Passion, the Crucifixion and
the Resurrection of Christ.

🏛 Palazzo della Ragione

Piazza delle Erbe. 📞 049 820 50 06.
⏰ 9am–7pm Tue–Sun (Nov–Feb: to
6pm). ⬤ 1 Jan, 1 May, 15 Aug, 25
& 26 Dec. 🎫 ♿ ℹ️

The "Palace of Reason", which
is also known as the Salone,
was built in 1218 to serve as
Padua's law court and council
chamber. The vast main hall
was originally decorated with
frescoes by Giotto, but fire
destroyed his work in 1420.
The Salone is breathtaking in
its sheer size. It is the largest
undivided medieval hall in
Europe, 80 m (260 ft) long,
27 m (90 ft) wide and 27 m
(90 ft) high. Frescoes painted
in 1420–25 by Nicola Miretto
cover its walls: the 333 panels
depict the months of the
year, with appropriate
gods, signs of the zodiac
and seasonal activities.
A 1466 copy of the huge
Gattamelata statue
(see p152) by Dona-
tello stands at one
end of the hall.

🏛 Caffè Pedrocchi

Via VIII Febbraio 15.
📞 049 878 12 31.
⏰ daily (Jun–Oct:
Tue–Sun).
Caffè Pedrocchi
opened in 1831, and became
famous throughout Italy as
the café that never closed its
doors. Today people come
as much to talk, play cards
or watch the world go by as
to eat or drink. The upstairs
rooms, decorated in florid
Moorish, Egyptian and other
styles, house a museum docu-
menting modern Italian history.

Padua: Cappella degli Scrovegni

ENRICO SCROVEGNI built this chapel in 1303, hoping thereby to spare his dead father, a usurer, from the eternal damnation in hell described by the poet Dante in his *Inferno*. The interior of the chapel is entirely covered with beautiful frescoes of scenes from the life of Christ, painted by Giotto between 1303 and 1305. As works of great narrative force, they exerted a powerful influence on the development of European art.

The Nativity
The naturalism of the Virgin's pose marks a departure from Byzantine stylization, as does the use of natural blue for the sky, in place of celestial gold.

Expulsion of the Merchants
Christ's physical rage, the cowering merchant and the child hiding his face show an animation that is characteristic of Giotto's style.

The Coretti
Giotto painted the two panels known as the Coretti as an exercise in perspective, creating the illusion of an arch with a room beyond.

View towards altar

West entrance   North side   Altar   South side   West entrance

GALLERY GUIDE

Due to the Cappella degli Scrovegni's small size, the number of visitors allowed in at any one time is strictly limited. Prior to entering, visitors are required to spend 15 minutes in a decontamination chamber, where multimedia, multilingual information on the chapel is provided. The visit itself is also restricted to 15 minutes. Advance booking is compulsory, either by phone or online (www.cappelladegliscrovegni.it), with a credit card payment.

KEY

☐ Episodes of Joachim and Anna

☐ Episodes from the Life of Mary

☐ Episodes from the Life and Death of Christ

☐ The Virtues and Vices

☐ The Last Judgment

The Last Judgment
This scene fills the entire
west wall of the chapel.
Its formal composition
is closer to Byzantine
tradition than some of
the other frescoes, with
parts probably painted
by assistants. A model
of the chapel is shown
(centre left, at the bottom)
being offered to the
Virgin by Scrovegni.

VISITORS' CHECKLIST

Piazza Eremitani. 049 201 00
20. to Piazzale Boschetti.
9am–7pm daily (Nov–Jan: to
6pm). public hols. Advance
booking compulsory.

Mary is Presented at the Temple
Giotto sets many scenes against an
architectural background, using the
laws of perspective to give a sense of
three dimensions.

Injustice
The Vices and
Virtues are painted
in monochrome.
Here Injustice is
symbolized by scenes
of war, murder
and robbery.

View towards entrance

Lament over the Dead Christ
Giotto's figures express their grief
in different ways: some huddle
together, another gestures wildly.

GIOTTO

The great Florentine artist Giotto
(1266–1337) is regarded as the
father of Western art. His work,
with its sense of pictorial space,
naturalism and narrative drama,
marks a decisive break with the
Byzantine tradition of the pre-
ceding 1,000 years. He is the first
Italian master whose name has
passed into posterity, and although
he was regarded in his lifetime as a
great artist, few of the works attributed
to him are fully documented. Some may have been
painted by others, but his authorship of the frescoes
in the Scrovegni Chapel need not be doubted.

Exploring Padua

Padua is a city of many attractions, with a rich history: this is reflected in the major museum complex which occupies a group of 14th-century monastic buildings attached to the church of the Eremitani, a reclusive Augustinian order. Next door is the Cappella degli Scrovegni (*see pp150–51*). Padua is, in addition, the setting for one of Italy's most important churches – the splendid Basilica di Sant'Antonio – and for one of the earliest universities to be founded in Italy.

⊞ Chiesa degli Eremitani and Museo Civico Eremitani

Piazza Eremitani. **☎** *049 820 45 51.*
Museum ○ *Tue–Sun.* **☒**
Chapel ○ *daily.*

The Eremitani church, built from 1276 to 1306, contains magnificent roof and wall tombs. Among them is that of Marco Benavides (1489–1582), a professor of law at the city university, whose Renaissance tomb was the work of Florentine architect Ammannati (1511–92). Celebrated frescoes (1454–7) by Mantegna, portraying scenes from the lives of St James and St Christopher, were destroyed during a bombing raid in 1944. Two scenes from this magnificent series survive in the Cappella Ovetari, south of the sanctuary: *The Martyrdom of St James* and *The Martyrdom of St Christopher.*

The Museo Civico Eremitani comprises a coin collection (which includes rare Roman medallions and an almost complete set of Venetian coinage), an archaeological section and an art gallery.

The rich archaeological collection contains interesting Roman tombs, fine mosaics and impressive life-size statues. Renaissance bronzes include the comical *Drinking Satyr* by Il Riccio (1470–1532).

The beautiful 14th-century Crucifix from the Cappella degli Scrovegni is in the Quadreria Emo Capodilista, as well as works by Giotto, and 15th- to 18th-century paintings from the Venetian and Flemish schools.

A 1st-century AD tomb in the archaeological collection

15th-century *Angels in Armour* by Guariento, Museo Civico Eremitani

🔒 Basilica di Sant'Antonio

Piazza del Santo.

This exotic church, with its minaret-like spires and Byzantine domes, is also known as Il Santo. It was built from 1232 to house the remains of St Anthony of Padua, a preacher who modelled himself on St Francis of Assisi. Although he was a simple man who rejected worldly wealth, the citizens of Padua built one of the most lavish churches in Christendom to serve as his shrine.

The influence of Byzantine architecture is clearly visible in the basilica's outline: a cone-shaped central dome rises above seven encircling domes; the façade combines Gothic and Romanesque elements.

Inside, the high altar features Donatello's magnificent reliefs (1444–5) on the miracles of St Anthony, and his statues of the Crucifixion, the Virgin and Paduan saints. The tomb of St Anthony, hung with offerings, lies in the north transept; large marble reliefs depicting the saint's life, carved in 1505–77 by various artists, adorn the walls around it. A lively fresco scene of the Crucifixion by Altichiero da Zevio (1380s) adorns the south transept.

♞ Statue of Gattamelata

Beside the entrance to the basilica stands one of the great works of the Renaissance: a statue of the mercenary soldier Gattamelata. This gritty portrait was created in 1443–52, in honour of a man who during his life did great service to the Venetian Republic. The artist Donatello won fame for the monument, the first equestrian statue made on such a large scale since Roman times.

The Basilica di Sant'Antonio, and Donatello's statue of Gattamelata

🐌 Scuola del Santo and Oratorio di San Giorgio

Piazza del Santo. 📞 049 875 52 35.
⬜ daily. 🏷

Five excellent frescoes, including the earliest documented paintings by Titian, are to be found in these two buildings. The Scuola del Santo contains two scenes from the life of St Anthony, which were painted by Titian in 1511. The works in the San Giorgio oratory were executed by Altichiero da Zevio and Jacopo Avenzo, who painted them in 1378–84.

🍂 Orto Botanico

Via Orto Botanico 15.
📞 049 827 21 19. ⬜ daily
(Nov–Mar: Mon–Sat am). 🏷 🅿 👶

Padua's botanical garden, one of the oldest in Europe (1545), still retains much of its original appearance. The gardens and hothouses were used to cultivate the first lilac trees (1568), sunflowers (1568) and potatoes (1590) to be grown in Italy.

🏛 Palazzo del Bo

Via VIII Febbraio 2. 📞 049 820 97 11. ⬜ for guided tours only.
Tue, Thu, Sat am, Mon, Wed, Fri pm. Times vary – phone to check. 🏷

The historic main university building originally housed the medical faculty, renowned throughout Europe. Among its famous teachers and students was Gabriele Fallopio (1523–62), after whom the Fallopian tubes are named.

Guided tours include the pulpit Galileo used when he taught physics here from 1592 until 1610 and the wooden anatomy theatre, built in 1594 and now the oldest surviving medical lecture theatre in the world.

The 16th-century anatomy theatre in the old medical faculty of the university's Palazzo del Bo, Padua

The Euganean Hills, formed by ancient volcanic activity

Euganean Hills ❽

🚉 🚌 to Terme Euganee, Montegrotto Terme. ℹ Viale Stazione 60, Montegrotto Terme (049 79 33 84).

THE CONICAL Euganean Hills, remnants of long-extinct volcanoes, rise abruptly out of the surrounding plain. Hot water springs bubble up out of the ground at Abano Terme and Montegrotto Terme where scores of establishments offer thermal treatments, ranging from mud baths to immersion in the hot sulphurated waters. Spa cures originated in Roman times; remains of the original baths and theatre are still visible at Montegrotto Terme.

🔒 Abbazia di Praglia

Via Abbazia di Praglia, Bresseo di Teolo. 📞 049 999 93 00.
⬜ Tue–Sun pm. ⬛ Jan, Easter, 25 Dec. 🎟 **Donations** welcome.

The Benedictine monastery at Praglia, 6 km (4 miles) west of Abano Terme, is a peaceful haven in the hills where the monks grow herbs and restore manuscripts. They lead guided tours of parts of the abbey and the church (1490–1548), noted for its beautiful cloister. There are also richly carved stalls in both the choir and the refectory, and paintings and frescoes by Zelotti, a 16th-century painter from Verona, in the dome of the church and the refectory.

🏛 Casa di Petrarca

Via Valleselle 4, Arquà Petrarca.
📞 0429 71 82 94. ⬜ Tue–Sun.
⬛ public hols. 🏷 🅿

The picturesque town of Arquà Petrarca, on the southern edge of the Euganean Hills, is named after Francesco Petrarca (1304–74). This medieval poet, known in English as Petrarch, spent the final years of his life here, in a house frescoed with scenes from his lyrical poems, overlooking a landscape of olive groves and vineyards. He lies buried in a simple sarcophagus in front of the church.

The Casa di Petrarca (part 14th century) in Arquà Petrarca

🏛 Villa Barbarigo

Valsanzibio. 📞 049 805 92 24.
⬜ Mar–Nov: 10am–1pm, 2pm–sunset daily. 🏷 👶 🅿

This 18th-century villa to the north of Arquà boasts one of the finest Baroque gardens in the Veneto. These were planned by Antonio Barbarigo in 1669, and are a grandiose mix of statuary, fountains, a maze, formal parterres, lakes and avenues of cypress trees.

The 16th-century Villa Foscari at Malcontenta, beside the Brenta Canal

Brenta Canal ❾

Padua and Venezia. **FS** *Venezia Mestre, Dolo, Mira.* **🚌** *to Mira, Dolo and Strà.* **Canal trips on *Il Burchiello:*** Padua. **📞** *049 820 69 10.* **W** www.ilburchiello.it 📧

OVER THE CENTURIES, in order to prevent the Venetian lagoon silting up, the rivers flowing into it were diverted. The river Brenta was canalized in two sections: the older branch, between Padua and Fusina (just west of Venice), dates back to the 1500s and flows for 36 km (22 miles). Its potential as a transport route was quickly realized and fine villas were built along its length. Many of these elegant buildings can still be admired today – the S11 road runs alongside most of the canal's length – and several of them are open to the public.

The 18th-century **Villa Nazionale** at Strà has an extravagant frescoed ceiling by Tiepolo. The **Barchessa Valmarana** at Mira (a pretty village) boasts 18th-century decorations. In the village of Malcontenta is **Villa Foscari**, or Villa Malcontenta, one of Palladio's loveliest villas *(see pp76–7)*. It was built in 1560 and the interior decorated with magnificent frescoes by Zelotti. These

villas may also be visited as part of an indulgent 8.5-hour guided tour from Padua, travelling to Venice (or, on alternate days, from Venice to Padua) along the river in a leisurely fashion on board the *Burchiello* motor launch – the cost for the one-way journey, however, is fairly prohibitive.

🚣 Barchessa Valmarana
Via Valmarana 11, Mira.
📞 *041 426 63 87.* ⏱ *mid-Mar–early Nov: Tue–Sun.* 📧 ♿ 🚫

🚣 Villa Nazionale
Via Pisani, Strà. **📞** *049 50 20 74.*
⏱ *Tue–Sun.* ● *1 Jan, 1 May, 25 Dec.*
📧 📷 *Sat & Sun (only in Italian).* 🚻

🚣 Villa Foscari
Via dei Turisti, Malcontenta.
📞 *041 547 00 12.* ⏱ *Tue & Sat am.*
● *Nov–Mar.* 📧

Treviso ❿

🚶 *81,700.* **🚌** **FS** **ℹ** *Piazzetta Monte di Pietà 8 (0422 54 76 32).* 🛒 *Tue & Sat am.*

DESPITE COMPARISONS with Venice, the lovely fortified city of Treviso has its own very distinctive character.

A good place to start a tour of the streets, some lined with attractive balconied houses beside willow-fringed canals, is **Calmaggiore**. The street links the Duomo with the Palazzo dei Trecento, the rebuilt 13th-century town hall.

The **Duomo** was founded in the 12th century but rebuilt several times. Inside, Titian's *Annunciation* (1570) vies for attention with the striking *Adoration of the Magi* fresco (1520) by Titian's arch-rival, Il Pordenone. More paintings by Titian and other artists of the Renaissance may be seen in the **Museo Civico**.

The fish market, which dates from medieval times, is held on an island in the middle of Treviso's river Sile; this allows the remains of the day's trading to be flushed away.

The bulky Dominican church of **San Nicolò**, nestling by the 16th-century city wall, contains interesting tombs and frescoes, including, on a wall of the chapter house, the first-ever depiction of spectacles in art. A magnificent tomb (1500) by Antonio Rizzo is framed by a fresco of pageboys (c.1500) by Lorenzo Lotto.

🏛 Museo Civico
Borgo Cavour 24. **📞** *0422 65 84 42.*
⏱ *Tue–Sun.* ● *public hols.* 📧

The houses of the medieval town of Treviso overlooking ancient canals

The façade and entrance to the Renaissance Palazzo dei Rettori in Belluno

South of the town are the ski resorts of the Alpe del Nevegal; in the summer a chair lift operates from Faverghera up the flank of the mountain to a height of 1,600 m (5,250 ft) offering extensive views.

🏛 **Museo Civico**
Piazza Duomo 16. 🕿 *0437 94 48 36.*
🕐 *May–Sep: Tue–Sun; Oct–Apr:*
Mon–Sat. 🈵 🗹 🛈

Conegliano ⓫

Treviso. 🏘 *35,000.* 🚉 🚌 🛈 *Via XX Settembre 61 (0438 212 30).* 🛒 *Fri.*

CONEGLIANO lies among Prosecco-producing vineyards, and winemakers from all over Italy learn their craft at Conegliano's renowned wine school. Via XX Settembre, the winding and arcaded main street, is lined with fine 15th- to 18th-century palazzi, many in the Venetian Gothic style or decorated with fading frescoes. The **Duomo** contains the town's one great work of art, an altarpiece painted by local artist Cima da Conegliano (1460–1518) depicting the *Virgin and Child with Saints* (1493).

A mythical statue on Conegliano's theatre

Reproductions of Cima's most famous works are on show in the **Casa di Cima**, the artist's birthplace. The detailed landscapes in the background of his paintings were based on the hills around the town; the same views can still be seen from the gardens surrounding the Castelvecchio (old castle).

🏛 **Casa di Cima**
Via Cima. 🕿 *0438 216 60 (phone in advance to arrange a visit).* 🈵

Belluno ⓬

🏘 *36,000.* 🚉 🚌 🛈 *Piazza Duomo 2 (0437 94 00 83).* 🛒 *Sat.*

PICTURESQUE BELLUNO, capital of Belluno province, serves as a bridge between the two different parts of the Veneto, with the flat plains to the south and the Dolomite peaks to the

north. Both are encapsulated in the views to be seen from the 12th-century **Porta Rugo** at the southern end of Via Mezzaterra, the main street of the old town. More spectacular still are the views from the bell tower of the 16th-century **Duomo** (subsequently rebuilt). The nearby baptistry houses a font cover with the figure of John the Baptist carved by Andrea Brustolon (1662–1732). Brustolon's works also grace the churches of San Pietro (on Via San Pietro) and Santo Stefano (Piazza Santo Stefano). North of Piazza del Duomo stands the city's most elegant building, the **Palazzo dei Rettori** (1491) – once home to the town's Venetian rulers – and the 12th-century **Torre Civica**, all that now survives of a medieval castle.

The **Museo Civico** contains paintings by Bartolomeo Montagna (1450–1523) and Sebastiano Ricci (1659–1734), and a notable archaeological section. North of the museum is Belluno's finest square, the **Piazza del Mercato**, with its arcaded Renaissance palaces and its fountain of 1410.

Cortina d'Ampezzo ⓭

Belluno. 🏘 *6,800.* 🚌 🛈 *Piazzetta San Francesco 8 (0436 32 31).* 🛒 *Tue am & Fri am.*

ITALY'S TOP SKI RESORT, much favoured by the smart set from Turin and Milan, is well supplied with restaurants and bars. Cortina is set amid the extremely dramatic scenery of the Dolomites (*see pp78–9*), which explains part of the resort's attraction: all around, crags and spires thrust their distinctive weather-beaten shapes above the trees.

Cortina benefits from better than average sports facilities, thanks to hosting the 1956 Winter Olympics. In addition to downhill and cross-country skiing, there is also a ski jump and a bobsleigh run for those who favour something more adventurous than usual, as well as an Olympic ice stadium, several swimming pools, tennis courts and riding facilities.

During the summer months, Cortina becomes an excellent base for walkers. Useful information on trails and guided walks is available from the tourist office or, during the summer, from the Guides' office opposite.

Corso Italia in Cortina d'Ampezzo, Italy's most important ski resort

Traditional copper pans on display in the Museo Carnico in Tolmezzo

Tolmezzo ⑭

🏛 *10,000.* 🚌 ℹ️ *Piazza XX Settembre 9 (0433 448 98).* 🔄 *Mon.*

TOLMEZZO IS THE CAPITAL of the Carnia region, named after the Celtic tribe that inhabited the area around the 4th century BC. The town is surrounded by the high peaks of the Carnic Alps, including the pyramidal Monte Amariana (1,906 m – 6,253 ft) to the east. The best place to begin a tour of the region is the **Museo delle Arti Popolari**, which has displays of local costumes, crafts, textiles and agriculture.

Southwest of the town, a scenic road climbs 14 km (8.5 miles) to the ski resort of **Sella Chianzutan**, a good base for walking in the summer. More resorts line the road, west of Tolmezzo, to **Ampezzo**, at which point a minor road heads north through the gorge of the River Lumiei. Following this road to the Ponte di Buso bridge and the **Lago di Sauris** is an excellent introduction to the majestic Carnic Alps.

Above this point the road is often impassable in winter, but in summer there are flower-filled meadows all along the road up to Sella di Razzo, and then back along the **Pesarina Valley**, via Comeglians and Ravascletto. Returning south, **Zuglio** was once the Roman town of Forum Iulii Carnicum, guarding the road over the pass. Today it is worth a detour for the remains of its Roman basilica, baths and forum.

🏛 Museo delle Arti Popolari

Via della Vittoria 2. 📞 *0433 432 33.* ⏱ *Tue–Sun (Aug: also on Mon).* ⬤ *1 Jan, 25 Dec.* 🈺 ♿ 🚫

Pordenone ⑮

🏛 *49,000.* 🚉 🚌 ℹ️ *Corso Vittorio Emanuele II 38 (0434 219 12).* 🔄 *Sat am & Wed.*

OLD PORDENONE consists of one long street, the **Corso Vittorio Emanuele**, lined with pretty arcaded houses of pink brick, some with the faded traces of decorative frescoes on their façades. The 13th-century **Palazzo Comunale** forms a striking conclusion to the street with its eccentrically shaped roofline of curves and minaret-like side towers, and its 16th-century clocktower. Opposite is the **Museo d'Arte**, housed in the 17th-century Palazzo Ricchieri, where works by the local artist Il Pordenone (1484–1539) are on display.

Around the corner stands the **Duomo**, which contains the lovely altar painting of the *Madonna della Misericordia* (1515) by Il Pordenone. The bell tower beside the Duomo is a fine example of Romanesque decorative brickwork.

🏛 Museo d'Arte

Corso Vittorio Emanuele 51. 📞 *0434 39 23 11.* ⏱ *Tue–Fri.* ⬤ *public hols.* 🈺 ♿ 🚫

Udine ⑯

🏛 *99,000.* 🚉 🚌 ℹ️ *Piazza I Maggio 7 (0432 29 59 72).* 🔄 *Sat.*

UDINE IS A CITY of varied and surprising architecture. In the centre lies **Piazza della Libertà**, where the Loggia del Lionello (1448–56), built of pink stone in Venetian Gothic style, stands beside the Art Deco Caffè Contarena. Opposite, the Renaissance symmetry of the Porticato di San Giovanni is interrupted by the Torre dell'Orologio (Clock Tower, 1527) crowned by two bronze Moors who strike the hours. Note also the fountain of 1542, the two 18th-century statues, and the column supporting the Lion of St Mark.

Beyond the **Arco Bollani**, a gateway designed by Palladio in 1556, steps lead up to a 26-m (85-ft) hill which offers sweeping views over the city. On the hill is the 16th-century castle, now the **Musei Civici e Galleria di Storia e Arte Antica**, which houses fine art and archaeology collections.

Southeast of Piazza Matteotti, where a small market is held, at the end of Via Savorgnana, stands the **Oratorio della Purità**, and the **Duomo** with its octagonal bell tower. Both contain important paintings and frescoes by Giambattista Tiepolo (1696–1770). More of Tiepolo's work can be seen in the **Palazzo Arcivescovile**, which the artist decorated with frescoes.

Lago di Sauris, an artificial lake lying in the Carnic Alps above Tolmezzo

The arcaded Porticato di San Giovanni on Piazza della Libertà, Udine

ENVIRONS: Outside Codroipo, 24 km (15 miles) west, rises the imposing **Villa Manin**. A road passes through the villa's grounds, so its massive size can be seen even when the house – once the retreat of Ludovico Manin, the last doge of Venice (1725–1802) – and its magnificent gardens are closed to the public.

🏛 Musei Civici e Galleria di Storia e Arte Antica
Castello di Udine. **📞** 0432 50 28 72. **🕐** Tue–Sat (Sun am). **🔴** 1 Jan, Easter, 1 May, 25 Dec. **🎫 ♿ 🚫**

🏛 Palazzo Arcivescovile
Piazza Patriarcato 1. **📞** 0432 250 03. **🕐** Wed–Sun. **🔴** 1 Jan, Easter, 25 Dec. **🎫 ♿ 🚹**

🏛 Villa Manin
Passariano. **📞** 0432 90 66 57. **🕐** Tue–Sun. **🔴** 1 Jan, 25 Dec. **🎫** for exhibitions only. **♿**

Cividale del Friuli ⑰

👥 11,000. **FS 🚌 ℹ** Corso Paolino d'Aquileia 4 (0432 73 14 61). **🔴** Sat.

A GATE IN THE medieval walls of Cividale leads down the main street and straight to the dramatic ravine of the River Natisone, which is spanned by the arch of the **Ponte del Diavolo** (Devil's Bridge).

Above the river's north bank stands the **Tempietto Longobardo** (Lombardic Chapel), a very rare example of an 8th-century church decorated with reliefs of saints, modelled in stucco. The town's history is traced in the excellent **Museo Archeologico Nazionale**,

which contains the excavated remains of buildings from a Roman town, and a collection of Lombardic items including jewellery, ivory and weapons.

Next door is the **Duomo**, rebuilt in 1453 after a fire, with its beautiful silver altarpiece (13th century). The **Museo Cristiano**, off the south aisle, contains sculptures from the original church: of particular interest is the altar donated by Ratchis, the Lombardic Duke of Friuli and later King of Italy (737–44), which is finely carved with scenes from the Life of Christ, including a charming Nativity. There is in addition the unusual baptismal font of Patriarch Callisto (737–56): this octagonal structure, with a roof supported by pillars, is decorated with symbols of the Evangelists.

The Lion of Venice above the entrance to Gorizia's castle

🏛 Tempietto Longobardo
Piazzetta San Biagio. **🕐** daily. **🎫 🚫**

Interior view of the Tempietto Longobardo in Cividale del Friuli

🏛 Museo Archeologico Nazionale
Palazzo dei Provveditori Veneti, Piazza del Duomo 1.
📞 0432 70 07 00. **🕐** daily.
🔴 1 Jan, 25 Dec. **🎫 ♿**
🏛 Museo Cristiano
Piazza del Duomo. **📞** 0432 73 11 44.
🕐 daily. **🔴** Sun am & public hols. **♿**

Gorizia ⑱

👥 37,000. **FS 🚌 ℹ** Palazzo della Regione, Via Roma 5 (0481 38 62 25). **🔴** Thu, Fri.

G ORIZIA WAS AT the centre of fierce fighting during both world wars and was split in two by the 1947 Treaty of Paris, leaving part in Italy, part in Yugoslavia (now Slovenia).

The town's arcaded streets and pastel-painted houses have been carefully restored following substantial damage during World War II. A visit to the modern Museo Provinciale della Grande Guerra (Museum of the Great War), housed in the basement of the **Museo Provinciale**, provides a fascinating introduction to the realities of war. The museum uses videos, photographs, and life-size mock-ups of trenches, latrines and gun emplacements to show the waste, squalor and heroism of war.

Rooms on the upper floor of the museum house temporary exhibitions and items from the town's art collection, which includes works by local artists.

On a mound nearby rises the castle, encircled by 16th-century fortifications. From here there are extensive views stretching over the town to the mountains beyond.

ENVIRONS: To the southwest of Gorizia, scenic country roads pass through the foothills of the **Carso**, a limestone plateau stretching down to Trieste. The plateau is dotted with fields enclosed by drystone walls, and gouged with tunnels, caves and underground rivers.

🏛 Museo Provinciale
Borgo Castello 13. **📞** 0481 53 39 26.
🕐 Tue–Sun. **🔴** 1 Jan, 25 Dec. **🎫 🚫**

The attractive harbourside at Grado, along the coast south of Aquileia

Aquileia ⑲

🏃 3,300. 🚌 ℹ️ *Via Julia Augusta* *(0431 91 94 91).* 🛥️ *Tue.*

AQUILEIA, now little more than a village but encircled by the ruins of palatial villas, baths, temples and market buildings, provides a poignant reminder of the lost splendour of the Roman Empire.

It was here that Emperor Augustus received Herod the Great, King of Judea, in 10 BC, and it was here too, in AD 381, that the early Christian church held a major council attended by the learned saints Ambrose and Jerome to settle doctrinal issues. In the 5th century, however, the town was abandoned following several sackings. Fortunately, substantial parts of the early Christian basilica have survived, which contain the town's particular treasure: ornate floor mosaics.

⛪ Basilica
Piazza Capitolo. 🕿 *0431 910 67.* ⬜ *daily.* ⬤ *during mass.* **Crypt** 🎫 ♿

The basilica was founded in about AD 313 and much of the original structure still survives, including the magnificent floor mosaics of the nave and **Cripta degli Scavi** below. The designs are a mixture of geometric patterns, biblical stories and scenes from everyday life in ancient Aquileia. There is a lively portrayal of the tale of Jonah, who was swallowed by an extraordinary sea monster: the fishing boats are also surrounded by a rich array of creatures from the deep, including wide-eyed dolphins and squid.

🏛️ Museo Archeologico Nazionale
Via Roma 1. 🕿 *0431 910 16.* ⬜ *daily.* ⬤ *public hols.* 🎫 ♿ Ø

The mosaics in the basilica demonstrate a tradition of craftsmanship that flourished

in the city from the 2nd century AD. Additional examples of mosaics and stone carvings from the Classical era (1st to 3rd centuries) are on display in this museum, together with glass, amber, and a collection of flies, beautifully worked in gold, that formed the adornment of a Roman matron's veil.

🏛️ Museo Paleocristiano
Località Monastero. 🕿 *0431 911 31.* ⬜ *daily.* ⬤ *1 Jan, 1 May, 25 Dec.* 🎫 ♿ Ø

This museum, which stands not far from Aquileia's ancient harbour beside the once-navigable River Natissa, focuses on the development of art during the early Christian era.

ENVIRONS: South of Udine, **Palmanova** is worth a visit for its remarkable octagonal layout and intact walls. The town was built in 1593 by the Venetians to commemorate the Battle of Lepanto.

Grado sits on a group of low islands in the middle of the Adriatic lagoon, attached to the mainland by a narrow causeway. The town grew into a port for Aquileia in the 2nd century and was used as a haven by Aquileia's citizens during the barbarian invasions. Today, Grado is a popular seaside resort. At the centre of the old town stands the **Duomo**, which contains 6th-century frescoes in the apse, similar to those covering the vaults of San Marco in Venice *(see pp106–9).* Nearby, in the little church of **Santa Maria delle Grazie**, there are yet more 6th-century mosaics.

SYMBOLISM IN EARLY CHRISTIAN ART

Christians were persecuted until their religion was granted official status by Constantine the Great in AD 313. Prior to this they had developed a language of secret symbols to express their beliefs, many of which can be seen in the mosaics and marble tomb chests of Aquileia. Many of these and other symbols later found their way into popular bestiaries and folk art.

Part of the 4th-century floor mosaic in the basilica at Aquileia

The Winged figure of Victory *holding a laurel wreath was a Classical symbol of triumph, and holiness. Later, it came to represent Christ's resurrection, and more generally, victory over death.*

Trieste 🄴

🏘 218,000. ✈ 🚆 ⛴
ℹ Piazza Unità d'Italia 4/b (040 347 83 12). 🔄 Tue–Sat.

TRIESTE IS AN atmospheric city, tucked up next to Slovenia, with a long, bustling harbour lined with handsome buildings and lapped by the waves of the Adriatic Sea.

🏛 Acquario Marino
Molo Pescheria 2. ☎ 040 30 62 01. 🔄 Tue–Sun (Nov–Mar: am only). ● public hols. 🅿 ♿
The city's aquarium is one of the most popular attractions in Trieste. It contains examples of the fascinating marine life in the Adriatic.

⚓ Castello di San Giusto
Piazza Cattedrale 3.
☎ 040 30 93 62. 🔄 daily.
● 1 & 6 Jan, 25 & 26 Dec. 🅿
Up above the harbour stands a hilltop castle built by Trieste's Venetian governors from 1368. It is set on a terrace that offers sweeping views over the Gulf of Trieste. The castle houses two museums containing Roman mosaics, and a collection of weapons and armour.

⛪ Basilica Paleocristiana
Via Madonna del Mare 11. ☎ 040 436 31. 🔄 10am–noon Wed.
Beside the castle lie the substantial ruins of the Roman basilica or law court built around AD 100. Note the stone magistrates' bench and throne.

⛪ Duomo
Piazza Cattedrale. ☎ 040 30 96 66.
🔄 daily.
In the church of **San Giusto**, the city's Duomo, magistrates' bench and throne of the Roman basilica were reinterpreted to become the seat of the bishop and clergy. Because the building was formed in the 14th century by linking two 5th-century churches that stood side by side, there are two thrones and benches here. The two apses are decorated with very fine 13th-century mosaics in the Venetian style.

🏛 Museo di Storia ed Arte ed Orto Lapidario
Via della Cattedrale 15. ☎ 040 31 05 00.
🔄 Tue–Sun.
● public hols. 🅿
The important archaeological collection held here provides fascinating evidence of Trieste's extensive trade links with the ancient Greek world.

13th-century mosaics in the apse of San Giusto, Trieste's Duomo

ENVIRONS: From **Villa Opicina**, just north of Trieste, sweeping views may be had over the city, its bay and south down the coast of Slovenia. A little beyond, at Borgo Grotta Gigante, lies the **Grotta del Gigante**, a huge cavern filled with stunning "organ pipe" formations and tall columns of stalagmites.

At Grignano, 8 km (5 miles) northwest of the city, stands the **Castello di Miramare**, a white castle set in lush green gardens beside the sparkling blue Adriatic. It was built by the Habsburg Archduke Maximilian in 1856–60 as his summer retreat, a few years before he was assassinated in Mexico. It is still furnished in contemporary style.

🏕 Grotta del Gigante
Borgo Grotta Gigante. ☎ 040 32 73 12. 🔄 Tue–Sun (Jul & Aug: daily). 🅿 🅿

⚓ Castello di Miramare
Miramare, Grignano. ☎ 040 22 41 43. 🔄 daily. ♿ 🅿 (castle only.)

The Castello del Miramare on the bay of Trieste

***The Tortoise** hiding in his shell represented darkness and ignorance, while the cockerel, who crows at dawn, signified light and enlightenment.*

***ICHTHUS, or fish**, was an acronym for Iesous CHristos THeou Uios Soter – Jesus Christ, Son of God, Saviour, in ancient Greek.*

***Colourful birds**, such as peacocks, symbolized immortality and the glorious transformation of the soul when it arrives in Heaven.*

TRENTINO-ALTO ADIGE

HE ITALIAN-SPEAKING Trentino – named after Trento, the regional capital – and the German-speaking Alto Adige or Südtirol (South Tyrol, the region bordering the upper reaches of the River Adige) differ dramatically in culture. However, they do share one feature in common: the majestic Dolomites that form the backdrop to every town and village, covered in snow for three months of every year and carpeted with exquisite Alpine plants for another three.

The region's mountains have been cut by glaciers into a series of deep, broad valleys. Many of these face south, so it remains unusually warm and sunny, even in winter. Travellers have passed up and down these valleys for generations – as confirmed by the extraordinary discovery, in 1991, of a 5,000-year-old man's body found emerging from the surface of a melting glacier in Alto Adige. The frozen corpse wore leather boots, stuffed with hay for warmth, and was armed with a copper ice pick.

The paths that Neolithic man once trod became major road networks under the Romans, when many of the region's cities were founded. By the Middle Ages, Alto Adige had established its very own distinctive culture under the Counts of Tyrol, whose land (later appropriated by the Habsburgs) straddled both sides of today's Italian/Austrian border. The Tyrolean nobility built the castles that still line the valleys and the mountain passes, in order to protect travellers from brigands.

Another ancient legacy is the tradition of hospitality to be found in the numerous guesthouses along the valleys. Many of these are built in the distinctive Tyrolean style, with beautiful timber balconies for making the most of the winter sun, and overhanging roof eaves to keep snow at a distance. Cosy in winter, with log fires and warming food, and offering marvellous views, they make the ideal base for enjoying the region's mountain footpaths and ski slopes.

Skiers enjoying the slopes around Monte Spinale, near Madonna di Campiglio, in Trentino

◁ **A typical view of the Dolomites between Bressanone and Ortisei, in Alto Adige**

Exploring Trentino-Alto Adige

Trentino-alto adige is a region where unspoiled nature is complemented by a wealth of sporting opportunities. The tributary valleys feeding into the Adige valley contain lakes, rivers and streams, and also woodland, vineyards and Alpine pasture full of butterflies, birds and flowers. Southeast of the region rise the distinctive limestone peaks of the Dolomites, while further north the area becomes more mountainous still, enclosed finally by the splendid heights of the Alps.

Via Ponte Aquila in Bressanone

SIGHTS AT A GLANCE

KEY

▦	Motorway
▬	Major road
▭	Minor road
▬	Scenic route
≈	River
✲	Viewpoint

0 kilometres   25

0 miles   10

Castel Tirolo above the town of Merano

View of the Dolomites from Madonna di Campiglio

GETTING AROUND

The region's main artery is the Brenner Pass road: it runs from Austria in the north, following the River Adige from Bolzano to Trento, and southwards on to Verona. Both the motorway and the main road beside it are among the busiest in Europe, and the valley roads can also be congested during the ski season. Winter driving can be hazardous, requiring special tyres and snow chains. An excellent rail and coach network serves the whole area.

SEE ALSO

Abbazia di Monte Maria, founded in the 12th century, near Malles Venosta

Malles Venosta ❶
MALS IM VINSCHGAU

🏃 4,600. 🚉 🚌 ℹ️ Via San Benedetto 1 (0473 83 11 90). 🚊 Wed.

MALLES VENOSTA sits in high border country, close to Switzerland and Austria, and was a customs point during the Middle Ages. The town has several Gothic churches, whose spires and towers give an appealing skyline, mirroring the jagged peaks that rise all around. The oldest is the tiny church of **San Benedetto**, a 9th-century Carolingian building on Via San Benedetto, with frescoes of its patrons.

ENVIRONS: The medieval **Castel Coira** (Churburg) rises at Sluderno (Schluderns), 4 km (2.5 miles) southeast of Malles. It now contains an excellent collection of weapons and armour.

Clinging to the mountainside 5 km (3 miles) north of Malles, just above the town of Burgusio (Burgeis), is the Benedictine **Abbazia di Monte Maria** (Marienberg), founded in the 12th century but enlarged in the 18th and 19th. The church's crypt shelters an outstanding series of 12th-century frescoes.

The glorious medieval town of **Glorenza** lies just 2 km (1.25 miles) south of Malles.

♣ Castel Coira
Churburg, Sluderno. 📞 0473 61 52 41. 🕐 20 Mar–Oct: Tue–Sun by guided tour only. 🚫

🏛️ Abbazia di Monte Maria
📞 0473 83 13 06. 🕐 May–Oct: Mon–Sat; Nov–Apr: groups by appt only. 🕐 public hols. 🚫 🚫

Merano ❷
MERAN

🏃 35,000. 🚉 🚌 ℹ️ Corso della Libertà 45 (0473 27 20 00). 🚊 Tue, Fri.

MERANO IS AN attractive spa town popular with Austrians, Germans and Italians. On Corso Libertà, a street of smart shops and hotels, stands the **Kurhaus** or Spa Hall built in 1914, now a concert venue. The 15th-century **Castello Principesco** was home to the Habsburg Archduke Sigismund and is still furnished in period style. Inviting gardens line the River Passirio, which winds its way through the town. The Passeggiata Lungo Passirio d'Inverno

The Art Nouveau façade of the Kurhaus in Merano

(Winter Walk) follows the north bank to the Roman bridge, Ponte Romano; the Passeggiata d'Estate (Summer Walk) on the south bank leads to the medieval Ponte Passirio.

ENVIRONS: The romantic 12th-century **Castel Tirolo** lies 4 km (2.5 miles) to the north. It hosts a museum of Tyrolean history.

The grounds of **Castel Trauttmansdorff** house a fascinating botanical garden.

♣ Castello Principesco
Via Galilei. 📞 0473 25 03 29. 🕐 Tue–Sun & public hols. 🕐 Jan–Feb. 🚫 🚫

♣ Castel Tirolo
Via Castello 24, Tirolo. 📞 0473 22 02 21. 🕐 mid Mar–Oct: Tue–Sun. 🕐 Nov–mid-Mar. 🚫 🚫 🚫 🚫

♣ Castel Trauttmansdorff
Via S. Valentino 51a. 📞 0473 23 57 30. 🕐 15 Mar–15 Nov: daily. 🚫 🚫 🚫 🚫

Vipiteno ❸
STERZING

🏃 5,600. 🚉 🚌 ℹ️ Piazza Città 3 (0472 76 53 25). 🚊 daily.

VIPITENO, SURROUNDED by mineral-rich valleys, is very Tyrolean in feel. On Via Città Nuova, lined with fine mansions, rise the Gothic **Palazzo Comunale**, containing Renaissance sculpture and paintings, and the Torre dei Dodici, symbol of the town. Wood carvings in the **Museo Multscher**

Wrought-iron si Vipiteno

are by Hans Multscher; the Bavarian sculptor came to Vipiteno in 1456–8 to carve the altar for the parish **church**, which lies just south of the town.

To the west, the charming **Val di Racines** includes waterfalls and a natural rock bridge.

🏛️ Palazzo Comunale
Via Città Nuova 21. 📞 0472 72 37 00. 🕐 Mon–Fri. 🕐 Fri am; public hols.

🏛️ Museo Multscher
Via della Commenda. 📞 0472 76 64 64. 🕐 Apr–Oct: Tue–Sat. 🕐 public hols. 🚫

The medieval castle dominating the town of Brunico

Brunico ❹
BRUNECK

🏠 *13,000.* FS 🚌 ℹ️ *Piazza Municipio 7 (0474 55 57 22).* 🛒 *Wed.*

THIS ATTRACTIVE TOWN, overlooked by the imposing form of its medieval **castle**, retains 14th-century fortifications and a network of narrow streets that can only be explored on foot. The church of **St Ursula**, to the northwest of St Ursula's Gate, contains a series of outstanding mid-15th-century altar reliefs of the Nativity. The **Museo Etnografico di Teodone** offers displays of traditional agricultural life and local costumes; this folklore museum also provides an ideal opportunity to visit a 16th-century farmhouse and barn.

St Ursula's Gate sundial, Brunico

🏛 **Museo Etnografico di Teodone**
Via Duca Diet 24, Teodone.
📞 *0474 55 20 87.* ⏰ *late Apr–Oct: Tue–Sat, Sun and public hols pm (Aug: also Mon).* ♿ 🚻

Bressanone ❺
BRIXEN

🏠 *18,000.* FS 🚌
ℹ️ *Viale Stazione 9 (0472 83 64 01).* 🛒 *Mon.*

THE NARROW MEDIEVAL alleys of Bressanone cluster around the cathedral and the palace of the prince-bishops who ruled the town for much of its history. The **Duomo**, on

Piazza del Duomo, was rebuilt in the 18th century but retains its 12th-century cloister, decorated with superb 15th-century frescoes. The lavish interiors of Palazzo Vescovile, the bishops' Renaissance palace, house the **Museo Diocesano**. It contains precious items from the Middle Ages, as well as the **Museo dei Presepi**, with its collection of wooden crib figures that are carved locally.

ENVIRONS: At Velturno (Feldthurns), just 8 km (5 miles) southwest, stands the Renaissance **Castello di Velturno**, the summer retreat of the rulers of Bressanone noted for its frescoed rooms. A little over 3 km (2 miles) north

of Bressanone lies the **Abbazia di Novacella**, a picturesque group of fortified monastic buildings with an outstanding series of cloister frescoes. Further north up the valley, at **Rio di Pusteria** (Mühlbach), the remains of a 16th-century fortified barrier can be seen to the east of the town. The barrier funnelled ancient travellers through the customs post that divided Tyrol from the Görz district.

High above Rio di Pusteria, to the southeast, looms the massive outline of the **Castello di Rodengo** (Rodeneck). The castle contains wonderful 13th-century frescoes showing battle scenes, the Last Judgment and courtly episodes from the *Iwein* romance by Hartmann von Aue, the medieval poet.

🏛 **Museo Diocesano** & 🏛 **Museo dei Presepi**
Palazzo Vescovile, Piazza Palazzo Vescovile 2. 📞 *0472 83 05 05.* ⏰ *mid-Mar–Oct: Tue–Sun; Dec & Jan: daily (Museo dei Presepi only).* ⏰ *24 & 25 Dec.* ♿
♣ **Castello di Velturno**
Velturno. 📞 *0472 85 55 25.* ⏰ *Mar–Nov: Tue–Sun.* ♿ ♿
⛪ **Abbazia di Novacella**
Varna. 📞 *0472 83 61 89.* ⏰ *Mon–Sat.* ⏰ *public hols.* ♿ ♿
♣ **Castello di Rodengo**
Rodengo. 📞 *0472 45 40 56.* ⏰ *mid-May–mid-Oct: Tue–Sun.* ♿ ♿

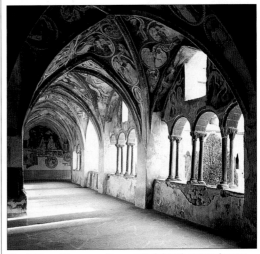

The cloisters of Bressanone Duomo with their 15th-century frescoes

The Baroque interior of the church of St Ulrich in Ortisei

Bolzano ❻

BOZEN

🏠 98,000. 🚉 🚌 🅸 *Piazza Walther 8 (0471 30 70 00).* 🚐 *Sat.*

Bolzano, the capital of the Alto Adige, is the gateway between the Italian-speaking Trentino region and the German-speaking Alto Adige or Südtirol, and has a marked Tyrolean atmosphere. The old centre, **Piazza Walther**, is dominated by the 15th-century Gothic **Duomo**, with its multicoloured mosaic-patterned roof and elaborate spire. The "wine door" inside the Duomo is carved with figures at work among vines and reflects the importance of wine to the local economy. In the middle of Piazza Walther is a statue of Walther von der Vogelweide, the 13th-century troubadour – born, according to legend, in this area. North of the square, the streets are lined with houses adorned with intricate gables, balconies and oriel windows. The out-door market, starting at Piazza Grano, forms an inviting array of local produce that continues along the arcaded Via dei Portici. This street continues to the **Museo Civico**, where South Tyrolean history is introduced through domestic interiors, wood carvings and costumes, while the modern **Museo Archeologico** houses

The Duomo spire, Bolzano

the famous 5,000-year-old "Iceman". The **Chiesa dei Domenicani** (Dominican church), on Piazza Domenicani, has 14th-century *Triumph of Death* frescoes and a frescoed cloister.

🏛 **Museo Civico**
Via Cassa di Risparmio 14.
📞 *0471 97 46 25.* 🕐 *for renovation until 2007.* 📷
🏛 **Museo Archeologico**
Via Museo 43. 📞 *0471 32 01 00.*
🕐 *Tue–Sun.* ⬤ *1 Jan, 1 May, 25 Dec.* 📷 🅾 🅿

Ortisei ❼

SANKT ULRICH

🏠 4,500. 🚌 🅸 *Via Rezia 1 (0471 79 63 28).* 🚐 *Fri.*

Ortisei is the prosperous main resort for the pretty Val Gardena and Alpe di Siusi region, and a major centre for

woodcarving; examples of local craftsmanship may be seen in local shops, in the **Museo della Val Gardena** (which also focuses on local archaeology), and in the church of **St Ulrich**.

To the south is the **Alpe di Siusi** (Seiser Alm) region, noted for its Alpine meadows, balconied farmsteads and onion-domed churches. The best way to explore this beautiful area is by cableway from Ortisei: to the northeast another cablecar runs to 2,518-m (8,260-ft) high Monte Seceda, and walks from here lead into the Odle Dolomites.

🏛 **Museo della Val Gardena**
Via Rezia 83. 📞 *0471 79 75 54.* 🕐 *Feb, Mar: Tue, Thu & Fri; Jun, Sep–mid-Oct: Tue–Fri; Jul, Aug: Sun–Fri.* 📷

Canazei ❽

🏠 1,800. 🚌 🅸 *Piazza Marconi (0462 60 11 13).* 🚐 *Sat (Jun–Sep).*

Located at the base of some of the highest and most awe-inspiring groups of peaks, Canazei is a good base for exploring the Dolomites. In summer, chair-lifts climb to viewpoints where the beauty of the encircling mountains can be appreciated to the full. The most popular viewpoints are Pecol and Col dei Rossi, reached by the Belvedere cableway from Via Pareda in Canazei: the cliffs of the Sella group are visible to the north, with Sasso Lungo to the west

Skiers enjoying views of the Dolomites above Canazei

and Marmolada, the highest of the Dolomites at 3,343 m (10,965 ft), to the south.

ENVIRONS: At **Vigo di Fassa**, 13 km (8 miles) southwest, the **Museo Ladino** focuses on the Ladin-speaking people of some of the valleys. Ladin – a Rhaeto-Romance language – is taught in local schools and the ancient traditions, costumes and music still thrive.

🏛 **Museo Ladino**
Via Milano 5, Pozzo di Fassa.
📞 0462 76 01 82. ⏰ Tue–Sat pm
(late Jun–mid-Sep: daily). 🎫 ♿ 📷

Cavalese ❾

🏠 3,600. 🚌 🛈 Via Fratelli
Bronzetti 60 (0462 24 11 11).
🔄 last Tue of month (not Jul).

The frescoed façade of the Palazzo della Magnifica Comunità

CAVALESE IS THE chief town in the Val di Fiemme, a pretty region of flower-filled aromatic pastures, delightful wooded valleys and Tyrolean architecture. At the centre of the town stands the **Palazzo della Magnifica Comunità**. Originally built in the 13th century, this was the seat of the medieval governing council which ruled the area as a semi-autonomous region. Today the panelled interiors contain medieval paintings by local artists, and an archaeology collection. Most visitors come for the excellent summer and winter resort facilities, and to climb, by cable car, to the 2,229 m (7,311 ft) top of **Alpe Cermis**, the mountain that rises to the south of the town.

ENVIRONS: The church in **Tesero**, the next village east, bears a 15th-century fresco by an unknown painter depicting

Vines growing on the terraced slopes of the Cembra valley

Sabbath-breakers. The church itself, dating back to 1450, has a flurry of Gothic vaulting, and a modern representation of the Crucifixion painted against a background of the village.

At **Predazzo**, about 13 km (8 miles) east, the **Museo Geologico e Mineralogico** explains the local geology.

🏛 **Palazzo della Magnifica Comunità**
Piazza Cesare Battisti 2.
📞 0462 34 03 65. ⏰ for
restoration. 📷
🏛 **Museo Geologico e Mineralogico**
Piazza Santi Filippo e Giacomo 1.
📞 0462 50 03 66.
⏰ for renovation.

San Martino di Castrozza ❿

🏠 470. 🚌 🛈 Via Passo Rolle 165
(0439 76 88 67).

THE RESORT OF San Martino occupies one of the most scenic and accessible valleys in the southern Dolomites, making it very popular with walkers and skiers. Cable cars rise to the peak of **Alpe Tognola** (2,163 m, 7,095 ft), southwest of the town, and up the **Cima della Rosetta** (2,609 m, 8,557 ft) to the east. Both offer magnificent views of the Pale di San Martino Dolomitic peaks, a stirring sight as the massive rock peaks, split by

Piramidi di Segonzano, near Cembra

glaciers, rise above a sea of green meadows and woodland. San Martino is almost entirely surrounded by forest, which once supplied the Venetian Republic with timber for ships. The forest is now protected, and as a result it is possible to see Alpine flowers, mushrooms, birds and other wildlife with relative ease.

Cembra ⓫

🏠 2,500. 🚌 🛈 Piazza Toniolli 2
(0461 68 31 10). 🔄 Wed.

THE WINE-PRODUCING town of Cembra nestles on the terraced slopes of a scenic valley of flower-filled villages. Some 6 km (4 miles) east of Cembra stand the **Piramidi di Segonzano**, a rare series of erosion pillars, some over 30 m (100 ft) high, each topped by a rock. The footpath to the pillars is well signposted, with informative noticeboards along the way explaining the formation of the bizarre columns, which are similar in appearance to giant termites' nests. Their setting amid bird-filled woodland makes the steep climb up to the site well worthwhile. A further reward is the fine view, from the top of the hill, along the Cembra valley and westwards as far as the Brenta group of Dolomites.

🏞 **Piramidi di Segonzano**
Strada Statale 612 to Cavalese.
⏰ daily.

The impressive falls of the Cascate di Nardis, Madonna di Campiglio

Madonna di Campiglio ⑫

🏠 *1,300.* 🚃 ℹ️ *Via Pradalago 4 (0465 44 20 00).* 🔵 *Jul–Aug: Tue & Thu.*

MADONNA DI CAMPIGLIO is the chief resort in the Val Meledrio. Nestling between the Brenta and Adamello groups of peaks, it makes the perfect base for walking or skiing amid the magnificent mountain terrain. Cableways radiate out from the town in every direction, giving easy access to the peaks.

ENVIRONS: The church at **Pinzolo**, 14 km (9 miles) south, has a well-preserved fresco depicting a *Dance of Death* (1539). The inevitable march of the figures, both rich and poor, is underlined by a text written in local dialect.

North of Pinzolo, the road west from Carisolo leads to the verdant and popular, yet unspoilt, **Val Genova**. About 4 km (2 miles) along the valley is the spectacular **Cascate di Nardis**, a waterfall that plunges down 90 m (300 ft). The two masses of rock at the bottom are said to be the forms of petrified demons.

Trento ⑬

🏠 *105,000.* 🚆 🚌 ℹ️ *Via Manci 2 (0461 98 38 80).* 🔵 *Thu.*

TRENTO, THE CAPITAL of the region to which it gave its name, is also the most attractive town in Trentino: it has a fine Romanesque cathedral and a richly decorated castle, and streets lined with handsome Renaissance mansions. Trento is noted as the venue for the **Council of Trent** (1545–63), set up by the Catholic Church to consider reforms that might encourage breakaway groups, in particular the German Protestants, to return to the fold. The reforms, which ushered in the period of the Counter-Reformation, were only partly successful.

The **Duomo**, site of some of the Council meetings, was built in robust Romanesque style from the 13th century. It was three centuries before it was completed, in 1515, but the builders maintained architectural harmony by ignoring Gothic and Renaissance styles entirely. The result is a church of unusual integrity, noble and assured. The Duomo stands on **Piazza Duomo**, the city's main square, which was first laid out by the Romans as their central market place or forum.

Inner courtyard of the Magno Palazzo

Trento's Roman name, Tridentum, is commemorated in the figure of Neptune who stands holding his trident at the top of the 18th-century fountain, which stands in the middle of the main square.

🏛️ **Museo Diocesano Tridentino**
Piazza Duomo 18. 📞 *0461 23 44 19.* 🕐 *Wed–Mon.* ⚫ *1 Jan, 25 Dec.*

This museum is housed in the **Palazzo Pretorio**, an imposing medieval building that stands on the eastern side of Piazza Duomo. Its contents include early ivory reliquaries, Flemish tapestries and paintings depicting the Council of Trent.

⚜️ **Castello del Buonconsiglio**
Via Bernardo Clesio 5. 📞 *0461 23 37 70.* 🕐 *Tue–Sun.* ⚫ *1 Jan, 1 Nov, 25 Dec.*

This large castle, built in the 13th century and later enlarged with additional buildings, is part of the defences of the town. Trento was an important frontier on the main road linking Italy to northern Europe, and thick walls still encircle the town.

The southern section of the castle consists of the magnificent **Magno Palazzo** (1530), built for the ruling prince-bishops of Trento, who were given extensive powers by the Holy Roman Emperor to foster loyalty and discourage defection to the pope. The lavish decoration (including frescoes of virile satyrs and nymphs by Gerolamo Romanino, 1531–2) speaks of huge wealth and a luxurious lifestyle. The fine rooms, now the setting for the **Museo Provinciale**, contain paintings, ceramics and 15th-century wood carvings, and prehistoric, Etruscan and Roman items. The **Torre dell'Aquila** (Eagle Tower) nearby contains frescoes painted around 1400. They depict the Months

Palazzo Pretorio and the Duomo in Trento's main square

The commanding form of the Ossario del Castel Dante in Rovereto

of the Year in charming detail: the month of January, for instance, has some delightful snowballing scenes.

ENVIRONS: Immediately to the west of Trento a scenic round-trip along a winding road leads up the north flank of **Monte Bondone** and back, via **Vezzano**, down the western slopes. The views along the route are magnificent, in particular from Vaneze and Vason. East of Trento, Pergine marks the start of the **Val Sugana**, a broad valley with attractive and popular lakes. In the hills north of Lake Levico lies the spa town of **Levico Terme**, distinguished by elegant Neo-Classical buildings set amid beautifully wooded parkland.

Rovereto ⑭

🏛 33,000. 🚉 🚌 🅸 Corso Rosmini 6 (0464 43 03 63). 🛒 Tue.

ROVERETO WAS at the centre of fierce fighting during World War I, after which the Venetian castle (built in 1416) that dominates the town was transformed into the **Museo Storico della Guerra**, a war museum. The displays include sections devoted to wartime humour, propaganda and spying. Near the entrance to the museum, stairs lead out on to the castle roof for a view of the imposing **Ossario del Castel Dante**.

Some distance away is the **Campana dei Caduti** (Bell of the Fallen), one of the largest bells in Italy, which was cast from melted-down cannons at the end of World War II and mounted in an imposing building above the town; it is rung daily at sunset.

Below the war museum stands the **Museo Civico**, with its collections on archaeology, art, natural history and folklore, while the Mario Botta-designed **Museo di Arte Contemporanea di Trento e Rovereto (MART)** showcases 20th-century Italian art.

ENVIRONS: A little over 8 km (5 miles) north of Rovereto is **Castel Beseno**, rising on a hill to the east. This enormous castle, by far the largest in the region, was built and rebuilt from the 12th century to the 18th to guard the junction of the three valleys. The ruins are undergoing restoration.

Five kilometres (3 miles) south of Rovereto, the main road passes through a valley littered with massive house-sized boulders created by landslips: these are known as Lavini di Marco or **Ruina Dantesca**, because they are mentioned in Dante's *Inferno* (XII, 4–9). Fossilized dinosaur footprints have recently been discovered there.

🏛 **Museo Storico della Guerra**
Via Castelbarco 7. 📞 0464 43 81 00.
🕐 Tue–Sun. ● 24, 25, 31 Dec, 1 Jan. ♿

🏛 **Museo Civico**
Borgo Santa Caterina 41.
📞 0464 43 90 55. 🕐 Tue–Sun.
● 1 Jan, Easter, 5 Aug, 25 Dec. ♿ ♿

🏛 **MART**
Corso Bettini 43. 📞 800 39 77 60.
🕐 Tue–Sun. ● public hols. ♿
♿ ♿ ♿ ♿

⚜ **Castel Beseno**
Besenello. 📞 0464 83 46 00. 🕐 Mar–Nov: Tue–Sun (Mon if public hols). ♿

Castello di Avio in its lush setting

Castello di Avio ⑮

Via Castello, Sabbionara d'Avio. 📞 0464 68 44 53. 🚉 to Vo, then 3-km (2-mile) walk. 🕐 Feb–mid-Dec: 10am–1pm, 2–6pm Tue–Sun (Oct–mid-Dec: to 5pm). ♿ ♿ ♿ ♿

CASTLES LINE THE Adige valley all the way to the Brenner Pass, but few are as accessible as the Castello di Avio, southwest of Ala. It was founded in the 11th century, considerably extended in the 13th, and today offers visitors far-reaching views. Among the numerous frescoes with secular themes is a rare series in the Casa delle Guardie (the Sentry House) depicting 13th-century battle scenes.

The extensive walls enclosing Castel Beseno above Rovereto

NORTHWEST ITALY

Northwest Italy at a Glance

THE NORTHWEST OF ITALY is made up of three very different geological characteristics: the jagged Alps, the flat plain, and the undulating shoreline of the Mediterranean. Within this varied landscape, some of it still wild and unspoilt, lie extremely rich and diverse vestiges of the area's substantial cultural heritage. The major sights, in the regions of Valle d'Aosta and Piedmont, Liguria and Lombardy, are shown on this map.

Valle d'Aosta

Parco Nazionale del Gran Paradiso

Basilica di Sant'Andrea, Vercelli

Mole Antonelliana, Turin

The Parco Nazionale del Gran Paradiso *is a beautiful wilderness, and the habitat of rare Alpine fauna and flora (see pp208–9).*

VALLE D'AOSTA AND PIEDMONT
(See pp202–21)

Piedmont

LIGURIA
(See pp222–35)

The capital of Piedmont *is Turin, an elegant and bustling city of splendid Baroque architecture. Its skyline is dramatically dominated by the Mole Antonelliana (see p216).*

San Remo *is a typical Riviera resort, with palm trees and a casino. The onion-domed outline of the Russian church adds an exotic flavour to the town (see p226).*

The casino, San Remo

The Basilica di Sant'Andrea *in Vercelli is an important Romanesque building, one of the earliest to use Gothic elements (see p220).*

◁ **Typical shuttered Ligurian façades in Santa Margherita Ligure**

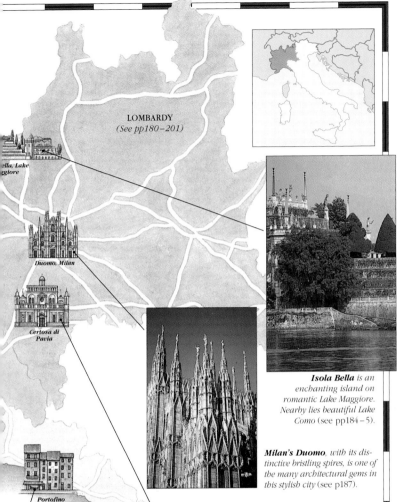

LOMBARDY
(See pp180–201)

ella, Lake
aggiore

Duomo, Milan

Certosa di
Pavia

Portofino

Isola Bella *is an*
enchanting island on
romantic Lake Maggiore.
Nearby lies beautiful Lake
Como (see pp184–5).

Milan's Duomo, *with its dis-*
tinctive bristling spires, is one of
the many architectural gems in
this stylish city (see p187).

Portofino *is*
one of Italy's most
exclusive resorts.
Nestling in a creek,
its pretty pastel-
coloured houses
surround a yacht-
filled harbour
(see p232).

The Certosa di Pavia, *a charming Carthusian*
monastery, includes a richly decorated Gothic
church with a magnificent Renaissance façade,
and a series of attractive cloisters (see pp196–7).

| 0 kilometres | 50 |
| 0 miles | 25 |

Regional Food: Northwest Italy

Grissini

RICHNESS AND HEARTINESS characterize the food of northwest Italy, an area dominated by the presence of the Alps. Here, unlike in the rest of Italy, butter is used in cooking as much as oil. The area is the home of rice growing in Italy, and risotto naturally features prominently on local menus, complementing the ubiquitous pasta dishes. Cheeses are also a speciality, as are truffles – which grow in the clay soil of Piedmont – and nuts of all types. Garlic, saffron, basil and wine are other favourite ingredients in the aromatic sauces. Grissini, the crisp breadsticks found on every restaurant table, originate in Turin.

Onion and Herb Focaccia is made from dough enriched with olive oil; it may also be baked plain, or with olives or tomato.

Green peppers

Red peppers

Orange peppers

Bagna Caôda

Spring onions

Celery

Yellow peppers

Bresaola, wafer-thin slices of cured raw beef, is served as an antipasto with olive oil and a squeeze of lemon.

Farinata is a flat bread made of oil and chickpea flour. It is relatively thin, similar to a pancake and eaten as a snack.

Bagna Caôda is an anchovy-based dip flavoured with garlic, olive oil, butter and sometimes truffles. It is served hot, fondue-style, and eaten with sliced raw vegetables which are dipped into it. It is a speciality of Piedmont.

Risotto alla milanese is a rich and delicious Milanese dish of rice, white wine, onion, saffron and grated Parmesan cheese.

Trenette al pesto, a Genoese speciality, consists of noodles with a sauce of basil, garlic, pine nuts, Parmesan and oil.

Pansôti with Walnut Sauce is Ligurian, spinach- and egg-filled pasta, with a sauce of nuts, garlic, herbs, ricotta cheese and olive oil.

Manzo brasato al Barolo *is a Piedmont dish of lean beef marinated in red wine and garlic, then stewed gently until tender.*

Cacciucco*, found on Livorno menus, is a rich stew of mixed fish and seafood cooked with wine, garlic and herbs.*

Costolette alla milanese *are veal cutlets dipped in egg and breadcrumbs, fried in butter and served with lemon.*

Ossobuco *is shin of veal with marrow bone in a tomato and wine sauce, with a hint of garlic, anchovy and lemon.*

Fagiano tartufato *– stuffed pheasant – is filled with white truffles and pork fat; it is then wrapped in bacon and roasted.*

Spezzatino di pollo *is a chicken quarter cooked with tomato sauce containing wine and, sometimes, truffles.*

CHEESE

The lush Alpine meadows in the northwest help to produce some of the finest cheeses in Italy. They include the blue-veined yet mild Gorgonzola; the delicate Mascarpone, a cream cheese much used in desserts; and Taleggio, a soft, creamy cheese to be eaten young, all from Lombardy. Fontina, a semi-hard cheese made in the Valle d'Aosta, has a nutty, slightly sweet taste.

Fontina   Taleggio

Gorgonzola

Spinaci alla Piemontese*, a side order, is a blend of spinach, anchovies, butter and garlic, with croutons.*

Amaretti *are light and delicious macaroon-type biscuits, usually taken with coffee, made from almonds and egg whites. They are often wrapped in pretty coloured paper.*

Torta di nocciole*, a Piedmontese nut tart, includes hazelnuts, eggs and butter among its ingredients.*

Zabaione *is a frothy concoction of egg, sugar and Marsala wine, accompanied by sponge fingers. It is served hot or cold.*

Panettone *from Milan is a light yeast cake which contains candied fruit. It is traditionally eaten at Christmas.*

The Wines of Northwest Italy

GRAPES ARE GROWN throughout the northwest – from the cliffs of Liguria to the steep mountainsides of Valle d'Aosta. The best wines, however, come from Piedmont, in particular the Langhe hills southwest of Turin, source of two of Italy's finest reds: the rich, powerful, long-lived Barolo and Barbaresco. Both of these are now showing the benefits of modern techniques and a renewed interest in high-quality wine making. Lighter, everyday red wines that go well with the local cuisine include Dolcetto and the popular Barbera. Another Piedmont speciality is sparkling *spumante*, Italians' instinctive choice whenever there is something around to celebrate.

Medieval illustration of a grape crusher

Castiglione Falletto in the heart of Piedm

Barbera d'Alba comes from the adaptable Barbera grape, which can grow on almost any slope. Its ubiquitous nature means that the wines it yields can be light and full of fruit, as well as dense, strong and full-flavoured. Good producers include Aldo Conterno, Voerzio, Pio Cesare, Altare, Gaja, Vaira and Vietti.

Dolcetto is grown in seven different areas. Dolcetto d'Alba has a delicious perfume and deep purple colour. Best drunk within one or two years, it ranges in flavour from fresh and fruity to the rich, concentrated plumminess of some of the top wines, such as those produced by Giuseppe Mascarello.

Barolo, prized the world over for its complex array of flavours and firm tannins, is made from the Nebbiolo grape and may take up to 20 years to mature. *Vigna Colonnello* is a top Barolo from Aldo Conterno, made only in the best years like 1993, 1990 and 1989.

The white truffle of Alba is an autumn speciality from the Langhe hills. Highly prized for its earthy scent, it is excellent with Barolo.

PIEDMONT

- Turin
- Chieri
- MONFERRATO
- Canale
- Barb
- Al
- Bra
- Saluzzo
- Barolo
- Cast
- Falle
- Dogliani
- Cuneo
- Mondovi
- LANG

KEY

☐	Barolo
☐	Barbaresco
☐	Other vineyard areas

0 kilometres   25

0 miles   15

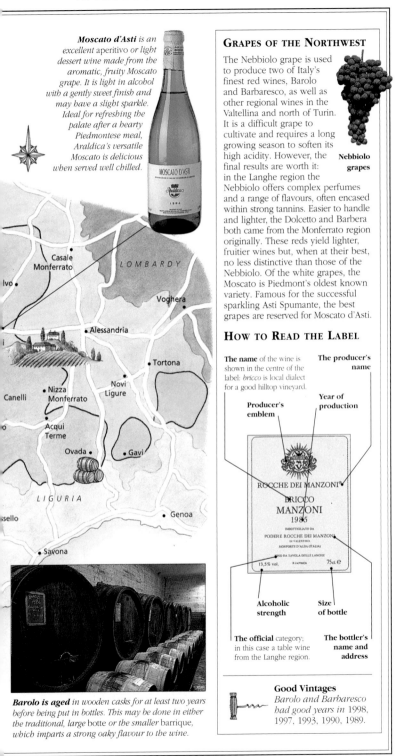

Moscato d'Asti is an excellent *aperitivo or light dessert wine made from the aromatic, fruity Moscato grape. It is light in alcohol with a gently sweet finish and may have a slight sparkle. Ideal for refreshing the palate after a hearty Piedmontese meal, Araldica's versatile Moscato is delicious when served well chilled.*

GRAPES OF THE NORTHWEST

The Nebbiolo grape is used to produce two of Italy's finest red wines, Barolo and Barbaresco, as well as other regional wines in the Valtellina and north of Turin. It is a difficult grape to cultivate and requires a long growing season to soften its high acidity. However, the final results are worth it: in the Langhe region the Nebbiolo offers complex perfumes and a range of flavours, often encased within strong tannins. Easier to handle and lighter, the Dolcetto and Barbera both came from the Monferrato region originally. These reds yield lighter, fruitier wines but, when at their best, no less distinctive than those of the Nebbiolo. Of the white grapes, the Moscato is Piedmont's oldest known variety. Famous for the successful sparkling Asti Spumante, the best grapes are reserved for Moscato d'Asti.

Nebbiolo grapes

HOW TO READ THE LABEL

The name of the wine is shown in the centre of the label: *bricco* is local dialect for a good hilltop vineyard.

The producer's name

Producer's emblem

Year of production

ROCCHE DEI MANZONI
BRICCO
MANZONI
1985
IMBOTTIGLIATO DA
PODERE ROCCHE DEI MANZONI
DI VALENTINO
MONFORTE D'ALBA (ITALIA)
VINO DA TAVOLA DELLE LANGHE
13,5% vol.   R 24/PROCH   75cl.℮

Alcoholic strength

Size of bottle

The official category; in this case a table wine from the Langhe region.

The bottler's name and address

Good Vintages

Barolo and Barbaresco had good years in 1998, 1997, 1993, 1990, 1989.

Barolo is aged in wooden casks for at least two years before being put in bottles. This may be done in either the traditional, large botte *or the smaller* barrique, *which imparts a strong oaky flavour to the wine.*

Understanding Architecture in Northwest Italy

Although the buildings of the northwest tend to be solid and imposing – a result partly of the more severe climate – there is no distinctive architectural stamp as there is around Venice, Florence or even in Rome. Instead, a variety of buildings in different styles, many borrowed or reinterpreted from elsewhere, are dotted across the area: enchanting medieval castles, outstanding Romanesque and Gothic buildings, unusual Baroque structures. The northwest is also rich in modern architecture – in terms of both design and materials – influenced by the region's industrial developments and its strong flair for innovative design, which also often draws its inspiration from earlier architectural styles.

**Castello Sforzesco,
1451–66 *(see p186)***

CHARACTERISTICS OF NORTHWEST ITALIAN ARCHITECTURE

Double row of defensive walls

Wooden balcony

Few windows

Massive square tower

Pointed turret

Battlements

***Castello di Fénis**, one of the finest castles in the Valle d'Aosta, is a 14th-century fortress with asymmetrical towers, turrets and crenellated walls. Frescoes adorn the interior (see p207).*

Alternating bands of marble

Rose window

Lions support columns and porch above

Elaborate carving

Rose window

Octagonal drum influenced by the Duomo in Florence

Highly ornate façade

***Cappella Colleoni**, Bergamo (1476), mixes rich, decorative elements in this early Renaissance masterpiece (see p193).*

Patterned marble design

***Monza's Duomo** (1390s) typifies the Lombard style of Romanesque architecture with its marble stripes and ornate carving (see p193).*

Massive scale

Ornate window surrounds

Rotunda

Balcony

Curved brickwork

***Palazzo Carignano** is perhaps the finest product of Turin's idiosyncratic Baroque school. Guarini's masterpiece (1679) boasts an extraordinary undulating brick façade and a fine rotunda (see p215).*

WHERE TO SEE THE ARCHITECTURE

The road to Aosta is flanked by numerous medieval castles *(see p206)* while inspirational Romanesque and Gothic churches are found in Lombardy – at Monza *(p193)*, Pavia *(p195)*, Milan *(pp186–193)*, and Como *(pp184–5)*. The 15th-century Certosa di Pavia *(pp196–7)* is a must, as well as the charming city of Mantova *(p199)*. Turin *(pp212–16)* is famous for its unique Baroque school, and Bergamo for its exuberance. Architecture from the last two centuries is best represented in Milan and Turin, and in Genoa some exciting new redevelopment projects are taking place.

Renzo Piano's mast structure (1992) in Genoa's redeveloped port

19TH–20TH CENTURY ARCHITECTURE

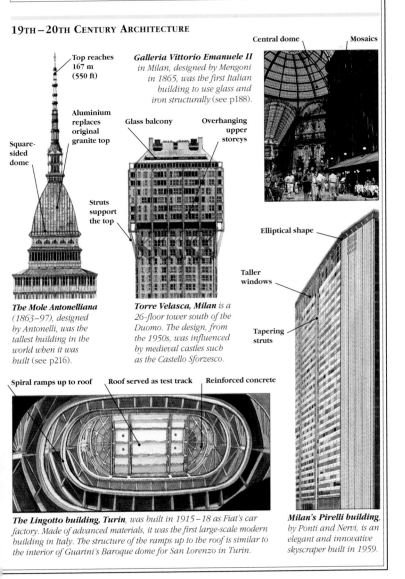

Top reaches 167 m (550 ft)

Aluminium replaces original granite top

Square-sided dome

Central dome

Mosaics

Galleria Vittorio Emanuele II in Milan, designed by Mengoni in 1865, was the first Italian building to use glass and iron structurally (see p188).

Glass balcony

Overhanging upper storeys

Struts support the top

The Mole Antonelliana *(1863–97), designed by Antonelli, was the tallest building in the world when it was built (see p216).*

Torre Velasca, Milan *is a 26-floor tower south of the Duomo. The design, from the 1950s, was influenced by medieval castles such as the Castello Sforzesco.*

Elliptical shape

Taller windows

Tapering struts

Spiral ramps up to roof

Roof served as test track

Reinforced concrete

The Lingotto building, Turin, *was built in 1915–18 as Fiat's car factory. Made of advanced materials, it was the first large-scale modern building in Italy. The structure of the ramps up to the roof is similar to the interior of Guarini's Baroque dome for San Lorenzo in Turin.*

Milan's Pirelli building, *by Ponti and Nervi, is an elegant and innovative skyscraper built in 1959.*

LOMBARDY

THE REGION OF LOMBARDY *stretches from the Alps, on the border with Switzerland, down through the romantic lakes of Como and Maggiore to the broad, flat plain of the River Po. It is an area of lakeside villas with azalea-filled gardens, of wealthy towns with imposing palazzi and highly decorated churches, and of efficient, modern industry and large-scale agriculture, the financial heart of Italy. At its centre stands Milan, the style-conscious capital of Lombardy.*

The region was named after the Lombards or Longobards, a barbarian tribe that invaded Italy in the 6th century AD. During the Middle Ages, Lombardy was part of the Holy Roman Empire, but not always loyal to its German emperors. The Lombards, who had a talent for banking and commerce, resented any outside interference with their prosperity.

The 12th century saw the rise of the Lega Lombarda, or Lombard League, a band of forceful separatists founded to counter the brutal imperialism of Frederick Barbarossa (their most modern incarnation was the Lega Nord political party). Power was seized by the region's great families, most notably the Visconti and the Sforza of Milan, from the 14th to the early 16th century. These dynasties also became great patrons of the arts, commissioning exquisite palaces, churches and artworks, many of which can still be seen. Bergamo, Mantova and Cremona – not to mention Milan itself – contain a remarkably rich array of art treasures. Here are such pinnacles of European civilization as the charterhouse at Pavia, Leonardo da Vinci's *Last Supper* and the magnificent paintings of the Pinacoteca di Brera in Milan.

Lombardy – famous as the birthplace of Virgil, Monteverdi, Stradivarius and Donizetti – today offers visitors the contrasting pleasures of lyrical lakeside landscapes (resorts on lakes Como and Maggiore have attracted poets, aristocrats and gamblers for centuries) and beautiful, bustling cities.

Strolling through Milan's enormous Galleria Vittorio Emanuele II

◁ **The peaceful shores of the beautiful Lake Como, southwest of Bellagio**

Exploring Lombardy

THE ENORMOUS PLAIN of the River Po runs through much of Lombardy, providing a landscape that is flat and perfectly suited to the consequent expansion of industry in the region. This is, however, also a region of great contrasts. To the north, in a still unspoilt setting in the foothills of the mountains, lie the lakes Como and Maggiore, as well as the dramatic valleys and peaks of the Parco Nazionale dello Stelvio around Bormio, Sondrio and Val Camonica. Further south, busy industrialized areas give way to huge tracts of agriculture dotted with towns of great beauty such as Cremona, Mantova and Pavia, which offer a rich and splendid array of artistic pleasures.

SIGHTS AT A GLANCE

SEE ALSO

• **Where to Stay** pp549–51

• **Where to Eat** pp584–6

Passo di Gavia in the Parco Nazionale dello
Stelvio on the eastern fringes of Lombardy

0 kilometres 25

0 miles 20

A view of Isola Bella on Lake Maggiore

The colourful façade of the
Cappella Colleoni in Bergamo

KEY

▰▰▰	Motorway
▰▰▰	Major road
▰▰▰	Minor road
▰▰▰	Scenic route
≈≈	River
✲	Viewpoint

GETTING AROUND

Milan has two international airports, which are obvious gateways
into northern Italy, and the vast and flat Lombard plain has its
advantages when it comes to transport: roads and railway lines
criss-cross it and make trips between the larger towns very easy.
The lakes, however, are better visited by car, as only two main
towns are served by trains, though there are bus and boat services
around the shores. The Parco Nazionale dello Stelvio and the
mountains are more remote still, but offer good tourist facilities.

Lake Como ●

S ET IN AN IDYLLIC LANDSCAPE of mountains and rugged
hillsides, Lake Como has for centuries attracted visitors
who come here to go boating, for walks in the hills, or
for relaxation and inspiration. The northern stretches,
in particular, are shrouded in an almost eerie calm. The
long and narrow lake, crafted
into a wishbone shape
by glacial erosion,
offers fine views
up to the Alps
and down to the
towns of Como
and Lecco.

View of the lake near Como

Villa Carlotta nestles among lush
gardens with lovely views.

Cernobbio was a
favourite resort of
the exiled Queen
Caroline of
England in the
early 19th
century.

The scenic route
just south of Bellagio
climbs a hill to offer
far-reaching lake views.

Menaggio is
one of a string
of popular
resorts lining the
west bank.

The northern stretches
are wilder and less
populated than the
southern part, offering
visitors great tranquillity.

Varenna, a ferry port, is
overlooked by a ruined
11th-century castle. At
Fiumelatte, just south,
there is a foaming stream,
the "river of milk".

Bellagio
*This delightful resort on
the cusp of the lake's two
arms has elegant lakeside
promenades and cafés.*

The southeastern arm
of the lake is also called
the Lago di Lecco.

Lecco, home to
the 19th-century
novelist, Manzoni.

Domaso
Gravedona
Còlico
S36
S38
Dervio
S340d
Menaggio
Varenna
Fiumelatte
Griante
Tremezzo
Bellagio
Mezzegra
Onno
S340
S36
S583
Cernobbio
S583
Lecco
Cernobbio
A9-E35
Como

0 kilometres   15

0 miles   10

Como
*The town, which gave its
name to the lake, boasts
a fine Duomo in mixed
Gothic and Renaissance styles,
with carvings on its façade.*

KEY

··· Car ferry route

••• Ferry route

△ Sailing and boating centre

ⓘ Tourist information

▬ Motorway

▬ Major road

▭ Minor road

※ Viewpoint

Tadoline's copy (1834) of Canova's *Cupid and Psyche* in Villa Carlotta

Exploring Lake Como

In the heart of **Como** lies the elegant Piazza Cavour. Nearby rises the beautiful 14th-century **Duomo**, with its 15th- and 16th-century reliefs and paintings, and fine tombs. The 18th-century dome is by Turin's famous Baroque architect, Juvarra. Next to the Duomo stand the 13th-century Broletto (town hall), charmingly striped in white, pink and grey, and the tall Torre del Comune. **Villa Carlotta** is an elegant 18th-century summerhouse, known for its gardens. In springtime, rhododendrons, camellias and azaleas burst into colour in this pretty setting. Inside, the villa houses a collection of sculptures.

Lecco, a small industrial town lying to the south of the lake's eastern arm, was home to the writer Alessandro Manzoni (1785– 1873). The author's childhood home, the **Villa Manzoni** is devoted to memorabilia of his life and works. In Piazza Manzoni, a monument depicts scenes from his most famous novel, *I Promessi Sposi (The Betrothed)* – set partly in 17th-century Lecco as well as Milan.

♨ Villa Carlotta
Tremezzo, Como. **(** *0344 404 05.* ◯ *Mar–Oct: 9–11:30am, 2–4:30pm daily.* 🎫
♨ Villa Manzoni
Via Guanella 1, Lecco. **(** *0341 48 12 47.* ◯ *9am–5:30pm Tue–Sun.* ◑ *1 Jan, Easter, 1 May, 15 Aug, 25 Dec.* 🎫

Lake Maggiore ➋

Verbania. **FS** 🚆 🚢 *Stresa, Verbania, Baveno & the islands.*
i *Piazza Marconi 16, Stresa (0323 301 50).* **W** *www.distrettolaghi.it*

LAKE MAGGIORE, the second largest Italian lake after Lake Garda, is a long expanse of water nestling right against the mountains and stretching into Alpine Switzerland; it is warmer in atmosphere and more romantic than Lake Como. The gently sloping shores are dotted with camellias, azaleas and verbena vegetation – from which the ancient lake derived its Roman name, Verbanus.

A huge copper statue of Cardinal Carlo Borromeo, the chief patron of the lake, stands in **Arona**, the town where he was born in 1538. It is possible to climb up and look out over the lake through his eyes and ears. Arona also boasts a ruined castle and a chapel, Santa Maria, dedicated to the Borromeo family.

Further up the western coast of the lake is **Stresa**, the chief resort and main jumping-off point for visits to the islands; the town is full of villas and verdant gardens, where many visitors take a stroll. Behind Stresa, a cable car ride away, rises Monte Mottarone, a snow-capped peak offering spectacular panoramic views of the

The statue of Carlo Borromeo in Arona

surrounding mountains, including Monte Rosa.

The **Borromean islands**, at the centre of the lake near Stresa, are small jewels of natural beauty augmented by artificial grottoes, architectural follies and landscaped parks. The **Isola Bella** is home to the 17th-century **Palazzo Borromeo** and its splendid garden of landscaped terraces, fountains, peacocks, statues and grottoes. Isola Madre is largely given over to a botanical garden. San Giovanni is the most exclusive and smallest of the isles, with a villa which once belonged to the conductor Arturo Toscanini (1867–1957).

The lake becomes quieter towards the Swiss border, but continues to be lined with attractive villas. The **Villa Taranto**, on the outskirts of Verbania, houses one of the best exotic botanical collections.

About 3 km (2 miles) west of **Cannobio**, a market town near Switzerland, is the dramatic gorge and tumbling waterfall of the Orrido di Sant'Anna, which can be reached by boat.

♨ Palazzo Borromeo
Isola Bella. 🚢 *from Stresa.* **(** *0323 305 56.* ◯ *mid Mar–Oct: daily.* 🎫
♨ Villa Taranto
Via Vittorio Veneto III, Verbania, Palanza. **(** *0323 55 66 67.* ◯ *Apr–Oct: daily.* 🎫 ♿

Isola Bella's 17th-century Palazzo Borromeo and garden on Lake Maggiore

Milan ❸

Detail from the Duomo

Cᴇɴᴛʀᴇ ᴏꜰ ꜰᴀꜱʜɪᴏɴ, business and finance, Milan has a bustling, businesslike feel about it. It is smart rather than attractive – a city of wealth as opposed to imagination and the heartland of the Italian economy. To the Goths, who took it over from the Romans, it was called "Mailand", the land of May, a place of warmth and inspiration. It has long been an important trading centre at the junction of transalpine routes, and a prize for powerful dynasties. Today, it is the best place to see Italy at its most cosmopolitan and stylish.

Portrait of a Young Woman by Pollaiuolo, Museo Poldi-Pezzoli

♣ Castello Sforzesco

Piazza Castello. **(** *02 88 46 37 00.* ◯ *9am–5:30pm Tue–Sun.* ● *public hols.* & W *www.milanocastello.it*

The first castle on this site was built by the Visconti family, but demolished when their reign ended in the mid-15th century. Milan's new ruler, Francesco Sforza, built in its place this Renaissance palace. The castle is based on a series of courtyards, the most beautiful of which, the Cortile della Rocchetta, is a graceful arcaded square designed by Bramante and Filarete. The palace now contains, together with sections on Applied Arts, Archaeology and Coins, the **Civiche Raccolte d'Arte Antica**. This fine collection of furniture, antiquities and paintings includes Michelangelo's unfinished sculpture, known as the

Michelangelo's *Rondanini Pietà* (c.1564) in the Castello Sforzesco

Rondanini Pietà. The canvases in the picture collection, dating from the Renaissance to the 18th century, are particularly impressive. Some rooms may be closed for restoration.

�识 Museo Poldi-Pezzoli

Via Alessandro Manzoni 12. **(** *02 79 48 89.* ◯ *Tue–Sun.* 𝄞 W *www.museopoldipezzoli.it*

Giacomo Poldi-Pezzoli was a wealthy nobleman who, on his death in 1879, bequeathed his magnificent art collection to the state. Its most famous painting is the 15th-century Renaissance *Portrait of a Young Woman* by Antonio Pollaiuolo, though there are also works by Piero della Francesca, Botticelli and Mantegna, among others. The applied arts section is richly endowed with fascinating items ranging from rugs and lace to glass, enamels and porcelain, as well as sculpture, jewellery and sundials, displayed in fine settings.

Sɪɢʜᴛꜱ ᴀᴛ ᴀ Gʟᴀɴᴄᴇ

Kᴇʏ

M	Metro station
P	Parking
🛈	Tourist information
✝	Church

♫ Teatro alla Scala

Piazza della Scala. **📞** 02 72 00 37 44.
Box Office 📞 02 86 07 75. **♿**
Museo Teatrale temporarily housed
at Corso Magenta 71. **📞** 02 469 12
49. **🕐** 9am–6pm Tue–Sun. **♿**
W www.teatroallascala.org

This Neo-Classical theatre,
known as La Scala, opened in
1778 and is one of the world's
most prestigious opera houses.
It has one of the largest stages
in Europe and hosts

The façade of the world-famous
Teatro alla Scala

⛪ Duomo

Piazza del Duomo. **📞** 02 86 46 34
56. **📷** for roof. **🕐** daily. **♿**

Situated at the very heart of
Milan is its giant cathedral, one
of the largest Gothic churches
in the world at 157 m (514 ft)
long and, at its widest point,
92 m (301 ft) across. It was
begun in the 14th century
under Prince Gian Galeazzo
Visconti but not completed
until more than 500 years later.

The building's most startling
feature is the extraordinary
roof, with its 135 spires and
innumerable statues and
gargoyles, and from which,
on a clear day, there are far-
reaching views to the Alps.

Below, the façade (under
restoration) boasts a
dazzling assortment of styles
from Gothic through to
Renaissance and Neo-Classical.
The bronze doors are faced
with bas-reliefs recounting
episodes from the life of the
Virgin and of Sant'Ambrogio,
and scenes retelling the
history of Milan. Note, around
the apse, the delicate Gothic
tracery of the windows.

Inside, the aisles are divided
by 52 giant pillars and lit from
all sides by remarkable stained
glass. Look out for
the Visconti family
symbol – a serpent
swallowing a man –
in the fine tracery of
the apse windows.
Among the many
tombs and statues is
a depiction of San
Bartolomeo Flayed,
carrying his skin.

The treasury,
beneath the main
altar, contains much
medieval gold and
silverwork. Excava-
tions have revealed
remains of the
original 4th-century
baptistry.

sumptuous
productions. An extra
200 standing tickets are put on
sale half an hour before each
performance. The **Museo Teatrale** houses sets and costumes
of past productions, portraits of
conductors and theatrical items
dating back to Roman times.
There is also a good view of
the auditorium, with its gilded
box galleries, *trompe-l'oeil*
effects and huge chandelier.

The Gothic Duomo, crowned with spires

Exploring Milan

IN ADDITION TO THE GREAT MONUMENTS in Milan, such as the cathedral and the castle, there is a host of varied and interesting museums, churches and civic buildings which provide an enthralling mix of old and new. This chic and busy metropolis offers plenty of opportunities for cultural activities, gastronomic adventures, designer-fashion shopping or just strolling about, Milan-style.

The glass ceiling and dome covering the Galleria Vittorio Emanuele II

🚇 Galleria Vittorio Emanuele II
Main entrances on Piazza del Duomo and Piazza della Scala.

This ornate shopping arcade, known as *il Salotto di Milano* (Milan's drawing room), was designed by the architect Giuseppe Mengoni in 1865. The galleria had a tragic start, however, as Mengoni fell to his death from the scaffolding not long before its inauguration in 1877 (a year before the arcade was actually finished). Tourists are nevertheless attracted to its stylish shops, cafés and restaurants, which include Il Salotto, said to serve the finest coffee in all Milan.

The galleria itself has a floor plan in the shape of a Latin cross, with an octagonal centre adorned with mosaics representing four continents (Europe, America, Africa and Asia), together with others representing Art, Agriculture, Science and Industry. Its finest feature is its metal and glass roof, crowned with a magnificent central dome. The roof was the first structure in Italy to use metal and glass in a structural way, rather than just decoratively. The floors are decorated with mosaics of the signs of the zodiac; tourists may be seen stepping on the genitals of Taurus the Bull, in order to bring good luck.

🏛 Museo del Duomo
Palazzo Reale, Piazza del Duomo 14.
[02 86 03 58 02. ☐ 10am–1:15pm, 3–6pm daily. ● public hols. 🖾

The museum is in the Palazzo Reale (Royal Palace), for centuries home to the Visconti and other rulers of Milan. It charts the history of the Duomo from its 14th-century origins (and the pre-existing church on its site) until the 1886 competition held to redesign its façade.

Among the exhibits there are 16th- and 17th-century wooden models of the cathedral, and many of the original medieval sculptures – including figures thought to be Gian Galeazzo Visconti and Galeazzo Maria Sforza. There are also stained-glass windows, paintings, tapestries and a pair of very elaborately carved choir stalls. Another section focuses on some of the 20th-century amendments to the cathedral.

🏛 Civico Museo d'Arte Contemporanea
Palazzo Reale, Piazza del Duomo 12.
[02 86 01 65. ● for restoration.
🖾 Galleria d'Arte Moderna Villa Reale, Via Palestro 16. [02 76 00 28 19. 🗹 9am & 11am Tue–Sun (compulsory whilst restoration underway).

The Museum of Contemporary Art (or CIMAC), on the second floor of the Palazzo Reale, is a refreshingly up-to-date gallery. Opened in 1984, it is still expanding, but the emphasis is heavily on Italian works: from the 19th century to pieces by members of the Futurist movement (Umberto Boccioni in particular), from abstract art to the more diverse productions of the present day. Look out for works by Carlo Carrà (1881–1966), Filippo De Pisis, Giorgio Morandi (1890–1964) and Tancredi, as well as those by more familiar artists such as Modigliani (1884–1920) and De Chirico (1888–1978). Among the non-Italian artists are Post-Impressionists (Van Gogh, Cézanne, Gauguin),

Still Life (1920) by Giorgio Morandi in the Museo d'Arte Contemporanea

Picasso – a bequest of 30 etchings – and Matisse, Klee, Mondrian and Kandinsky.

During restoration work, this collection is on display at the Galleria d'Arte Moderna.

🏛 Pinacoteca Ambrosiana

Piazza Pio XI 2. **02 80 69 21.** ⭘ *Tue–Sun.* 🌐 **W** www.ambrosiana.it

The recently renovated Ambrosiana is home to the magnificent library of Cardinal Federico Borromeo, whose 30,000 manuscripts, including a 5th-century illustrated *Iliad*, early editions of Dante's *Divine Comedy* (1353) and Leonardo's *Atlantic Codex* (15th century), survive to this day.

The building also houses an interesting art gallery, originally bequeathed by Borromeo on his death in 1618. The collection of paintings and sculpture attests to the cardinal's broad-ranging if slightly quirky taste, and now ranges from 14th-century pieces to works of the early 19th century. Among the canvases are the *Portrait of a Musician* by Leonardo da Vinci (1452–1519) and the *Portrait of a Young Woman*, attributed to his pupil, Ambrogio da Predis. Other masterpieces include the *Madonna of the Canopy* by Botticelli (15th century), a cartoon version of Raphael's Vatican fresco, *The*

Fruit Basket (c. 1596) by Caravaggio in the Pinacoteca Ambrosiana

School of Athens (16th century), and Caravaggio's *Fruit Basket* (the first painting in Italy to have a still life as its subject). There is also a strong collection of Venetian art, with paintings by Tiepolo, Titian, Giorgione and Bassano, and panel paintings by the late 15th-century Lombard painter, Bergognone.

🔒 San Satiro

Via Torino 19. **02 87 46 83.** ⭘ *daily.*

This unassuming church, its full title Santa Maria presso San Satiro, is one of the most beautiful Renaissance buildings in Milan. It stands on the site of

a 9th-century sanctuary, little of which remains apart from the Cappella della Pietà (off the left aisle), beside an 11th-century bell tower.

The interior seems to be in the shape of a Greek cross, but this is an illusion created by various *trompe-l'oeil* effects in stucco, as space restrictions led Bramante (who was entrusted with its construction in the late 1400s) to choose a T-shaped plan. Above the altar is a 13th-century fresco. An octagonal baptistry containing terracottas lies off the right aisle. The church's façade was finished only in the 19th century.

DESIGNER FASHION IN MILAN

Italians are famous for the attention they pay to their self-image, and here in Milan, Italian chic can be seen in the cluster of top-name shops which occupy the Quadrilatero, the parallelogram of streets delineated by Via Montenapoleone, Via Sant'Andrea, Via della Spiga and Borgospesso. Unlike the Paris fashion scene, which concentrates on flamboyant, often outrageous new designs for women, Milan is more understated in its stylishness: well-cut suits, elegant accessories, chic but wearable shoes. In a sense, the Quadrilatero merely reflects an up-market version of the fashions seen in the streets of any town in Italy: the values of style and comfort are the same; only the astronomical prices serve as a reminder that this is the shopping terrain of the glamorous and very well-heeled.

Dress by Prada

Via Montenapoleone, focus of Milan's smartest shops

Milan: Pinacoteca di Brera

MILAN'S FINEST art collection is held in an imposing
17th-century building, the Palazzo di Brera. This is
where, in the 18th century, the Accademia di Belle Arti
was founded; the picture collection developed alongside
the academy. Inside the Brera hang some of the finest
examples of Italian Renaissance and Baroque painting,
including works by Piero della Francesca, Mantegna,
Canaletto, Bellini, Raphael, Tintoretto, Veronese and
Caravaggio. The collection also includes 20th-century
works by some of Italy's most famous modern artists.

★ Dead Christ by Mantegna
*The subtle lighting and dramatic
perspective of this lamentation by
Mantegna (1430–1506) make it one
of his greatest masterpieces.*

GALLERY GUIDE
*The collection is
displayed in 38 rooms,
and was first built up by
paintings from
churches, later from
acquisitions. Not all
of it is permanently on
view – this is due to
restoration work and
research.*

Twin staircases lead up to
the first-floor entrance of
the Pinacoteca.

The Kiss *(1859)*
*Francesco Hayez's painting is
one of the most reproduced
works of Italian 19th-century
art. Patriotic and sentimental,
it became a symbol of the
optimism surrounding the
unification of Italy.*

The bronze statue
(1809) by Canova de-
picts Napoleon as a
demi-god with Victory
wings in his hand.

Works by
Rubens and Van
Dyck represent
some of the non-
Italian artists
on show.

KEY TO FLOORPLAN

- ☐ 15th- to 16th-century
  Italian painting
- ☐ 16th- to 17th-century Dutch
  and Flemish painting
- ☐ 17th-century Italian painting
- ☐ 18th- to 19th-century
  Italian painting
- ☐ 20th-century Italian
  painting and sculpture
- ☐ Non-exhibition space

Mother and Son
(1917)
The metaphysical paintings of Carlo Carrà show a dream world full of strange and obscure symbols.

VISITORS' CHECKLIST

Via Brera 28. **C** *02 72 26 31; 02 89 42 11 46.* **M** *Lanza, Montenapoleone & Duomo.* **🚌** *60, 61.* **🕐** *8:30am–7:30pm Tue–Sun (last adm: 1 hr before closing).* **🚫** *1 Jan, 1 May, 25 Dec.* **♿ 🔊** **W** *www.brera.beniculturali.it*

Portrait of Moisè Kisling
Modigliani's angular portrait of 1915 reflects his interest in African sculpture.

Twinned columns support the arcades in the courtyard.

The stone façade presents a regular and slightly austere appearance.

Madonna della Candeletta (c.1490)
This painting by Carlo Crivelli was the central part of a polyptych. It is richly detailed with much distinctive ornamentation.

Main entrance from Via Brera

STAR PAINTINGS

★ **Dead Christ by Mantegna**

★ **Marriage of the Virgin by Raphael**

★ **Marriage of the Virgin by Raphael**
This graceful altarpiece was painted in 1504. The circular temple is signed with the artist's name.

Milan: Southwest of the Centre

S OME OF MILAN'S FINEST TREASURES are to be found in its
religious buildings: the ancient monasteries and
churches make up some very fine architectural ensembles
in themselves, as well as incorporating important ruins
and relics dating back to Roman times. It is also in Milan
that one of the most famous images in the world is to be
found: Leonardo's evocative masterpiece, the *Last Supper*.

**The entrance to Sant'Ambrogio,
flanked by unequal bell towers**

🛉 Sant'Ambrogio

Piazza Sant'Ambrogio 15.
📞 02 86 45 08 95. 🕐 9:30am–
noon, 2:30–6pm daily. ♿
W www.santambrogio-basilica.it

Sant'Ambrogio, or St Ambrose,
the patron saint of Milan, was
so eloquent that bees were said
to fly into his mouth, attracted
by his honey tongue. As bishop
of Milan in the 4th century, he
worked hard to avoid a schism
in the church. This is the basilica that he began building in
AD 379, though today most of
it is 10th-century Romanesque.
A medieval gateway leads to
the bronze doors of the
entrance, flanked by two bell
towers. Inside, note the fine
rib vaulting and pulpit, and
the striking 9th-century altar

decorated with gold, silver
and precious gems. In a
chapel off the south aisle, fine
mosaics line a stunning cupola.
Down in the crypt lies the
tomb of Sant'Ambrogio himself.
   Above the portico, a small
museum contains architectural
fragments, tapestries and
paintings relating to the church.

🛉 San Lorenzo Maggiore

Corso di Porta Ticinese. 📞 02 89 40
41 29. 🕐 8:30am–12:30pm, 2:30–
6:30pm daily. 📷 for the Cappella.

This church contains the most
important collection of Roman
and early Christian remains in
Milan. The octagonal basilica
was built in the 4th century,
above what was probably a
Roman amphitheatre, and
subsequently rebuilt in the
12th and 16th centuries.
   In front of the church stands
a row of 16 Roman columns
and, in commemoration of his
Edict, a statue of the Emperor
Constantine. Fine 4th-century
mosaics adorn the Cappella di
Sant'Aquilino, a Romanesque
chapel, which also contains
two early Christian sarcophagi.
Other Roman architectural elements, incorporated into the
building of this church, are in
a chamber below the chapel.

**San Lorenzo Maggiore viewed
from the northeast**

🛉 Santa Maria delle Grazie

Piazza Santa Maria delle Grazie 2.
📞 02 498 75 88. **Cenacolo** 📞 02
89 42 11 46 (booking compulsory –
up to 60 days in advance). 🕐 8:15am–
6:45pm Tue–Sun. 🌑 public hols. 📷
♿ W www.cenacolovinciano.it

This beautiful 15th-century
Renaissance convent, its lovely
apse and calm small cloister
designed by Bramante, contains
one of the key images of western civilization: the *Cenacolo
(Last Supper)* by Leonardo da
Vinci. The image captures the
moment at which Christ tells
His disciples that one of them
will betray Him. The Christ
figure is unfinished: Leonardo
did not consider himself to be
worthy enough to complete it.
   The artist also spurned the
standard fresco technique of
painting on wet plaster, apply-
ing tempera to the dry wall
instead. The result has deterio-
rated badly: the paint is flaking
off, and restoration has proved
difficult. The painting is now
protected by a filtering system.

Leonardo da Vinci's *Last Supper* (1495–7) adorning the refectory wall of Santa Maria delle Grazie

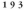

THE EDICT OF MILAN

Milan was colonised by the Romans in 222 BC, and quickly grew to be an important city at the junction of various trading routes. As the Roman Empire grew and then split into two, emperors began to neglect Rome for the better-placed Mediolanum (literally, city in the middle of the plain). It was here that Emperor Constantine declared his edict of AD 313, in which Christianity was officially recognized, thus effectively making it the religion of the empire. The emperor is said to have been converted following a vision, but by the 4th century adopting Christianity was the only way to unite the now disparate empire.

Emperor Constantine

Monza ❹

Milano. 🏛 125,000. 🚉 🚌 🚹 *Palazzo Comunale, Piazza Carducci (039 32 32 22).* 🛒 *Thu & Sat.* 🌐 *www.promonza.monza.net*

THESE DAYS MONZA is merely a satellite of Milan, famous for its international Formula One **Autodromo**, which lies inside a vast park on the edge of Monza. The park also has an elegant Rococo hunting lodge, the Villa Reale, and a golf course. At one time, however, Monza was one of the most important towns in Lombardy: Theodolinda, the 6th-century Lombard queen, built its first cathedral and bequeathed her treasure to the town.

In the town centre is the **Duomo**, with its notable green and white 14th-century façade and beautiful 15th-century frescoes portraying Theodolinda's life. Behind the high altar is the small Iron Crown, believed to have belonged to Emperor Constantine: it is prized for

the iron strip, said to have been one of the nails from the cross of Christ. More local treasures may be found in the Duomo's **Museo Serpero**, including a silver hen standing over seven tiny chicks – which symbolize Lombardy and the seven provinces it ruled – and a relic said to be John the Baptist's tooth.

🏎 **Autodromo**
Parco di Monza. 📞 *039 248 21.* ⭘ *daily.* ● *public hols.* 🅿️ ♿
🏛 **Duomo**
Piazza Duomo. 📞 *039 32 34 04.* **Museo Serpero** ⭘ *9–11:30am, 3–5:30pm Tue–Sat; 10:30am– noon, 3–5:30pm Sun.* 📷

Bergamo ❺

🏛 *150,000.* 🚉 🚌 🚹 *Vicolo Aquila Nera 2 (035 24 22 26).* 🛒 *Mon.* 🌐 *www.apt.bergamo.it*

BERGAMO IS A DELIGHTFUL hilltop town that owes much of its artistic inspiration and architectural splendour to the influence of Venice, which ruled it from the 15th to the late 18th century. The town is divided into two distinct parts: Bergamo Alta crowning the hill, with its cluster of attractive medieval and Renaissance buildings, and the more modern Bergamo Bassa below.

The jewel of the upper town is **Piazza Vecchia**, containing one of the most appealing architectural ensembles in the region. Its buildings include the 12th-century Torre del Comune with its fine clock and curfew bell that rings daily at 10pm, the late 16th-century Biblioteca Civica and the attractive 12th-century Palazzo della Ragione, or law courts, adorned with a statue of the lion of Venice.

The arcades of the Palazzo della Ragione lead to Piazza del Duomo, the square of the Neo-Classical Duomo, which is dominated by the façade of the **Cappella Colleoni** (see p178). The chapel was built

Detail from the Cappella Colleoni

Leonello d'Este (c.1440) by Pisanello in the Accademia Carrara, Bergamo

in 1476 to house the tomb of Bergamo's famous political leader, Bartolomeo Colleoni. It is flanked by two 14th-century buildings: an octagonal baptistry and the porch leading to the Romanesque basilica of Santa Maria Maggiore. The basilica's austere exterior contrasts with its Baroque interior, which contains the tomb of Gaetano Donizetti (1797–1848), the operatic composer who was born in Bergamo.

The **Galleria dell' Accademia Carrara** is the highlight of Bergamo Bassa, a major picture gallery with a fine collection of works by Venetian masters and local artists, as well as masterpieces from the rest of Italy: 15th-century works by Pisanello, Crivelli, Mantegna, Giovanni Bellini and Botticelli; 16th-century paintings by Titian, Raphael and Perugino; 18th-century canvases by Tiepolo, Guardi and Canaletto. Major artists represented from the rest of Europe include Holbein, Dürer, Brueghel and Velázquez.

🏛 **Galleria dell'Accademia Carrara**
Via S Tomaso 82a. 📞 *035 39 96 43.* ⭘ *Apr–Sep: 10am–1pm, 3–6:45pm; Oct–Mar: 9:30am–1pm, 2:30– 5:45pm Tue–Sun.* ● *public hols.* 📷

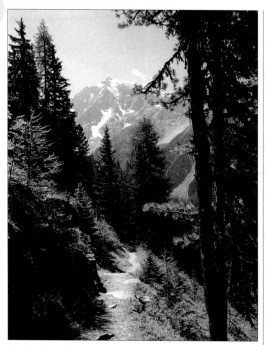

A leafy pathway through the Parco Nazionale dello Stelvio

Parco Nazionale dello Stelvio ⑥

Trento, Bolzano, Sondrio & Brescia.
🚌 from Bormio to Santa Caterina & Madonna dei Monti.
ℹ Via Roma 131b (0342 90 33 00).
🌐 www.valtellinaonline.com

THE STELVIO, Italy's largest national park, is the gateway from Lombardy to the glacier-strewn Dolomite mountains stretching into Trentino-Alto Adige. The glaciers are dotted with more than 50 lakes, and dominated by craggy peaks such as Gran Zebrù, Cevedale and Ortles – the tallest mountain here at 3,905 m (12,811 ft).

For walkers, the area provides virtually unlimited hiking, and access to remote areas populated by ibexes, marmots, chamois and eagles. The only real population centre in the Lombardy part of the park is at **Bormio**, which boasts plenty of winter and summer sports facilities, and is a good base from which to explore the area. The town's **Giardino**

Botanico displays some of the species of mountain plants found in the region.

🌸 **Giardino Botanico Alpino Retia**
Via Sertorelli, Località Rovinaccia, Bormio. 🕿 0342 90 16 54. ◯ May–Sep: daily. 🌐 www.stelviopark.it

Val Camonica ⑦

Brescia. 🚆 🚌 Capo di Ponte. ℹ Via Briscioli, Capo di Ponte (0364 420 80). 🌐 www.proloco.capo-di-ponte.bs.it

THIS ATTRACTIVE BROAD valley formed by a glacier is the setting for an extraordinary

series of prehistoric rock carvings. These form an astonishing outdoor mural from the Lago d'Iseo to Capo di Ponte and beyond, and the valley has been declared a cultural protection zone by UNESCO. More than 180,000 engravings from the Neolithic era until early Roman times have been discovered; the best are in the **Parco Nazionale delle Incisioni Rupestri**. Do not miss the Naquane rock, carved with nearly 1,000 figures from the Ice Age. The **Centro Camuno** focuses on the Roman settlement in the valley.

🏛 **Centro Camuno in Studi Preistorici**
Via Marconi 7, Capo di Ponte.
🕿 0364 420 91. ◯ Mon–Fri. 🚻
🏛 **Parco Nazionale delle Incisioni Rupestri**
Capo di Ponte. 🕿 0364 421 40.
◯ 8:30am–4:30pm Tue–Sun.
● Nov–Feb: noon–1pm Tue–Sun; 1 Jan, 1 May, 25 Dec.

Lago d'Iseo ⑧

Bergamo & Brescia. 🚆 🚢 Iseo.
ℹ Lungolago Marconi 2, Iseo (030 98 02 09). 🌐 www.apt.brescia.it

THIS GLACIATED LAKE lying in wine-producing country is surrounded by tall mountains and waterfalls and boasts a mini-mountain of its own, in the form of the island of Monte Isola. Along the shores of the lake are a clutch of fishing villages such as Sale Marasino and Iseo itself. From Marone, on the east bank of the lake, a road leads to the village of **Cislano**, about 5 km (3 miles) away. Here, extraordinary spire-like rock formations rise from the ground, each spire

Prehistoric engraving of a mounted hunter and stag in the Val Camonica

The partly Renaissance Ponte Coperto, straddling the River Ticino at Pavia

topped by a boulder. These distinctive erosion pillars, one of the strangest and most beautiful natural wonders in Lombardy, are known locally as the "Fairies of the Forest".

Brescia ⑨

🚹 190,000. 🚆 🚌 **ℹ** Corso Zanardelli 38 (030 434 18). 🗓 Sat. 🌐 www.apt.brescia.it

LOMBARDY'S SECOND city after Milan boasts a rich artistic heritage, ranging from Roman temples to the triumphalist Mussolini-era architecture of its main square, Piazza Vittoriale. The major sights include the Roman ruins around Piazza del Foro, consisting of the **Tempio Capitolino** – a three-part Capitoline temple, now incorporating a museum – and a theatre; the **Pinacoteca Civica Tosio Martinengo**, containing works by Raphael, Lorenzo Lotto and local artists; and the **Duomo** on Piazza Paolo VI, with its 11th-century core and white 17th-century exterior. One of the relics in the Duomo is the banner from the *Carroccio*, or sacred ox cart, which served as a symbol for the medieval Lega Lombarda. **Piazza della Loggia**, where the market is held, is named after the Renaissance loggia, built partly by Palladio. The 18th-century church of San Nazaro e San Celso on Via Bronzoni contains an altarpiece by Titian.

♫ Tempio Capitolino
Via Musei 57a. **[** 030 460 31. **●** for restoration. 🏛
🏛 Pinacoteca Civica Tosio Martinengo
Piazza Moretto 4.
[030 377 49 99. **◯** Tue–Sun. **◯** 1pm–2:30pm (winter); 1 Jan, 1 May, 1 Nov, 25 Dec. 🏛 🚻

Lodi ⑩

Milano. 🚹 40,000. 🚆 🚌 **ℹ** Piazza Broletto 4 (0371 42 13 91). 🗓 Tue, Thu, Sat & Sun. 🌐 www.apt.lodi.it

THIS IS A CHARMING medieval town of pastel-coloured houses with wrought-iron gateways, pretty courtyards and gardens. Just off Piazza della Vittoria, the arcaded square on which the 12th-century Duomo stands, is the fine Renaissance church of the **Incoronata**. The magnificent octagonal interior is entirely decorated with wall paintings and gilding, and crowned with a dome. One of the chapels has 15th-century works by Bergognone.

Pavia ⑪

🚹 81,000. 🚆 🚌 **ℹ** Via Fabio Filzi 2 (0382 221 56). 🗓 Wed & Sat. 🌐 www.apt.pavia.it

DURING PAVIA'S golden age, the city was the Lombards' capital, and later witnessed coronations of Charlemagne and Frederick Barbarossa. Even after it lost its

The Roman Tempio Capitolino in Brescia

status to Milan in 1359, Pavia remained an important city, and great Romanesque churches, tall towers and other monuments still reflect this.

As well as the Charterhouse *(see pp196–7)* just north of Pavia, there is the sandstone **Basilica di San Michele** off Corso Garibaldi. The building was founded in the 7th century but largely rebuilt in the 12th after being struck by lightning. Its façade is decorated with symbols and friezes of fantastic animals, and inside there are intricate carvings on the columns; a chapel to the right of the main altar contains a 7th-century silver crucifix.

In the town centre, around Piazza della Vittoria, are several ancient monuments, including the medieval **Broletto** (town hall), with its 16th-century façade, and the recently renovated **Duomo**, originally begun in 1488 and worked on in turn by Amadeo, Leonardo da Vinci and Bramante. The dome was added in the 1880s. The 11th-century tower that stood next to it collapsed suddenly in 1989. Crossing the river is the **Ponte Coperto**, a Renaissance covered bridge with a consecrated church half-way along it. The bridge was rebuilt after World War II.

Pavia is also the site of one of Europe's oldest (1361) and most respected universities, now residing around a series of Neo-Classical courtyards off Strada Nuova. This road continues northwards to the 14th-century castle, now home to the **Museo Civico**.

Northwest of Piazza Castello is the 12th-century church, **San Pietro in Ciel d'Oro**. It no longer boasts the fine gilded ceiling after which it is named, but does still contain a magnificent shrine to St Augustine, whose bones were allegedly brought to Pavia in the 8th century. The body of the philosopher Boëthius (c.480–524) is buried down in the crypt.

🏛 Museo Civico
Castello Visconteo, Viale 11 Febbraio. **[** 0382 338 53. **◯** Tue–Sun (Tue–Fri: am only). **●** public hols. 🏛

Certosa di Pavia ⑫

THE CHARTERHOUSE 8 km (5 miles) north of Pavia is the
pinnacle of Renaissance architecture in Lombardy,
a gloriously decorated Carthusian monastery built over
200 years. Conceived as a monument to Gian Galeazzo
Visconti, the Milanese ruler who founded the complex
in 1396, this shrine was created by
the great 15th-century craftsman
Giovanni Antonio Amadeo, among
others, who used innovative
techniques of relief work
and multicoloured
decoration. The Certosa
is still home to Carthusian
monks, who are under
a strict vow of silence.

The choir stalls
(15th century)
are deeply carved
and inlaid with
intricate marquetry.

The tomb of Gi
Galeazzo Visco
(1351–1402
in the so
transe

Pietra Dura Altar
*Several of the 17th-
century altars in the
chapels have lavish
designs worked in
semi-precious stones
("pietra dura").*

The grilles date
from c.1660.

The side chapels are
richly decorated with
marble, *trompe l'oeil*
frescoes and ornate
altars and altarpieces.

The interior
of the church is
largely Gothic.

★ Frescoes by Bergognone (*c.1488–93*)
*This striking portrait of Christ is one of
several frescoes by Bergognone in the
transept and chapels, together with an
altar painting of Sant'Ambrogio.*

Tomb of Ludovico il Moro and Beatrice d'Este
*This realistic marble portrait of Ludovico and his
child bride was begun by Cristoforo Solari in
1497, some 11 years before Ludovico's death.*

Great Cloister
This huge cloister is reached through the Small Cloister. It is framed on three sides by the two-storey monks' cells, each backed by a small garden. A hatch beside the door permits food to be delivered without any communication.

VISITORS' CHECKLIST

Viale del Monumento, Pavia.
☎ 0382 221 56. 🚌 from Pavia.
🚆 Certosa. Both followed by 1 km (half a mile) walk. 🕐 9–11:30am, 2:30–5pm (to 6pm May–Sep) Tue–Sun & Mon public hols (last adm: 30 mins before closing). **Donation** to guide. 📷
🚻 ♿ 🎫 Ⓦ www.apt.pavia.it

Monk's cell

The New Sacristy is painted with colourful ceiling frescoes.

This delightful, arcaded Small Cloister, with fine terracotta ornamentation, contains a small garden, planted in formal designs.

★ Renaissance Façade
The 15th-century lower part of the façade is profusely decorated with statues and carvings of Roman emperors, saints (here St Peter), apostles and prophets. The upper part dates from 1500.

Main entrance to the Certosa

★ Altarpiece by Perugino
The six-panel altarpiece was painted in 1496 but now only one panel – that depicting God the Father – is original; it is flanked by two paintings by Bergognone.

STAR FEATURES

★ Renaissance Façade

★ Altarpiece by Perugino

★ Frescoes by Bergognone

The Duomo on Piazza del Comune, Cremona

Cremona ⑬

🏛 76,000. 🚇 🚌 ℹ️ Piazza del
Comune 5 (0372 232 33). 🎪 Wed
& Sat. 🌐 www.aptcremona.it

CREMONA, A MAJOR agricultural
market, is most famous
for music, thanks to native sons
such as the composer Claudio
Monteverdi (1567–1643) and
the violin-maker Stradivarius
(1644–1737). The town itself
is dominated by the beautiful
Piazza del Comune.

The main attraction is the
exuberant part-Romanesque
Duomo, and its bell tower –
said to be the tallest medieval
tower in Italy – known as the
Torrazzo; the two are linked
by a Renaissance loggia. The
wonderful façade is dominated
by the large 13th-century rose
window and by a number of
intricate touches, including a
small portico with statues of
the Virgin and saints. Inside,
the Duomo is sumptuously
decorated with magnificent
early 16th-century frescoes and
Flemish tapestries, as well as
paintings in the side chapels.
The top of the Torrazzo offers
sweeping views. Outside the
Duomo, note the pulpit where
itinerant preachers, including
San Bernardino of Siena, used
to speak to onlookers.

Next to the Duomo stands
an octagonal 12th-century
baptistry, while on the other
side of the piazza rise the

arcades of the
late 13th-century
Loggia dei Militi
where the town's
lords once met,
now a war
memorial.

The **Palazzo del
Comune** is the
other major build-
ing on the square.
It was rebuilt
in the 1200s.

The **Museo
Civico**, housed
in a 16th-century
palazzo, contains
paintings, wood
carvings, the cathe-
dral's treasure,
ceramics, a section
on archaeology
and four rare
violins: one each
by Guarnieri del
Gesù, Andrea and Niccolò
Amati, and Stradivarius. The
building also includes the
Museo Stradivariano, which
displays drawings, models
and violins that were made
by Stradivarius himself.

On the eastern outskirts of
the town, on the road to Casal-
maggiore, lies the Renaissance
church of **San Sigismondo**. It
was here that Francesco Sforza
married Bianca Visconti in
1441, and the church was subsequently rebuilt (from 1463)
in honour of the event. The
interior is richly decorated with

16th-century paintings, altarpieces and frescoes by artists
of the Cremona school (Campi
family, Gatti and Boccaccino).

⛪ Torrazzo
Piazza del Comune.
🕐 Easter–1 Nov: daily. 🏷

🏛 Palazzo del Comune
Piazza del Comune. 📞 0372 40 72 50.
🕐 9am–6pm Tue–Sat; 10am–6pm
Sun. ● public hols. 🏷 🚻

**🏛 Museo Stradivariano &
🏛 Museo Civico**
Via Ugolani Dati 4. 📞 0372 200 73.
🕐 9am–6pm Tue–Sat; 10am–6pm
Sun. ● public hols. 🏷 🚻

Sabbioneta ⑭

Mantova. 🏛 4,600. 🚌 from
Mantova. ℹ️ Piazza d'Armi (0375
22 10 44). 🎪 Wed am. 📋 apply to
the tourist information centre. 🏷

SABBIONETA is the result of a
delightful experiment in the
theory of Renaissance architecture. It was built by Vespasiano
Gonzaga Colonna (1531–91) as
an ideal city, and within its
hexagonal walls is a perfect
gridwork arrangement of
streets and buildings designed
on a human scale. The finest
buildings include the splendid
Teatro All'Antica designed by
Scamozzi, the Palazzo Ducale
and the frescoed Palazzo del
Giardino, which may be visited
as part of a tour of the town.

ANTONIO STRADIVARI AND HIS VIOLINS

Cremona is where the violin was
developed. The instrument-
maker Andrea Amati made
the first ones in the 1530s,
and they soon became
popular with the royal
courts throughout Europe
because of their superior
tone to the medieval fiddle.

It was Antonio Stradivari,
known as Stradivarius
(1644–1737) – the pupil
of Andrea Amati's grandson

**19th-century engraving
of Antonio Stradivari**

Niccolò – who raised the level of craftsmanship to genius.
He used to go walking in the forests of the Dolomites in
search of the perfect wood for his instruments. Stradivarius
produced more than 1,100 violins in his workshop, of
which more than 400 exist to this day and remain
unrivalled by modern techniques or equipment. The main
stopping-off points on a Stradivarius tour of Cremona are
the Museo Stradivariano, the Museo Civico, and the great
man's tombstone on Piazza Roma.

The ceiling of the Camera degli Sposi, by Mantegna, in the Palazzo Ducale

Mantova ⓯

🏛 55,000. 🚊 🚌 🛈 *Piazza Andrea Mantegna 6 (0376 32 82 53).* 🚌 *Thu.* 🅦 *www.aptmantova.it*

MANTOVA (MANTUA) IS A striking if stern-looking place of fine squares and aristocratic architecture, bordered on three sides by lakes formed by the swollen banks of the River Mincio. The climate can be humid as a result, but Mantova more than makes up for it with a keen sense of cultural history: it was the birthplace of the poet Virgil and playground for three centuries of the Gonzaga dukes. It was also the refuge where Shakespeare sent Romeo into exile from Verona, and the setting for Verdi's opera *Rigoletto*. These links are all celebrated in street names, signposts and monuments around the town. The theatrical connections are enhanced by the 18th-century **Teatro Accademico Bibiena**, on Via Accademia, which Mozart's father thought was the finest he had ever seen.

Mantova is focused on three attractive main squares: Piazza dell'Erbe, Piazza del Broletto, named after the 13th-century building adorned with a statue of the poet Virgil, and the cobbled Piazza Sordello. On one side of Piazza Sordello is the **Duomo**, with an 18th-century façade and fine interior stuccoes by Giulio Romano (c.1492–1546); on another side, the forbidding façade of the Palazzo Bonacolsi, with its tall prison tower. Piazza dell'Erbe

is dominated by the **Basilica di Sant'Andrea** (15th century), designed largely by Alberti, the early Renaissance architect and theorist, and now flanked by an arcade of shops. The square is also notable for the appealing 11th-century Rotonda di San Lorenzo, and the part-13th-century Palazzo della Ragione with its 15th-century clock tower.

Detail from the 15th-century clock tower on Piazza dell'Erbe

🏛 Palazzo Ducale
Piazza Sordello. ☏ *0376 22 48 32.* 🕐 *8:45am–7:15pm (last adm 6pm) Tue–Sun.* ⬤ *1 Jan, 1 May, 25 Dec.* 📷 *0376 32 82 53 (by request).* 📷
Camera degli Sposi ☏ *0412 41 18 97 (bookings compulsory).*
The highlight of Mantova is the Palazzo Ducale, the vast, 500-room home of the Gonzaga family which covers the northeastern corner of the town and incorporates Castello San Giorgio (a 14th-century fortress),

a basilica, and the palace proper. The many works of art include an unfinished series of 15th-century frescoes by Pisanello, retelling episodes from the Arthurian legends; a large portrait by Rubens (17th century) of the ducal family in the Salone degli Arcieri; and – most absorbing of all – the frescoes by Mantegna in the **Camera degli Sposi** (1465–74). These portray Lodovico Gonzaga and members of his family and court in all their magnificence *(pp200–201)*. The entire room is decorated with images of people, animals and fantastic landscapes, and completed by a light-hearted *trompe l'oeil* ceiling of figures, putti and a blue sky.

🏛 Palazzo Tè
Viale Tè. ☏ *0376 32 32 66.* 🕐 *Mon pm, Tue–Sun.* ⬤ *1 Jan, 1 May, 25 Dec.* 📷 🚻
At the other end of town stands the early 16th-century Palazzo Tè, built by Giulio Romano for the Gonzaga family as a base from which they could go horse riding. Here the artworks conspire with the architecture to produce striking effects: in the **Sala dei Giganti**, for instance, the frescoed Titans seem to be tearing down the very pillars of the room. Also remarkable is the **Sala di Amore e Psiche**, decorated with erotic scenes from Apuleius' *Golden Ass* and said to celebrate Federico II's love for his mistress. Other rooms are lavishly painted with horses and Zodiac signs.

The 13th-century façade of Palazzo Ducale overlooking Piazza Sordello

15th-century fresco, by Mantegna, from the Camera degli Sposi in the Palazzo Ducale ▷

VALLE D'AOSTA AND PIEDMONT

P IEDMONT AND THE NEIGHBOURING VALLE D'AOSTA *are – apart from Turin and its cultural splendours – essentially countryside. To the north lie the Alps, with ski resorts such as Courmayeur, and the wild stretches of the Parco Nazionale del Gran Paradiso. To the south lie the vineyard-clad hills around Barolo, and seemingly end-less fields of grain and rice, used in the local dish, risotto.*

The northwest is also rich in culture. From the 11th century to the 18th, both the verdant Valle d'Aosta and Piedmont were part of the French-speaking princi-pality of Savoy and enjoyed the influences of both sides of the Alpine divide. Even today, French and dialectal variants are still spoken in the remote valleys of Piedmont and in much of the Valle d'Aosta. It was only under Duke Eman-uele Filiberto in the 16th century that the region was brought definitively into the Italian sphere of influence; and later it was to play the key role in the Risorgimento *(see pp58–9)*, the ambitious movement that united Italy under a king from Piedmont. The ves-tiges of this history are to be found in the medieval castles of the Valle d'Aosta and the extraordinary clusters of chapels known as *sacri monti* dotted around the foothills of the Alps. Piedmont also spawned a school of painting, which is in evidence in the small parish churches and excellent fine art collections in the region. The most impres-sive architecture in the northwest, however, is un-doubtedly to be found in Turin, a much underrated and surprisingly elegant Baroque city which boasts, among other things, one of the best Egyptian museums in the world. Piedmont is also known for its indus-try – Fiat in Turin, Olivetti in Ivrea, Ferrero in Alba – but it has not for-gotten its agricultural roots, and food and drink play an important role in the life of the region: the hills of south-ern Piedmont produce many of the great Italian red wines.

Traditional pavement café in the heart of Turin

◁ The 13th-century Châtelard castle in the Valle d'Aosta

Exploring Valle d'Aosta and Piedmont

THE VAST FLAT PLAIN of the Po, covered with the watery expanse of rice fields around Vercelli and Novara, eventually gives way, in the west, to the majestic heights of the Alps. Turin, the largest city in the area and the capital of Piedmont, stands at the edge of the plain, nestling almost in the shadow of the mountains. Further northwest, attractive Alpine valleys headed by dramatic peaks provide the setting for the traditional villages, ancient towns and castles around Aosta. The Parco Nazionale del Gran Paradiso is an unspoilt tract of breathtaking scenery.

Rice fields around Vercelli

SIGHTS AT A GLANCE

Turin, the capital of Piedmont, in the valley of the Po

GETTING AROUND

The Fréjus Pass and the Mont Blanc Tunnel link France with northwest Italy, while the tunnel under the Simplon or Sempione Pass provides a direct rail route from Switzerland. From the rest of Italy there are excellent motorway connections across the plain to Turin and up to Aosta. The region is well served with rail links, and buses connect the main towns and outlying resorts. Getting around the mountains is more difficult, making the car the best method of transport.

St Pierre castle in the Valle d'Aosta

SEE ALSO

- *Where to Stay* pp551–4
- *Where to Eat* pp586–8

0 kilometres 25

0 miles 20

KEY

▰▰▰	Motorway
▬▬	Major road
▭▭	Minor road
▱▱▱	Scenic route
〰	River
☆	Viewpoint

Monte Bianco ❶

Aosta. **FS** *Pré-St-Didier.* **🚌** *Courma-yeur.* **ℹ** *Piazzale Monte Bianco 13, Courmayeur (0165 84 20 60).*

MONTE BIANCO – Mont Blanc as it is also known – the tallest mountain in the Alps at 4,810 m (15,780 ft), dominates the western Aosta valley and its attractive all-year resort, **Courmayeur**. A series of cable car rides from Entrèves, 5 km (3 miles) further north, leads to Chamonix. Passing its highest point (3,842 m, 12,606 ft) at Aiguille du Midi, it offers a spectacular view. From Pré-St-Didier, below Courmayeur, the **Little St Bernard Pass**, with its small glaciers, forests and ravines, can be explored.

Colle del Gran San Bernardo ❷

Aosta. **FS** **🚌** *Aosta.* **ℹ** *Strada Statale Gran San Bernardo 13, Etroubles (0165 785 59).* **◷** *daily.* **W** *www.gransanbernardo.net*

THE GREAT ST BERNARD pass is synonymous with the hardy mountain rescue dogs that have been trained locally by Catholic monks since the 11th century. The **Monks' Hospice**, founded around 1050 by St Bernard of Aosta, lies just over the Swiss border (bring your passport), on the shores of a lovely lake; the dogs are still being trained here.

The pretty Great St Bernard valley itself includes the town of Etroubles, set in a forest of conifers, the hamlet of St-Oyen with its pretty parish church, and the resort of St-Rhémy-en-Bosses.

A St Bernard dog

🏛 Monks' Hospice
Colle San Bernardo, Switzerland. **📞** *00 41 277 87 12 36.* **◷** *daily.*

Monte Cervino ❸

Aosta. **FS** **🚌** *Breuil-Cervinia.* **ℹ** *Via Guido Rey 17, Breuil-Cervinia (0166 94 91 36).* **W** *www.montecervino.it*

THE DISTINCTIVE triangular peak of Monte Cervino (the Matterhorn) rises to 4,478 m (14,691 ft) and is easily recognizable. Below the mountain lies a scattering of attractive villages like Antey-St-André, Valtournanche (which gave its name to the valley) and the resort of **Breuil-Cervinia**. From Breuil a cable car rises to the Plateau Rosa (3,480 m, 11,418 ft) offering dramatic views of the surrounding mountains. This entire area is a paradise for both skiers and walkers.

Monte Rosa ❹

Aosta. **FS** *Verrès.* **🚌** *St-Jacques.* **ℹ** *Route Varasc, Champoluc (0125 30 71 13).* **W** *www.aiatmonterosa.com*

MONTE ROSA, Italy's second highest mountain, overlooks the picturesque Ayas and Gressoney valleys. The rolling lower Ayas valley is dominated by the ruins of the 11th-century **Castello di Graines**. Higher up, the resort of Champoluc has a cable car connection with the striking **Testa Grigia** (3,315 m/10,877 ft). The Gressoney valley is home to the Walser people, who speak an obscure German dialect. At the bottom of the valley, north of Pont-St-Martin, lies **Issime**: the 16th-century church here has a fresco of the Last Judgment on its façade.

⚜ Castello di Graines
Graines, Strada Statale 506.

MEDIEVAL CASTLES AND FORTS IN THE VALLE D'AOSTA

The mountains alone provided insufficient protection to the fragmented kingdoms that covered the Valle d'Aosta in the Middle Ages. The medieval lords, who ruled ruthlessly over their small domains, built castles to enforce their often fragile power. Of the many built, 70 castles survive in some form to this day. You will pass a number of them if you drive into Italy by the Mont Blanc tunnel; they stretch from Aosta to Pont-St-Martin.

Originally Aosta castles were designed to be defensive and threatening, such as the looming tower of **Montmayer**, perched high on a huge rock by the Valgrisenche valley. Nearby, the equally forbidding dark tower of **Ussel** throws a melancholy, brooding watchfulness over the valley.

Fénis and **Verrès** represent an important shift in the function of the feudal castle. Both Fénis, a splendid 14th-century showpiece *(see p178)*, and Verrès were not just import-ant military outposts but also examples of palatial opulence and good living. **Issogne** too furthered this luxurious trend with its elaborate frescoes, loggias and fountains.

Decoration was also important to Vittorio Emanuele II, owner of **Sarre**, who turned the halls of his fortress into a plush hunting lodge. The owners of **Châtelard**, set in some of the highest vineyards in Europe, placed fine wine production alongside military aims.

The strategically sited 14th-century castle at Verrès

The 12th-century cloister, with 40 carved columns of darkened marble, in Sant'Orso

Aosta **5**

🏛 37,000. **FS** 🚌 **ℹ** Piazza Chanoux 8 (0165 23 66 27). 🗓 Tue. **W** www.regione.vda.it

LYING ON A PLAIN surrounded by dramatic mountains, the town of Aosta provides a remarkable mixture of ancient culture and spectacular scenery. The Romans captured it from Salassian Gauls in 25 BC, and Aosta is still dotted with fine Roman architecture built in honour of Emperor Augustus – indeed the town was once called *Augusta Praetoria*, and its name only evolved into Aosta over the centuries. The medieval town was later fortified by the Challant family and then by the Dukes of Aosta, who added towers to the old Roman walls.

Modern Aosta is a bustling crossroads for local industries and tourists on their way to the mountains. The centre, however, still consists of a delightful grid of large squares and surprising architectural treasures, which justify Aosta's nickname of "Rome of the Alps".

🏛 Roman Ruins
Roman Theatre, Via Baillage. 🗓 9am–8pm daily (to 6:30pm Oct–Feb). **Amphitheatre**, Convento di San Giuseppe, Via dell'Anfiteatro. **📞** 0165 26 20 89. 🗓 daily, phone convent ahead. 🖼 🚻 **Roman Forum**, Piazza Giovanni XXIII. ⬤ for restoration.
During Roman times, entry to Aosta was over the **bridge** to the east of the town (beyond the modern bridge) and through the **Arch of Augustus**. This triumphal arch is today marred by a roof added in the 18th century. Ahead stands

the **Porta Pretoria**, its double row of stone arches flanked by a medieval tower; the gateway originally stood about 2.5 m (8 ft) higher than at present. Equally well preserved is the town's **Roman Theatre**, with a section of its 20-m (65-ft) high façade. The elliptical **Amphitheatre**, a little to the north, is reached through the convent of San Giuseppe. In the old town, next to the cathedral, lies the **Roman Forum**, or market place, with its huge cryptoporticus: the function of this impressive underground gallery remains the object of speculation.

Detail of a medieval mosaic on the floor of Aosta's Cattedrale

🏛 Cattedrale
Piazza Giovanni XXIII. 🗓 daily. **Museo del Tesoro** **📞** 0165 404 13. 🗓 Apr–Sep: 9–11:30am, 3–5:30pm Tue–Sat (Sun am only); Oct–Mar: 8:30–11:30am, 3–5.30pm Sun. 🖼
This relatively modest shrine to St John the Baptist was first built in the 12th century, but has been altered many times

since. The interior is Gothic, with finely carved 15th-century choir stalls, and floor mosaics. Next door, the **Museo del Tesoro** contains a rich collection of statuettes and reliquaries, and a number of impressive medieval tombs.

🏛 Sant'Orso
Via Sant'Orso. **📞** 3498 04 12 39. 🗓 daily. 🚻
East of the town walls is the architectural highlight of Aosta: a medieval complex of church buildings. Sant'Orso itself has an unusual Gothic façade with a thin, tall portal. The interior has 11th-century frescoes, a crypt of the same date holding the tomb of St Orso, patron saint of Aosta, and a beautiful **cloister** with columns and capitals carved into highly detailed figures and animals.

ENVIRONS: The castle at **Fénis** (*see p206*), 12 km (8 miles) east, is one of the few castles in the Aosta valley with a well-preserved interior, including beautiful frescoes and wooden galleries. **Issogne**, 38 km (23 miles) southeast, is the setting for another highly decorated castle, remodelled around 1490. It is filled with frescoes and decorative motifs, including a wrought-iron fountain in the shape of a pomegranate tree.

🏰 Castello di Fénis
Fénis. **📞** 0165 76 42 63. 🗓 daily. ⬤ 1 Jan, 25 Dec; Tue (winter). 🖼
🏰 Castello di Issogne
Issogne. **📞** 0125 92 93 73. 🗓 daily. ⬤ 1 Jan, 25 Dec; Wed (winter). 🖼

Some of the impressive ruins standing in the Roman Forum in Aosta

Parco Nazionale del Gran Paradiso ⑥

A BREATHTAKING WILDERNESS of dramatic mountains and lush meadows, the Gran Paradiso is Italy's foremost national park, created in 1922 from part of a former royal hunting reserve of the House of Savoy. It is mainly a summer resort for walkers due to its unspoiled scenery, rare wildlife and unusual Alpine flowers, though there is also cross-country skiing during the winter months. The king of the park is the ibex, a relative of the goat family all but extinct in the rest of Europe. The park is also prized by naturalists for its chamois, ptarmigan, golden eagles, rare butterflies and marmots.

Castello di Aymavilles
The 18th-century core of this castle is framed by medieval corner towers.

Goletta Waterfall
is an impressive cascade near the Lago di Goletta.

Male Ibex
The ibex lives largely above the tree line. Groups are often seen around Col Lauson at dawn and dusk, and also around Pont in June.

Val di Rhêmes-Notre-Dame
This peaceful and broad valley offers magnificent scenery with waterfalls and fast-flowing streams running from the glacier at its head.

Cascata di Lillaz
This tall, dramatic waterfall, situated a little to the east of the rustic village of Lillaz, is best observed after the spring snow melt.

Cogne is the main resort and a good base from which to explore the park. Maps of the park's routes and footpaths are available here.

Lillaz is sedate and off the beaten track, while Valnontey and Cogne are two of the busiest resorts.

★ **Paradisia Alpine Garden**
The botanic garden contains a collection of Alpine plants, including the delicate "twinflower".

VISITORS' CHECKLIST

Piemonte and Valle d'Aosta. ⓘ Segreteria Turistica, Via Umberto I 1, Noasca (0124 90 10 70). Other information offices at Ceresole Reale & Cogne. ◯ daily. Ⓕ Aosta & Pont Canavese. 🚌 from Aosta or Pont Canavese to the different valleys. ⚑ **Paradisia Alpine Garden**, Valnontey, Cogne. ⓒ 0165 741 47. ◯ mid-Jun–mid-Sep: daily. 🅿 ♿ Ⓦ www.pngp.it Ⓦ www.parks.it

---

STAR SIGHTS

★ **Paradisia Alpine Garden**

★ **Valnontey**

0 kilometres 5

0 miles 5

★ **Valnontey**
This lovely valley, after which the resort is named, provides dramatic views of glaciers and easy access to various footpaths.

KEY

ⓘ Tourist information

═ Main road

☙ Viewpoint

The small resort of Ceresole Reale
under winter snow

Lake Ceresole Reale **7**

Torino. 🚌 to Ceresole Reale. 🛈 Corso
Vercelli 1, Ivrea (0125 61 81 31);
Comune di Ceresole (0124 95 32 00).
🔲 www.canavese-vallilanzo.it

O**N THE SOUTHERN,** Piedmont
side of the extensive Parco
Nazionale del Gran Paradiso
(see pp208–9) lies the small
resort of Ceresole Reale, on the
shores of a spectacular mountain lake. The route from
Cuorgnè goes through the
rolling countryside of the Canavese and follows the S460
along a narrow gorge with a
cascading stream. At **Noasca**,
a spectacular waterfall may be
seen high above the houses.
Ceresole Reale lies in a basin
surrounded by meadows and
forests of larch, and framed by
mountains – the Gran Paradiso
range to the north, Levanna
to the southwest – which are
reflected in the clear waters
of the lake. The lake itself is
actually a dammed reservoir,
providing energy to supply
Turin with electricity. This
nevertheless unspoiled corner
is a good base for walking,
climbing and hiking, and also
offers facilities for skiing
during the winter.

Via Lattea **8**

Torino. 🚆 Oulx. 🚌 to Sauze d'Oulx.
🛈 Via Louset, Sestriere (0122 75 54
44). 🔲 www.sestriere.it

T**HE CLOSEST RING** of mountain
resorts to Turin, and as a
consequence popular for
weekend excursions, is known
colloquially as the Via Lattea
or "milky way". Villages like
Bardonecchia and **Sauze
d'Oulx** preserve traditional old
stone and wood buildings that
have been a feature of the
region for centuries. The small
church in Bardonecchia has, in
addition, a fine 15th-century
carved choir. In contrast, the
super-modern complex at
Sestriere has been purpose-
built to accommodate skiers in
winter and hikers in summer.
From Bardonecchia a chair-
lift operates some of the way
up **Punta Colomion**, which
rises immediately to the south
of the resort. The summit, at
2,054 m (6,738 ft), offers fine
views, and numerous hiking
and walking possibilities.

Susa **9**

Torino. 🏛 7,000. 🚆 🚌 🛈 Corso
Inghilterra 39 (0122 62 24 70). 🛒 Tue.
🔲 www.prosusa.it

T**HIS ATTRACTIVE** mountain
town flourished in Roman
times: the **Arch of Augustus**,
built in 8 BC commemorates
the alliance between the local

The impressive part-Roman
gateway, Porta Savoia, in Susa

Gaulish chieftain and the
Emperor Augustus. Other relics
from the Roman period include
two arches of an aqueduct,
sections of an amphitheatre
and traces of the old town
walls. **Porta Savoia**, an imposing Roman gateway dating
from the 4th century, was
remodelled in the Middle Ages.
Most of the historic centre
of the town is medieval, including the castle of Countess
Adelaide and the **Duomo**,
both originally 11th century.
The Duomo, much altered
since then, houses a polyptych (c.1500) attributed to
Bergognone, and a precious
14th-century Flemish triptych
portraying the *Virgin and
Saints*. South of the town lies
the Gothic church of **San
Francesco**, surrounded by an
area of early medieval houses.

A street in the traditional village of Bardonecchia, on the Via Lattea

Carved capitals on the Porta dello Zodiaco at the Sacra di San Michele

Sacra di San Michele ⑩

Strada Sacra San Michele. ☎ 011 93 91 30. 🚌 Jul–Aug from Avigliana & Turin. ◷ 9:30am–12:30pm, 3–6pm Tue–Sun (Nov–Mar: to 5pm). Phone to arrange group visits. 🖳 www.sacradisanmichele.com

THIS SOMEWHAT forbidding abbey complex is perched on a ridge halfway up Monte Pirchiriano, at 962 m (3,156 ft). Its monastic community was founded around the year 1000, possibly on the site of a previous sanctuary, though the exterior looks every bit as much a fortress as the spiritual refuge that it was for 600 years.

During its prime, the abbey attracted pilgrims on their way to Rome, and as a result it grew enormously wealthy and powerful, controlling over 100 other abbeys in Italy, France and Spain. It was subsequently looted several times, despite being fortified, before falling into decline and eventually being suppressed in 1662.

The sanctuary is reached by climbing 154 steep steps hewn out of the rock, which offer wonderful views over the surrounding countryside and up to the Alps. At the very top of this stairway, known as the Scalone dei Morti (Stairway of the Dead), is the Romanesque Porta dello Zodiaco, a doorway carved with creatures and symbols relating to the signs of the Zodiac. Beyond the doorway a few more steps lead into the church itself, which dates from the 12th–13th centuries and incorporates traces of an earlier building. The interior houses 15th- and 16th-century paintings and frescoes, and a 16th-century triptych by the Piedmontese artist Defendente Ferrari. The crypt holds the tombs of the early dukes and princes of the House of Savoy-Carignano.

Avigliana ⑪

Torino. 🏠 9,500. 🚆 🚌 ℹ Piazza de Popolo 2 (011 932 86 50). 🗓 Thu. 🖳 www.montagnedoc.it

ON A FINE DAY, this small town perched beside two glacier-fed lakes and encircled by tall mountains looks breathtakingly beautiful. Avigliana is overlooked by a castle, first erected in the mid-10th century but now in ruins, which was once the home of the Counts of Savoy. Until the early 15th century the town was one of their favourite bases.

The medieval houses here are largely unspoiled, particularly in the two main *piazzas*, Santa Maria and Conte Rosso. Other buildings of note are the Casa della Porta Ferrata and the 15th-century Casa dei Savoia, both on Via XX Settembre.

The church of San Giovanni (13th–14th century) contains early 16th-century paintings by Defendente Ferrari.

Pinerolo ⑫

Torino. 🏠 36,000. 🚆 🚌 ℹ Viale Giolitti 7–9 (0121 79 55 89). 🗓 Wed & Sat. 🖳 www.montagnedoc.it

PINEROLO LIES in an attractive setting beside hills at the confluence of the Lemina and Chisone valleys. The town was the capital of the Acaia family, a branch of the House of Savoy, and in the 14th and 15th centuries it was known for the cultural atmosphere that prevailed here under the family's patronage. However, the town enjoyed none of the stability of Turin: it was occupied by the French five times between the 15th and 18th centuries. During the 17th century the French demolished many of the town's ancient buildings in order to make Pinerolo a defensive stronghold; among the political prisoners allegedly held here was the notorious "Man in the Iron Mask". Today the town is a busy centre of commerce.

A number of monumental buildings do remain, however. The **Duomo**, at the centre of the town, was remodelled in Gothic style in the 15th–16th centuries and has a fine portal and an impressive bell tower. Via Principi d'Acaia climbs up to the 14th-century palace of the Princes of Acaia, and to the 15th-century church of **San Maurizio**, where the Acaia princes are buried; beside it rises a 14th-century bell tower.

The medieval arcades surrounding Piazza Conte Rosso in Avigliana

Turin ⑬

MENTION TURIN (Torino) and most people will think of industry and prosperity. It is certainly an economic powerhouse but it is also a town of grace and charm, with superb Baroque architecture and excellent museums, set against the dramatic scenery of the foothills of the Alps. Turin is also, of course, home to the famous Turin Shroud, the Fiat car company, and the Juventus football team. The 2006 Winter Olympics will be held here.

Exploring Turin

Though settled by the Romans (**Porta Palatina** is an impressive 1st-century AD relic), and the seat of a university since the Middle Ages, Turin came into its own only after 1563, when Emanuele Filiberto of Savoy moved his capital here. Three centuries of prosperity ensued. Turin then became the base for Italy's unification movement and, from 1861 to 1865, the capital of the newly united country. Subsequently its main power

The Fiat car factory logo

was economic. In 1899 the Agnelli family created the car company **Fiat** (Fabbrica Italiana Automobili Torino), which grew to be one of the biggest in Europe. After World War II, Turin attracted thousands of poor Italians from the south who came to work in its factories. Though there have been social conflicts and labour disputes as a result, managers and workers unite over football: the Juventus team is owned by the much-revered Agnelli family.

Statue of Emperor Augustus in front of the Roman Porta Palatina

🏠 Duomo

Piazza San Giovanni. 📞 011 436 15 40. ⭕ daily. ♿

The cathedral, built in 1497–8 and dedicated to St John the Baptist, is the only example of Renaissance architecture in

TURIN TOWN CENTRE

0 metres   500

0 yards   500

KEY

P   Parking

i   Tourist information

✝   Church

FS   Railway station

The 15th-century Duomo, with the Cappella della Sacra Sindone beyond

Turin. The sober square bell tower, which predates the rest of the church by 30 years, stands in refreshing contrast to Turin's sumptuous Baroque buildings; its top was designed by Filippo Juvarra in 1720. Inside, the Duomo is heavy with statuary and paintings. On the right side of the church is the **Cappella della Sacra Sindone** (Chapel of the Holy Shroud), which is actually incorporated into the Palazzo Reale *(see p216)*. The chapel is a remarkable feat, designed by Guarino Guarini (1624–83), with an extraordinary mesh-like cupola; the exterior view is equally eccentric. On top of the altar is the urn containing the famous Shroud itself.

♛ Palazzo Madama
Piazza Castello. ◯ *Tue–Sun.*
Turin's main square once contained a medieval castle which incorporated elements of the original Roman city walls. The castle was later enlarged and remodelled, and a new façade by Juvarra was added, at the request of a royal widow, in the 18th century. The Palazzo Madama – as it was subsequently renamed – now sits in the centre of the square with a stately, balustraded façade.

   The interior, with its grand staircase and first floor, both designed by Juvarra, is home to the

Museo Civico d'Arte Antica. This extensive collection contains treasures ranging in date from the Graeco-Roman era to the 19th century. The display includes the famous and mysterious *Portrait of an Unknown Man* by Antonello da Messina (15th century) among the paintings and sculptures, and reproductions of the Duc de Berry's beautiful *Book of Hours* from c.1420. Other sections contain displays of glass, jewellery, textiles and furniture. The museum will be closed for renovation until 2005.

The façade of the Palazzo Madama, designed by Filippo Juvarra in 1718–21

THE TURIN SHROUD

The most famous – and most dubious – holy relic of them all is kept in Turin's Duomo. The shroud, said to be the winding-sheet in which the body of Christ was wrapped after His crucifixion, owes its fame to the fact that the shroud bears the imprint of a crucified man with a wound in his side, and bruises from what might have been a crown of thorns.

   The shroud is one of the most famous medieval relics. Its early history is unclear, but the House of Savoy was in possession of it around 1450, and had it displayed in Guarini's chapel from 1694. The "original" shroud – which sits in a silver casket inside an iron box within a marble coffer inside the urn on the chapel altar – is not on view, though a replica is, together with a welter of scientific explanations as to the shroud's possible origins. In 1988, however, the myth of the shroud was exploded: a carbon-dating test showed that it dates back no further than the 12th century. The shroud nevertheless remains an object of religious veneration.

Detail of the mysterious 12th-century Turin Shroud

Exploring Turin

THE CITY OF TURIN IS BLESSED with numerous interesting museums, which are housed in splendid palazzi and civic buildings. The centre itself is relatively small, with broad, straight streets, often bordered with historic cafés and shops, which are pleasant places to stroll along. The city is also famous for its innovative cuisine and boasts some of the country's finest restaurants.

G Ferrari's *St Peter and a Donor* (16th century), Galleria Sabauda

Granite statue of Ramses II (13th century BC) in the Museo Egizio

🏛 Museo Egizio

Via Accademia delle Scienze 6. 📞 011 561 77 76. 🕐 8:30am–7:30pm Tue–Sun. ● *1 Jan, 25 Dec.* 🈯 🅰
W www.museoegizio.org

Turin owes its magnificent Egyptian Museum – one of the most important in the world – largely to the Piedmont-born Bernardo Drovetti, who was stationed in Egypt as French Consul General at the time of the Napoleonic Wars. It was the booty he brought back that formed the basis of this very fine collection of Egyptian arti-

facts. On the ground floor, the items on display include monumental sculptures and reconstructed temples; upstairs, there are collections of papyrus and everyday objects. Among the most impressive sculptures are a black granite Ramses II (13th century BC, or 19th dynasty), the slightly earlier Amenophis II, and the basalt figure of Gemenef-Har-Bak, a vizier from the 26th dynasty. The Sala della Nubia contains a reconstruction of the 15th-century BC **Rock Temple of Ellessiya**.

Extraordinary wall and tomb paintings are displayed on the upper floor, together with items of daily use such as the tools used for measuring, weaving, fishing and hunting. The 14th-century BC Tomb of Kha and Merit, complete with the food, tools and ornaments buried with them for the afterlife, is particularly fascinating. The papyrus collection is beautiful and of enormous interest to scholars: these documents have been vital to modern understanding of Egyptian language, customs and history – one document, the *Papiro dei Re* (Royal Papyrus), crucially lists all the pharaohs up to the 17th dynasty, with their dates.

🏛 Galleria Sabauda

Via Accademia delle Scienze 6. 📞 011 54 74 40. 🕐 8:30am–7:30pm Tue, Fri–Sun (opens 2pm Wed & 10am Thu). 🈯 🅰

The Palazzo dell'Accademia delle Scienze, the building by Guarini in which the Egyptian Museum is housed, is also home to the House of Savoy's main painting collection. The top two floors are the setting for a stunning array of works by Italian, French, Flemish and Dutch masters.

The collection was originally begun in the second half of the 15th century, and has been expanded over the centuries since. It is grouped in regional schools and contains a section on Piedmontese painting: this includes masterpieces by Gaudenzio Ferrari (c.1480–1546) and two early 16th-century paintings by Defendente Ferrari. Among works of particular interest from other Italian schools are Antonio and Piero Pollaiuolo's 15th-century *Tobias and the Archangel*

Detail from an 18th-dynasty papyrus Book of the Dead, Museo Egizio

Raphael, and the *Ritratto di Gentiluomo* (portrait of a nobleman) by Bronzino. Bellini, Mantegna, and Veronese are among other Italian artists represented.

The section on Dutch and Flemish art includes works such as Jan Van Eyck's *St Francis* (15th century) and Rembrandt's *Old Man Sleeping* (17th century), as well as portraits by Van Dyck, which include a study of Charles I's children, and his *Principe Tommaso di Savoia-Carignano* (1634). Among the French works on display are 17th-century landscape paintings by Claude Lorrain and Poussin.

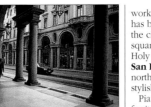

Spacious arcades on Turin's Via Roma

🜛 Palazzo Carignano

Via Accademia delle Scienze 2.
☎ 011 562 11 47. ◯ 9am–7pm Tue–Sun. ● 1 Jan, 25 Dec. 🈺 ♿

The main façade of Palazzo Carignano by Guarini

This Baroque palazzo is not only Guarini's masterpiece, it is arguably the finest building in Turin, with its magnificent brick façade and ornate rotunda. It was built in 1679 for the Carignano family – an offshoot of the main House of Savoy and ancestors of the Italian kings – but came into its own in the 19th century when the first king of Italy, Vittorio Emanuele II was born here in 1829. After Italy was unified in 1861 by a series of referenda, the former royal residence was used as the first national parliament building.

The palazzo is now home to the **Museo Nazionale del Risorgimento**, which through paintings and a collection of artifacts (housed in the rooms where history was made), tells the story of unification. It introduces Mazzini, Cavour and Garibaldi – key figures in the Risorgimento (*see pp58–9*).

🜛 Via Roma

Running through the historic centre, Turin's main street leads from Piazza Castello (north) through Piazza San Carlo to the distinctive arched façade of Stazione Porta Nuova (south). Via Roma is a magnificent concourse lined with stylish shops and shaded arcades, interrupted only by cobbled squares, crisscrossed by tramlines. A grid pattern of side streets branches off either side of Via Roma, revealing additional shopping arcades.

🜛 Piazza San Carlo

The ensemble of Baroque architecture on this square halfway along Via Roma has earned it the nickname of "Turin's drawing room". At its southern end are the twin churches of Santa Cristina and San Carlo; both were built in the 1630s, though **Santa Cristina** has a Baroque façade, crowned with statues, which was designed by Juvarra in the early 18th century.

At the centre of the square stands a 19th-century statue of Emanuele Filiberto. The

work, by Carlo Marocchetti, has become an emblem of the city. At the corners of the square, frescoes depict the Holy Shroud. The **Galleria San Federico**, in the square's northwestern corner, is a stylish shopping arcade.

Piazza San Carlo is known for its society cafés. In one such establishment, in 1786, Antonio Benedetto Carpano invented the drink known as vermouth, which is still very popular in Turin today.

🜛 Pinacoteca Giovanni e Marella Agnelli

Lingotto, Via Nizza 230.
☎ 011 006 20 08. ◯ 9am–7pm Tue–Sun. 🈺 ♿ 🅿 🖵 🍴
🌐 www.pinacotecaagnelli.it

Standing on the site of a former Fiat factory, this museum holds paintings by the likes of Modigliani, Matisse and Picasso, as well as two statues by Canova.

🌿 Parco del Valentino

Corso Massimo D'Azeglio. ◯ daily.
Borgo Medioevale ☎ 011 443 17 01. ◯ 9am–7pm Tue–Sun (to 8pm Apr–Oct). **Orto Botanico** ☎ 011 661 24 47. ◯ Apr–Sep: Sat & Sun. 🈺 ♿

This park contains the **Borgo Medioevale**, a complex of buildings resembling a medieval village and castle, which was built for an exhibition in the late 1880s. The buildings show different types of design and construction, based on traditional houses and castles that can be found scattered throughout Piedmont and in the Valle d'Aosta.

The **Orto Botanico**, beside the medieval complex, is an impressive botanical garden in a pleasant setting.

Looking south across the elegant Piazza San Carlo, "Turin's drawing room"

Turin: Symbols of the City

TURIN'S ARCHITECTURE MIRRORS the city's transition from monarchic power to industrial power. Witness the ostentation of the Baroque apartments of the Savoy royal family; and contrast them with the futuristic Mole Antonelliana, a tall structure which heralded the dawn of the modern industrial age. Much of Turin's history in the 20th century has been dominated by the motor car: Fiat made Turin its home and, despite some industrial unrest, the city's workers replied by rewarding it with success. For the curious, Turin's motor museum is worth a visit, as it maps out the history of Italian car design.

The 19th-century tower, Mole Antonelliana, dominating Turin

🎭 Mole Antonelliana
Via Montebello 20. 📞 011 81 25 16.
Museo del Cinema
📞 011 812 56 58. 🕐 9am–6:45pm Tue–Sun (to 9:45pm Sat). 🎫
🌐 www.museonazionaledelcinema.it
This building is the Turin equivalent of the Eiffel Tower in Paris: an unmissably tall landmark that serves no clear purpose except perhaps to act as a signature for the city. It looks like a glorified lightning conductor: indeed in 1954 an electric storm struck down the top 47 m (155 ft), which was later replaced. The 167-m (550-ft) Mole, by Alessandro Antonelli (1798–1888), was meant to be a synagogue, but the city finished it in 1897 and used it to house the Risorgimento museum. The Mole ("massive structure") – for a time the tallest building in the world – became a symbol of

Inside the dome of San Lorenzo

Italian unity. It houses the Cinema Museum, designed with the help of British director Peter Greenaway.

🎭 Palazzo Reale
Piazzetta Reale. 📞 011 436 14 55.
🕐 8:30am–6:30pm Tue–Sun (further areas of the palace open Sat & Sun pm).
🔴 25 Dec. 🎫 ⚑ 👶 ♿
The Palazzo Reale was the seat of the Savoy royal family from 1660 until the unification of Italy in 1861. Behind the austere façade, designed by Amedeo di Castellamonte, lie richly decorated state apartments; the ceilings were painted by Morello, Miel and Seyter in the 17th century. The many splendid furnishings, tapestries and ornaments date from the 17th to the 19th centuries; they include the elaborate Chinese Cabinet, the Alcove Room, the lavishly decorated Throne Room, and the innovative Scala delle Forbici, or Scissor Stairs, created by Juvarra in 1720. Behind the palace are extensive gardens, which extend northwards.

To the left of the main entrance is **San Lorenzo**. This fine Baroque building, begun in 1634, is by architect Guarino Guarini, its ornate interior boasting another of his extraordinary, geometric domes.

🏛 Armeria Reale
Piazza Castello 191. 📞 011 54 38 89.
🕐 daily. 🔴 1 Jan, 15 Aug, 25 Dec.
🎫 🌐 www.artito.arti.beniculturali.it
One wing of the Palazzo Reale, on the northern side of the main square, provides the splendid setting for one of the most extensive and breathtaking collections of arms and armoury in the world.

The armoury originally belonged to the House of Savoy, and was opened to the public in 1837. The fine rooms, such as the splendid Galleria Beaumont, designed by Juvarra in 1733, hold treasures ranging in date from Roman and Etruscan times to the 19th century. The collection has some particularly magnificent medieval and Renaissance items from some of the greatest armourers and gunsmiths in the world, including a pistol of Charles V. One section is devoted largely to Oriental arms and armour.

The adjoining but separate Royal Library contains a collection of drawings and manuscripts, including a self-portrait by Leonardo da Vinci.

ENVIRONS: About 3 km (2 miles) out of the city centre is the colossal hall built in the 1960s for the **Museo dell'Automobile**. Founded in 1933, it now houses over 150 veteran, vintage and classic cars. The collection includes glorious Bugattis, Maseratis, Lancias,

A lavishly decorated gallery in the 17th-century Palazzo Reale, a royal home until unification

Fiats and also a number of fine foreign cars. The first petrol-driven car made in Italy (1896) is kept here, as well as the first Fiat (1899) and the 1929 Isotta Fraschini *coupé de ville* that was used to transport Gloria Swanson in the Hollywood film *Sunset Boulevard*. Note also that a large number of the sports cars from the 1950s have the steering wheel on the right – ie British – side: this brief trend was in deference to the great British car makers such as Aston Martin.

Designs from 1949 for the Ferrari 166 MM

There is also a library and a documentation centre which are both open to the public.

⌂ Museo dell'Automobile
Corso Unità d'Italia 40. **C** *011 67 76 66.* **○** *Tue–Sun (till late Thu & Sun).* **●** *1 Jan, 25 Dec.* **⌧ &**
w *www.museoauto.org*

Stupinigi **⑭**

Piazza Principe Amedeo 7, Stupinigi. **C** *011 358 12 20.* **☐** *63 to P. Caio Mario & then 41.* **○** *10am–5pm Tue– Sun (Nov–Mar: 9:30am–4pm).* **⌧ &**

An interior view of the 18th-century Palazzina di Caccia di Stupinigi

I N 1729–30 THE ARCHITECT Filippo Juvarra (1676–1736) designed the magnificent hunting lodge of Stupinigi – known as the Palazzina di Caccia di Stupinigi – at a beautiful location 9 km (5 miles) southwest of Turin. It was created for Vittorio

Amedeo II and is one of the very finest hunting lodges, built on an impressive scale, reminiscent of the palace of Versailles in France.

The dynamic and complex plan incorporates semicircles and an octagon, with the main block consisting of a dome rising above a circular building from which wings jut out, not unlike the arms of a windmill.

The mass of the central section is lightened by balustrading topped with urns and figures, while the dome is crowned with an 18th-century bronze figure of a stag.

The huge interior includes rooms sumptuously decorated with *trompe l'oeil* paintings and frescoes on a hunting theme – the 18th-century *Triumph of Diana*, for instance, in the main *salone*. About 40 of those rooms house the interesting **Museo d'Arte e di Ammobiliamento**, a museum specializing in 17th- and 18th-century furniture and furnishings. Many of the ornate items on display in these rooms were originally kept in other former royal residences.

Outside there are extensive grounds, which feature an elegant combination of spectacular broad avenues, parkland and colourful formal parterres.

Basilica di Superga **⑮**

Strada Basilica di Superga 73, Comune di Torino. **C** *011 898 00 83.*
FS *Sassi.* **☐** *79 fr Sassi.* **○** *May–Sep: 9am–noon, 3–6pm; Oct–Apr: 10am–noon, 3–5pm.* **●** *8 Sep.*
Tombs **●** *Fri, public hols.* **Donation**.

O N A HILL to the east of Turin, reachable by car or by railway, stands the superb Baroque basilica of Superga, built by Juvarra in 1717–31. The commission came from Duke Vittorio Amedeo II, in fulfilment of a vow made to the Virgin Mary in 1706 while the French were besieging the duke and his army in Turin.

The beautiful yellow and white façade is dominated by a large portico designed like a Classical temple, with a 65 m- (213 ft-) high dome immediately beyond. It is flanked by twin bell towers on either side. The interior is magnificent, decorated in light blue and yellow, and contains numerous fine paintings and carvings.

Underneath the basilica lies the great mausoleum which houses the tombs of the kings, princes and princesses of Savoy from the 18th and 19th centuries. Turin's 1949 aircrash victims, including the city's football team, are also remembered on a plaque behind the basilica.

One of the other benefits of visiting the basilica is seeing the views over Turin.

The imposing façade of the 18th-century Baroque Basilica di Superga designed by Filippo Juvarra

The 17th-century Basilica dell'Assunta dominating Sacro Monte, Varallo

Santuario d'Oropa ⑯

Via Santuario d'Oropa 480, Comune di Biella. **C** 015 2555 1203. **FS** Biella. ⬛ from Biella. ◯ 8am–noon daily. ⬛ **Chiesa Vecchia** ◯ 2–7pm. **Chiesa Nuova** ◯ 2–6pm. **W** www.santuariodoropa.com

PERCHED ABOVE the wool town of Biella stands the tranquil church and hospice complex of Oropa, a series of three squares surrounded by pale buildings with stone-shingled roofs, cut into the forested hillside.

The sanctuary, which dates largely from the 17th and 18th centuries, was founded in the 4th century by Sant' Eusebio, Bishop of Vercelli. It was intended as a hospice for the poor, and to honour the "Black Madonna" which he had brought back from the Holy Land. The Madonna, said to be the work of St Luke himself, is the object of some of the most important pilgrimages in the region.

The statue of the Madonna is kept in the restored **Chiesa Vecchia** (Old Church), whose façade was designed by Filippo Juvarra (1676–1736). Beyond it, at the top of the complex, rises the imposing mass of the Neo-Classical **Chiesa Nuova** (New Church), which was begun in 1885 but completed only in 1960.

Behind this church, a foot-path leads to the cable car up to Monte Mucrone, from where there is good walking country-side. On a hill southwest of the complex stand 16 chapels, a dozen of which date from between 1620 and 1720. They contain frescoed scenes which depict the life of the Virgin.

Domodossola ⑰

Verbania. 🏠 20,000. **FS** ⬛ **H** Stazione entrance, Piazza Matteotti 24 (0324 24 82 65). ⬛ Sat. **W** www.prodomodossola.it

AT THE CENTRE of this pretty mountain town of Roman origin lies the **Piazza Mercato**, or market square, framed by attractive arcades and houses dating from the 15th and 16th centuries. The good-value produce at the local market attracts people even from France and Switzerland.

The Ossola valley, where the town lies, sits in an Alpine landscape of pasture and forest sliced by rivers and streams. Pretty villages north of the town include **Crodo**, with its cold-water mineral spas, and **Baceno**, where the 14th–16th-century church contains fine frescoes and wood carvings.

Further north, the Anti-gorio and Formazza valleys are planted with fig trees and vineyards. Just before La Frua, spectacular water-falls from the River Toce drop about 145 m (475 ft) when the waters are not being harnessed for power. The idyllic Valle Vigezzo, east of Domodossola, also offers breathtaking views.

Varallo ⑱

Vercelli. 🏠 7,900. **FS** ⬛ **H** Corso Roma 38 (0163 56 00 49 and 0163 545 91). ⬛ Tue.

THE SMALL TOWN and tourist resort of Varallo lies half-way up the attractive Sesia valley, and boasts a remarkable church, **Santa Maria delle Grazie**. The late 15th-century church is notable for its beautiful frescoed wall depicting the Life of Christ and *trompe l'oeil* architectural elements; the paintings are the work of Gaudenzio Ferrari (1484–1546).

A long stairway behind the church (and also a cableway) climbs up to the even more extraordinary **Sacro Monte**, a religious community built at an altitude of about 610 m (2,000 ft). This "Sacred Mount" was founded as a sanctuary of the New Jerusalem in 1486 and sponsored by the Archbishop of Milan, San Carlo Borromeo.

The Basilica dell'Assunta, with a 19th-century façade, is set in a tranquil courtyard with palm trees and a fountain; the interior is a riot of ornate Baroque architecture. Dotted around it are over 40 chapels representing the sacred sites of Jerusalem, with statues and painted figures positioned in front of frescoed backdrops painted by Gaudenzio Ferrari, Tanzio da Varallo and others.

Christ Condemned (16th century) in a chapel at Varallo's Sacro Monte

The interior of the church of San Giulio in the middle of Lake Orta

Lake Orta ⑲

Novara. FS ▭ ⏢ Orta. ℹ Via
Panoramica, Orta San Giulio (0322 90
56 14). W www.distrettolaghi.it

LAKE ORTA IS ONE of Italy's
least visited lakes – unjustly,
as it is delightfully set among
the foothills of the Alps.
    The lake's main resort is **Orta
San Giulio**, a small town with
a historic centre containing
handsome palazzi, and houses
decorated with wrought-iron
balconies. In the lakeside
Piazza Principale stands the
Palazzo della Comunità, a
frescoed building of 1582
resting on arcades. At the top
of a mound stands the 15th-
century church of **Santa Maria
Assunta** (rebuilt in the 17th
century), with a Romanesque
doorway and an interior that
is richly decorated with 17th-
century frescoes and paintings.
    Above Orta San Giulio is
the sanctuary of **Sacro Monte**,
built from 1591 to 1770 and
dedicated to St Francis of
Assisi. A winding path, offering lovely views of the lake,

climbs to the church. The path
is lined by 21 chapels, most of
them Baroque, in which frescoes and life-size figure groups
by various artists depict scenes
from the life of St Francis.
    In the middle of the lake
rises the picturesque **Isola San
Giulio**. The island was said to
have been liberated from
snakes and monsters by the
4th-century Christian preacher
Julius, from whom the island's
name derives. The basilica here
is notable for its 12th-century
black marble pulpit decorated
with wild animals and birds,
and for the 15th-century frescoes – including one attributed
to Gaudenzio Ferrari, of the
Virgin and Child Enthroned.

Novara ⑳

🚶 105,000. FS ▭ ℹ Baluardo
Quintino Sella 40 (0321 39 40 59).
🛒 Mon, Thu & Sat.
W www.turismonovara.it

**Fresco detail of a horseman (17th century)
by Morazzone in San Gaudenzio, Novara**

NOVARA HAS DISTANT origins
as the Roman city of
Nubliaria – meaning "surrounded in mist". Nowadays its
delightful arcaded streets and

squares, and historic buildings,
exude a quiet affluence. Many
of the most important buildings
stand around Piazza della
Repubblica. They include the
beautiful Renaissance courtyard
of the **Broletto** (town hall),
with its graceful 15th-century
red-brick arcades and covered
stairway. The buildings now
house a small **Museo Civico**,
comprising an archaeological
section and a picture gallery.
    Across the piazza rises the
Duomo, rebuilt by the architect Alessandro Antonelli in
around 1865 in Neo-Classical
style, with a huge central
doorway. The interior contains
dramatic Renaissance paintings
of the Vercelli school and
Flemish tapestries, as well as
the remains of an earlier
sanctuary on this site: these
include the frescoed 12th-
century chapel of San Siro and
the 15th-century cloisters. The
octagonal **Baptistry** next door
dates in part from the 5th
century and is painted
with medieval
frescoed scenes of the
terrible Apocalypse.
    A few streets away
stands the church of
San Gaudenzio. It
is strikingly crowned
by an elongated four-
tiered dome and spire,
designed by Antonelli,
and reminiscent of his
Mole Antonelliana in
Turin *(see p216)*. At the
top of the spire, which
is 121 m (400 ft) high,
is a statue of San
Gaudenzio himself.
    Inside, the late 16th-
century church contains a fine
collection of Renaissance and
Baroque paintings by artists
from Piedmont: these include
a notable 17th-century battle
scene by Tanzio da Varallo,
a 16th-century altarpiece by
Gaudenzio Ferrari, and a fresco
painting by Pier Francesco
Morazzone (c.1572–1626).

🏛 **Museo Civico**
Via Fratelli Rosselli 20. 📞 0321 62 30
21. 🕐 Apr–Oct: 10am–1pm, 4–7pm;
Nov–Mar: 9am–noon, 3–6pm Tue–Sun.
⬤ public hols. 🌐 ♿ W www.
comune.novara.it
🔒 **Baptistry**
Piazza della Repubblica. 📞 0321 66 16
71. 🕐 ask at the Curia Arcivescovile.

View across Lake Orta to the Isola San Giulio

Vercelli ㉑

🏠 *50,000.* 🚆 ⬛ ℹ️ *Viale Garibaldi 90 (0161 25 78 88).*
🗓️ *Tue & Fri.*

VERCELLI IS THE RICE capital of Europe, set in a vast plain of paddy fields that give rise to millions of plates of risotto each year. The paddies provide a sight of shimmering sheets of water stretching far into the distance. Vercelli itself also developed its own school of painting in the 16th century, and has one major architectural treasure, the 13th-century **Basilica di Sant'Andrea**.

The Basilica, standing just across from the railway station, is famous as the first example of Italian architecture to be influenced by the Gothic style of northern France – note the beautiful vaulted nave and the flying buttresses, typical Gothic elements. Overall, however, the Basilica remains a stunning achievement in Romanesque architecture, built from 1219 to 1227 as part of an abbey for the papal legate Cardinal Guala Bicheri. The façade, curiously, changes colour halfway up, the blue-grey of the lower part turning to red and white in the twin towers; these are linked by a double arcade. A carving attributed to Antelami (12th century) adorns the central lunette.

The three-aisled interior is gently illuminated through rose windows. The muted decoration is largely focused on the vaulting, which is supported by tall, slender shafts. Off the north side is the simple 13th-century cloister, beautifully framed by arcades rising from clustered columns.

Vercelli's other important historic buildings are not far away, including the imposing 16th-century **Duomo**, the **Ospedale Maggiore** (13th century), and the church of **San Cristoforo**, with frescoes and a particularly fine Madonna (both c.1529) painted by Gaudenzio Ferrari.

The **Museo Civico Borgogna** is the best place to admire the masterpieces of the Vercelli school. The main shopping street, Corso Libertà, has a handful of attractive 15th-century houses and courtyards.

🏛️ **Museo Civico Borgogna**
Via Antonio Borgogna 8. 📞 *016125 27 76.* 🕐 *Tue–Fri pm, Sat & Sun am.* ⬛ *1 Jan,15 Aug, 1 Nov, 25 Dec.* 🚫
📷 🌐 *www.museoborgogna.it*

The 13th-century cloisters of the Basilica di Sant'Andrea in Vercelli

Asti ㉒

🏠 *74,000.* 🚆 ⬛ ℹ️ *Piazza Alfieri 29 (0141 53 03 57).* 🗓️ *Wed & Sat.*
🌐 *www.terredasti.it*

MOST OFTEN ASSOCIATED only with sweet *spumante* (sparkling) wine, Asti is in fact at the centre of Italy's most

Detail of the carving on the 15th-century porch at the entrance to the Duomo in Asti

prestigious wine region *(see pp176–7)* and also a tranquil and noble city of medieval towers, elegant churches and warm red roofs.

Just north of the main railway station lies the Piazza del Campo del Palio, the largest square in Asti and formerly the site of its annual horse race, now in Piazza Alfieri. The race, held towards the end of September to coincide with the local wine fair, rivals the Palio in Siena *(see p331)* for outrageous horsemanship and medieval pageantry.

Beyond this square lies the triangular-shaped **Piazza Alfieri**. A statue here commemorates the local poet and dramatist Vittorio Alfieri (1749–1803), in whose honour both this square and the main street were renamed.

Corso Alfieri runs the entire length of the old city centre. At its eastern end stands the 15th-century church of **San Pietro in Consavia**, with its terracotta decoration, 17th-century frescoes, and attractive cloister. Beside it is the circular Romanesque **baptistry** which dates from the 10th–12th centuries; it was once the church of the knights of the Order of St John of Jerusalem, who had their headquarters here.

West of Piazza Alfieri is the **Collegiata di San Secondo** (13th–15th century), named after Asti's patron saint, which houses a Renaissance polyptych by Gandolfino d'Asti and 15th-century frescoes. The area around the western section of Corso Alfieri contains a few of the medieval towers for which the town was once famous; they include the Torre dei Comentini, the very elegant

The watery expanses of the rice fields around Vercelli

Torre Troyana and, at the far end, the Torre Ropa. This was built on the ruins of a tower in which San Secondo, a Roman soldier, was held. The nearby 14th-century Gothic **Duomo** has a 15th-century porch and, inside, 18th-century frescoes, and two 12th- to 13th-century carvings on the west corner of the transept.

Cuneo

🚶 56,000. 🚉 ℹ️ *Via Roma 28 (0171 69 32 58).* 🛒 *Tue.*
🌐 www.cuneotourism.com

CUNEO DERIVES ITS NAME from *cumeo*, meaning wedge-shaped, which describes the sliver of land that the town occupies at the confluence of two rivers, the Gesso and the Stura di Demonte. In early November the town hosts the regional cheese fair, with unusual local cheese varieties.

The town centres on a large square, **Piazza Galimberti**, with its old arcades, where the traders come to hawk their wares every Tuesday. Much of the town was rebuilt in the 18th and 19th centuries, providing Cuneo with wide, tree-lined boulevards, though the impressive viaduct that takes the railway line into town dates from the 1930s. The deconsecrated 13th-century church of **San Francesco** has a fine 15th-century portal.

Market day in the enormous Piazza Galimberti at the centre of Cuneo

The Castello di Casotto in the hills above the resort of Garessio

The 18th-century church of **Santa Croce** has a concave façade by Francesco Gallo.

Cuneo is a good base for exploring the pretty local valleys, such as the Valle Stura, where rare flowers grow.

Bossea Caves

Località Bossea, Comune Frabosa Soprana. ☎️ *0174 34 92 40.*
🚉 *Mondovì.* 🚌 *from Mondovì.*
🕐 *daily for guided tours only.*
🌐 www.grottadibossea.it

SOME 25 KM (16 miles) south of Mondovì, near the end of a scenic route which follows the valley of the Torrente Corsaglia up into the Maritime Alps, are the caves of Bossea, some of the finest in Italy. The series of caves contains remarkable stalactite columns and shapes that have formed over many thousands of years. Guided tours lead through different chambers – some of them surprisingly vast – following the underground rivers and lakes. The skeleton of a pre-historic bear, *Ursus spelaeus*, which was discovered here, is also on display.

Bring a sweater – the temperature rarely rises above 9° C (50° F).

Garessio

Cuneo. 🚶 4,000. 🚉 ℹ️ *Piazza Carrara 137 (0174 811 22).* 🛒 *Fri.*
🌐 www.garessio.net

ONE OF THE PRETTIER resorts of the Maritime Alps, Garessio is no more than a sprinkling of houses spread out over the hills, surrounded by woods of chestnut trees. It is also a popular spa.

According to legend, the waters here have miraculous powers: in about AD 980 an octogenarian nobleman found instant relief from his kidney and circulatory problems by drinking the mineral-rich water. Since then, the waters have been drunk for their remedial properties – linked in particular with the relief of diuretic and digestive problems – and for their refreshing taste.

ENVIRONS: About 10 km (4 miles) west of Garessio stands the **Castello di Casotto**, the dramatically sited summer palace used by the House of Savoy. The royal family used to come here to enjoy the local mineral water, the attractive scenery and the exceptionally pure air of the hills.

The town of **Ormea**, 12 km (7 miles) southwest, is interesting for its ruined 11th-century castle, its church with late 14th-century Gothic frescoes, and its attractive houses.

♣ **Castello di Casotto**
Garessio. ☎️ *0174 35 11 31.*
🕐 *9am–noon, 2:30–6pm daily.*

LIGURIA

L IGURIA IS A LONG, THIN COASTAL STRIP *nestling at the foot of vine-covered mountains. Here pastel-coloured houses bask in the Mediterranean sun, while their gardens, flourishing in the mild climate, are a riot of colourful plants. In contrast with resorts like Portofino and even San Remo, the bustling city of Genoa, for centuries a trading port of immense power, is the only major population centre.*

Genoa has a long history as a seafaring power, achieving greatness first as a trading post with ancient Greece and Phoenicia, and later, as the capital of a small commercial empire that at one stage eclipsed even Venice. The great sea admiral Andrea Doria came from Genoa, as did the 15th-century explorer of the Americas, Christopher Columbus.

Genoa's rise began in the 12th century, when it succeeded in beating the Saracen pirates that plagued the Ligurian coast. Thereafter, the maritime republic prospered, profiting from the Crusades to set up trading posts in the Middle East and marshalling its naval might to humble its rivals. The golden age lasted from the 16th to the mid-17th century, and included the glorious reign of Andrea Doria who enriched the city by financing the wars of Genoa's European allies through the offices of the city's bank. Factionalism among the ruling aristocracy, however, and foreign conquest, by the French in 1668 and the Austrians in 1734, led to the region's decline. It was only in the early 19th century, with unification fervour spreading thanks to native son Giuseppe Mazzini and the revolutionary Garibaldi, that Liguria ever recaptured a glimpse of its former prominence. Today, sheltered by the steep slopes that rise from the sea, faded, elegant mansions lie along the coast, particularly in San Remo, where aristocrats came to spend the winter at the end of the 19th century.

Green shutters and rich ochre walls characterize the houses of Portofino

◁ Rugged cliffs tumble into the sea along Liguria's Riviera Levante

Exploring Liguria

LIGURIA DIVIDES NEATLY into two parts. The western coastline, known as the Riviera Ponente, is a thin strip of coastal plain stretching across to the French border, while the eastern coastline, or Riviera Levante, is more rugged and picturesque, descending directly into the sea. Between the two lengths of coast lies the region's capital and biggest port, Genoa (Genova). The faded elegance of the tranquil coastal villages contrasts with this cramped and busy port which snakes along the coast, hemmed in between the sea and the mountains rising steeply behind it.

Stag motif of the city of Cervo, above the cathedral doors

Genoese street market selling fruit and vegetables

KEY

▬▬ Motorway

▬▬ Major road

▭▭ Minor road

▬▬ Scenic route

〰 River

⁎ Viewpoint

0 kilometres   25

0 miles   10

Nice
Monaco

Alessandr

DEGO   SASSELLO   ARE

Cuneo   ALBISO

SAVONA

CALIZZANO

MONTE GALERO

GROTTE DI TOIRANO ⑧

MONTE MONEGA   ALBENGA ⑦

ALPI MARITTIME   ALASSIO

MONTE PIETRAVECCHIA   TRIORA

DOLCEACQUA ③   BUSSANA VECCHIA ⑤   CERVO ⑥

BALZI ROSSI ①   IMPERIA

② ①   SAN REMO ④

VILLA HANBURY

RIVIERA DI PONENTE

The smart resort of San Remo on the Riviera Ponente, west of Genoa

SEE ALSO

• **Where to Stay** pp554–5

• **Where to Eat** pp589–90

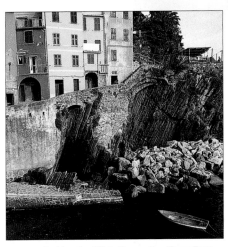

Houses wedged into the cliffs in Riomaggiore, Cinque Terre

GETTING AROUND

If you keep to the coast, transport in Liguria is straightforward. The A10–E80 motorway, becoming the A12–E80 at Genoa, and a mainline railway hug the shore from the French border to Tuscany. The main stations along the route are at Ventimiglia, San Remo, Imperia, Savona, Genoa and La Spezia. There are good road and rail links between Genoa and Milan and Turin. Access to inland Liguria is harder because of the mountains. Bus services link many of the coastal towns with the prettiest hill villages. You can explore some of the countryside by car by following the smaller routes, such as the S28 from Imperia towards Garessio in Piedmont, the S334 from Albisola or the S456 from Voltri towards Milan.

The spectacular gardens of the Villa Hanbury near Ventimiglia

Balzi Rossi ❶

Imperia. 🚉 *Ventimiglia & Mentone.*
🚌 *from Ventimiglia to Ponte San Luigi & then a ten-minute walk.*

A N UNASSUMING promontory is the setting for some of the most important caves in northern Italy. Guided tours lead through the traces of the cave-dwelling civilization of pre-Iron Age Liguria. The caves contain excavated burial sites where the dead were adorned with sea-shells. The **Museo Nazionale dei Balzi Rossi** contains tools, weapons and stone-etched female figures dating from 100,000 years ago. There is also a reproduction of an etching of a horse found in one of the caves.

🏛 **Museo Nazionale dei Balzi Rossi**
Via Balzi Rossi 9. 📞 *0184 381 13.*
🕐 *8:30am–7:30pm Tue–Sun.*
🔴 *1 Jan, 1 May, 25 Dec.* 🐾

Villa Hanbury ❷

Corso Monte Carlo 43, Località La Mortola. 📞 *0184 22 95 07.* 🚉
Ventimiglia. 🚌 *from Ventimiglia.*
🕐 *9:30am–4pm (to 5pm Mar–mid-Jun & 6pm mid-Jun–Sep) daily.* 🐾
🌐 *www.cooperativa-omnia.com*

I N 1867 THE ENGLISH botanist Sir Thomas Hanbury and his brother bought this villa on the Mortola promontory. They took full advantage of the exceptionally mild and sunny Ligurian climate to establish a garden of exotic plants along the sloping pathways of the enchanting seaside villa.

The collection, gathered by Hanbury on trips to Africa and Asia, has grown to number more than 3,000 varieties of tropical flora including rubber trees, palms and wild cacti.

The garden is now run by the state and is one of the most impressive botanical gardens in Italy. Even winter sees a wealth of colour and vegetation here.

Dolceacqua ❸

Imperia. 🏘 *1,800.* 🚉 🚌 ℹ *Via Barberis Colomba 3 (0184 20 66 66).*
🔵 *Thu.* 🌐 *www.dolceacqua.it*

T HIS PRETTY wine-producing village, 8 km (5 miles) north of Ventimiglia, is built on either side of the churning River Nervia, its two halves joined by an arching 33-m (108-ft) medieval stone bridge. The highlight is the ruined **castle** (12th–15th century) inhabited for a while in the 16th century by the powerful Doria family from Genoa. The

two square towers at the front dominate the village. The terraced vineyards in the surrounding hills produce bunches of grapes for general consumption as well as for a robust red wine known as Rossese or vino di Dolceacqua.

San Remo ❹

Imperia. 🏘 *60,000.* 🚉 🚌 ℹ
Largo Nuvoloni 1 (0184 590 59). 🔵
Tue & Sat. 🌐 *www.rivieradeifiori.org*

The Casinò Municipale in San Remo, completed in 1906

S AN REMO IS a pleasant resort of faded elegance. The composer Tchaikovsky, Alfred Nobel (the father of modern explosives) and the nonsense poet Edward Lear all stayed in the stuccoed mansions of the palm-lined seafront avenue, the Corso Imperatrice. The focus of the town, then as now, is the Casino. A little further down the Corso stands the ornate Russian Orthodox church of San Borilio.

The old town, La Pigna (fir cone), is a huddle of narrow lanes with medieval houses and pastel-coloured shutters. A coach service goes from San Remo to San Romolo, a small village 786 metres (2,579 ft) above sea level that offers beautiful views of the area.

An enchanting flower market is held on Corso Garibaldi (6–8am, Jun–Oct), while the Italian Song Festival takes place here in February.

Bussana Vecchia ❺

Imperia. Off San Remo–Arma di Taggià road.

B USSANA VECCHIA is a marvel-lously atmospheric ghost town. In February 1887 an earthquake shook the village,

The village of Dolceacqua with its medieval bridge and ruined castle

reducing its Baroque church and surrounding houses to ruins. (One survivor, Giovanni Torre del Merlo, went on to invent the ice-cream cone.)

The town was rebuilt closer to the sea and since then the original village has been taken over by artists, who have restored some interiors, providing a venue for summer concerts and exhibitions.

Cervo ❻

Imperia. 🦶 *1,200.* FS 🚌
ℹ *Piazza Santa Caterina 2 (0183 40 81 97).* 🚃 *Thu.*

CERVO IS THE PRETTIEST of the many old seafront villages just east of Imperia, with a narrow complex of streets and houses rising dramatically up from the shingle beach. At the top of the village stands the concave Baroque façade of **San Giovanni Battista**. In front of the church, in July and August, they hold charming chamber orchestra performances. The church is also known as the *"dei corallini"*, after the coral fishing which once brought prosperity for the local people. Now Cervo is an unassuming but characteristic Ligurian holiday resort, with unspoilt hotels near the beach.

San Giovanni Battista at Cervo

Spectacular rock formations in the grottoes of Toirano

Albenga ❼

Savona. 🦶 *21,000.* FS 🚌 ℹ *Viale Martiri della Libertà 1 (0182 55 84 44).* 🚃 *Wed.* Ⓦ *www.inforiviera.it*

UNTIL THE Middle Ages, the Roman port of Albium Ingaunum played an important maritime role.

The 5th-century Baptistry at Albenga

The sea, however, gradually moved further out, leaving the town, now called Albenga, stranded on the Centa River. Most striking now is its Romanesque brick architecture, in particular the three 13th-century towers clustered around the cathedral of **San Michele**. The cathedral's interior was restored to its medieval form in the late 1960s. To the south is an intriguing 5th-century **Baptistry** with a ten-sided exterior and octagonal interior. Inside, the original 5th-century blue and white mosaics of doves represent the 12 apostles. To the north of the cathedral is the small Piazza dei Leoni, named after its three stone lions imported from Rome.

In a 14th-century palace on Piazza San Michele is the **Museo Navale Romano** founded in 1950 following the salvage of a Roman ship that had sunk offshore around 100–90 BC. The museum contains ancient amphorae as well as exhibits salvaged from more recent shipwrecks.

🏛 **Baptistry**
Piazza San Michele. 🔔 *0182 512 15.* ◑ *Tue–Sun.* ● *1 Jan, Easter, 25 Dec.* 📷

🏛 **Museo Navale Romano**
Piazza San Michele 12. 🔔 *0182 512 15.* ◑ *Tue–Sun.* ● *1 Jan, Easter, 25 Dec.* 📷

Grotte di Toirano ❽

Piazzale delle Grotte, Toirano. 🔔 *0182 980 62.* 🚌 *from Albenga to Borghetto Santo Spirito.* FS *to Borghetto Santo Spirito or Loano then bus.* ◑ *9:30am– noon, 2–5pm daily.* ● *mid-Dec–25 Dec.* 📷 Ⓦ *www.toiranogrotte.it*

BENEATH the delightful medieval hill-town of Toirano lies a series of extra-ordinary caves containing relics of Paleolithic life dating from 100,000 BC.

Guided tours through the **Grotta della Basura** (Witch's Cave) reveal remarkable prehistoric human and animal footprints, and a collection of ancient bear bones and teeth in the "bear cemetery".

The **Grotta di Santa Lucia**, which can also be visited by guided tour, reveals the full beauty of the luminous yellow and grey stalactites and stalag-mites that have formed here over thousands of years.

The **Museo Preistorico della Val Varatella** at the entrance to the Grotta della Basura has a small display of finds from the caves, as well as a model of a prehistoric bear.

🏛 **Museo Preistorico della Val Varatella**
Piazzale delle Grotte. 🔔 *0182 980 62.* ◑ *for restoration.*

Street-by-Street: Genoa ❾

THERE IS SOMETHING refreshingly rough-edged about Genoa (Genova in Italian), Italy's most important commercial port. In contrast to the genteel resorts along the neighbouring coast, the narrow streets of the old town are the haunts of sailors and streetwalkers.

With its natural harbour and the mountains to protect it, Genoa rose to prominence as a sea-based power. During the 16th century Andrea Doria cemented Genoa's importance, and also proved an astute patron of the arts.

\ **Palazzo Bianco**

Piazza San Matteo
The houses and church of San Matteo were built by the Doria family in 1278. Palazzo Quartara has a bas relief of St George above the doorway.

PIAZZA CAMPETTO

VIA DI SCURRERIA

PIAZZA SAN MATTEO

SALITA SAN MA

VIA ARCHIVESCOVATO

← **The port and Palazzo Reale**

San Lorenzo
The black and white striped Gothic façade of the Duomo dates from the early 13th century.

VIA SAN LORENZO

PIAZZA MATTEOTTI

Palazzo Ducale
Once the seat of the doges of Genoa, this elegant building with its two fine 16th-century courtyards and arcades now contains a major arts and cultural centre.

SALITA POLLAIUOLI

PIAZ ERBE

San Donato has a splendid 12th-century octagonal bell tower.

VICO TRE RE MAGI

Sant'Agostino
The 13th-century church and convent were bombed during World War II, but the bell tower remains. The cloisters now house sculpture like this fragment from the tomb of Margaret of Brabant by Pisano (1312).

KEY

– – – Suggested route

0 metres   100

0 yards   100

Church of Gesù

This Baroque church, built between 1589 and 1606, is also known as the church of Santi Ambrogio e Andrea.

VISITORS' CHECKLIST

640,000. ✈ Cristoforo Colombo 6 km (4 miles) W.
FS Stazione Principe, Piazza Acquaverde. ⚓ Stazione Marittima, Ponte dei Mille.
ℹ Area Porto Antico (010 253 06 71); Stazione Principe (010 246 26 33). 🗓 Mon, Wed & Thu.
🎉 24 Jun: San Giovanni Battista; Jul: Ballet Festival; Oct: Fiera Nautica. 🌐 www.apt.genova.it

Piazza De Ferrari is the site of the Neo-Classical Banco di Roma and the Accademia, as well as the restored Teatro Carlo Felice.

The bronze fountain in Piazza De Ferrari was constructed in 1936.

Porta Soprana
The eastern gateway to the city has curved outer walls and stands close to the site of Christopher Columbus's house.

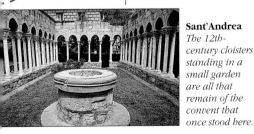

Sant'Andrea
The 12th-century cloisters standing in a small garden are all that remain of the convent that once stood here.

19th-century lion guarding the steps leading to the Duomo

🔒 San Lorenzo (Duomo)

Piazza San Lorenzo. 📞 010 26 57 86.
🕐 daily. **Museo del Tesoro**
📞 010 247 18 31. 🕐 9–11:30am, 3–5:30pm Mon–Sat. 📷

The Duomo, with its black and white striped exterior, blends many architectural styles, from the 12th-century Romanesque side portal of San Giovanni to the Baroque touches of some of its side chapels. The three portals at the west end are in French Gothic style.

The most sumptuous of the chapels is dedicated to St John the Baptist, patron saint of the city; it includes a 13th-century sarcophagus that once held the venerated saint's relics.

Steps lead down from the sacristy to the **Museo del Tesoro di San Lorenzo**. It houses such treasures as the Roman green glass dish said to have been used at the Last Supper, and a blue chalcedony plate on which the head of John the Baptist was allegedly served up to Salome.

🚢 The Port

Aquarium *Ponte Spinola.* 📞 010 234 51. 🕐 9:30am–7:30pm Mon–Wed, Fri (to 10:30pm Thu & 8:30pm Sat–Sun) (Jul–Aug: to 11pm daily). 📷 🔲 🍴
🌐 www.acquariodigenova.it

The port is the heart of Genoa and the origin of its wealth and power as a seafaring city state in the 11th and 12th centuries. It is a workaday place, ringed by busy roads and 1960s wharves and office buildings.

Among the vestiges of its medieval glory is the **Lanterna** lighthouse (restored in 1543) near the Stazione Marittima. In the old days fires would be lit at the top of the Lanterna to guide ships into port. Today, regeneration of the port is in part due to the Renzo Piano-designed conference centre (*see p179*) and the **Aquarium**, one of the largest in Europe and an ideal place to sample the richness of marine life.

Exploring Genoa

VISITORS ARE WELL REWARDED when they explore Genoa – a city proud of its history and legends. The palaces of the Via Balbi and Via Garibaldi, and the paintings and sculptures dotted around the city in churches and museums, are among the finest in northwestern Italy. The environs, too, provide scenic and relaxing locations for excursions along the coast or in the steep hills behind.

The courtyard of the University on Via Balbi

⚑ Sant'Agostino
Piazza Sarzano 35. **(** 010 251 12 63. ☐ on request only.
Museo di Architettura e Scultura Ligure ☐ 9am–7pm Tue–Fri, 10am–7pm Sat–Sun. ● public hols. 🎫 ♿

The Gothic church of Sant'Agostino was begun in 1260, but bombed to pieces in World War II. It is now deconsecrated and all that remains of the original building is the fine Gothic bell tower, decorated with coloured tiles. The monastery, of which the church of Sant'Agostino was

once a part, was also bombed. What remained were two ruined cloisters – one of which forms the only triangular building in Genoa. The cloisters have recently been reconstructed and converted into the **Museo di Architettura e Scultura Ligure**. It contains the city's collection of architectural pieces and fragments of sculpture, as well as frescoes – all salvaged from Genoa's other destroyed churches. The finest piece is a magnificent fragment from the tomb of Margaret of Brabant. Margaret, who died in 1311, was the wife of Emperor Henry VII who invaded Italy in 1310. Carved by Giovanni Pisano around 1313, the sculptures from her tomb were restored and repositioned in 1987. The figures, whose garments are arranged in simple folds, seem to be helping Margaret to lay down to rest.

🏛 Palazzo Reale
Via Balbi 10. **(** 010 271 01. ☐ Tue–Sun (Tue & Wed am only). ● 1 Jan, 25 Apr, 1 May, 25 Dec. 🎫 ♿

This austere-looking residence, used by the Kings of Savoy from the 17th century onwards, has a highly ornate Rococo interior – notably its ballroom and its Hall of Mirrors. Among the paintings are works by Parodi and Carlone and a *Crucifixion* by Van Dyck. The lovely garden, which slopes down towards the old port, includes an intriguing cobblestone mosaic around the central fountain, depicting houses and animals.

Opposite the palace is the old **University** (1634) designed by the architect Bartolomeo Bianco, as was much of Via Balbi. The large building brilliantly overcomes Genoa's hilly topography, and is constructed on four levels.

🏛 Palazzo Bianco
Via Garibaldi 11. **(** 010 557 22 03. ☐ 9am–7pm Tue–Fri, (from 10am Sat–Sun). 🎫 **Palazzo Rosso**
(010 247 63 51. ☐ 9am–7pm Tue–Fri, (from 10am Sat–Sun). 🎫

The Palazzo Bianco is situated on Genoa's most beautiful street, **Via Garibaldi**, where there are numerous fine 16th-century mansions and palazzi. The Palazzo Bianco contains the city's prime collection of paintings, including the works of many Genoese artists such as Luca Cambiaso, Bernardo Strozzi, Domenico Piola and Giovanni Benedetto

---

CHRISTOPHER COLUMBUS IN GENOA

A portrait of Columbus, Villa Doria in Pegli

The name of Christopher Columbus, the explorer of the New World, is in evidence all over Genoa. His statue greets you as soon as you emerge in Piazza Acquaverde from Porta Principe railway station; various public buildings bear his name; even the airport is called Aeroporto Cristoforo Colombo. In the 17th-century Palazzo Belimbau, built on top of the old city walls, is a series of frescoes by the Genoese artist Tavarone celebrating the explorer's life and you can see three of his letters in the Sala del Sindaco in Palazzo Tursi (the city hall) on Via Garibaldi. It is not certain whether Columbus (c.1451– 1506) was born in Genoa, in Savona 15 km (9 miles) to the west or outside Italy altogether. However, city registers mention his father, a weaver, and different family homes within the city. The small ivy-clad house next to the Porta Soprana may have been Columbus's childhood home, where he first discovered his passion for the sea.

The house where Columbus may have lived

The romantic gardens at Villa Durazzo-Pallavicini in Pegli

Castiglione. Better-known artists include Filippino Lippi (a lovely *Madonna with Saints*), Van Dyck, Veronese and Rubens. Across the street in the **Palazzo Rosso** are more paintings, including works by Dürer and Caravaggio, as well as ceramics and furniture. Upstairs in the *piano nobile* the rooms are adorned with 17th-century frescoes by Genoese artists such as de Ferrari and Piola.

⚰ Staglieno Cemetery
Piazzale Resasco, Staglieno. ☎ 010 87 01 84. ◯ daily. ● public hols. ♿

Fine tomb architecture from the huge Staglieno Cemetery

This grandiose cemetery, just over the hills northeast of Genoa along the Bisagno River, is so big (160 ha, 395 acres) that it has its own internal bus system. Founded in 1844, its tombs and monuments make up an eerie city of miniature cathedrals, Egyptian temples and Art Nouveau palaces. Its most famous resident is Giuseppe Mazzini, the Genoese revolutionary who died not far from Pisa in 1872.

ENVIRONS: Until World War II, **Pegli**, 6 km (4 miles) west of the city centre, was a popular weekend retreat for rich Genoese. Now it forms part of the city, but maintains an air of tranquillity thanks to its parks and two villas, the 19th-century **Villa Durazzo-Pallavicini** and the 16th-century **Villa Doria**. The latter houses a naval history museum celebrating Genoa's glorious past: you can see compasses, astrolabes, globes, model ships and a portrait of Columbus, ascribed to Ghirlandaio, probably dating from 1525. An archaeological museum in the Villa Durazzo-Pallavicini relates the pre-Roman history of the Ligurian coast. The villa's garden is landscaped with romantic grottoes, pavilions and fountains.

Nervi, 8 km (5 miles) to the east of the city, is another former resort town, famous for its seafront promenade, the **Passeggiata Anita Garibaldi** (named after Garibaldi's wife). The walk follows a route that has been cut into the rock face, giving panoramic views of the coast. The lush **Parco Municipale** is another feature of Nervi. It once formed the grounds of two aristocratic

villas – the Villa Serra and the Villa Gropallo. The former, on Via Capolungo, now houses the **Galleria d'Arte Moderna** featuring modern Italian painting. The **Villa Luxoro** on Via Aurelia is notable for its collection of clocks, fabrics, furniture and lace. The area is also famous as Garibaldi's departure point when he set off for Sicily with his *Mille* (the famous "Thousand" men) to bring about the unification of Italy. A large monument at Quarto dei Mille, about 3 km (2 miles) back towards the city, marks the place where the volunteers met in May 1860 to follow the intrepid revolutionary (*see pp58–9*). **Villa Grimaldi** houses a permanent sculpture and art exhibition showing late 18th- and early 19-century works by Fattori, Boldi and Messina.

🏛 Galleria d'Arte Moderna
Villa Serra, Via Capolungo 3, Nervi.
☎ 010 372 60 25. ◯ Tue–Sun. ♿

🏛 Villa Doria
Piazza Bonavino 7, Pegli. ☎ 010 696 98 85. ◯ Tue–Sat (am only). ● public hols. ♿ ♿

🏛 Villa Durazzo-Pallavicini
Via Pallavicini 11, Pegli. ☎ 010 66 68 64. ◯ 9am–7pm (Nov–Feb: 10am–5pm) Tue–Sun. ● public hols. ♿ ♿

🏛 Villa Grimaldi
Via Capolungo 9, Nervi.
☎ 010 32 23 96. ◯ daily.

🏛 Villa Luxoro
Via Mafalda di Savoia 3, Nervi.
☎ 010 32 26 73. ◯ Tue–Sat am. ● public hols. ♿

Pini (c.1920) by Rubaldo Merello in the Galleria d'Arte Moderna at Nervi

Pastel-coloured houses near the pebbly beach at Camogli

Camogli ⑩

Genova. 🏛 6,500. 🚉 🚌 ⛴
ℹ Via XX Settembre 33 (0185 77
10 66). ⛴ Wed. 🅆 www.camogli.it

Built on a pine-wooded
slope, Camogli is a fishing
village where sea-shells
adorn the pastel-painted
house walls, and the smell
of frying fish wafts out from
the small restaurants into
the streets. Near the pebble
beach and fishing port is
the medieval Castello della
Dragonara.

Camogli celebrates its
famous festival of the
Blessing of the Fish on the
second Sunday of May when
sardines are fried in a huge
pan 4 m (13 ft) in diameter.
The fish is distributed free
to all-comers.

Portofino Peninsula ⑪

Genova. 🚌 ⛴ Portofino.
ℹ Via Roma 35 (0185 26 90 24).
🅆 www.portofinobayarea.com

Portofino is the most
exclusive harbour and
resort town in Italy, crammed
with the yachts of the
wealthy. You can reach
Portofino by road (cars
are not allowed into the
village), or boat, from the
resort of Santa Margherita
Ligure. Above the town are

the church of **San Giorgio**,
containing relics said to be
of the dragon-slayer, and
a castle.

On the other side of the
peninsula, which you have
to reach on foot (a two-hour
walk) or by boat,
is the **Abbazia di
San Fruttuoso**,
named after a
3rd-century saint
whose followers
were ship-
wrecked here
and, according
to legend,
protected by
three lions. The
white abbey
buildings, set
among pines and olive trees,
date mostly from the 11th
century, although the imposing
Torre dei Doria was added
500 years later. You can take
a boat to try to locate the
Cristo degli Abissi, a bronze
statue of Christ that sits on the

sea bed near San Fruttuoso,
protecting sailors. Further
west along the coast is Punta
Chiappa, a rocky promontory
famous for the changing
colours of the surrounding sea.

🔒 **Abbazia di San Fruttuoso**
San Fruttuoso. 📞 0185 77 27 03.
🕐 Jun–Sep: 10am–6pm daily; Oct,
Mar–May: 10am–4pm Tue–Sun; Dec–
Feb: 10am–4pm Sat–Sun. ⬤ Nov. 🈲

Rapallo ⑫

Genova. 🏛 30,000. 🚉 🚌 ⛴ ℹ
Lungomare Vittorio Veneto 7 (0185 23
03 46). ⛴ Thu. **Cable car** 📞 0185
27 34 44. 🅆 www.apttigullio.liguria.it

Historians know Rapallo as
the place where two post-
World War I treaties were
signed, while film buffs might
recognize it from the 1954
movie *The Barefoot Contessa*,
which was shot here. Rapallo
was also a haven for writers
such as DH Lawrence and Ezra
Pound. Its villas still have a
patrician feel to
them, as do the
riding stables, golf
course and tennis
courts. The palm-
lined esplanade
ends in a small
16th-century
castle, in which
art exhibitions are
occasionally held.
A cable car from
the centre of the
village goes up
to the 16th-century **Santuario
di Montallegro**, which houses
a Byzantine icon said to
possess miraculous powers.

**The 16th-century castle
jutting into Rapallo harbour**

🔒 **Santuario di Montallegro**
Montallegro. 📞 0185 23 90 00.
🕐 9am–12:30pm, 3–5:30pm daily.

Large yachts moored in Portofino's famous harbour

The dramatic coastline near Corniglia in the Cinque Terre

Cinque Terre ⑬

La Spezia. **FS** *to all towns.* **⛴** *Monterosso, Vernazza.* **ℹ** *Via del Molo, Monterosso (0187 81 70 59) (summer only); Via del Santuario 83, Riomaggiore (0187 92 06 33).* **W** *www.parconazionalecinqueterre.it*

THE CINQUE TERRE is a stretch of rocky coastline on the Riviera di Levante that extends from Monterosso al Mare to Riomaggiore at its southeastern tip. The name refers to five self-contained villages that seem to dramatically cling to the very edge of vertiginous cliffs: Monterosso al Mare, Vernazza, Corniglia, Manarola and Riomaggiore. The villages were once only accessible by sea and today there is still no road that links them all. An ancient footpath known as the Sentiero Azzurro follows the coast, joining the villages and offering wonderful views of the distinctive green terraced vineyards that produce the local dry white Cinque Terre wines.

These days the five villages suffer from some depopulation. The largest, **Monterosso al Mare**, on the northwestern edge of the Cinque Terre, overlooks a wide bay with its own sandy beach. **Vernazza**, further down the coast, has streets linked by steep steps or *arpaie*. **Corniglia**, perched at the pinnacle of rocky terraces, seems untouched by the passage of time, as does **Manarola**, which is linked by the famous Via dell'Amore, or Lovers' Lane, to **Riomaggiore**, a 15-minute walk away.

The best way to visit the villages is by boat (from La Spezia, Lerici or Porto Venere) or by train (La Spezia–Genoa railway line).

Portovenere ⑭

La Spezia. **👥** *4,600.* **🚌** **⛴**
ℹ *Piazza Bastreri (0187 79 06 91).* **📅** *Mon.* **W** *www.portovenere.it*

NAMED AFTER VENUS herself, Portovenere is one of the most romantic villages on the Ligurian coast with its cluster of narrow streets lined with pastel-coloured houses. In the upper part of the village is the 12th-century church of **San Lorenzo**. A sculpture over the doorway here depicts the martyrdom of the saint who was roasted alive on a grill.

Above the doorway of San Lorenzo in Portovenere

On the stone promontory that curls out into the sea is the small, black-and-white 13th-century church of **San Pietro**. From here, or from the 16th-century castle on top of the cliffs on the northwestern side of the village, there are superb views of the Cinque Terre and the small island of Palmaria, about 400 m (1,300 ft) offshore.

Lerici ⑮

La Spezia. **👥** *13,000.* **🚌 ⛴ ℹ** *Via Biagini 2 (0187 96 73 46).* **📅** *Sat am.* **W** *www.aptcinqueterre.sp.it*

THIS STRETCH OF COAST, along the Gulf of La Spezia or Poets' Gulf, was once popular with such literati as Yeats and DH Lawrence. The village of San Terenzo, across the bay from Lerici, was where the poet Shelley spent the last four years of his life. It was from his home, the Casa Magni, that he set out in 1822 on a voyage to meet Leigh Hunt in Livorno. Tragically, he was shipwrecked near Viareggio and drowned.

Lerici, once a small fishing village and now a popular resort, sits on the edge of a beautiful bay overlooked by pastel-coloured houses. The forbidding medieval **Castello di Lerici** (13th century), built by the Pisans and later passed to the Genoese, dominates the holiday villas below. Today it houses a museum of geo-paleontology and is a venue for art exhibitions and concerts.

♟ Castello di Lerici
Piazza San Giorgio. **📞** *0187 96 90 42.* **◯** *daily.* **●** *Mon; 9–26 Dec.* **📷**

The harbour of Vernazza in the Cinque Terre

A stunning view of Manarola on the Sentiero Azzurro, Cinque Terre ▷

CENTRAL ITALY

Central Italy at a Glance

THE CENTRAL REGIONS of Italy are popular with visitors because they offer a range of beautiful landscapes and towns rich in culture and history, including outstanding churches, towers and palaces. Emilia-Romagna is home to the impressive Po Delta that provides a haven for wildlife. Tuscany is dominated by Florence, one of Italy's most celebrated centres. Umbria and Le Marche offer gentle pastoral countryside and picturesque hilltowns. The major sights of this rewarding area are shown here.

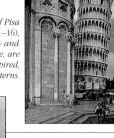

The Leaning Tower *of Pisa and the Duomo (see pp314–16), splendid examples of 12th- and 13th-century architecture, are decorated with Arabic-inspired, complex geometric patterns.*

Leaning Tower of Pisa

TUSC
(See pp3

FLORENCE
(See pp262–303)

Duomo, Campanile and Baptistry

The Duomo *and the Baptistry, set in the heart of Florence, dominate the city (see pp272–4). The dome dwarfs many surrounding buildings.*

Palazzo Pitti

The Uffizi *contains a superb collection of Florentine art from Gothic to High Renaissance and beyond (see pp278–81).*

The Palazzo Pitti, begun in 1457 for the banker Luca Pitti, became the main residence of the Medici. It now houses their treasures (see pp294–5).

| 0 kilometres | 1 |
| 0 miles | 0.5 |

| 0 kilometres | |
| 0 miles | 25 |

◁ **Autumn colour in Tuscany, in the hills of the Val d'Orcia, south of Siena**

The church of San Vitale in Ravenna is a gem of Byzantine art and architecture (see p260). It contains brilliantly preserved mosaics from the 6th century.

EMILIA-ROMAGNA
(See pp246–61)

San Vitale, Ravenna

The Palazzo Ducale in Urbino was built by Duke Federico, the town's 15th-century ruler, to plans by Laurana (see pp360–61). This Renaissance palace now houses the Galleria Nazionale delle Marche.

SAN MARINO

NCE
nset)

Palazzo Ducale, Urbino

LE MARCHE
(See pp354–63)

UMBRIA
(See pp338–53)

Duomo, Siena

Basilica of San Francesco, Assisi

Siena, a medieval town steeped in tradition, centres around the Campo, the large piazza shaped like a scallop shell (see pp328–33). The lively horse race, the Corsa del Palio, is held here in July and August.

Giotto's fresco cycle from the Basilica of San Francesco in Assisi was executed in the 13th century (see pp344–7). The church is visited by thousands of pilgrims each year.

Regional Food: Central Italy

THE FOOD OF TUSCANY, UMBRIA and Le Marche is simple but often hearty. Packed with flavour, it is based on peasant cooking that relies heavily on olive oil, tomatoes, beans, hams and salamis. With Bologna, Italy's gastronomic capital, as its main city, Emilia-Romagna tends to have more elaborate dishes, using ingredients such as cream, interesting meats – including game, Parma ham and mortadella – and good-quality cheeses. Fresh fish and seafood is available along the coasts, but is often more expensive than meat.

Artichoke

Balsamic vinegar *from Modena in Emilia-Romagna is renowned throughout the world. Aged for up to fourteen years in oak barrels, the dark, smooth vinegar is used to flavour soups, stews and salad dressings.*

Wild boar salami

Mortadella

Cooked ham (prosciutto cotto)

Parma ham (prosciutto crudo)

Cured meats and hams *form an important part of the cuisine of central Italy. The most famous is Parma ham from Emilia-Romagna, where the pigs are fattened on the whey left over from making Parmesan cheese.*

Panzanella, *a refreshing summer salad, is made of juicy tomatoes, onion, garlic and oil-soaked bread, garnished with fresh basil.*

Tortelloni, *a larger version of tortellini, may be stuffed with meat or cheese and served with a rich sauce.*

Liver paste

Tomato paste

Olive paste

Anchovy paste

Crostini *are delicious snacks made from rounds of toast topped with anchovy, olive, liver or tomato paste. Bruschetta is grilled bread rubbed with garlic and drizzled with olive oil.*

Spaghetti al Ragù *is a traditional dish from Bologna. The pasta is topped with a generous portion of beef and tomato sauce.*

Cannelloni *is another form of stuffed pasta. Large pasta tubes may be filled with meat or cheese and spinach, and then coated with tomato or bechamel sauce before being baked.*

Baccalà *is a simple, flavourful dish of dried salt cod prepared with garlic and garnished with parsley. In Tuscany, tomatoes are often added.*

Bistecca alla Fiorentina, *grilled over an open fire, is a large, tender steak that can be seasoned with oil and herbs and garnished with fresh lemon.*

Scottiglia di Cinghiale *is prepared with wild boar chops. This dish is particularly popular in the Maremma area of southern Tuscany.*

Torta di Limone *is one of the richer desserts that come from Emilia-Romagna. It is prepared with lemons and fresh cream.*

Torta di Riso *is a traditional Tuscan dessert consisting of rice cake served with a simple fruit sauce and seasonal fruit.*

Pecorino

Parmesan

Cheeses *are used in many recipes, but may also be served with fruit as a main course or at the end of a meal.*

Panforte

Panforte *is a dense, dark cake spiced with cinnamon and cloves. Ricciarelli are made from ground almonds, orange peel and honey.*

Cantucci *are sweet Tuscan biscuits often served together with vin santo, a traditional dessert wine.*

Ricciarelli

MUSHROOMS AND TRUFFLES

Wild mushrooms are considered a great delicacy in central Italy, and a range of fresh and dried mushrooms is frequently used in cooking. Fresh mushrooms are available in the autumn when restaurants are often packed with locals tasting seasonal mushroom dishes. Prized black truffles *(tartufi neri)* with a rich flavour and firm texture are expensive and used sparingly, as are funghi porcini. Porcini may be served grilled as a main course, used on pizza, in stuffed pasta or served as a vegetable dish, sautéed gently with garlic.

Chanterelle
(Cantarello or Gallinaccio)

Field blewit
(Agarico nudo)

Parasol
(Mazza da Tamburo)

Boletus edulis
(Porcini)

Oyster
(Ostrica)

Black truffle
(Tartufo nero)

The Wines of Central Italy

Roman mosaic of a bird eating grapes

VINEYARDS ARE SEEN EVERYWHERE in Central Italy, from the rolling cypress-fringed hills of Tuscany to the flatter, Lambrusco-producing plains of Emilia-Romagna. The finest red wines are made in the hills of southeastern Tuscany: Chianti Classico, Brunello di Montalcino and Vino Nobile di Montepulciano. Today's innovative mix of modern and traditional techniques is steadily improving the quality of much of the region's wine.

Chianti Classico is the heart of the Chianti zone. Chianti may be light and fruity or dense and long-lived – price is the usual guide. Rocca delle Macie is very reasonably priced.

Vernaccia di San Gimignano is a Tuscan white wine with a long, distinguished history. Traditionally a golden, often oxidized wine, it is now also produced in a fresher style, for early drinking. Teruzzi e Puthod make consistently good Vernaccia.

Parma

Moderna

Bologna

E M I L I A - R O M A G N A

Pistoia

Lucca

Florence

Pisa

Greve

Vino Nobile di Montepulciano is made from the same grapes as Chianti. It can be of superior quality, hence its claim to be a "noble wine". The vineyards are set around the delightful hilltop village of Montepulciano.

San Gimignano

Siena

T U S C A N Y

Montepu

Montalcino

Brunello di Montalcino is made from Sangiovese, Brunello being its local name. Its firm tannins may need up to ten years to soften before the rich, spicy flavours are revealed. Rosso di Montalcino, on the other hand, can be enjoyed much younger.

SUPER-TUSCANS

During the 1970s innovative wine makers set out to create new, individual wines even though under the existing rules they would be labelled as simple table wine. A trend which started with Antinori's Tignanello (a Sangiovese-Cabernet Sauvignon blend), this approach has reinvigorated Tuscan wine, to produce some exciting variations.

SASSICAIA 1999

BOLGHERI SASSICAIA

Sassicaia, a red wine made from the Cabernet Sauvignon grape

```
0 kilometres        50
0 miles        25
```

Chianti estate at Badia a Passignano in Tuscany

KEY

- Chianti
- Chianti Classico
- Vernaccia di San Gimignano
- Brunello di Montalcino
- Vino Nobile di Montepulciano
- Orvieto Classico
- Orvieto
- Verdicchio dei Castelli di Jesi
- Lambrusco

Verdicchio is a dry white wine from Le Marche with a crisp, slightly salty taste. In recent years the introduction of the single vineyard Verdicchio, such as Umani Ronchi's CaSal di Serra, has won much acclaim.

Orvieto Classico is a popular Umbrian white wine. This fresh, dry (Secco) version from the Antinori estate is a good example of a modern-style Orvieto. The wine also comes in a sweeter form, known as Abboccato.

GRAPES OF CENTRAL ITALY

The versatile Sangiovese grape dominates wine making in Central Italy. It is the main grape in Chianti, in Vino Nobile di Montepulciano, in Brunello di Montalcino, and in many of the new-style Super-Tuscan wines. Of the established whites, Trebbiano and Malvasia head the list. Imported varieties such as white Chardonnay and red Cabernet Sauvignon are playing an increasing role, often being used to complement and enhance native varieties.

Sangiovese grapes

HOW TO READ THE LABEL

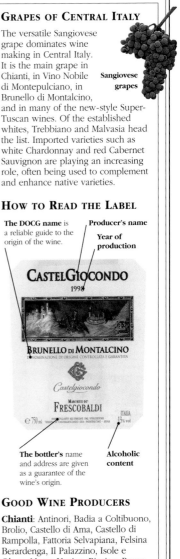

The DOCG name is a reliable guide to the origin of the wine.

Producer's name

Year of production

The bottler's name and address are given as a guarantee of the wine's origin.

Alcoholic content

GOOD WINE PRODUCERS

Chianti: Antinori, Badia a Coltibuono, Brolio, Castello di Ama, Castello di Rampolla, Fattoria Selvapiana, Felsina Berardenga, Il Palazzino, Isole e Olena, Monte Vertine, Riecine, Rocca delle Macie, Ruffino, Tenuta Fontodi.
Brunello di Montalcino: Argiano, Altesino, Caparzo, Castelgiocondo, Costanti, Il Poggione, Villa Banfi.
Vino Nobile di Montepulciano: Avignonesi, Le Casalte, Poliziano. In **Umbria**: Adanti, Lungarotti.

Good Chianti Vintages
2000, 1999, 1997, 1995, 1993, 1990, 1988, 1985, 1983, 1975, 1971, 1970.

Understanding Architecture in Central Italy

CENTRAL ITALY has countless fine Renaissance buildings, many of them concentrated in and around Florence. Their clear lines, elegant simplicity and harmonious proportions came out of a re-evaluation of the past. Turning their backs on the Gothic style, the architects of the Renaissance returned to Classical Rome for inspiration. Most of the large buildings had been started by the late 15th century, paid for by the Catholic Church or by powerful noble families, such as the Medici of Florence.

The Palazzo Ducale in Urbino (begun 1465)

RELIGIOUS BUILDINGS

Arched bays trisect the façade.

Pope Pius II's coat of arms

One of 12 roundels by Luca della Robbia

Small circular windows

Square plan topped by small dome

Symmetrical floorplan is based on a Greek cross.

Harmonious proportions

Pienza's Duomo was built by Bernardo Rossellino in 1459 for Pope Pius II as part of his vision of the ideal Renaissance city (see p323).

The Pazzi Chapel of Santa Croce in Florence (1433) is one of Brunelleschi's most famous works, decorated with terracotta roundels by Luca della Robbia (see pp276–7).

Santa Maria della Consolazione in Todi, begun in 1508, owes much to the ideas of the architect Bramante (see p349).

TOWN AND COUNTRY HOUSES

The cornice was designed to cast a shadow over the face of the palace around midday.

Square windows are found only on the ground floor.

Wedge-shaped masonry

Strong horizontal line

The Palazzo Strozzi in Florence (1489–1536) is typical of many Tuscan city palaces (see p318). The three storeys are given equal importance, and the massive rusticated stonework conveys the impression of strength and power (see p285).

WHERE TO SEE THE ARCHITECTURE

The simple canons of the Renaissance were interpreted differently away from the hotbed of artistic thought and cultural endeavour of Florence, which has the greatest number of churches and palaces. Alberti's Tempio Malatestiano at Rimini *(see p258)* evokes the sobriety of ancient Roman architecture yet seeks to

Vista in the Boboli Gardens, Florence

reinterpret it in his own unique fashion. Urbino's Palazzo Ducale *(pp360–61)* perfects the grace and polish of the era and is a truly noble period residence. On a smaller scale are the planned Renaissance centres of elegant towns such as Ferrara *(p253)*, Pienza *(p323)* and Urbania *(p359)*. All three centres are examples of enlightened patronage, and pay homage to the art of antiquity.

The weight of the lantern prevents the dome from springing apart.

Timber ribs provide the main support.

Outer shell

Inner shell

The top edge of the frieze divides the façade in two.

Classical triangular pediment

Volute connects the lower and upper parts.

The Duomo in Florence *is crowned by the revolutionary dome (1436) by Brunelleschi, which had to be built without scaffolding due to its size. The timber structure is covered by an inner and outer shell (see pp272–3).*

The façade of Santa Maria Novella *in Florence (1458–70) was designed by Leon Battista Alberti. He incorporated some of the existing Gothic features into an overall design typical of the Renaissance (see pp288–9).*

The villa at Poggio a Caiano *(1480) was redesigned in the Renaissance by Giuliano da Sangallo (see p318). The graceful, curved staircase was added around 1802.*

Clock, a later addition

Classical frieze

Colonnade derived from a Classical temple

Classical portico

EMILIA-ROMAGNA

EMILIA-ROMAGNA *is the heartland of central Italy, a broad corridor through the hills and plains of the Po Valley that marks the watershed between the cold north of the Alps and the hot Mediterranean south. With its rich agricultural land, historical cities and thriving industry, it is one of the most prosperous areas in Italy.*

Most of the major towns in Emilia-Romagna lie near the Via Aemilia, a Roman road built in 187 BC that linked Rimini on the Adriatic coast with the garrison town of Piacenza. Prior to the Romans, the Etruscans had ruled from their capital, Felsina, located on the site of present-day Bologna. After the fall of Rome, the region's focus moved to Ravenna, which became a principal part of the Byzantine Empire administered from Constantinople.

During the Middle Ages pilgrims heading for Rome continued to use the Via Aemilia. Political power, however, passed to influential noble families – the Malatesta in Rimini, the Bentivoglio in Bologna, the d'Este in Ferrara and Modena, and the Farnese in Parma and Piacenza. Great courts grew up around the families, attracting poets such as Dante and Ariosto, as well as painters,

sculptors and architects whose works still grace the medieval centres of these towns. Cobbled together from separate Papal States in 1860, modern Emilia-Romagna was given its present borders in 1947. Emilia, the western part of the region, is traditionally associated with a more northern outlook and a tendency towards the left in politics. Romagna, on the other hand, has recently witnessed an increase in the support for right-wing parties calling for political independence from Rome.

The entire region has a reputation as a great gastronomic centre. Agriculture has long thrived on the Po's alluvial fringes, earning the Pianura Padana (Po Plain) epithets such as the "bread basket" and "fruit bowl" of Italy. Pigs still outnumber humans in many areas, and some of the country's most famous staples – Parma ham and Parmesan cheese – originate here.

The medieval Palazzo del Comune in Ferrara

◁ The Fontana del Nettuno (Neptune's Fountain) in Bologna

Exploring Emilia-Romagna

Emilia-Romagna is a chequerboard of fields and plains between the Po river to the north and the forest-covered Apennine mountain slopes to the south. The best place to begin a tour of the region is centrally situated Bologna. Modena, its long-time rival, boasts one of the country's loveliest Romanesque cathedrals. Parma has a more provincial feel and Ferrara, too, has an easygoing air. Castell'Arquato offers a taste of the smaller villages that dot the hills south of the Po.

Piazza Cavalli, Piacenza's central square

Reed-lined shores along the Po Delta

SIGHTS AT A GLANCE

GETTING AROUND

Excellent road and rail links, aided by mostly flat terrain, make this region quick and easy to get around. Bologna is connected by the A1–E35 to Florence and by the A13 to Ferrara and Venice. The busy A1–E35 links Bologna to Milan via Piacenza, Fidenza and Parma. The A15–E31 connects Parma with La Spezia, and the A21–E70 joins Piacenza and Cremona. Fast, frequent train services run along almost parallel routes.

The beach at Cesenatico, north of Rimini on the Adriatic coast

KEY

▬▬	Motorway
▬▬	Major road
▬▬	Minor road
▬▬	Scenic route
≈	River
☀	Viewpoint

0 kilometres 25

0 miles 20

The 13th-century Palazzo Pretorio in Castell'Arquato

Piacenza ❶

🏠 *105,000.* FS 🚌 **ℹ** *Piazza Cavalli 7 (0523 32 93 24).* 🛒 *Wed & Sat.*

PIACENZA TRACES its history back to Roman times. Located near the Po, it served as a fortified camp protecting the Emilian plain from invasion. The centre is still based on the Roman plan.

Piacenza has a pleasantly understated old centre full of fine medieval and Renaissance buildings. Pride of place goes to two bronze equestrian **statues** in the central Piazza Cavalli, the work of the 17th-century sculptor Francesco Mochi, a pupil of Giam-bologna. Lauded as master-pieces of Baroque sculpture, the statues represent Alessandro Farnese, a soldier of fortune, and his son, Ranuccio: both were rulers of 16th-century Piacenza.

Behind the statues is the red-brick **Palazzo del Comune**, also known as "Il Gotico", an evocatively battlemented Lombard-Gothic palace begun at the end of the 13th century. It is one of Italy's most beautiful medieval buildings.

The **Duomo**, at the end of Via XX Settembre, has a rather leaden Lombard-Romanesque exterior (begun in 1122), and a 14th-century campanile. The interior features Guercino's painted cupola and medieval frescoes. There are also frescoed saints near the main door, painted to resemble members of the congregation.

The **Museo Civico** offers an eclectic mixture of sculpture and paintings – the star among these is the *Madonna and Child with John the Baptist* by Botticelli (1444–1510). There is also an armoury and archaeology section. The highlight here is the so-called *Fegato di Piacenza*, an Etruscan bronze representation of the sheep livers once used by priests for divination, inscribed with deities' names.

🏛 **Museo Civico**
Palazzo Farnese, Piazza Cittadella. 📞 *0523 32 82 70.* 🕐 *Tue–Sun (Tue–Thu am only).* ⬤ *public hols.* ♿

Castell'Arquato ❷

Piacenza. 🏠 *4,500.* 🚌 **ℹ** *Viale Remondini 1 (0523 80 30 91).* 🛒 *Mon.*

TUCKED INTO THE FOLDED hills between Fidenza and Piacenza, Castell'Arquato is one of the prettiest villages in the countryside south of the Po. Day visitors come at the weekends to escape Emilia's larger cities, thronging the restaurants and bars around the beautiful **Piazza Matteotti**. The best medieval building on the piazza is the 13th-century **Palazzo Pretorio**, a Romanesque basilica. The impressive **Rocca Viscontea** (14th century), a former fortress, is on Piazza del Municipio. It is partly closed for restoration. The village's hilltop site offers good views, particularly over the verdant Arda valley to the east.

Fidenza ❸

Parma. 🏠 *23,000.* FS 🚌 **ℹ** *Piazza Duomo 2 (0524 840 47).* 🛒 *Wed & Sat.*

LIKE MANY TOWNS hugging the line of the Po, Fidenza owed its early prominence to the Via Aemilia (the old Roman road). The town assumed greater importance as a medieval way station for pilgrims en route to Rome. Today Fidenza is visited for its superb **Duomo** on Piazza Duomo (13th century), a composite piece of architecture that embraces Lombard, Gothic and transi-tional Romanesque elements. The most immediately eye-catching feature is the opulent façade, probably created by the craftsmen who worked with Benedetto Antelami on Parma's Duomo. Inside, the walls are dotted with fragments of medieval frescoes, while the crypt contains the relics of San Donnino, the Duomo's patron.

Detail from façade of Duomo in Fidenza

Interior of Parma Baptistry

Parma 4

175,000. 🚋 🚌 ℹ Via Melloni 1a (0521 21 88 89). 🗓 Wed & Sat; Thu (flea market).
W turismo.comune.parma.it/turismo/

F EW ITALIAN TOWNS are as prosperous as Parma, not only a byword for fine food and good living but also a treasure trove of excellent paintings, superlative sculpture and fine medieval buildings. It boasts one of Italy's top opera houses and a panoply of elegant shops and first-rate bars and restaurants.

The Lombard-Romanesque **Duomo** on Piazza Duomo, among the greatest in northern Italy, is renowned for the painting that fills its main cupola, the *Assumption* (1526–30) by Antonio da Correggio. The nave is adorned with the work of Correggio's pupils. The south transept features a carved frieze of *The Deposition* (1178) by Benedetto Antelami, who was also responsible for much of the exquisite **Baptistry** (1196) just south of the cathedral. The reliefs inside and outside the latter – particularly those describing the months of the year – are among the most important of their age in Italy.

East of the Duomo is the church of **San Giovanni Evangelista** (rebuilt 1498–1510) whose dome features a fresco (c.1520) of the *Vision of St John at Patmos* by Correggio. Frescoes by Parmigianino can be seen here and in the 16th-century church of **Madonna della Steccata** on Via Dante.

🏛 Palazzo Pilotta
Piazzale della Pilotta 15. **Galleria**
📞 0521 23 33 09.
🕐 Tue–Sun am. 💷 ᕃ
Museo 📞 0521 23 37 18. 🕐 Tue–Sun am. 💷
This vast palace was built for the Farnese family during the 1500s and rebuilt after bomb damage from World War II. It comprises several parts, including the **Teatro Farnese** (1628), a copy of Palladio's ravishing theatre in Vicenza, built entirely of wood.

Both Correggio and Parmigianino are represented in the palace's **Galleria Nazionale**, which also houses works by Fra Angelico, El Greco and Bronzino, and two paintings by Ludovico Carracci: the *Apostles at the Sepulchre* and the *Funeral of the Virgin* (both late 16th century).

The **Museo Archeologico Nazionale**, on the lower floor, has exhibits from Velleia, an Etruscan necropolis, and from prehistoric sites in the hills around Parma.

🏛 Camera di Correggio
Via Melloni. 📞 0521 23 33 09.
🕐 Tue–Sun. 💷 ᕃ
Originally the refectory of the Benedictine convent of San Paolo, this room was frescoed by Correggio in 1518 with mythological scenes.

Campanile and Baptistry in Parma

THE MAKING OF PARMESAN CHEESE AND PARMA HAM

No cheese is as famous or as vital to Italy's cuisine as Parmesan *(Parmigiano).* There are two types: the superior Parmigiano-Reggiano and the lower-quality Grana. The cheese is made using techniques that have barely altered in centuries. Partially skimmed milk is added to whey, to promote fermentation, and rennet is used to curdle the milk. The cheese is then salted and shaped. Parmesan is not only used in cooking but is delicious eaten on its own, or with pears – an Italian speciality.

Shop selling Parmesan cheese and Parma ham

Parma ham owes its excellence to techniques perfected over many years and to the special conditions in which it is cured. It is made from pigs fattened on whey left over from the making of Parmesan cheese. The meat has a character that requires little more than salt and pepper to produce the famous *prosciutto crudo.* The breezy hills of Langhirino, south of Parma, are ideal for curing the hams, which are aged for up to ten months. Each ham is branded with the five-pointed crown of the old Duchy of Parma.

Flora by Carlo Cignani (1628–1719) in the Galleria Estense in Modena

Modena ⑤

🏛 175,000. 🚊 🚌 ℹ *Via Scudari 12 (059 20 66 60)*. 🗓 *Mon.* 🌐 *www.comune.modena.it/infoturismo*

To MOST ITALIANS Modena means fast cars, for both Ferrari and Maserati have factories in its industrial outskirts, and opera, since this is the birthplace of Luciano Pavarotti. Monuments to an earlier age, however, make this one of Emilia's most enticing historic destinations. A thriving colony since Roman times, the city rose to medieval prominence on the back of its broad agricultural hinterland and the arrival in 1598 of the d'Este nobles from Ferrara. This family continued to rule the city until the 18th century.

🔒 Duomo

Corso Duomo. 📞 *059 21 60 78.* 🗓 *daily.* **Torre Ghirlandina** 🗓 *Apr–Oct: 10am–1pm, 3–7pm Sun.*

Modena's superlative **Duomo** rises alongside the old Roman Via Aemilia (now Via Emilia). One of the region's greatest Romanesque buildings, it was founded by Countess Matilda of Tuscany, ruler of Modena in the 11th century. It was designed by Lanfranco and dedicated to San Geminiano, the city's patron saint, whose stone coffin lies under the choir. Its most noticeable feature is the **Torre Ghirlandina**, a perilously leaning tower begun at the same time as the Duomo and completed two centuries later. It once housed the *Secchia*, a wooden bucket whose 1325 theft from Bologna allegedly sparked a war between the two cities. It also inspired Tassoni's 17th-century mock epic poem *La Secchia Rapita* (The Stolen Bucket), and became the symbol of a rivalry between the cities.

The large reliefs on the Duomo's main (west) façade are the work of the 12th-century sculptor Wiligelmus. The highlight of the rather severe interior is a large carved *tribuna* (rood screen) decorated with 12th-century scenes from the Passion.

🏛 Palazzo dei Musei

Largo di Porta Sant'Agostino 337. **Galleria Estense** 📞 *059 439 57 11.* 🗓 *8:30am–7:30pm Tue–Sun.* ● *1 Jan, 1 May, 25 Dec.* ♿ **Biblioteca Estense** 📞 *059 22 22 48.* 🗓 *Mon–Sat (Sat am only).* ● *public hols.*

Northwest of the Duomo, and reached through an attractive warren of old streets, is the Palazzo dei Musei. Formerly an arsenal and workhouse, it is now home to the city's best museums and galleries. Its finest section is the **Galleria Estense**, given over to the d'Este private art collection, which was transferred here when the city of Ferrara, the family's former dominion, became part of the Papal States. Most of the paintings are by Emilian and Ferrarese artists (notably Reni and the Carracci) but there are also works by Velázquez, Tintoretto, Bernini and Veronese.

Among the permanent displays in the **Biblioteca Estense**, the d'Este Library, are a 1481 edition of Dante's *Divine Comedy*, and dozens of fascinating maps and diplomatic letters, many dating back centuries. A map dated 1501 was among the first to show the 1492 voyage by Columbus to the New World. The jewel of the collection is the magnificent illuminated Borso d'Este Bible, with gloriously decorated pages containing over 1,200 miniatures by 15th-century artists of the Ferrara school, most notably Taddeo Crivelli and Franco Russi.

The Torre Ghirlandina in Modena

ENVIRONS: The **Ferrari** factory, 20 km (12 miles) to the south, was founded by Enzo Ferrari in 1945. The FIAT-owned manufacturer now produces around 2,500 cars annually. The **Galleria Ferrari** has a small exhibition featuring memorabilia, classic engines and many vintage cars.

🏛 Galleria Ferrari

Via Dino Ferrari 43, Maranello. 📞 *0536 94 32 04.* 🗓 *9:30am–6pm daily.* ● *1 Jan, 25 Dec.* 📷♿

Ferrari 250 SWB, produced between 1959 and 1962

Ferrara ❻

🏛 *140,000.* **FS** 🚇 **ℹ** *Castello Estense, Largo Castello (0532 20 93 70).* 🗓 *Mon & Fri.*

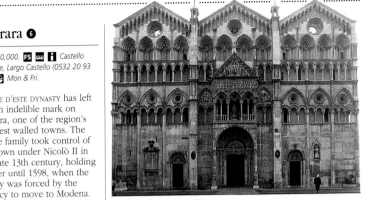

Façade of the Duomo in Ferrara

THE D'ESTE DYNASTY has left an indelible mark on Ferrara, one of the region's greatest walled towns. The noble family took control of the town under Nicolò II in the late 13th century, holding power until 1598, when the family was forced by the papacy to move to Modena.

♠ Castello Estense

Largo Castello. **🕻** *0532 29 92 33.* 🕐 *daily.* ● *public hols.* 🔯
The family's dynastic seat, with its moats, towers and battlements (begun 1385), looms over the town centre. Ferrante and Giulio d'Este were

The impressive medieval Castello Estense in Ferrara

incarcerated in its draughty dungeons for plotting to overthrow Alfonso I d'Este. Parisina d'Este, wife of the ruthless Nicolò III, was executed here for having an affair with Ugo, her illegitimate stepson.

🏛 Palazzo del Comune

Piazza Municipale.
Bronze statues of Nicolò III and Borso d'Este, one of Nicolò's reputed 27 children, adorn this medieval palace (begun 1243). Both are copies of the 15th-century originals by Leon Battista Alberti.

🏛 Museo della Cattedrale

Via San Romano. **🕻** *0532 76 12 99.* 🕐 *Tue–Sun.* ● *Easter, 25 Dec.*
Donation.
Ferrara's 12th-century Duomo is a Romanesque-Gothic hybrid designed by Wiligelmus. Fine reliefs on the façade depict

scenes from the Last Judgment. The excellent **museum** (in a deconsecrated church opposite the cathedral) contains a fine set of marble reliefs of the *Labours of the Months* (late 12th century), two painted organ shutters (1469) of *St George* and the *Annunciation* by Cosmè Tura, and the *Madonna of the Pomegranate* (1408) by Jacopo della Quercia.

🏛 Palazzo Schifanoia

Via Scandiana 23. **🕻** *0532 641 78.* 🕐 *Tue–Sun.* ● *public hols.* 🔯
This d'Este summer retreat, begun in 1385, is famous for its Salone dei Mesi (Room of the Months), decorated with beautiful 15th-century murals by Tura and other Ferrarese painters with scenes of the different months. The commissioner, Borso d'Este, appears in many of the panels.

🏛 Museo Archeologico Nazionale

Palazzo di Ludovico il Moro, Via XX Settembre 122. **🕻** *0532 662 99.* 🕐 *Tue–Sun.* ● *public hols.* 🔯 🔸
The most interesting exhibits here are artifacts that were excavated from Spina, a Greco-Etruscan trading post near Comacchio on the Po Delta.

🏛 Palazzo dei Diamanti

Corso Ercole d'Este 21. **🕻** *0532 20 58 44.* 🕐 *Tue–Sun am, Thu pm.* ● *1 Jan, 1 May, 25 Dec.* 🔯
Named after the diamond motifs on its façade, this palace houses a modern art gallery, a museum devoted to the Risorgimento, and the Pinacoteca Nazionale, which contains works from leading exponents of the local Renaissance school.

THE D'ESTE FAMILY DYNASTY

During their medieval heyday, the d'Este family presided over one of Europe's leading courts, combining the roles of blood-crazed despots with enlightened Renaissance patrons. Nicolò III, for example, had his wife and her lover brutally murdered. Alfonso I (1503–34) married Lucrezia Borgia, descendant of one of Italy's most notorious families, while Ercole I (1407–1505) attempted to poison a nephew who tried to usurp him (and eventually had him executed). At the same time the d'Este court attracted writers like Petrarch, Tasso and Ariosto, and painters such as Mantegna, Titian and Bellini. Ercole I also rebuilt Ferrara, creating one of Europe's finest Renaissance cities.

Portrait of Alfonso I d'Este by Titian (c.1485–1576)

Street-by-Street: Bologna ❼

Detail of façade from San Petronio

THE HISTORIC city centre of Bologna is a handsome ensemble of brick buildings and charming porticoed streets. Medieval palaces are clustered around the two central squares, Piazza Maggiore and Piazza del Nettuno, flanked to the south by the churches of San Petronio and San Domenico. The university of Bologna is the oldest in Europe and the venerable Archiginnasio was its first official building. Further afield, the skyline is etched by the Asinelli and Garisenda towers, and by the campanile of Santo Stefano.

Fontana di Nettuno
The famous Neptune fountain (1566) was designed by Tommaso Laureti and decorated with magnificent bronze figures by Giambologna.

The Palazzo del Podestà (13th century) was remodelled in 1484.

Tourist information

Railway station
↑ **Ferrara**

← **Modena**

VIA UGO BASSI

VIA DELL'INDIPENDENZA

VIA RIZZOLI

VIA IV NOVEMBRE

PIAZZA MAGGIORE

VIA OREFICI

CA

★ San Petronio
The Martyrdom of St Sebastian *(15th century) in the Cappella di San Sebastiano is by Lorenzo Costa of the Ferrarese School.*

Archiginnasio

VIA D'AZEGLIO

VIA DELL'ARCHIGINNASIO

VIA FARINI

Piazza Cavour
The flagged medieval streets and shady porticoed buildings found in this pleasant piazza are typical of Bologna's elegant city centre.

PIAZZA CAVOUR

VIA DE

VIA GARIBALDI

STAR SIGHT
★ San Petronio

San Domenico
(1251) is dedicated to St Dominic, who is buried here in a magnificent tomb.

San Giacomo Maggiore
The Triumph of Death *fresco
by Costa (1483–6) adorns
the Cappella Bentivoglio.*

🔒 **San Giacomo Maggiore**
Piazza Rossini. 📞 051 22 59 70.
🕐 daily.

This Romanesque-Gothic
church, begun in 1267 but
altered substantially since, is
visited mainly for the Cappella
Bentivoglio, a superb family
chapel founded by Annibale
Bentivoglio in 1445 and consecrated in 1486. Pride of place
naturally goes to a portrait
with subtle characterization of
the patrons by Lorenzo Costa
(1460–1535), who was also
responsible for the frescoes of
the *Apocalypse,* the *Madonna
Enthroned* and the *Triumph
of Death.* The chapel's altarpiece, depicting the
*Virgin and Saints
with Two Angel
Musicians* (1488),
is the work of
Francesco Francia.
The Bentivoglio
family is further
glorified in the tomb
of Anton Galeazzo
Bentivoglio (1435)
opposite the chapel.
It was among the
last works of the
noted Sienese
sculptor, Jacopo
della Quercia. The
Oratory of Santa
Cecilia features
frescoes on the lives
of Santa Cecilia and
San Valeriano by Costa and
Francesco Francia (1504–6).

Pinacoteca
Nazionale

Museo di
Anatomia
Umana
Normale

VIA ZAMBONI

VIA BENEDETTO XIV

Ravenna

VIA SAN VITALE

STRADA MAGGIORE

PIAZZA DI
PORTA
RAVEGNANA

VIA SANTO STEFANO

VIA CASTIGLIONE

Firenze

**Torri degli
Asinelli e
Garisenda**
*The colossal towers
are two of the few
remaining towers
begun by Bologna's
important families
in the 12th century.*

Abbazia di Santo Stefano
*The Fontana di Pilato, or
Pilate's fountain, in the
courtyard features a basin
with Lombard inscriptions
from the 8th century.*

KEY

– – – Suggested route

0 metres   150
0 yards   150

**The Bentivoglio tomb (1435) by
Jacopo della Quercia**

Exploring Bologna

MONUMENTS TO BOLOGNA's rich cultural heritage are scattered across the city, from the leaning towers and the church of San Petronio in the old centre to the Pinacoteca Nazionale in the university district.

♛ Torri degli Asinelli e Garisenda

Piazza di Porta Ravegnana. ○ *daily.* 📷

The famous Torri Pendenti, or leaning towers – Torre degli Asinelli and Torre Garisenda – are among the few survivors of the original 200 that once formed the skyline of Bologna. Both were begun in the 12th century, though there were probably earlier towers on the site – Dante mentioned a pair of towers here in his *Inferno*. Torre Garisenda was shortened as a safety measure within only a few years of its construction, and still leans some 3 m (10 ft) from the vertical. At 97 m (318 ft) tall, Torre Asinelli is the fourth highest tower in Italy after those in Cremona, Siena and Venice. Its 500-step ascent offers fine views over Bologna's pantiled rooftops to the hills beyond.

⛪ Abbazia di Santo Stefano

Via Santo Stefano 24.

【 051 22 32 56. ○ *daily.*

Santo Stefano is a curious collection of four medieval churches (originally seven) jumbled together under one roof. The 11th-century church of the Crocifisso provides little

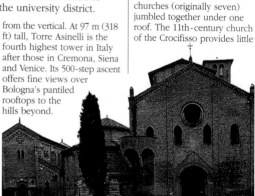

Exterior of the Abbazia di Santo Stefano

⛪ SAN PETRONIO

Piazza Maggiore. 【 051 22 21 12. ○ *daily.* ⛫

Dedicated to the city's 5th-century bishop, this church ranks among the greatest of Italy's brick-built medieval buildings. Founded in 1390, it was originally intended to be larger than St Peter's in Rome, but its size was scaled down when the church authorities diverted funds to the nearby Palazzo Archiginnasio. The resulting financial shortfall left the church decidedly lopsided, with a row of columns on its eastern flank that were intended to support an additional internal aisle. The project's financial profligacy, nonetheless, was said to have been instrumental in turning Martin Luther against Catholicism.

The altarpiece of the *Martyrdom of St Sebastian* is from the late Ferrarese School.

The pink and white interior adds to the overall light and airy effect.

The canopied main portal features beautiful biblical reliefs (1425–38) by Jacopo della Quercia.

Gothic Interior
The interior is airy, with graceful pillars supporting the roof. Twenty-two chapels, shielded by screens, open off the nave. In 1547 the Council of Trent (see p168) was temporarily moved here due to the plague.

Entrance

Unfinished upper façade

The meridian line was traced in 1655 by the astronomer Gian Domenico Cassini. It is 67 m (219 ft) long.

The stained-glass windows (1464–6) in this chapel are by Jacob of Ulm.

more than a corridor to polygonal San Sepolcro, the most appealing of the quartet. Also dating from the 11th century, its centrepiece is the tomb of St Petronius, a marvellously overstated affair modelled on the Holy Sepulchre of Jerusalem. The courtyard contains the so-called Fontana di Pilato, an 8th-century basin.

Santi Vitale e Agricola dates originally from the 5th century, making it the oldest church in the city. It was rebuilt in the 8th and 11th centuries. Inside are the sarcophagi of Saints Vitalis and Agricola, martyred in the 4th century. Santa Trinità features a small museum of minor paintings and religious artifacts, including wooden statues of the *Adoration of the Magi* painted by Simone dei Crocifissi (c.1370).

Bell tower

Choir Stalls
The exquisite inlaid choir stalls of the Chapel of the Holy Sacrament were made by Raffaello da Brescia in 1521.

🏛 Pinacoteca Nazionale

Via delle Belle Arti 56.
📞 *051 421 19 84.*
🕐 *Tue–Sun.*
🔴 *1 Jan, 1 May, 15 Aug, 25 Dec.* 🎫 ♿

Bologna's principal art gallery, and one of northern Italy's most important collections, stands on the edge of the city's university district, a bustling area of bars, bookshops and cheap restaurants. The gallery is mainly dedicated to work by Bolognese painters, notably Vitale da Bologna, Guido Reni, Guercino and the Carracci family. Members of the Ferrarese School are also represented, in particular Francesco del Cossa and Ercole de' Roberti. The two highlights are Perugino's *Madonna in Glory* (c.1491) and Raphael's famous *Ecstasy of St Cecilia*, painted around 1515, both artists having worked in Bologna.

The *Ecstasy of St Cecilia* (c.1515) by Raphael in Bologna's Pinacoteca Nazionale

🏛 Museo di Anatomia Umana Normale

Palazzo Poggi, Via Zamboni 33. 📞 *051 209 93 60.* 🕐 *Mon–Fri by appt.* 🔴 *1 Jan, Easter, 1 May, 25 Dec, public hols.*

Although well off the standard tourist itineraries, the Museum of Human Anatomy is one of the more memorable of Bologna's smaller museums. The collection includes occasionally gruesome visceral waxworks and numerous models of organs, limbs and flayed bodies. Sculpted rather than made from casts, they have an artistic as well as scientific appeal. The models were used as medical teaching aids until the 19th century. The contents of the museum recently moved to Palazzo Poggi, which also contains the Museo Cartageographica.

⛪ San Domenico

Piazza di San Domenico 13.
📞 *051 640 04 11.* 🕐 *daily.* ♿

Bologna's San Domenico can lay claim to being the most important of Italy's many Dominican churches. Begun in 1221, after St Dominic's death, it was built to house the body of the saint, who died here and lies buried in a tomb known as the Arca di San Domenico. A magnificent composite work, the tomb's statues were executed by Nicola Pisano; the reliefs of scenes from the *Life of St Dominic* were the work of Nicola Pisano and his assistants; the canopy (1473) is attributed to Nicola di Bari; while the figures of the angels and Saints Proculus and Petronius are early works by Michelangelo. The reliquary (1383) behind the sarcophagus contains St Dominic's head.

Arca di San Domenico in the Basilica di San Domenico

Fresco of Malatesta and St Sigismund (1451) by Piero della Francesca in the Tempio Malatestiano, Rimini

Faenza ❽

Ravenna. 🏛 54,000. 🚆 🚌
🛈 Piazza del Popolo 1 (0546 252 31).
🚹 Tue, Thu & Sat.

FAENZA IS SYNONYMOUS with the **faïence** ceramic-ware to which it gave its name. Renowned across Europe for over 500 years, the pottery, with its distinctive blue and ochre colouring, is still made in countless small factories around the town.

The highlight of Faenza is the **Museo Internazionale delle Ceramiche**, one of the largest ceramic collections in Italy. Its exhibits feature not only examples of local ware, but also pottery from other countries and other periods, including Roman ceramics and medieval majolica. There is also a section devoted to the modern ceramic art of Picasso, Matisse and Chagall.

🏛 **Museo Internazionale delle Ceramiche**
Viale Baccarini 19. 📞 0546 69 73 11.
🕐 Apr–Oct: Tue–Sun; Nov–Mar: Tue–Sun (Tue–Fri am only). 🌑 1 Jan, 1 May, 15 Aug, 25 Dec. 🚹 📷

Rimini ❾

🏛 130,000. 🚆 🚌 🛈 Piazzale Fellini 3 (0541 569 02). 🚹 Wed & Sat.
🅆 www.riminiturismo.it

RIMINI WAS ONCE a quaint seaside resort, whose charms were celebrated in the early films of Federico Fellini (1920–93), the director born and raised here. Today it is the largest beach resort in Europe. The seafront, which stretches unbroken for almost 15 km (9 miles), is lined with clubs, bars and restaurants. The crowded beaches are clean and well groomed, though entrance fees are charged at private beaches.

The town's old quarter, by contrast, is pleasantly quiet. Its charming cobbled streets gather around **Piazza Cavour**, dominated by the 14th-century **Palazzo del Podestà**. Rimini's finest building is the **Tempio Malatestiano**, built as a Franciscan church but converted in 1450 by Leon Battista Alberti, the great Florentine architect, into one of Italy's great Renaissance monuments. The work was commissioned by Sigismondo Malatesta (1417–68), a descendant of Rimini's ruling medieval family, and reputedly one of the most evil and

debauched men of his time. Ostensibly designed as a chapel, the Tempio became little more than a monument to Malatesta. Inside are sculptures by Agostino di Duccio and a fresco (1451) by Piero della Francesca of Malatesta kneeling before St Sigismund (1451).

The entwined initials of Malatesta and his fourth wife, Isotta degli Atti, provide a recurring decorative motif, and there are reliefs depicting scenes of bacchanalian excess and oddities such as strangely posed elephants (a Malatesta family emblem). All this led Pope Pius II to condemn the building as "a temple of devil-worshippers", and to burn Malatesta's effigy for acts of "murder, violation, adultery, incest, sacrilege and perjury".

ENVIRONS: Further along the coast, the resorts become relatively quieter. **Cesenatico**, 18 km (11 miles) north, offers all the usual facilities yet the beaches are less crowded.

🚆 **Tempio Malatestiano**
Via IV Novembre. 📞 0541 242 44.
🕐 8am–12:30pm, 3:30–6pm Mon–Sat; 9am–1pm, 3:30–7pm Sun. 🚹

Ravenna ❿

🏛 90,000. 🚆 🚌 🛈 Via Salara 8–12 (0544 354 04). 🚹 Wed & Sat.
🅆 www.turismo.ravenna.it

MOST PEOPLE VISIT Ravenna for its superb mosaics from the Byzantine period (see pp260–61), but the town itself is a surprisingly pleasant medley of old streets, fine shops and peaceful piazzas.

Façade of the Renaissance Tempio Malatestiano in Rimini

Piazza del Popolo, Ravenna's central square

The **Museo Nazionale** features a wide range of icons, paintings and archaeological displays. The best place to relax and take a break from sightseeing is Piazza del Popolo, a lovely ensemble of medieval buildings.

🏛 **Museo Nazionale**
Via Fiandrini. 📞 0544 344 24.
🕐 Tue–Sun. 📷 ♿

Po Delta ⓫

Ferrara. 🚆 Ferrara Ostellata. 🚌 to Goro or Gorino. 🚢 from Porto Garibaldi, Goro & Gorino. 🛈 Piazza Folegatti 28, Comacchio (0533 31 01 61). **Parco Delta del Po** 📞 0533 31 40 03. 🌐 www.parcodeltapo.it

THE PO IS ITALY'S longest river. Its vast basin covers some 15 per cent of the country and supports around a third of the nation's population. Although ravaged in many places by industrial pollution, at its finest it offers beautifully subtle landscapes – rows of poplar trees across misty fields and vistas over the shifting sands of its vast delta, an estuary of marshes, dunes and islands.

The immense **Parco Delta del Po** is a national park stretching for 600 sq km (234 sq miles), all the way to the Veneto. Wetland areas such as the **Valli di Comacchio** north of Ravenna have long been nature reserves, a winter home to thousands of breeding and migrating birds. Ornithologists gather here to see gulls, coots, bean geese and black terns, and far rarer species such as the white egret, hen harrier and pygmy cormorant. **Comacchio**, the nearest settlement, comprises 13 tiny islands connected by bridges. It is one of several fishing villages in the area, and its most famous catch is eels, often caught using methods, like water gates, that date back as far as Roman times.

Other nature reserves include the **Bosco della Mesola**, a tract of ancient woodland planted by the Etruscans and cared for by generations of monks. You can walk or cycle through it, with excellent opportunities for seeing large herds of deer.

For a good look at the entire region, follow the S309 – part of the old Via Romea pilgrimage trail to Rome – that runs north to south through some 100 km (62 miles) of the park. Numerous smaller lanes branch off into the wilderness. There are also boat trips to some of the delta's more remote corners: key departure points include the villages of Ca' Tiepolo, Ca' Vernier and Taglio di Po. Most areas also offer the possibility of hiring bicycles. The 125-km (78-mile) ride along the right bank of the Po is popular with cyclists.

Hen harrier, found in the Po Delta

The peaceful landscape along the banks of the river in the Po Delta

A Tour of Ravenna

Rᴀᴠᴇɴɴᴀ ʀᴏsᴇ ᴛᴏ ᴘᴏᴡᴇʀ in the 1st century BC under the Emperor Augustus, who built a port and naval base at nearby Classe, currently the site of a major excavation project. As Rome's power declined, Ravenna was made the capital of the Western Empire (AD 402), a role it retained during the Ostrogoth and Byzantine rule in the 5th and 6th centuries. Ravenna is renowned for its early Christian mosaics – the town had converted to Christianity in the 2nd century AD. The mosaics span the years of Roman and Byzantine rule, offering comparisons between Classically inspired designs and later Byzantine motifs.

Mosaic detail from San Vitale

The Good Shepherd ②
This mosaic adorns the tiny Mausoleo di Galla Placidia. Begun in 430, this exquisite building probably never received the remains of Placidia, wife of a barbarian emperor.

San Vitale ①
San Vitale's apse mosaics (526–547) show Christ, San Vitale (being handed a martyr's crown), two angels and Bishop Ecclesius, who began the church (see pp46–7).

Baptism of Jesus ③
The 5th-century Battistero Neoniano (Neonian Baptistry) is named after the bishop who may have commissioned its decoration, including this beautiful mosaic. It was built near the remains of a Roman bathhouse and is Ravenna's oldest monument.

Battistero degli Ariani ⑤
The cupola of this late 5th-century baptistry has a mosaic showing the Apostles ringed around a centrepiece depicting the Baptism of Christ.

Sant'Apollinare Nuovo ⑥
This glorious 6th-century church, named after Ravenna's first bishop, is dominated by two rows of mosaics. Both show processions of martyrs and virgins bearing gifts for Christ and the Virgin.

Tomba di Dante ④
Dante's wanderings around Italy after his exile from Florence eventually brought him to Ravenna, where he died in 1321. A lamp in his sepulchre (1780) is fed by oil given by the city of Florence.

KEY

- - - Suggested route

P Parking

Tourist information

0 metres 200
0 yards 200

FLORENCE

LORENCE IS A VAST AND BEAUTIFUL *monument to the Renaissance, the artistic and cultural reawakening of the 15th century. Writers such as Dante, Petrarch and Machiavelli contributed to its proud literary heritage, though it was the paintings and sculptures of artists such as Botticelli, Michelangelo and Donatello that turned the city into one of the world's greatest artistic capitals.*

While the Etruscans had long settled the hills around Fiesole, Florence first sprang to life as a Roman colony in 59 BC. Captured by the Lombards in the 6th century, the city later emerged from the Dark Ages as an independent city state. By the 13th century a burgeoning trade in wool and textiles, backed by a powerful banking sector, had turned the city into one of Italy's leading powers. Political control was wielded first by the guilds, and later by the Florentine Republic. In time, power passed to leading noble families, of which the most influential were the Medici, a hugely wealthy banking dynasty. Florence, and later Tuscany, remained under the family's almost unbroken sway for three centuries. During this time the city was at the cultural and intellectual heart of Europe, its cosmopolitan atmosphere and wealthy patrons providing the impetus for a period of unparalleled artistic growth. Artists, sculptors and architects flocked to the city, filling its streets, churches and palaces with some of the world's greatest Renaissance works. By 1737 the Medici had died out, leaving the city under Austrian (and briefly Napoleonic) control until Italian Unification in 1860. Between 1865 and 1871 Florence was the capital of the new Kingdom of Italy. In recent history its streets and artistic heritage were ravaged by the Arno floods of November 1966.

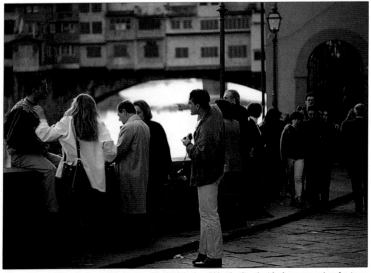

Florentines strolling in front of Ponte Vecchio (1345), the old bridge lined with shops spanning the Arno

◁ **The dome of Florence's Duomo, completed in 1436, designed by Brunelleschi**

Exploring Florence

H ISTORIC FLORENCE is a surprisingly compact area, and the majority of the sights described on the following pages can easily be reached on foot. Most visitors head for the Duomo, the city's geographical and historical focus, ideally placed to explore the Campanile, Baptistry and Museo dell'Opera del Duomo. To the south is Piazza della Signoria, long the city's political heart, flanked by the Palazzo Vecchio, Florence's town hall, and the Uffizi, one of Italy's leading art galleries. To the east lies the church of Santa Croce, home to frescoes by Giotto and the tombs of some of Florence's greatest men. To the west stands Santa Maria Novella, the city's other great church, also adorned with fresco-filled chapels. Across the Ponte Vecchio and the Arno – the river that bisects the city – is the district of Oltrarno, dominated by Santo Spirito and the vast Pitti

Bell tower, Palazzo Vecchio

Palace, containing galleries with works by great Renaissance artists including Raphael and Titian.

GETTING AROUND

Florence has an excellent bus service, including electric buses, making public transport convenient. The compact city centre, a restricted traffic area, is best negotiated on foot.

KEY

Street-by-Street: Around San Marco pp266–7

Street-by-Street: Around the Duomo pp270–71

Street-by-Street: Around Piazza della Repubblica pp284–5

Street-by-Street: Around Oltrarno pp292–3

FS Railway station

P Parking

i Tourist information

— City walls

Ponte Vecchio with Ponte Santa Trìnita in the foreground

LOCATOR MAP

SIGHTS AT A GLANCE

Churches
Cappella Brancacci
  pp290–91 **25**
Cappelle Medicee **19**
Convento di San Marco **2**
Duomo and Baptistry
  pp272–4 **7**
Ognissanti **24**
Orsanmichele **8**
Santissima Annunziata **3**
Santa Croce **10**
Santa Felìcita **28**
San Lorenzo **18**
Santa Maria Novella **21**
San Miniato al Monte **30**
Santo Spirito **26**

Buildings, Monuments and Squares
Mercato Centrale **20**
Palazzo Antinori **22**
Palazzo Davanzati **16**
Palazzo Rucellai **23**
Palazzo Strozzi **17**
Palazzo Vecchio **15**
Piazza della Signoria **14**
Piazzale Michelangelo **29**
Ponte Vecchio **12**
Spedale degli Innocenti **5**

Museums and Galleries
Bargello **9**
Galleria dell'Accademia **1**
Museo Archeologico **4**
Museo dell'Opera del
  Duomo **6**
Museo di Storia della
  Scienza **11**
Palazzo Pitti pp294–5 **27**
Uffizi pp278–81 **13**

SEE ALSO

0 metres   500

0 yards   500

Street-by-Street: Around San Marco

THE BUILDINGS in this part of Florence once stood on the fringes of the city, serving as stables and barracks. The Medici menagerie of lions, elephants and giraffes was housed here. Today it is a student quarter and the streets are often busy with young people attending the university or the Accademia di Belle Arti, the world's oldest art school, founded in 1563.

Santissima Annunziata
This fine Renaissance church has an opulent Baroque interior ❸

Palazzo Pandolfini was designed by Raphael in 1516.

★ Convento di San Marco
The Annunciation (c.1445) is an example of Fra Angelico's exquisite fresco decoration ❷

Sant'Apollonia features a fresco of the *Cenacolo* (Last Supper) by Andrea del Castagno (1450).

Luigi Cherubini (1760–1842), the Florentine composer, trained at the Conservatorio.

Galleria dell'Accademia
This detail is from a 14th-century altarpiece, the Madonna and Saints, *by an unnamed master* ❶

KEY

– – – Suggested route

```
0 metres        50
0 yards         50
```

Giambologna's statue of Duke Ferdinando I was cast by Tacca in 1608.

LOCATOR MAP
See Florence Street Finder map 2

Spedale degli Innocenti
Opened in 1444, the city orphanage by Brunelleschi was decorated with cameos by Andrea della Robbia ❺

The Giardino dei Semplici was opened in 1543.

Museo Archeologico
Many of the Etruscan objects in the museum were originally in the Medici collections ❹

VIA GINO CAPPONI

STAR SIGHTS

★ **Convento di San Marco**

★ **Galleria dell'Accademia**

Part of the 15th-century *Cassone Adimari* by Lo Scheggia in the Accademia

Galleria dell'Accademia ❶

Via Ricasoli 60. **Map** 2 D4. 🄲 *055 238 86 09 (information); 055 29 48 83 (reservations).* ⏰ *8:15am–6:50pm Tue–Sun (extended hours in the summer).* ⬤ *Mon, public hols.*

THE ACADEMY OF FINE ARTS, founded in 1563, was the first school established in Europe specifically to teach the techniques of drawing, painting and sculpture. The art collection displayed here was formed in 1784 to provide material for students to study and copy.

The most famous work is Michelangelo's *David* (1504), a colossal (5.2 m/ 17 ft) nude of the biblical hero who killed the giant Goliath. The sculpture was commissioned by the city for Piazza della Signoria, but it was moved to the Accademia for safekeeping in 1873. One copy now stands in its original position *(see pp282–3)* and a second is on Piazzale Michelangelo. The *David* established Michelangelo, at the age of 29, as the foremost sculptor of his time.

Michelangelo's other masterpieces in the Accademia include the *Quattro Prigioni* (the Four Prisoners), sculpted between 1521 and 1523 and intended to adorn the tomb of Pope Julius II. The statues

Michelangelo's *David*

were presented to the Medici family in 1564 by the artist's nephew, Leonardo. The muscular figures struggling to free themselves from the stone are among the most dramatic of Michelangelo's works. The statues were then moved to the Grotta Grande in the Boboli Gardens, where casts of the originals can now be seen.

The Accademia also contains an important collection of paintings by 15th- and 16th-century Florentine artists, among them Filippino Lippi, Fra Bartolomeo, Bronzino and Ridolfo del Ghirlandaio. The major works include the *Madonna del Mare* (Madonna of the Sea), attributed to Botticelli (1445–1510), and *Venus and Cupid* by Jacopo Pontormo (1494–1556), based on a preparatory drawing by Michelangelo. Also here is an elaborately painted wooden chest, the *Cassone Adimari* (1440–45) by Lo Scheggia, the stepbrother of Masaccio. Originally part of a wealthy bride's trousseau, it is decorated with details of Florentine life, clothing and architecture. A scene of the bridal party appears on the chest in front of the Baptistry.

The Salone della Toscana (Tuscany Room) features more modest paintings and sculptures by 19th-century members of the Accademia and plaster models by the sculptor, Lorenzo Bartolini.

The light and airy former library, designed by Michelozzo

Convento di San Marco ❷

Piazza di San Marco. **Map** 2 D4. 📞 055 28 76 28 (information). 🕗 7am–noon, 4–8pm. 🏛 **Museo di San Marco** 📞 055 238 86 08; 055 29 48 83 (reservations). 🕗 8:15am–1:50pm (later Sat, Sun). ● 1 Jan, 1 May, 25 Dec, 2nd & 4th Mon and 1st, 2nd & 5th Sun of each month. 🖼 ♿ 🚫

T HE CONVENT OF SAN MARCO was founded in the 13th century and enlarged in 1437 when Dominican monks from nearby Fiesole moved there at the invitation of Cosimo il Vecchio. He paid a considerable sum to have the convent rebuilt by his favourite architect, Michelozzo, whose simple cloisters and cells provide the setting for a remarkable series of devotional frescoes (c.1438–45) by Florentine painter and Dominican friar Fra Angelico. The convent and art collections form the **Museo di San Marco**.

Michelozzo's magnificent **Chiostro di Sant'Antonino** was named after the convent's first prior, Antonino Pierozzi (1389–1459), who later became the Archbishop of Florence. Most of the faded frescoes in this cloister describe scenes from the saint's life by Bernardino Poccetti. The panels in the corner are by Fra Angelico. A door in the right side of the cloister leads to the **Ospizio dei Pellegrini** (Pilgrims' Hospice). Today it houses the museum's free-standing paintings, including two famous masterpieces: Fra Angelico's moving *Deposition* (c.1435–40), an altarpiece painted for the church of Santa Trinità, and the *Madonna dei Linaiuoli*, commissioned by the Linaiuoli (flaxworkers' guild) in 1433.

In the courtyard, right of the convent's former bell, is the vaulted **Sala Capitolare** (Chapter House), decorated with a noted but over-restored *Crucifixion and Saints* (1440) painted by Fra Angelico.

Covering one wall of the small **Refettorio** (refectory) is a fresco of the *Last Supper* (c.1480) by Domenico Ghirlandaio. Stairs from the courtyard lead to the first floor, where you suddenly see Fra Angelico's *Annunciation* (c.1440), thought by many to be among the city's most beautiful Renaissance

A detail from Fra Angelico's poignant *Deposition* (c. 1440)

paintings. Beyond, ranged around three sides of the cloister, are the **Dormitory Cells**. These 44 tiny monastic cells are frescoed with scenes from *The Life of Christ* by Fra Angelico and assistants (1439–45). The cells numbered 1 to 11 are generally attributed to Fra Angelico personally, as is the lovely fresco of the Madonna and Saints on the right of the corridor (see p28).

Cells 12–14 were once occupied by Savonarola, the zealous Dominican monk who became Prior of San Marco in 1491. Among other deeds, Savonarola incited Florentines to rebel against the Medici and was responsible for the burning of many works of art. Denounced as a heretic, he was burned at the stake in Piazza della Signoria in 1498.

Along the third corridor lies an airy colonnaded hall, formerly a public **library** designed by Michelozzo in 1441 for Cosimo il Vecchio. Beyond it lie two cells (38 and 39) which were used by Cosimo when he went on retreat here. Each is decorated with two frescoes (the other cells have only one), and they are both larger than any of the neighbouring rooms.

Fra Angelico's allegorical fresco, the *Mocking of Christ* (c. 1442), showing Jesus blindfolded and being struck by a Roman guard

The Birth of the Virgin (1514) by del Sarto in Santissima Annunziata

Santissima Annunziata ❸

Piazza della Santissima Annunziata. **Map** 2 E4. 055 239 80 34. 7:30am–12:30pm, 4pm–6:30pm daily.

FOUNDED BY the Servite order in 1250, the church of the Holy Annunciation was later rebuilt by Michelozzo between 1444 and 1481. Its atrium contains frescoes by the Mannerist artists Rosso Fiorentino, Andrea del Sarto and Jacopo Pontormo. Perhaps the finest of its panels are *The Journey of the Magi* (1511) and *The Birth of the Virgin* (1514) by Andrea del Sarto.

The heavily decorated, dark interior has a frescoed ceiling completed by Pietro Giambelli in 1669. Here is one of the city's most revered shrines, a painting of the Virgin Mary begun by a monk in 1252 but miraculously completed by an angel, according to devout Florentines. Newly-wed couples traditionally visit the shrine (on the left as you enter the church) to present a bouquet of flowers to the Virgin and to pray for a long, fruitful and fecund marriage.

A door from the north transept leads to the **Chiostrino dei Morti** (Cloister of the Dead), so called because it was originally used as a burial ground. Today it is best known for del Sarto's beautiful fresco, *The Madonna del Sacco* (1525).

The church is situated on the northern flank of **Piazza della Santissima Annunziata**, one of the finest Renaissance squares in Florence. Designed by Brunelleschi, the delicate nine-bay arcade fronts the Spedale degli Innocenti to its right, while at the centre of the square stands a bronze equestrian statue of Duke Ferdinando I. Started by Giambologna, it was finished in 1608 by his assistant Pietro Tacca (who designed the square's bronze fountains).

Museo Archeologico ❹

Via della Colonna 36. **Map** 2 E4. 055 235 75. 8:30am–2pm Tue–Sun (to 7pm Tue & Thu); 2–7pm Mon. 1 Jan, 1 May, 25 Dec.

THE ARCHAEOLOGICAL MUSEUM in Florence is in a palazzo built by Giulio Parigi for the Princess Maria Maddalena de' Medici in 1620. It now exhibits an outstanding collection of Etruscan, Greek, Roman and Egyptian artifacts, although parts of the collection are being restored following the flood in 1966. The first floor contains a splendid series of Etruscan bronzes as well as the famous *Chimera* (4th century BC), a mythical lion with a goat's head imposed on its body and a serpent for a tail. Equally impressive is the 1st-century *Arringatore* bronze

Etruscan warrior, Museo Archeologico

found near Lake Trasimeno in Umbria. It is inscribed with the name of Aulus Metellus. A large section on the second floor is dedicated to Greek vases, notably the famed François Vase, found in an Etruscan tomb near Chiusi.

Spedale degli Innocenti ❺

Piazza della Santissima Annunziata 12. **Map** 2 E4. 055 249 17 08. 8:30am–2pm Thu–Tue. 1 Jan, Easter, 25 Dec.

Part of Brunelleschi's arcaded loggia, Spedale degli Innocenti

NAMED AFTER Herod's biblical Massacre of the Innocents, the "Hospital" opened in 1444 as Europe's first orphanage. Part of the building is still used for this purpose. Brunelleschi's arcaded loggia is decorated with glazed terracotta roundels, added by Andrea della Robbia around 1498, showing babies wrapped in swaddling bands. At the left end of the portico you can see the *rota*, a rotating stone cylinder on which anonymous mothers could place their unwanted children and ring the bell for them to be admitted to the orphanage.

Within the building lie two elegant cloisters: the **Chiostro degli Uomini** (Men's Cloister), built between 1422 and 1445 and decorated with *sgraffito* roosters and cherubs, and the smaller Women's Cloister (1438). A small upstairs gallery contains a handful of fine works, including terracottas by della Robbia and pictures by Botticelli, Piero di Cosimo and Domenico Ghirlandaio.

Street-by-Street: Around the Duomo

WHILE MUCH OF FLORENCE was rebuilt during the Renaissance, the eastern part of the city retains a distinctly medieval feel. With its maze of tiny alleys, it is an area that would still be familiar to Dante (1265–1321), whose birthplace allegedly lay somewhere among these lanes. The poet would recognize the church of Santa Maria de' Cerchi where he first glimpsed Beatrice, as well as the gaunt outlines of the Bargello. He would also be familiar with the Baptistry, one of the city's oldest buildings, though he would not know the Campanile nor the Duomo, whose foundations were laid in the poet's old age.

Stained glass window from the Duomo

★ Duomo and Baptistry
The exteriors of the Duomo and Baptistry are richly decorated with marbles and reliefs, such as this detail from the Duomo's façade **7**

The Loggia del Bigallo (1358) is where abandoned children were once left. They were then sent to foster homes if they remained unclaimed.

Orsanmichele
The church's niche carvings depict patron saints of trade guilds, such as this copy of Donatello's St George **8**

PIAZZA DI SAN GIOVANNI

PIAZZA DEL DUOMO

VIA DELL OCHE

VIA DE' MEDICI

VIA S. ELISABETTA

VIA ROMA

VIA D. SPEZIALI

VIA DE' CALZAIUOLI

VIA D. TAVOLINI

VIA DE' CERCHI

V. DE' LAMBERTI

V.D. CIMATORI

CALIMALA

VIA PORTA ROSSA

VIA DE

KEY

– – – Suggested route

0 metres   100

0 yards   100

Via dei Calzaiuoli, lined with smart shops, is the city's liveliest street.

Piazza della Signoria ↓

Museo dell'Opera del Duomo

Works from the Duomo, Campanile and Baptistry are displayed in this museum **6**

Pegna sells a range of fine wines, oil and honey.

VIA FOLCO PORTINARI

VIA DELL' ORIUOLO

LOCATOR MAP
See Florence Street Finder map 6

Carving from Luca della Robbia's choir loft in the Museo dell'Opera

Museo dell'Opera del Duomo **6**

Piazza del Duomo 9. **Map** 2 D5 (6 E2).
055 230 28 85. 9am–7:30pm
daily (to 1:30pm Sun & public hols)
(last adm: 40 mins before closing).
1 Jan, Easter, 25 Dec.

THE CATHEDRAL Works Museum has reopened after extensive remodelling and now a series of rooms is dedicated to the history of the Duomo. The main ground-floor room holds statues from Arnolfo di Cambio's workshop which were once placed in the cathedral's niches. Nearby is Donatello's *St John*. A new room contains 14th- and 15th-century religious paintings and reliquaries.

Michelangelo's *Pietà* has pride of place on the staircase. The hooded figure of Nicodemus is widely believed to be a self-portrait.

The first room on the upper floor contains two choir lofts, dating to the 1430s, by Luca della Robbia and Donatello. Carved in crisp white marble and decorated with coloured glass and mosaic, both depict children playing musical instruments and dancing. Other works by Donatello in this room are his statue of *La Maddalena* (1455) and several Old Testament figures.

The room to the left contains an exhibition of the tablets which used to decorate the bell tower. A lower level houses examples of the tools used by Brunelleschi's workmen and a copy of di Cambio's original cathedral façade.

Badia Fiorentina, the abbey church founded in 978, is home to *The Virgin Appearing to St Bernard* (1485) by Filippino Lippi.

BORGO DEGLI ALBIZI

VIA DE' GIRALDI

VIA DEL PROCONSOLO

VIA DEL PRESTO

VIA DE PANDOLFINI

VIA DELL' ACQUA

ALIGHIERI

Casa di Dante, a restored medieval house, is reputedly Dante's birthplace.

PIAZZA DI S. FIRENZE

★ **Bargello**
The city's old prison is home to a rich collection of applied arts and sculpture, including this figure of Mercury by Giambologna (1564) **9**

STAR SIGHTS

★ **Duomo and Baptistry**

★ **Bargello**

Duomo and Baptistry ●

RISING ABOVE THE heart of the city, the richly-decorated Duomo – Santa Maria del Fiore – and its orange-tiled dome have become Florence's most famous symbols. Typical of the Florentine determination to lead in all things, the cathedral is Europe's fourth largest church, and to this day it still remains the city's tallest building. The Baptistry, with its celebrated bronze doors, may date back to the 4th century, making it one of Florence's oldest buildings. The Campanile, designed by Giotto in 1334, was completed in 1359, 22 years after his death.

Sir John Hawkwood by Paolo Uccello, in the Duomo

Campanile
At 85 m (276 ft), the Campanile is 6 m (20 ft) shorter than the dome. It is clad in white, green and pink Tuscan marble.

Gothic windows

The Neo-Gothic marble façade echoes the style of Giotto's Campanile, but was only added in 1871–87.

★ Baptistry
Colourful 13th-century mosaics illustrating the Last Judgment *decorate the ceiling above the octagonal font, where many famous Florentines, including Dante, were baptized. The doors are by Andrea Pisano (south) and Lorenzo Ghiberti (north, east).*

North Doors

East Doors
(See p274)

Main entrance

South Doors

Campanile Reliefs
Copies of reliefs by Andrea Pisano on the Campanile's first storey depict the Creation of Man, and the Arts and the Industries. The originals are kept in the Museo dell'Opera del Duomo (see p271).

The top of the dome offers spectacular views over the city.

★ Dome by Brunelleschi
Brunelleschi's dome, finished in 1463, was the largest of its time to be built without scaffolding. The outer shell is supported by a thicker inner shell that acts as a platform for it.

The *Last Judgment* frescoes (1572–4) by Vasari were completed by Zuccari.

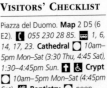

VISITORS' CHECKLIST

Piazza del Duomo. **Map** 2 D5 (6 E2). 055 230 28 85. 1, 6, 14, 17, 23. **Cathedral** 10am–5pm Mon–Sat (3:30 Thu, 4:45 Sat), 1:30–4:45pm Sun. **Crypt** 10am–5pm Mon–Sat (4:45pm Sat). **Baptistry** noon–7pm Mon–Sat, 8:30am–2pm Sun. **Dome** 8:30am–7pm Mon–Sat (5:40pm Sat). **Campanile** 8:30am–7:30pm daily. **All buildings** 1 Jan, Easter, 8 Jun, 15 Aug, 25 Dec. www.operaduomo.firenze.it

Bricks were set between marble ribs in a self-supporting herringbone pattern – a technique Brunelleschi copied from the Pantheon in Rome.

Chapels at the East End
The three apses, crowned by smaller copies of the dome, have five chapels each. The 15th-century stained glass is by Ghiberti.

Entrance leading to the dome

The marble sanctuary around the High Altar was created by Baccio Bandinelli in 1555.

Marble Pavement
The colourful, intricately inlaid pavement (16th century) was designed in part by Baccio d'Agnolo and Francesco da Sangallo.

Dante Explaining the Divine Comedy (1465)
This painting by Michelino shows the poet outside Florence against a backdrop of Purgatory, Hell and Paradise.

STAR FEATURES

★ **Dome by Brunelleschi**

★ **Baptistry**

The East Doors of the Baptistry

Lorenzo Ghiberti's famous bronze Baptistry doors were commissioned in 1401 to mark the city's deliverance from the plague. Ghiberti was chosen to make a set of new doors after a competition that involved seven leading artists, including Donatello, Jacopo

Ghiberti's winning panel

della Quercia and Brunelleschi. The trial panels by Ghiberti and Brunelleschi are so different from Florentine Gothic art of the time, notably in the use of perspective and individuality of figures, that they are often regarded as the first works of the Renaissance.

"GATE OF PARADISE"

Having spent 21 years working on the North Doors, Ghiberti was commissioned to make the East Doors (1424–1452). Michelangelo enthusiastically dubbed them the "Gate of Paradise". The original ten relief panels showing scriptural subjects are now exhibited in the Museo dell'Opera del Duomo *(see p271)*; those on the Baptistry are copies.

Abraham and the Sacrifice of Isaac
The jagged modelled rocks symbolizing Abraham's pain are carefully arranged to emphasize the sacrificial act.

Joseph Sold into Slavery
Ghiberti, a master of perspective, formed the architectural elements in shallower relief behind the figures to create the illusion of depth in the scene.

KEY TO THE EAST DOORS

1	2
3	4
5	6
7	8
9	10

1 Adam and Eve are Expelled from Eden
2 Cain Murders his Brother, Abel
3 The Drunkenness of Noah and his Sacrifice
4 Abraham and the Sacrifice of Isaac
5 Esau and Jacob
6 Joseph Sold into Slavery
7 Moses Receives the Ten Commandments
8 The Fall of Jericho
9 The Battle with the Philistines
10 Solomon and the Queen of Sheba

Detail of carvings by Donatello on the wall of Orsanmichele

Orsanmichele ❽

Via dell'Arte della Lana. **Map** 3 C1 (6 D3). ☐ *9am–noon (to 1pm Sun), 4–6pm daily.* ■ *1st and last Mon of each month, 1 Jan, 1 May, 25 Dec.*

B UILT IN 1337 as a grain market, Orsanmichele was later converted into a church which took its name from *Orto di San Michele*, a monastic garden long since vanished. The arcades of the market became windows, which are today bricked in, but the original Gothic tracery can still be seen. The decoration was entrusted to Florence's major *Arti* (guilds). Over 60 years they commissioned sculptures of their patron saints to adorn the 14 exterior niches, though today many of the figures are copies. Among the sculptors were Lorenzo Ghiberti, Donatello and Verrocchio.

The beautifully tranquil interior contains an opulent 14th-century altar by Andrea Orcagna, a *Virgin and Child* by Bernardo Daddi (1348) and a statue of the *Madonna and Child with St Anne* by Francesco da Sangallo (1522).

Bargello ❾

Via del Proconsolo 4. **Map** 4 D1 (6 E3). 🕻 *055 238 86 06.* 🚌 *14, A.* ◐ *8:15am–1:50pm Tue–Sun.* ● *1 Jan, 1 May, 25 Dec.* 📷 ∅ ♿

F LORENCE'S second-ranking museum after the Uffizi, the Bargello contains a wonderful medley of applied arts and Italy's finest collection of Renaissance sculpture.

Begun in 1255, the fortress-like building was initially the town hall (making it the oldest seat of government in the city), but later became a prison and home to the chief of police (the *Bargello*). It also became known for its executions, which took place in the main courtyard until 1786, when the death sentence was abolished by Grand Duke Pietro Leopoldo. Following extensive renovation, the building opened as one of Italy's first national museums in 1865.

The key exhibits range over three floors, beginning with the Michelangelo Room, superbly redesigned after extensive damage during the 1966 flood. Three contrasting works by Michelangelo lie dotted around the room, the most famous a tipsy-looking *Bacchus* (1497), the sculptor's first large free-standing work. Close to it is a powerful bust of *Brutus* (1539–40), the only known portrait bust by Michelangelo, and a beautifully delicate circular relief depicting the *Madonna and Child* (1503–5). Countless works by other sculptors occupy the same room. Among them is an exquisite *Mercury* (1564) by the Mannerist genius, Giambologna, as well as several virtuoso bronzes by the sculptor and goldsmith Benvenuto Cellini (1500–71).

Across the courtyard, full of fragments and the coats of arms of the Bargello's various incumbents, two more rooms contain exterior sculptures removed from sites around the city. The courtyard's external staircase leads to the first floor, which opens with a wonderfully eccentric

Brunelleschi's Sacrifice of Isaac (1402) in the Bargello

Donatello's David (c.1430) in the Bargello

bronze menagerie by Giambologna. To the right is the Salone del Consiglio Generale, a cavernous former courtroom that contains the cream of the museum's Early Renaissance sculpture. Foremost among its highlights is Donatello's heroic *St George* (1416) – the epitome of "youth, courage and valour of arms" in the words of Vasari. Commissioned by the Armourers' Guild, the statue was brought here from Orsanmichele in 1892. At the centre of the room, in direct contrast, is Donatello's androgynous *David* (c.1430), famous as the first free-standing nude by a Western artist since antiquity. Among the room's more easily missed works, tucked away on the right wall, are two reliefs depicting *The Sacrifice of Isaac* (1402). Created by Brunelleschi and Lorenzo Ghiberti respectively, both were entries in the competition to design the Baptistry doors.

Beyond the Salone, the Bargello's emphasis shifts to the applied arts, with room after room devoted to rugs, ceramics, silverware and a host of other beautiful *objets d'art*. The most celebrated of these rooms is the Salone del Camino on the second floor, which features the finest collection of small bronzes in Italy. Some are reproductions of antique models, others are small copies of Renaissance statues. Giambologna, Cellini and Antonio del Pollaiuolo are among those represented.

Bacchus (1497) by Michelangelo

Santa Croce ⑩

Work BEGAN AROUND 1294 on the Gothic church of Santa Croce, which contains tombs and monuments of famous Florentines, such as Michelangelo, Galileo and Machiavelli, as well as radiant early 14th-century frescoes by Giotto and his pupil Taddeo Gaddi. In the cloister alongside the church stands the Cappella de' Pazzi (Pazzi Chapel), a Renaissance masterpiece designed by Filippo Brunelleschi.

Tomb of Leonardo Bruni (1447)
Rossellino's effigy of this great humanist was unusual in its sensitive realism and lack of monumental pomp.

Annunciation by Donatello (15th century)

Tomb of Michelangelo (1570)
Vasari's tomb figures represent Painting, Sculpture and Architecture.

Tomb of Machiavelli

The Neo-Gothic façade by Niccolò Matas was added in 1863.

Tomb of Galileo

Entrance

Exit

Tree of Life by Taddeo Gaddi

Refectory

Cimabue's Crucifixion
Badly damaged in the flood of 1966, this 13th-century masterpiece is among the highlights of the collection, as is Taddeo Gaddi's magnificent Last Supper (c.1355–60).

★ Cappella de' Pazzi
Brunelleschi's domed chapel with Classical proportions was begun in 1443. The roundels (c.1442–52) are by Luca della Robbia.

The Neo-Gothic campanile
was added in 1842, after the
original was destroyed in
1512 by lightning.

The Cappella Baroncelli,
frescoed by Taddeo Gaddi
between 1332 and 1338,
contains the first true night
scene in Western art.

Sacristy

★ **Cappella Bardi Frescoes**
*Giotto frescoed the Bardi
and Peruzzi chapels to the
right of the high altar
between 1315 and 1330.
This touching scene from
the left-hand wall of the
chapel shows* The Death
of St Francis *(1317).*

STAR FEATURES

★ **Cappella Bardi
Frescoes**

★ **Cappella de' Pazzi**

Museo di Storia della Scienza ⓫

Piazza de' Giudici 1. **Map** 4 D1
(6 E4). 🔲 055 26 53 11. ◯ winter:
9:30am–5pm Mon–Wed & Sat (to
1pm Tue); summer: 9:30am–5pm
Mon–Sat (to 1pm Tue & Sat).
● public hols. 🎫 🎦

THIS LIVELY and superbly
presented museum devotes
two floors to various scientific
themes, illustrating each with
countless fine displays and a
panoply of old and beautifully
made scientific instruments. It
is also something of a shrine
to the Pisa-born
scientist Galileo
Galilei (1564–
1642), and
features two
of his tele-
scopes, as
well as
large-scale
reconstructions
of his experiments
into motion,
velocity and acceleration.
These are sometimes
demonstrated by the
attendants. Other
exhibits come from
the Accademia del Cimento
(Academy for Experimen-
tation), founded in 1657 by
Grand Duke Ferdinand II
in memory of Galileo.

The first few rooms are
devoted to astronomical,
mathematical and navigational
instruments, with galleries
concentrating on Galileo,
telescopes and optical games.
Some of the best exhibits are
in room 7, which is crammed
with early maps, globes and
astrolabes, the antique micro-
scopes, thermometers and
barometers are located in
the rooms beyond. On the

**Astrolabe,
Museo di Storia
della Scienza**

second floor there are some
fine old clocks, mathematical
instruments, calculators, a
horrifying collection of
19th-century surgical
instruments, and some
graphic anatomical models.

Ponte Vecchio ⓬

Map 4 D1 (6 E4).

PONTE VECCHIO, the oldest
surviving bridge in the city,
was built in 1345, the last in a
succession of bridges and fords
on the site that dated back to
Roman times. Designed by
Giotto's pupil Taddeo
Gaddi, it was
originally the
domain of
blacksmiths,
butchers and
tanners (who
used the river for
disposing of waste).
They were reviled
for their noise and
stench and were evicted
in 1593 by Duke
Ferdinando I –
replaced by jewellers
and goldsmiths. The
elevated Corridoio Vasariano
runs along the eastern side of
the bridge, above the shops.
Giorgio Vasari designed the
corridor in 1565 to allow the
Medici family to move about
their residences without
having to mix with the public.
This was the city's only bridge
to escape destruction during
World War II and visitors
today come as much to admire
the views as to browse among
the antique shops and
specialized jewellery shops. A
bust of the famous goldsmith
Benvenuto Cellini stands in
the middle of the bridge.

Ponte Vecchio viewed from the Ponte Santa Trìnita

Uffizi ⑬

THE UFFIZI, Italy's greatest art gallery, was built in 1560–80 to house offices (*uffici*) for Duke Cosimo I. The architect Vasari used iron as reinforcement, enabling his successor, Buontalenti, to create an almost continuous wall of glass on the upper storey. This was used as a gallery for Francesco I to display the Medici art treasures. In the 19th century the gallery's ancient objects were moved to the archaeological museum and sculpture to the Bargello, leaving a priceless collection of paintings. There are plans to double the entire exhibition space by 2007.

Main staircase

Entrance hall

Entrance

Buontalenti staircase

Corridor ceilings are frescoed with 1580s "grotesques" inspired by Roman grottoes.

Bacchus (*c.1589*) Caravaggio's early work depicts the god of wine as a pallid, debauched youth. The mood of dissipation is echoed in the decaying fruit, one of Western art's earliest still-life paintings.

Annunciation (*1333*) The Sienese painter Simone Martini was strongly influenced by French Gothic art, and this is one of his masterpieces. The two saints are by Martini's pupil and brother-in-law, Lippo Memmi.

GALLERY GUIDE

Ancient Greek and Roman sculptures are in the corridor around the inner side of the horseshoe-shaped building. The paintings are hung in a series of rooms off the main corridor, in chronological order, to show the development of Florentine art from Gothic to Renaissance and beyond. Many well-known paintings are in rooms 7–18. Five new rooms opened in 2004. To avoid the queues, book your ticket in advance. Pick up a gallery guide to stay ahead of any layout changes.

Ognissanti Madonna (*c.1310*) Giotto's grasp of spatial depth and substance in this altarpiece was a milestone in the mastery of perspective.

KEY TO FLOORPLAN

- ☐ East Corridor
- ☐ West Corridor
- ☐ Arno Corridor
- ☐ Gallery rooms 1–45
- ☐ Non-exhibition space

VISITORS' CHECKLIST

Loggiata degli Uffizi 6. **Map** 4 D1
(6 D4). 055 238 86 51 (info);
055 29 48 83 (reservations). B,
23. 8:15am–6:50pm Tue–Sun
(extended hours in summer). Last
adm: 45 mins before closing.
1 Jan, 25 Dec.
www.uffizi.firenze.it

The Duke and Duchess of Urbino (c.1465–70)
*Piero della Francesca's portraits of Federico da Montefeltro
and his wife Battista Sforza were painted after Battista died
aged 26. Her portrait was probably based on her death mask.*

The Tribune,
decorated in
red and gold,
contains the
works most
valued by
the Medici.

The Birth of Venus (c.1485)
*Botticelli shows the goddess of love flanked by
Zephyrus, god of the west wind, who blows
the risen Venus to shore on a half-shell. The
myth may symbolize the birth of beauty
through the divine fertilization of matter.*

The Holy Family (1507)
*Michelangelo's paint-
ing, the first to break
with the convention
of showing Christ
on the Virgin's lap,
inspired Mannerist
artists through its
expressive handling
of colour and posture.*

Vasari's Classical Arno
façade (begun 1560)

The Vasari Corridor
is a passageway
across the Arno to
the Pitti Palace.

**The Venus of
Urbino** (1538)
*Titian's sensuous nude,
inspired by Giorgione's
Sleeping Venus, may in
fact be a portrait of a
courtesan deemed
sufficiently beautiful
to be a goddess.*

Exploring the Uffizi

T HE UFFIZI offers not only the chance to see the
world's greatest collection of Italian Renaissance
paintings, but also the opportunity to enjoy masterpieces
from as far afield as Holland, Spain and Germany.
Accumulated over the centuries by the Medici, the
collection was first housed in the Uffizi in 1581, and
eventually bequeathed to the Florentine people by
Anna Maria Lodovica, the last of the Medici.

Madonna and Child with Angels
(1455–66) by Fra Filippo Lippi

GOTHIC ART

P AST THE STATUES and antiquities of room 1, the Uffizi
proper opens in style with
three altarpieces of the *Maestà*,
or Madonna Enthroned, by
Giotto, Duccio and Cimabue,
some of Italy's greatest 13th-
century painters. Each work
marks a stage in the development of Italian painting away
from the stilted conventions
of Byzantium to the livelier
traditions of Gothic and
Renaissance art. The shift is
best expressed in Giotto's
version of the subject (known
as the *Ognissanti Madonna*),
where new feeling for depth
and naturalistic detail is shown
in the range of emotion
displayed by the saints and
angels, and by the carefully
evoked three-dimensionality
of the Virgin's throne.

Giotto's naturalistic influence
can also be seen among the
paintings of room 4, which is
devoted to the 14th-century
Florentine School, an interesting counterpoint to the Sienese
paintings of Duccio and his
followers in room 3. Among
the many fine paintings here
are works by Ambrogio and
Pietro Lorenzetti, and Simone
Martini's *Annunciation*.

Room 6 is devoted to
International Gothic, a highly
decorative style that represented the height of Gothic
expression. It is exemplified
by Gentile da Fabriano's
exquisite, glittering *Adoration
of the Magi* painted in 1423.

EARLY RENAISSANCE

A NEW UNDERSTANDING of
geometry and perspective
during the 15th century
increasingly allowed artists
to explore the complexities
of space and depth. None
became more obsessed with
these new compositional
possibilities than Paolo

Uccello (1397–1475), whose
picture of *The Battle of San
Romano* (1456) in room 7
is one of the gallery's most
fevered creations.

Room 7 also contains two
panels from 1460 by Piero
della Francesca, another artist
preoccupied with the art of
perspective. The panels,
which are among the earliest
Renaissance portraits, depict
the Duke and Duchess of
Urbino on one side and
representations of their
virtues on the other.

While such works can seem
coldly experimental, Fra
Filippo Lippi's *Madonna and
Child with Angels* (1455–66),
in room 8, is a masterpiece of
warmth and humanity. Like

Sandro Botticelli's allegorical painting, *Primavera* **(1480)**

many Renaissance artists, Lippi uses a religious subject to celebrate earthly delights such as landscape and feminine beauty. A similar approach is apparent in the works of Botticelli, whose famous paintings in rooms 10–14 are for many the highlight of the gallery. In *The Birth of Venus*, for example, Venus takes the place of the Virgin, expressing a fascination with Classical mythology common to many Renaissance artists. The same is true of the *Primavera* (1480), which breaks with Christian religious painting by illustrating a pagan rite of spring.

Detail from *The Annunciation* (1472–5) by Leonardo da Vinci

HIGH RENAISSANCE AND MANNERISM

ROOM 15 FEATURES works attributed to the young Leonardo da Vinci, notably a sublime *Annunciation* (1472–5), which reveals hints of his still emerging style, and the *Adoration of the Magi* (1481), which remained unfinished when he left Florence for Milan to paint *The Last Supper* (1495–8).

Room 18, better known as the Tribune, was designed in 1584 by Buontalenti in order to accommodate the best-loved pieces of the Medici collection. Its most famous work is the so-called Medici Venus (1st century BC), a Roman copy of a Greek statue deemed to be the most erotic in the ancient world. The copy proved equally salacious and was removed from Rome's Villa Medici by Cosimo III to keep it from corrupting the city's art students. Other highlights in

room 18 include Agnolo Bronzino's portraits of *Cosimo I* and *Eleonora di Toledo*, both painted around 1545, and Pontormo's *Charity* (1530) and the portrait of *Cosimo il Vecchio* (1517).

Rooms 19 to 23 depart from the gallery's Florentine bias, demonstrating how rapidly Renaissance ideas and techniques spread beyond Tuscany. Painters from the German and Flemish schools are well represented, together with painters from Umbria like Perugino, but perhaps the most captivating works are the paintings by Venetian and northern Italian artists such as Mantegna, Carpaccio, Correggio and Bellini.

Room 25, which returns to the Tuscan mainstream, is dominated by Michelangelo's *Holy Family* or Doni Tondo (1456), notable for its vibrant colours and the Virgin's unusually twisted pose. The gallery's only work by Michelangelo, it was to prove immensely influential with the next generation of painters, especially Bronzino (1503–72), Pontormo (1494–1556) and Parmigianino (1503–40). The last of these was responsible for the *Madonna of the Long Neck* (c.1534) in room 29. With its contorted anatomy, unnatural colours and strange composition, this painting is a masterpiece of the style that came to be called Mannerism. Earlier, but no less remarkable masterpieces in rooms 26 and 28 include Raphael's sublime

Madonna of the Goldfinch (1506) by Raphael

Madonna of the Long Neck (c.1534) by Parmigianino

Madonna of the Goldfinch (1506) and Titian's notorious *Venus of Urbino* (1538), censured by Mark Twain as the "foulest, the vilest, the obscenest picture the world possesses". Others hold it to be one of the most beautiful nudes ever painted.

LATER PAINTINGS

VISITORS, already sated by a surfeit of outstanding paintings, are often tempted to skim through the Uffizi's final rooms. The paintings in rooms 30 to 35 – which are mainly from the Veneto and Emilia-Romagna – are mostly unexceptional, but the gallery's last rooms (41–45) contain important paintings. Room 41 has works by Rubens and Van Dyck. Room 44, dedicated to Rembrandt and northern European painting, features Rembrandt's *Portrait of an Old Man* (1665) and two self-portraits of the artist as a young and old man (painted in 1634 and 1664, respectively). New rooms on the ground floor hold works by Caravaggio. These include *Medusa* (1596–8), painted for a Roman cardinal; *Bacchus* (c.1589), one of the artist's earliest works; and the *Sacrifice of Isaac* (c.1590), whose violent subject is belied by the painting's gentle background landscape. The new rooms also hold works by Guido Reni.

Piazza della Signoria ⑭

PIAZZA DELLA SIGNORIA and Palazzo Vecchio have been at the heart of Florence's political and social life for centuries. The great bell once used to summon citizens to *parlamento* (public meetings) here, and the square has long been a popular promenade for both visitors and Florentines. The piazza's statues (some are copies) commemorate the city's major historical events, though its most famous episode is celebrated by a simple pavement plaque near the loggia: the execution of the religious leader Girolamo Savonarola who was burnt at the stake.

Savonarola (1452–98)

David
This copy of the famous Michelangelo statue symbolizes triumph over tyranny. The original (see p267) stood in the piazza until 1873.

Heraldic Frieze
The crossed keys on this shield represent Medici papal rule.

Salone dei Cinquecento (1495)
This vast chamber contains a statue of Victory by Michelangelo and frescoes by Vasari describing Florentine triumphs over Pisa and Siena.

Sala dei Gigli

Fontana di Nettuno,
Ammannati's fountain (1575) of the Roman sea god surrounded by water nymphs commemorates Tuscan naval victories.

The Marzocco is a copy of the heraldic lion of Florence carved by Donatello in 1420. The original is in the Bargello (see p275).

★ Palazzo Vecchio *(completed 1332)*
This Republican frieze over the palace entrance is inscribed with the words, "Christ is King", implying that no mortal ruler has absolute power.

★ The Rape of the Sabine Women by Giambologna
(1583) The writhing figures in Giambologna's famous statue were carved from a single block of flawed marble.

The Uffizi

The Loggia dei Lanzi
(1382), designed by Orcagna, is named after the Lancers, the bodyguards of Cosimo I who were billeted here.

Roman statues, possibly of emperors, line the Loggia.

★ Perseus by Cellini
This bronze statue (1554) of Perseus beheading Medusa was intended to warn Cosimo I's enemies of their probable fate.

Palazzo Vecchio ⑮

Piazza della Signoria (entrance on via della Ninna). **Map** 4 D1 (6 D3). 📞 *055 276 84 65.* 🚌 *A, B.* 🕙 *9am–7pm daily (to 2pm Thu) (extended hours in summer). Last adm: 45 mins before closing.* 🚫 *1 Jan, Easter, 1 May, 15 Aug, 25 Dec.* 💶 🚻 ***Secret Itineraries & Children's Museum** (by reservation only).* 📞 *055 276 82 24.*

THE "OLD PALACE" still fulfils its original role as town hall. It was completed in 1322 when a huge bell, used to call citizens to meetings or warn of fire, flood or enemy attack, was hauled to the top of the imposing bell tower. While retaining much of its medieval appearance, the interior was remodelled for Duke Cosimo I in 1540. The redecoration was undertaken by Vasari, who incorporated bombastic frescoes (1563–5) of Florentine achievements. Michelangelo's *Victory* statue (1525) graces the Salone dei Cinquecento, which also has a tiny study decorated by Florence's leading Mannerist painters in 1569–1573. Other highlights include the Cappella di Eleonora, painted by Bronzino (1540–45); the loggia, with its views over the city; the Sala dei Gigli (Room of Lilies) with Donatello's *Judith and Holofernes* (c.1455) and frescoes of Roman heroes by Ghirlandaio (1485); as well as the recently opened museum for children and the secret rooms and passageways.

A copy of Verrocchio's Putto fountain in Vasari's courtyard

STAR FEATURES

★ Palazzo Vecchio

★ Perseus by Cellini

★ The Rape of the Sabine Women by Giambologna

Street-by-Street: Around Piazza della Repubblica

Underlying the street plan of modern Florence is the far older pattern of the ancient Roman city. Nowhere is this more evident than in the grid of narrow streets around Piazza della Repubblica, site of the old Roman forum. This pivotal square housed the city's main food market until the 1860s, when redevelopment tidied up the area, and added the triumphal arch that now stands in today's café-filled square.

Santa Trìnita has frescoes by Ghirlandaio on the Life of St Francis (1486), depicting events that took place in this area. Here, a child is revived after falling from the Palazzo Spini-Ferroni.

Palazzo Spini-Ferroni

Ponte Santa Trìnita was built in wood in 1290 and then rebuilt by Ammannati in 1567 to celebrate the defeat of Siena.

KEY

– – – Suggested route

0 metres	200
0 yards	200

Palazzo Strozzi
This monumental palazzo dominates the square ⓱

Santi Apostoli was reputedly founded by Charlemagne.

Palazzo Davanzati
Frescoes with exotic birds decorate the Sala dei Pappagalli, which was once the dining room of this 14th-century palazzo ⓰

Piazza della Repubblica, which dates from the 19th century, is lined by some of Florence's oldest and best known cafés.

Mercato Nuovo, the "New Market" (1547), now deals mainly in souvenirs.

Palazzo di Parte Guelfa was the headquarters of the Guelphs, the dominant political party of medieval Florence.

Ponte Vecchio
(See p277)

Detail of a frieze illustrating a medieval romance in Palazzo Davanzati

Palazzo Davanzati ⑯

Via Porta Rossa 13. **Map** 3 C1 (5 C3).
📞 *055 238 86 10.* ⬤ *for renovation.*

THIS WONDERFUL MUSEUM, also known as the Museo dell'Antica Casa Fiorentina, uses original fittings and furniture to recreate a typical well-to-do 14th-century town house. Due to structural problems, the museum is currently closed to the public, but a small exhibition, including photographs and a few items from the museum, has been organized in the entrance of the building.

Pelting holes in the vaulted ceiling of the entrance court-yard were designed to drop missiles on unwanted visitors. In one corner of the inner courtyard is a well and a pulley system to raise buckets of water to each floor – something of a luxury since most medieval households had to fetch their water from a public fountain.

Palazzo Strozzi ⑰

Piazza degli Strozzi. **Map** 3 C1 (5 C3).
Piccolo Museo di Palazzo Strozzi ⬤ *for restoration.*

SHEER SIZE accounts for the impact of the Palazzo Strozzi, and although it is only three storeys high, each floor exceeds the height of a normal palazzo. It was commissioned by the wealthy banker Filippo Strozzi, who had 15 buildings demolished to make way for the palazzo. He hoped it would rival the Medici palaces elsewhere in the city. Strozzi died in 1491, just two years after the first stone was laid.

Work on the building continued until 1536, with three major architects contributing to its design – Giuliano da Sangallo, Benedetto da Maiano and Simone del Pollaiuolo (also known as Cronaca). The exterior, built of huge rusticated masonry blocks, remains unspoiled. Look out for the original Renaissance torch-holders, lamps and the rings for tethering horses that still adorn the corners and façades. A small museum off the courtyard records the building's history, but the palace is now primarily used as an exhibition venue and has been host to some world-class art exhibitions.

Exterior of Palazzo Strozzi, with masonry block rustication

San Lorenzo ⑱

SAN LORENZO was the parish church of the Medici family, and in 1419 Brunelleschi was commissioned to rebuild it in the Classical style of the Renaissance. Almost a century later Michelangelo submitted some plans for the façade, and began work on the Medici tombs in the Sagrestia Nuova. He also designed a library, the Biblioteca Mediceo-Laurenziana, to house the family's collection of manuscripts. The lavish family mausoleum, the Cappella dei Principi, was started in 1604.

Cappella dei Principi
The Medici mausoleum, behind the high altar, was begun in 1604 by Matteo Nigetti, and forms part of the Cappelle Medicee.

The huge dome by Buontalenti echoes that of the Duomo *(see pp272–3).*

The Old Sacristy was designed by Brunelleschi and decorated by Donatello.

Campanile

Biblioteca Staircase
Michelangelo's Mannerist staircase, one of the artist's most innovative designs, was built by Ammannati in 1559.

Michelangelo designed the desks and ceiling of the Biblioteca, where exhibitions of Medici manuscripts are often held.

The cloister garden is planted with box hedges, pomegranate and orange trees.

The Martyrdom of St Lawrence
Bronzino's vast Mannerist fresco of 1659 is a bravura, choreographed study of the human form, rather than a reverential response to the agony of the saint.

Entrance to church

VISITORS' CHECKLIST

Piazza di San Lorenzo. **Map** 1 C5
(6 D1). 🚌 7, 10, 11, 12, 25, 31,
32, 33. **Basilica** 📞 055 21 66 34.
⏱ 10am–5pm Mon–Sat. 🚫 ✝
Biblioteca 📞 055 21 44 43. ⏱
9am–1pm Mon–Sat. 🚫 pub hols.

A simple stone slab marks
the unostentatious grave of
Cosimo il Vecchio
(1389–1464), founder
of the Medici dynasty.

The Cappelle Medicee
complex comprises the
Cappella dei Principi and its
crypt, the Sagrestia Nuova
(*see p287*).

Pulpits by Donatello
*The bronze pulpits in the
nave were Donatello's last
works. Completed by his
pupils in 1460, the reliefs
capture the flinching pain of
Christ's Passion and the
glory of the Resurrection.*

**St Joseph and Christ
in the Workshop**, a
striking work showing
the young Christ with
his father, is by Pietro
Annigoni (1910–88),
one of the few modern
artists whose work is
seen in Florence.

Michelangelo submitted
several designs for the
façade of San Lorenzo, but
it remains unfinished.

**The Tomb of the Duke of Nemours
(1520–34) by Michelangelo in the
Cappelle Medicee's New Sacristy**

Cappelle Medicee ⑲

Piazza di Madonna degli Aldobrandini. **Map** 1 C5 (6 D1). 📞 055 238
86 02; 055 29 48 83 (reservations).
🚌 many routes. ⏱ 8:15am–4:50pm
daily (1:50pm public hols). Last adm:
30 mins before closing. 🚫 1st, 3rd,
& 5th Mon of each month, 2nd & 4th
Sun, 1 Jan, 1 May, 25 Dec. 🚫 ♿

THE MEDICI CHAPELS divide
into three distinct areas.
Beyond the entrance hall lies
a low-vaulted crypt, a suitably
subdued space for the brass-
railed tombs of many lesser
members of the Medici
family. From here steps lead
to the octagonal **Cappella dei
Principi** (Chapel of Princes),
a vast family mausoleum
begun by Cosimo I in 1604.
The ceiling is garishly frescoed
and the walls are smothered
in huge swathes of semi-
precious *pietre dure* (inlaid
stone). Spaced around the

walls are the tombs of six
Medici Grand Dukes. A corridor leads to Michelangelo's
New Sacristy, designed as a
counterpoint to Brunelleschi's
Old Sacristy in San Lorenzo.
Three groups of statues, all
carved by Michelangelo
between 1520 and 1534, stand
around the walls: that on
the near left hand wall is *The
Tomb of the Duke of Urbino*
(grandson of Lorenzo the
Magnificent). Opposite is *The
Tomb of the Duke of Nemours*
(Lorenzo's third son). Close
to the unfinished *Madonna
and Child* (1521) is the simple
tomb containing Lorenzo the
Magnificent and his murdered
brother, Giuliano (died 1478).

Mercato Centrale ⑳

Piazza del Mercato Centrale. **Map** 1 C4
(5 C1). ⏱ 7am–2pm Mon–Sat.

AT THE HEART of the San
Lorenzo street market is
the bustling Mercato Centrale,
Florence's busiest food
market. It is housed in a vast
two-storey building of cast-
iron and glass, built in 1874
by Giuseppe Mengoni.
   The ground floor stalls sell
meat, poultry, fish, salamis,
hams, cheeses and excellent
olive oils. There are also
Tuscan takeaway foods such as
porchetta (roast suckling pig),
lampredotto (pig's intestines)
and *trippa* (tripe). Fresh fruit,
vegetables and flowers are sold
on the top floor: look out for
wild mushrooms and truffles
in the autumn, and broad
beans, peas and baby
artichokes in early spring.

Yellow courgette flowers and other vegetables in the Mercato Centrale

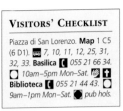

Santa Maria Novella ㉑

THE CHURCH of Santa Maria Novella was built by the Dominicans between 1279 and 1357. The lower Romanesque part of its façade was incorporated into one based on Classical proportions by the pioneering Renaissance architect Leon Battista Alberti in 1456–70. The Gothic interior contains superb frescoes, including Masaccio's powerful *Trinity*. The famous Green Cloister, frescoed with perspective scenes by Paolo Uccello, and the dramatically decorated Spanish Chapel now form a museum.

The arcade arches are emphasized by grey and white banding.

Monastic buildings

The Nave
The piers of the nave are spaced closer together at the altar end. This trick of perspective creates the illusion of an exceptionally long church.

Cappellone degli Spagnuoli, the chapel used by the Spanish courtiers of Eleonora of Toledo, has frescoes of salvation and damnation.

Chiostro Verde takes its name from the green base used in Uccello's frescoes, which were sadly damaged by the 1966 floods.

Trinity by Masaccio
This pioneering fresco (c.1428) is renowned as a masterpiece of perspective and portraiture. The kneeling figures flanking the arch are the painting's sponsors, judge Lorenzo Lenzi and his wife.

Entrance

Entrance to museum

Cappella Strozzi
The 14th-century frescoes by Nardo di Cione and his brother Andrea Orcagna were inspired by Dante's epic poem, The Divine Comedy.

The Strozzi Tomb is
by Benedetto
da Maiano
(1493).

**Cappella di
Filippo Strozzi**
features Filippino
Lippi's frescoes of St John
raising Drusiana from the dead
and St Philip slaying a dragon.

Cappella Tornabuoni
*Ghirlandaio's famous fresco
cycle,* The Life of John the
Baptist *(1485), peoples the
biblical episodes with
Florentine aristocrats in
contemporary dress.*

Ghirlandaio's *Madonna della Misericordia* (1472) in Ognissanti

Palazzo Antinori ㉒

Via de' Tornabuoni. **Map** 1 C5 (5 C2).
⬤ to the public. **Cantinetta
Antinori** 📞 055 29 22 34. ⏰
12:30–2:30pm, 7–10:30pm Mon–Fri.

Palazzo antinori was built
in 1461–6 and is one of
the finest small Renaissance
palazzi in Florence. It was
acquired by the Antinori in
1506 and has remained with
the family ever since. The
dynasty owns many estates
all over Tuscany and Umbria,
producing a range of wines,
oils and liqueurs that can be
sampled – along with fine
Tuscan dishes – in the wine
bar off the main courtyard,
called the Cantinetta Antinori.

Palazzo Rucellai ㉓

Via della Vigna Nuova 16. **Map** 1 C5
(5 B2). ⬤ to the public. **Archivio
Alinari** Largo Fratelli Alinari 15.
📞 055 239 51. ⏰ 9am–6pm
Mon–Fri. ⬤ public hols. 🚫

Built in 1446–57, this is
one of the most ornate
Renaissance palaces in the
city. It was commissioned
by Giovanni Rucellai,
whose enormous wealth
derived from the import of
a rare and costly red dye
made from lichen found
only on Majorca. The dye
was called *oricello*, from which
the name Rucellai is derived.
Giovanni commissioned
several buildings from the
architect Leon Battista Alberti,
who designed this palace as a
virtual textbook illustration of
the major Classical orders.

The palazzo used to house
the Museo Alinari, but the
collection has recently moved
to Largo Alinari 15 and is now
known as the Archivio Alinari.
The Alinari brothers began
taking pictures of Florence in
the 1840s. They supplied high-
quality prints, postcards and
art books to foreigners who
flocked to Florence in the 19th
century. The museum offers
a vivid insight into the social
history of Florence at that time.

Ognissanti ㉔

Borgo Ognissanti 42. **Map** 1 B5 (5 A2).
📞 348 645 0390. ⏰ 8:30am–
12:30pm, 3:30–5:30pm Mon–Fri;
9:30–10:30am, 3:30–5pm Sat & Sun
(to 6pm Sun). ⬤ first and last Mon
of each month. 🚫

Ognissanti, or All Saints,
was the parish church of
the Vespucci, one of whose
members, the 15th-century
navigator Amerigo, gave his
name to the New World. The
young Amerigo is depicted in
Ghirlandaio's fresco of the
Madonna della Misericordia
(1472) in the second chapel
on the right between the Virgin
and the man in the red cloak.
Amerigo realized that the land
discovered by Columbus was
a new continent and made
two voyages there. His letters
enabled cartographers to draw
the first maps of the new land.
Ognissanti is also the burial
place of Botticelli. His fresco
of *St Augustine* (1480) is on
the south wall. Alongside the
church is a cloister and refectory with Ghirlandaio's fresco
of *The Last Supper* (1480).

Cappella Brancacci ㉕

T HE CHURCH of Santa Maria del Carmine is famous for the Brancacci Chapel, which contains frescoes on *The Life of St Peter* commissioned by the Florentine merchant Felice Brancacci around 1424. Although the paintings were begun by Masolino in 1425, many of the scenes are by his pupil, Masaccio (who died before completing the cycle) and by Filippino Lippi, who completed the work in 1480. Masaccio's revolutionary use of perspective, his narrative drama and the tragic realism of his figures placed him in the vanguard of Renaissance painting. Many great artists, including Leonardo and Michelangelo, later visited the chapel to study his pioneering work.

In every scene, St Peter is distinguished from the crowds as the figure in the orange cloak.

St Peter Healing the Sick
Masaccio's realistic portrayal of cripples and beggars was revolutionary in his time.

The grouping of stylized figures in Masaccio's frescoes reflects his interest in the sculpture of Donatello.

Masaccio's simple style allows us to focus on the figures central to the frescoes without distracting detail.

Expulsion of Adam and Eve
Masaccio's ability to express emotion is well illustrated by his harrowing portrait of Adam and Eve being driven out of the Garden of Eden, their faces wracked by misery, shame and the burden of self-knowledge.

KEY TO THE FRESCOES: ARTISTS AND SUBJECTS

☐ Masolino

☐ Masaccio

☐ Lippi

| 1 | 2 | 3 | 7 | 8 | 9 |
| 4 | 5 | 6 | 10 | 11 | 12 |

1 Expulsion of Adam and Eve
2 The Tribute Money
3 St Peter Preaching
4 St Peter Visited by St Paul
5 Raising the Emperor's Son;
   St Peter Enthroned
6 St Peter Healing the Sick

7 St Peter Baptizing the Converts
8 St Peter Healing the Cripple;
   Raising Tabitha
9 Temptation of Adam and Eve
10 St Peter and St John Giving Alms
11 Crucifixion; Before the Proconsul
12 The Release of St Peter

VISITORS' CHECKLIST

Piazza del Carmine. **Map** 3 A1 (5 A4). 055 238 21 95; 055 29 48 83 (reservations). D. 10am–5pm Mon, Wed–Sat, 1–5pm Sun. Tue, public hols.

Masolino's *Temptation of Adam and Eve* is gentle and decorous, in contrast with the emotional force of Masaccio's painting on the opposite wall.

Woman in a Turban
The freshness of Masaccio's original colours is seen in this rediscovered roundel, hidden behind the altar for 500 years.

St Peter is depicted against a background of Florentine buildings.

Two Figures
Masolino's work tends to be more formal, less naturalistic and less animated than that of Masaccio.

Before the Proconsul
Filippino Lippi was called in to complete the cycle of frescoes in 1480. He added this emotional scene showing the Proconsul sentencing St Peter to death.

Street-by-Street: Oltrarno

Medici coat of arms

FOR THE MOST PART, the Oltrarno is a homely area of small houses, quiet squares and shops selling antiques, bric-a-brac and foodstuffs. The Via Maggio, a busy thoroughfare, breaks this pattern, but step into the side streets and you escape the bustle to discover a corner of old world Florence. The restaurants serve authentic, reasonably priced food, and the area is full of studios and workshops restoring antique furniture. Among the things to see are Santo Spirito and Palazzo Pitti, one of the city's largest palaces, whose medley of museums contains an art collection second only to that of the Uffizi.

Santo Spirito
Brunelleschi's simple church was completed after the architect's death ㉖

Ponte Santa Trinita

Cenacolo di Santo Spirito, the old refectory of a monastery that once stood here, contains a dramatic fresco attributed to Orcagna (c.1360).

Palazzo Guadagni (1500) was the first in the city to be built with a rooftop loggia, setting a trend among the aristocracy.

Palazzo di Bianca Cappello (1579) is covered in ornate *sgraffito* work and was the home of the mistress of Grand Duke Francesco I.

Masks and murals are handmade at this shop, Frieze of Papier Mâché.

LOCATOR MAP
*See Florence Street Finder
maps 3, 5*

The 16th-century fountain
and gargoyle in Piazza de' Frescobaldi were
designed by Buontalenti, as was the façade
(1593–4) of the nearby church of Santa Trìnita.

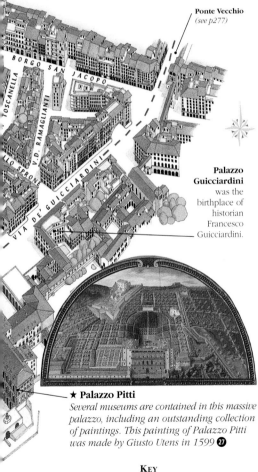

Ponte Vecchio
(see p277)

BORGO SAN JACOPO

TOSCANELLA

V. D. RAMAGLIANTI

LLO SPRONE

VIA DE' GUICCIARDINI

**Palazzo
Guicciardini**
was the
birthplace of
historian
Francesco
Guicciardini.

★ **Palazzo Pitti**
*Several museums are contained in this massive
palazzo, including an outstanding collection
of paintings. This painting of Palazzo Pitti
was made by Giusto Utens in 1599* ㉗

KEY

– – – Suggested route

STAR SIGHTS

★ Palazzo Pitti

0 metres   100

0 yards   100

Santo Spirito ㉖

Piazza di Santo Spirito. **Map** 3 B2
(5 B4). D. 055 21 00 30.
10am–noon, 4–5:30pm Mon–Fri,
4–5:30pm Sat & Sun. Wed pm.

THE AUGUSTINIAN foundation
of this church dates from
1250. The present building,
dominating the northern end
of the pretty Piazza di Santo
Spirito, was designed by the
architect Brunelleschi in 1435,
but not completed until the
late 15th century. The unfinished, modest façade was
added in the 18th century.

Inside, the harmony of the
proportions has been somewhat spoiled by the elaborate
Baroque baldacchino and the
High Altar, which was finished
in 1607 by Giovanni Caccini.
The church has 38 side
altars, decorated with 15th-
and 16th-century Renaissance
paintings and sculpture,
among them works by
Cosimo Rosselli, Domenico
Ghirlandaio and Filippino
Lippi. The latter painted a
magnificent *Madonna and
Child* (1466) for the Nerli
Chapel in the south transept.

In the north aisle, a door
beneath the organ leads to
a vestibule with an ornate
coffered ceiling. It was
designed by Simone del
Pollaiuolo, more commonly
known as Cronaca, in 1491.
The sacristy adjoining the
vestibule, in which 12 huge
columns are crammed into a
tiny space, was designed by
Giuliano da Sangallo in 1489.

**Interior of Santo Spirito with
colonnaded aisle**

Palazzo Pitti ②

T HE PALAZZO PITTI was originally built for the banker Luca Pitti. The huge scale of the building, begun in 1457 and attributed to Brunelleschi, illustrated Pitti's determination to outrival the Medici family through its display of wealth and power. Ironically, the Medici later purchased the palazzo when building costs bankrupted Pitti's heirs. In 1550 it became the main residence of the Medici, and subsequently all the rulers of the city lived here. Today the richly decorated rooms exhibit countless treasures from the Medici collections.

The Three Ages of Man (c.1510), attributed to Giorgione

GALLERIA PALATINA

T HE PALATINE GALLERY, which forms the heart of the Pitti museum complex, contains countless masterpieces by artists such as Botticelli, Titian, Perugino, Andrea del Sarto, Tintoretto, Veronese, Giorgione and Gentileschi. The works of art, accumulated by the Medici family and the house of Habsburg-Lorraine, are still hung much as the grand dukes wished, regardless of subject or chronology. The gallery consists of 11 main salons, the first five of which are painted with allegorical ceiling frescoes glorifying the Medici. Begun by Pietro da Cortona in 1641, they were completed in 1665

by his pupil Ciro Ferri. Room 1 (Sala di Venere) contains Antonio Canova's statue of the *Venus Italica* (1810), commissioned by Napoleon to replace the *Venus de' Medici* (which was to be taken to Paris). Room 2 (Sala di Apollo) features Titian's *Portrait of a Gentleman* (1540), perhaps the finest of several paintings by the artist in the gallery. Still finer pictures adorn rooms 4 and 5, including some by Perugino, Andrea del Sarto and a host of paintings by Raphael. The most beautiful of the last group are

Judith (1620–30) by Artemisia Gentileschi

Raphael's High Renaissance *Madonna della Seggiola* or Madonna of the Chair (c.1514–15), and the *Donna Velata* or Veiled Woman (c.1516), whose model was reputedly the artist's mistress. Other paintings in the remaining gallery rooms include Fra Filippo Lippi's lovely *Madonna and Child*, painted in the mid-15th century, and Caravaggio's *The Sleeping Cupid* (1608).

Madonna of the Chair (c.1515) by Raphael

Galleria Palatina

The Museo degli Argenti, or the silverware museum, also displays precious *objets d'art.*

The Boboli Gardens

Brunelleschi designed the palace façade, which was eventually extended to three times its original length.

Entrance to museums and galleries

Appartamenti Reali

The Galleria d'Arte Moderna is a 30-room gallery featuring paintings from the years 1784 to 1924.

The Palmieri Rotonda by Giovanni Fattori (1825–1908)

APPARTAMENTI REALI

THE ROYAL APARTMENTS on the first floor of the south wing of the palazzo were built in the 17th century. They are decorated with frescoes by various Florentine artists, a series of portraits of the Medici by the Flemish painter Justus Sustermans, who worked at the court between 1619 and 1681, and a group of 18th-century Gobelins tapestries. In the late 18th and early 19th centuries, the apartments were revamped

The Throne Room of the Appartamenti Reali

Galleria del Costume

Piazza della Signoria depicted in precious stones

in Neo-Classical style by the Dukes of Lorraine when they succeeded the Medici dynasty as the rulers of Florence.

The apartments are lavishly appointed with ornate gold and white stuccoed ceilings and rich decoration, notably the walls of the Parrot Room, which are covered with an opulent crimson fabric detailed with a bird design. The Tapestry Rooms are hung with 17th- and 18th-century tapestries of French, Belgian and Italian manufacture. The apartments reflect the tastes of three distinct historical periods.

OTHER COLLECTIONS

THE MUSEO degli Argenti (Silverware Museum) is housed in rooms formerly used by the Medici as summer apartments. The family's lavish taste is reflected in the vast array of precious objects on display. These embrace beautiful examples of Roman glassware, ivory, carpets, crystal, amber, and fine works by Florentine and German goldsmiths. Pride of place goes to 16 *pietre dure* vases (decorated with hard and semi-precious inlaid stones), once owned by Lorenzo the Magnificent.

The Galleria del Costume, which opened in 1983, reflects the changing taste in the courtly fashion of the late 18th century up to the 1920s.

The highlights of the Galleria d'Arte Moderna (Modern Art Gallery) are the wonderful paintings of the *Macchiaioli* (spot-makers), who were a group of Tuscan artists with a style very similar to that of the French Impressionists.

THE BOBOLI GARDENS

A copy of Giambologna's *Oceanus Fountain* (1576)

The Boboli Gardens, a lovely place to escape the rigours of sightseeing, were laid out for the Medici after they bought the Palazzo Pitti in 1549. An excellent example of stylized Renaissance gardening, they were opened to the public in 1766. The more formal parts of the garden, nearest the palazzo, consist of box hedges clipped into symmetrical geometric patterns. These lead to wilder groves of ilex and cypress trees, planted to create a contrast between artifice and nature. Countless statues adorn the gardens, particularly along the Viottolone, an avenue of cypress trees planted in 1637. High above the gardens stands the Forte di Belvedere, designed by Buontalenti in 1590 for the Medici Grand Dukes.

The Virgin from *The Annunciation* (1528) by Pontormo

Santa Felicita ㉘

Piazza di Santa Felìcita. **Map** 3 C2 (5 C5). 🚌 D. 📞 055 21 30 18. ⏰ 9am–noon, 3–6pm Mon–Sat; 4:30–6pm Sun. ♿

T HERE HAS BEEN a church on this site since the 4th century. The present structure, begun in the 11th century, was remodelled in 1736–9 by Ferdinando Ruggieri, who retained Vasari's earlier porch (added in 1564) as well as many of the church's original Gothic features.

The Capponi family chapel to the right of the entrance contains two works by Jacopo da Pontormo: *The Deposition* and *The Annunciation* (1525–28). The frescoes' strange composition and remarkable colouring make them two of Mannerism's greatest masterpieces.

Piazzale Michelangelo ㉙

Piazzale Michelangelo. **Map** 4 E3. 🚌 12, 13.

O F ALL THE GREAT Florentine viewpoints – such as the Duomo and Campanile – none offers such a magnificent panorama of the city as

Piazzale Michelangelo. Laid out in the 1860s by Giuseppe Poggi, and dotted with copies of Michelangelo's statues, its balconies attract many visitors and the inevitable massed ranks of souvenir sellers. However, this square remains an evocative spot, especially when the sun sets over the Arno and distant Tuscan hills.

San Miniato al Monte ㉚

Via del Monte alle Croci. **Map** 4 E3. 📞 055 234 27 31. 🚌 12, 13. ⏰ Apr–Sep: 8am–7:30pm daily; Oct–Mar: 8am–noon, 3–6pm Mon–Sat (3–6pm Sun). 🔴 public hols. ♿

S AN MINIATO is one of the most beautiful Romanesque churches in Italy. Begun in 1018, it was built over the shrine of San Miniato (St Minias), a rich Armenian merchant beheaded for his beliefs by Emperor Decius in the 3rd century. The façade, begun around 1090, has the geometric marble patterning typical of Pisan-Romanesque architecture. The statue on the gable shows an eagle carrying a bale of cloth, the symbol of the powerful Arte di Calimala (guild of wool importers), who financed the church in the Middle Ages. The 13th-century mosaic

The façade of the church of San Miniato al Monte

shows Christ, the Virgin and St Minias. The same protagonists appear in the apse mosaic inside the church, which sits above a crypt supported by columns salvaged from ancient Roman buildings. The floor of the nave is covered with seven mosaic panels of animals and signs of the Zodiac. These mosaics date back to 1207.

Other highlights include Michelozzo's free-standing Cappella del Crocifisso (1448) and the Renaissance Cappella del Cardinale del Portogallo (1480) with terracotta roundels (1461) on the ceiling by Luca della Robbia. There is a fresco cycle of *Scenes from the Life of St Benedict* by Spinello Aretino in the sacristy, which was completed in 1387.

Ponte Vecchio and the Arno from the heights of Piazzale Michelangelo

FLORENCE STREET FINDER

MAP REFERENCES given for sights in the Florence section refer to the maps on the following pages. Where two references are provided, the one in brackets relates to the large-scale maps, 5 and 6. References are also given for Florence hotels (*see pp557–9*) and restaurants (*see pp591–3*), and for useful addresses in the *Travellers' Needs* and *Survival Guide* sections at the back of the book. The map below shows the area of Florence covered by the *Street Finder*. The symbols used for sights and other features on the *Florence Street Finder* maps are listed below. Streets in Florence have double sets of numbers: red numbers are for businesses, and black or blue for domestic residences.

SCALE OF MAPS 1–2 & 3–4

0 metres   250

0 yards   250

1:12,000

SCALE OF MAPS 5–6

0 metres   150

0 yards   150

1:7000

0 kilometres   1

0 miles   0.5

KEY TO STREET FINDER

▦ Major sight	ℹ Tourist information
▦ Place of interest	✚ Hospital with casualty unit
FS Railway station	▣ Police station
🚌 Bus terminus	⛪ Church
P Parking	✡ Synagogue

⊠ Post office
⌁ Railway line
One-way street
City walls
Pedestrianized street

SEE PAGES 5, 6 FOR ENLARGEMENT OF THIS AREA

A · 1 · 5 · B · C

LUNGARNO · SODERINI · V. D. VIGNA NUOVA · VIA DEL PURGATORIO · V. DE' ANSELMI

PIAZZA CARLO GOLDONI · Palazzo Corsini · LUNGARNO CORSINI · PIAZZA DEGLI STROZZI · Palazzo Strozzi · Orsan

Palazzo Strozzi · PIAZZA DE' DAVANZATI · Mercato Nuov · V. P.TA ROSSA

BORGO SAN FREDIANO · Pescaia di S. Rosa · PIAZZA DI CESTELLO · San Frediano in Cestello · Santa Trinita · P. DI S. TRINITA · Palazzo Bartolini-Salimbeni · Palazzo Davanzati · Palazzo Spini-Ferroni · Palazzo di Parte Guelfa · Santi Apostoli · San ai

PIAZZA DI VERZAIA · VIA LUDOVICO ARIOSTO · BORGO SAN FREDIANO · VIA LORENZO BARTOLINI · VIA DI MONTE · PIAZZA DEL TIRATOIO · Pescaia di S. Rosa · PIAZZA NAZARIO SAURO · LUNGARNO GUICCIARDINI · Ponte alla Carraia · Ponte S. Trinita · Ponte Vecchio · LUNGARNO D. ACCIAIUOLI

PIAZZA DI VERZAIA · PIAZZA DE' NERLI · VIA SAN GIOVANNI · VIA DEI CARDATORI · VIA DEI TESSITORI · VIA DEL DRAGO D'ORO · BORGO DELLA STELLA · LUNGARNO DI SANTO SPIRITO

PIAZZA PIATTELLINA · PIAZZA DEL CARMINE · VIA SANTA MONACA · VIA SANT'AGOSTINO · MAFFIA · Santo Spirito · PIAZZA DE' FRESCOBALDI · BORGO SAN JACOPO

Cappella Brancacci (Santa Maria del Carmine) · Cenacolo di Santo Spirito · VIA DELLO SPRONE · PIAZZA DELLA PASSERA · Santa Felicita · Ponte Vecchio

PIAZZA TORQUATO TASSO · VIA DELL'ORTO · VIA DI CAMALDOLI · VIA DELLA CHIESA · VIA DEL CAMPUCCIO · PIAZZA DI SANTO SPIRITO · VIA DE' VELLUTI · VIA DE' GUICCIARDINI · PIAZZA DE' PITTI

GIARDINO TORRIGIANI · VIA FRANCESCO PETRARCA · VIA VILLANI · VIA MINIMA · VIA GIANO DELLA BELLA · VIA DELLE CALDAIE · VIA MAZZETTA · VIA SANT'AGOSTINO · **Palazzo Pitti** · PIAZZA DI SAN FELICE

VIA SANTA MARIA · ROMANA · Museo La Specola

VOLGA · VIA FRANCESCO PETRARCA · VIA DEL CASONE · VIA IPPOLITO PINDEMONTE · VIA VINCENZO MONTI · V. DE' MORI · V. SERUMIDO · VIA DEL BOBOLINO · GIARDINO DI BOBOLI · Forte di Belvedere

VIA UGO FOSCOLO · VIA PIETRO METASTASIO · PIAZZA DELLA CALZA · PIAZZALE DELLA PORTA ROMANA · VIA DEL MASCHERINO · VIA D. MADONNA D. PACE · VIA DEL BOBOLINO

VIA GIOVANNI PRATI · VIA DELLE CAMPORA · VIA SENESE · VIA CANTAGALLI · VIA DANTE DEL CASTIGLIONE · VIALE NICCOLÒ MACHIAVELLI · FARINATA DEGLI UBERTI · VIA MICHELE DI LANDO · VIA DI SAN LEONA

V. DI SANT'ILARIO A COLOMBAIA · VIA SENESE · VIA DANTE DEL CASTIGLIONE · VIALE DEL POGGIO · VIA BENEDETTO DA FOIANO · VIALE NICCOLÒ MACHIAVELLI · VIA DI SAN LEONARDO

V. PAOLO MASCAGNI · VIA SENESE · PIAZZALE GALILEO · VIALE

VIA LORENZO BELLINI · VIA BENEDETTO CASTELLI · VIA LORENZO MAGALOTTI · VIALE DEL POGGIO IMPERIALE · V.LE EVANGELISTICA TORRICELLI · VIA DI SAN LEONARDO · VIA V. VIVIANI · VIALE

VIA GIOVANNI ALFONSO BORELLI · VIALE DEL GELSOMINO · VIA LEONARDO XIMENES · VIA DI SAN LEONARDO · VIA GUGLIELMO RIGHINI

A · B · C

TUSCANY

RENOWNED FOR ITS ART, *history and evocative landscape, Tuscany is a region where the past and present merge in pleasant harmony. Hill-towns gaze across the countryside from on high, many encircled by Etruscan walls and slender cypress trees. Handsome palaces testify to the region's wealth while medieval town halls indicate a long-standing tradition of democracy and self-government.*

In the countryside, among the vineyards and olive groves, there are hamlets and farmhouses, as well as fortified villas and castles that symbolize the violence and intercommunal strife that tore Tuscany apart during the Middle Ages. Several imposing castles and villas were built for the Medici family, the great patrons of the Renaissance who supported eminent scientists, such as Galileo.

Northern Tuscany, and the heavily populated plain between Florence and Lucca, is dominated by industry, with intensively cultivated land between the cities and the wild mountainous areas.

The area centred around Livorno and Pisa is now the region's economic hub. Pisa, at the height of its powers, dominated the western Mediterranean from the 11th to the 13th centuries.

Its navy opened up extensive trading routes with North Africa, and brought to Italy the benefits of Arabic scientific and artistic achievement. During the 16th century the Arno estuary began to silt up, ending Pisan power.

At the heart of central Tuscany lies Siena, which was involved in a long feud with Florence. Its finest hour came with its victory in the Battle of Montaperti in 1260, but it was devastated by the Black Death in the 14th century and finally suffered a crushing defeat by Florence in the siege of 1554–5.

Northeastern Tuscany, with its mountain peaks and woodland, provided refuge for hermits and saints, while the east was home to Piero della Francesca, the early Renaissance painter whose timeless and serene works are imbued with an almost religious perfection.

A timeless view and way of life in Casole d'Elsa, near San Gimignano in central Tuscany

◁ **The complex architecture of Pisa's Duomo (begun in 1063) and the Leaning Tower (begun in 1173)**

Exploring Tuscany

Tuscan cities such as Florence, Siena and Pisa, together with smaller towns like Lucca, Cortona and Arezzo, contain some of Italy's most famous artistic treasures. Medieval villages such as San Gimignano, with its famous towers, or Pienza, a tiny Renaissance jewel, sit at the heart of the glorious pastoral countryside for which the region is equally renowned. Elsewhere landscapes range from the spectacular mountains of the Alpi Apuane to the gentle hills of Chianti.

SIGHTS AT A GLANCE

View of Cortona in eastern Tuscany

| 0 kilometres | 25 |
| 0 miles | 20 |

Cypress trees, a classic feature of the Tuscan landscape

Verona
Venezia
Bologna

PRATO

10

ARTIMINO

11   Arno   **13** FIESOLE

FLORENCE

VALLOMBROSO

SANSEPOLCRO

15

RADDA IN
CHIANTI

24

**SAN
GIMIGNANO**

MONTERCHI

14   **AREZZO**

23

MONTERIGGIONI

22 SIENA

CORTONA

16

21

CRETE SENESI

Perugia

GETTING AROUND

Motorways or fast dual
carriageways link Florence,
the hub of Tuscany's road and
rail network, to Siena, Pisa, Lucca
and the south. The Via Aurelia
and A12–E80 motorway serve
the Tuscan coast. Rural roads,
however, can be slow and
winding. Rail links are good,
and connect most major towns.

26

SAN GALGANO

PIENZA

18 MONTE PULCIANO

19

20

MONTALCINO

CHIUSI

17

MONTE
AMIATA

MAREMMA

31

SOVANA

29

PITIGLIANO

30

AMONE

MARSILIANA

MONTE
RGENTARIO   ORBETELLO

32

Roma

KEY

▬▬▬	Motorway
▬▬▬	Major road
▬▬▬	Minor road
▬▬▬	Scenic route
≈	River
⚘	Viewpoint

Carrara ❶

Massa Carrara. 🏛 70,000. **FS** 🚌
ℹ️ *Viale XX Settembre (localitá
Stadio) (0585 84 44 03).* 🐟 *Mon.*

INTERNATIONALLY renowned for
its marble quarries, Carrara's
almost flawless white stone
has been prized for centuries
by famous sculptors from
Michelangelo to Henry Moore
(the stone for Michelangelo's
David came from Carrara). The
region's 300 or more quarries
date back to Roman times,
making this one of the oldest
industrial sites in continuous
use in the world. Many of the
town's marble-sawing mills
and workshops welcome
visitors, offering them the
chance to see the ways in
which marble and quartz are
worked. These techniques –
along with marble artifacts old
and new – can be seen at the
Museo Civico del Marmo.

Local marble is put to good
use in the town's **Duomo** in
Piazza del Duomo, particularly
in the fine Pisan-Romanesque
façade with its delicate rose
window. The cathedral square
also contains Michelangelo's
house, used by the sculptor

A quarry in the marble-bearing hills around Carrara

during his visits to select blocks
of marble. The town has some
lovely corners to explore, in
particular the elegant Piazza
Alberica. Most visitors head
for the stone quarries that are
open to the public at nearby
Colonnata and at **Fantiscritti**
(take one of the regular town
buses or follow the signs to
the "Cave di Marmo"). The
latter features a small museum
with displays of various marble
quarrying techniques.

🏛 **Museo Civico del Marmo**
Viale XX Settembre. **C** *0585 84 57
46.* ◻ *Mon–Sat.*

Garfagnana ❷

Lucca. **FS** 🚌 *Castelnuovo di
Garfagnana.* ℹ️ *Castelnuovo di
Garfagnana (0583 64 43 54).*

A LOVELY VERDANT, silent
valley wedged between
the Orecchiella mountains
and the Alpi Apuane, the
Garfagnana region can be
explored from **Seravezza**,
Barga or **Castelnuovo di
Garfagnana**. While the town
of Barga makes the prettiest
base, thanks to its tawny
stone cathedral and charming
streets, Castelnuovo is more
convenient for drives and
walks in the surrounding
mountains. **San Pellegrino in
Alpe** in the Orecchiella has a
fascinating folklore museum,
the **Museo Etnografico**. It is
easily seen in conjunction with
the **Orto Botanico Pania di
Corfino** at the headquarters
of the **Parco dell'Orecchiella**
at Pania di Corfino, with its
collection of local Alpine trees.

To the west is the Parco
Naturale delle Alpi Apuane, an
area whose spectacular jagged
peaks and wooded valleys are
criss-crossed by hiking trails
and scenic mountain roads.

🏛 **Museo Etnografico**
Via del Voltone 15, San Pellegrino in
Alpe. **C** *0583 64 90 72.* ◻ *Tue–
Sun (Jul–Aug: daily).* 🖼️
🌿 **Parco dell'Orecchiella**
Centro Visitatori, Orecchiella.
C *0583 61 90 98.* ◻ *Jul–Aug:
daily; Jun & Sep: Sat–Sun; Apr–May
& Oct–Nov: Sun.* ♿
🌿 **Orto Botanico Pania
di Corfino**
Parco dell'Orecchiella. **C** *0583 64 49
11.* ◻ *May–Sep: Sun (Jul–Aug: daily).*

The Parco Naturale delle Alpi Apuane on the edge of the Garfagnana

One of many seaside cafés lining the waterfront in the popular beach resort of Viareggio

Bagni di Lucca ❸

Lucca. ▓ 7,400. ▒ ▐ Via Umberto 13 (0583 88 88 81). ▣ Wed & Sat.

ALL OVER TUSCANY there are hot springs of volcanic origin, like Bagni di Lucca. The Romans first exploited the springs and built bath complexes with army veterans, who settled in towns including Florence and Siena, could relax. More spas came into prominence in the Middle Ages and the Renaissance, and have continued to be recommended for relieving a variety of ailments, such as arthritis.

Tuscan spas really came into their own in the early 19th century when Bagni di Lucca reached its heyday as one of Europe's most fashionable spas, frequented by emperors, kings and aristocrats. Visitors came not only for thermal cures, but also for the **Casino** (1837), one of Europe's first licensed gambling houses. These days the town is rather sleepy, and its main sights are the 19th-century monuments, including the Neo-Gothic **English Church** (1839) on Via Crawford and the **Cimitero Anglicano** (Protestant Cemetery) on Via Letizia.

ENVIRONS: Southeast of Bagni di Lucca lies another popular spa town, **Montecatini Terme**. Developed in the 18th century, this town is one of the most interesting with a wide range of spa architecture, from Neo-Classical to Art Nouveau spa establishments.

Viareggio ❹

Lucca. ▓ 55,000. ▐▌ ▒ ▐ Viale Carducci 10 (0584 96 22 33). ▣ Thu.

KNOWN FOR ITS CARNIVAL, held in January and early February, this is also the most popular of the resorts on the Versilia coast. Its famous "Liberty" (Art Nouveau) style of architecture can be seen in the grand hotels, villas and cafés built in the 1920s after the resort's original boardwalk and timber chalets went up in flames in 1917. The finest example of the architecture is the **Gran Caffè Margherita** at the end of Passeggiata Margherita, designed by the prolific father of Italian Art Nouveau, Galileo Chini.

Torre del Lago Puccini ❺

Lucca. ▓ 11,000. ▐▌ ▒
▐ Viale Kennedy 2 (0584 35 98 93).
▣ Fri, & Sun.

A GLORIOUS AVENUE of lime trees, the Via dei Tigli, connects Viareggio with Torre del Lago Puccini, once the home of the opera composer Giacomo Puccini (1858–1924). He and his wife are buried in their former home, now the **Museo Villa Puccini**, a small museum that features the piano on which the maestro composed many of his works. Equal prominence is given to the villa's original fittings, including the gun room that housed Puccini's hunting rifle. **Lago Massaciuccoli**, a nature reserve for rare and migrant birds, provides a pretty backdrop for open-air performances of Puccini's works.

🏛 **Museo Villa Puccini**
Piazzale Belvedere Puccini 226.
▐ 0584 34 14 45. ◯ daily
(winter: Tue–Sun). ▨ ♿

Near Puccini's lakeside home at **Torre del Lago Puccini**

Street-by-Street: Lucca **6**

Lucca's regular grid of streets still follows the pattern of the former Roman colony founded in 180 BC. Great, solid ramparts, built in the 16th to 17th century, help to shut out traffic, making the city a pleasant place to explore on foot. San Michele in Foro – one of the town's many fine Pisan-Romanesque churches – stands on the site of the Roman forum (*foro*), the city's main square laid out in ancient times. It is still Lucca's main square today.

San Frediano / Palazzo Pfanner

Tourist information

Casa di Puccini

Giacomo Puccini (1858–1924), composer of some of the world's most popular operas, including La Bohème, *was born in this house.*

VIA CALDERIA

VIA BUIA

VIA S. LUCIA

VIA FILLUNGO

PIAZZA A SAN MICHELE

VIA VENETO

VIA ROMA

VIA SANTA CRO

VIA BECCHERIA

VIA CENAMI

Piazza Napoleone

This sprawling square is named after Napoleon, whose sister, Elisa Baciocchi, ruled Lucca from 1805 to 1815.

PIAZZA NAPOLEONE

VIA XX SETTEMBRE

VIA DEL BATTISTERO

PIAZZA DEL GIGLIO

VIA DEL DUOMO

Railway station

PIAZZA SAN MARTINO

PIAZZA ANTELMINELLI

★ San Michele in Foro

The extraordinary Pisan-Romanesque façade (11th to 14th century) has three tiers of twisted or carved columns, each one different from the rest.

San Giovanni

The Museo dell'Opera del Duomo, a new museum, features treasures removed from San Martino.

STAR SIGHTS

★ **San Martino**

★ **San Michele in Foro**

KEY

– – – Suggested route

0 metres   300

0 yards   300

Apostles from the mosaic on the façade of San Frediano in Lucca

In Via Fillungo, Lucca's main shopping street, several shop fronts are decorated with Art Nouveau details.

Anfiteatro Romano

SANT'ANDREA

VIA ANASTASIO

Torre dei Guinigi

VIA SANTA CROCE

VIA GUINIGI

PIAZZA SERVI

Villa Bottoni

Pinacoteca Nazionale

LISNERI

VIA DELL'ARCIVESCOVADO

Giardino Botanico

San Martino

Lucca's beautiful 11th-century Duomo is one of the outstanding examples of the exuberant Pisan-Romanesque style.

San Frediano

Piazza San Frediano. ☐ daily.
San Frediano's striking façade features a colourful 13th-century mosaic, *The Ascension*, a fine prelude to the church's wonderfully atmospheric interior. Pride of place goes to a splendid Romanesque font on the right, its sides carved with scenes from the Life of Christ and the story of Moses. Note the scene of Moses and his followers (dressed as medieval knights) as they pass through the divided Red Sea. In the second chapel in the north aisle, Aspertini's frescoes (1508–9) tell the story of Lucca's precious relic, the Volto Santo – a carving said to date from the time of the Crucifixion. The fine altarpiece (1422) in the fourth chapel of San Frediano's north aisle is by Jacopo della Quercia.

San Michele in Foro

Piazza San Michele. ☐ daily.
Built on the site of the old Roman forum (*foro*), San Michele's rich mixture of twisted marble columns and Cosmati work (inlaid marble) adorns one of the most exuberant Pisan-Romanesque façades in Tuscany. Built between the 11th and 14th centuries, its decoration is overwhelmingly pagan. Only the huge winged figure of St Michael on the pediment marks this out as a church. The interior has little of

interest except for the beautiful painting of *Saints Helena, Jerome, Sebastian and Roch* by Filippino Lippi (1457–1504).

Casa di Puccini

Via di Poggio. C 0583 58 40 28.
☐ daily (Oct–May: Tue–Sun).
● 1 Jan, 25 Dec.
The fine 15th-century house in which Giacomo Puccini (1858–1924) was born is now a shrine to the great opera composer. It contains portraits of Puccini, costume designs for his operas and the piano he used when composing his last opera, *Turandot*.

Via Fillungo

Lucca's principal shopping street winds its way through the heart of the city towards the Anfiteatro Romano. A good place to stroll, its northern end has several shops with Art Nouveau ironwork, and halfway down lies the deconsecrated church of San Cristoforo, built in the 13th century, with a lovely interior.

One of the many bars and shops along Via Fillungo

Exploring Lucca

Lucca's peaceful narrow lanes wind among the medieval buildings, opening suddenly to reveal churches, tiny piazzas, and many other reminders of the city's long history, including a Roman amphitheatre.

Medieval buildings mark the outline of Lucca's old Roman amphitheatre

♩ Anfiteatro Romano

Piazza del Anfiteatro.

Roman *Lucca* was founded in 180 BC, and stones from the ancient Roman amphitheatre have been ransacked over the centuries to build churches and palaces, leaving only a handful of original fragments studded into today's arena-shaped Piazza del Mercato. Slum housing clogged the piazza until 1830, when it was cleared on the orders of Marie Louise, the city's Bourbon ruler of that time. It was then that the amphitheatre's original shape was revealed, a graphic and evocative reminder of Lucca's rich Roman heritage. Low archways at the piazza's cardinal points mark the gates through which beasts and gladiators would once have entered the arena.

⛪ Museo dell'Opera del Duomo

Piazza Antelminelli 5. ☎ 0583 49 05 30. ◯ daily. 🎫 ♿

The museum, housed in the former Archbishop's Palace (14th century), displays the treasures of the Duomo of San Martino. These include the 11th-century carved stone head

♦ SAN MARTINO

Piazza San Martino. ☎ 0583 95 70 68. ◯ daily. 🎫 for sacristy.

Lucca's cathedral was built after the campanile, hence the façade's cramped and asymmetric appearance. The main portals contain remarkable 13th-century carvings by Nicola Pisano and Guidetto da Como. The Tempietto inside houses a painting by Tintoretto and the Volto Santo, a revered 13th-century effigy once believed to have been carved at the time of the Crucifixion.

Façade
The cathedral façade is decorated with Romanesque sculptures and colonnading (1204).

The campanile was begun in 1060 as a defensive tower.

Ghirlandaio's painting of The *Madonna and Saints* (1449–94) is in the Sacristy.

Domed chapels encircling the apse

Romanesque blind arcades and carved capitals

Tomb of Ilaria del Carretto
This beautiful portrait in marble by Jacopo della Quercia (1405–6) is of the youthful bride of Paolo Guinigi.

Matteo Civitali's marble Tempietto (1184)

Circular clerestory windows, in the nave and above the aisle roof, illuminate the church's unusually tall nave.

Nicola Pisano (1200–78) carved the *Journey of the Magi* and *Deposition* on the left portal.

Baroque gods and goddesses in the garden of the Palazzo Pfanner

of a king, removed from the cathedral façade, and a rare 12th-century Limoges casket, possibly created for a relic of St Thomas à Becket. The Croce dei Pisani, made by Vincenzo di Michele in 1411, is a sublime masterpiece of the goldsmith's art. It shows Christ on the Tree of Redemption, surrounded by angels, the Virgin, St John and the other Evangelists.

🏶 Palazzo Pfanner

Gardens 【 *340 923 30 85.*
◯ *Mar–Oct: daily; Nov–Feb: by appt.*
This elegant, imposing house (1667) has a beautiful outside staircase. It also boasts one of Tuscany's most delightful formal gardens. Laid out in the 18th century, the garden's central avenue is lined with Baroque statues of the gods and goddesses of ancient Roman mythology. The garden can also be viewed while walking along the ramparts.

The house itself contains a collection of court costume of the 18th and 19th centuries. Many garments are made of silk, whose production accounted for much of Lucca's medieval wealth.

🏶 Ramparts

One of the pleasures of visiting Lucca is strolling along the ramparts – the magnificent city walls, whose tree-lined promenade offers some entrancing views of the city.

Work on the ramparts began around 1500, when advances in military technology made the old medieval defences ineffective. On their completion in 1645, the walls were some of the most advanced of their time. One of their most curious features was the open space that lay beyond them, and which survives to this day, cleared to prevent the enemy taking cover in trees and undergrowth. Ironically, the walls never actually had to be defended, and they were eventually converted into a public park in the early 19th century.

Romanesque lion in the Museo Nazionale Guinigi

Part of the imposing 17th-century ramparts that encircle Lucca

🔒 Santa Maria Forisportam

Piazza di Santa Maria Forisportam.
◯ *daily.*
This church was built at the end of the 12th century, beyond the Roman walls of Lucca. Its name, Forisportam, means "outside the gate". The unfinished marble façade, in Pisan-Romanesque style, has blind arcading. Above the central portal is a relief of the *Coronation of the Virgin* (17th century). The interior was redesigned in the early 16th century, resulting in the nave and transepts being raised. The fourth altar of the south aisle contains a painting of *St Lucy*, and the north transept has an *Assumption*, both by Guercino (1591–1666).

🏛 Museo Nazionale di Villa Guinigi

Via della Quarquonia. 【 *0583 49 60 33.* ◯ *Tue–Sun (Sun am only).*
● *1 Jan, 1 May, 25 Dec.* 🅿
This massive Renaissance villa was built in 1418 for Paolo Guinigi, leading light of the noble family who ruled Lucca in the early 15th century. A familiar landmark of the city is the battlemented tower, the Torre dei Guinigi, with oak trees growing at the top. It offers good views over the city and the Apuan Alps. The garden features traces of a Roman mosaic, together with a pride of Romanesque lions removed from the city's walls.

Inside, the museum's first floor is devoted to sculptures and archaeological displays. The highlights are works by Matteo Civitali, Jacopo della Quercia and fine Romanesque reliefs removed from several of Lucca's churches. Most of the paintings in the gallery on the floor above are by minor local artists, with the exception of two works by Fra Bartolomeo (c.1472–1517): *God the Father with Saints Catherine and Mary Magdalene* and the *Madonna della Misericordia.* The floor also has furnishings, church vestments and choir stalls from Lucca's cathedral, inlaid with marquetry views of the city carved in 1529.

Pisa ❼

Inlaid marble, Duomo façade

For much of the Middle Ages, Pisa's powerful navy ensured its dominance of the western Mediterranean. Trading links with Spain and North Africa in the 12th century brought vast mercantile wealth and formed the basis of a scientific and cultural revolution that is still reflected in Pisa's splendid buildings – especially the Duomo, Baptistry and Campanile (Leaning Tower). Pisa's decline began in 1284, with its defeat by Genoa, and was hastened by the silting up of the harbour. The city fell to the Florentines in 1406, but suffered its worst crisis in 1944 when it fell victim to Allied bombing.

A detail from the Duomo pulpit

The Baptistry, Duomo and Leaning Tower in Pisa's Campo dei Miracoli

🏛 Leaning Tower
See p316. W *www.opapisa.it (reservations).* ☑ *Visits last 40 mins. No children under 8 allowed.* ♿

🏛 Duomo and Baptistry
Piazza Duomo. ☎ *050 56 05 47.* ◯ *daily (Duomo: pm only on Sun).* W *www.opapisa.it*

Pisa's famous Leaning Tower is now the best-known building in the Campo dei Miracoli (Field of Miracles). Originally, however, it was intended as a campanile to complement the Duomo, which was begun by Buschetto in 1064. Today the Duomo stands as one of the

finest Pisan-Romanesque buildings in Tuscany, its wonderful four-tiered façade a medley of creamy colonnades and intricate blind arcades. Buschetto's tomb is in the left arch of the façade. Other important features of the exterior include the Portale di San Ranieri (leading to the south transept) and the bronze doors (1180), decorated with reliefs cast by Bonanno Pisano, the first architect of the Leaning Tower. Inside, the highlights are the carved pulpit (1302–11) by Giovanni Pisano, the *Tomb of Emperor Henry VII* (1315) by Tino da Camaino,

and a mosaic of *Christ in Majesty* in the apse, completed by Cimabue in 1302.

The circular Baptistry was begun in 1152 along Romanesque lines, and finished a century later (the delay caused by a shortage of money) in a more ornate Gothic style by Nicola and Giovanni Pisano. The former was responsible for the marble pulpit (1260) in the interior, carved with reliefs of the *Nativity*, the *Adoration of the Magi*, the *Presentation*, the *Crucifixion* and the *Last Judgment*. The pillars that support the pulpit feature statues of the Virtues. The inlaid marble font (1246) is by Guido da Como.

⚰ Camposanto
Piazza dei Miracoli. ☎ *050 56 05 47.* ◯ *daily.* ● *1 Jan, 25 Dec.*

The Camposanto (cemetery) is the fourth element in the Campo dei Miracoli's lovely ensemble. Begun in 1278 by Giovanni di Simone, the vast marble arcades of this long, rectangular building are said to enclose soil from the Holy Land. Bombs in World War II all but destroyed its once famous frescoes, leaving only traces of *The Triumph of Death* (1360–80). Nearby is the Orto Botanico, one of Europe's oldest botanical gardens.

A fresco from the *Triumph of Death* cycle in the Camposanto

Santa Maria della Spina alongside the River Arno in Pisa

🏛 Museo dell'Opera del Duomo

Piazza del Duomo 6.
📞 050 56 05 47. 🕐 daily. 🎫 ♿
Housed in the cathedral's 13th-century former Chapter House, this excellent modern museum displays exhibits removed over the years from the Duomo, Baptistry and Camposanto. Among the highlights is an imposing 10th-century hippogriff (half horse, half griffin). Cast in bronze by Moorish craftsmen, this statue was looted by Pisan adventurers during the wars against the Saracens. There are also works by both Nicola and Giovanni Pisano, notably Giovanni's ivory *Virgin and Child* (1300), carved for the Duomo's high altar. Other exhibits include paintings, Roman and Etruscan remains, and ecclesiastical treasures.

10th-century bronze hippogriff

🏛 Museo Nazionale di San Matteo

Lungarno Mediceo, Piazza San Matteo 1. 📞 050 54 18 65.
🕐 9am–7pm Tue–Sun. 🎫
This museum is located on the banks of the Arno in San Matteo, an elegantly fronted medieval convent that in the 1800s also served as a prison. Much of the building has been closed for years – several of the rooms have no numbers and some of the exhibits are poorly labelled. Nevertheless, the museum presents a unique opportunity to examine the complete sweep of Pisan and Florentine art from the 12th to the 17th centuries.

The first rooms are devoted to sculpture and early Tuscan paintings. The best exhibits include a 14th-century polyptych by Francesco Traini of *Scenes from the Life of St Dominic*, Simone Martini's fine polyptych of *The Madonna and Saints* (1321), and a 14th-century statue of the *Madonna del Latte*, attributed to Andrea Pisano, another member of Pisa's talented school of medieval sculptors. The half-length statue, in gilded marble, shows Christ feeding at his mother's breast. In room 6 are some of the highlights of the museum, including Masaccio's *St Paul* (1426), Gentile da Fabriano's radiant 15th-century *Madonna of Humility*, and Donatello's reliquary bust of *San Rossore* (1424–7). Additional rooms contain paintings by Guido Reni, Benozzo Gozzoli, Rosso Fiorentino, and an important picture of *Christ* attributed to Fra Angelico (c.1395–1455).

⚓ Santa Maria della Spina

Lungarno Gambacorti. 📞 050 53 24 74. 🕐 by permission only.
The roofline of this tiny church, located just beyond the Ponte Solferino, bristles with spiky Gothic pinnacles, miniature spires and niches sheltering statues of apostles and saints. The decoration reflects the history of the church, which was built between 1230 and 1323 to house a thorn *(spina)* from Christ's Crown of Thorns, the gift of a Pisan merchant. The church was once even closer to the Arno, but was rebuilt on the present site in 1871 to protect it from flooding.

🏛 Piazza dei Cavalieri

The huge building on the north side of this square is the Palazzo dei Cavalieri, home to one of Pisa University's most prestigious colleges: the Scuola Normale Superiore. Designed by Vasari in 1562, the building, which is covered in exuberant black and white *sgraffito* decoration (designs scratched into wet plaster), served as the headquarters of the Cavalieri di Santo Stefano, an order of knights created by Cosimo I in 1561. The imposing statue outside depicts Cosimo I.

The Virgin and Child (1321) by Simone Martini in the Museo Nazionale

The Leaning Tower of Pisa

BEGUN IN 1173 on sandy silt subsoil, the Leaning Tower (Torre Pendente) started to tilt even before the third storey was finished in 1274. Despite the shallow foundations, construction continued and the structure was completed in 1350. The tower's apparent flouting of the laws of gravity has attracted many visitors over the centuries, including the Pisan scientist Galileo, who climbed to the top to conduct his experiments on the velocity of falling objects. After recent engineering interventions that decreased the lean by 38 cm (14 in), the tower is once again safe and open to the public.

Galileo Galilei (1564–1642)

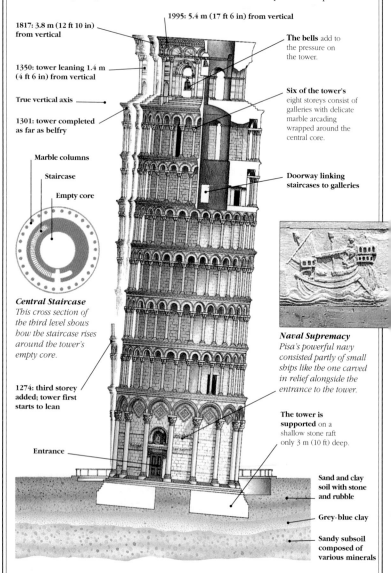

1995: 5.4 m (17 ft 6 in) from vertical

1817: 3.8 m (12 ft 10 in) from vertical

1350: tower leaning 1.4 m (4 ft 6 in) from vertical

True vertical axis

1301: tower completed as far as belfry

Marble columns

Staircase

Empty core

The bells add to the pressure on the tower.

Six of the tower's eight storeys consist of galleries with delicate marble arcading wrapped around the central core.

Doorway linking staircases to galleries

Central Staircase
This cross section of the third level shows how the staircase rises around the tower's empty core.

1274: third storey added; tower first starts to lean

Entrance

Naval Supremacy
Pisa's powerful navy consisted partly of small ships like the one carved in relief alongside the entrance to the tower.

The tower is supported on a shallow stone raft only 3 m (10 ft) deep.

Sand and clay soil with stone and rubble

Grey-blue clay

Sandy subsoil composed of various minerals

Vinci ❽

Florence. 🏛 *1,500.* 🚌 🏢 *Wed.*

FAMOUS AS THE BIRTHPLACE of Leonardo da Vinci (1452–1519), this hilltop town celebrates the genius in the **Museo Leonardiano**, housed in the 13th-century castle. Among the displays are wooden models of Leonardo's machines and inventions, most of them based on drawings from his notebooks, shown alongside these. These include a bicycle, his conception of a car, an armoured tank and even a machine-gun.

🏛 Museo Leonardiano
Castello dei Conti Guidi.
📞 *0571 560 55.* ⏰ *daily.* 🎫

Model bicycle based on designs by Leonardo, Museo Leonardiano

Pistoia ❾

🏛 *93,000.* 🚆 🚌 🅸 *Palazzo dei Vescovi, Piazza del Duomo (0573 216 22).* 🛍 *Wed & Sat.*

PISTOIA'S CITIZENS were once known for violence and intrigue, a reputation grounded in the medieval disputes between the city's rival factions, the Bianchi and Neri (Whites and Blacks). Their favoured weapon was a tiny, locally made dagger known as a *pistola*. Long a centre of metalwork, everything from buses to mattress springs are now made here. In the centre, several fine historic buildings are preserved.

🏛 Duomo
Piazza del Duomo. ⏰ *daily.*
Piazza del Duomo, Pistoia's main square, is dominated by the Duomo (San Zeno) and its bulky 12th-century campanile, originally built as a watchtower in the city walls. The interior of the Duomo is

Detail of frieze (1514–25) by Giovanni della Robbia, Ospedale del Ceppo

rich in funerary monuments. The finest of these, in the south aisle, is the tomb of Cino da Pistoia. He was a friend of Dante and fellow poet, and is depicted in a relief (1337) lecturing to a class of young boys.

Nearby is the chapel of St James and its extraordinary silver altar decorated with more than 600 statues and reliefs. Although the earliest of these dates from 1287, the altar was not completed until 1456. One of the craftsmen involved was Brunelleschi, who began his career as a silversmith before turning to architecture. Also in the Piazza del Duomo is the octagonal Baptistry, completed in 1359.

🏛 Ospedale del Ceppo
Piazza Giovanni XXIII.
This hospital and orphanage, founded in 1277, was named after the *ceppo* (hollowed-out tree trunk) that was used to collect donations for its work. The main façade features coloured terracotta panels (1514–25) by Giovanni della Robbia illustrating the *Seven Works of Mercy*. The portico is by Michelozzo.

The Pisan-Romanesque façade of Pistoia's Duomo (San Zeno)

🏛 Cappella del Tau
Corso Silvano Fedi 70.
📞 *0573 322 04.* ⏰ *Mon–Sat am.*
The Cappella del Tau (1360) is so called because the monks who built it wore on their cloaks the letter T (*tau* in Greek), symbolizing a crutch and their work with the sick and disabled. Inside there are frescoes by Niccolò di Tommaso on *The Creation* and the *Life of St Anthony Abbot* (1370). Two doors down, the **Palazzo Tau** has work by Marino Marini, Pistoia's best-known 20th-century artist.

The Fall (1372) by Niccolò di Tommaso in the Cappella del Tau

🏛 San Giovanni Fuorcivitas
Via Cavour. ⏰ *daily.*
Built in the 12th to 14th centuries, the striking church of San Giovanni Fuorcivitas (literally "St John Outside the City") once stood beyond the city walls. Its north flank is clad in banded marble and there is a Romanesque relief of the Last Supper over the portal. Inside, the holy water stoup, carved in marble with figures of the Virtues, is by Giovanni Pisano (1245–1320). A masterly pulpit, carved in 1270 with scenes from the New Testament, is by Guglielmo da Pisa. Both are among the finest works of this period, when artists were reviving the art of carving.

Prato ❿

🏛 170,000. 🚉 ℹ *Piazza delle Carceri 15 (0574 241 12).* 🚢 *Mon.*

WHILE TEXTILE factories gird Prato's outskirts, the city centre retains several important churches and museums. The **Duomo** (begun 1211) is flanked by the Pulpit of the Holy Girdle (1434–8), designed by Donatello and Michelozzo, used once a year to display a girdle, reputedly given to Thomas the Apostle before the Assumption of the Virgin. Inside the Duomo is *The Life of John the Baptist* (1452–66) by Fra Filippo Lippi, and a fresco cycle (1392–5) by Agnolo Gaddi.

Other sights include the **Museo Civico**, **Santa Maria delle Carceri**, a Renaissance church in Piazza delle Carceri; the **Castello dell' Imperatore**, a fortress built by Emperor Frederick II in 1237; the **Centro per l'Arte Contemporanea Pecci**; and the **Museo del Tessuto**, which traces the history of Prato's textile industry.

🏛 **Museo Civico**
Palazzo Pretorio, Piazza del Comune. 🗹 *0574 61 63 02.* ⬤ *for restoration.*
♣ **Castello dell'Imperatore**
Piazza delle Carceri. ◯ *Wed–Mon.*
🏛 **Centro per l'Arte Contemporanea Pecci**
Viale della Repubblica 277. 🗹 *0574 53 17.* ◯ *Wed–Mon.* 🅦 *www.centropecci.it*
🏛 **Museo del Tessuto**
Piazza del Comune. 🗹 *0574 61 15 03.* ◯ *Mon, Wed–Sat.*

Madonna del Ceppo by Fra Filippo Lippi in Prato's Museo Civico

Buontalenti's Villa di Artimino, or "Villa of a Hundred Chimneys"

Artimino ⓫

Prato. 🏛 *400.* 🚉

A SMALL FORTIFIED hamlet, Artimino is remarkable for the unspoiled Romanesque church of **San Leonardo**. Outside the walls lies the **Villa di Artimino**, designed by Buontalenti in 1594 for Grand Duke Ferdinando I. Also known as the "Villa of a Hundred Chimneys" – after the chimney pots crowding the roofline – it houses the **Museo Archeologico Etrusco**, a collection of archaeological exhibits.

ENVIRONS: For lovers of Pontormo's paintings, the church of **San Michele** in Carmignano, 5 km (3 miles) north of Artimino, contains *The Visitation* (1530). East of here lies the villa of **Poggio a Caiano**. Built in 1480 by Giuliano da Sangallo for Lorenzo de' Medici *(see p245)*, it was the first Italian villa to be designed in the Renaissance style.

🏛 **Villa di Artimino**
Viale Papa Giovanni 23.
Villa 🗹 *055 871 81 24.* ◯ *by appt.*
Museum 🗹 *055 871 80 81.* ◯ *9:30am–12:30pm daily.* 🅖
🏛 **Poggio a Caiano**
Piazza Medici. 🗹 *055 87 70 12.* ◯ *Tue–Sun.* 🅖 🅖

San Miniato ⓬

Pisa. 🏛 *3,900.* 🚉 ℹ *Piazza del Popolo 3 (0571 427 45).* 🚢 *Tue.*

THIS HILLTOP TOWN manages to remain aloof from the vast industrial sprawl of the Arno valley. Its key building

is the semi-derelict Rocca (castle), built for Frederick II, German Holy Roman Emperor, in the 13th century. Close by stands the **Museo Diocesano**, which is home to a *Crucifixion* (c.1430) attributed to Filippo Lippi, a terracotta bust of Christ attributed to Verrocchio (1435–88), and the *Virgin of the Holy Girdle* by Andrea del Castagno (c.1417–57). Next door, the red-brick Romanesque façade of the **Duomo** dates from the 12th century. Its strange inset majolica plates, evidence of trade with Spain or North Africa, probably represent the North Star and the constellations of Ursus Major and Minor (all three were key points of reference for early navigators).

🏛 **Museo Diocesano**
Piazza Duomo. 🗹 *0571 41 82 71.* ◯ *10am–1pm, 3–7pm Tue–Sun (Nov–Mar: to 6pm).* 🅖

Façade of the Duomo in San Miniato

Fiesole ⓭

Florence. 🏛 *15,000.* 🚉 ℹ *Via Portigiani 3/5 (055 59 87 20).* 🚢 *Sat.*

FIESOLE STANDS IN rolling hilly countryside 8 km (5 miles) north of Florence. Idyllically situated among olive groves, it is a popular retreat from the city thanks to its hilltop position which attracts cool breezes. Founded in the 7th century BC, the original Etruscan colony was a powerful force in central Italy, only

A view over the hills and rooftops of Fiesole from Via di San Francesco

surrendering its supremacy after the foundation of Florence (1st century BC).

The recently restored **Duomo** of San Romolo in Piazza Mino da Fiesole was begun in 1028. It has a massive bell tower and a bare Romanesque interior. Behind the Duomo, an archaeological area contains the remains of a 1st-century BC **Roman theatre**, traces of **Etruscan walls** from the 4th century BC, and the **Museo Faesulanum**, with a collection of bronzes, ceramics and jewellery dating from the Bronze Age.

Via di San Francesco, a steep lane offering lovely views, leads to the Franciscan friary of **San Francesco** (14th century) and the interesting 9th-century church of **Sant'Alessandro**, with a Neo-Classical façade.

Via Vecchia Fiesolana leads to the hamlet of **San Domenico**, where the 15th-century church of the same name contains a painting of the *Madonna with Angels and Saints* (c.1430) by Fra Angelico and the Chapter House contains a fresco of *The Crucifixion* (c.1430), also by him. Close by, on the Via della Badia dei Roccettini, is the **Badia Fiesolana**, a pretty Romanesque church with a striped marble façade and interior of local grey sandstone, *pietra serena*.

🏛 **Museo Faesulanum**
Via Portigiani 1. 📞 055 594 77.
⏰ daily (Oct–Mar: Wed–Mon). 🎫

Arezzo ⑭

🏃 92,000. 🚉 ℹ️ Piazza della Repubblica 82 (0575 208 39). 🚌 Sat.

Arezzo is one of Tuscany's wealthiest cities, its prosperity based on a thriving jewellery industry. Although much of its medieval centre was destroyed during World War II, resulting in extensive rebuilding and many medieval alleys being replaced by broad avenues, the city preserves some outstanding sights: foremost are Piero della Francesca's famous frescoes in the church of **San Francesco** *(see pp320–21)*. Close to the church on Corso Italia, the main street, stands the **Pieve di Santa Maria**, which boasts one of the most ornate Romanesque façades in the region. To its rear stretches the steeply sloping **Piazza Grande**, flanked by an arcade (1573) designed by Vasari, and by

the **Palazzo della Fraternità dei Laici** (1377–1552). The latter features a *Madonna* relief by Bernardo Rossellino. The huge **Duomo** to the north is best known for its 16th-century stained glass and a small fresco of *Mary Magdalene* by Piero della Francesca (1416–92). The **Museo del Duomo** features three wooden crucifixes, dating from the 12th and 13th centuries, a bas relief of *The Annunciation* (1434) by Rossellino and paintings by Vasari. More works by Vasari can be seen in the **Casa di Vasari**, a house built by the artist in 1540. Still more frescoes by him are displayed in the **Museo d'Arte Medioevale e Moderna**, a museum that is famed for its excellent collection of majolica pottery.

The **Fortezza Medicea**, a ruined Medici castle built by Antonio da Sangallo during the 16th century, has fine views.

🏛 **Museo del Duomo**
Piazzetta del Duomo 13. 📞 0575 239 91. ⏰ Thu–Sat am by appt. 🎫

🏠 **Casa di Vasari**
Via XX Settembre 55. 📞 0575 40 90 40. ⏰ Wed–Mon.

🏛 **Museo d'Arte Medioevale e Moderna**
Via di San Lorentino 8. 📞 0575 40 90 50. ⏰ Tue–Sun. 🎫

🏰 **Fortezza Medicea**
Parco il Prato. 📞 0575 37 76 66.
⏰ daily. 🎫

The monthly antiques market held in Arezzo's Piazza Grande

Arezzo: San Francesco

THE 13TH-CENTURY CHURCH of San Francesco houses one of Italy's greatest fresco cycles, the *Legend of the True Cross* (1452–66), Piero della Francesca's masterpiece. The scenes, on the walls of the choir, are now visible again after a long restoration. They describe the history of the Cross used to crucify Christ, from sprig to Tree of Knowledge, to its use as a bridge during the reign of Solomon, and ultimately its discovery by Helena, mother of Constantine, the first Christian emperor.

A Group of Onlookers
These figures kneel in wonder while Heraclius returns the True Cross to Jerusalem.

Excavation of the Cross
The town, meant to be Jerusalem, gives a fair representation of 15th-century Arezzo.

The Cross returns to Jerusalem.

KEY TO FRESCOES

1 The Death of Adam; a sprig from the Tree of Knowledge is planted over his grave; 2 The Queen of Sheba visits Solomon and foresees that a bridge made from the Tree will be used to crucify the greatest king in the world; 3 Solomon, assuming he is the greatest king in the world, orders the bridge to be buried; 4 The Annunciation: Christ's death is foreshadowed in the panel's cruciform structure; 5 Constantine has a vision of the Cross and hears a voice saying "In this sign you shall conquer"; 6 Constantine defeats his rival Maxentius; 7 The Levite Judas is tortured and reveals the location of the True Cross; 8 Three crosses are dug up; Constantine's mother Helena recognizes the True Cross; 9 The Persian king Chosroes is defeated after stealing the Cross; 10 The True Cross is returned to Jerusalem.

The Defeat of Chosroes depicts the defeat of a Persian king who had stolen the Cross.

Judas reveals where the Cross is hidden.

Painted Crucifix
The 13th-century Crucifix forms the focal point of the fresco cycle. The figure at the foot of the Cross represents St Francis, to whom the church is dedicated.

The Death of Adam
Piero's vivid portrayal of Adam and Eve in old age shows an adept treatment of anatomy. He was one of the first Renaissance artists to paint nude figures.

VISITORS' CHECKLIST

Piazza San Francesco. **(** 0575 90 04 04 *(booking mandatory).* **○** 9am–6pm Mon–Sat (to 5:30pm Sat); 1–5:30pm Sun. **✝ ⚙ ♿**

The prophets appear to play no part in the narrative cycle; their presence may be for purely decorative reasons.

The buildings in the fresco reflect the newly fashionable styles of Renaissance architecture.

The wood of the Cross is buried in a pit.

Constantine dreams of the Cross on the eve of battle against rival emperor Maxentius.

Constantine leads his cavalry into battle.

The Queen of Sheba recognizes the wood of the Cross.

Solomon's Handshake
The handshake between the Queen of Sheba and Solomon, King of Israel, portrays 15th-century hopes for a union between the Orthodox and Western churches.

Piero's *The Resurrection* (1463) in Sansepolcro

Sansepolcro ⑮

Arezzo. 🏛 *16,000.* 🚌 ℹ *Piazza Garibaldi 2 (0575 74 05 36).* 🛒 *Tue, Sat.*

SANSEPOLCRO is the birthplace of Piero della Francesca (1410–92). The town's **Museo Civico** contains two of his masterpieces: *The Resurrection* (1463) and the *Madonna della Misericordia* (1462). It also has a 15th-century *Crucifixion* by Luca Signorelli. In the church of **San Lorenzo** on Via Santa Croce there is a *Deposition* in the Mannerist style by Rosso Fiorentino (1494–1541).

Another renowned painting by Piero della Francesca, the *Madonna del Parto* (1460), can be seen at Via Reglia 1 in Monterchi, 13 km (8 miles) southwest of Sansepolcro.

🏛 **Museo Civico**
Via Aggiunti 65. ☎ *0575 73 22 18.* ◯ *daily.* ● *public hols.* 📷

Cortona ⑯

Arezzo. 🏛 *23,000.* 🚆 🚌 ℹ *Via Nazionale 42 (0575 63 03 52).* 🛒 *Sat.*

CORTONA WAS FOUNDED by the Etruscans and apart from being one of the oldest hill-towns in Tuscany, it is also one of the most scenic. A major power in the Middle Ages, it was able to hold its own against Siena and Arezzo. Today it is a charming maze of old streets and medieval

buildings, like the **Palazzo Comunale** on Piazza Signorelli. The town's early history is traced in the **Museo dell'Accademia Etrusca**, which contains Etruscan artifacts and a wide variety of Egyptian and Roman remains. The small **Museo Diocesano** features several fine paintings, in particular a *Crucifixion* by the Renaissance artist Pietro Lorenzetti, a *Deposition* (1502) by Luca Signorelli, and a sublime *Annunciation* (c.1434) by Fra Angelico. Signorelli, born in Cortona, is buried in the church of **San Francesco** (built in 1245), which contains an *Annunciation* painted in Baroque style by Pietro da Cortona, another native artist. The **Madonna del Calcinaio** (1485), a gem of Renaissance architecture, is located on the southern outskirts of town.

The 13th-century Palazzo Comunale in Cortona

🏛 **Museo dell'Accademia Etrusca**
Palazzo Casali, Piazza Signorelli 9. ☎ *0575 63 04 15.* ◯ *daily (except Mon in winter).* 📷
🏛 **Museo Diocesano**
Piazza del Duomo 1. ☎ *0575 628 30.* ◯ *Tue–Sun.* 📷

Chiusi ⑰

Siena. 🏛 *10,000.* 🚆 🚌 ℹ *Piazza Duomo 1 (0578 22 76 67).* 🛒 *Tue.*

CHIUSI IS NOW a largely modern town, but in the past it was one of the most powerful cities in the Etruscan league, reaching the height of its influence in the 7th and 6th centuries BC *(see p41)*. Numerous Etruscan tombs lie dotted in the surrounding countryside, the source of the exhibits in the town's **Museo Nazionale Etrusco**. Founded in 1871, the museum is packed with cremation urns, vases decorated with black figures and Bucchero ware, burnished to resemble bronze.

The Romanesque **Duomo** in Piazza del Duomo incorporates recycled Roman pillars and capitals. The wall decorations in the nave, resembling frescoes, were painted by Arturo Viligiardi in 1887. There is a Roman mosaic underneath the high altar. Visits can be made to several Etruscan tombs under the town from the **Museo della Cattedrale**, a museum in the cloister of the Duomo that also features displays of Roman, Lombardic and medieval sculpture from the region.

🏛 **Museo Nazionale Etrusco**
Via Porsenna 17. ☎ *0578 201 77.* ◯ *9am–2pm daily (to 1pm Sun).* 📷
🏛 **Museo della Cattedrale**
Piazza del Duomo. ☎ *0578 22 64 90.* ◯ *daily.* 📷

Etruscan frieze in the Museo Nazionale Etrusco in Chiusi

Pienza's Piazza Pio II, designed by Bernardo Rossellino (1459)

Montepulciano ⑱

Siena. 🏘 *14,000.* 🚌 ℹ️ *Via di Gracciano 59 (0578 75 73 41).* 🛒 *Thu.* 🌐 *www.prolocomontepulciano.it*

THIS IS ONE of Tuscany's highest hill-towns, its walls and fortifications offering broad views over Umbria and southern Tuscany, and the vineyards providing the Vino Nobile wine that has made its name famous. The streets are brimming with Renaissance palazzi. The main street, the Corso, climbs to the **Duomo** (1592–1630), the setting for one of the masterpieces of the Sienese School, the *Assumption* (1401) by Taddeo di Bartolo. The High Renaissance church, **Tempio di San Biagio** (1518–34), lies off the road to Pienza.

Pienza ⑲

Siena. 🏘 *2,300.* 🚌 ℹ️ *Corso il Rossellino 59 (0578 74 90 71).* 🛒 *Fri.*

PIENZA IS A delightful village whose intimate little centre was almost completely re-designed in the 15th century by Pope Pius II. Born as Aeneas Sylvius Piccolomini in 1405, when the village was known as Corsignano, he became a leading Humanist scholar and philosopher. Elected pope in 1458, he decided to rebuild his birthplace, renaming it Pienza in his own honour. The Florentine architect and sculptor, Bernardo Rossellino, was commissioned to build a cathedral, papal palace and town hall (all completed in the three years from 1459 to 1462), but the grander scheme for a planned model Renaissance town was never realized. Some idea of what might have been, however, can still be gained from the **Palazzo Piccolomini**, the former papal palace, which continued to be inhabited by Pius's descendants until 1968. The rooms open to the public include Pius's bedroom and library, though the highlight of a visit is the superb panorama from the loggia and arcaded courtyard at the palace's rear.

Pleasant walks and more great views can be had from the village walls. The airy **Duomo** *(see p244)* next door contains six altarpieces of the *Madonna and Child*, each commissioned from the leading Sienese painters of the day. Rossellino was forced to build the Duomo on a cramped site with poor foundations, and cracks appeared in the building before it was even completed. Today the church's eastern end suffers from severe subsidence.

🏛 **Palazzo Piccolomini**
Piazza Pio II. ℂ *0578 74 85 03.* ◯ *mid-Dec–mid-Nov: Tue–Sun.* 🎟 ✄ *every 30 mins.*

Montalcino ⑳

Siena. 🏘 *5,100.* 🚌 ℹ️ *Costa del Municipio 1 (0577 84 93 31).* 🛒 *Fri.*

HILLTOP MONTALCINO sits at the heart of vineyards that produce Brunello, one of Italy's finest red wines. It can be sampled in the Enoteca (wine shop) situated in the 14th-century **Fortezza** with its impressive ramparts. The town's timeless streets are a pleasure to wander, and there are some buildings of interest. On the way from the fortress into town is the monastery of Sant' Agostino and its 14th-century church with an attractive rose window and, just beyond, the Palazzo Vescovile. On Piazza del Popolo the slim tower of the Palazzo Communale, constructed in the 13th and 14th centuries, stands tall above the town.

♣ **Fortezza**
Piazzale della Fortezza. ℂ *0577 84 92 11.* 🎟 *for ramparts.*
Enoteca ◯ *Apr–Oct: 9am–8pm daily; Nov–Mar: 9am–6pm daily.*

The Tempio di San Biagio on the outskirts of Montepulciano

The landscape of the Crete Senesi

Crete Senesi ㉑

Asciano. **FS** 🚌 **ℹ** *Corso Matteotti 18 (0577 71 95 10).*

To the south of Siena and central Tuscany is the area known as the Crete Senesi, which is characterized by round clay hillocks eroded by heavy rain over the centuries. Dubbed the "Tuscan desert", it is almost completely barren. Cypress and pine trees, planted to provide windbreaks along roads and around isolated farm houses, are an important feature in this empty, primeval landscape. Shepherds tend flocks of sheep here; the milk is used to produce the strongly flavoured *pecorino* cheese that is popular throughout Tuscany.

Siena ㉒

See pp328–33.

Monteriggioni ㉓

Siena. 🕍 *7,000.* 🚌 **ℹ** *Pro Loco (0577 30 48 10).* 🕐 *Jun–Aug.*

Monteriggioni is a gem of a medieval hilltop town. It was built in 1203 and ten years later became a garrison town. It is completely encircled by high walls with 14 heavily fortified towers, built to guard the northern borders of Siena's territory against invasion by Florentine armies.

Dante used Monteriggioni as a simile for the deepest abyss at the heart of his *Inferno*, which compares the town's "ring-shaped citadel… crowned with towers" with giants standing in a moat. The perfectly preserved walls are best viewed from the Colle di Val d'Elsa road. Within the walls, the sleepy town consists of a large piazza, a pretty Romanesque church (on the piazza), a few houses, a couple of craft shops, restaurants, and shops selling many of the locally produced Castello di Monteriggioni wines.

ENVIRONS: West of Monteriggioni by 3 km (2 miles) lies the former Cistercian Abbey of **Abbadia dell' Isola** (12th century). This Romanesque church was largely rebuilt in the 18th century, after the cupola fell apart. It contains frescoes by Taddeo di Bartolo and Vincenzo Tamagni and a Renaissance altarpiece.

San Gimignano ㉔

See pp334–5.

Volterra ㉕

Pisa. 🕍 *13,000.* 🚌 **ℹ** *Via Giusto Turazza 2 (0588 861 50).* 🛒 *Sat.* 🌐 *www.provolterra.it*

Like many Etruscan cities, Volterra is situated on a high plateau, offering fine views over the surrounding hills. In many places the ancient Etruscan walls still survive. The **Museo Guarnacci** contains one of the best collections of Etruscan artifacts in Italy. Of special interest is the group of over 600 cinerary urns, made from alabaster or terracotta, many of which were gathered from local tombs.

The **Palazzo dei Priori**, the medieval seat of government on Piazza dei Priori, is the oldest of its kind in Tuscany. It was begun in 1208 and there are 14th-century frescoes inside. The Pisan-Romanesque **Duomo**, located on Piazza San Giovanni, has a fine 13th-century pulpit with sculptured panels.

Detail from the pulpit in Volterra's Duomo

Volterra's excellent art gallery and museum, the **Pinacoteca e Museo Civico**, features works by Florentine artists. *Christ in Majesty* (1492) by Ghirlandaio shows Christ hovering above an idealized Tuscan landscape. Luca Signorelli's *Virgin and Child with Saints* (1491) states his debt to Roman art through the reliefs on the base of the Virgin's throne. Painted in the same year, his *Annunciation* is a beautifully balanced composition. Another highlight is Rosso Fiorentino's Mannerist painting, *The Deposition* (1521).

The city is famous for its craftsmen who have been carving elaborate statues and *objets d'art* from locally mined alabaster for 2,500 years.

The beautifully preserved walls of Monteriggioni in central Tuscany

The ruined abbey at San Galgano, surrounded by dense woodland

🏛 **Museo Guarnacci**
Via Don Minzoni 15. 📞 0588 863 47.
⏱ daily. ⬤ 1 Jan, 25 Dec. 🈺
🏛 **Pinacoteca e Museo Civico**
Via dei Sarti 1. 📞 0588 875 80.
⏱ daily. ⬤ 1 Jan, 25 Dec. 🈺

San Galgano 🄦

Siena. 🚌 from Siena. 📞 0577 75
66 11. **Abbey & oratory** ⏱ daily.

The remote Cistercian abbey at San Galgano lies in a superb setting. San Galgano (1148–81) was a brave but dissolute knight who turned to God, renouncing the material world. When he tried to break his sword against a rock as a symbol of his rejection of war, it was swallowed by the stone. This he interpreted as a sign of God's approval. He built a hut on a hill above the abbey (the site of today's beehive-shaped chapel at **Montesiepi**, built c.1185). Here he later died a hermit. Pope Urban III declared him a saint and an example to Christian knights.

The abbey, begun in 1218, is Gothic in style, reflecting the French origins of the Cistercian monks who designed it. They avoided contact with the outside world and divided their lives between prayer and labour. Despite an emphasis on poverty, the monks became wealthy from the sale of wood, and by the middle of the 14th century the abbey

was corruptly administered and gradually fell into decline.

In the late 14th century, the English mercenary Sir John Hawkwood sacked the abbey and by 1397 the abbot was its sole occupant. It was eventually dissolved in 1652.

St Galgano's sword stands embedded in a stone just inside the door of the circular **oratory**. The 14th-century stone walls of the side chapel are covered with worn frescoes showing scenes from Galgano's life by Ambrogio Lorenzetti (1344).

Massa Marittima 🄧

Grosseto. 🏘 9,500. 🚌 🛈 Amatur,
Via Todini 3–5 (0566 90 27 56).
🔵 Wed.

Set in the Colline Metallifere (metal-bearing hills) where lead, copper and silver ores were mined as early as Etruscan times, Massa Marittima is far from being a grimy industrial town. Excellent examples of Romanesque architecture survive from the period when the town became an independent republic (1225–1335). The Romanesque-

Gothic **Duomo** in Piazza Garibaldi is dedicated to St Cerbone, a 6th-century saint whose story is sculpted in stone above the main portal. Inside the building, the *Maestà* is attributed to Duccio (c.1316).

The **Museo della Miniera** (museum of mining) is located partially inside a former mine shaft and has exhibits that explain mining techniques, tools and minerals.

The **Museo Archeologico e Pinacoteca** has material from Paleolithic to Roman times. Other attractions are the Fortezza Senese and the Torre della Candeliera.

🏛 **Museo della Miniera**
Via Corridoni. 📞 0566 90 22 89. ⏱
by 📷 Tue–Sun (Jul & Aug: daily). 🈺
🏛 **Museo Archeologico e Pinacoteca**
Palazzo del Podestà, Piazza Garibaldi.
📞 0566 90 22 89. ⏱ Tue–Sun. 🈺

View across the rooftops of Massa Marittima

Denuded hillocks of clay in the Crete Senesi area southeast of Siena ▷

Street-by-Street: Siena ㉒

**Unicorn
Contrada**

Sɪᴇɴᴀ's ᴘʀɪɴᴄɪᴘᴀʟ sɪɢʜᴛs cluster in the maze of narrow streets and alleys around the fan-shaped Piazza del Campo. One of Europe's greatest medieval squares, the piazza sits at the heart of the city's 17 *contrade*, a series of parishes whose ancient rivalries are still acted out in the twice-yearly Palio (*see p331*). Loyalty to the *contrada* of one's birth is fierce, and as you wander the streets you will see the parishes' animal symbols repeated on flags, plaques and carvings. Siena's hilly position also means that city walks offer delightful hidden corners and countless sudden views.

The Duomo dominating Siena's skyline

Bus station ↑

Railway station ↙

Via della Galluzza leads to the house of St Catherine.

The Baptistry has fine frescoes and a font with reliefs by Donatello, Jacopo della Quercia and Ghiberti.

★ Duomo
Striped black and white marble pillars, surmounted by a carved frieze of the popes, support the Duomo's vaulted ceiling, painted blue with gold stars to resemble the night sky.

Each tier of the Duomo's bell tower has one more window than the floor below.

VIA D. GALLUZZA

PIAZZA INDIPENDENZA

VIA DI DIACCETO

VIA DI FONTEBRANDA

VIA DI CITTA

VIA DEI PELLEGRINI

VIA FRANCIOSA

PIAZZA SAN GIOVANNI

VIC. D. CAMPANE

VIA DEL FUSARI

VIA DEL POGGIO

VIA DI CITTA

PIAZZA DEL DUOMO

VIA DEL CAPITANO

Museo dell'Opera del Duomo
Duccio's Maestà, one of the greatest Sienese paintings, was paraded around Siena's streets on its completion in 1311, and influenced the city's painters for decades to come.

Kᴇʏ

– – – Suggested route

0 metres	300
0 yards	300

Loggia della Mercanzia

Built in 1417, the arcade is where Siena's medieval merchants and money dealers carried out their business.

VISITORS' CHECKLIST

🚶 60,000. 🚉 Piazzale Rosselli.
🚌 Piazza S. Domenico. 🛈 Piazza del Campo 56 (0577 28 05 51).
🛒 Wed. 🎏 2 Jul, 16 Aug: Palio; Jul: Settimana Musicale Chigiana (classical music). 🌐 www. terresiena.it

🏛 Piazza del Campo

Italy's loveliest piazza occupies the site of the old Roman forum, and for much of Siena's early history was the city's principal marketplace. It began to assume its present shape in 1293, when the Council of Nine, Siena's ruling body at the time, began to acquire land with a view to creating a grand civic piazza. The red brick paving was begun in 1327 and completed in 1349, its distinctive nine segments designed to reflect the authority of the Council of Nine and to symbolize the protective folds of the Madonna's cloak. The piazza has been the focus of city life ever since, a setting for executions, bullfights and the twice-yearly drama of the Palio *(see p331)*, a festival centred around a bareback horse race. Cafés, restaurants and fine medieval palazzi now line the Campo's fringes, dominated by the **Palazzo Pubblico** (1297–1342) and **Torre del Mangia**, built in 1348 *(see p330)*. This imposing ensemble tends to overshadow the little **Fonte Gaia** on the piazza's northern edge. The fountain is a 19th-century copy of an original carved by Jacopo della Quercia in 1409–19. Its reliefs depict the *Virtues*, *Adam and Eve*, and the *Madonna and Child* (the originals are on the rear loggia of the Palazzo Pubblico). The fountain's water is still supplied by a 500-year-old aqueduct.

The **Logge del Papa**, or Pope's colonnade, was built in honour of Pius II in 1462.

VIA BANCHI DI SOTTO

VIA DI PANTANETO

VIA MALAVOLTI

PIAZZA DEL CAMPO

VIA DEL PORRIONE

VIA DI SALICOTTO

PIAZZA DEL MERCATO

VIA DUPRÈ

Tourist information

Drummer in Siena's Palio

Fonte Gaia

These reliefs are 19th-century copies of originals by Jacopo della Quercia.

★ **Palazzo Pubblico**

The graceful Gothic town hall was completed in 1342. At 102 m (330 ft), the bell tower, Torre del Mangia, is the second highest medieval tower ever built in Italy.

STAR SIGHTS

★ **Duomo**

★ **Palazzo Pubblico**

The Piazza del Campo and Fonte Gaia from the Torre del Mangia

Exploring Siena

ONCE A CAPITAL to rival Florence, Siena is Italy's prettiest medieval town, still endowed with the grandeur of the age in which it was at its peak (1260–1348). Begin an exploration of its historic centre in Piazza del Campo and the surrounding maze of medieval alleys.

Lorenzetti's *Allegory of Good Government* (1338), Palazzo Pubblico

🏛 Palazzo Pubblico

Piazza del Campo 1. **C** *0577 29 22 63.* **Museo Civico & Torre del Mangia** ◯ *daily.* 🖼

Although it continues in its ancient role as Siena's town hall, the Palazzo Pubblico's medieval rooms, some decorated with paintings of the Sienese School, are open to the public. The **Museo Civico** is housed here. The main council chamber, or Sala del Mappamondo, is named after a map of the world painted by Ambrogio Lorenzetti in the early 14th century. One wall is covered by Simone Martini's recently restored fresco of the *Maestà* (1315), which depicts the Virgin in Majesty as the Queen of Heaven, attended by the Apostles, saints and angels. Opposite is a fresco (attributed to Simone Martini, but possibly later) of the mercenary *Guidoriccio da Fogliano* (1330). The walls of the chapel alongside are covered with frescoes of the *Life of the Virgin* (1407) by Taddeo di Bartolo, and the choir stalls

(1428) are decorated with wooden panels inlaid with biblical scenes. The Sala della Pace contains the famous *Allegory of Good and Bad Government* (1338–40), a pair of frescoes by Ambrogio Lorenzetti. They form one of the most important series of secular paintings from the Middle Ages. In the *Good Government* fresco civic life flourishes, while the *Bad Government*, presided over by a demon, reveals rubbish-strewn streets and ruins.

The Sala del Risorgimento is covered with late 19th-century frescoes illustrating the events leading up to the unification of Italy under King Vittorio Emanuele II.

In the palace courtyard is the entrance to the magnificent **Torre del Mangia**, the palace's huge bell tower. Rising 102 m (330 ft), it is a prominent feature of

Siena's skyline. Built by the brothers Muccio and Francesco di Rinaldo between 1338 and 1348, it was named after the first bell-ringer, whose idleness led to the nickname *Mangiaguadagni* (literally "eat the profits"). There are 505 steps to the top of the tower, which has wonderful views.

🏛 Santuario e Casa di Santa Caterina

Costa di Sant'Antonio.
C *0577 24 73 93.* ◯ *daily.*

Siena's patron saint, Catherine Benincasa (1347–80), was the daughter of a tradesman. At the age of eight she devoted herself to God and had many visions, as well as later receiving the stigmata (wounds of Christ). Like her namesake, St Catherine of Alexandria, she was believed to have been betrothed to the Christ child in a vision – a scene which inspired many artists. Her eloquence per-suaded Pope Gregory XI to return the seat of the papacy to Rome in 1376, after 67 years of exile in Avignon. St Catherine died in Rome and was canonized in 1461.

Today Catherine's house is surrounded by chapels and cloisters. Among them is the Church of the Crucifixion, which was built in 1623 in her orchard to house the late 12th-century Crucifixion, in front of which she received the stigmata in 1375. The house is decorated with paintings of events from her life by artists including her contemporaries Francesco Vanni and Pietro Sorri.

Cloister of Santuario e Casa di Santa Caterina, birthplace of Siena's patron saint

⚜ Palazzo Piccolomini

Via Banchi di Sotto 52. 📞 *0577 24 71 45.* 🕐 *Mon–Sat am.* ⬤ *1–15 Aug.*

Siena's most imposing private palazzo was built for the wealthy Piccolomini family in the 1460s by the Florentine architect and sculptor Bernardo Rossellino. It now contains the Sienese state archives, account books and taxation documents dating back to the 13th century. Some of the leading artists of their day were employed to paint the wooden bindings used to enclose the tax and account records. The paintings, now on display in the Sala di Congresso, often show scenes of Siena itself, bristling with towers, or episodes from the city's past.

Other records include a will attributed to Boccaccio and the council's contract with Jacopo della Quercia for the Fonte Gaia *(see p329).*

A detail from Martini's *Blessed Agostino Novello* (c.1330)

⛪ Pinacoteca Nazionale

Via San Pietro 29. 📞 *0577 28 11 61.* 🕐 *daily.* ⬤ *Sun, Mon pm.* 🎫 ♿

This fine gallery, which is housed in the 14th-century Palazzo Buonsignori, contains an unsurpassed collection of paintings by artists of the Sienese School. Arranged in chronological order, from the 13th century through to the Mannerist period (1520–1600), highlights include Duccio's *Madonna dei Francescani* (1285) and Simone Martini's masterpiece *The Blessed Agostino Novello and Four of His Miracles* (c.1330). Pietro Lorenzetti's *Two Views*, from the 14th century, are early examples of landscape painting, and Pietro da Domenico's *Adoration of the Shepherds* (1510) shows how the art of

The austere exterior of the church of San Domenico (begun 1226)

Siena remained visibly influenced by its Byzantine roots long after the naturalism of the Renaissance had reached across the rest of Europe.

🔒 San Domenico

Piazza San Domenico. 🕐 *daily.*

The preserved head of the city's patroness, St Catherine of Siena (1347–80), can be seen in a gilded tabernacle on the altar of a chapel dedicated to her in the huge, barn-like Gothic church of San Domenico (begun 1226). The chapel itself was built in 1460 for this purpose and is dominated by Sodoma's frescoes (1526), to the right and left of the altar, which show Catherine in states of religious fervour. The church has the only portrait of St Catherine considered authentic, painted by her friend Andrea Vanni.

THE SIENESE PALIO

The Palio is Tuscany's most celebrated festival and it occurs in the Campo each year on 2 July and 16 August at 7pm. It is a bareback horse race first recorded in 1283, but it may have had its origins in Roman military training. The jockeys represent ten of Siena's 17 *contrade* (districts); the horses are chosen by the drawing of lots and are blessed at the local *contrada* churches. Preceded by days of colourful pageantry, costume processions and heavy betting, the races themselves last only 90 seconds each. Thousands of spectators crowd into the piazza to watch the race, and rivalry between competitors is intense. The winner is rewarded with a silk *palio* (banner). Festivities for the winners can last for weeks.

A *contrada* symbol

The Sienese displaying their flag-throwing skills before the Palio

Siena: Duomo

A symbol of
the Risen Christ
on the façade

SIENA'S DUOMO (1136–1382) is one of Italy's greatest cathedrals, a spectacular mixture of sculpture, paintings and Pisan-influenced Romanesque-Gothic architecture. Had 14th-century plans to create a new nave come to fruition, the building would have become the largest church in Christendom. In the event the plan came to nothing, abandoned when the plague of 1348 virtually halved the city's population. Among the Duomo's treasures are sculptural masterpieces by Nicola Pisano, Donatello and Michelangelo, a fine inlaid pavement and a magnificent fresco cycle by Pinturicchio.

Baptismal Font
This Renaissance font by della Quercia, Ghiberti and Donatello stands in the Baptistry.

Pulpit Panels
Carved in 1265–8 by Nicola Pisano, with help from Arnolfo di Cambio and his son Giovanni, the panels on the octagonal pulpit depict scenes from the Life of Christ.

In the nave, black and white marble pillars support the vault.

Chapel of St John the Baptist

The north aisle contains sculptures by Michelangelo of Saints Peter, Pius, Gregory and Paul (1501–4).

Inlaid Marble Floor
The Massacre of the Innocents *is one of a series of scenes in the inlaid marble floor. The marble is usually uncovered during September each year.*

Piccolomini Library
Pinturicchio's frescoes (1509) portray the life of the Piccolomini pope, Pius II. Here he presides at the betrothal of Frederick III to Eleonora of Portugal.

The Museo dell'Opera del Duomo occupies the side aisle of the unfinished nave, which was roofed over to house the museum.

The Campanile was added in 1313.

Archway leading to the Baptistry

Façade gives indication of planned size of nave

The unfinished nave, if completed, would have measured 50 m (162 ft) in length and 30 m (97 ft) in breadth.

Entrance to Duomo

The doors were built in 1284–97, the rest of the façade a century later.

VISITORS' CHECKLIST

P. del Duomo. ☎ 0577 28 30 48. ▦ *Pollicino*. ◷ 7:30am–7:30pm Mon–Sat, 1:30–7pm Sun (Nov–mid-Mar: to 5pm Mon–Sat). ✝

Piccolomini Library ◷ 9am–7:30pm daily (exc Sun am) (Nov–mid-Mar: 10am–1pm, 2–5pm). ✎

🏛 Museo dell'Opera del Duomo

Piazza del Duomo 8. ☎ 0577 28 30 48. ◷ daily (Nov–mid-Mar: only am). ● public hols. ✎

Part of this museum is devoted to items removed from the Duomo, including a tondo of a *Madonna and Child*, probably by Donatello, as well as several badly eroded Gothic statues by Giovanni Pisano and Jacopo della Quercia. The highlight is Duccio's huge *Maestà* (1308–11), one of the Sienese School's finest works. It depicts the Madonna and Child on one side, and scenes from the Life of Christ on the other. It was originally placed on the Duomo's high altar, where it replaced the striking *Madonna of the Large Eyes* (1220–30) by an anonymous Sienese painter, also in the museum.

Statues from the Duomo now on show in the Museo dell'Opera

🏰 Fortezza Medicea

Viale Maccari. **Fortezza** ◷ daily. **Enoteca** ☎ 0577 28 84 97. ◷ noon–1am Mon–Sat (to 8pm Mon). ✎

This huge red-brick fortress was built for Cosimo I by Baldassarre Lanci in 1560, following Siena's defeat by the Florentines in the 1554–5 war. After an 18-month siege, during which more than 8,000 Sienese died, the town's banking and wool industries were suppressed by the Florentine masters and all major building work ended.

The fortress now houses the Enoteca Italica, a wine shop offering visitors the chance both to taste and to buy from a comprehensive list of quality wines from all over Italy.

Façade Statues

Many façade statues have been replaced by copies; the originals are in the Museo dell'Opera del Duomo.

Street-by-Street: San Gimignano ❷

T HE THIRTEEN TOWERS that dominate San
Gimignano's majestic skyline were built by
noble families in the 12th and 13th centuries,
when the town's position – on the main pilgrim
route from northern Europe to Rome – brought
it great prosperity. The plague of 1348, and the
diversion of the pilgrim route, led to its decline
as well as its preservation. Today only one of
the towers, the Torre Grossa, is open to the
public. For a small town, San Gimignano is
rich in works of art, good shops and restaurants.

San Gimignano's famous skyline, almost
unchanged since the Middle Ages

Collegiata
*This 11th-century
church's interior
is full of frescoes,
including* The
Creation *(1367)
by Bartolo di
Fredi.*

Palazzo del Popolo
*The council chamber of the town
hall (1288–1323) features a
large* Maestà *(1317)
by Lippo Memmi.*

**The Annunciation
by Ghirlandaio**
*This painting,
completed in 1482,
is located in a
courtyard loggia
alongside the
Collegiata.*

Via San Giovanni
is lined with shops
selling local goods.

Sant'Agostino

Tourist
information

VIA SAN MATTEO

VIA CAPASSI

VIA DIACCETO

PIAZZA
NOMI

PIAZZA
DEL
DUOMO

PIAZZA
DELLA
CISTERNA

VIA DELLA COSTERELLA

VIA DI QUERCECCHIO

VIA BERIGNANO

VIA SAN GIOVANNI

Bus station

**Among the Piazza del
Duomo's** historic buildings
is the Palazzo Vecchio
del Podestà (1239),
whose tower is
probably the
town's oldest.

**Piazza della
Cisterna**
*This square is
named after
the well at its
centre and
is the heart
of the old
town.*

**The Museo
Civico** provides
access to the tallest of the
town's 13 remaining towers.

KEY

— — — Suggested route

0 metres   250
0 yards   250

🏛 Museo Civico

Palazzo del Popolo, Piazza del Duomo.
📞 0577 94 03 40. **Museum &
tower** ☐ daily (winter: Tue–Sun). 🎫
Frescoes in the courtyard of
this museum feature the coats
of arms of city mayors and
magistrates, as well as a 14th-
century *Virgin and Child* by
Taddeo di Bartolo.

The first public room is
the Sala di Dante, where an
inscription recalls a visit by
the poet in 1300. The walls
are covered with hunting
scenes and a huge *Maestà*
fresco (1317) by Lippo
Memmi. The floor above has
an art collection, which
includes excellent works
by Pinturicchio, Bartolo
di Fredi, Benozzo Gozzoli
and Filippino Lippi. The
famous *Wedding Scene*
frescoes by Memmo di
Filippucci (early 14th
century) show a couple
sharing a bath and going
to bed – an unusual
record of life in 14th-
century Tuscany.

🏛 Collegiata

Piazza del
Duomo. ☐ daily.
This 12th-century
Romanesque church
contains a feast of
frescoes. In the
north aisle the
frescoes comprise
26 episodes from
the Old Testament
(1367) by Bartolo di Fredi.
The opposite wall features
scenes from the *Life of Christ*
(1333–41) by Lippo Memmi,
while at the back of the church

**Bartolo di Fredi's
Christ, Sant'Agostino**

**The ceiling of the Collegiata,
painted with gold stars**

there are scenes from the *Last
Judgment* painted by Taddeo
di Bartolo. Frescoes (1475) by
Ghirlandaio adorn both the
tiny Chapel of Santa Fina and
the nearby loggia.

🏛 Sant'Agostino

Piazza Sant'Agostino. ☐ daily.
Consecrated in 1298, this
church has a simple façade,
contrasting markedly with the
heavily decorated Rococo
interior (c.1740) by Vanvitelli.
Above the main altar is
the *Coronation of the
Virgin* by Piero del
Pollaiuolo, dated
1483. The choir is
entirely covered in
a cycle of frescoes
of *The Life of St
Augustine* (1465)
executed by the
Florentine artist
Benozzo Gozzoli.
In the Cappella di San
Bartolo, on the right of the
main entrance, is an elaborate
marble altar completed by
Benedetto da Maiano in 1495.

**Fresco from the early 14th-century *Wedding Scene* cycle by
Memmo di Filippucci in the Museo Civico**

Elba ❷❽

Livorno. 🏘 30,000. ⛴ Portoferraio
🚌 ℹ Calata Italia 26 (0565 91 46
71). 🛒 Portoferraio: Fri.

Elba's most famous resident
was Napoleon, who spent
nine months here after the
fall of Paris in 1814. Today
Italy's third largest island is
mainly populated by holidaymakers, who come by ferry
from Piombino, 10 km (6
miles) away on the mainland.
The main town is Porto-
ferraio, with an old port
and a modern seafront of
hotels and fish restaurants.

The landscape of the island
is varied. On the west coast,
which tends to be a little
quieter, there are sandy
beaches suitable for all water
sports. The east coast, centred
on the town of Porto Azzurro,
the island's second port, is
more rugged, with high cliffs
and stony beaches. Inland,
olive groves and vineyards
line hillsides, and vegetation
covers the mountains. A good
way to see the interior is to
take the road from Marciana
Marina to the old medieval
village of Marciana Alta. Close
by, a minor road leads to a
cable car that runs to Monte
Capanne (1,018 m/3,300 ft),
a magnificent viewpoint.

Marciana Marina on Elba

Sovana ❷❾

Grosseto. 🏘 100. ℹ Amatur,
Sorano (0564 61 70 08).

Sovana is one of southern
Tuscany's prettiest villages.
Its single little street ends in
Piazza del Pretorio, home to

the ancient church of Santa
Maria, which contains frescoes
and a 9th-century altar canopy.
A lane beyond leads through
olive groves to the Romanesque Duomo, filled with
reliefs and carvings from an
earlier church on the site. Some
fine Etruscan tombs lie in the
surrounding countryside, many
of them clearly signed and
easily visited from the village.

Maremma ❸❶

Grosseto. ℹ Maremma Centro Visite,
Alberese (0564 40 70 98). **Marginal
Areas** 🚌 to entrances from Alberese.
🕐 daily. 🎫 📷 **Inner Park Areas** 🚌
from Alberese to tour departure point.
🕐 9am–1 hr before sunset Wed, Sat,
Sun, public hols. 🎫 only Jun–Sep:
walking tours at 7am (4 hrs) & 4pm
(3 hrs). 📷 🖥 www.parks.it

The Etruscans,
followed by the
Romans, were the first
to cultivate the marshes
and low hills of the
Maremma. Following the
collapse of the Roman Empire,
however, the area fell prey to
flooding and malaria, twin
scourges that left it virtually
uninhabited until the 18th
century. The land has since
been reclaimed, the irrigation
canals unblocked and farming
developed on the fertile soil.
The stunning Parco Naturale
della Maremma was set up in
1975 to preserve the area's
native flora and fauna, and to
prevent development on one
of Italy's few pristine stretches
of coastline. Entrance to much
of the park is restricted to
access on foot or by a park
bus from Alberese. Other more
marginal areas, however, such
as the excellent beach at
Marina di Alberese and the
countryside around Talamone
in the south, are easier to see.

View over Pitigliano and the town's dramatic cliffs and caves

Pitigliano ❸❶❓

Grosseto. 🏘 4,400. 🚌 ℹ Piazza
Garibaldi 51 (0564 61 71 11). 🛒 Wed.

Pitigliano is spectacularly
situated high above the
cave-riddled cliffs of the Lente
valley. Its maze of tiny
medieval streets includes a
small Jewish ghetto, formed
in the 17th century by Jews

Irrigated salt marsh

Trappola

Fiume Ombrone

P Ma Alb

Beaches

The Ombrone estuary is a mixture
of pines, marsh and dunes and is
home to birds such as the flamingo,
sea eagle, roller and bee-eater.

KEY

══	Roads
▨▨	Paths
⋯	Canals and rivers
▬ ▬	Itineraries

0 kilometres   2

0 miles   1

fleeing from Catholic persecution. The **Palazzo Orsini** has its water supply brought in by an impressive aqueduct, built in 1545. It houses the **Museo Zuccarelli** with its small exhibition of work by artist Francesco Zuccarelli (1702–88), who lived locally. He also painted two of the altarpieces in the medieval **Duomo** in Piazza San Gregorio. The **Museo Etrusco** contains finds from ancient local settlements.

🏛 **Museo Zuccarelli**
Palazzo Orsini, Piazza della Fortezza Orsini 4. 📞 0564 61 60 74.
🕐 Mar–Jul: Tue–Sun; Aug: daily; Sep–Dec: Sat & Sun. 🎫

🏛 **Museo Etrusco**
Piazza della Fortezza Orsini.
📞 0564 61 40 74. 🕐 Tue–Sun.

Monte Argentario ②

Grosseto. 👥 13,000. 🚌 ℹ Corso Umberto I 55, Porto Santo Stefano (0564 81 42 08). 🛒 Tue.

Mㅣᴏɴᴛᴇ ᴀʀɢᴇɴᴛᴀʀɪᴏ was an island until the early 1700s, when the shallow waters separating it from the mainland began to silt up, creating two sandy spits of land, known as *tomboli*, which enclose the Orbetello lagoon. Today the lagoon hosts a beautiful nature reserve. **Orbetello** itself, a lively and relatively unspoilt little town, was linked to the island in 1842, when a dyke was constructed from the mainland. The harbour towns of **Porto Ercole** and **Porto Santo Stefano** are up-market

Porto Ercole, Monte Argentario

resorts, busy with visitors in summer. Interior roads – notably the Strada Panoramica – offer peaceful drives past rocky coves and bays.

Entry tickets are sold at Alberese's park headquarters.

Wild Boar
The most impressive of the Maremma's many wild animals is the indigenous wild boar, a smaller creature than the Eastern European boar found elsewhere in Tuscany.

San Rabano, a ruined Cistercian abbey (12th century), is close to the park's highest point.

Pine nuts for cooking are still collected from the park's woodlands.

The Uccellina Hills are crowned by old Spanish watchtowers, pinewoods and scented *macchia*.

Birds of prey, such as the hobby and peregrine, hunt in more remote parts of the park.

- Spergolaia

Alberese 🏛 🅿 ℹ

Pratini

rre di lmarino

Torre dell' Uccellina

Torre di Collelungo

FS **Stazione di Alberese**

San Rabano

Unspoilt coastline

Marked Footpaths
Several gentle footpaths are marked around the park, but in practice you can wander almost at will among most of its dunes and pinewoods.

Rocca di Talamone 🅿

Stazione di Talamone FS

This fishing village is set against pretty countryside.

• Talamone

UMBRIA

LONG DISMISSED AS *Tuscany's "gentler sister", Umbria has recently emerged from the shadow of its more famous western neighbour. Forming an expanse of gentle pastoral countryside and high mountain wilderness, the picturesque region has been dubbed the "Green Heart of Italy". Umbria is also well known for the beauty and profusion of its medieval hill-towns.*

The region was inhabited in the 8th century BC by the Umbrians, a peaceable farming tribe, and later colonized by the Etruscans and Romans. In the Middle Ages, the Lombards established a dukedom centred around Spoleto. By the 13th century much of the region was scattered with independent city-states, most of them eventually absorbed by the Papal States, where they remained until Italian unification in 1860.

Today the old towns are Umbria's chief glory. In Perugia, the region's capital, and the smaller centres of Gubbio, Montefalco and Todi, there are numerous Romanesque churches, civic palaces, vivid fresco cycles and endless medieval nooks and crannies. Spoleto, renowned for its summer arts festival, blends grandiose medieval monuments with Roman remains and some of Italy's oldest churches. The surrounding Vale of Spoleto is a chequerboard of agricultural countryside and fascinating traditional villages.

Assisi, the birthplace of St Francis, contains the Basilica di San Francesco, frescoed in part by Giotto. At Orvieto, magnificently situated on its volcanic crag, there are Etruscan remains and one of Italy's finest Romanesque-Gothic cathedrals.

Umbria's oak woods, ice-clear streams and rich soils yield many delicacies. Chief among these are trout and truffles, olive oils to rival those of Tuscany, prized lentils from Castelluccio, cured meats from Norcia and tangy mountain cheeses. A variety of well-regarded wines are produced from the vineyards of Torgiano and Montefalco.

A shop in Norcia selling a selection of Italy's finest hams, sausages and salamis

◁ A street scene in the ancient town of Todi

Exploring Umbria

A SSISI AND SPOLETO, Umbria's loveliest towns, are the most convenient and charming bases for exploring the region. Both these medieval gems are unmissable, as is the old centre of Perugia, the region's capital, and the alluring hill-towns of Gubbio, Spello, Montefalco and Todi. Umbria's landscapes are as compelling as its towns, from the eerie wastes of the Piano Grande and the mountain splendour of the Monti Sibillini national park (best reached from Norcia) to the gentler countryside of the Valnerina and the beach-fringed shores of Lake Trasimeno.

SIGHTS AT A GLANCE

SEE ALSO

Olive harvest in the Umbrian countryside near Orvieto

GETTING AROUND

Excellent road, rail and bus links exist in the region. The A1 from Florence passes Orvieto, which is linked to Todi by the S448. The S75 connects Perugia, Assisi and Spello, then the S3 continues to Trevi, Spoleto and Terni. Rome–Florence trains serve Orvieto, and Rome–Ancona trains serve Spoleto, with branch lines connecting Perugia, Spello and Assisi.

The hill-town of Castelluccio, east of Norcia, and the Monti Sibillini

A side street in the medieval town of Gubbio in northern Umbria

KEY

▬▬▬	Motorway
▬▬▬	Major road
▬▬▬	Minor road
▬▬▬	Scenic route
≈≈	River
☀	Viewpoint

0 kilometres 25

0 miles 15

Gubbio ❶

Perugia. 🏛 *33,000.* 🚊 *Fossato di Vico-Gubbio.* 🚌 ℹ️ *Piazza Oderisi 6 (075 922 06 93).* 🛒 *Tue.*

Gubbio vies with Assisi for the title of Umbria's most medieval town. The beauty of its twisting streets and terra-cotta-tiled houses is enhanced by the forest-swathed Apennines. Founded by the Umbrians in the 3rd century BC as Tota Ikuvina, it assumed greater prominence in the 1st century AD as a Roman colony (Eugubium). It emerged as an independent commune in the 11th century having spread up the slopes of Monte Ingino. From 1387 to 1508 Gubbio was ruled from Urbino by the Dukes of Montefeltro.

The 13th-century **Duomo** is distinguished by a wagon-vaulted ceiling whose curved arches symbolize hands in prayer. Medieval Via dei Consoli leads to the 13th-century **Palazzo del Bargello** – a stone-faced building formerly the headquarters of the chief of police. Also here is the **Fontana dei Matti** (Fountain of the Mad), named after the tradition that anyone who walks around it three times will go insane.

Macabre legends surround the walled-up **Porte della Morte** (Doors of Death) that can be seen in Via dei Consoli and elsewhere in the town. Reputedly used for the passage of coffins from houses, the doors, once tainted, were sealed and never used again. Their purpose was probably defensive. In the lower town, the church of **San Francesco** (1259–82) is known for 17 faded

Façade of the Palazzo dei Consoli in Gubbio

The interior of Perugia's San Pietro, rebuilt in the 15th century

frescoes showing scenes from the *Life of the Virgin* (1408–13) by Ottaviano Nelli. Opposite is the **Tiratoio** (Weavers' Loggia). Wool was stretched out to dry in its shady arcade. West of here are the ruins of a 1st-century AD Roman amphitheatre.

🏛 Palazzo dei Consoli
Piazza Grande. 📞 *075 927 42 98.* ⏰ *10am–1pm, 3–6pm daily (Nov–Mar: 10am–1pm, 2–5pm).* ⬤ *1 Jan, 1, 14 & 15 May, 25 Dec.* 💶
Dominating the skyline of Gubbio is this mighty civic palace, begun in 1332 by Gattapone. Its Salone dell'Arengo houses the Museo Civico, best known for the Eugubine Tablets (250–150 BC). Discovered in 1444, the seven bronze slabs are inscribed with Etruscan and Roman characters, probably a phonetic translation of prayers and rituals from the ancient Umbrian and Etruscan languages. Upstairs a small art gallery contains works by local painters.

One of the Eugubine Tablets in Gubbio

🏛 Palazzo Ducale
Via Federico da Montefeltro. 📞 *075 927 58 72.* ⏰ *8:30am–7pm Thu–Tue.* ⬤ *1 Jan, 1 May, 25 Dec.* 💶 ♿
Attributed to Francesco di Giorgio Martini, this palace was built in 1470 for the Montefeltro as a copy of the family home in Urbino *(see pp360–61)*. It also has a pretty Renaissance courtyard.

Assisi ❷

See pp344–5.

Perugia ❸

🏛 *160,000.* 🚊 🚌 ℹ️ *Piazza IV Novembre 3 (075 572 33 27).* 🛒 *daily.* 🌐 *www.umbria2000.it*

Perugia's old centre hinges around the pedestrianized Corso Vannucci, named after the local painter Pietro Vannucci (Perugino). At its northern end is Piazza IV Novembre, dominated by the **Fontana Maggiore**, a 13th-century fountain by Nicola and Giovanni Pisano. To the rear rises the 15th-century **Duomo**, its entrance flanked by a statue of Pope Julius II (1555) and a pulpit built for Siena's San Bernardino (1425). Its Cappella del Santo Anello contains the Virgin's "wedding ring", a weighty piece of agate said to change colour according to the character of the person wearing it. The third pillar in the south nave holds a Renaissance painting of the *Madonna delle Grazie* by Gian Nicola di Paolo. The figure is credited with miraculous powers, and mothers bring newly baptized children to kneel before it. Buried in the transepts are Popes Urban IV and Martin IV.

Away from the Corso is the **Oratorio di San Bernardino** (1457–61) on Piazza San Francesco, with a colourful façade by Agostino di Duccio.

Beyond the old city walls on Borgo XX Giugno stands **San Pietro**, Perugia's most extravagantly decorated church. Founded in the 10th century and rebuilt in 1463, the best feature of the fine interior is the wooden choir (1526).

Piazza Giordano Bruno is home to **San Domenico** (1305–1632), Umbria's largest church, which is known for the Gothic tomb of Benedict XI (c.1304) and decoration by Agostino di Duccio.

🏛 Museo Archeologico Nazionale dell'Umbria

San Domenico, Piazza Giordano Bruno. 📞 075 572 71 41. ⬤ daily (Mon pm only). ⬤ 1 Jan, 1 May, 25 Dec. 🅰 ♿ Housed in the cloisters of San Domenico, this museum exhibits prehistoric, Etruscan and Roman artifacts.

🏛 Palazzo dei Priori

Corso Vannucci 19. 📞 075 572 42 07. ⬤ daily. ⬤ 1 Jan, 1 May, 25 Dec & 1st Mon each month. ♿ **Collegio del Cambio** ⬤ daily. 🅰 The monumental walls and bristling crenellations of this palace mark it as Umbria's finest public building (see pp50–51). Among its fine rooms is the Sala dei Notari (c.1295), the former lawyers' hall, vividly frescoed with scenes from the Old Testament – the work of a follower of Pietro Cavallini. The raised doorway is guarded by a pair of large bronzes made in 1274: a Guelph lion and a griffin, the medieval

Medieval street in Perugia

emblem of Perugia. The Sala di Udienza del Collegio della Mercanzia, built around 1390, was formerly used by the Merchants' Guild. This room is late Gothic in style, with exquisite panelling and 15th-century inlaid wood.

Also in the palace is the **Collegio del Cambio**, Perugia's former money exchange, which was begun in 1452. This room was used by the Bankers' Guild. Its walls are covered with superlative frescoes (1498–1500) by Perugino, works that are devoted to a mixture of Classical and religious scenes. A glum self-portrait scowls down from the centre of the left wall, while the hand of Perugino's pupil Raphael may be evident in some panels on the right wall.

Entrance of Palazzo dei Priori, Perugia

🏛 Galleria Nazionale dell'Umbria

Palazzo dei Priori, Corso Vannucci 19. 📞 075 574 12 47. ⬤ daily. ⬤ 1st Mon of month, 1 Jan, 25 Dec. 🅰 Umbria's greatest collection of paintings is displayed here on the third floor of the palace. Most of the works are 13th- to 18th-century paintings by local artists, but the highlights are altarpieces by Piero della Francesca and Fra Angelico.

Lake Trasimeno ❹

Perugia. 🚉 🚌 Castiglione del Lago. ℹ Piazza Mazzini 10, Castiglione del Lago (075 965 24 84). 🌐 www.umbria2000.it

Edged with low hills and gentle farming country, this is Italy's fourth-largest lake. Its miles of placid water and reed-lined shores have a tranquil, melancholy beauty.

Drainage of the lake began under the Romans, but today the lake is gently drying up of its own accord. The town of **Castiglione del Lago**, jutting out on a fortified promontory, has an easy-going atmosphere and small sandy beaches. The 16th-century **castle** is used for summer concerts. The church of **Santa Maria Maddalena**, begun in 1836, has a fine *Madonna and Child* (c.1500) by Eusebio di San Giorgio.

Like Castiglione, **Passignano sul Trasimeno** offers boat trips to **Isola Maggiore**. The island's charming village is known for lace-making.

Colourful façade of Perugia's Oratorio di San Bernardino

THE BATTLE OF LAKE TRASIMENO

In 217 BC the Romans suffered one of their worst ever military defeats on the shores of Lake Trasimeno. The Carthaginian general, Hannibal, lured the Romans (who were led by the consul Flaminius) into a masterful ambush close to present-day Ossaia (Place of Bones) and Sanguineto (Place of Blood). Some 16,000 legionaries perished, hacked down on the lake's marshy fringes. Hannibal, by contrast, lost only 1,500 men. Today you can explore the battlefield, which includes over 100 mass graves found near Tuoro sul Trasimeno.

19th-century engraving of General Hannibal

Assisi: Basilica di San Francesco

THE BURIAL PLACE of St Francis, this basilica was begun in 1228, two years after the saint's death. Over the next century its Upper and Lower Churches were decorated by the foremost artists of their day, among them Cimabue, Simone Martini, Pietro Lorenzetti and Giotto, whose frescoes on the *Life of St Francis* are some of the most renowned in Italy. The basilica, which dominates Assisi, is one of the great Christian shrines and receives vast numbers of pilgrims throughout the year.

The campanile was built in 1239.

Faded paintings by Roman artists line the walls above Giotto's *Life of St Francis*.

The choir (1501) features a 13th-century stone papal throne.

St Francis *Cimabue's simple painting (c.1280) captures the humility of the revered saint, who stood for poverty, chastity and obedience.*

★ Frescoes by Lorenzetti *The bold composition of Pietro Lorenzetti's fresco, entitled* The Deposition *(1323), is based around the truncated Cross, focusing attention on the twisted figure of Christ.*

Steps to the Treasury

The crypt contains the tomb of St Francis.

Lower Church *Side chapels were created here in the 13th century to accommodate the growing number of pilgrims.*

STAR FEATURES

★ **Frescoes by Giotto**

★ **Frescoes by Lorenzetti**

★ **Cappella di San Martino**

Upper Church
The soaring Gothic lines of the 13th-century Upper Church symbolized the heavenly glory of St Francis. This style also influenced later Franciscan churches.

The façade and its rose window are early examples of Italian Gothic.

Entrance to Upper Church

Entrance to Lower Church

★ Frescoes by Giotto
The Ecstasy of St Francis *is one of 28 panels that make up Giotto's cycle on the* Life of St Francis *(c.1290–95).*

★ Cappella di San Martino
The frescoes in this chapel on the Life of St Martin *(1315) are by the Sienese painter Simone Martini. This panel shows the* Death of the Saint. *Martini was also responsible for the fine stained glass in the chapel.*

VISITORS' CHECKLIST

Piazza San Francesco.
[075 819 00 84.] FS *Assisi.*
⊙ 6:30am–7pm daily.

Assisi ❷

Perugia. 25,000. FS 🚌 🅸
Piazza del Comune 22 (075 81 25 34).
⊟ *Sat.* W www.umbria2000.it

THIS BEAUTIFUL medieval town, with its geranium-hung streets, lovely views and fountain-splashed piazzas, is heir to the legacy of St Francis (c.1181–1226), who is buried in the **Basilica di San Francesco**. Sadly the town suffered serious damage during the earthquake of September 1997, but restoration was relatively swift – completed in approximately two years. The tourist office can give information on which sights are open to visitors.

Piazza del Comune, Assisi's main square, is dominated by the columns of the **Tempio di Minerva**, a Roman temple-front from the Augustan age. The Palazzo Comunale, opposite, is home to the **Pinacoteca Comunale**, an art gallery with works by local medieval artists.

Down Corso Mazzini lies the **Basilica di Santa Chiara**, the burial place of St Clare – Francis's companion and the founder of the Poor Clares (an order of nuns). One of its chapels contains the crucifix that is said to have bowed its head and ordered Francis to "Repair God's church". It came from **San Damiano**, a sublime church set amid olive groves south of the Porta Nuova.

The **Duomo (San Rufino)**, built during the 12th and 13th centuries, has a superb Romanesque façade. Inside is a small museum of paintings, and there are archaeological items in the crypt. From the Duomo, Via Maria delle Rose leads to the **Rocca Maggiore** (rebuilt in 1367), an evocative if much-restored castle.

Thirteenth-century **San Pietro**, on Piazza San Pietro, is a simple and carefully restored Romanesque church. The nearby **Oratorio dei Pellegrini**, a 15th-century pilgrims' hospice, contains well-preserved frescoes by Matteo da Gualdo.

Giotto's fresco, *St Francis Appearing to the Friars at Arles* (c.1295), in the Basilica di San Francesco, Assisi ▷

Orvieto ❺

Terni. 🏛 22,000. 🚇 🚌
ℹ *Piazza Duomo 24 (0763 34
17 72).* 🛒 *Thu & Sat.*

PERCHED ON A A 300-m (984-
ft) plateau, Orvieto looks
down over a vineyard-spotted
plain. Visitors flood into the
town to admire the **Duomo**,
among the greatest of Italy's
Romanesque-Gothic cathedrals.

The tiny 14th-century church
of **San Lorenzo in Arari** is at
the end of Via Scalza. Its walls
feature frescoes describing the
martyrdom of St Lawrence,
who was grilled to death. The
altar is made from an Etruscan
sacrificial slab. Via Malabranca
leads to **San Giovenale** at
Orvieto's western tip, a church
that is beautifully and almost
completely covered in detailed
frescoes from the 15th and
16th centuries. It offers broad
views over the surrounding
countryside. **Sant'Andrea**,
in Piazza della Repubblica,
is distinguished by a

curious 12-sided
campanile, part of
the original 12th-
century building.

🏛 Museo dell'
Opera del Duomo
Piazza Duomo. 📞 *0763
34 35 92.* 📅 *Tue, Thu,
Sat, Sun, hols.* ●
*partially, for restoration.
Nov–Feb: Mon.*
This interesting
little museum
contains an eclectic
collection of treasures given
to the Duomo. Among the
highlights are paintings by
Lorenzo Maitani (died 1330)
and sculptures by Andrea
Pisano (c.1270–1348).

🏛 Museo Archeologico
Faina & Museo Civico
Piazza Duomo 29. 📞 *0763 34 15 11.*
◯ *daily.* ● *1 Jan, 25 Dec; Oct–Mar:
Mon.* 🎫 🖼 🛒 🚻
The first of these two museums
has a well-known, low-key
collection of Etruscan remains
including many Greek vases

View into the Pozzo di San Patrizio in Orvieto

that were found in Etruscan
tombs in the area. The Museo
Civico contains ancient Greek
artifacts, as well as Etruscan
copies of Greek works.

🏛 Museo d'Arte Moderna
"Emilio Greco"
Palazzo Soliano, Piazza Duomo. 📞
0763 34 46 05. ◯ *daily.* 🎫 *allows
entry at Pozzo di San Patrizio.* 🚻
This museum is devoted to
the modern Sicilian sculptor,
Emilio Greco, who made the
bronze doors (1964–70) of
the Duomo in Orvieto.

🔒 DUOMO OF ORVIETO
Piazza Duomo. 📞 *0763 34 11 67.*
◯ *daily.* 🚻
Some 300 years in the
building, Orvieto's
Duomo (begun 1290),
with its breathtaking
façade, is one of Italy's
greatest cathedrals. It
was inspired by the
Miracle of Bolsena
in which real blood
from a consecrated
host supposedly fell
on the altar cloth
of a church in
nearby Bolsena.

**Carved
choir stalls**

The exterior is characterized
by horizontal bands of white
travertine and blue-grey basalt.

**14th-century
rose window
by Orcagna**

**The reliquary
of the Corporal**
contains the altar
cloth from Bolsena.

Cappella del Corporale
This chapel contains Lippo Memmi's
Madonna dei Raccomandati *(1320).
There are also frescoes (1357–64) by
Ugolino di Prete Ilario of the* Miracle of
Bolsena *and* Miracles of the Sacrament.

**Bronze
doors by Emilio
Greco (1964–70)**

🚰 Pozzo di San Patrizio

Viale San Gallo. 📞 *0763 34 37 68.*
⏰ *daily.* 🔴 *1 Jan, 25 Dec.* 🎫 *allows entry at Museo d'Arte Moderna.*

This well was commissioned in 1527 by Pope Clement VII and designed by the Florentine architect Antonio da Sangallo to provide the town with a water supply in case of attack. Two 248-step staircases drop into its dank interior, cleverly arranged as a double helix (spiral) so as not to intersect. The 62-m (203-ft) shaft, built from tufa blocks and bricks, took ten years to complete.

🏛 Necropoli Etrusca – Crocefisso del Tufo

Strada Statale 71 to Orvieto Scalo, km 1,600. 📞 *0763 34 36 11.* ⏰ *8:30am–7pm (Oct–Mar: to 5pm) daily.* 🎫 🔷

This Etruscan necropolis from the 6th century BC has burial chambers built of blocks of tufa. Etruscan letters, thought to be the names of the deceased, are inscribed on the tombs.

Cappella Nuova
Luca Signorelli's great fresco cycle of the Last Judgment (1499–1504) features prominently in this chapel. Fra Angelico and Benozzo Gozzoli worked here before Signorelli.

The Façade
There are detailed carvings (c.1320–30) at the base of its four main pilasters. By Lorenzo Maitani, they depict scenes from the Old and New Testaments, including hell and damnation.

View of the hill-town of Todi in southern Umbria

Todi ➏

Perugia. 🏠 *17,000.* 🚉 🚌
ℹ *Piazza del Popolo 38 (075 894 33 95).* 🛒 *Sat.*

LOOKING DOWN over the Tiber valley from its hilltop eyrie, Todi is one of the most strikingly situated of Umbria's famous hill-towns. An ancient Etruscan, and then Roman settlement, it still preserves an uncorrupted medieval air, with several tiny churches, three austere public palaces and many sleepy corners.

Most people are drawn here by the **Piazza del Popolo**, the main square, flanked by the lovely plain-faced **Duomo**. Built in the 13th century on the site of a Roman temple to Apollo, it has a dusky interior and one of Umbria's finest choirs (1521–30). Note Ferraù da Faenza's huge painting (1596) on the rear wall, a less than totally successful copy of Michelangelo's *Last Judgment*, and the altarpiece at the end of the right aisle by Giannicola di Paolo (a follower of Perugino).

Also flanking the piazza are the **Palazzo dei Priori** (1293–1337) and the linked **Palazzo del Capitano** (1290) and **Palazzo del Popolo** (1213). In the Palazzo del Capitano, distinguished by its redoubtable medieval interior, lies the **Museo**

Etrusco-Romano. The museum contains a collection of local Etruscan and Roman artifacts. There are altarpieces and sacred objects in the **Pinacoteca Comunale**, also housed in the palace.

A few steps from the piazza rises **San Fortunato** (1292–1462), named after Todi's first bishop, with a florid Gothic doorway (1415–58). The high vaulted plan is based on German Gothic "hall" churches and the "barn" churches of Tuscany, characterized by a low-pitched vault, polygonal apse and naves and aisles of equal height. The choir (1590) is superb, but the church's most famous work is the *Madonna and Child* (1432) by Masolino da Panicale (fourth chapel on the right). The crypt contains the tomb of Jacopone da Todi (c.1228–1306), a noted medieval poet and mystic.

To the right of the church are some shady gardens, from which a path (past the tiny castle) drops through the trees to emerge in front of **Santa Maria della Consolazione** (1508–1607), near the N79. One of central Italy's finest Renaissance churches, and based on a Greek cross, it may have been built to a plan by Bramante. The stark, chill interior is overshadowed by the harmonious exterior.

🏛 Museo Etrusco-Romano and Pinacoteca Comunale

Palazzi Comunali. 📞 *075 894 41 48.* ⏰ *Tue–Sun (Apr: daily).* 🎫 🔷

Santa Maria della Consolazione in Todi

Spoleto ⑦

Perugia. 🚶 *38,000.* 🚉 🚌
ℹ️ *Piazza della Libertà 7
(0743 23 89 11).* 🛒 *Tue & Fri.*
🌐 *www.comune.spoleto.it*

FOUNDED BY THE UMBRIANS, Spoleto was one of central Italy's most important Roman colonies, a prominence maintained by the Lombards, who in the 7th century made it the capital of one of their three Italian dukedoms. After a spell as an independent city state, in 1354 Spoleto fell to the papacy.

Spoleto, within its wooded setting, is the loveliest of the Umbrian hill-towns. Its urbane atmosphere is enhanced by its superb monuments and by the Festival dei Due Mondi, one of Europe's leading arts festivals held annually in June and July.

At the southern end of Piazza del Mercato is the **Arco**

di Druso, a 1st-century AD Roman arch. It is flanked by the church of **Sant'Ansano**, whose crypt is covered in frescoes that may date from the 6th century. Via Aurelio Saffi, at the piazza's northern end, leads to **Sant'Eufemia**. This utterly simple 10th-century Romanesque church is known for its matroneum (women's gallery), once used to segregate the congregation.

A short way beyond, the fan-shaped Piazza del Duomo opens out to reveal Spoleto's 12th-century **Duomo**, graced with an elegant façade. Filling the apse of the Baroque interior is a great, newly restored fresco cycle. The final work of Fra Lippo Lippi, from 1467–9, it describes episodes from the *Life of the Virgin*. The Cappella Erioli is adorned with Pinturicchio's unfinished *Madonna and Child* (1497).

The best of the exceptional churches in the lower town is 4th-century **San Salvatore**, located in the main cemetery, a spot suited to the church's eerie sense of antiquity. Nearby stands **San Ponziano**, fronted by a captivating three-tiered Romanesque façade typical

Façade of San Pietro in Spoleto

of Umbria. It has a 10th-century crypt, supported by odd little columns and decorated with Byzantine frescoes.

Romanesque **San Gregorio** in Piazza Garibaldi dates from 1069, but its cramped façade and stolid campanile incorporate fragments of Roman buildings. Inside is a raised presbytery and a lovely multi-columned crypt. Well-preserved patches of fresco dot the walls. Some 10,000 Christian martyrs are supposedly buried near the church. They were reputedly slaughtered in the town's Roman **amphitheatre**, traces of which can be seen in the barracks on Via del Anfiteatro.

🌉 Ponte delle Torri

This magnificent 14th-century aqueduct, the "bridge of towers", is 80 m (262 ft) high. Designed by Gattapone (from Gubbio), it is the town's single most famous monument.

Ponte delle Torri, Spoleto

ROMANESQUE CHURCHES IN UMBRIA

Umbria's church-building tradition had its roots in ancient Roman basilicas and in the chapels built over the shrines of its many saints and martyrs. The region's Romanesque façades are usually divided into three tiers, often with three rose windows arranged above a trio of arched portals. The three doors usually correspond to the interior's nave and two aisles, which derive from the simple barn-like plan of Roman basilicas. Inside, the presbytery is often raised in order to allow for the building of a crypt, which usually contained the relics of a saint or martyr. Many of the churches took centuries to build, or were repeatedly modified over time, often acquiring elements of Gothic, Baroque or Renaissance styles.

San Lorenzo di Arari in Orvieto takes its name from an Etruscan altar (arari). This 14th-century church has a very simple façade (see p348).

12th-century campanile

Renaissance portico

Spoleto's Duomo (1198) has eight rose windows, a mosaic (1207) and a Renaissance portico (1491). The tower was built from old Roman remains.

From the bridge, there are views of the bastions of the **Rocca Albornoz**, a huge papal fortress built in 1359–64, also by Gattapone. Across the bridge a path leads to the Strada di Monteluco and the church of **San Pietro**, famous for the fascinating 12th-century carvings on its façade.

Rocca Albornoz
Piazza San Simone. 0743 47 07.
daily. compulsory.

Pinacoteca Comunale
Palazzo Comunale, Piazza del Municipio. 0743 21 81.
Tue–Sun. 1 Jan, 25 Dec.
Spoleto's art gallery has four beautifully appointed rooms with works by Perugino and his Spoletan protégé, Lo Spagna (c.1450–1528), including a painting of the Madonna and Child with Saints.

Montefalco 8

Perugia. 4,900. Mon.

MONTEFALCO, whose name (Falcon's Mount) draws inspiration from its lofty position and sweeping views, is the best of the fascinating villages in the Vale of Spoleto. Criss-crossed by streets almost too narrow for cars, it takes less than five minutes to walk through the village. Yet you might happily spend a morning here, most of it in the polished, new **Museo Civico** housed in the former church

A panel from Gozzoli's fresco cycle (1452) in Montefalco's Museo Civico

of San Francesco. Its highlight is Benozzo Gozzoli's *Life of St Francis* (1452), a radiant fresco cycle that borrows heavily from Giotto's cycle in Assisi *(see pp344–7)*. Other painters represented here are Perugino, Tiberio d'Assisi and Nicolò Alunno, all leading medieval Umbrian artists.

The simple Gothic church of **Sant'Agostino** (begun 1279) on Corso Mameli is dotted with frescoes from the 14th–16th centuries. The church also contains three mummies.

In the main square local wines on sale include the rich, red Sagrantino di Montefalco. Just outside the town walls, the church of **Sant'Illuminata** is covered with charming frescoes, the work of the local 16th-century artist Francesco

Melanzio. About 2 km (1 mile) beyond, the prettily situated church of **San Fortunato** is decorated with frescoes by Gozzoli and Tiberio d'Assisi.

ENVIRONS: The village in the Vale of Spoleto with the most spectacular setting is **Trevi**. The churches of **San Martino** (16th century), on Passeggiata di San Martino, and **Madonna delle Lacrime** (1487–1522), south of Trevi on the road into the village, contain paintings by Perugino and Tiberio d'Assisi, among others.

Museo Civico di San Francesco
Via Ringhiera Umbra 9. 0742 37 95 98. Mar–Oct: daily; Nov–Feb: Tue–Sun.
1 Jan, 25 Dec.

The Duomo (1253) in Assisi is a fine example of the three-tiered façades found across central Italy (see p345). It has a pointed arch and a row of arcading.

11th-century campanile
Carved figures

Rose window
Rounded portal

Todi's Duomo was begun in the 12th century, but work on its windows and portals continued until the 17th century (see p349).

18th-century rose window

San Michele (c.1195) in Bevagna has a beautiful portal that combines both Romanesque and old Roman fragments (see p352).

Spello ⓥ

Perugia. 🏠 *8,000*. FS 🚌
ℹ️ *Piazza Matteotti 3 (0742 30
10 09)*. 🚌 *Wed*.

SPELLO IS ONE of the better
known villages in the Vale
of Spoleto. It is renowned for
a fresco cycle by Pinturicchio
in the Cappella Baglioni of
the church of **Santa Maria
Maggiore** (12th–13th century)
on Via Consolare. Executed
around 1500, the frescoes
depict scenes from the New
Testament. Towards the centre
of the village is the Gothic
church of **Sant'Andrea** (13th
century) on Via Cavour. This
road becomes Via Garibaldi,
which leads to **San Lorenzo**,
a Baroque gem of a church
dating from the 12th century.
   Spello also boasts Roman
ruins from the age of Augustus:
the **Porta Consolare** at the
end of Via Consolare, and the
twin-towered **Porta Venere**
by Via Torri di Properzio.
   The road to Assisi over
Monte Subasio offers stunning views from the top of
the mountain above Spello.

ENVIRONS: The least known
village in the Vale of Spoleto
is **Bevagna**. Like Spello, it
sprang to life as a way-station
on the Via Flaminia (the
Roman road that ran through
this part of Umbria). The
medieval Piazza Silvestri is
the setting for two
Romanesque
churches.

The lofty peaks of the Monti
Sibillini in eastern Umbria

San Silvestro (1195) is the
more atmospheric of the pair,
thanks to its shadowy interior
and ancient crypt, but **San
Michele** (late 12th century)
has an elegant portal, famed
for the little gargoyles on either
side. Both churches are the
work of Maestro Binello.

Monti Sibillini ⓦ

Macerata. FS *Spoleto*. 🚌 *Visso*. ℹ️
*Largo Giovanni Battista Antinori 1, Visso
(0737 97 27 11)*. W *www.sibillini.net*

RECENTLY AWARDED national
park status, the Monti
Sibillini in eastern Umbria
provide the region's wildest
and most spectacular scenery.
A range 40 km (25 miles) long,
the mountains form part of
the Apennines, a chain that
runs the length of the Italian
peninsula. **Monte
Vettore** is the
loftiest

point, and the peninsula's
third highest; it stands at
2,476 m (8,123 ft), a great
whale-backed peak close to
the cave of the mythical sybil
that gave the region its name.
   Good maps and trails make
this a superb walking area,
while drivers can follow hair-
pin roads to some of Italy's
most magical landscapes.
Chief of these is the **Piano
Grande**, a huge upland plain
surrounded by a vast amphitheatre of mountains. Bare
but for flocks of sheep and
bedraggled haystacks, the plain
blazes with wild flowers in
spring and with lentils later in
the year. The only habitation
is **Castelluccio**, a beautiful,
neglected mountain village
now being restored. It can be
reached by road from Norcia
and Arquata del Tronto.

**Shop front in Norcia displaying
the town's varied meats**

Norcia ⓧ

Perugia. 🏠 *4,700*. 🚌 ℹ️ *Piazza
San Benedetto (0743 82 81 73)*.
🚌 *Thu*.

THE BIRTHPLACE of St
Benedict, Norcia is a
robust mountain town and an
excellent base for exploring
Valnerina and Monti Sibillini.
One of Italy's culinary capitals,
it is renowned for truffles and
for some of Italy's best hams,
sausages and salamis. Indeed,
the Italian word for a pork
butcher's *(norcineria)* derives
from the name of the town.
   Norcia's main sights are in
Piazza San Benedetto. On
the eastern flank, the church
of **San Benedetto** has a 14th-
century portal adorned with
statues of Benedict and his
sister (Santa Scolastica). Legend
claims that the church marks
the site of Benedict's birth –

Pinturicchio's *Annunciation* (c.1500) in Spello's Santa Maria Maggiore

The 8th-century monastery of San Pietro in Valle, set in the beautiful Valnerina

indeed there are the remains of a 5th-century building in the crypt. However, the church was more likely to have been built over the site of an old Roman temple, since the forum of the Roman colony of Nursia once occupied this spot.

Left of the church stands the newly renovated **Palazzo Comunale**, a monument to the town's period as a free commune during the 13th and 14th centuries. On the opposite side of the square rises the **Castellina** (1554), a blunt papal fortress designed by Vignola to help impose order on an unruly mountain district. The **Duomo** (1560), to the left of the Castellina, has been ravaged by earthquakes over the centuries. Indeed, Norcia has been the victim of successive earthquakes and its houses are low and heavily

buttressed with thick walls to protect them from further damage. **Sant'Agostino** on Via Anicia features a range of good 16th-century frescoes. A little way beyond, the **Oratorio di Sant'Agostinaccio** in Piazza Palatina contains a superb 17th-century ceiling. Via Umberto shelters the **Edicola** (1354), a strange tabernacle believed to have been carved for a Holy Week procession.

Valnerina ⑫

Perugia. FS *Spoleto, then bus.* ⓗ *Piazza Garibaldi 1, Cascia (0743 711 47).*

THE VALNERINA (Little Valley of the River Nera) curves through a broad swathe of eastern Umbria, draining the mountains around Norcia and the Sibillini before emptying into the Tiber. It is edged with craggy, tree-covered slopes and dotted with upland villages and fortified hamlets.

The high spot is **San Pietro in Valle**, an idyllically situated monastery in the hills above the village of Colleponte. Founded in the 8th century, it is one of the few surviving memorials to the Lombards, whose central Italian duchy had its capital in Spoleto. The main body of the monastery church dates from this period, as does the high altar. The nave walls are covered in a wealth of 12th-century frescoes. Some of the best Romanesque carvings in Umbria can be found here.

More popular than the monastery are the **Cascate delle Marmore** near Terni, among Europe's highest waterfalls at 165 m (541 ft). Created by the Romans during drainage work, their waters are now diverted to produce hydroelectric power on all but a few special days. You can view the falls from Marmore village or the S209.

🏛 **San Pietro in Valle**
Località Ferentillo, Terni. ◖ *0744 78 03 16.* ◻ *daily.*
🏞 **Cascate delle Marmore**
7 km (4 miles) along S209 Valnerina, Terni. ◻ *sporadically. Ask at tourist information.*

Piazza San Benedetto and the church of San Benedetto in Norcia

LE MARCHE

··

Tucked away *in a remote corner between the Adriatic Sea and the Apennine mountains, Le Marche (the Marches) is an enchanting rural patchwork of old towns, hill country and long, sandy beaches. In pre-Christian times the area was settled by the Piceni, a tribe eventually assimilated by the Romans.*

In the 4th century BC, exiles from Magna Graecia colonized much of the region. The most notable town was Ancona, also the northernmost point of Greek influence on the Italian peninsula. During the early Middle Ages the region marked the edge of the Holy Roman Empire, giving rise to its present name (*march* meant border area).

The region's historical peak was reached in the 15th century under Federico da Montefeltro, whose court at Urbino became one of Europe's leading cultural centres. Much of Urbino's former grandeur survives, particularly in Federico's magnificent Renaissance Palazzo Ducale, now home to a regional art collection. Ascoli Piceno is almost as enchanting as Urbino, its central Piazza del Popolo among the most evocative old squares in Italy. Smaller towns like San Leo and Urbania and the republic of San Marino also boast fine medieval monuments.

Today probably as many people come to Le Marche for its beaches and towns as for its hilly, unspoilt interior. Especially beautiful are the snowcapped peaks of the Monti Sibillini, situated in magnificent walking and skiing country.

Regional cuisine encompasses the truffles and robust cheeses of the mountains, tender hams and salamis, *olive ascolane* (olives stuffed with meat and herbs) and *brodetto*, fish soup made in several versions up and down the coast. Dry, white Verdicchio is the best known wine, although more unusual names, such as Bianchello del Metauro, are gaining in popularity.

A field of poppies and olive trees in the heart of Le Marche's countryside

◁ **Medieval gates and ramparts surrounding the hilltop republic of San Marino**

Exploring Le Marche

THE MEDIEVAL TOWNS of Urbino and Ascoli Piceno are the highlights of the region, but the rolling hills of the interior contain an abundance of smaller towns and all but undiscovered villages. San Leo, with its dramatic fortress, is one of the best. Most of the countryside is a pretty mixture of woods and remote hills, rising in the west to the majestic Monti Sibillini. Ancona and the attractive town of Pèsaro are the pivotal points of the vast coastline.

SAN LEO ❶
SAN MARINO ❷
GRADARA
PESARO ❸
FANO ❹
MONTEFELTRO
S72
Rimini
S16
MONTE CARPEGNA
S258
Foglia
S243
S3
E78
URBINO ❺
FOSSOMBRONE
S424
URBANIA ❻
Metauro
Cesano
Arezzo
E78
APPENNINO
S257
MONTE PETRANO
S360
GROTTE DI FRASASSI ❼
FABRIANO
S361
APPENNINO
Foligno
Assisi
Perugia
Terni

Rolling countryside between Loreto and Ascoli Piceno

KEY

▰▰	Motorway
▰▰	Major road
▰▰	Minor road
▰▰	Scenic route
≈	River
☼	Viewpoint

View of Ascoli Piceno, one of the prettiest towns in Le Marche

SIGHTS AT A GLANCE

Ancona **9**
Ascoli Piceno **12**
Conero Peninsula **10**
Fano **4**
Grotte di Frasassi **7**
Jesi **8**
Loreto **11**
Pèsaro **3**
San Leo **1**
San Marino **2**
Urbania **6**
Urbino pp360–61 **5**

The rocky reef near Portonovo on the Conero Peninsula

GETTING AROUND

The A14–E55 provides easy access to the coastal resorts. Dual-carriageway spurs from the A14–E55 lead to Jesi, Urbino and Ascoli Piceno, but north-south roads in the interior can be slow. Bus services are generally good, but in the interior can be infrequent. The railway service along the coast is excellent, with a good service through the heart of the region, though it can be slow.

A market scene in Fano

SEE ALSO

- *Where to Stay* pp564–5

- *Where to Eat* pp597–8

MAR ADRIATICO

SENIGALLIA
S16
ANCONA
9
S16
A14–E55
CONERO
PENINSULA
10
8
JESI
Musone
LORETO
11
S7
RECANATI
MACERATA
S77
S361
SAN SEVERINO
MARCHE
S77
TOLENTINO
FERMO
S210
Tenna
S78
A14–E55
S16
S433
SAN BENEDETTO
DEL TRONTO
PARCO NAZIONALE
DEI MONTI SIBILLINI
S78
SA
MONTE
SIBILLA
Tronto
12
ASCOLI PICENO
Teramo

0 kilometres   25

0 miles   10

The bell tower of the Duomo rising above the village of San Leo

San Leo ❶

Pèsaro. 🛈 Piazza Dante 14
(0541 91 63 06). 🚌 from Rimini,
change at Villanova.

FEW CASTLES are as impressive as the great **fortress** that towers over the village of San Leo. Dante used this crag-top site as a model for the landscapes of *Purgatorio*, while Machiavelli considered the citadel to be the finest piece of military architecture in Italy. Its rocky ramparts once contained the Mons Feretrius, a Roman temple dedicated to Jupiter.

An earlier Roman fortress on the site became a papal prison in the 18th century. Its most famous inmate was the larger-than-life Conte di Cagliostro. A swindler, womanizer, necromancer, quack and alchemist, Cagliostro was imprisoned for heresy in the 1790s. His cell was specially built so that its window faced the village's two churches. It is still visible, together with a small picture gallery, state rooms, and the majestic Renaissance ramparts, built by Francesco di Giorgio Martini for the dukes of Montefeltro in the 15th century.

The captivating village has a quaint cobbled square with a superb 9th-century **Pieve** (parish church). Built partly with stone from the ruined Mons Feretrius, the church was raised over the site of a 6th-century chapel.

Just behind lies the 12th-century **Duomo**, a fine Romanesque building with Corinthian capitals and Roman columns from the Mons Feretrius. The lid of St Leo's sarcophagus is in the crypt. Ancient pagan carvings can be seen on the wall behind the altar.

⚓ Fortress
Via Leopardi. 🕿 0541 91 63 02.
🕐 9am–6pm daily. 📷

San Marino ❷

🏛 26,000. 🚌 San Marino Città (fr
Rimini). 🛈 Contrada Omagnano 20,
San Marino (0549 88 23 90).
🔲 www.visitsanmarino.com

EUROPE'S OLDEST republic, tiny San Marino was reputedly founded by St Marinus, a 4th-century monk and stonemason forced to flee the religious persecution of the Emperor Diocletian. With him was St Leo, founder of the nearby town of San Leo. Situated on the slopes of Monte Titano, the country has its own mint, stamps, football team – even its own 1,000-strong army. It is also famous for Formula One racing.

There are no customs formalities in this small country, whose borders are just 12 km (7 miles) apart at the widest point. Sadly, the capital, **San Marino**, is overrun with visitors and souvenir stalls for much of the year. Garibaldi, who sought shelter here after fleeing Venice in 1849, is honoured by a monument in Piazza Garibaldi. **Borgomaggiore**, the largest town, lies at the foot of Monte Titano, with a cable car to the capital above.

Pèsaro ❸

🏛 85,000. 🚃 🚌 🛈 Piazza
della Libertà 11 (0721 693 41).
🗓 Tue & 1st Thu of month.

Detail of the *Coronation of the Virgin* by Bellini (c.1470) in the Musei Civici

ONE OF THE ADRIATIC'S larger seaside resorts, Pèsaro has managed to retain a stylish air. Behind the promenade and the wall of white stucco hotels is a lively, attractive medieval area.

The art gallery of the **Musei Civici** contains Giovanni Bellini's sumptuous polyptych, the *Coronation of the Virgin* (c.1470). The museum also features Renaissance ceramics.

The **Museo Archeologico Oliveriano** presents historical displays from Roman remains to Iron Age artifacts from the necropolis of nearby Novilara.

The best of the town's churches is **Sant'Agostino** on Corso XI Settembre, remarkable for its choir stalls, each a patchwork of inlaid landscapes and narrative scenes.

Pèsaro is also a point of musical pilgrimage. In 1792 the composer Gioacchino Rossini was born here. His home, **Casa Rossini**, contains

Duty-free shop in San Marino

memorabilia, while his piano and some original manuscripts lie in the **Conservatorio Rossini**. His operas are performed in the **Teatro Rossini** in Piazza Lazzarini during the annual August music festival.

🏛 **Musei Civici**
Piazza Mosca 29. 📞 0721 312 13.
🕐 Tue, Wed am; Thu–Sun. 🈂

🏛 **Museo Archeologico Oliveriano**
Via Mazza 97. 📞 0721 333 44.
🕐 Mon–Sat am. ♿

🏛 **Casa Rossini**
Via Rossini 34. 📞 0721 38 73 57.
🕐 Tue–Sun. 🈂

🏛 **Conservatorio Rossini**
Piazza Olivieri 5. 📞 0721 336 70.
🕐 Mon–Sat am, but phone first to arrange. ● public hols.

Fano ❹

Pèsaro. 🏘 54,000. 🚉 🚌 ⛴
ℹ Via Cesare Battisti 10 (0721 80 35 34). 🈂 Wed & Sat.

A**NCIENT FANO** stands out from the string of beach resorts south of Pèsaro, thanks to its fine old centre and historic monuments. Named after Fanum Fortunae, a pagan temple to the goddess Fortuna, it became the terminus of the Via Flaminia (an important consular road from Rome) and the largest Roman colony on the Adriatic coast. The **Arco d'Augusto** (AD 2), on Via Arco d'Augusto, is Fano's most significant ancient monument, having narrowly escaped destruction at the hands of Federico da Montefeltro in 1463. He destroyed its upper section while besieging the town as a papal *condottiere*.

The 16th-century **Fontana della Fortuna**, in Piazza XX Settembre, is dedicated to the goddess Fortuna. The large **Palazzo Malatesta** that rises up to its rear was built around 1420 and enlarged in 1544 for Fano's rulers, the Rimini-based Malatesta family. Inside is the small **Museo Civico** and the **Pinacoteca Malatestiana**, with works by Guercino, Guido Reni and the Venetian artist, Michele Giambono.

🏛 **Museo Civico and Pinacoteca Malatestiana**
Piazza XX Settembre.
📞 0721 82 83 62. 🕐 Tue–Sun.
● 1 Jan, 25 & 26 Dec. 🈂

Entrance to the Palazzo Ducale in Urbania

Urbino ❺

See pp360–61.

Urbania ❻

Pèsaro. 🏘 7,200. 🚌
ℹ Corso Vittorio Emanuele 21 (0722 31 72 11). 🈂 Thu.

U**RBANIA, WITH ITS** elegant arcaded centre, takes its name from Pope Urban VIII (1623–44), who entertained the notion of converting the old medieval village known as Castel Durante into a model Renaissance town.

Its chief attraction is a monument from an earlier age, the huge **Palazzo Ducale**, built by the dukes of Montefeltro as one of several residential alternatives to the Palazzo Ducale in nearby Urbino. It was begun in the 13th century, and then rebuilt in the 15th and 16th centuries. Beautifully situated alongside the Metauro river, it houses a small art gallery, a modest museum, old maps and globes, and the remnants of Duke Federico's famous library.

🏛 **Palazzo Ducale**
Palazzo Ducale. 📞 0722 31 31 51.
🕐 Tue–Sun (Oct–Mar: ask at library). ● public hols. 🈂

Fontana della Fortuna in Fano

Urbino: Palazzo Ducale

ITALY'S MOST BEAUTIFUL Renaissance palace was
built for Duke Federico da Montefeltro, ruler
of Urbino (1444–82). He was a soldier, but also
a man of the arts, and his palace, with its library,
paintings and refined architecture, is a tribute
to courtly life and to the artistic and intellectual
ideals of the Renaissance. The Palazzo Ducale
houses the Galleria Nazionale delle Marche.

**★ The Flagellation by
Piero della Francesca**
*Dramatic perspective creates an
unsettling effect in this 15th-century
painting of the scourging of Christ.*

Towers attributed to Laurana

**The palace rising
above Urbino**

**The simple
east side** of
the palace was
designed by Maso di
Bartolomeo before 1460.

Cortile d'Onore
*This early Renaissance
courtyard was designed by
the Dalmatian-born artist
Luciano Laurana (1420–79).*

M
entra

The Libr
was one
Europe's
in its day

Ideal City
*Attributed to Luciano
Laurana, this 15th-century
painting of an imaginary
Renaissance city is notable
for its measured perspective
and lack of people.*

★ Studiolo
The former study of Federico da Montefeltro is decorated with intarsia (inlaid wood), some of it designed by Botticelli.

Duke Federico by Pedro Berruguete
The duke, shown here with his son in this 15th-century painting, was always portrayed in left profile after an injury to his face.

VISITORS' CHECKLIST

Piazza Duca Federico 13. 0722 32 26 25. Piazza del Merca-tale. Summer: 8:30am–2pm Mon, 8:30am–7:15pm Tue–Sun. Phone for winter schedule. Last adm: 60 mins before closing. 1 Jan, 25 Dec. www.marcheturismo.it

Hanging garden

The rooms in this wing are known as the Appartamento della Duchessa.

★ La Muta by Raphael
The Mute Woman may be a portrait of Maddalena Doni, a Florentine noblewoman.

STAR EXHIBITS

★ **The Flagellation by Piero della Francesca**

★ **La Muta by Raphael**

★ **Studiolo**

Urbino ❺

Pèsaro. 16,000. Piazza Rinascimento 1 (0722 26 13). Sat.

AMID URBINO'S TANGLE of medieval and Renaissance streets stands the Neo-Classical **Duomo**, on Piazza Federico, built in 1789. Of special interest is the painting of the *Last Supper* by Federico Barocci (c.1535–1612). The **Museo Diocesano** contains a collection of ceramics, glass and religious artifacts.

Urbino's famous son, the painter Raphael (1483–1520), lived in the **Casa Natale di Raffaello**. It has a highly evocative interior, especially the kitchen and courtyard.

In Via Barocci stands the medieval **Oratorio di San Giuseppe**, known for its *presepio* (Christmas crib), and the 14th-century **Oratorio di San Giovanni Battista**, whose interior is smothered in 15th-century frescoes of the *Crucifixion* and the *Life of John the Baptist* by Giacomo and Lorenzo Salimbeni.

The 15th-century **Fortezza dell'Albornoz** on Viale Bruno Buozzi is the defensive focus of Urbino's surviving 16th-century walls and bastions.

Museo Diocesano
Piazza Pascoli 2. 0722 28 50. Mon–Sat (Oct–Mar: ask Duomo custodian).
Casa Natale di Raffaello
Via di Raffaello 57. 0722 32 01 05. daily (Sun am only). 1 Jan, 25 Dec.

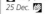

A street scene in the medieval town of Urbino

Fresh seafood and fishing boats in the harbour at Ancona

Grotte di Frasassi ⓻

Ancona. 📞 *0732 972 11.* 🚆 *Genga San Vittore Terme.* ⏱ *9am–6pm. Guided tours only (1 hr 20 mins).* 🚫 *1 Jan, 10–30 Jan, 4 Dec, 25 Dec.*

Some of europe's largest publicly accessible caverns lie in the cave network gouged out by the River Sentino south-west of Jesi. Of the vast net-work of 18 km (11 miles), an area of about 1,000 m (3,281 ft) is open to the public. The colossal **Grotta del Vento** is large enough to contain Milan cathedral – its ceiling extends to a height of 240 m (787 ft). This cavern has been used for a range of experiments, from sensory deprivation to an exploration of the social consequences of leaving a group of people alone in its depths for long periods.

Jesi ⓼

Ancona. 🏘 *41,000.* 🚆 🚌 ℹ *Piazza della Repubblica 11 (0731 597 88).* 🛒 *Wed & Sat.*

Perched on a long, rocky ridge, Jesi lies in the heart of the verdant hill country where Verdicchio is produced. A crisp, white wine renowned for centuries, Verdicchio is bottled in unique containers – glass models of the terracotta amphorae once used to export the wine to ancient Greece. No wine is made in Jesi itself, but there are many vineyards in the surrounding countryside.

Housed in the town's 18th-century Palazzo Pianetti is the **Pinacoteca e Musei Civici**, which contains fine late-period paintings by Lorenzo Lotto. Almost as alluring as the gallery's paintings, however, is the great central salon – an orgy of Rococo decoration that once formed the centrepiece of the Palazzo Pianetti. The nearby **Palazzo della Signoria** features an interesting little collection of archaeological finds, while beyond the old town's Renaissance walls stands the 14th-century church of **San Marco**, known for its collection of well-preserved Giottesque frescoes.

🏛 **Pinacoteca e Musei Civici**
Via XV Settembre. 📞 *0731 53 83 43.* ⏱ *Tue–Sun.*
🏛 **Palazzo della Signoria**
Piazza Colocci. 📞 *0731 53 83 45.* ⏱ *call to check times.*

Ancona ⓽

🏘 *98,000.* ✈ 🚆 🚌 ⛴ ℹ *Via Thaon de Revel 4 (071 35 89 91).* 🛒 *Tue & Fri.* 🌐 *www.turismo.marche.it*

The capital of le marche and its largest port (with ferries to and from Greece and Croatia), Ancona dates back to at least the 5th century BC, when it was settled by Greek exiles from Siracusa. Its name derives from *ankon* (Greek for elbow), a reference to the rocky spur that juts into the sea to form the town's fine natural harbour.

Heavy bombing during World War II destroyed much of the medieval town. The 15th-century **Loggia dei Mercanti** (merchants' exchange) on Via della Loggia survives as a monument to the town's medieval heyday.

Just north of the loggia is the Romanesque church of **Santa Maria della Piazza**, with a lovely façade. The nearby **Pinacoteca Comunale F Podesti e Galleria d'Arte Moderna** includes canvases by Titian and Lorenzo Lotto. In the **Museo Archeologico Nazionale delle Marche** there are displays of Greek, Gallic and Roman art. The **Arco di Traiano**, by the harbour, was erected in AD 115 and is one of Italy's better preserved Roman arches.

An impressive cavern in the cave system of the Grotte di Frasassi

The beach at the village of Sirolo on the Conero Peninsula

🏛 Pinacoteca Comunale F Podesti e Galleria d'Arte Moderna

Via Pizzecolli 17. **📞** 071 222 50 41. **⏰** Tue–Sat daily (Sun pm & Mon am). **🎫** public hols. 🚫 ♿

🏛 Museo Archeologico Nazionale delle Marche

Palazzo Ferretti, Via Ferretti 1. **📞** 071 207 53 90. **⏰** Tue–Sun (Oct–May am only). **🎫** 1 Jan, 25 Dec. 🚫 ♿

Conero Peninsula ⑩

Ancona. 🚉 🚢 Ancona. 🚌 from Ancona to Sirolo or Numana. **ℹ** Via Thaon de Revel 4, Ancona (071 35 89 91).

THE BEAUTIFUL cliff-edged Conero Peninsula is the only natural feature to disturb the almost unbroken line of beaches along the coast of Le Marche. Easily accessible from Ancona to the north, it is a semi-wild area known for its scenery, its wines (notably Rosso del Conero) and for a collection of coves, beaches and picturesque little resorts.

The best of these resorts is **Portonovo**, above whose beach stands **Santa Maria di Portonovo**, a pretty 11th-century Romanesque church mentioned by Dante in Canto XXI of *Paradiso*. **Sirolo** and **Numana** are busier and more commercialized, but you can escape the crowds by hiking the flower-swathed slopes of Monte Conero, which stands at 572 m (1,877 ft), or by taking a boat trip to the smaller beaches beyond the resorts.

Loreto ⑪

Ancona. 🏘 11,000. 🚉 🚌 **ℹ** Via Solari 3 (071 97 02 76). 🛒 Fri.

LEGEND HAS IT that in 1294 the house of the Virgin Mary (**Santa Casa**) miraculously up-rooted itself from the Holy Land and was brought by angels to a laurel grove (*loreto*) south of Ancona. Each year several million pilgrims visit the

Santa Casa in Loreto

Santa Casa in Loreto and its **Basilica**. Begun in 1468, the latter was designed and built in part by Renaissance architects Bramante, Sansovino and Giuliano da Sangallo. Its paintings include works by Luca Signorelli. The **Museo-Pinacoteca** has 16th-century paintings by Lorenzo Lotto.

🔔 Basilica and Santa Casa

Piazza Santuario. **📞** 071 97 01 04. **⏰** daily. ♿

🏛 Museo-Pinacoteca

Palazzo Apostolico. **📞** 071 97 77 59. **⏰** Tue–Sun daily. **🎫** Easter, 1 May, 15 Aug. 🚫

Ascoli Piceno ⑫

🏘 54,000. 🚌 **ℹ** Piazza del Popolo 17 (0736 25 30 45). 🛒 Wed & Sat.

THIS ALLURING TOWN takes its name from the Piceni, a tribe eventually conquered by the Romans in 89 BC. The gridiron plan of Roman Asculum Picenum is visible in the streets today, but it is the town's medieval heritage that attracts most visitors.

The enchanting **Piazza del Popolo** is dominated by the 13th-century **Palazzo dei Capitani del Popolo**, whose façade was designed by Cola dell'Amatrice, and the church of **San Francesco**, a large and faintly austere Gothic ensemble built between 1262 and 1549.

Via del Trivio leads north to a medieval district overlooking the River Tronto. Along Via Cairoli lies the 13th-century Dominican church of **San Pietro Martire**. Opposite is the church of **Santi Vincenzo e Anastasio** (11th century), with an ancient crypt built over a spring said to cure leprosy.

Around Piazza dell'Arringo is the 12th-century **Duomo**, spoiled by a Baroque overlay. Its Cappella del Sacramento contains a polyptych by the 15th-century artist Carlo Crivelli. The **Pinacoteca Civica** has more works by Crivelli and by Guido Reni, Titian and Alemanno. The **Museo Archeologico** contains Roman, Piceni and Lombard artifacts.

🏛 Pinacoteca Civica

Palazzo Comunale, Piazza Arringo. **📞** 0736 29 82 13. **⏰** daily. **🎫** 1 Jan, 25 Dec. 🚫 ♿

🏛 Museo Archeologico

Palazzo Panighi, Piazza Arringo. **📞** 0736 25 35 62. **⏰** daily. **🎫** 1 Jan, 1 May, 25 Dec. 🚫 ♿

A view of the medieval town of Ascoli Piceno

ROME AND LAZIO

Rome and Lazio at a Glance

T HE FIRST SETTLEMENTS IN THE REGION can be traced back to the early Etruscan civilization in northern Lazio. Rome grew to rule a vast empire and, as the empire began to divide, the region became the centre of the Christian world. Artists and architects flocked to work for the popes and their families, notably in the Renaissance and Baroque periods when some magnificent architectural works were created. The legacy of this uninterrupted history can be seen all over the city and the surrounding area.

St Peter's, with its majestic dome by Michelangelo, is a magnificent and sumptuous 16th-century basilica (see pp408–9).

Piazza Navona, flanked by cafés, contains three Baroque fountains, including the colossal Fontana dei Quattro Fiumi, one of Bernini's finest works (see p389).

St Peter's

PIAZZA NAVONA (See pp386–9)

Fontana dei Quattro Fiumi

THE VATICAN AND TRASTEVERE (See pp404–19)

Santa Maria in Trastevere, probably the first Christian church in Rome, holds some remarkable mosaics such as this detail from Cavallini's Life of the Virgin which dates from 1291 (see p418).

Santa Maria in Trastevere

LAZIO (See pp444–55)

Cerveteri tombs

ROME (See main map)

Cerveteri is one of the many necropolises left by the Etruscan civilization in northern Lazio. The larger tumulus tombs often contained frescoes and utensils useful for the afterlife (see p450).

| 0 kilometres | 15 |
| 0 miles | 10 |

◁ Bernini's allegorical Fountain of the Four Rivers at the centre of Piazza Navona

The Pantheon, built between AD 118–125, is a marvel of Roman engineering with its huge dome hidden behind the Classical portico (see p394).

SEE ALSO

- **Where to Stay** pp565–9
- **Where to Eat** pp599–602

NORTHEAST ROME
(See pp396–403)

Santa Maria Maggiore's richly decorated interior blends different architectural styles, such as this baldacchino from the 18th century (see p403).

Santa Maria Maggiore

Pantheon

THE ANCIENT CENTRE
(See pp372–85)

Capitoline Museums

Colosseum

San Giovanni in Laterano

AVENTINE AND LATERAN
(See pp420–27)

San Giovanni in Laterano, the Cathedral of Rome, incorporates the elaborate Corsini Chapel built in the 1730s (see p426).

The Capitoline Museums have held treasures of the Classical world since the Renaissance, including this colossal 4th-century head of Constantine (see pp376–7).

0 metres   750

0 yards   750

The Colosseum was constructed in AD 80 by Emperor Vespasian. His aim was to gain popularity by staging deadly gladiatorial combats and wild animal fights for public viewing (see p383).

Regional Food: Rome and Lazio

THE TRADITIONAL *cucina romanesca* has always relied on fresh seasonal produce from the nearby countryside bought in the local markets. Mushrooms, in autumn, and artichokes, in spring, are served in dozens of different ways, and the *mesticanza*, a fresh mix of salad leaves including the peppery *rughetta* (rocket) and *puntarelle* (curly endive shoots), is also delicious when it is in season in the summer months. Many of the genuinely Roman dishes are highly seasoned with onions, garlic, rosemary, sage and bay leaves. The typical Roman meat dish, based on the so-called *quinto quarto* (fifth quarter) – head, tail, trotters and so on – is flavoured with olive oil, herbs, *pancetta* (bacon) and *guanciale* (pig's cheek) and is a culinary delight. *Pecorino*, a tangy sheep's milk cheese, is often sprinkled onto dishes as seasoning and the blander *ricotta* is a filling for pizzas as well as the Roman dessert *torta di ricotta*.

Sage leaves

Supplì di Riso *are fried rice croquettes stuffed with mozzarella. They are typically Roman and make an excellent snack.*

Filetti di Baccalà*, deep-fried cod fillets which were originally a Jewish speciality, have become a feature of Roman cuisine.*

Batter-fried artichoke hearts

Batter-fried courgette flowers

Gnocchi alla Romana*, small semolina dumplings, can be eaten with tomato sauce or just with butter.*

An antipasto *starts the meal and is usually a selection of appetizers based on the vegetables that are in season. The vegetables may be fresh, grilled or preserved in aromatic oils or vinegar. Artichoke hearts and courgette flowers are excellent in spring, and are used in a variety of dishes, including the fritto misto, a selection of local ingredients fried in batter.*

Risotto alla Romana *is a rice dish made with a sauce of liver, sweetbreads and Marsala, a fortified wine from Sicily.*

Bucatini all'Amatriciana *is hollow spaghetti-like pasta with bacon, tomatoes and onion sprinkled with pecorino cheese.*

Spaghetti alla Carbonara*, devised in Rome, is made with bacon, eggs, Parmesan cheese and, if desired, black pepper.*

***Coda alla Vaccinara** is a traditional Roman dish made from braised oxtail served with herbs and a tomato sauce.*

***Torta di Ricotta**, a popular dessert from Rome, is a delicious cheesecake filled with ricotta, Marsala and lemon.*

***Saltimbocca alla Romana** is a tasty dish of veal with ham and sage. It can also be served rolled and skewered.*

***Fave al Guanciale** are young spring broad beans, simmered in olive oil with pig's cheek (guanciale) and onion.*

WHAT TO DRINK IN ROME AND LAZIO

Vines thrive in the warm climate and fertile land of Lazio, keeping up the wine-producing tradition that was started around the hills of Rome over 2,000 years ago by the ancient Romans. Today, wine is usually drunk with meals as a matter of course and the region offers abundant supplies of inexpensive dry white wine for the city's restaurants and cafés. Of local bottled white wines, Frascati is the best known, but Castelli Romani, Marino, Colli Albani and Velletri are very similar in style. All are made from one grape variety, the Trebbiano, though better quality versions contain a dash of Malvasia for perfume and flavour. Local red wine is rarer and most reds come from other parts of Italy. As well as the usual range of digestives and apéritifs, such as Campari, beer is also widely available and the popular Italian lager is Nastro Azzurro. Fruit juices are also good and bars squeeze fresh orange juice *(spremuta)*. Rome's drinking water, another debt to the ancient Romans, is particularly good, fresh and sweet, and in abundant supply.

Frascati, the best known local white

***Torre Ercolana**, one of the few red wines produced in Lazio, is made in small quantities and generally regarded as one of the region's best wines. It is made from both the local Cesanese grapes and the more robust Cabernet, and should be kept to age for at least five years.*

***Drinking water** in Rome, unlike many other Mediterranean cities, is excellent. The city benefits from a constant supply of fresh drinking water, piped down from the hills through a system of pipes and aqueducts that has changed very little since ancient Roman times. At regular intervals throughout the city, ornate fountains pump delicious fresh water for general use as well as for drinking. Only if there is a sign saying* acqua non potabile *is the water not safe to drink.*

One of Rome's many fresh water drinking fountains

***Coffee** is almost more important to Roman life than wine. Take espresso for a shot of neat strong black coffee at any time of the day, sit with a milky cappuccino for breakfast or mid-afternoon, or take a caffelatte in a glass for extra milk.*

Espresso

Cappuccino

Caffelatte

Understanding Architecture in Rome and Lazio

THE ARCHITECTURE of Imperial Rome, a combination of Etruscan and Classical Greek styles, gradually developed new and uniquely Roman forms based on the arch, the vault and the dome. During the early Christian period simple, rectangular basilicas were built, forms which by the 12th century had been incorporated into the stark Romanesque style. The Renaissance, inspired by the example of Florence, saw a return to Classical ideals of simplicity and harmonious proportions, though it was to be in the flamboyance of the 17th-century Baroque that Rome once again found great architectural expression.

The extravagant Baroque style of the Fontana di Trevi, Rome

FROM ETRUSCAN TO CLASSICAL ROME

The Podium made the temple more prominent.

The arch became a feature of Roman architecture.

A portico was a porch with columns.

Reliefs were scavenged from earlier monuments.

Three naves divided the interior of the basilica.

Etruscan temples, based on Greek models, inspired early Roman architecture. A front portico was the only entrance.

The Arch of Constantine (AD 315) is typical of triumphant Imperial Roman architecture (see p379). It stands at a colossal 25 m (82 ft).

Early Christian basilicas (4th century) were based on a rectangular floorplan.

FROM RENAISSANCE TO BAROQUE

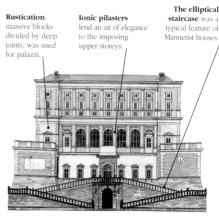

Doric columns recall Classical architecture.

Bramante adopted the circular form of ancient temples.

Rustication, massive blocks divided by deep joints, was used for palazzi.

Ionic pilasters lend an air of elegance to the imposing upper storeys.

The elliptical staircase was a typical feature of Mannerist houses.

The Tempietto at San Pietro in Montorio, Rome (1502) is a model of Renaissance architecture: simple and perfectly proportioned (see p419).

Palazzo Farnese at Caprarola, a pentagonal building completed in 1575 (see p449), combines some Mannerist tricks of architecture with the strict geometric proportions characteristic of the Renaissance.

WHERE TO SEE THE ARCHITECTURE

A walk through the back streets of the centre of Rome will reveal masterpieces of virtually every architectural age. The most ancient treasures are seven obelisks stolen from Egypt. One stands on the back of Bernini's elephant *(see p394)*. Highlights from Ancient Rome include triumphal arches and temples such as the Pantheon *(see p394)*. Romanesque elements survive in the church of San Clemente *(see p425)*, while the Renaissance finds expression in the dome of St Peter's *(see pp408–9)*. Magnificent Baroque treasures dot the entire city, in particular flamboyant fountains that adorn the squares. Outside the city the outstanding sights are the late Renaissance villas such as Caprarola *(see p449)*.

Part of Bernini's elephant supporting an ancient Egyptian obelisk

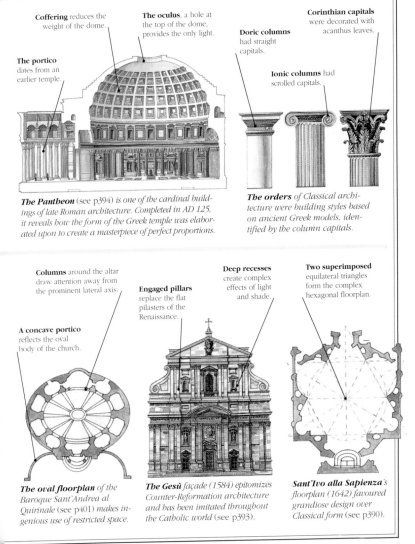

Coffering reduces the weight of the dome.

The oculus, a hole at the top of the dome, provides the only light.

The portico dates from an earlier temple.

Corinthian capitals were decorated with acanthus leaves.

Doric columns had straight capitals.

Ionic columns had scrolled capitals.

The Pantheon (see p394) *is one of the cardinal buildings of late Roman architecture. Completed in AD 125, it reveals how the form of the Greek temple was elaborated upon to create a masterpiece of perfect proportions.*

The orders *of Classical architecture were building styles based on ancient Greek models, identified by the column capitals.*

Columns around the altar draw attention away from the prominent lateral axis.

A concave portico reflects the oval body of the church.

Engaged pillars replace the flat pilasters of the Renaissance.

Deep recesses create complex effects of light and shade.

Two superimposed equilateral triangles form the complex hexagonal floorplan.

The oval floorplan *of the Baroque Sant'Andrea al Quirinale* (see p401) *makes ingenious use of restricted space.*

The Gesù *façade (1584) epitomizes Counter-Reformation architecture and has been imitated throughout the Catholic world* (see p393).

Sant'Ivo alla Sapienza's *floorplan (1642) favoured grandiose design over Classical form* (see p390).

THE ANCIENT CENTRE

THE CAPITOL, the southern summit of the Capitoline Hill, was the symbolic centre of the Roman world and home to the city's three most important temples. These were dedicated to the god Jupiter Optimus Maximus, protector of Rome, Minerva, goddess of wisdom and war, and Juno Moneta, a guardian goddess. Below the Capitol lies the Forum, once the focus of political, social, legal and commercial life; the Imperial Fora, built when Rome's population grew; and the Colosseum, the centre of entertainment. Overlooking the Forum is the Palatine Hill, where Romulus is said to have founded Rome in the 8th century BC, and emperors lived for over 400 years.

Capitoline Wolf with Romulus and Remus

SIGHTS AT A GLANCE

Churches
Santa Maria in Aracoeli ❸

Museums and Galleries
Capitoline Museums pp376–7 ❶

Historic Piazzas
Piazza del Campidoglio ❷

Ancient Sites and Buildings
Arch of Constantine ❿

Colosseum p383 ❾
Forum of Augustus ❺
Forum of Caesar ❼
Mamertine Prison ❻
Palatine pp384–5 ⓫
Roman Forum pp380–81 ❽
Trajan's Forum and Markets ❹

GETTING THERE

The Capitoline is in walking distance of Piazza Venezia, the hub of the city bus routes, while the Forum, Colosseum and Palatine are close to Metro Colosseo. Buses 87 and 186 link Piazza Venezia and the Colosseum with Corso Rinascimento, in the heart of the *centro storico*.

KEY

▨	Street-by-Street: The Capitoline Hill *pp374–5*
Ⓜ	Metro station
ℹ	Tourist information

0 metres	250
0 yards	250

◁ **View of the Colosseum rising behind the Forum**

Street-by-Street: The Capitoline Hill

T HE CAPITOL, citadel of ancient Rome, was
designed by Michelangelo in the 16th
century. He was responsible for the
trapezoid Piazza del Campidoglio as
well as the Cordonata, the broad
flight of steps leading up to it. The
piazza is flanked by Palazzo Nuovo
and Palazzo dei Conservatori,
housing the Capitoline Museums,
with their fine collections of
sculpture and paintings. It is also
well worth walking behind the
museums to the
Tarpeian Rock, for a
fine view of the Forum
lying below.

The Victor Emmanuel Monument was begun in 1885
and inaugurated in 1911 in honour of Victor Emmanuel II,
the first king of unified Italy.

San Marco, dedicated to
the patron saint of Venice,
has splendid 9th-century
mosaics in the apse.

PIAZZA VENEZIA

Palazzo Venezia,
once the home of
Mussolini, now holds
a museum of fine and
decorative arts. Exhibits
include this medieval
gilt and enamel angel.

**The Aracoeli
Staircase** was
completed in
1348 to
commemorate
the end of the
plague.

The Cordonata is
presided over by the
colossal statues of Castor
and Pollux.

VIA DEL TEATRO DI MARCELLO

★ **Capitoline Museums**
*The collections of art and
ancient sculpture include this
statue of the
Emperor Marcus
Aurelius, a replica
of which stands in
the centre of the
piazza* ❶

STAR SIGHT

★ Capitoline Museums

KEY

‒ ‒ ‒ Suggested route

---

0 metres	75
0 yards	75

Santa Maria in Aracoeli

The brick façade hides treasures such as this 15th-century fresco of the Funeral of San Bernardino by Pinturicchio ❸

NORTHEAST ROME

THE ANCIENT CENTRE

Tevere

AVENTINE AND LATERAN

LOCATOR MAP
See Rome Street Finder map 3

Palazzo Nuovo was made into a public museum in 1734.

PIETRO IN CARCERE

Palazzo Senatorio, the splendid Renaissance seat of the city government, is built on the ruins of the ancient Tabularium.

Piazza del Campidoglio
Michelangelo designed the geometric paving and the façades of the buildings ❷

Palazzo dei Conservatori

VIA DEL TEMPIO DI GIOVE

The Temple of Jupiter, represented on this coin, was dedicated to Jupiter Optimus Maximus, the most important of the Roman gods. He was believed to have the power to protect or destroy the city.

The Tarpeian Rock is a cliff from which traitors were believed to have been thrown to their death in ancient Rome.

Steps to the Capitoline

Capitoline Museums ❶

See pp376–7.

Piazza del Campidoglio ❷

Map 3 B5. 🚌 40, 64, 70, 75.

Wᴴᴇɴ ᴇᴍᴘᴇʀᴏʀ ᴄʜᴀʀʟᴇs ᴠ announced he was to visit Rome in 1536, Pope Paul III Farnese asked Michelangelo to give the Capitoline a face-lift. He redesigned the piazza, renovated the façades of its palaces and built a new stair-case, the Cordonata. This gently rising ramp is now crowned with the massive statues of Castor and Pollux.

Santa Maria in Aracoeli ❸

Piazza d'Aracoeli. **Map** 3 B5.
☎ 06 679 81 55. 🚌 64, 70, 75.
🕐 9am–12:30pm, 3–6pm daily.

Tʜɪs ᴄʜᴜʀᴄʜ sᴛᴀɴᴅs on the site of the Temple of Juno on the northern summit of the Capitoline Hill, and dates back at least to the 6th century. The church is famous today for its ornate gilded ceiling and a very fine series of frescoes by Pinturicchio, dating from the 1480s. They depict scenes from the life of San Bernardino of Siena. The miracle-working *Santo Bambino* figure was stolen in 1994 but has been replaced by a replica.

The marble staircase and austere façade of Santa Maria in Aracoeli

Capitoline Museums: ❶
Palazzo Nuovo

A COLLECTION of Classical sculptures has been kept on the Capitoline Hill since Pope Sixtus IV donated a group of bronze sculptures to the city in 1471. Paintings as well as sculpture are now housed in two palaces designed by Michelangelo. The Palazzo Nuovo, first opened to the public in 1734 by Pope Clement XII, contains a fine selection of Greek and Roman sculptures.

LOCATOR MAP

Discobolus
The twisted torso was part of a Greek statue of a discus thrower. An 18th-century sculptor turned him into a wounded warrior.

Mosaic of the Doves
This 1st-century AD naturalistic mosaic once decorated the floor of Hadrian's Villa at Tivoli (see p452).

Alexander Severus as Hunter
In this marble of the 3rd century AD, the emperor's pose is a pastiche of the mythical hero, Perseus, holding up the head of Medusa the Gorgon after he had killed her.

Stairs to ground floor

Stairs to first floor

Courtyard

Hall of the Philosophers
The hall contains Roman copies of portrait busts of Greek politicians, scientists and poets. These adorned the homes of wealthy Romans.

Main entrance

Dying Galatian
Great compassion is conveyed in this Roman copy of a Greek work of the 3rd century BC.

KEY TO FLOORPLAN

☐	Ground floor
☐	First floor
☐	Second floor
☐	Non-exhibition space

Palazzo dei Conservatori

T HE PALAZZO DEI CONSERVATORI was the seat of the city's magistrates during the late Middle Ages. Its frescoed halls are still used occasionally for political meetings and the ground floor houses the municipal registry office. While much of the palazzo is given over to sculpture, including fragments of a huge sculpture of Constantine, the art galleries on the second floor hold works by Veronese, Tintoretto, Caravaggio, Van Dyck and Titian.

VISITORS' CHECKLIST

Musei Capitolini, Piazza del Campidoglio. **Map** 3 B5.
06 39 96 78 00.
40, 63, 64, 70, 75, 81, 87 and many other routes through Piazza Venezia.
9am–8pm Tue–Sun.
1 Jan, 1 May, 25 Dec.
entrance ticket is valid for both museums.
W www.museicapitolini.org

St John the Baptist
Caravaggio's sensual portrait (1595–6) of the young saint caressing a sheep is a highly unorthodox image of Christ's forerunner.

Medusa
This bust by Bernini of the mythological Medusa is in Room 5.

Second-floor art gallery

Stairs to first floor

Stairs to ground floor

Roman Garden

First floor

Courtyard

Main entrance

The Rape of the Sabine Women
Pietro da Cortona glamorized the mass abduction of Sabine women by the Romans in this painting of 1629.

Spinario
This is a charming bronze sculpture from the 1st century BC of a boy trying to remove a thorn from his foot.

Trajan's Forum and Markets ❹

Map 3 B4. **Trajan's Forum**, Via dei Fori Imperiali. ◐ *to the public.* **Trajan's Markets**, Via IV Novembre. ☎ *06 679 00 48.* ◯ *9am–5:30pm Tue–Sun (to 4:30pm in winter).* ◐ *public hols.* 🖼 🅿 ♿

TRAJAN BEGAN to build his forum in AD 107 to commemorate his final conquest of Dacia (present day Romania) after successful campaigns in AD 101–2 and 105–6. His new forum was the most ambitious yet, with a vast colonnaded open space centring on an equestrian statue of the emperor, a huge basilica, and two big libraries. Dominating the ruins today is **Trajan's Column**, which originally stood between the two libraries.

Trajan's Column

Spiralling up its 30 m (98 ft) high stem are minutely detailed scenes from the Dacian campaigns, beginning with the Romans preparing for war and ending with the Dacians being ousted from their homeland. The subtly modelled reliefs were designed to be seen from viewing platforms on the libraries, and are consequently difficult to interpret from ground level. If you want to examine the scenes in detail there are casts in the Museo della Civiltà Romana *(see p432).* The **market** complex, which is situated directly behind the forum, was begun slightly earlier. Like the forum it was probably designed by Apollodorus of Damascus, and was the

Via Biberatica, the main street through Trajan's Markets

ancient Roman equivalent of the modern shopping centre. There were around 150 shops selling everything from oriental silks and spices to fruit, fresh fish and flowers. It was also here that the *annone*, or corn dole, was distributed. This was a free ration of corn given to Roman men, a practice which was introduced in the Republic by politicians who wanted to buy votes and prevent unrest during periods of famine.

RECONSTRUCTION OF TRAJAN'S MARKETS

Cross vaulting

The Main Hall had 12 shops on two storeys. The corn ration was distributed from the upper floor.

Amphorae, used for storing wine and oil, were discovered on the upper corridor.

The terrace has a good view of Trajan's Forum.

The shops on the ground floor were cool, and probably sold vegetables, fruit and flowers.

Staircase

Via Biberatica is named after the drinking inns that once lined it.

Large hall with semi-domed ceiling

Forum of Augustus ❺

Piazza del Grillo 1. **Map** 3 B5.
🚍 87, 186. ⭘ by appt. 🎫 includes entry to Trajan's Markets.

THE FORUM of Augustus, which once stretched from a high wall at the foot of sleazy Suburra to the edge of Caesar's Forum, was built to celebrate Augustus's victory in 41 BC over Brutus and Cassius, the assassins of Julius Caesar. As a consequence the temple in its centre was dedicated to Mars the Avenger. The temple, with its cracked steps and four Corinthian columns, is easily identified. Originally it had a statue of Mars that looked very like Augustus, but in case anyone failed to notice the resemblance, a colossal statue of the emperor himself was placed against the wall of the Suburra quarter.

19th-century engraving of the Mamertine Prison

Mamertine Prison ❻

Clivo Argentario 1. **Map** 3 B5. 📞 06 69 94 10 20. 🚍 84, 85, 87, 175, 186. ⭘ 9am–12:30pm, 2:30–6:30pm (2–5pm in winter) daily. **Donation**.

BELOW THE 16th-century church of San Giuseppe dei Falegnami is a dank dungeon in which, according to Christian legend, St Peter and St Paul were imprisoned. They are said to have caused a spring to bubble up into the

Podium of the Temple of Mars the Avenger, Forum of Augustus

cell, and to have used the water to baptize two prison guards. The prison was in an old cistern with access to the city's main sewer (the Cloaca Maxima). The lower cell was used for executions, and corpses were thrown into the sewer. However, the inmates, who received no food, often died of starvation.

Forum of Caesar ❼

Via del Carcere Tulliano. **Map** 3 B5. 📞 06 399 67 00. 🚍 84, 85, 87, 175, 186, 810, 850. ⭘ by appt only.

THE FIRST of Rome's Imperial fora was built by Julius Caesar to relieve congestion in the Roman Forum when Rome's population boomed. He spent a fortune – most of it booty from his recent conquest of Gaul – buying up and demolishing houses on the site. Pride of place went to a temple dedicated in 46 BC to Venus Genetrix (Venus the Ancestor) as Caesar claimed to be descended from the goddess. The temple contained statues of Caesar and Cleopatra as well as of Venus, but all that remains today is a platform and three Corinthian columns. The forum was once enclosed by a double colonnade, under which was sheltered a row of shops. However, this burned down in AD 80 and was rebuilt by Domitian and Trajan. The latter also added the Basilica

Argentaria – which became an important financial exchange – as well as shops and a heated public lavatory.

Roman Forum ❽

See pp380–81.

Colosseum ❾

See p383.

Arch of Constantine ❿

Between Via di San Gregorio and Piazza del Colosseo. **Map** 7 A1.
🚍 75, 85, 87, 110, 175, 673, 810.
🚋 3. Ⓜ Colosseo.

THIS TRIUMPHAL ARCH is one of Imperial Rome's last monuments, built in AD 315, a few years before Constantine moved the capital of the Empire to Byzantium. It was built to celebrate Constantine's victory in AD 312 over his co-emperor Maxentius at the Battle of the Milvian Bridge. Constantine attributed the victory to a dream in which he was told to mark his men's shields with *chi-rho*, the first two Greek letters of Christ's name. Christian tradition prefers a version in which the emperor has a vision of the Cross, mid-battle. There is nothing Christian about the arch: most of the reliefs were from earlier pagan monuments.

Palatine ⓫

See pp384–5.

The north side of the Arch of Constantine

Roman Forum ●

IN THE EARLY REPUBLIC, the Forum was a
chaotic place, with food stalls and brothels
as well as temples and the Senate House. By
the 2nd century BC it was decided that Rome
required a more salubrious centre, and the
food stores were replaced by business
centres and law courts. The Forum
remained the ceremonial centre
of the city under the Empire,
with emperors renovating
old buildings and erecting
new temples and
monuments.

**Arch of
Septimius Severus**
*This triumphal arch
was erected in AD 203,
the 10th anniversary
of Emperor Septimius
Severus' accession.*

**The Temple of Antoninus
and Faustina** is now
incorporated into the
church of San
Lorenzo in
Miranda.

The Rostra was the
orator's tribune from
which speeches
were made.

**Temple
of Saturn**

VIA DELLA CURIA

VIA SACRA

The Curia, or
ancient Roman
Senate House,
has been
reconstructed.

Basilica Julia
*Named after Julius
Caesar, who began its
construction in 54 BC,
this was the seat of the civil
magistrates court.*

Basilica Aemilia
was a meeting hall
for business and
money exchange.

**Temple
of Vesta**

Temple of Castor and Pollux
*Although there has been a temple
here since the 5th century BC, the
columns and elaborate cornice
date from AD 6 when the
temple was rebuilt.*

STAR SIGHTS

★ **House of the Vestal
Virgins**

★ **Basilica of Constan-
tine and Maxentius**

★ **House of the
Vestal Virgins**
*The priestesses who
tended the sacred
flame in the Temple
of Vesta lived here.
The house was a
large rectangular
building around a
central garden.*

0 metres		75
0 yards		75

★ Basilica of Constantine and Maxentius

The basilica's three vast barrel vaults are all that remain of the Forum's largest building. Like other basilicas, it was used for the administration of justice and conducting business.

The Temple of Romulus, now part of the church of Santi Cosma e Damiano which stands behind it, retains its original 4th-century bronze doors.

Arch of Titus

This arch was erected by Emperor Domitian in AD 81 to commemorate the sack of Jerusalem by his father Vespasian and brother Titus, 13 years earlier.

Antiquarium Forense
This small museum contains finds from the Forum. Exhibits range from Iron Age burial urns to this frieze of Aeneas from the Basilica Aemilia.

VIA DEI FORI IMPERIALI

VIA SACRA

VIA SACRA

Colosseum

The Temple of Venus and Rome was built in AD 135, and was largely designed by Hadrian.

Palatine

Santa Francesca Romana
The Romanesque bell tower of Santa Francesca Romana towers over one of a number of churches built among the ruins of the Forum.

THE VESTAL VIRGINS

The cult of Vesta, the goddess of fire, dates back to at least the 8th century BC. Romulus and Remus were allegedly born of the Vestal priestess Rhea and the god Mars. Six virgins kept the sacred flame of Vesta burning in her circular temple. The girls, who came from noble families, were selected when they were between six and ten years old, and served for 30 years. They had high status and financial security, but were buried alive if they lost their virginity and whipped by the high priest if the sacred flame died out. Although they were permitted to marry after finishing their service, few did so.

Honorary statue of a Vestal Virgin

Exploring the Roman Forum

To APPRECIATE THE LAYOUT of the Roman Forum before wandering through its confusing patchwork of ruined temples, triumphal arches and basilicas, it is best to view the whole area from the Capitoline Hill above. From there you can make out the more substantial ruins, and the course of the Via Sacra (Sacred Way), the route followed through the Forum by religious and triumphal processions making their way up to the Capitol to give thanks at the Temple of Jupiter (see p375).

Corinthian columns of the Temple of Castor and Pollux

The Main Sights

The first building you come to on entering the Forum is the **Basilica Aemilia**. A rectangular hall built in 179 BC, it was a meeting place for moneylenders, businessmen and tax collectors. Although little more remains of it than a pastel marble pavement fringed with column stumps, you can still find splashes of verdigrised bronze, reputedly the remains of coins which melted when the Visigoths invaded Rome and burnt down the basilica in the 5th century.

Inside the Curia – the stark brick building next to the basilica – are the **Plutei of Trajan**, relief panels commissioned by either Trajan or Hadrian to decorate the Rostra, the public oratory platform. On one panel are piles of books holding tax records, which Trajan had destroyed in order to free citizens from debts. The **Arch of Septimius Severus** is the best preserved of the Forum's monuments. The marble relief panels depict the military triumphs of the emperor in Parthia (modern-day Iran and Iraq) and Arabia.

The **Temple of Saturn** was the focus of the annual Saturnalia celebrations, when, for up to a week in December, schools closed, slaves dined with their masters, presents were exchanged and a fair and market were held.

Soaring above the remains of the Basilica Julia are three delicately fluted columns and a finely carved slab of entablature taken from the **Temple of Castor and Pollux**. This striking relic is dedicated to the twin brothers of Helen of Troy, who were supposed to have appeared at the battle of Lake Regillus in 499 BC, aiding the Romans in their defeat of the Etruscans.

The elegant circular **Temple of Vesta** was one of ancient Rome's most sacred shrines and was dedicated to the goddess of the hearth. The flame, kept alive by the Vestal Virgins, symbolized the perpetuity of the state and its extinction prophesied doom for the city. The building was

Restored section of Temple of Vesta

partly reconstructed in 1930, but the circular form goes back to the Latin mud huts which originally occupied the site. Just behind the **House of the Vestal Virgins**, the living quarters of the priestess and the Vestals. This enormous complex of 50 rooms was once annexed to the Temple. Best preserved are the rooms overlooking a pretty courtyard, ornamented with statues of Vestals, ponds of waterlilies and rose trees.

On the other side of the Forum lie the impressive remains of the **Basilica of Constantine**. It was begun in AD 308 by Maxentius, and is therefore also known as the Basilica of Maxentius.

Constantine completed it after he defeated his rival at the battle of Milvio in AD 312. The stark remains of the huge arches and ceilings give an indication of the original scale and grandeur of the forum's public buildings. Three enormous coffered vaults remain, which originally measured up to 35 m (115 ft) and were faced with marble. The interior walls, which held niches for statues, were also covered with marble below and stucco above. Remains of a spiral staircase which once led to the roof can be found scattered on the ground.

The basilica's apse and hexagonal arches were often used as models by Renaissance architects striving to recreate a Classical symmetry and nobility in their work. They include Michelangelo, who allegedly studied the basilica's architecture when working on the dome of St Peter's.

Central courtyard of the House of the Vestal Virgins

Colosseum **9**

Gladiator's shield

Rome's greatest amphitheatre was commissioned by Emperor Vespasian in AD 72. Deadly gladiatorial combats and wild animal fights were staged by emperors and wealthy citizens, largely to gain popularity. Slaughter was on a huge scale: at the inaugural games in AD 80, over 9,000 wild animals were killed. The Colosseum could hold up to 55,000 people, who were seated according to rank.

The Velarium, a huge sailcloth awning which sheltered spectators from the sun, was supported by poles on the upper storey.

VISITORS' CHECKLIST

Piazza del Colosseo.
Map 7 B1. **C** 06 39 96 77 00.
75, 81, 85, 87, 117, 175, 673, 810. **M** Colosseo.
3 to Piazza del Colosseo.
9am–1 hour before sunset daily. 1 Jan, 25 Dec. limited.

Internal Corridors
These allowed the large and often unruly crowd to move freely and be seated quickly.

The Colossus of Nero
This gilt bronze statue from Nero's palace, over which the Colosseum was built, may have given the amphitheatre its name.

Entry routes and stairs led to seats at the various levels. The emperor and consul had their own, separate entrances.

Corinthian columns

Ionic columns

Doric columns

The arena floor covered a network of lifts and cages for wild animals.

Entrances

Doric, Ionic and Corinthian Tiers
The tiers inspired many Renaissance architects, who also plundered the building, using its travertine to build palaces and part of St Peter's.

Roman Gladiators
These were originally soldiers in training. Their combat became a sport, and slaves, prisoners of war or criminals were forced to fight men or wild animals to the death.

Emperor Vespasian
He ordered the Colosseum to be built on the site of Nero's palace, to dissociate himself from the hated tyrant.

Palatine

THE PALATINE, once the residence of emperors and aristocrats, is the most pleasant of Rome's ancient sites. The ruins range from the simple house in which Augustus is thought to have lived, to the Domus Flavia and Domus Augustana, the public and private wings of a luxurious palace built by Domitian.

Statue of the Goddess Cybele

The Huts of Romulus, indicated by holes left by the supporting posts, were reputedly founded by Romulus in the 9th century BC.

Temple of Cybele, Goddess of fertility

The House of Augustus is thought to have been the public part of the emperor's modest home.

★ House of Livia
Many of the wall paintings have survived in the private quarters of the house where Augustus is believed to have lived with his wife Livia.

★ Domus Flavia
The courtyard of the Domus Flavia was lavishly paved with coloured marble. The Roman poets praised this villa as the most splendid.

Domus Augustana was the private home of the emperors.

STAR SIGHTS

★ Domus Flavia

★ House of Livia

Emperor Septimius Severus
During his reign (AD 193–211), he extended the Domus Augustana and built an impressive bath complex.

0 metres		75
0 yards		75

Cryptoporticus
This underground gallery, elaborately decorated with stuccoed walls, was built by Emperor Nero.

The courtyard of the Domus Flavia was lined by Domitian with mirror-like marble, so he could spot would-be assassins.

The exedra of the stadium may have housed a balcony.

Forum entrance

Stadium
Part of the Imperial palace, this enclosure may have been used by the emperors as a private garden.

The Palace of Septimius Severus
This extension of the Domus Augustana projected beyond the hillside, supported on giant arches.

A HISTORY OF THE PALATINE HILL

Romans of the Decadence by Thomas Couture (1815–79)

The Founding of Rome
According to legend the twins Romulus and Remus were brought up on the Palatine by a wolf. Here Romulus, having killed his brother, is said to have founded the village that was destined to become Rome. Traces of mud huts dating back to the 8th century BC have been found on the hill, lending archaeological support to the legend.

The Republic
By the 1st century BC the Palatine was the most desirable address in Rome and home to the leading citizens of the Republic. Its residents, including the erotic poet Catullus and the orator Cicero, were notoriously indulgent, and their villas were magnificent dwellings with doors of ivory, floors of bronze and frescoed walls.

The Empire
Augustus was born on the Palatine in 63 BC, and lived there in a modest house after becoming emperor. The hill was therefore an obvious choice of abode for future emperors. Domitian's ambitious house, the Domus Flavia (1st century AD), and its private quarters, the Domus Augustana, remained the official residence of future emperors (who were referred to as *Augustus*) for more than 300 years.

AROUND PIAZZA NAVONA

HE AREA around Piazza Navona, known as the *centro storico*, has been inhabited for at least 2,000 years. Piazza Navona stands above an ancient stadium; the Pantheon has been a temple since AD 27; and the Theatre of Marcellus in the Ghetto has been converted into exclusive

Detail of an 18th-century street shrine

flats. The area's heyday began in the 15th century, when the papacy returned to Rome. Throughout the Renaissance and Baroque eras princes, popes and cardinals settled here, as did the artists and artisans they commissioned to build and adorn lavish palaces, churches and fountains.

SIGHTS AT A GLANCE

Churches and Temples
Chiesa Nuova ❻
Gesù ⓭
La Maddalena ⓴
Sant'Ignazio di Loyola ⓱
Sant'Ivo alla Sapienza ❷
San Luigi dei Francesi ❸
Santa Maria sopra Minerva ⓯
Santa Maria della Pace ❺

Museums and Galleries
Palazzo Doria Pamphilj ⓮
Palazzo Spada ❿

Ancient Sites and Buildings
Area Sacra di Largo Argentina ⓬
Pantheon ⓰

Historic Buildings
Palazzo Altemps ❹
Palazzo della Cancelleria ❼
Palazzo Farnese ❾

Historic Piazzas and Areas
Campo de' Fiori ❽
Ghetto and Tiber Island ⓫
Piazza Colonna ⓲
Piazza di Montecitorio ⓳
Piazza Navona ❶

GETTING THERE
Corso Vittorio Emanuele II and Corso Rinascimento are main bus arteries, but only minibus 116 runs in the *centro storico*.

KEY

Street-by-Street: Around Piazza Navona pp388–9

Street-by-Street: Around the Pantheon pp392–3

P Parking

i Tourist information

0 metres 250

0 yards 250

◁ **Piazza Navona, with the Fontana del Moro (1653) and the 17th-century church of Sant'Agnese in Agone**

Street-by-Street: Around Piazza Navona

NO OTHER PIAZZA in Rome can rival the theatricality of Piazza Navona. The luxurious cafés are the social centre of the city, and day and night there is always something going on in the pedestrian area around the three flamboyant Baroque fountains. The Baroque is also represented in many of the area's churches. To discover an older Rome, walk along Via del Governo Vecchio to admire the façades of Renaissance buildings, browse in the fascinating antiques shops and lunch in one of the many trattorias.

The Torre dell'Orologio by Borromini (1648) formed part of the Oratorio dei Filippini.

Chiesa Nuova
This church was rebuilt in 1575 for the order founded by San Filippo Neri ❻

The Vatican

VIA DEL CORALLO

VIA DEL GOVERNO VECCHIO

VIA DI PARIONE

At the Oratorio dei Filippini (1637) biblical stories were sung and the congregation responded with a chorus: the origin of the oratorio.

Via del Governo Vecchio preserves a large number of fine Renaissance houses.

CORSO VITTORIO EMANUELE II

PIAZZA DI PASQUINO

VIA DI SANT

Santa Maria della Pace
This Renaissance church has frescoes of the Four Sibyls by Raphael and a refined courtyard by Bramante. The Baroque portico is by Pietro da Cortona ❺

STAR SIGHTS

★ **Piazza Navona**

Pasquino is a 3rd-century BC Hellenistic statue of Menelaus. Romans have been hanging satirical verses at its feet since the 16th century.

Palazzo Braschi, a late 18th-century building designed by Cosimo Morelli, has a splendid balcony overlooking the piazza.

Palazzo Pamphilj

Fontana del Moro

Campo de' Fiori

Sant'Andrea della Valle, begun in 1591, has a flamboyant Baroque façade flanked by angels with outstretched wings by Ercole Ferrata. The church is the setting of the first act of Puccini's *Tosca*.

KEY

― ― ― Suggested route

0 metres   75

0 yards   75

Sant'Agnese in Agone
by Borromini (1657) is allegedly built on the site where, in AD 304, the young St Agnes was exposed naked to force her to renounce her faith.

LOCATOR MAP
See Rome Street Finder map 2

Fontana dei Quattro Fiumi

San Luigi dei Francesi
This church, which was completed in 1589, is best known for three paintings by Caravaggio ❸

PIAZZA NAVONA
CORSIA AGONALE
VIA DEL SALVATORE
CORSO DEL RINASCIMENTO
VIA DEGLI STADERARI
VIA DEI SEDIARI

Palazzo Madama,
the seat of the Italian Senate, was originally built for the Medici family in the 16th century, on the site of one of their banks.

Sant'Ivo alla Sapienza
This tiny domed church is one of Borromini's most original creations. He worked on it between 1642 and 1650 ❷

★ Piazza Navona
The piazza is lined with palaces and pavement cafés, and punctuated by flamboyant Baroque fountains ❶

Largo di Torre Argentina

Piazza Navona ❶

Map 2 F3. 🚌 40, 46, 62, 64, 81, 87, 116, 492, 628.

ROME'S MOST BEAUTIFUL Baroque piazza follows the shape of a 1st-century AD stadium built by Domitian, which was used for athletic contests *(agones)*, chariot races and other sports. Traces of the stadium are still visible below the church of Sant'Agnese in Agone, which is dedicated to a virgin martyred on the site for refusing to marry a pagan.

The piazza began to take on its present appearance in the 17th century, when Pope Innocent X, whose family palazzo was on the piazza, commissioned a new church, palace and fountain. The fountain, the Fontana dei Quattro Fiumi, is Bernini's most magnificent, with statues of the four great rivers of the world at that time (the Nile, the Plate, the Ganges and the Danube) sitting on rocks below an obelisk. Bernini also designed the muscle-bound Moor in the Fontana del Moro, though the present statue is a copy. Until the 19th century, the piazza was flooded in August by stopping the fountain outlets. The rich would splash around in carriages, while street urchins paddled. Even today the piazza remains the social centre of the city.

Symbolic figure of the River Nile on Bernini's Fontana dei Quattro Fiumi

Sant'Ivo alla Sapienza ❷

Corso del Rinascimento 40. **Map** 2 F4.
📞 06 686 49 87. 🚌 40, 46, 64, 70, 81, 87, 116, 186, 492, 628. ⏰ 10am–4:30pm Mon–Sat (to 1pm Sat), 9am–noon some Sun. ● Jul–Aug. ♿

H IDDEN IN the courtyard of Palazzo della Sapienza, seat of the old University of Rome, Sant'Ivo's spiral belfry is nevertheless a distinctive landmark on Rome's skyline. Built by Borromini in 1642–60, the church is astonishingly complex, an ingenious combination of concave and convex surfaces. The work spanned the reigns of three popes, and incorporated in the design are their emblems: Urban VIII's bee, Innocent X's dove and olive branch and the star and hills of Alexander VII.

San Luigi dei Francesi ❸

Via Santa Giovanna d'Arco.
Map 2 F3 & 12 D2. 📞 06 688 27 1. 🚌 70, 81, 87, 116, 186, 492, 628. ⏰ 8:30am–12:30pm, 3:30–7pm daily. ● Thu pm. 🚫

T HE FRENCH NATIONAL church in Rome, San Luigi is a 16th-century building, best known for three magnificent canvases by Caravaggio in the Cerasi chapel. Painted between 1597 and 1602, these were Caravaggio's first significant religious works: *The Calling of St Matthew, Martyrdom of St Matthew* and *St Matthew and the Angel*. The first version of this last was initially rejected because it depicted the saint as an old man with dirty feet.

Detail from Caravaggio's *The Calling of St Matthew* (1597–1602) in San Luigi dei Francesi

Side relief of the Ludovisi Throne, on display in the Palazzo Altemps

Palazzo Altemps ❹

Via di Sant'Apollinare 46. **Map** 2 F3.
📞 06 39 96 77 00. 🚌 70, 81, 87, 115, 280, 628. ⏰ 9am–7:45pm Tue–Sun. 🎧 📷 📱 ♿

A N EXTRAORDINARY collection of Classical sculpture is housed in this branch of the Museo Nazionale Romano *(see p402)*. Restored as a museum during the 1990s, the palazzo was originally built for Girolamo Riario, nephew of Pope Sixtus IV in 1480. In the popular uprising that followed the pope's death in 1484, the building was sacked and Girolamo fled the city. In 1568 Cardinal Marco Sittico Altemps bought the palazzo, it was renovated in the 1570s by Martino Longhi the Elder, who added the obelisk-crowned belvedere and marble unicorn.

The Altemps family were avid collectors; the courtyard and its staircase are lined with ancient sculptures, which complement the Ludovisi sculptures. One of the highlights is the marble statue *Galata's Suicide*, a copy of the bronze original, in the Salone del Camino. Also on the first floor is the Greek, 5th-century BC Ludovisi Throne, a carved relief shows Aphrodite.

Galata's Suicide in the Palazzo Altemps

Santa Maria della Pace ❺

Vicolo del Arco della Pace 5.
Map 2 E3. 📞 06 686 11 56. 🚌 46, 62, 64, 70, 81, 87, 116, 492, 628. ⏰ 10am–12:45pm Tue–Fri. ♿

N AMED BY POPE Sixtus IV to celebrate the peace he hoped to bring to Italy, this church dates from the 1480s and contains a beautiful fresco by Raphael. Bramante's refined cloister was added in 1504, while the façade was designed in 1656 by Pietro da Cortona.

Chiesa Nuova ❻

Piazza della Chiesa Nuova. **Map** 2 E4.
📞 06 687 52 89. 🚌 46, 64.
⏰ 8am–noon, 4:30–7pm daily. ♿

S AN FILIPPO NERI commissioned this church in 1575 to replace the dilapidated one his Order had been given by Pope Gregory XIII. Neri required his followers to humble themselves, and set aristocratic young men to work as labourers on the church. Against his wishes, the nave, apse and dome were richly frescoed after his death by Pietro da Cortona. There are three paintings by Rubens around the altar. The first versions were rejected, so Rubens repainted them on slate, placing the originals above his mother's tomb.

Palazzo della Cancelleria ❼

Piazza della Cancelleria. **Map** 2 E4.
📞 06 69 89 34 91. 🚌 46, 62, 64, 70, 81, 87, 116, 492. ⏰ by appt only.

A SUPREME EXAMPLE of the confident delicacy of early Renaissance architecture, this palazzo was begun in 1485, and was allegedly financed by the gambling proceeds of Raffaele Riario, a nephew of Pope Sixtus I. In 1478 Riario was involved in the Pazzi conspiracy against the Medici, and when Giovanni de' Medici became Pope Leo XIII in 1513, he took belated revenge, seizing the Riario palace and turning it into the papal chancellery.

Tiber Island, with Ponte Cestio, built in 46 BC, linking it to Trastevere

Campo de' Fiori ❽

Map 2 F4. 🚌 116 & routes to Corso Vittorio Emanuele II.

CAMPO DE' FIORI (field of flowers), was one of the liveliest and roughest areas of medieval and Renaissance Rome. Cardinals and nobles mingled with fishmongers and foreigners in the piazza's market; Caravaggio killed his opponent after losing a game of tennis on the square; and the goldsmith Cellini murdered a business rival nearby. Today, the area continues to be a hub of secular activity. The colourful market, trattorias and down-to-earth bars retain the original animated atmosphere.

In the Renaissance the piazza was surrounded by inns, many of which were owned by the 15th-century courtesan Vannozza Catanei, mistress of Pope Alexander VI.

The square was also a place of execution. The statue in its centre is the philosopher Giordano Bruno, burned at the stake for heresy on this spot in 1600 for suggesting the earth moved around the sun.

Palazzo Farnese ❾

Piazza Farnese. Map 2 E5. 🚌 23, 116, 280 & routes to Corso Vittorio Emanuele II. ⬤ to the public.

ORIGINALLY CONSTRUCTED for Cardinal Alessandro Farnese, who became Pope Paul III in 1534, this palazzo was started by Antonio da Sangallo the Younger, and continued after his death by Michelangelo, who created the cornice on the façade and the courtyard's third storey.

The palace, now the French Embassy, is closed to the public, but when the chandeliers are lit at night you may be able to glimpse the ceiling of the Galleria, an illusionistic masterpiece (1597–1603) by Annibale Carracci based on Ovid's *Metamorphoses*.

Palazzo Spada ❿

Piazza Capo di Ferro 13. Map 2 F5. 📞 06 686 11 58. 🚌 23, 116, 280 & routes to Largo di Torre Argentina. ⬤ 9am–7pm Tue–Sun. ⬤ 1 Jan, 1 May, 25 Dec. ♿ 🚫 🔲 ♿ 🅆 www.galleriaborghese.it

A STUCCO extravaganza studded with reliefs of illustrious Romans, this palazzo was built in 1550, but bought in 1637 by Cardinal Bernardino Spada. A keen patron of the arts, he commissioned Borromini to create an illusionistic tunnel that appears four times longer than it is. The cardinal's art collection, in the Galleria Spada, includes works by Guercino, Dürer and Artemisia Gentileschi.

Ghetto and Tiber Island ⓫

Map 3 A5 & 6 D1. 🚌 23, 63, 280, 780 and routes to Largo di Torre Argentina.

THE FIRST JEWS came to Rome as traders in the 2nd century BC and were greatly appreciated for their financial and medical skills during the Roman Empire. Persecution began in the 16th century, when Pope Paul IV forced all of the Jews to live within a walled enclosure, an area later to form the hub of the present-day Ghetto.

Today Via del Portico d'Ottavia, the district's main street, leads to Rome's central synagogue, passing restaurants and shops selling Roman Jewish food. Ponte Fabricio links the Ghetto with Tiber Island, a centre of healing since 293 BC when a Temple to Aesculapius was founded. The island is now home to a hospital.

Fruit stalls at Campo de' Fiori's lively morning market

Street-by-Street: Around the Pantheon

THE MAZE OF NARROW STREETS around the Pantheon is a mixture of lively restaurants and cafés, and some of Rome's finest sights. This is also the city's financial and political district, home to Parliament, government offices and the stock exchange. The Pantheon itself, with its awe-inspiring domed interior, has long been a symbol of the city.

Sant'Ignazio di Loyola
This church has a superb illusionistic ceiling painted by Andrea Pozzo in 1685 ⓱

The Temple of Hadrian now forms the façade of the Stock Exchange.

★ **Palazzo Doria Pamphilj**
Among the masterpieces in the art gallery of this vast family palazzo is this Salomé by Titian painted in 1516 ⓮

Piazza della Minerva centres on Bernini's outlandish sculpture of an elephant supporting an Egyptian obelisk.

PIAZZA DI SANT'IGNAZIO

VIA DI SANT'IGNAZIO

VIA DEL SEMINARIO

PIAZZA DEL COLLEGIO ROMANO

VIA DELLA GATTA

PIAZZA DELLA ROTONDA

VIA DEL PIÈ DI MARMO

PIAZZA DELLA MINERVA

VIA DEL GESÙ

VIA DEL PLEBISCITO

Santa Maria sopra Minerva
This is one of Rome's few Gothic churches, with works by Michelangelo, Bernini and Filippino Lippi ⓯

★ **Pantheon**
The Pantheon, a temple to "all the gods", is Rome's best-preserved ancient building. It was built in the 1st century AD, probably to a design by Emperor Hadrian ⓰

KEY

– – – Suggested route

LOCATOR MAP
See Rome Street Finder map 3

Via della Gatta is overlooked by this marble statue of a cat *(gatta)* that gives the narrow street its name.

The Pie' di Marmo, an ancient marble foot, is probably part of a giant statue from the temple to the Egyptian goddess Isis.

Palazzo Altieri incorporates the hovel of an old woman who refused to allow her house to be demolished when this palace was built in the 17th century.

Gesù
Built in the late 16th century, this Jesuit church served as a model for the Order's churches throughout the world **⑬**

STAR SIGHTS

★ **Pantheon**

★ **Palazzo Doria Pamphilj**

0 metres 75
0 yards 75

Area Sacra di Largo Argentina ⑫

Largo di Torre Argentina. **Map** 2 F5.
🚌 40, 46, 62, 64, 70, 81, 87, 186, 492. 🅿 with permit only (see p614).

T HE REMAINS of four temples were discovered in the 1920s at the centre of Largo Argentina, now a busy bus terminus and traffic junction. They date from the era of the Republic, and are among the oldest found in Rome. For the purpose of identification, they are known as A, B, C and D. The oldest (temple C) dates from the early 3rd century BC. It was placed on a high platform preceded by an altar and is typical of Italic temple plans as opposed to the Greek model. Temple A is from the 3rd century BC, but in medieval times the small church of San Nicola di Cesarini was built over its podium and the remains of its two apses are still visible. The column stumps to the north belonged to a great portico, known as the Hecatostylum (portico of 100 columns). In Imperial times two marble latrines were built here – the remains of one are visible behind temple A. Behind temples B and C, near Via di Torre Argentina, are the remains of a great platform of tufa blocks. These have been identified as part of the Curia of Pompey, a rectangular building where the Senate met, and where Julius Caesar was assassinated by Brutus, Cassius and their followers on 15 March 44 BC.

Area Sacra, with the ruins of circular temple B

Baroque *Triumph of Faith over Idolatry* by Pierre Legros, Gesù

Gesù ⑬

Piazza del Gesù. **Map** 3 A4.
📞 06 69 70 01. 🚌 H, 46, 62, 64, 70, 81, 87, 186, 492, 628 & other routes. 🅿 6am–12:30pm, 4–7:15pm daily.

B UILT BETWEEN 1568 and 1584, the Gesù was Rome's first Jesuit church. The Jesuit order was founded in Rome in 1537 by a Basque soldier, Ignatius Loyola, who became a Christian after he was wounded in battle. The order was austere, intellectual and heavily engaged in missionary activity and religious wars.

The much-imitated design of the Gesù typifies Counter-Reformation architecture, with a large nave with side pulpits for preaching to crowds, and a main altar as the centrepiece for the mass. The illusionistic decoration on the nave ceiling and dome was added by Il Baciccia in the 17th century.

The nave depicts the *Triumph of the Name of Jesus* and its message is clear: faithful, Catholic worshippers will be joyfully uplifted to heaven while Protestants and heretics are flung into the fires of hell. The message is reiterated in the Cappella di Sant'Ignazio, a rich display of lapis lazuli, serpentine, silver and gold. The Baroque marble by Legros, *Triumph of Faith over Idolatry*, shows a female "Religion" trampling on the head of the serpent Idolatry, while in Théudon's *Barbarians Adoring the Faith*, an angel aims a kick towards a decrepit old barbarian couple entangled with a snake.

Palazzo Doria Pamphilj

Piazza del Collegio Romano 2. **Map** 3 A3. 06 679 73 23. 64, 81, 85, 117, 119, 492. 10am–5pm Fri–Wed. 1 Jan, Easter, 1 May, 15 Aug, 25 Dec. by appt for private apartments.

PALAZZO DORIA PAMPHILJ is a vast edifice whose oldest parts date from 1435. When the Pamphilj family took over in 1647 they built a new wing, a splendid chapel and a theatre.

The family art collection has over 400 paintings dating from the 15th–18th centuries, including a portrait of Pope Innocent X by Velázquez and works by Titian, Guercino, Caravaggio and Claude Lorrain. The opulent rooms of the private apartments retain many of their original furnishings, including Brussels and Gobelins tapestries, Murano chandeliers and a gilded crib.

Velázquez's *Pope Innocent X* (1650)

Santa Maria sopra Minerva

Piazza della Minerva 42. **Map** 3 A4. 06 679 39 26. 116 & many other routes. 7am–7pm daily.

ONE OF ROME'S rare Gothic buildings, this church was built in the 13th century over what were thought to be the ruins of a Temple of Minerva. It was a stronghold of the Dominicans, who produced some of the Church's most infamous inquisitors, and who tried the scientist Galileo in the adjoining monastery.

Inside, the church has a superb collection of art and sculpture, ranging from 13th-century Cosmatesque tombs to

Interior of the Pantheon, burial place for Italian monarchs

a bust by Bernini. Highlights include Antoniazzo Romano's *Annunciation* featuring Cardinal Juan de Torquemada, uncle of the vicious Spanish Inquisitor, and the Carafa Chapel whose frescoes by Filippino Lippi have recently been restored.

In the Aldobrandini Chapel are the tombs of the 16th-century Medici popes, Leo X and his cousin Clement VII, and near the steps of the choir is a stocky *Risen Christ*, begun by Michelangelo.

The church also contains the tombs of many famous Italians, such as St Catherine of Siena who died in 1380 and Fra Angelico, the Dominican friar and painter, who died in 1455. Outside, Bernini's spectacular sculpture of an elephant holds an obelisk on its back.

Simple vaulted nave of Santa Maria sopra Minerva

Pantheon

Piazza della Rotonda. **Map** 3 A4. 06 68 30 02 30. 116 & many routes. 8:30am–7:30pm daily (9am–6pm Sun). 1 Jan, 1 May, 25 Dec.

THE PANTHEON, the Roman "temple of all the gods", is the most extraordinary and best preserved ancient building in Rome. The first temple on the site was a conventional rectangular affair erected by Agrippa between 27 and 25 BC; the present structure was built and possibly designed by Emperor Hadrian in AD 118.

The temple is fronted by a massive pedimented portico screening what appears to be a cylinder fused to a shallow dome. Only from the inside can the true scale and beauty of this building be appreciated: a vast hemispherical dome equal in radius to the height of the cylinder giving perfectly harmonious proportions to the building. A circular opening, the *oculus*, lets in the only light.

In the 7th century Christians claimed to be plagued by demons as they passed by, and permission was given to make the Pantheon a church. Today it is lined with tombs, ranging from a restrained monument to Raphael to huge marble and porphyry sarcophagi holding the bodies of Italian monarchs.

Sant'Ignazio di Loyola ⓱

Piazza di Sant'Ignazio. **Map** 3 A4.
🕻 06 679 44 06. 🚌 117, 119, 492.
🕐 7:30am–12:30pm, 3–7:30pm
daily. ✝

Tʜɪs ᴄʜᴜʀᴄʜ was built by Pope Gregory XV in 1626 in honour of St Ignatius of Loyola, founder of the Society of Jesus (Jesuits) and the man who most embodied the zeal of the Counter-Reformation.

Together with the Gesù (see p393), Sant'Ignazio forms the nucleus of the Jesuit area of Rome. It is one of the most extravagant Baroque churches and its vast interior is plated with precious stones, marble, stucco and gilt, creating a thrilling sense of theatre. The church has a Latin-cross plan, with an apse and many side chapels. A cupola was planned but never built, as the nuns from a nearby convent objected that it would obscure the view from their roof garden. Instead the space was filled by a perspective painting of a dome on a flat disc.

Even more striking is the illusionistic ceiling created by the Jesuit artist Andrea Pozzo in 1685, a propagandist extravaganza extolling the success of Jesuit missionaries throughout the world. Above four women, representing Asia, Europe, America and Africa, lithe angels and beautiful youths are sucked into a heaven of fluffy clouds.

Detail from the AD 180 Column of Marcus Aurelius, Piazza Colonna

Piazza Colonna ⓲

Map 3 A3. 🚌 95, 116, 492.

Hᴏᴍᴇ ᴛᴏ Palazzo Chigi, official residence of the prime minister, Piazza Colonna is dominated by and named after the majestic Column of Marcus Aurelius. This was erected after the death of Marcus Aurelius in AD 180 to commemorate his victories over the barbarian tribes of the Danube. It is clearly an imitation of Trajan's Column (see p378) with scenes from the emperor's wars spiralling in reliefs up the column. The 80-year lapse between the two works produced a great artistic change: the wars of Marcus Aurelius are rendered with simplified pictures in stronger relief, sacrificing Classical proportions for the sake of clarity and immediacy.

Piazza di Montecitorio ⓳

Map 3 A3. **Palazzo di Montecitorio**
🕻 06 676 01. 🚌 116. 🕐 10am–6pm 1st Sun of month.

Tʜᴇ ᴏʙᴇʟɪsᴋ in the centre of Piazza Montecitorio formed the spine of a giant sundial brought back from Egypt by Augustus. It vanished in the 9th century, and was rediscovered under medieval houses during the reign of Julius II (1503–13).

The piazza is dominated by the rugged façade of Palazzo di Montecitorio, designed by Bernini and completed in 1697, after his death, by Carlo Fontana. It has been the seat of Italy's Chamber of Deputies since the late 19th century.

La Maddalena's stuccoed façade

La Maddalena ⓴

Piazza della Maddalena. **Map** 3 A3.
🕻 06 679 77 96. 🚌 116 & many other routes. 🕐 8am–noon, 5–7:30pm daily.

Sɪᴛᴜᴀᴛᴇᴅ ɪɴ a small piazza near the Pantheon, the Maddalena's Rococo façade, built in 1735, epitomizes the love of light and movement of the late Baroque. The façade has been restored, despite the protests of Neo-Classicists who dismissed its painted stucco as icing sugar.

The diminutive dimensions of the church did not deter 17th- and 18th-century decorators from filling the interior with paintings and ornaments from the floor to the top of the elegant cupola.

Baroque illusionistic ceiling by Andrea Pozzo in Sant'Ignazio di Loyola

NORTHEAST ROME

Lion fountain in Piazza del Popolo

THIS AREA stretches from the exclusive shopping streets around Piazza di Spagna to the Esquiline Hill, once bourgeois, but now a poor, often seedy area full of early Christian churches. The Piazza di Spagna and Piazza del Popolo district grew up in the 16th century, when the increase in the influx of pilgrims was such that a road was built to channel them as quickly as possible to the Vatican. About the same time, the Quirinal Hill became the site of a papal palace. When Rome became capital of Italy in 1870, Via Veneto became a lavish residential area, and the Esquiline was covered with apartments for the new civil servants.

SIGHTS AT A GLANCE

Churches
Sant'Andrea al Quirinale ❼
San Carlo alle Quattro Fontane ❽
Santa Maria della Concezione ❿
Santa Maria Maggiore ⓯
Santa Maria del Popolo ❸
Santa Maria della Vittoria ⓫
San Pietro in Vincoli ⓮
Santa Prassede ⓭

Museums and Galleries
Museo Nazionale Romano ⓬
Palazzo Barberini ❾

Ancient Sites and Buildings
Ara Pacis ❹
Mausoleum of Augustus ❺

Historic Buildings
Villa Medici ❷

Piazzas and Fountains
Piazza di Spagna and the Spanish Steps ❶
Trevi Fountain ❻

GETTING THERE
Metro stations Repubblica, Barberini and Spagna (line A) cover the area between Termini and Piazza del Popolo. Bus 16 runs from Termini to Santa Maria Maggiore and down Via Merulana.

KEY

Street-by-Street: Piazza di Spagna pp398–9

FS Railway station

M Metro station

P Parking

i Tourist information

--- City walls

0 metres 250

0 yards 250

◁ The Spanish Steps with their spring display of azaleas

Street-by-Street: Piazza di Spagna

T̲HE NETWORK OF NARROW STREETS around Piazza di
Spagna forms one of the most exclusive areas in
Rome, drawing droves of tourists and Romans to the
elegant shops around Via Condotti. The square and its
nearby coffee houses have long attracted those who
want to see and be seen. In the 18th century the area
was full of hotels for frivolous aristocrats doing the
Grand Tour, as well as artists, writers and composers,
who took the city's history and culture more seriously.

Caffè Greco is an 18th-century
café once frequented by writers
and musicians such as Keats,
Goethe, Byron, Liszt and Wagner.

Trinità dei Monti is a
16th-century church at
the top of the Spanish
Steps. There are fine
views of Rome from
the stairway.

**Babington's Tea
Rooms**, founded
by two English
spinsters in
1896, still
serves
English
teas.

Spagna

**★ Piazza di
Spagna and the
Spanish Steps**
*These have been at the
heart of tourist Rome
since the 18th century* ❶

**The Keats-Shelley
Memorial House**,
where the poet Keats
died in 1821, is now a
museum honouring
English Romantic poets.

**The Colonna dell'
Immacolata**, erected
in 1857, commemorates
Pope Pius IX's doctrine
of the Immaculate
Conception.

**The Collegio
di Propaganda
Fide**, built for
the Jesuits in
1662, has a
superb façade
designed
by Francesco
Borromini.

KEY

− − − Suggested route

0 metres   75

0 yards   75

LOCATOR MAP
See Rome Street Finder map 3

Sant'Andrea delle Fratte
contains two angels by
Bernini (1669) made for
Ponte Sant'Angelo, which Pope
Clement X thought
too lovely to expose
to the weather.

The Fontana della Barcaccia at the
foot of the Spanish Steps

Piazza di Spagna and the Spanish Steps ❶

Map 3 A2. 🚌 *116, 117.* Ⓜ *Spagna.*

SHAPED LIKE a crooked bow
tie, and surrounded by
muted, shuttered façades,
Piazza di Spagna is crowded
all day and (in summer) most
of the night. The most famous
square in Rome, it takes its
name from the Palazzo di
Spagna, built in the 17th
century to house the Spanish
Embassy to the Holy See.

The piazza has long been
the haunt of foreign visitors
and expatriates. In the 18th
and 19th centuries the square
stood at the heart of the city's
main hotel district. Some of
the travellers came in search
of knowledge and inspiration,
although most were more
interested in collecting statues
to adorn their family homes.

When the Victorian novelist
Charles Dickens visited, he
reported that the Spanish

Steps were crowded with
models dressed as Madonnas,
saints and emperors, hoping
to attract the attention of
foreign artists.

The steps were built in the
1720s to link the square with
the French church of Trinità
dei Monti above. The French
wanted to place a statue of
Louis XIV at the top, but the
pope objected, and it was not
until the 1720s that the Italian
architect Francesco de Sanctis
produced the voluptuous
Rococo design which satisfied
both camps. The Fontana
Barcaccia, sunk into the
paving at the foot of the steps
due to low water pressure,
was designed by Bernini's
less famous father, Pietro.

Villa Medici ❷

Accademia di Francia a Roma,
Viale Trinità dei Monti 1.
Map 3 B1. ☎ *06 679 83 81.*
🚌 *117.* Ⓜ *Spagna.* 🎟 📷 *only.*

SUPERBLY POSITIONED on the
Pincio Hill, this 16th-
century villa has retained the
name that it assumed when
Cardinal Ferdinando de'
Medici bought it in 1576. It
is now home to the French
Academy, which was founded
in 1666 to give artists the
chance to study in Rome.
From 1803 musicians were
also allowed to study here:
both Berlioz and Debussy
were students.

The villa is only open for
exhibitions, but the formal
gardens, with a gorgeously
frescoed pavilion, and copies
of ancient statues, can be
visited in certain months.

19th-century engraving of the inner façade of the Villa Medici

STAR SIGHT

★ **Piazza di Spagna and
the Spanish Steps**

Pinturicchio's fresco of the *Delphic Sibyl* (1509) in Santa Maria del Popolo

Santa Maria del Popolo ❸

Piazza del Popolo 12. **Map** 2 F1.
📞 06 361 08 36. 🚌 95, 117, 119,
490, 495, 926. Ⓜ Flaminio.
🕐 7am–noon, 4–7pm Mon–Sat;
7:30am–1:30pm, 4:30–7:30pm Sun.

SANTA MARIA DEL POPOLO was one of the first Renaissance churches in Rome, commissioned by Pope Sixtus IV della Rovere in 1472. Lavish endowments by Sixtus's descendants and other powerful families have made it one of Rome's greatest artistic treasures.

Shortly after Sixtus died in 1484, Pinturicchio and his pupils frescoed two chapels (first and third right) for the della Rovere family. On the altar of the first chapel there is a lovely *Nativity* from 1490 that depicts a stable at the foot of a Classical column.

In 1503 Sixtus IV's nephew Giuliano became Pope Julius II and had Bramante build a new apse. Pinturicchio was called in again to paint its vaults with Sibyls and Apostles framed in an intricate tracery of freakish beasts.

In 1513 Raphael created the Chigi chapel (second left) for the wealthy banker Agostino Chigi. The design is an audacious Renaissance fusion of the sacred and profane; there are pyramid-like tombs and a ceiling mosaic of God holding the signs of the zodiac describing Chigi's horoscope. Raphael died before the chapel was finished and it was completed by Bernini who added the dynamic statues of Daniel and Habakkuk. In the Cerasi chapel, left of the altar, there are two realistic works painted by Caravaggio in 1601: the *Conversion of St Paul* and the *Crucifixion of St Peter*. The artist uses daringly exaggerated lighting effects and foreshortening techniques to intensify the dramatic effect.

Detail of the Ara Pacis frieze

Ara Pacis ❹

Via di Ripetta. **Map** 2 F2. 📞 06 68
80 68 48. 🚌 70, 81, 117, 119, 186,
628. ⬤ for restoration.

PAINSTAKINGLY reconstructed over many years from scattered fragments, the exquisitely carved Ara Pacis (Altar of Peace) celebrates the peace created throughout the Mediterranean by Emperor Augustus. Commissioned by the Senate in 13 BC and completed four years later, the altar stands in a square enclosure of Carrara marble, carved with realistic reliefs of such quality that experts think the craftsmen may have been Greek.

The reliefs on the north and south walls depict a procession that took place on 4 July, 13 BC, in which the members of the emperor's family can be identified, including Augustus's grandson, Lucius, who is the toddler clutching at the skirts of his mother, Antonia. The site is now housed in a building by architect Richard Meier.

Mausoleum of Augustus ❺

Piazza Augusto Imperatore. **Map**
2 F2. 📞 06 67 10 38 19. 🚌 81,
117, 492, 628, 926. ⬤ by appt only:
permit needed (see p614). 🔲 🔲

NOW JUST A WEEDY mound ringed with cypresses and strewn with litter, this was once the most prestigious burial place in Rome. Augustus had the mausoleum built in 28 BC, the year before he became sole ruler, as a tomb for himself and his descendants. The circular building was 87 m (270 ft) in diameter with two obelisks (now in Piazza del Quirinale and Piazza dell' Esquilino) at the entrance. Inside were four concentric passageways linked by corridors where urns holding the ashes of the Imperial family were placed, including those of Augustus who died in AD 14.

Trevi Fountain ❻

Piazza di Trevi. **Map** 3 B3. 🚌 116 &
many other routes.

NICOLA SALVI'S theatrical design for Rome's largest and most famous fountain was completed in 1762. The central figures are Neptune, flanked by two Tritons, one trying to

Rome's largest and most famous fountain, the Trevi

master an unruly sea-horse, the other leading a quieter beast, symbolizing the two contrasting moods of the sea.

The site originally marked the terminal of the Aqua Virgo aqueduct, built by Augustus' right-hand man and son-in-law, Agrippa, in 19 BC to channel water to Rome's new bath complexes. One of the reliefs on the first storey shows a young girl, Trivia, after whom the fountain may have been named. She is said to have first shown the spring, 22 km (14 miles) from the city, to thirsty Roman soldiers.

The dome of San Carlo alle Quattro Fontane, by Borromini

Interior, Sant'Andrea al Quirinale

Sant'Andrea al Quirinale ❼

Via del Quirinale 29. **Map** 3 C3.
📞 06 48 90 31 87. 🚌 116, 117.
🕐 8am–noon, 4–6pm Wed–Mon.
🔴 Aug pm. 🚫

Sant'Andrea was designed for the Jesuits by Bernini and executed by his assistants between 1658 and 1670. The site was wide but shallow, so Bernini took the radical step of pointing the long axis of his oval plan towards the sides, and leading the eye round to the altar by means of a strong horizontal cornice. At the altar he combined sculpture and painting to create a theatrical crucifixion of Sant'Andrea (St Andrew); the diagonally crucified saint on the altarpiece looks up at a stucco effigy of himself ascending to the lantern, where the Holy Spirit and cherubs await him in heaven.

San Carlo alle Quattro Fontane ❽

Via del Quirinale 23. **Map** 3 C3.
📞 06 488 32 61. 🚌 116 & routes to Piazza Barberini. Ⓜ Barberini.
🕐 10am–1pm, 3–6pm Mon–Sat; 10am–1pm Sun.

In 1638, Borromini was commissioned by the Trinitarians to design a church and convent on a tiny cramped site at the Quattro Fontane crossroads. The church, so small that it is said it would fit inside one of the piers of St Peter's, is designed with bold, fluid curves on both the façade and interior to give light and life to the diminutive building. The dome, with its concealed windows, illusionistic coffering and tiny lantern designed to make it look higher than it really is, is a cunning feature.

Palazzo Barberini ❾

Via delle Quattro Fontane 13. **Map** 3 C2. 📞 06 328 10. 🚌 52, 53, 61, 62, 63, 80, 95, 116, 175, 492, 590. Ⓜ Barberini. 🕐 8:30am–7:30pm Tue–Sun. 🔴 public hols. 🚫 💳 ♿ (lift). 🌐 www.galleriaborghese.it

When Maffei Barberini became Pope Urban VIII in 1623, he decided to build a grand family palazzo. Designed by Carlo Maderno as a typical country villa on the fringes of the city, it now overlooks Piazza Barberini, where traffic hurtles around Bernini's Triton fountain. Maderno died shortly after the foundations had been laid, and Bernini and Borromini took over.

The most dazzling room is the Gran Salone, with an illusionistic ceiling frescoed by Pietro da Cortona in 1633–9. The palazzo also houses part of the Galleria Nazionale d'Arte Antica with works by Titian, Filippo Lippi, Caravaggio and Artemisia Genti-leschi. The most famous is a portrait of a courtesan, reputedly Raphael's lover, *La Fornarina*, said to be a baker's daughter, although not painted by the artist himself.

Ceiling fresco detail in Palazzo Barberini (1633)

Santa Maria della Concezione ❿

Via Veneto 27. **Map** 3 C2. 📞 06 487 11 85. 🚌 52, 53, 61, 62, 63, 80, 95, 116, 175. Ⓜ Barberini. **Crypt** 🕐 9am–noon, 3–6pm Fri–Wed. 🎦

Below this unassuming church on Via Veneto is a crypt decked with the dismembered skeletons of 4,000 Capuchin monks. They form a macabre reminder of the transience of life, with vertebrae wired together to make sacred hearts and crowns of thorns, and, in one chapel, the poignant skeleton of a tiny Barberini princess.

Santa Maria della Vittoria ⓫

Via XX Settembre 17. **Map** 4 D2. 📞
06 482 61 90. 🚌 *61, 62, 84, 175,
910.* Ⓜ *Repubblica.* 🕐 *8:30–11am
(to 10am Sun), 3:30–6pm daily.*

SANTA MARIA DELLA VITTORIA is
an intimate Baroque church
with a lavish, candlelit interior.
Inside the Cornaro chapel is
one of Bernini's most ambitious sculptures, the *Ecstasy of
St Teresa* (1646). The physical
nature of St Teresa's ecstasy is
apparent as she appears collapsed on a cloud with her
mouth half open and eyes
closed, struck by the arrow of
a smiling angel. Ecclesiastical
members, past and present,
of the Venetian Cornaro family,
who commissioned the chapel,
sit in boxes as if watching and
discussing the scene being
played out in front of them.

**Bernini's *Ecstasy of St Teresa* in
Santa Maria della Vittoria**

Museo Nazionale Romano ⓬

Palazzo Massimo, Largo di Villa Peretti
1 (1 of 5 sites). **Map** 4 E3. 📞 *06 481
55 76.* 🚌 *all routes to Termini.*
Ⓜ *Repubblica.* 🕐 *9am–7:45pm
Tue–Sun.* 🎟 *ticket valid for all sites.*
🔲 ♿ 📷 ✍

FOUNDED IN 1899, the Museo
Nazionale Romano –
one of the world's leading
museums of Classical art –
houses most of the antiquities
found in Rome since 1870,
as well as important older

collections.
During the
1990s it
underwent
a major
reorganization
and now has
five branches:
the Palazzo
Altemps *(see
p390)*; the
Baths of
Diocletian;
the Aula
Ottagona,
the Crypta;
Balbi, and
the Palazzo
Massimo.
In the latter,
exhibits dating
from the 2nd
century BC to
the late 4th century AD are
displayed in a series of rooms
over three floors. Highlights
include the *Quattro Aurighe*
mosaics from a villa in northern Rome, the breathtaking
series of frescoes from Livia's
summer villa, and the famous
statue of her husband, the
Emperor Augustus.

Santa Prassede ⓭

Via Santa Prassede 9a. **Map** 4 D5.
📞 *06 488 24 56.* 🚌 *16, 70, 71,
75, 714.* Ⓜ *Vittorio Emanuele.*
🕐 *7:30am–noon, 4–6:30pm daily.* ♿

THE CHURCH was founded by
Pope Paschal II in the 9th
century and decorated by
Byzantium artists with the most
important, glittering mosaics in
Rome. In the apse Christ stands
between Santa Prassede and
her sister, dressed as Byzantine
empresses, among white-robed
elders, lambs, feather-mop
palms and bright red poppies.
The Cappella di San Zeno is
even lovelier, a jewel-box of

9th-century mosaic, Santa Prassede

**One of the finely detailed Quattro Aurighe mosaics
on display at the Museo Nazionale Romano**

a mausoleum, built by Pope
Paschal II for his mother,
Theodora. Her square halo
shows that she was still alive
when the mosaic was created.

San Pietro in Vincoli ⓮

Piazza di San Pietro in Vincoli.
Map 4 D5. 📞 *06 488 28 65.*
🚌 *75, 84, 117.* Ⓜ *Colosseo.*
🕐 *7am–12:30pm, 3:30–7pm daily
(Oct–Mar: to 6pm).* ♿

THE CHURCH'S NAME means
St Peter in Chains, so called
because it houses what are said
to be the chains with which
St Peter was shackled in the
Mamertine Prison *(see p379).*
According to tradition, one set
of chains was sent to Constantinople by Empress Eudoxia;
when it was returned to Rome
some years later it miraculously fused with its partner.
    San Pietro is now best known
for the Tomb of Julius II, commissioned from Michelangelo
by the pope in 1505. Much to
the artist's chagrin, Julius soon
became more interested in the
building of a new St Peter's and
the tomb project was laid to
one side. After the pope died
in 1513, Michelangelo resumed
work on the tomb, but had
only completed the statues of
the *Dying Slaves* (now in found
in Paris and Florence) and
Moses when he was called
away to paint the *Last Judgment* in the Sistine Chapel.

Santa Maria Maggiore ⑮

A CONFIDENT BLEND of architectural styles, ranging from Early Christian to late Baroque, Santa Maria is also famous for its superb mosaics. Founded in about AD 420, it retains the original colonnaded triple nave, lined with panels of rare 5th-century mosaics. The Cosmatesque marble floor and bell tower are medieval, as are the spectacular mosaics on the triumphal arch and in the loggia. The lavish coffered ceiling is Renaissance; the façades, domes and chapels Baroque.

VISITORS' CHECKLIST

Piazza di Santa Maria Maggiore.
Map 4 E4. **(** 06 48 31 95.
🚌 16, 70, 71, 714. 🚋 14.
M Cavour. ⬭ 7am–7pm daily.
✝

Coronation of the Virgin
This is one of the wonderful 13th-century mosaics in the apse by Jacopo Torriti.

Bell tower

Tomb of Cardinal Rodriguez
This Gothic tomb, which dates from 1299, contains magnificent marblework by the Cosmati.

5th-century mosaics

18th-century façade by Ferdinando Fuga

13th-century mosaics

Cappella Paolina
Flaminio Ponzio, architect of the Villa Borghese, designed this sumptuous chapel in 1611 for Pope Paul V who is buried here.

Column in Piazza Santa Maria Maggiore
In 1611 a bronze of the Virgin and Child was added to this ancient marble column which came from the Basilica of Constantine.

Cappella Sistina
This chapel was built for Pope Sixtus V (1584–7) by Domenico Fontana and was opulently covered with ancient marble. It houses the pope's tomb.

THE VATICAN AND TRASTEVERE

VATICAN CITY, the world capital of Catholicism, is the world's smallest state. It occupies 43 ha (106 acres) within high walls watched over by the Vatican guard. It was the site where St Peter was martyred (c.AD 64) and buried, and it became the residence of the popes who succeeded him. The papal palaces, next to the great basilica of St Peter's, are home to the Sistine Chapel

Pope Urban VIII's coat of arms in St Peter's

and the eclectic collections of the Vatican Museums, as well as being the residence of the pope. Neighbouring Trastevere is quite different, a picturesque old quarter, whose inhabitants consider themselves to be the only true Romans. Sadly, the proletarian identity of the place is in danger of being destroyed by the proliferation of trendy restaurants, clubs and shops.

SIGHTS AT A GLANCE

GETTING THERE

The quickest way to the Vatican is by Metro Line A to Ottaviano San Pietro, just north of Piazza San Pietro. The 40 and 64 buses link it with Termini. Trastevere is a short walk from Campo de' Fiori across Ponte Sisto.

Churches
San Francesco a Ripa ❾
San Pietro in Montorio and the Tempietto ❿
Santa Cecilia in Trastevere ❽
Santa Maria in Trastevere ❼
St Peter's pp408–9 ❷

Museums and Galleries
Palazzo Corsini and Galleria Nazionale d'Arte Antica ❺
Vatican Museums pp410–17 ❸

Historic Buildings
Castel Sant'Angelo ❶
Villa Farnesina ❹

Parks and Gardens
Botanical Gardens ❻

KEY

A Tour of the Vatican *pp406–7*

P Parking

ℹ Tourist information

— City walls

0 metres 250
0 yards 250

◁ **View of St Peter's with the Ponte Sant'Angelo in the foreground**

A Tour of the Vatican

Crucifix in
the Vatican

THE VATICAN, a sovereign state since February 1929, is ruled by the pope, Europe's only absolute monarch. About 500 people live here and, as well as accommodation for staff and ecclesiasts, the city has its own post office, banks, currency, judicial system, radio station, shops and a daily newspaper, *l'Osservatore Romano*.

★ St Peter's
Most of the great architects of the Renaissance and Baroque had a hand in the design of the Basilica of St Peter's, the most famous church in Christendom (see pp408–9).

Vatican Radio broadcasts in 20 languages throughout the world from this tower, part of the 9th-century Leonine Wall.

★ Sistine Chapel
Michelangelo frescoed the ceiling with scenes from Genesis (1508–12), and the altar wall with the Last Judgment (1534–41). The chapel is used by cardinals when electing a new pope (see p414).

The Papal Audience Chamber

Information office

PIAZZA DEL SANT'UFFIZIO

PIAZZA
PIO XI

★ Raphael Rooms
Raphael frescoed this suite in the early 16th century. Works like The School of Athens *established his reputation, to equal that of his contemporary Michelangelo (see p417).*

Piazza San Pietro was laid out by Bernini between 1656 and 1667.

To Via della Conciliazione

This staircase leading down from the museums, designed in 1932 by Giuseppe Momo, is in the form of a double helix, consisting of two spirals: one to walk up and one to walk down.

LOCATOR MAP
See Rome Street Finder map 1

Entrance to Vatican Museums

★ **Vatican Museums**
This marble group of the Laocoön (AD 1) is one of many prestigious works of art in the Vatican (see p410).

The Cortile della Pigna is named after a bronze pine cone from an ancient fountain.

VIA DI PORTA ANGELICA

The Vatican Gardens, open for guided tours, make up a third of the Vatican's territory.

0 metres   75
0 yards   75

Castel Sant'Angelo ❶

Lungotevere Castello. **Map** 2 D3.
📞 06 39 96 76 00. 🚌 23, 34, 280.
🕐 9am–8pm Tue–Sun (last entry 7pm). ● 1 Jan, 25 Dec. 🎫 🔲 📷
🔲 ♿

T**HE MASSIVE FORTRESS** of Castel Sant'Angelo takes its name from the vision of the Archangel Michael by Pope Gregory the Great in the 6th century as he led a procession across the bridge, praying for the end of the plague.

The castle began life in AD 139 as the Emperor Hadrian's mausoleum. Since then it has been a bridgehead in the Emperor Aurelian's city wall, a medieval citadel and prison, and a place of safety for popes during times of political unrest. A corridor links it with the Vatican Palace, providing an escape route for the pope. From dank cells to fine apartments of Renaissance popes, the museums cover all aspects of the castle's history, including the Sala Paolina, with illusionistic frescoes (1546–8) by Pellegrino Tibaldi and Perin del Vaga and the Courtyard of Honour.

St Peter's ❷

See pp408–9.

Vatican Museums ❸

See pp410–17.

View of Castel Sant'Angelo from the Ponte Sant'Angelo

St Peter's ❷

Catholicism's most sacred shrine, the sumptuous, marble-caked basilica of St Peter's draws pilgrims and tourists from all over the world. It holds hundreds of precious works of art, some salvaged from the original 4th-century basilica built by Constantine, others commissioned from Renaissance and Baroque artists. The dominant tone is set by Bernini, who created the baldacchino twisting up below Michelangelo's huge dome. He also created the Cathedra in the apse, with four saints supporting a throne that contains fragments once thought to be relics of the chair from which St Peter delivered his first sermon.

Dome of St Peter's
The 136.5 m (448 ft) high dome, designed by Michelangelo, was not completed in his lifetime.

Baldacchino
Commissioned by Pope Urban VIII in 1624, Bernini's extravagant Baroque canopy stands above St Peter's tomb.

A staircase of 537 steps leads to the summit of the dome.

The church is 186 m (615 ft) long.

Entrance to Historical Artistic Museum and Sacristy

The Papal Altar stands over the crypt where St Peter is reputedly buried.

HISTORICAL PLAN OF THE BASILICA OF ST PETER'S

St Peter was buried in AD 64 in a necropolis near the site of his crucifixion in the Circus of Nero. In AD 324 Constantine constructed a basilica over the tomb. The old church was rebuilt in the 15th century, and throughout the 16th and 17th centuries various architects developed the existing structure. The new church was inaugurated in 1626.

KEY

▢	Circus of Nero
▢	Constantinian
▢	Renaissance
▢	Baroque

Monument to Pope Alexander VII
Bernini's last work in St Peter's was finished in 1678 and shows the Chigi pope among the allegorical figures of Truth, Justice, Charity and Prudence.

The Grottoes
A fragment of this 13th-century mosaic by Giotto, salvaged from the old basilica, is now in the Grottoes, where many popes are buried.

Two minor cupolas by Vignola (1507–73)

The foot of St Peter by Arnolfo di Cambio, 13th century, has worn thin from the touch of pilgrims over the centuries.

Michelangelo's Pietà
Protected by glass since an attack in 1972, the Pietà was created in 1499 when Michelangelo was only 25.

VISITORS' CHECKLIST

Piazza San Pietro. **Map** 1 B3. **[**
06 69 88 37 12 *(sacristy)*; 06 69
88 16 62 *(tourist info)*. ⊟ 23, 40,
49, 64, 81, 492. **M** *Ottaviano
San Pietro*. **Basilica** ◻ *Apr–Sep:
7am–7pm daily (mid-Oct–Mar:
to 6pm)*. ✝ ♿ ◲ **Treasury**
◻ *Apr–Sep: 9am–6:15pm daily
(Oct–Mar: to 5:15pm)*. ◲
Grottoes ◻ *Apr–Sep:
7am–6pm daily (Oct–Mar: 5pm)*. ◲
Dome ◻ *8am–5pm daily.* ◲
Papal audiences: *Usually Wed
at 10am in Piazza San Pietro or
in the Papal Audience Chamber.
Tickets (free) from Prefecture of
the Pontifical Household.* **FAX** *06
69 88 58 63.* ◻ *9am–1pm
Mon–Sat; or write to: Prefettura
della Casa Pontificia, 00120 Città
del Vaticano. The pope appears at
noon Sun to bless the crowd
in Piazza San Pietro.*

From this Library window, the pope blesses the faithful gathered in the piazza below.

Façade by Carlo Maderno (1614)

The Holy Door is used only in Holy Years.

Filarete Doors
These bronze doors from the old basilica were decorated with biblical reliefs by Filarete between 1439 and 1445.

Markings on the floor of the nave show how other churches compare in length.

Entrance

Atrium by Carlo Maderno

Piazza San Pietro
On Sundays, religious festivals and special occasions such as canonizations, the pope blesses the crowds from a balcony.

Vatican Museums ❸

Home to the Sistine Chapel and Raphael Rooms as well as to one of the world's most important art collections, the Vatican Museums are housed in palaces originally built for Renaissance popes such as Julius II, Innocent VIII and Sixtus IV. Most of the later additions were made in the 18th century, when priceless works of art accumulated by earlier popes were first put on show.

Etruscan Museum
The Etruscan collection includes a woman's gold clasp (fibula) from the 7th-century BC Regolini-Galassi tomb at Cerveteri, north of Rome.

Gallery of Maps
The Siege of Malta is one of 40 maps of the Church's territories, frescoed by the 16th-century cartographer Ignazio Danti on the gallery's walls.

Gallery of the Candelabra

Raphael Rooms
This is a detail of the Expulsion of Heliodorus from the Temple, one of many frescoes painted by Raphael and his pupils for Julius II's private apartments (see p417).

Gallery of Tapestries

Stairs down

Upper floor

Sistine Chapel *(see p414)*

Sala dei Chiaroscuri

Raphael Loggia

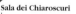

Borgia Apartment
Pinturicchio and his assistants frescoed these rooms for Alexander VI in 1492–95.

GALLERY GUIDE
The museum complex is vast: the Sistine Chapel is 20–30 minutes' walk from the entrance, so allow plenty of time. There is a strict one-way system, and it is best to be selective or choose one of four colour-coded itineraries, which vary from 90 minutes to a five-hour marathon.

Modern religious art on view here was sent to the popes by artists worldwide, such as Bacon, Ernst and Carrà.

Gregorian Profane Museum

Pio-Clementine Museum
The finest of the Vatican's Classical statues are on display here, like the Apollo Belvedere, *a Roman copy in marble of a 4th-century BC Greek bronze.*

Stairs up to Etruscan Museum

Entrance

VISITORS' CHECKLIST

Città del Vaticano (entrance in Viale Vaticano). **Map** 1 B2.
📞 06 69 88 38 60. 🚌 49 to entrance, 23, 81, 492, 990.
Ⓜ *Ottaviano San Pietro, Cipro Musei Vaticani.* 🕐 8:45am–4:45pm Mon–Fri (Nov–Feb: to 1:45pm); 8:45am–1:45pm Sat, last Sun of month. Last entry: 90 mins before closing. ⬤ religious and public hols. Special permit required for Raphael Loggia, Vatican Library, Lapidary Gallery & Vatican Archives. 🎟 free last Sun of month. ♿ special routes.
🔲 🍴 📷 Ⓦ www.vatican.va

Cortile Ottagonale

Lower floor

Braccio Nuovo

Chiaramonti Museum

The Lapidary Gallery
contains inscriptions from pagan and Christian catacombs, but is closed to the public.

Egyptian Museum
The collection of Egyptian artifacts includes this painted bas-relief from a 2400 BC tomb. The museum was organized by Father Ungarelli, a 19th-century Egyptologist.

Pio-Christian Museum
Early Christianity adopted Classical images so that its doctrines could be more easily understood. This 4th-century statue of Christ as the Good Shepherd derives from the pastoral figure of the shepherd.

Pinacoteca
The Vatican's art gallery has 15th- to 19th-century works, and is particularly strong on the Renaissance. This unfinished painting of St Jerome *by Leonardo da Vinci reveals his mastery of anatomy.*

KEY TO FLOORPLAN

■	Egyptian and Assyrian art
☐	Greek and Roman art
☐	Etruscan art
☐	Early Christian and medieval art
☐	15th- to 19th-century art
☐	Modern religious art
☐	Lapidary Gallery
☐	Non-exhibition space

Exploring the Vatican's Collections

THE VATICAN'S GREATEST TREASURES are its superlative Greek and Roman antiquities, together with the magnificent artifacts excavated from Egyptian and Etruscan tombs during the 19th century. Some of Italy's greatest artists, such as Raphael, Michelangelo and Leonardo da Vinci, are represented in the Pinacoteca (art gallery) and parts of the former palaces, where they were employed by popes to decorate sumptuous apartments and galleries.

Head of an athlete in mosaic from the Baths of Caracalla, AD 217

EGYPTIAN AND ASSYRIAN ART

THE EGYPTIAN COLLECTION contains finds from 19th- and 20th-century excavations in Egypt, as well as statues that were brought to Rome in Imperial times. There are also Roman imitations of Egyptian art from Hadrian's Villa (see p452) and from temples in Rome devoted to Egyptian gods and goddesses, such as Isis and Serapis.

The genuine Egyptian works, displayed on the lower floor next to the Pio-Clementine Museum, include statues, mummies, mummy cases and a Book of the Dead. One of the main treasures is a colossal granite 13th-century statue of Queen Mutuy, the mother of Rameses II, which was found on the site of the Horti Sallustiani gardens near Via Veneto. Also noteworthy are the head of a statue of Montuhotep IV (20th century BC), the beautiful mummy case of Queen Hetepheres, and the tomb of Iri, who was the guardian of the Pyramid of Cheops. This dates back to the 22nd century BC.

Roman copy of the Greek *Doryphoros*

GREEK, ETRUSCAN AND ROMAN ART

THE GREATER PART of the Vatican Museums is dedicated to Greek and Roman art. However, the Etruscan Museum houses a superb collection of Etruscan (see p40) and pre-Roman artifacts from Etruria and the Greek colonies of southern Italy. Here, the most famous exhibits are the gold jewellery and bronze throne, bed and funeral cart, found in the 650 BC Regolini-Galassi tomb in Cerveteri (see p450).

Prize Greek and Roman pieces form the nucleus of the Pio-Clementine Museum. These include high-quality Roman copies of 4th-century BC Greek statues, such as the *Apoxyomenos* (an athlete wiping his body after a race) and the *Apollo del Belvedere*. The splendid *Laocoön* (1st century AD), originally from Rhodes, was found in 1506 in the ruins of Nero's Golden House. Works such as these inspired Michelangelo and other Renaissance artists. The much smaller Chiaramonti Museum is lined with ancient busts, and its extension, the Braccio Nuovo, has a 1st-century BC statue of Augustus from the villa of his wife Livia. It is based on the *Doryphoros* (spear-carrier) by the 5th-century BC Greek sculptor

Polyclitus. There is also a Roman copy of this on display opposite. The Gregorian Profane Museum, housed in a new wing, follows the evolution of Roman art from reliance on Greek models to a recognizably Roman style.

In this museum, original Greek works include large marble fragments from the Parthenon in Athens. Among the Roman pieces are two reliefs, the *Rilievi della Cancelleria*, commissioned by Domitian in AD 81 to glorify the military parades of his father, Emperor Vespasian. There are also fine Roman floor mosaics, two from the Baths of Caracalla (see p427), and one, in the Round Room, dated 3rd century AD, from the Baths of Otricoli in Umbria.

In the Vatican Library is the 1st-century AD *Aldobrandini Wedding*, a beautiful Roman fresco depicting a bride being prepared for her marriage.

Roman mosaic from the Baths of Otricoli, Umbria, in the Round Room

EARLY CHRISTIAN AND MEDIEVAL ART

THE MAIN COLLECTION of early Christian antiquities is in the Pio-Christian Museum, which contains inscriptions and sculpture from catacombs and early Christian basilicas. The sculpture consists chiefly of reliefs from sarcophagi, though the most striking work is a free-standing 4th-century statue of the *Good Shepherd*. The sculpture's chief interest lies in the way it blends Biblical episodes with pagan mythology. The idealized pastoral figure of the shepherd became Christ himself, while bearded philosophers turned into the Apostles.

The first two rooms of the Pinacoteca are dedicated to late medieval art, mostly wooden altarpieces painted in tempera. The outstanding work is Giotto's *Stefaneschi Triptych* of about 1300 which decorated the main altar of the old St Peter's.

The Vatican Library has a number of medieval treasures including reliquaries, textiles, enamels and icons.

Pietà (c.1471–4) by the Venetian artist Giovanni Bellini in the Pinacoteca

Detail of Giotto's *Stefaneschi Triptych* (1330) in the Pinacoteca

15TH- TO 19TH-CENTURY ART

MANY RENAISSANCE popes were connoisseurs of the arts who considered it their duty to sponsor the leading painters, sculptors and goldsmiths of the age. The galleries around the Cortile del Belvedere were decorated by great artists between the 16th and the 19th centuries.

The Gallery of Tapestries is hung with tapestries woven in Brussels to designs by students of Raphael. The Apartment of Pope Pius V has beautiful 15th-century Flemish tapestries, and the Gallery of Maps is frescoed with 16th-century maps of ancient and contemporary Italy.

Alongside the Raphael Rooms *(see p417)* are the Room of the Chiaroscuri and Pope Nicholas V's private chapel. This was frescoed between 1447 and 1451 by Fra Angelico. Also worth seeing is the Borgia Apartment, decorated in the 1490s by Pinturicchio and his pupils for the Borgia pope, Alexander VI. Another set of fascinating frescoes can

Pinturicchio's *Adoration of the Magi* (1490), Borgia Apartment

be found in the Loggia of Raphael, but a visit here requires special permission.

The Pinacoteca has many important Renaissance works. Highlights from the 15th century are a fine *Pietà* by Giovanni Bellini, part of his *Coronation of the Virgin* altarpiece in Pèsaro *(see p358)*; and Leonardo da Vinci's unfinished *St Jerome*, discovered, after being long lost, in two halves. One was being used as a coffer lid in an antique shop, the other as the seat of a stool in a shoemaker's. Exceptional pieces from the 16th century include eight tapestry cartoons, the *Transfiguration* and *Madonna of Foligno* by Raphael, in a room devoted to the artist; a *Deposition* by Caravaggio; an altarpiece by Titian; and *St Helen* by Veronese, which shows the saint as a gorgeously dressed aristocrat.

Sistine Chapel: The Ceiling

MICHELANGELO FRESCOED the ceiling for Pope Julius II between 1508 and 1512, working on specially designed scaffolding. The main panels, which chart the Creation of the World and Fall of Man, are surrounded by subjects from the Old and New Testaments – except for the Classical Sibyls who are said to have foreseen the birth of Christ. In the 1980s the ceiling was restored revealing colours of an unsuspected vibrancy.

Libyan Sibyl

The pagan prophetess reaches for the Book of Knowledge. Like most female figures Michelangelo painted, the beautiful Libyan Sibyl was probably modelled on a man.

Illusionistic architecture

Creation of the Sun and Moon

Michelangelo depicts God as a dynamic but terrifying figure commanding the sun to shed light on the earth.

KEY TO CEILING PANELS

GENESIS: 1 God Dividing Light from Darkness; 2 Creation of the Sun and Moon; 3 Separating Waters from Land; 4 Creation of Adam; 5 Creation of Eve; 6 Original Sin; 7 Sacrifice of Noah; 8 The Deluge; 9 Drunkenness of Noah.

ANCESTORS OF CHRIST: 10 Solomon with his Mother; 11 Parents of Jesse; 12 Rehoboam with Mother; 13 Asa with Parents; 14 Uzziah with Parents; 15 Hezekiah with Parents; 16 Zerubbabel with Parents; 17 Josiah with Parents.

PROPHETS: 18 Jonah; 19 Jeremiah; 20 Daniel; 21 Ezekiel; 22 Isaiah; 23 Joel; 24 Zechariah.

SIBYLS: 25 Libyan Sibyl; 26 Persian Sibyl; 27 Cumaean Sibyl; 28 Erythrean Sibyl; 29 Delphic Sibyl.

OLD TESTAMENT SCENES OF SALVATION: 30 Punishment of Haman; 31 Moses and the Brazen Serpent; 32 David and Goliath; 33 Judith and Holofernes.

Original Sin
This shows Adam and Eve tasting the forbidden fruit from the Tree of Knowledge, and their expulsion from Paradise. Michelangelo represents Satan as a snake with the body of a woman.

The Ignudi are athletic male nudes whose significance is uncertain.

The lunettes are devoted to frescoes of the ancestors of Christ, like Hezekiah.

RESTORATION OF THE SISTINE CEILING

The recent restorers of the Sistine Chapel used computers, photography and spectrum technology to analyse the fresco before cleaning began. They separated Michelangelo's work from that of later restorers and discovered that the restorers had attempted to clean the ceiling with materials ranging from bread to retsina wine. The new restoration revealed the familiarly dusky,

A restorer cleaning the Libyan Sibyl

eggshell-cracked figures to have creamy skins, lustrous hair and to be dressed in brightly-coloured, luscious robes: "a Benetton Michelangelo" mocked one critic, claiming that a layer of varnish which the artist had added to darken the colours had been removed. However, after examining the work, most experts agreed that the new colours probably matched those painted by Michelangelo.

Sistine Chapel: The Walls

THE MASSIVE WALLS of the Sistine Chapel, the main chapel in the Vatican Palace, were frescoed by some of the finest artists of the 15th and 16th centuries. The 12 paintings on the side walls, by artists including Perugino, Ghirlandaio, Botticelli and Signorelli, show parallel episodes from the life of Moses and of Christ. The decoration of the chapel walls was completed between 1534 and 1541 by Michelangelo, who added the great altar wall fresco, the *Last Judgment*.

KEY TO THE FRESCOES: ARTISTS AND SUBJECTS

The Last Judgment

☐ Perugino   ☐ Botticelli   ☐ Ghirlandaio

☐ Rosselli   ☐ Signorelli   ☐ Michelangelo

1 Baptism of Christ in the Jordan
2 Temptations of Christ
3 Calling of St Peter and St Andrew
4 Sermon on the Mount
5 Handing over the Keys to St Peter
6 Last Supper
7 Moses's Journey into Egypt
8 Moses Receiving the Call
9 Crossing of the Red Sea
10 Adoration of the Golden Calf
11 Punishment of the Rebels
12 Last Days of Moses

THE LAST JUDGMENT BY MICHELANGELO

REVEALED IN 1993 after a year's restoration, the *Last Judgment* is considered to be the masterpiece of Michelangelo's mature years. It was commissioned by Pope Paul III Farnese, and required the removal of some earlier frescoes and two windows over the altar. A new wall was erected which slanted inwards to stop dust settling on it. Michelangelo worked alone on the fresco for seven years, until its completion in 1541.

The painting depicts the souls of the dead rising up to face the wrath of God, a subject that is rarely used for an altar decoration. The pope chose it as a warning to Catholics to adhere to their faith in the turmoil of the Reformation. In fact the work conveys the artist's own tormented attitude to his faith. It offers neither the certainties of Christian orthodoxy, nor the ordered view of Classicism.

In a dynamic, emotional composition, the figures are caught in a vortex of motion. The dead are torn from their graves and hauled up to face Christ the Judge, whose athletic, muscular figure is the focus of all the painting's movement.

Christ shows little sympathy for the agitated saints around him, clutching the instruments of their martyrdom. Neither is any pity shown for the damned, hurled down to the demons in hell. Here Charon, pushing people off his boat into the depths of Hades, and the infernal judge Minos, are taken from Dante's *Inferno*. Minos has ass's ears, and is a portrait of courtier Biagio da Cesena, who had objected to the nude figures in the fresco. Michelangelo's self-portrait is on the skin held by the martyr St Bartholomew.

Souls meeting the wrath of Christ in Michelangelo's *Last Judgment*

Raphael Rooms

POPE JULIUS II'S PRIVATE APARTMENTS were built above those of his hated predecessor, Alexander VI, who died in 1503. Julius was impressed with Raphael's work and chose him to redecorate the four rooms *(stanze)*. Raphael and his pupils began in 1508, replacing works by better-known artists, including Raphael's teacher, Perugino. The new frescoes quickly established the young artist's reputation in Rome, but the project took 16 years to complete and he died before it was finished.

Detail from Raphael's *The Mass of Bolsena* (1512)

HALL OF CONSTANTINE

THE FRESCOES IN THIS room were started in 1517 and completed in 1525, five years after Raphael's death, and are largely the work of the artist's pupils. The theme of the decoration is the triumph of Christianity over paganism, and the four major frescoes show scenes from the life of Constantine, the first Christian emperor. These include the *Vision of the Cross* and the emperor's victory over his rival, Maxentius, at *The Battle of the Milvian Bridge*, for which Raphael had provided a preparatory sketch.

ROOM OF HELIODORUS

RAPHAEL DECORATED this private antechamber between 1512 and 1514. The main frescoes all contain thinly veiled references to the protective powers of the papacy. The room's name refers to the fresco on the right, *The Expulsion of Heliodorus from*

the Temple, showing Heliodorus felled by a horseman as he tries to rob the Temple in Jerusalem. It alludes to Pope Julius II's victory over foreign armies in Italy. *The Mass of Bolsena* on the left wall refers to a miracle that occurred in 1263, in which a priest who doubted the doctrine of the Holy Host was said to have seen blood issue from it at the moment of sacrifice.

ROOM OF THE SEGNATURA

COMPLETED BETWEEN 1508 and 1511, the frescoes here are the most harmonious in the series. The scheme followed by Raphael, dictated by Pope Julius II, reflected the Humanist belief that there could be perfect harmony between Classical culture and Christianity in the search for truth. The most famous work, *The School of Athens*, centres on the debate about truth between the Greek philosophers Plato and Aristotle. Raphael depicted some of his contemporaries as philosophers, including Leonardo da Vinci, Bramante and Michelangelo.

KEY TO FLOORPLAN

① Hall of Constantine

② Room of Heliodorus

③ Room of the Segnatura

④ Room of the Fire in the Borgo

ROOM OF THE FIRE IN THE BORGO

THIS WAS ORIGINALLY the dining room, but when the decoration was completed under Pope Leo X, it became a music room. All the frescoes exalt the reigning pope by depicting events in the lives of his 9th-century namesakes, Leo III and IV. The main frescoes were designed by Raphael, but finished by his assistants between 1514 and 1517. The most famous, *The Fire in the Borgo*, shows a miracle of 847, when Pope Leo IV put out a fire by making the sign of the cross. Raphael draws a parallel between this and the legendary flight of Aeneas from Troy, recounted by Virgil. Aeneas appears in the foreground, carrying his father Anchises on his back.

The School of Athens (1511) showing philosophers and scholars

Villa Farnesina ➍

Via della Lungara 230. **Map** 2 E5.
📞 06 68 02 72 68. 🚌 23, 280.
🕐 9am–1pm Mon–Sat. 📷 🚫

T HE FABULOUSLY WEALTHY
Sienese banker Agostino
Chigi commissioned this villa
in 1508 from his fellow
Sienese Baldassare Peruzzi.
Chigi's main home was across
the Tiber, and the villa was
designed purely for lavish
banquets. Artists, poets,
cardinals, princes and the
pope himself were entertained
here in magnificent style.
Chigi also used the villa for
sojourns with the courtesan
Imperia, who allegedly inspired one of the *Three Graces*
painted by Raphael in the
Loggia of Cupid and Psyche.
  The simple, harmonious
design of the Farnesina, with
a central block and projecting
wings, made it one of the first
true villas of the Renaissance.
Peruzzi decorated some of
the interiors himself, such as
the Sala della Prospettiva
upstairs, in which the illusionistic frescoes create the
impression of looking out
over 16th-century Rome
through a marble colonnade.
  Other frescoes, by Sebastiano
del Piombo and Raphael and
his pupils, illustrate Classical
myths, while the vault of the
main hall, the Sala di Galatea,
is adorned with astrological
scenes showing the position
of the stars at the time of
Chigi's birth. After his death
the business collapsed, and in
1577 the villa was sold off to
the Farnese family.

**Raphael's *Three Graces* in the
Villa Farnesina**

**Queen Christina of Sweden's
bedroom in the Palazzo Corsini**

Palazzo Corsini and Galleria Nazionale d'Arte Antica ➎

Via della Lungara 10. **Map** 2 D5.
📞 06 68 80 23 23. 🚌 23, 280.
🕐 8:30am–1:45pm Tue–Sat,
8:30am–7pm Sun (last adm: 30 mins
before closing). 🕐 1 Jan, 1 May, 15
Aug, 25 Dec. 📷 🚫 🔇 📷 🔒
W www.galleriaborghese.it

B UILT FOR Cardinal Domenico
Riario in 1510–12, the
Palazzo Corsini has numbered
Bramante, the young Michelangelo, Erasmus and the
mother of Napoleon among
its guests. Queen Christina of
Sweden died here in 1689.
The palazzo was rebuilt by
Ferdinando Fuga, who
planned the façade to be
viewed from an angle, as Via
della Lungara is too narrow
for a full frontal view.
  When the palazzo was
bought by the state in 1893,
the Corsini family donated
their collection of paintings,
which formed the core of the
national art collection, and
was soon augmented. The
collection is now split between
Palazzo Barberini and Palazzo
Corsini. Although the best
works are in the Barberini,
there are paintings by Van
Dyck, Rubens, Murillo, and,
notably, an androgynous
St John the Baptist (c.1604)
by Caravaggio and a *Salome*
(1638) by Reni. The strangest
work is a portrait of the rotund
Queen Christina as the goddess
Diana by J Van Egmont.

Botanical Gardens ➏

Largo Cristina di Svezia 24. **Map** 2 D5.
📞 06 49 91 71 06. 🚌 23, 280. 🕐
9:30am–6:30pm (Oct–Mar: 5:30pm)
Tue–Sat. ● public hols, Aug. 📷 🔒

S EQUOIAS, PALM TREES, orchids
and bromeliads are among
the 7,000 plants from all over
the world represented in the
Botanical Gardens (Orto
Botanico). Indigenous and
exotic species are grouped to
illustrate their botanical families and their adaptation to
different climates and eco-
systems. There are also some
curious plants like the ginkgo
that have survived almost
unchanged from earlier eras.

**Palm trees in the Botanical
Gardens, Trastevere**

Santa Maria in Trastevere ➐

Piazza Santa Maria in Trastevere.
Map 5 C1. 📞 06 581 48 02.
🚌 H, 23, 280. 🕐 7am–9pm daily.
🔒 🔒

S ANTA MARIA IN TRASTEVERE
was probably the first
Christian place of worship in
Rome, founded by Pope
Callixtus I in the 3rd century,
when emperors were still
pagan and Christianity a
minority cult. According to
legend, it was built on the
site where a fountain of oil
had miraculously sprung up
on the day that Christ was
born. The basilica became
the focus of devotion to the
Madonna, and although
today's church, and its
remarkable mosaics, date
largely from the 12th and
13th centuries, images of the

Apse mosaic of the *Coronation of the Virgin*, Santa Maria in Trastevere

Virgin continue to dominate. The façade mosaics probably date from the 12th century, and show Mary, Christ and ten lamp-bearing women. Inside in the apse is a stylized 12th-century *Coronation of the Virgin*, and below, a series of realistic scenes from the life of the Virgin by the 13th-century artist Pietro Cavallini. The oldest image of the Virgin is a 7th-century icon, the *Madonna di Clemenza*, which depicts her as a Byzantine empress flanked by a guard of angels. It sits above the altar in the Cappella Altemps.

Santa Cecilia in Trastevere ❽

Piazza di Santa Cecilia. **Map** 6 D2.
📞 06 589 92 89. 🚌 H, 23, 44, 280. ⏰ 9:30am–12:30pm, 4–6:30pm daily.
Cavallini fresco ⏰ 10:15am–12:15pm daily.

ST CECILIA, aristocrat and patron saint of music, was martyred here in AD 230. After an unsuccessful attempt to suffocate her by locking her in the hot steam bath of her house for three days, she was beheaded. A church was built, possibly in the 4th century, on the site of her house (still to be seen beneath the church, along with the remains of a tannery). Her body was lost, but it turned up again in the Catacombs of San Callisto *(see p432)*. In the 9th century it was reburied here by Pope Paschal I, who rebuilt the church.

A fine apse mosaic survives from this period. The altar canopy by Arnolfo di Cambio and the fresco of *The Last Judgment* by Pietro Cavallini can be reached through the adjoining convent; they date from the 13th century, one of the few periods when Rome had a distinctive artistic style.

In front of the altar is a delicate statue of St Cecilia by Stefano Maderno, which is based on sketches made of her perfectly preserved relics when they were briefly disinterred in 1599.

San Francesco a Ripa ❾

Piazza San Francesco d'Assisi 88. **Map** 6 D2. 📞 06 581 90 20. 🚌 H, 23, 44, 75, 280. ⏰ 7am–noon, 4–7pm Mon–Sat; 7am–1pm, 4–7:30pm Sun. ♿

ST FRANCIS OF ASSISI lived here in a hospice when he visited Rome in 1219 and his stone pillow and crucifix are preserved in his cell. The church was built by a follower, a local nobleman called Rodolfo Anguillara, who is

Bernini's *Ecstasy of Beata Ludovica Albertoni*, San Francesco a Ripa

portrayed on his tombstone wearing the Franciscan habit.

Entirely rebuilt in the 1680s by Cardinal Pallavicini, the church is rich in 17th- and 18th-century sculptures. Not to be missed in the Altieri chapel (fourth left, along the nave) is Bernini's exquisite late work, the *Ecstasy of Beata Ludovica Albertoni* (1674).

San Pietro in Montorio and the Tempietto ❿

Piazza San Pietro in Montorio 2. **Map** 5 B1. 📞 06 581 39 40. 🚌 44, 75, 100. ⏰ 8:30am–noon, 4–6pm daily. **Tempietto** ⏰ 9:30am–12:30pm, 2–4pm (4–6pm in summer) Tue–Sun.

Bramante's circular Tempietto at San Pietro in Montorio

THE TEMPIETTO, a diminutive masterpiece of Renaissance architecture completed by Bramante in 1502, stands in the courtyard of San Pietro in Montorio. The name means "little temple" and its circular shape echoes early Christian *martyria*, chapels built on the site of a saint's martyrdom. This was erroneously thought to be the spot in Nero's Circus where St Peter was crucified. Bramante ringed the chapel with Doric columns, a Classical frieze and fine balustrade.

AVENTINE AND LATERAN

THIS IS ONE of the greenest parts of the city, taking in the Celian and Aventine Hills, as well as the very congested area around San Giovanni in Laterano. The Celian, now scattered with churches, was a fashionable place to live in Imperial Rome. Some of the era's splendour is still apparent in the ruins of the Baths of Caracalla.

Mosaic fragment, Baths of Caracalla

Behind the Baths rises the Aventine Hill, a peaceful, leafy area, with the superb basilica of Santa Sabina, and lovely views across the river to Trastevere and St Peter's. In the valley below, cars and Vespas skim around the Circus Maximus, following the ancient charioteering track, while to the south lies Testaccio, a lively working-class district.

SIGHTS AT A GLANCE

Churches
San Clemente **6**
San Giovanni in Laterano **7**
Santa Maria in Cosmedin **2**
Santa Maria in Domnica **3**
Santi Quattro Coronati **5**
Santa Sabina **11**
Santo Stefano Rotondo **4**

Ancient Sites and Buildings
Baths of Caracalla **8**
Temples of the Forum Boarium **1**

Monuments and Tombs
Protestant Cemetery **10**
Pyramid of Caius Cestius **9**

KEY

Street by Street: Piazza della Bocca della Verità *pp422–3*

FS Railway station

M Metro station

P Parking

— Tourist information

GETTING THERE
Bus 95 runs from Piramide to Piazza della Bocca della Verità. The Celian is near Metro Colosseo and Circo Massimo; tram 3 and buses 81, 160 and 715 are all good routes to the Aventine area.

0 metres   250
0 yards   250

◁ **Pines and orange trees in the Aventine's Parco Savelli, with the dome of St Peter's in the distance**

Street-by-Street: Piazza della Bocca della Verità

THE SITE OF ROME'S FIRST PORT and its busy cattle market, this is an odd little corner of the city, stretching from the heavily trafficked road running along the Tiber to the southern spur of the Capitoline Hill, a place of execution from ancient times until the Middle Ages. Although best known for the Bocca della Verità (Mouth of Truth) in Santa Maria in Cosmedin, which is supposed to snap shut on the hands of liars, there are many other sites in the area, notably two temples from the Republican era. In the 6th century

The Casa dei Crescenzi, studded with ancient fragments, incorporates the ruins of a 10th-century tower built by the powerful Crescenzi family to guard the river Tiber.

the area became home to a Greek community who founded the churches of San Giorgio in Velabro and Santa Maria in Cosmedin.

Sant'Omobono stands on an archaeological site where finds date back to the 6th century.

★ **Temples of the Forum Boarium**
These two buildings are the best preserved of Rome's Republican temples ❶

Ponte Rotto, as this forlorn ruined arch in the Tiber is called, simply means "broken bridge". Built in the 2nd century BC, its original name was the Pons Aemilius.

The Fontana dei Tritoni, built by Carlo Bizzaccheri in 1715, shows the strong influence of Bernini.

★ **Santa Maria in Cosmedin**
The Bocca della Verità, *a medieval drain cover, is set into the portico* ❷

KEY

– – – Suggested route

0 metres   75
0 yards   75

San Giovanni Decollato belonged to a confraternity that encouraged condemned prisoners to repent.

(map labels) VIA DI SAN GIOVANNI DECOLLATO · LUNGOTEVERE DEI PIERLEONI · TEVERE · PONTE PALATINO · PIAZZA DELLA BOCCA DELLA VERITÀ · VIA DELLA GREC

Santa Maria della Consolazione was named after an image of the Virgin placed here in 1385 to give consolation to the condemned.

THE ANCIENT CENTRE

NORTHEAST ROME

AVENTINE AND LATERAN

San Teodoro is a circular church on the edge of the Palatine with exceptional 6th-century apse mosaics.

San Giorgio in Velabro, a 7th-century basilica, was damaged in an explosion in 1994, and has now been restored.

Arco degli Argentari

VIA DEI FIENILI

VIA DI SAN TEODORO

The 4th-century Arch of Janus, a four-faced marble-plated arch at the edge of the Forum Boarium market, was an ideal place for merchants and customers to do business in the shade.

VIA DEI CERCHI

STAR SIGHTS

★ Santa Maria in Cosmedin

★ Temples of the Forum Boarium

Temples of the Forum Boarium ❶

Piazza della Bocca della Verità.
Map 6 E1. 🚌 23, 44, 81, 95, 160, 170, 280, 628, 715, 716.

THESE WONDERFULLY well-preserved Republican temples are at their best in moonlight, standing in their grassy enclave beside the Tiber sheltered by umbrella pines. During the day, they look less romantic, stranded in a sea of traffic. They date from the 2nd century BC, and were saved from ruin by being consecrated as Christian churches in the Middle Ages by the Greek community then living in the area. The rectangular temple, formerly known as the Temple of Fortuna Virilis, was probably dedicated to Portunus, the god of rivers and ports. Set on a podium it has four Ionic travertine columns fluted at the front and 12 half-columns embedded in the tufa wall of the *cella* – the room that housed the image of the god. In the 9th century the Temple was converted into the church of Santa Maria Egiziaca, after a 5th-century prostitute who re-formed and became a hermit.
  The smaller circular Temple, which is made of solid marble and surrounded by 20 fluted columns, was dedicated to Hercules, though it was long believed to be a Temple of Vesta because of its similarity to the one in the Forum.

The Ionic façade of the Republican era Temple of Portunus

Apse mosaic from the 9th century of the Virgin and Child in Santa Maria in Domnica

Santa Maria in Cosmedin ❷

Piazza della Bocca della Verità. **Map 6 E1.** 📞 *06 678 14 19.* 🚌 *23, 44, 81, 95, 160, 170, 280, 628, 715, 716.* ⏰ *9am–6pm daily (10am–noon, 3–5pm winter).* 🕆 ♿ 🖵

THIS BEAUTIFUL church was built in the 6th century on the site of the ancient city's food market. The Romanesque bell tower and portico were added during the 12th century. In the 19th century a Baroque façade was removed and the church restored to its original simplicity. It contains many fine examples of Cosmati work, in particular the mosaic pavement, the raised choir, the bishop's throne, and the canopy over the main altar.

Set into the wall of the portico is the Bocca della Verità (Mouth of Truth), a grotesque marble face, thought to have

The nave of Santa Maria in Cosmedin with its Cosmati floor

been an ancient drain cover. Medieval tradition had it that the jaws would snap shut on liars – a useful way of testing the faithfulness of spouses.

Santa Maria in Domnica ❸

Piazza della Navicella 12. **Map 7 B2.** 📞 *06 700 15 19.* 🚌 *81, 117, 673.* Ⓜ *Colosseo.* ⏰ *winter: 9am–noon, 3:30–6pm daily; summer: 4–7pm daily.* ♿

SANTA MARIA IN DOMNICA was probably founded in the 7th century, and renovated in the 9th century. By this time the Romans had lost the art of making mosaics, so Pope Paschal I imported mosaicists from Byzantium. They created an exquisite apse mosaic showing the Virgin, Child and angels in a delicate garden of paradise. Paschal I is kneeling at the Virgin's feet wearing a square halo, indicating that he was alive when it was made.

In 1513 Andrea Sansovino added a portico decorated with lions' heads, a punning homage to Pope Leo X.

Santo Stefano Rotondo ❹

Via di Santo Stefano Rotondo 7. **Map 9 B2.** 📞 *06 42 11 99.* 🚌 *81, 117, 673.* ● *for restoration (call for details).* 🚫

SANTO STEFANO ROTONDO was built between 468 and 483 on a circular plan with four chapels in a

cruciform shape. Its circular inner area is enclosed by two concentric corridors. A third, outer corridor was demolished on the orders of Leon Battista Alberti in 1453. In the 1500s Niccolò Pomarancio, Antonio Tempesta and others covered the walls with 34 frescoes detailing the martyrdoms of saints.

Cloister of Santi Quattro Coronati

Santi Quattro Coronati ❺

Via dei Santi Quattro Coronati 20. **Map 7 C1.** 📞 *06 70 47 54 27.* 🚌 *85, 117, 850.* 🚋 *3.* ⏰ *6:30am–12:30pm, 3:30–7:45pm daily.* **Cloister & Chapel of St Sylvester** *pm only.* ♿

THIS FORTIFIED convent was built in the 4th century to house the relics of four Persian stonemasons, martyred after they refused to make a statue honouring the pagan god Aesculapius. It was rebuilt after invading Normans set fire to it in 1084.

Highlights are a delightful garden cloister and the Chapel of St Sylvester, where 12th-century frescoes recount the legend of Constantine's conversion to Christianity.

San Clemente ⊙

In 1857 FATHER MULLOOLY, the Irish Dominican prior of San Clemente, began excavations beneath the existing 12th-century basilica. Directly underneath he and his successors discovered a 4th-century church, and below that a number of ancient Roman buildings. Both basilicas are dedicated to St Clement, the fourth pope. On the lowest level is a temple devoted to the cult of Mithras, a mystical all-male religion imported from Persia which rivalled Christianity for popularity.

VISITORS' CHECKLIST

Via di San Giovanni in Laterano.
Map 7 B1. 📞 06 774 00 21.
🚌 85, 87, 117, 186, 810, 850.
Ⓜ Colosseo. 🚋 3. 🕐 9am–12:30pm, 3–6pm daily (from 10am Sun). 💶 to excavations.
🚻 ⏸ 🔲

Cappella di Santa Caterina
Recently restored frescoes by the 15th-century artist Masolino da Panicale show scenes from the life of St Catherine of Alexandria.

Entrance

Apse Mosaic
The 12th-century Triumph of the Cross *includes finely detailed animals and acanthus leaves.*

12th-century basilica

Paschal Candlestick
This splendid 12th-century spiralling candlestick, striped with glittering multi-coloured mosaic, is the work of the Cosmati.

18th-century façade

Piscina

Schola Cantorum

4th-century basilica

Temple of Mithras

Life of San Clemente
Faded frescoed episodes from the life of the fourth pope decorate the lower church. This one tells the story of a boy found alive in his tomb under the sea.

Triclinium
An altar to the god Mithras, showing him slaying a bull, stands in the dank triclinium, a room used for ritual banquets by cult members.

San Giovanni in Laterano ❼

S AN GIOVANNI, the cathedral of Rome, was founded by
Emperor Constantine in the early 4th century. It has
been rebuilt several times, notably in 1646 when
Borromini restyled the interior, but retains its original
basilica form. Before the papacy
moved to Avignon in 1309, the
adjoining Lateran Palace was
the official papal residence.
The present structure dates
from 1589, but older parts
survive, like the Scala Santa
(Holy Staircase) which Christ is
said to have climbed at his trial.

VISITORS' CHECKLIST

Piazza di San Giovanni in
Laterano. **Map** 8 D2. 06 69
88 64 52 (church); 06 69 88 64
33. 16, 81, 85, 87, 650.
3. San Giovanni. **Cathedral
& Cloisters** 7am–6:45pm daily
(Oct–Mar: to 6pm). **Museum**
9am–1pm Mon–Sat.
Baptistry 7:30am–
12:30pm, 4–7:30pm daily.

Baptistry
*Though much restored,
the octagonal baptistry
contains some beautiful
5th-century mosaics.*

North façade

East Façade
*The main entrance, on
the east façade (1735), is
adorned with statues of
Christ and the Apostles.*

Apse

**Museum
entrance**

**Lateran
Palace**

Papal Altar
*The Gothic baldacchino,
which rises over the papal
altar, is decorated with
14th-century frescoes.*

**On Maundy
Thursday** the
pope, as Bishop of
Rome, gives a blessing
from the loggia of the
city's main cathedral.

The Corsini Chapel
was built in the 1730s
for Pope Clement XII
Corsini, who lies
buried in a porphyry
tomb from the
Pantheon.

**Main
entrance**

Cloisters
*Built by the Vassalletto family in about 1220,
the cloisters are remarkable for their twisted
columns and inlaid marble mosaics.*

Boniface VIII Fresco
*Possibly by Giotto, this
fragment shows the pope
announcing the Holy Year
of 1300, which attracted
around two million pilgrims.*

Part of one of the gymnasia in the Baths of Caracalla

Baths of Caracalla ❽

Viale delle Terme di Caracalla 52.
Map 7 A3. 📞 06 39 96 77 00. 🚌
160, 628. 🚋 3. 🕐 9am–1 hr before
sunset Tue–Sun, 9am–2pm Mon.
🌙 1 Jan, 25 Dec. 🚫 🔲 🔲

R EARING UP at the foot of the
Aventine Hill are the
monolithic red-brick ruins of
the Baths of Caracalla. Begun
by Emperor Septimius Severus
in AD 206, and completed by
his son Caracalla in AD 217,
they remained in use until the
6th century, when the Goths
sabotaged the city's aqueducts.

Going for a bath was one of
the social events of the day in
ancient Rome. Large com-
plexes such as Caracalla, with
a capacity for 1,600 bathers,
were not simply places to have
a natter and get washed, but
also areas which offered an
impressive array of facilities:
art galleries, gymnasia,
gardens, libraries, conference
rooms, lecture rooms and
shops selling food and drink.

A Roman bath was a long
and complicated business,
beginning with a form of
Turkish bath, followed by a
spell in the *caldarium*, a large
hot room with pools of water
to moisten the atmosphere.
Then came the lukewarm
tepidarium, followed by a
visit to the large central
meeting place known as the
frigidarium, and finally a
plunge into the *natatio*, an
open-air swimming pool. For
the rich, this was followed by
a rub-down with scented
woollen cloth.

Most of the rich marble
decorations of the baths were
scavenged by the Farnese

family in the 16th century to
adorn the rooms of Palazzo
Farnese *(see p391)*. There are,
however, statues and mosaics
from the Baths in the Museo
Nazionale Archeologico in
Naples *(see pp474–5)* and in
the Vatican's Gregorian
Profane Museum *(see p412)*.

So dramatic is the setting
that until recently it was the
regular venue for the open-air
opera season in August.

Pyramid of Caius Cestius ❾

Piazzale Ostiense. **Map** 6 E4.
🚌 23, 95, 280. 🚋 3. Ⓜ *Piramide*.

C AIUS CESTIUS was a wealthy
but unimportant 1st-
century BC *praetor*, or senior
magistrate. At the time,
inspired by the Cleopatra
scandals, there was a craze
for all things Egyptian, and
Caius decided to commission
himself a pyramid as a tomb.
Set into the Aurelian Wall
near Porta San Paolo, it is
built of brick and faced with
white marble; according to an
inscription, it took just 330
days to build in 12 BC.

**The Pyramid of Caius Cestius on
Piazzale Ostiense**

Protestant Cemetery ❿

Cimitero Acattolico, Via di Caio
Cestio. **Map** 6 E4. 📞 06 574 19 00.
🚌 23, 280. 🚋 3. 🕐 9am–4:30pm
(Oct–Mar: to 3:30pm) Tue–Sat,
9am–2pm Sun. Last adm: 30 mins
before closing. **Donation**.

N ON-CATHOLICS have been
buried in this cemetery
behind the Aurelian Wall since
1738. In the oldest part (on the
left as you enter) is the grave
of the poet John Keats, who
died in 1821 in a house on
Piazza di Spagna *(see p398)*.
He wrote his own epitaph:
"Here lies one whose name
was writ in water". Close by
rest the ashes of Percy Bysshe
Shelley, who drowned in 1822.

The interior of Santa Sabina

Santa Sabina ⓫

Piazza Pietro d'Illiria 1. **Map** 6 E4.
📞 06 57 94 06 00. 🚌 23, 44, 95,
170, 781. 🕐 6:30am–12:45pm,
3:30–7pm daily. ♿

H IGH ON THE AVENTINE stands
an early Christian basilica,
founded by Peter of Illyria in
AD 425 and later given to the
Dominican order. It was restored to its original simplicity in
the early 20th century. Light fil-
ters through 9th-century windows on to a nave framed by
pale Corinthian columns.
Above the main door is a blue
and gold 5th-century mosaic
inscription to Peter. In the side
portico outside is a 5th-century
panelled door carved with biblical scenes, notably one of the
oldest images of the Crucifixion (top left-hand corner).

Further Afield

IT IS WELL WORTH making the effort to see some of Rome's outlying sights. Highlights are the Villa Giulia, home to a magnificent Etruscan museum, and the Museo Borghese on the splendid Villa Borghese estate, with its extraordinary collection of virtuoso statues by Bernini. Other sights range from ancient churches and catacombs to the more modern suburb of EUR, a strange architectural medley begun by Mussolini in the 1930s.

KEY

▨	Central Rome
☐	Suburbs
══	Motorway
──	Major road
──	Minor road
──	City walls

10 km = 6 miles

Villa Borghese ❶

Map 3 B1. ▤ 52, 53, 88, 95, 116, 490. ▤ 3, 19. **Park** ◯ dawn–sunset daily.

THE VILLA AND ITS PARK were designed in 1605 for Cardinal Scipione Borghese, the sybaritic nephew of Pope Paul V. An extravagant patron of the arts, he amassed one of Europe's finest collections of paintings, statues and antiquities, many of which are still displayed in the villa which he built especially to house his antique sculptures.

The **park** was one of the first of its kind in Rome, its formal gardens divided by avenues and graced with statues. It contained 400 newly planted trees, garden sculpture by Bernini's father, Pietro, along with many ingenious fountains, "secret" flower gardens, enclosures of exotic animals and birds, and even a grotto with artificial rain. There was also a speaking robot and a trick

chair, which trapped anyone who sat in it. At first the grounds were open to the public, but after a visitor was shocked by the collection of erotic paintings, Paul V decided to keep the park private.

In 1773 work began on redesigning the park in the wilder, Romantic style made fashionable by landscape artists like Claude Lorrain and Poussin. Over the next few

Temple of Aesculapius, an 18th-century folly, at the Villa Borghese

years mock-Classical temples, fountains and *casine* (summer-houses) were added. In 1901, the park and villa were acquired by the state, and in 1911 the area was chosen as the site for the International Exhibition. Pavilions were built by many of the world's nations, the most impressive of which is the **British School at Rome** by Edwin Lutyens. In the northeastern corner of the park lie the Museo Zoologico and a small redeveloped zoo, known as the Bioparco, where the emphasis is on conservation. Today the estates of the Villa Borghese, Villa Giulia and the Pincio gardens form one vast park, with the **Giardino del Lago**, at its centre, named after an artificial boating lake. Its main entrance is marked by an 18th-century copy of the Arch of Septimius Severus, while on the lake's island is a fake Ionic temple to the Greek god of health, Aesculapius, designed by the 18th-century architect Antonis Aspurucci.

A circular Temple of Diana folly lies between the Porta Pinciana, at the top of Via Veneto, and Piazza di Siena, a grassy amphitheatre which hosts Rome's international horse show in May. Its umbrella pines inspired the composer Ottorino Respighi to write *The Pines of Rome* (1924). The open-air opera season is also held in the park.

To the northwest of the park is the Galleria Nazionale d'Arte Moderna, which houses a large but somewhat uninspiring collection of 19th- and 20th-century paintings.

Sacred and Profane Love by Titian (1514), in the Galleria Borghese

Museo e Galleria Borghese ➋

Villa Borghese, Piazzale Scipione Borghese 5. **⟮** 06 328 10. **🚍** 52, 53, 116, 910. **🚋** 3, 19. **◯** 9am– 7:30pm Tue–Sun (reservations needed for Sat & Sun). **●** public hols. 🖼 🚫 🏠 📷 👜 ♿

SCIPIONE BORGHESE's villa was designed in 1605 as a typical Roman country house, with its wings projecting into the surrounding gardens. It was built by Flaminio Ponzio, Pope Paul V's architect, and was used by Scipione for entertaining guests and for displaying his impressive collection of paintings and sculpture. Between 1801 and 1809 Prince Camillo Borghese, husband to Napoleon's sister Pauline, unfortunately sold many of the family paintings

to his brother-in-law, and swapped 200 of Scipione's Classical statues for an estate in Piedmont. These statues are still in the Louvre and, as a consequence, the remaining antique Classical collection is less interesting than it might once have been. However, the hedonistic cardinal was an enthusiastic patron of the arts and the sculptures he commissioned from artists such as the young Bernini now rank among his most famous works.

The eight rooms of the ground floor of the Villa Borghese are set around a central hall, the Salone. The most famous statue is one of Bernini's finest works, *Apollo and Daphne* (1624) in room 3, which shows the nymph Daphne with bay leaves sprouting from her outstretched fingers, roots growing from her toes and rough bark enfolding her smooth body, as she begins to metamorphose into a laurel tree to escape being abducted by the god Apollo. Abduction is also the theme of *The Rape of Proserpina*, again by Bernini, in room 4. Depicting Pluto, the god of the under-world, carrying Proserpina, daughter of Ceres, off to be his bride, the sculpture is a virtuoso piece in which Bernini contrasts the taut musculature of Pluto with the soft yielding flesh of Proserpina, whose thigh dimples in his iron grip.

The third famous Bernini piece, which dates from 1623, is *David* in room 2. The artist captures the tensed, grimacing youth the moment before he releases the stone that slew Goliath. It is said that Pope Urban VIII held a mirror up to Bernini so that the sculptor could model David's face on his

Detail of *Rape of Proserpina* by Bernini (1622), Museo Borghese

own. In the next alcove is the Villa Borghese's most infamous work – a sculpture, executed in 1805 by Canova, of Pauline Borghese as *Venus Victrix* (Venus the Conqueror). The semi-naked Pauline reclining on a chaise-longue shocked those who saw it and Pauline's husband kept the statue locked away, even denying Canova access to it.

The next room holds a selection of antiquities, notably a Roman copy of a plump *Bacchus* by the 4th-century BC Greek sculptor Praxiteles, and fragments of a 3rd-century AD mosaic found on one of the Borghese estates in Torrenova, showing gladiators battling with wild animals.

The Galleria Borghese, on the upper floor, houses some superb Baroque and Renaissance paintings, which could formerly be seen at the Complesso San Michele in Trastevere while the gallery was closed for renovation. Works includes Raphael's masterpiece, the *Deposition*, various works by Caravaggio, the graceful *Danäe* by the 16th-century artist Correggio, as well as works by Pinturicchio, Barocci, Rubens and Titian.

Bernini's *Apollo and Daphne* (1624)

Villa Giulia ❸

THIS VILLA WAS BUILT in 1550 as a country retreat for Pope Julius III. Designed by Vignola and Ammannati, with contributions by Michelangelo and Vasari, it was intended for entertaining guests of the Vatican, such as Queen Christina of Sweden, rather than as a permanent home. The gardens were planted with 36,000 trees and peppered with pavilions and fountains. Villa Giulia also used to house an outstanding collection of sculptures: 160 boats filled with statues and ornaments were sent to the Vatican after the death of Pope Julius III in 1555.

Since 1889 the villa has been home to the Museo Nazionale Etrusco, an impressive collection of pre-Roman antiquities from central Italy.

VISITORS' CHECKLIST

Piazzale di Villa Giulia 9.
📞 06 322 65 71.
🚌 52, 95. 🚋 3, 19.
🕐 8:30am–7:30pm Tue–Sun.
⛔ 1 Jan, 1 May, 25 Dec.
Concerts in July. 🎫
🎧 with seven days' notice.
📷 🚫 📖 ♿ 🏛

Rooms 24–29 contain finds from the Ager Faliscus, an area between the Tiber and Lake Bracciano, in particular temples from Falerii Vetere, the principal Faliscan town.

Ficoroni Cist
Engraved and beautifully illustrated, this 4th-century BC bronze marriage coffer held mirrors and other body care implements.

Rooms 11–18, the Antiquarium collection, display domestic and votive objects and ceramics, including the Chigi vase from 6th-century BC Corinth.

Room 19 exhibits finds from the Castellani collection, including early 6th-century ceramics and bronzes.

Spiralled Faliscan Crater
Painted in the free style of the 4th century BC, this spiral-handled vase was used to hold wines or oil. The Falisci were an Italic tribe influenced by the Etruscans.

Ninfeo (Nympheum)

Husband and Wife Sarcophagus
This 6th-century BC tomb from Cerveteri shows a deceased couple banqueting in the afterlife. Their tender expression bears witness to the skill of Etruscan artists.

Rooms 30–34 exhibit finds from various sites including the Temple of Diana at Nemi.

KEY TO FLOORPLAN

☐ Ground floor

▨ First floor

☐ Non-exhibition space

Rooms 1–10 are arranged by site, starting with Vulci (most importantly articles from the Warrior's Tomb) and including Bisenzio, Veio and Cerveteri.

Entrance

Apse mosaic in Sant'Agnese, showing the saint flanked by two popes

Sant'Agnese fuori le Mura ❹

Via Nomentana 349.
[06 861 08 40. **[]** 36, 60, 84, 90.
[] 9am–noon, 4–6pm Tue–Sat,
4–6pm Sun, 9am–noon Mon.
[] to catacombs. **[] []**

SANT'AGNESE FUORI LE MURA
was built in the 4th century
above the crypt of the 13-year-
old martyr St Agnes, and
although much altered it
retains the form of the original
basilica. According to legend it
was founded by Constantine's
daughter Constantia, who was
cured from leprosy after
sleeping beside Agnes's tomb.

In the 7th-century apse
mosaic, St Agnes appears as a
bejewelled Byzantine empress
in a stole of gold and a violet
robe. Tradition has it that she
appeared like this eight days
after her death holding a white
lamb. On 21 January two lambs
are blessed in the church and
a vestment called a *pallium* is
woven from their wool, to be
given to a new archbishop.

Santa Costanza ❺

Via Nomentana 349. **[** 06 861
08 40. **[]** 36, 60, 84, 90. **[]** 9am–
noon, 4–6pm Tue–Sat, 4–6pm Sun,
9am–noon Mon. **[] [] []**

THIS CIRCULAR church was
built in the early 4th
century as a mausoleum
for Emperor Constantine's
daughters, Constantia and
Helena. The dome and its
drum are supported by an
arcade that rests on 12
magnificent pairs of granite
columns, while the encircling
ambulatory has a barrel-
vaulted ceiling decorated with
the world's earliest surviving
Christian mosaics. Dating
from the 4th century, they are
thought to have been copied
from a secular Roman floor
and include flowers, animals
and birds. There is even a
charming scene of a Roman
grape-harvest, though the
wine is said by Christians
to represent Christ's blood.

In a niche on the far side
of the church is a replica of
Constantia's ornate porphyry
sarcophagus, carved with
cherubs crushing grapes.
The original was moved to
the Vatican Museums in 1790.

Circular interior of the 4th-
century church of Santa Costanza

The sanctity of Constantia
is somewhat debatable.
Described by the historian
Marcellinus as a fury incarn-
ate, constantly goading her
equally unpleasant husband,
Hannibalianus, to violence, her
canonization was probably the
result of some confusion with a
saintly nun of the same name.

Via Appia Antica ❻

[] 118, 218, 760.

Cypresses lining the Via Appia

THE FIRST PART of the Via
Appia was built in 312 BC
by Appius Claudius Caecus. In
190 BC, when it was extended
to the ports of Taranto and
Brindisi, the road became
Rome's link with its empire in
the East. It was the route
taken by the funeral proces-
sions of the dictator Sulla (78
BC) and Emperor Augustus
(AD 14), and it was along this
road that St Paul was led as a
prisoner to Rome in AD 56.
The church of Domine Quo
Vadis? marks the spot where
St Peter is said to have met
Christ when fleeing Rome.

The road is lined with
ruined family tombs, decaying
monuments, and collective
burial places (*columbaria*).
Beneath the fields on either
side lies a maze of catacombs,
including those of San Callisto
and San Sebastiano.

Catacombs ❼

Via Appia Antica 126. 🚐 *118, 218,
660.* **San Callisto** 📞 *06 513 01 51.*
🕐 *8:30am–noon, 2:30–5:30pm
Thu–Tue (to 5pm in winter).* ⬤ *1 Jan,
Feb, Easter, 25 Dec.* 🖼️ ⛪ 📷 📷 ∅

I N BURYING THEIR DEAD in
underground cemeteries
outside the city walls, the
early Christians were simply
obeying the laws of the time.
They were not forced to use
them because of persecution,
as later popular myth has
suggested. Many saints were
buried here, and the catacombs later became shrines
and places of pilgrimage.

Today several catacombs
are open to the public. The
vast Catacombs of San Callisto,
hewn from volcanic tufa,
contain niches, or *loculi,* which
held two or three bodies, as
well as the burial places of
several early popes. Close by,
walls in the Catacombs of San
Sebastiano are covered in
graffiti invoking St Peter and
St Paul, whose remains may
once have been moved here.

**Engraving of Christian ceremony in
Catacombs of San Callisto (AD 50)**

EUR ❽

🚐 *170, 671, 714.* Ⓜ *EUR Fermi,
EUR Palasport.* **Museo della Civiltà
Romana** *Piazza G Agnelli 10.*
📞 *06 592 60 41.* 🕐 *9am–6:15pm
Tue–Sat, 9am–1:30pm Sun & public
hols.* ⬤ *1 Jan, 1 May, 25 Dec.* 🖼️

T HE ESPOSIZIONE UNIVERSALE di
Roma (EUR), a suburb to
the south of the city, was originally built for an international
exhibition, a kind of "Work

**EUR's Palazzo della Civiltà del
Lavoro, the "Square Colosseum"**

Olympics", that was planned
for 1942, but never took place
because of the outbreak of war.
The architecture was intended
to glorify Fascism, and as a
result the bombastic style of the
buildings can look overblown
and rhetorical to modern
eyes. Of all the buildings the
best known is probably the
Palazzo della Civiltà del Lavoro
(the Palace of the Civilization
of Work), an unmistakable
landmark for people arriving
from Fiumicino airport.

The scheme was eventually
completed in the 1950s.
Despite the area's dubious
architecture, EUR has been a
planning success, and people
are still keen to live here. As
well as residential housing,
the vast marble halls along
the wide boulevards are also
home to a number of government offices and museums.
Best among the latter is the
Museo della Civiltà Romana,
famous for its casts of the
reliefs from the Column
of Trajan, and for a
large scale

model depicting 4th-century
Rome with all the buildings
which then stood within the
Aurelian walls. The south of
the suburb features a lake
and shady park, and the huge
domed Palazzo dello Sport,
built for the 1960 Olympics.

San Paolo fuori
le Mura ❾

Via Ostiense 186. 🚐 *23, 128, 170,
670, 761, 766, 769.* Ⓜ *San Paolo.*
📞 *06 541 03 41.* 🕐 *7am–7pm
daily (to 6:30pm in winter).*
Cloister ⬤ *1–3pm.* ⛪ ♿ 📷

T ODAY'S CHURCH is a faithful
if soulless reconstruction
of the great 4th-century basilica destroyed by fire in 1823.
Only a few fragments of the
earlier church survived, most
notably the cloister (1241),
with its pairs of colourful inlaid columns, considered one
of the most beautiful in Rome.

Elsewhere, the church's
triumphal arch is decorated
on one side with heavily
restored 5th-century mosaics,
and on the other with mosaics
by Pietro Cavallini originally on
the façade. The equally fine
mosaics (1220) in the apse
represent the figures of Christ
with St Peter, St Andrew, St
Paul and St Luke.

The single most outstanding
work of art is the fine marble
canopy over the high altar, the
work of Arnolfo di Cambio
(1285), with the possible
assistance of Pietro Cavallini.
Below the altar is the *confessio*
where it is alleged St Paul
was once buried. To its right
is an impressive Paschal
candlestick dating from the
12th century by Nicolò di
Angelo and Pietro
Vassalletto.

19th-century mosaic on façade of San Paolo fuori le Mura

ROME STREET FINDER

MAP REFERENCES given with sights described in the Rome chapters relate to the maps on the following pages. Map references are also given for hotels *(see pp542–75)* and restaurant listings *(see pp578–609)* and for useful addresses in the *Travellers' Needs* and *Survival Guide* sections at the back of the book. The first figure in the map reference tells you which Street Finder map to turn to, and the letter and number which follow refer to the grid reference on that map. The small map below shows the area of Rome covered by each of the eight maps and the corresponding map number is given in black. All the major sights are sketched out on the maps, and symbols, listed in the key below, are used to indicate the location of other important buildings.

1

The Vatican and Trastevere

2 **3**

Northeast Rome

4

Around Piazza Navona

The Ancient Centre

5

6 **7**

Aventine and Lateran

8

0 kilometres 2

0 miles 1

KEY AND SCALE FOR STREET FINDER PAGES

▢	Major sight	**P**	Parking	⊠	Post office
▢	Place of interest	**i**	Tourist information	=	Railway line
FS	Railway station	✚	Hospital with casualty unit		One-way street
M	Metro station	▣	Police station	—	City walls
▤	Bus terminus	✝	Church		
▥	Tram terminus	✡	Synagogue		

0 metres 250

0 yards 250

Rome Bus Routes

Flaminio **M** 95

Santa Maria del Popolo

117-119

628-926

490-492
913-990
991-999

990

23

M Lepanto

VIA COLONNA

Tevere

VIA DEL BABUINO

VIA D. RIPETTA

117-119

117-119

VIA DEL CORSO

M Ottaviano

VIA COLA DI RIENZO

81-590

VIA CICERONE

81-590

70-186
280-913

490-492

32

32-81

23-49-492-990

PIAZZA DEL RISORGIMENTO

Musei Vaticani

23

VIA PORCARI

34-49-492-990

VIA CRESCENZIO

23-34

34-49
87-926
990

PIAZZA CAVOUR

81

81-590-628-926

VIA TOMACELLI

628

VIA CON

119-590
628

49

CITTÀ DEL VATICANO

VIA DEI CORRIDORI

62

29-62

34

Castel Sant'Angelo

280

70-87
186-492
913-926

Ponte Cavour

San Pietro

PIAZZA SAN PIETRO

VIA AURELIA

87-492

49

913

PIAZZA SILVES

BORGO S. SPIRITO

Ponte Umberto I

LT. MARZIO

628

116

34-46-64-98
881-916-982-46B

VIA D. PORTA CAVALLEGGERI

64

Ponte Pr. Amedeo

280

46B-98-870
881-982

70-87-116-186
204-492

52-53-61
71-80-85
160-850

62-63-95-1
160-175-10

VIA DELLA STAZIONE DI S. PIETRO

64

870

116

CORSO D. RINASCIMENTO

PIAZZA D. ROTONDA

116

64

870

23-280-870

23-280-870

VIA GIULIA

116

CORSO VITTORIO EMANUELE II

30-70-81-87-116
186-204-492-628

116

116

Pantheon

VIALE ALDO FABRIZI

Ponte Mazzini

41

40-46-62-64-916

LUNGOTEVERE TEBALDI

116

116

30-40-46-62-63
64-70-81-87-186
492-628-810-916

LGO TORRE ARGENTINA

H

Villa Farnesina

23-280

LT. D. FARNESINA

23-280

H

PIAZ VENE

716
781

Gianicolo

870

870

Ponte Sisto

LT. D. VALLATI

VIA ARENULA

63-780-H

H-23-63-280-780

63

62-63-95-1

Villa Doria Pamphilj

Ponte Garibaldi

Isola Tiberina

Ponte Palatino

LT. D. CENCI

Santa Maria in Trastevere

LT. D. ANGUILLARA

23-280

44

VIA DI SAN PANCRAZIO

44-870-871

44-75

VIALE DI TRASTEVERE

44-75

44-75

LUNGOTEVERE AVENTINO

23-44-280

870

44-75

44-871

44-710-870-871

75

23-30-44-95-170-280-716-781

VIA DANDOLO

0 metres 250

0 yards 250

75

780-H

Ponte Sublicio

Tevere

95-170

95-170

VIA MARMORATA

23-30-75-280-716

KEY TO BUS MAP

64 — Bus route

46 — Start/end of bus route (*capolinea*)

➤ Direction

M Metro station

▣ Railway station

\\ Tunnel

▪ Major sight

170-719-781

780-H

288-766
773-774
786-871

170-781

Ponte Testaccio

VIA MANUZIO

719

673-719

VIA ZABAGLIA

95

170-781

60

280

Piramide **M**

23-673-716

Stazione Trastevere

LAZIO

YING BETWEEN the Apennines and the Tyrrhenian Sea, Lazio is a varied region of volcanic lakes, mountains, ravines, vineyards and olive groves. Before the rise of Rome, it was populated by the Etruscans and various Italic tribes, including the Latins, after whom the region is named. Besides rich archaeological sites, Lazio also offers skiing and swimming and water sports in the lakes and sea.

Lazio was inhabited at least 60,000 years ago, although the first signs of a substantial civilization date back to the 10th century BC. By the 7th century BC a flourishing Etruscan and Sabine civilization based on trade and agriculture existed in the north, while the region's southern margins were colonized by the Latins, Volsci and Ernici. History mingles with myth in the writings of Virgil, who describes how Aeneas landed in Lazio where he married the daughter of the king of the Latins. Romulus and Remus (legendary founders of Rome) were descendants of this alliance.

With the rise of Rome as a power, the Etruscan and Latin peoples were, in time, overwhelmed and the focus of the region turned to the city of Rome. Great roads and aqueducts extended out of the city like spokes of a wheel, and wealthy patricians built lavish villas in the surrounding countryside. The early Middle Ages saw the rise of the Church's temporal power and, with the foundation of monasteries at Subiaco and Montecassino, Lazio became the cradle of western monasticism, and eventually part of the Papal States. In the 16th and 17th centuries, wealthy papal families competed with one another to build luxurious villas and gardens, hiring some of the best architects of the Renaissance and Baroque.

Throughout its history, however, Lazio has been eclipsed and neglected by Rome. The Pontine marshes were a malaria-ridden swamp until the 1920s, when Mussolini had them drained and brought new roads and agricultural improvements to the area.

Looking out over Caprarola during the early evening *passeggiata*

◁ **Vignola's graceful Renaissance parterre gardens and fountains in Villa Lante, Viterbo**

Exploring Lazio

Much of Lazio's landscape was formed by the eruption of four volcanoes which showered the area with lava. Lakes formed in the craters, and the soil, rendered fertile by the lava, nourished vines, olives, fruit and nut trees. The volcanic activity also left Lazio with hot springs, notably around Tivoli, Viterbo and Fiuggi. Rome dominates the area, dividing the wooded hills of the north from the reclaimed Pontine marshes in the south. Swimming and sailing are possible in lakes Bracciano, Bolsena and Albano, while Lazio's best beaches lie between Gaeta and Sabaudia in the Parco Nazionale del Circeo.

SIGHTS AT A GLANCE

SEE ALSO

The Tolfa hills southwest of Lake Bracciano

KEY

▓▓▓	Motorway
▬▬▬	Major road
▬▬▬	Minor road
▬▬▬	Scenic route
≈≈	River
☀	Viewpoint

The old quarter overlooking the beach at Sperlonga

GETTING AROUND

Rome's two international airports at Fiumicino and Ciampino serve the region. The main motorways are the *Autostrada del Sole* Firenze–Roma (A1) and Roma–Napoli (A1–E45), and the Roma–L'Aquila (A24–E80). The ring road *(raccordo anulare)* around Rome connects the motorways and main roads.

The Lazio bus service, COTRAL, serves all the main towns with changeover points for the smaller locations in Rome and at Latina, Frosinone, Viterbo and Rieti. Train routes into the region from other Italian cities are efficient, although within Lazio the services are slower and less frequent.

Palestrina's terraces climbing up the hill

Ascoli Piceno

AMATRICE

Terni

S260

RIETI

L'Aquila

FARFA

PARCO NATURALE REGIONALE DEI MONTI SIMBRUINI

TIVOLI

SUBIACO

PALESTRINA

FRASCATI

Lago Albano

FIUGGI

MONTI ERNICI

ANAGNI

SORA

CASAMARI

POSTA FIBRENA

FROSINONE

MONTECASSINO

NINFA

SERMONETA

FOSSANOVA

CASSINO

LATINA

Caserta Napoli

PARCO NAZIONALE DEL CIRCEO

TERRACINA

SPERLONGA

GAETA

GOLFO DI GAETA

Pozzuoli

ISOLE PONZIANE

0 kilometres 15

0 miles 10

Carved loggia of the Palazzo Papale, Viterbo

Tuscania ❶

Viterbo. 🚶 7,500. 🚌 ℹ️ *Piazza Basile (0761 43 63 71).* 🛒 *Fri am.*

T USCANIA'S TRIM WALLS and towers are visible from afar on the empty low-lying plains between Viterbo and Tarquinia. Although shaken by an earthquake in 1971, its medieval and Renaissance buildings have since been carefully reconstructed. Just outside the city walls, on the rocky Colle San Pietro, two remarkable churches dating from the Lombard-Romanesque period occupy the site of Tuscana, a major Etruscan centre conquered by Rome in 300 BC. **Santa Maria Maggiore**, at the foot of the hill, has a typically Lombard-Romanesque asymmetric façade with blind arcades and a bold rose

Façade of San Pietro, Tuscania

window. Over the central door lies a simple marble Madonna and Child, framed by abstract motifs and biblical scenes. Inside, a rare 12th-century full-immersion baptism font stands in the aisle. The Lombard-Romanesque church of **San Pietro**, on top of the hill, is a striking building of ochre-hued tufa and white marble details. It stands on a grassy piazza, along with two medieval towers and a bishop's palace. The façade features an intricately inlaid rose window flanked by strange reliefs, including three-headed bearded demons. The interior is true to its 8th-century form, with squat columns, toothed arches, capitals carved with stylized plants and a Cosmati floor. Below the church lies a strange mosque-like crypt.

Viterbo ❷

🚶 60,000. 🚊 🚌 ℹ️ *Ex Porta Romana Station (0761 30 47 95).* 🛒 *Sat.*

V ITERBO WAS AN important Etruscan centre before falling to the Romans in the 4th century BC. Its heyday, however, came in the 13th century when it briefly became the papal seat (1257–81). During World War II it was devastated, but the austere grey stone medieval core, still encircled by walls, and many of the town's churches, have been carefully restored.

In **San Pellegrino**, Viterbo's oldest and best preserved quarter, medieval houses with towers, arches and external staircases line narrow streets running between little piazzas decorated with fountains.

On Piazza San Lorenzo the 12th-century **Duomo** boasts an elegant black and white striped bell tower, a solemn 16th-century façade and a stark Romanesque interior. The adjacent 13th-century **Palazzo Papale**, with a finely carved loggia, was built for popes during their visits to the city.

The town's civic buildings border the main square, Piazza del Plebiscito. The most interesting is the 15th-century **Palazzo dei Priori**, frescoed inside by Baldassare Croce with scenes from the town's history and mythological past.

Outside the city walls, on Viale Capocci, the Romanesque **Santa Maria della Verità** has wonderful 15th-century frescoes by Lorenzo da Viterbo.

Villa Lante's small but splendid Renaissance gardens, considered Vignola's masterpiece

ENVIRONS: The **Villa Lante**, northeast of Viterbo, was begun in 1562 by Vignola for Cardinal Gambara. The main attractions are the outstanding Renaissance gardens and fountains. Be careful not to be a victim of a 16th-century practical joke: many of the fountains will sprinkle people without warning.

🏛 **Palazzo dei Priori**
Piazza Plebiscito. ▪ 0761 34 81. ○ daily. ● public hols. ♿ ▯
🏛 **Villa Lante**
Bagnaia. ▪ 0761 28 80 08. ○ Tue–Sun. ● 1 Jan, 1 May, 25 Dec. ▨ ♿ to gardens.

The main façade of the pentagonal Palazzo Farnese at Caprarola

Montefiascone ❸

Viterbo. 🏠 13,000. 🚉 🚌 ℹ Largo Plebiscito 1 (0761 83 20 60). 🖪 Wed.

Carved 11th-century capital in San Flaviano, Montefiascone

THIS PRETTY TOWN is perched on the edge of a defunct volcanic crater between the shores of Lake Bolsena, over which there are splendid views, and the Via Cassia. It is dominated by the octagonal bulk of its cathedral, **Santa Margherita**, whose dome, created in the 1670s by Carlo Fontana, is second only in size to St Peter's.

On the town's outskirts, along the Via Cassia towards Orvieto, lies **San Flaviano**, a lovely double-decker building with a 12th-century church oriented east over an 11th-century church pointing west. Inside are some fine 14th-century frescoes and freely carved capitals, thought to have been inspired by the traditions of Etruscan art.

ENVIRONS: The popular lake-side beach resort of **Bolsena**, 15 km (9 miles) north on Lake Bolsena, has a medieval castle, as well as boats to the islands of Bisentina and Martana.

Bomarzo ❹

Parco dei Mostri, Bomarzo.
▪ 0761 92 40 29. 🚉 to Viterbo. 🚌 from Viterbo (not Sun or public hols). ○ 8am–sunset. ▨ ♿

THE SACRO BOSCO beneath the town of Bomarzo was created between 1522 and 1580 by Duke Vicino Orsini as a bizarre memorial to his late wife. Far from designing a meticulous Renaissance garden, Orsini embraced the artificiality and distortion of the Mannerist period by creating lop-sided buildings and sculpting huge boulders of stone into fantastic creatures and vast allegorical monsters.

One of the bizarre stone monsters in Bomarzo's Sacro Bosco

Caprarola ❺

Viterbo. 🏠 4,900. 🚌 ℹ Via Filippo Nicolai 2 (0761 64 61 57). 🖪 Tue.

PERHAPS THE GRANDEST of the country villas created during the 17th century by the wealthy families of Rome, **Palazzo Farnese** (see p370) is the focal point of the medieval village of Caprarola. Designed by Vignola, it was built between 1559 and 1575 and takes its star-shape from the foundations of a large pentagonal fortress designed by Antonio da Sangallo the Younger half a century earlier. On the main floor, reached by an elaborately stuccoed spiral staircase, the rooms were frescoed, largely by the Zuccari brothers in 1560, with scenes depicting heroic episodes from the life of Hercules and the Farnese family.

ENVIRONS: Created, according to legend, by the god Hercules ramming his club into the ground, **Lago di Vico**, 4 km (3 miles) west of Caprarola, in fact occupies the remnants of a volcanic crater. An idyllic enclave, the lake is encircled by the wooded slopes of the Cimini Hills (much of which is a nature reserve). A scenic road runs around the lake, and the best place for swimming is on the southeast shore.

🏛 **Palazzo Farnese**
Caprarola. ▪ 0761 64 60 52. ○ Tue–Sun. ● 1 Jan, 1 May, 25 Dec. ▨

Etruscan tumulus tombs from the necropolis at Cerveteri

Tarquinia ❻

Viterbo. 🚌 15,000. 🚆 🛈 Piazza Cavour 1 (0766 84 92 82). 🛒 Wed.

ANCIENT TARQUINIA (Tarxuna) was one of Etruria's most important centres. It occupied a strategic position to the north-east of the present town, on a ridge dominating the coastal plain, until the 4th century BC when it fell to Rome.

Tarquinia itself is worth a wander for its crumbling medi-eval churches and spacious main square, though the main reason to visit is the **Museo Archeologico e Necropoli**, which has one of Italy's better collections of Etruscan finds. Relaxed, reclining statues of the deceased adorn the sarcophagi on the ground floor, but the star attraction, on the mezza-nine, is a group of terracotta winged horses dating from the 4th century BC.

On a hilltop 2 km (1 mile) southeast of town are the frescoed tombs of the **necro-polis** dug into the soft volcanic tufa. There are almost 6,000

Dancers from the 4th-century BC frescoed Tomba del Triclinio in the Museo Archeologico, Tarquinia

tombs but only about 15 can be visited at a time. The frescoes that decorate them, designed to remind the dead of life, range from frenetic dancing figures in the Tomba delle Leonesse to the diners reclining in the Tomba dei Leopardi.

🏛 **Museo Archeologico e Necropoli**
Piazza Cavour. 🕿 0766 85 60 36. 🕐 Tue–Sun. 🔴 1 Jan, 1 May, 25 Dec. 🌠 ♿

Cerveteri ❼

Roma. 🚌 30,000. 🚆 🚌 🛈 Piazza Risorgimento (06 99 55 19 71). 🛒 Fri.

IN THE 6TH century BC Cerveteri (ancient Kysry) was one of the most populated and culturally rich towns of the Mediterranean, trading with Greece and controlling a large area along the coast. The **necropolis**, a city of the dead 2 km (1 mile) outside town, is a network of streets lined with tombs dating from the 7th to the 1st century BC. Some of the larger tumulus tombs, like the Tomba degli Scudi e delle Sedie, are arranged like houses with rooms, doors and corridors. The Tomba dei Rilievi is decor-ated with plaster reliefs of tools, pets and myth-ological figures. Although the

best finds from the necropolis are in museums such as the Vatican Museums, Villa Giulia and the British Museum in London, some can be seen in the small **Museo Nazionale Cerite** in the centre of town.

ENVIRONS: There are more traces of the Etruscans to be seen at **Norchia**, where the tombs are carved out of a rock face, and **Sutri**, whose amphi-theatre is one of the few relics of the living Etruscans.

⋔ **Necropolis**
Via delle Necropoli. 🕿 06 994 00 01. 🕐 Tue–Sun. 🔴 public hols. 🌠
🏛 **Museo Nazionale Cerite**
Piazza Santa Maria. 🕿 06 994 13 54. 🕐 Tue–Sun. 🔴 public hols. 🌠

Lake Bracciano ❽

Roma. 🚆 🚌 Bracciano. 🛈 P. IV Novembre 6, Bracciano (06 99 84 00 34).

Medieval Anguillara on Lake Bracciano

BRACCIANO is a large lake famous for its fish, and popular for water sports and lakeside lunches.

Medieval **Anguillara**, to the south, is the prettiest of the lakeside towns with romantic views over the water. The main town, **Bracciano**, on the east shore, is dominated by the Orsini-Odescalchi fortress, a pentagonal 15th-century structure with frescoes by Antoniazzo Romano and other Tuscan and Umbrian artists.

⛫ **Castello Orsini-Odescalchi**
Piazza Mazzini 14. 🕿 06 99 80 23 79. 🕐 Tue–Sun. 🔴 1 Jan, 25 Dec. 🌠

Ostia Antica ⑨

Viale dei Romagnoli 717, Ostia. 📞
06 56 35 80 99. Ⓜ *Piramide, then*
🚇 *from Porta San Paolo to Ostia
Antica.* **Excavations & Museum**
⏱ *9am–1 hr before sunset Tue–Sun.*
⛔ *1 Jan, 1 May, 25 Dec.* ♿

FOR OVER 600 years Ostia
was Rome's main port
and a busy trading
centre, until the 5th
century AD when a dis-
astrous combination of
malaria and commercial
competition brought
the town into decline.
Silt preserved
its buildings and
it now lies 5 km
(3 miles) inland.

    The ruins of Ostia
give a vivid idea of life
in Classical times. The
main thoroughfare, the
Decumanus Maximus, runs
through the Forum, which
houses Ostia's largest temple,
the **Capitol**, and past the
restored **theatre**, still used for
open air concerts in summer.
The road is lined with baths,
shops and multi-storey
buildings. There is even a
Thermopolium, or bar, with
a marble counter and paintings
advertising food and drink.

**The building
material** for the
houses was
brick, left plain or
covered in mural
decoration.

**The internal
courtyard** has
remained a feature
of Italian housing.

**Ruins of shops and offices along
the Decumanus Maximus**

Balcony

Apartments
or single rooms
were rented out.

OSTIA APARTMENTS
Much of Ostia's population
lived in blocks of flats, such
as this building, based on the
Casa di Diana (2nd century AD).

Shops
occupied the
ground floor
of the block.

The bar served
wine and snacks.

Frascati and the Castelli Romani ⑩

Roma. 🚇 🚌 *Frascati.* ℹ *Piazza Marconi 1, Frascati (06 942 03 31).* **Villa
Aldobrandini Gardens** ⏱ *Mon–Fri
with permission from tourist office only.*

THE ALBAN HILLS have long
been a country retreat for
Romans. In Classical times they
were scattered with villas; in
the Middle Ages with fortified
castles (hence the name); and
in the 16th and 17th centuries
with luxurious country residences and their spectacular
parks and gardens. During
World War II German defences
were based in the Alban hills
and many Castelli towns were
damaged by Allied bombs.
Although partly protected by
a nature reserve, the hilltop
towns are popular day-trip
destinations as well as being
famous for their white wine.

Frascati's central piazza is a
belvedere overlooked by the
Villa Aldobrandini, a majestic
17th-century building set in
a splendid park of secret
grottoes, fountains and statues.
    The fortified Abbazia di San
Nilo in **Grottaferrata**, 3 km
(2 miles) south, was founded
in 1004 and contains some
lovely 17th-century frescoes by
Domenichino in the chapel.

Overlooking Lake Albano,
6 km (4 miles) south, **Castel
Gandolfo** is the site of the
pope's summer palace. When
in residence the pope addresses
the crowd from the balcony.
    Gathered around a sturdy
9th-century castle, and famed
for its strawberries, **Nemi**, 10
km (6 miles) southeast, looks
down onto the glassy dark
blue waters of Lake Nemi.

The forested shores around the small, volcanic Lake Nemi

Tivoli, a favourite place to escape the heat of the Roman summer

Tivoli ⓫

Roma. 🏛 *57,000*. 🚇 🚌 🛈 *Largo Garibaldi (0774 33 45 22)*. 🚆 *Wed*.

Hill-town Tivoli, now probably the most popular excursion from Rome, was once a favoured resort of the ancient Romans, attracted by its fresh water and sulphur springs, and beautiful countryside. The temples that once covered Tivoli's hilltop are still visible in places. Some are half buried in medieval buildings, others, such as the Temples of Sibyl and Vesta, inside the gardens of the Sibilla restaurant (on Via Sibilla), are relatively intact.

Splendours from around the world reproduced in Hadrian's Villa

The town's most famous sight is the **Villa d'Este**, a sumptuous country residence created in the 16th century by Pirro Ligorio for Cardinal Ippolito d'Este from the shell of a Benedictine monastery. It is known primarily for its gardens, steeply raked on terraces, and studded with spectacular, if somewhat faded and moss-hung, fountains. Although suffering from reduced water-pressure and polluted water due to centuries of neglect, the gardens give a vivid impression of the frivolous luxury enjoyed by the papal families. Highlights include the Viale delle Cento Fontane and the Fontana dell'Organo Idraulico, which, thanks to a hydraulic system, can play music. At the other end of town, the **Villa Gregoriana**, now a hotel, is set in a lush wooded valley where paths wind down into a deep ravine.

ENVIRONS: About 5 km (3 miles) west of Tivoli are the ruins of **Hadrian's Villa**. Easily seen in conjunction with a visit to the town, this is one of the largest and most spectacular villas ever built in the Roman Empire (it once covered an area greater than the centre of Imperial Rome).

Hadrian was an inveterate traveller and his aim in creating the villa was to reproduce some of the wonders he had seen around the world. The Stoa Poikile, for example, a walkway around a rectangular pool and garden, recalls the painted colonnade of the Stoic philosophers in Athens, while the Canopus evokes the grand sanctuary of Serapis in

Alexandria. There are also ruins of two bath complexes, a Latin and a Greek library, a Greek theatre, and a private study on a little island known as the Teatro Marittimo.

Today the rambling ruins, full of shady nooks and hidden corners, make a lovely place to relax, picnic or explore.

🏛 **Villa d'Este**
Piazza Trento 1. 📞 *0774 31 20 70*. ⬜ *Tue–Sun*. ⬤ *1 Jan, 1 May, 25 Dec*. 🎫

🏛 **Villa Gregoriana**
Piazza Massimo. ⬤ *for restoration*.

🏛 **Hadrian's Villa**
Villa Adriana. 📞 *0774 53 02 03*. ⬜ *daily*. ⬤ *1 Jan, 1 May, 25 Dec*. 🎫

Palestrina ⓬

Roma. 🏛 *18,000*. 🚌 🛈 *Palazzo Barberini, Via Barberini (06 957 31 76)*.

Mosaic fragment of Nile in flood, Archaeological Museum, Palestrina

Medieval Palestrina grew up over the terraces of a huge temple dedicated to the goddess Fortuna Primigenia, the mother of all gods. The temple, founded in the 8th century BC and rebuilt in the 2nd century BC by Sulla, housed one of the most important oracles of ancient times. The terraces of the sanctuary, littered with fragments of columns and porticoes, lead up to the curved **Palazzo Barberini**. Built over the site of a circular temple, it now houses the **Museo Nazionale Archeologico**, best known for a 1st-century BC mosaic portraying the Nile in flood.

🏛 **Museo Nazionale Archeologico**
Via Barberini. 📞 *06 953 81 00*. ⬜ *daily*. ⬤ *1 Jan, 1 May, 25 Dec*. 🎫

Subiaco ⑬

Roma. 🏛 *9,000.* 🚌 ℹ️ ♿ *Via Cadorna 59 (0774 82 20 13).* 🚌 *Sat.*

IN THE 6th century, weary of the decadence of Rome, St Benedict left the city to become a hermit in a cave above Subiaco. Others joined him, and eventually there were 12 monasteries in the area.

Only two now survive: **Santa Scolastica**, dedicated to Benedict's sister, is organized around three cloisters, one Renaissance, one early Gothic and the third Cosmatesque. Higher up, the 12th-century **San Benedetto** is a more rewarding destination. Overhanging a deep gorge, it comprises two churches built on top of each other. The upper is decorated with 14th-century Sienese frescoes; the lower, built over several levels, incorporates the original cave where Benedict spent three years after fleeing Rome.

🛕 **Santa Scolastica**
3 km (2 miles) E of Subiaco.
☎ *0774 824 21.* ⭕ *daily.* 🚫 ♿
🛕 **San Benedetto**
3 km (2 miles) E of Subiaco.
☎ *0774 850 39.* ⭕ *daily.* 🚫 ♿

Montecassino ⑭

Cassino. ☎ *0776 31 15 29.*
🚆 *Cassino then bus.*
⭕ *9am–noon, 3:30–6pm daily (Nov–Mar: to 5pm).*

THE ABBEY of Montecassino, mother church of the Benedictine order and a centre of medieval art, was founded in 529 by St Benedict. By the 8th century it was an important centre of learning, and by the 11th century had become one of the richest monasteries in Europe.

In 1944 it was a German stronghold and a target for Allied bombs. Most of the complex was devastated, including the lavish Baroque church, but the walls remained intact and the abbey withstood for three months before falling to the Allies. The adjoining war cemeteries commemorate the 30,000 soldiers killed.

THE MONASTERIES OF LAZIO

Rose window, Fossanova

St Benedict founded the Abbey of Montecassino around 529 and there wrote his famous Rule. Based on the principles of prayer, study and manual labour, this became the fundamental monastic code of western Europe. The Cistercian Order, an offshoot of the Benedictines, came to Italy from Burgundy in the 12th century. The Cistercians were followers of St Bernard, whose creed was based on austerity and self-sufficiency, qualities which were reflected in the simple, early Gothic architecture of their monasteries. Their first abbey was at Fossanova. Other Cistercian abbeys in Lazio include Valvisciolo (northeast of Sermoneta) and San Martino in Cimino (near Lago di Vico).

The Abbey of Montecassino, destroyed during World War II, was rebuilt as a replica of its 17th-century predecessor.

The Abbey of San Benedetto, Subiaco, was founded in the 11th century over St Benedict's cave. A staircase carved in the rock leads to the grotto where he preached to shepherds.

The Abbey of Casamari, 14 km (8 miles) east of Frosinone, was founded by Benedictine monks in 1035 and handed over to the Cistercians who rebuilt it in 1203.

The abandoned medieval village of Ninfa, now a beautiful garden

Anagni ⑮

Frosinone. 🏘 *20,000.* FS 🚌
ℹ *Piazza Innocenzo III (0775 72 78 52).* 🛒 *Wed.*

ACCORDING TO LEGEND Saturn founded five towns in southeast Lazio, including Anagni, Alatri and Arpino. This area is now known as La Ciociaria, from *ciocie*, the bark clogs worn in the area until about 30 years ago.

Before the Romans conquered this part of Lazio it was inhabited by several different tribes: the Volsci, the Sanniti, and the Hernici. Little is known of them, apart from the extraordinary walls with which they protected their settlements. In later years these were believed to have been built by the Cyclops, a mythical giant, which gave them their present name of Cyclopean walls.

Anagni was the most sacred Hernician centre until its destruction by the Romans in 306 BC. In the Middle Ages it was the birthplace and family seat of several popes, an era from which many buildings survive, most notably Boniface VIII's 13th-century mullion-windowed palace.

The beautiful Romanesque **Duomo**, Santa Maria, built over the ancient Hernician acropolis, boasts a fine Cosmati mosaic floor from the 13th century as well as 14th-century Sienese frescoes. The crypt of San Magno is frescoed with one of the most complete surviving cycles of the 12th and 13th centuries.

ENVIRONS: Alatri, perched on an olive-covered slope 28 km (17 miles) east of Anagni, was an important Hernician town. It preserves an impressive double set of Cyclopean walls, 2 km (1 mile) long and 3 m (10 ft) high, from its 7th-century BC acropolis. In the medieval town below the walls is the Romanesque church of Santa Maria Maggiore, greatly restored in the 13th century.

Arpino, 40 km (25 miles) east of Alatri, is a bustling town with a medieval core, and was the birthplace of the

An unusual pointed arch in the Cyclopean walls at Arpino

Roman orator, Cicero. About 3 km (2 miles) above Arpino, at the site of the ancient town of Civitavecchia, is a tremendous stretch of Cyclopean walls which includes a rare gateway with a pointed arch.

Sermoneta and Ninfa ⑯

Latina. FS *Latina Scalo.* 🚌 *from Latina.* ℹ *Via Duca del Mare 19, Latina (0773 69 54 04).* **Ninfa** 📞 *0773 63 39 35 & 06 687 30 56 (for group bookings).* 🕐 *Apr–Oct: 1st Sat & Sun of the month (call for further dates).* ♿

SERMONETA IS A LOVELY hilltop town overlooking the Pontine Plains, with narrow cobbled streets winding around medieval houses, palaces and churches. The **Duomo** has a fine 15th-century panel by Benozzo Gozzoli showing the Virgin cradling Sermoneta in her hands. At the top of the town rises the moated fairy-tale Castello Caetani, frescoed with mythological scenes by a pupil of Pinturicchio.

In the valley below lies the abandoned medieval village of **Ninfa**, converted into lush gardens by the Caetani family in 1921. Streams and waterfalls punctuate the picturesque garden laid out among crumbling buildings.

Terracina ⓱

Latina. 👥 40,000. 🚆 🚌 🛈 *Via Leopardi (0773 72 77 59).* 🔄 *Thu.*

ROMAN TERRACINA was an important commercial centre on the Via Appia (the Appian Way). Today it is a popular seaside resort, with a fascinating collage of medieval buildings and Roman ruins in its historic centre, perched on the slopes of the Ausonian Hills. The more modern part of town by the sea is full of restaurants, bars and hotels.

Bombing during World War II uncovered many of the town's ancient structures, notably a stretch of the Appian Way and the original paving of the Roman Forum in Piazza del Municipio. The 11th-century **Duomo** was built in the shell of a Roman temple, and is still entered by the temple's steps. The medieval portico is adorned with a lovely 12th-century mosaic and the interior preserves the 13th-century mosaic pavement. Next

Duomo at Terracina with original Roman steps

door, the modern town hall houses the **Museo Archeologico**, devoted to local Greek and Roman finds.

About 3 km (2 miles) above the town are the podium and foundations that once supported the Temple of Jove Anxur, dating back to the 1st century BC. This huge arcaded platform is illuminated at night and offers vertiginous views of Terracina and its bay.

🏛 Museo Archeologico
Piazza Municipio. 📞 *0773 70 73 13.* 🕐 *Tue–Mon am.* ⬤ *public hols.* 🎫

Sperlonga ⓲

Latina. 👥 4,000. 🚌 🛈 *Corso San Leone 22 (0771 55 70 00).* 🔄 *Sat.*

SPERLONGA IS a popular seaside resort surrounded by sandy beaches. The old town sits on a rocky promontory, a picturesque labyrinth of whitewashed buildings, narrow alleyways, piazzettas and balconies offering an occasional glimpse of the sea below. It is now full of bars, restaurants and boutiques. The modern part of town lies down on the seafront.

The area around Sperlonga was a favourite retreat for the ancient Romans during the hot summer months. They built villas along the coast, and converted natural caves in the nearby cliffs into places to dine and relax.

In 1957 archaeologists excavating the huge complex of Tiberius's luxury villa, 1 km (half a mile) on the southern outskirts of town, found some marvellous 2nd-century BC Hellenistic sculptures in a large cave open to the sea. These sculptures, representing

12th-century bell tower at Gaeta

incidents from Homer's *Odyssey*, are thought to be by the same artists from Rhodes (where the Emperor Tiberius once lived) who were responsible for the Laocoön *(see p407)*. They are displayed, along with other local finds, in the **Museo Archeologico Nazionale** which is part of the archaeological zone.

🏛 Zona Archeologica
Via Flacca. 📞 *0771 54 80 28.* 🕐 *daily.* ⬤ *1 Jan, 25 Dec.* 🎫

Gaeta ⓳

Latina. 👥 22,000. 🚌 🛈 *Via Emanuele Filiberto 5 (0771 46 11 65).* 🔄 *Wed.*

ACCORDING TO VIRGIL, Gaeta was named after Aeneas's wet nurse Caieta, who was allegedly buried here. The town sits on the southern headland of the gulf of Gaeta, under Monte Orlando. The historic centre is dominated by a mighty Aragonese castle and the pinnacles of mock-Gothic San Francesco. To the north, the modern quarter links Gaeta to the bay of Serapo, a picturesque beach resort.

Gaeta's most beautiful feature is the **Duomo**'s elegant late Romanesque bell tower, its lofty summit topped by a roof of coloured ceramic tiles. On the seafront lies the tiny 10th-century church of **San Giovanni a Mare**, with faded frescoes, a hemispherical dome and a sloping floor to let the sea flow out after flooding.

Stretches of sandy beach along the coast between Gaeta and Terracina

SOUTHERN ITALY

Southern Italy at a Glance

Visitors to SOUTHERN ITALY find a rich array of archaeological remains. Although those of the Romans at Pompeii are high on everyone's list, Greek ruins litter Sicily and the southern coast and there are mysterious ancient structures, called *nuraghe*, in Sardinia. Campania, Puglia and Sicily are admired for their architecture, while across the south there are magnificent landscapes, abundant wildlife and endless opportunities for outdoor activities. The cuisine alone, with its eclectic heritage and diversity of tastes, provides the excuse to dawdle on the coast or in the mountain villages.

Abruzzo

Parco Nazion. d'Abruzzo

The Parco Nazionale d'Abruzzo, *a vast unspoilt wilderness, is home to wolves, bears and many species of birds (see pp490–91).*

Su Nuraxi at Barumini, *built around 1500 BC, is the most celebrated of Sardinia's mysterious stone nuraghe sites (see p533).*

Su Nuraxi

SARDINIA
(See pp528–35)

The cloister decoration at Monreale cathedral is a legacy of Sicily's Arabic past, with elaborate columns adorned with fine mosaics and splendid sculpted capitals (see pp514–5).

Monreale cathedral

Temple of Cor

Sicily's Valley of the Temples at Agrigento *contains some of the best ruins outside Greece. Mostly Doric in construction and style, they date from the 5th and 6th centuries BC (see p520).*

0 kilometres   100

0 miles   50

◁ **Vines and citrus trees growing along Campania's scenic Costiera Amalfitana (Amalfi Coast)**

The Museo Archeologico Nazionale in Naples is one of Italy's most important museums. It houses the treasures of Pompeii, including sculptures, vases and everyday artifacts which provide a detailed glimpse of Roman life (see pp474–5).

ABRUZZO, MOLISE AND PUGLIA
(See pp484–497)

Molise

NAPLES AND CAMPANIA
(See pp466–483)

Museo Archeologico Nazionale

Puglia

Pompeii

Basilicata

Santa Croce

BASILICATA AND CALABRIA
(See pp498–505)

Pompeii's Roman ruins include streets, houses and an amphitheatre (see pp478–9).

Calabria

The church of Santa Croce in Lecce is an excellent example of the exuberant Lecce Baroque style, from its elaborate rose window to the intricately carved capitals (see pp496–7).

Mount Etna

SICILY
(See pp506–527)

Mount Etna, one of the world's largest volcanoes, is still active, with lava erupting from fissures that dot its flanks. The nearby city of Catania has suffered repeatedly from volcanic damage (see p523).

Regional Food: Southern Italy

S OUTHERN ITALIAN FOOD is as varied as the landscape, each region having its own specialities.
While pasta, for example, is eaten throughout
Italy, nothing matches the handmade *orecchiette*
of Puglia. Think of Naples, and wafer-thin
pizza springs to mind. Sicilian food is
both rustic and voluptuous. Across the
south, the dishes are enlivened with
seafood, fruity green olive oil and dry
white wine and, together with fresh green
vegetables and huge, bursting tomatoes, account for
one of the most enviably healthy diets in Europe.

**Dried
chillies**

*Some of Italy's best olives
come from Puglia. Green and
black olives may be served
in piquant oil and garlic.*

**Grilled
swordfish**

Squid   **Anchovies**

*A dish of simply cooked
seafood* (frutti di mare) *may
also contain mussels* (cozze),
oysters (ostriche), *prawns*
(gamberetti) *or octopus*
(polpi) – *moistened
with olive oil and a
dash of lemon juice to
enhance the flavours.*

Prawns

Roasted red pepper

**Char-grilled
courgette**

**Grilled
tuna**

Lobster   **Mussels**

*Sliced vegetables
brushed with olive oil
and lightly grilled are
often served as an
antipasto* (appetizer).

*Pizza Napoletana
is a simple thin pizza
topped with tomato, garlic,
basil and anchovies.*

**Marinated
artichoke
hearts**

**Char-grilled
aubergine**

Maccheroncini con le sarde,
*a Sicilian classic, contains sar-
dines, fennel, raisins, pine nuts,
breadcrumbs and saffron.*

Pesce spada (swordfish steak),
*grilled or pan-fried with lemon
and oregano, is a favourite in
Campania, Puglia and Sicily.*

Agnello arrosto *(juicy roast
lamb) is a Sardinian speciality,
roasted on a spit or in casseroles
with rosemary and thyme.*

Sicilian cassata is ice cream made with ricotta cheese, candied fruit, pistachios, sugar and chocolate in a sponge cake.

Nougat is a sweet Sardinian speciality that can be made simply with nuts, or flavoured with chocolate.

Cannoli

Sicilian almond biscuits

Many biscuits and cakes are made in honour of a religious festival or saint's day. They might be deep-fried in oil, soaked in honey, encrusted with almonds or stuffed with ricotta, like the tube-shaped cannoli *biscuits much favoured in Sicily.*

TYPICAL SOUTHERN SEASONINGS

The food of the south is simple but often served with aromatic herbs like oregano, rosemary, basil, mint, sage and thyme, as well as garlic, capers, sundried tomatoes, anchovies and sardines.

Rosemary

Oregano   **Capers**

Sardines   **Sundried tomatoes**

SOUTHERN CHEESES

Cheese exists in almost infinite varieties. Delicate mozzarella di bufala, made with buffalo milk, is delicious eaten on its own. Scamorza, a similar spun cheese, is exceptional – especially from Basilicata. It is also served smoked. Hard-textured Provolone can be mild or piquant, while ricotta, from sheep's milk, is creamy.

Provolone   **Scamorza**

Ricotta   **Mozzarella**   **Smoked Scamorza**

WINE

The south's sunny hillsides have produced wine since the Bronze Age. Puglia produces more wine than any other region in Italy, and Sicily boasts some of the south's finest wines. Good producers include Regaleali, Rapitalà, Corvo and Donnafugata. Marsala, a classic dessert wine also from Sicily *(see p518)*, was devised in the 18th century and made famous by Admiral Nelson. Pellegrino is an excellent producer.

Sicilian white wine   **Sweet Marsala**

OLIVE OIL

Some of the finest olive oils *(olio di oliva)* in Italy come from the south. The words *extra vergine* (extra virgin) refer to the pure, unblended oil from the first pressings of the olives. A variation is chilli oil *(olio santo)*, soaked with red chilli peppers, resulting in a rich, spicy oil with a red hue.

Chilli oil (Olio santo)   **Olive oil (Olio di oliva)**

Understanding the Architecture of Southern Italy

THE ROMANESQUE STYLE of southern Italy owes much to the Normans, who in the 11th century brought from France both form and style in architecture and sculpture. In the southeast, the style has hefty Byzantine overtones; in Sicily it is characterized by strong traditional Islamic motifs and a love of rich colour, pattern and ornamentation. These elements surface later in Sicily's Baroque style and are allied to a dynamism that originates in the Baroque of

Baroque carving on Bagheria's Villa Palagonia

Rome – though in Sicily it is more vivacious. Neapolitan Baroque is more sophisticated and displays a greater interest in the creative use of space.

BYZANTINE AND ROMANESQUE FEATURES

Lateral towers

Interlacing arches

Multicoloured marble

Glass and plaster mosaics on gold

Rich ornamentation

Interlacing arches

Cefalù, *begun in 1131 by Roger II, is one of Sicily's great Norman cathedrals (see p519). Its west front exhibits many northern Romanesque features, such as the massive towers.*

Christ Pantocrator, *a Byzantine apse mosaic (c.1132), adorns the Cappella Palatina (see p510).*

The east end *of the Norman cathedral of Monreale, founded in 1172 by William II, is built of multicoloured materials with interlacing arches (see pp514–15).*

BAROQUE FEATURES

Massive scale of stairway

Sweeping view down corridor

Bold statue of lion

Lifelike putti

Brilliant realism of drapery

Caserta's Palazzo Reale, *a sumptuous royal palace begun by Charles III in 1752, is characterized by its monumental scale (see p480). The richly decorated interior is prefaced by several huge entrances and impressive staircases offering views. The enormous building was designed by Luigi Vanvitelli.*

Giacomo Serpotta's *stucco reliefs (c.1690) in Palermo's Oratorio di Santa Zita illustrate Sicilians' love of exuberant decoration (see p513).*

WHERE TO SEE THE ARCHITECTURE

The best places to see Romanesque architecture are Puglia and the cathedral cities of northwestern Sicily. Puglia's best churches are those at Trani *(see p493)* and nearby Canosa, Molfetta and Bitonto; Ruvo di Puglia *(p494)*, San Leonardo di Siponto on the Gargano Peninsula and Martina Franca, near Alberobello. The Baroque style of the south is epitomized by the villas, palaces

The Duomo portal in Ruvo di Puglia

and churches of Naples and Sicily, and by the deeply encrusted ornamentation found on church façades in Lecce *(pp496–7)*, in Puglia. In Sicily, the Baroque of Palermo *(pp510–13)*, Bagheria *(p516)*, Noto, Modica and Ragusa *(p527)* and Siracusa *(pp526–7)* is well known. Less so are churches at Piazza Armerina *(p521)*, Trapani *(p516)*, Palazzolo Acreide, close to Siracusa, and Acireale, near Catania.

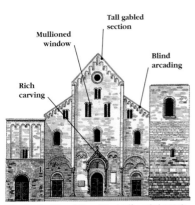

Rich carving · **Mullioned window** · **Tall gabled section** · **Blind arcading**

Bari's Basilica di San Nicola *(founded 1087) was the model for subsequent churches in Puglia (see p494). Based on Norman architecture, its façade is flanked by towers and divided vertically into three, reflecting the tripartite nature of its plan.*

Half columns · **Rose window** · **Blind arcading**

The façade of Troia cathedral *(1093–1125) owes its design to Pisan architecture and its rich ornamentation to Byzantine and Arab models (see pp492–3).*

Carved scroll · **Protruding columns**

The façade *of Siracusa's Duomo, begun in 1728 by Andrea Palma, is animated by broken or curved elements (see pp526–7).*

Three-tiered structure · **Central bell tower** · **Curved surface**

San Giorgio in Ragusa *(1744) has a façade by Gagliardi with layers of ornamentation culminating in the tower (see p527).*

Stone-carved decoration

Lecce's Chiesa del Rosario *(begun 1691) was built by Lo Zingarello of soft local sandstone in the Lecce Baroque style of profuse carving (see pp496–7).*

The Ancient Greeks in Southern Italy

SOME OF THE BEST ruins of the ancient Greek world are in Southern Italy. Syracuse, Selinunte, Segesta and Gela are among the better known Sicilian sites while those on the mainland include Croton, Locri and Paestum. Magna Graecia is the collective name given to these scattered colonies of ancient Greece, the earliest of which were founded in the Naples area in the 11th century BC. Many great figures of the age – including Pythagoras, Archimedes and Aeschylus – lived in these far-flung settlements, and it was here that the ancient winemaker's art flourished. Artifacts from this age are exhibited in the excellent archaeological museums of Naples, Syracuse and Taranto.

Ancient Herakleia (Herculaneum) was named after its patron deity, the mighty Hercules. It was buried by the eruption of Mount Vesuvius in AD 79 (see p479).

KYME
Cuma

NEAPOLIS
Napoli

HERAKLEI
Ercolano

POSEIDONIA
Paestum

EL
Ve

Poseidonia (today's Paestum), was the city of Poseidon, God of the Sea. Its ruins, dating from the 6th century BC, include the hulks of two of the finest Doric temples in Europe (see pp482–3).

Mount Etna was believed to be the forge of Hephaistos (Vulcan) – God of Fire – or the Cyclops, the one-eyed giant (see p523).

Tyndaris was one of the last Greek cities founded on Sicily.

LIPARA
Lipari

TYNDARI
Tindar

PANORMOS
Palermo

SOLUS
Soluto

ERYX
Erice

EGESTA
Segesta

HIMERA
Himera

Eryx, founder of the town, was the son of Aphrodite and Poseidon.

SELINUS
Selinunte

Valley
of the
Temples

HENNA
Enna

KATA
Cata

MEGARA HYBLA
Meg

The legendary founder of Agrigento was Daedalus, who created wings for himself and his son, Icarus, so they could fly.

AKRAGAS
Agrigento

GELA
Gela

Mus
Archeolog
Region
Paolo O

Gela was prosperous under the rule of Hippocrates in the 5th century BC.

Egesta (built 426–416 BC) was colonized by the Elymians who may have originated at Troy. Among the ruins of this town are a half-completed temple and a theatre (see p518). Ancient Greeks used theatres for plays and cultural entertainment rather than combat.

0 kilometres   100

0 miles   50

Aeschylus, the dramatist, died in Gela in 456. Considered the father of Greek tragedy, his plays include Seven Against Thebes, Women of Aetna and Prometheus Bound.

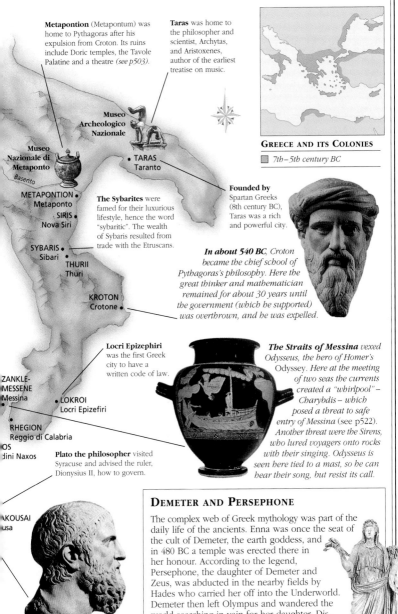

Metapontion (Metapontum) was home to Pythagoras after his expulsion from Croton. Its ruins include Doric temples, the Tavole Palatine and a theatre *(see p503)*.

Taras was home to the philosopher and scientist, Archytas, and Aristoxenes, author of the earliest treatise on music.

Museo Archeologico Nazionale

Museo Nazionale di Metaponto

• TARAS Taranto

METAPONTION • Metaponto

The Sybarites were famed for their luxurious lifestyle, hence the word "sybaritic". The wealth of Sybaris resulted from trade with the Etruscans.

SIRIS • Nova Siri

SYBARIS • Sibari

THURII Thurii

KROTON Crotone •

ZANKLE-MESSENE Messina •

• LOKROI Locri Epizefiri

RHEGION Reggio di Calabria

dini Naxos

AKOUSAI usa

GREECE AND ITS COLONIES

☐ *7th–5th century BC*

Founded by Spartan Greeks (8th century BC), Taras was a rich and powerful city.

In about 540 BC, Croton became the chief school of Pythagoras's philosophy. Here the great thinker and mathematician remained for about 30 years until the government (which he supported) was overthrown, and he was expelled.

Locri Epizephiri was the first Greek city to have a written code of law.

The Straits of Messina *vexed Odysseus, the hero of Homer's Odyssey. Here at the meeting of two seas the currents created a "whirlpool" – Charybdis – which posed a threat to safe entry of Messina (see p522). Another threat were the Sirens, who lured voyagers onto rocks with their singing. Odysseus is seen here tied to a mast, so he can hear their song, but resist its call.*

Plato the philosopher visited Syracuse and advised the ruler, Dionysius II, how to govern.

The mathematician and inventor, Archimedes, was born in Syracuse c.287 BC. His inventions included the famous Archimedean screw, and various weapons to stave off the Romans (see pp526–7).

DEMETER AND PERSEPHONE

The complex web of Greek mythology was part of the daily life of the ancients. Enna was once the seat of the cult of Demeter, the earth goddess, and in 480 BC a temple was erected there in her honour. According to the legend, Persephone, the daughter of Demeter and Zeus, was abducted in the nearby fields by Hades who carried her off into the Underworld. Demeter then left Olympus and wandered the world searching in vain for her daughter. Discovering that Zeus had allowed the abduction to happen, Demeter put a blight on Sicily: it would remain barren until Persephone returned. Finally Hades allowed her return from the Underworld, but only for a few months of each year – from spring to autumn. Demeter, satisfied with the result, ensured that Sicily became the most fertile place on earth.

Sculpture of Persephone

NAPLES AND CAMPANIA

THE CAPITAL OF CAMPANIA, *Naples is one of the few European cities of the ancient world that has never been completely extinguished. Founded by Greeks, it was embellished and enlarged by the Romans and in subsequent centuries was the much-prized booty of foreign invaders and Imperialists – most prominently the Normans, Hohenstaufen, French and Spanish.*

Naples today is a chaotic yet spectacular metropolis sprawling noisily and dirtily around the edge of the beautiful Bay of Naples. To one side is Mount Vesuvius; facing from the sea are the pretty islands of Capri, Ischia and Procida. Pompeii and Herculaneum, lying in the shadow of the volcano that destroyed them, contain the most revealing Roman ruins in Italy.

For centuries Naples has dominated the Italian south – the *Mezzogiorno*, or land of the midday sun. Unemployment, poverty and crime are a problem – Camorra-related crime is as deep-seated here as the Mafia is in Sicily – but there is also an attractive, rude ebullience.

The ancient history of Campania is linked to the Etruscans and the Greeks, whose gigantic ruins can be seen at Paestum. Next came a time of great prosperity under the Romans; archaeological evidence of this still exists at Benevento, Santa Maria Capua Vetere and Pozzuoli.

The hinterland, with its rich, well-cultivated plains, is eclipsed by the Amalfi coastline with its breathtaking views and the dramatic seaboard of the Cilento. The mountainous interior, remote and unvisited, contains small towns that were settled by the Greeks, developed by the Romans and often abandoned in the wake of malaria and Saracen attacks.

A glimpse into the narrow streets of Naples' Quartieri Spagnoli (Spanish Quarter)

◁ The old fishing quarter on the island of Procida in the Bay of Naples

Exploring Naples and Campania

THE MAIN CENTRE FROM WHICH to explore Campania is the anarchic metropolis of Naples (Napoli). To the north, verdant plains sweep down to Santa Maria Capua Vetere. To the east is the lonely, mountainous province of Benevento. Tragic, earthquake-ravaged Avellino and its province lurk on a plain beyond Vesuvius. The northern coastline is not as enticing as the Roman ruins lining it at such places as Cuma. The Costiera Amalfitana, south of Naples, is stunning. Beyond the tip of the Sorrentine Peninsula and along the Cilento coast there is good swimming, as on Capri, Ischia and Procida in the Gulf of Naples.

SIGHTS AT A GLANCE

Benevento **5**
Capri **9**
Caserta **4**
Costiera Amalfitana **6**
Ischia and Procida **10**
Naples (Napoli) pp470–77 **1**
Paestum **8**
Pompeii pp478–9 **2**
Salerno **7**
Santa Maria Capua Vetere **3**

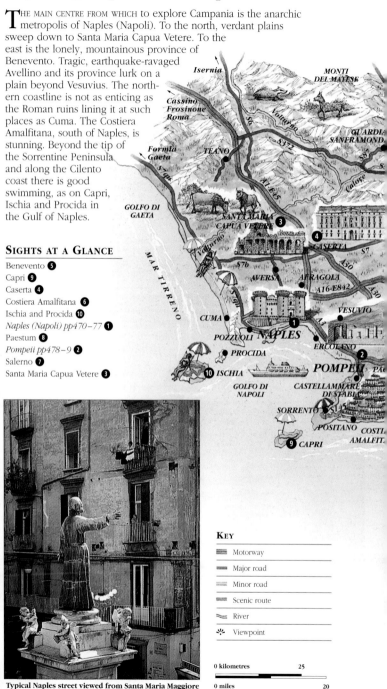

Typical Naples street viewed from Santa Maria Maggiore

KEY

▰▰▰	Motorway
▰▰▰	Major road
▰▰▰	Minor road
▰▰▰	Scenic route
≈≈	River
☼	Viewpoint

0 kilometres   25

0 miles   20

View of the Costiera Amalfitana from the hilltown of Ravello

GETTING AROUND

Northern Campania is easily accessible from Naples on the A1. The A16 heads east towards Puglia. Salerno and the Cilento can be reached on the A3. Branching off the A3, the S18 heads deep into the Cilento. To reach its coast, take the S267. The villages of the Costiera Amalfitana (Amalfi coast) lie along the scenic S163, accessed via the S145. The islands of Capri, Ischia and Procida are accessible by boat from Mergellina and the Molo Beverello in Naples, Sorrento, Positano, Amalfi and Salerno. Campania's main towns and sights are linked by railway. The bus service is comprehensive but infrequent in the interior of the Cilento.

SEE ALSO

Naples ❶

THE COMPACT CENTRE of Naples, filled with palaces, churches, convents and monasteries, revolves around just a few streets. From the Piazza del Plebiscito, Via Toledo (also called Via Roma) proceeds north towards Piazza Dante. To the east, narrow Via del Tribunale and Via San Biagio dei Librai penetrate the historic and noisy heart of the

San Gennaro, protector of Naples

View of the Bay of Naples and Mount Vesuvius

city, the *Spaccanapoli* (split Naples). South of Palazzo Reale is the Santa Lucia district. To the west is the port of Mergellina and overlooking the city is the Vomero district.

Exploring Northeast Naples

Many of the city's gems of art and architecture can be found here, including the Museo Archeologico Nazionale and its Roman treasures from Herculaneum and Pompeii. The buildings provide a wide range of architectural styles from the French-Gothic of the Duomo to the Florentine-Renaissance style of the Porta Capuana.

Tomb of Ladislas, San Giovanni a Carbonara

Renaissance monuments, including Marco and Andrea da Firenze's masterpiece, the Tomb of Ladislas, behind the church's high altar. Built to house the body of King Ladislas of Naples (1386–1414), who enlarged the church, the tomb is a three-storey confection of statues and arches topped by an equestrian figure.

🏠 San Giovanni a Carbonara

Via Carbonara 5. ☏ 081 29 58 73.
◯ 8am–noon, 4:30–8:30pm Mon–Sat, 8am–2pm Sun.
A great and rare success story in the annals of Neapolitan building restoration, San Giovanni a Carbonara (built 1343) is open again after suffering damage in 1943, long closure and pitiful neglect. Within are glorious medieval and

The beautiful Renaissance gate of Porta Capuana

⚜ Castel Capuano and Porta Capuana

Piazza Enrico de Nicola.
Begun by Norman King William I and completed by Frederick II, Castel Capuano was a royal palace until 1540, when it became the Court of Justice. Today it functions as a courthouse.
Nearby, between the Aragonese towers of the Capua Gate and facing a market, is a rare sculpture in the Florentine-Renaissance manner. Created by Giuliano da Maiano (and finished in 1490 by Luca Fancelli) as a defensive gate, Porta Capuana is perhaps Italy's finest Renaissance gateway.

0 metres　　250
0 yards　　　250

SIGHTS AT A GLANCE

KEY

M	Metro station
▦	Funicular
ℹ	Tourist information
✝	Church

Interior of the Duomo

✝ Duomo

Via Duomo 147. ☎ 081 44 90 97. ○ daily (Sun: am only).
Built between 1294 and 1323, the Duomo of San Gennaro lies behind a mostly 19th-century façade. The nave is lined with ancient columns, and there is an array of monuments to past rulers, along with paintings by Lanfranco and Domenichino.

The Duomo houses the relics of San Gennaro, patron saint of Naples (martyred AD 305). The ornate Cappella San Gennaro holds his head, within a silver-gilt bust, and phials of his congealed blood, which miraculously liquefies three times a year (on the first Sunday in May, 19 Sep and 16 Dec). According to tradition, if the blood should fail to liquefy, the city will have bad luck. The Cappella Carafa, a Renaissance masterpiece built from 1497 to 1506, contains the saint's tomb.

Accessible from the Duomo's north aisle is the Basilica di Santa Restituta, founded in the 4th century on the site of a former Temple of Apollo, and rebuilt in the 14th century. It has ceiling paintings by Luca Giordano (1632–1705) and a 5th-century baptistry.

VISITORS' CHECKLIST

▦ 1,300,000. ✈ Capodichino 4 km (2.5 miles) NW. ▥ Centrale, P. Garibaldi. ▦ P. Garibaldi. ⚓ Stazione Marittima, Molo Beverello & Mergellina. ℹ P. del Gesù Nuovo (081 551 27 01), Stazione Centrale. ○ daily. ⚑ San Gennaro: 19 Sep. Ⓦ www.inapoli.it

✝ Monte della Misericordia

Via Tribunali 253. ☎ 081 44 69 44. ○ 9am–12:45pm Mon–Sat (gallery open Tue, Thu & Sat. Adm charge).
The 17th-century octagonal church belonging to this charitable foundation houses Caravaggio's huge *Seven Acts of Mercy* (1607). The art gallery houses important works of art including paintings by Luca Giordano and Mattia Preti.

✝ Cappella Sansevero

Via Francesco de Santis 19. ☎ 081 551 84 70. ○ Wed–Mon (only am on Sun). ▦ ∅ ♿ (to church only.)
This small 16th-century chapel is the burial sepulchre of the Princes of Sangro di Sansevero. It possesses both Christian and Masonic symbolism, giving the chapel an unusual character.

Remarkable 18th-century sculpture fills the chapel. Antonio Corradini's ironic *Modesty* is a voluptuous female, carefully veiled. *The Resurrection of the Prince*, by an unknown artist, is mirrored by that of Christ, above the altar. Giuseppe Sammartino's *The Dead Christ* is an alabaster figure beneath a marble veil, and is a work of breathtaking technical virtuosity.

Eccentric Prince Raimondo, an 18th-century alchemist, is associated with the chapel. He performed gruesome experiments on human bodies, for which he was excommunicated. The results of some of his experiments can be seen in the crypt.

Sammartino's *The Dead Christ* (1753) in the Cappella Sansevero

Exploring Central Naples

THE PART OF SANTA LUCIA bordered by Via Duomo to the east, Via Tribunali to the north, Via Toledo (Roma) to the west and the water to the south, is the old heart of Naples. Especially rich in 14th- and 15th-century churches, the area offers visitors an abundance of sights.

Interior of San Gregorio Armeno

🏛 San Lorenzo Maggiore
Via Tribunali 316. ☎ 081 45 49 48.
Church ◯ 9am–5pm Mon–Sat,
9:30am–1:30pm Sun and pub hols.
🅿 🚹 Excavations ◯ as above.
This mainly 14th-century Franciscan church (with an 18th-century façade) was built during the reign of Robert the Wise of Anjou. The storyteller Giovanni Boccaccio (1313–75) reputedly based the character Fiammetta on King Robert's daughter Maria, whom he

The simple Gothic interior of San Lorenzo Maggiore, looking down the nave to the apse

saw here on Easter Eve, 1334. For Naples, San Lorenzo Maggiore is a rare Gothic edifice. Its nave and the apse ambulatory have a magnificent period simplicity. The church houses medieval tombs including the Gothic tomb of Catherine of Austria, who died in 1323, by a pupil of Giovanni Pisano. Excavations in the monastic cloister, where the lyric poet and scholar Petrarch (see p153) once stayed, have found the remains of a Roman basilica. There are also important Greek and medieval excavations.

🏛 San Gregorio Armeno
Via San G Armeno 1. ☎ 081 552 01 86. ◯ am daily.
Benedictine nuns still preside over this church. The convent attached to it earned a reputation for luxury since the nuns, traditionally from noble families, were accustomed to lavish living, which continued here. The sumptuous Baroque interior of the church sports frescoes by the prolific Luca Giordano. The cloister

is a haven in a neighbourhood noisy with vendors of Neapolitan crib figures *(presepi)*, whose many workshops line the Via San Gregorio Armeno.

🏛 Museo Filangieri
Palazzo Cuomo, Via Duomo 288.
☎ 081 20 31 75.
◯ for restoration. 🅿
The 15th-century Renaissance Palazzo Cuomo houses the Museo Filangieri. Founded in 1881, the original museum collections put together by Prince Gaetano Filangieri were destroyed during World War II. The new collection contains interesting and varied objects, including porcelain, embroidery, manuscripts, Italian and Spanish arms, objects from local archaeological excavations and paintings by such artists as Luca Giordano, Ribera and Mattia Preti.

🏛 Sant'Angelo a Nilo
Piazzetta Nilo. ☎ 081 551 62 27.
◯ am daily.

Renaissance tomb of Cardinal Brancaccio, Sant'Angelo a Nilo

This 14th-century church contains a fine work of Renaissance sculpture: the Tomb of Cardinal Rinaldo Brancaccio. Designed by Michelozzo, it was sculpted in Pisa, and then shipped to Naples upon completion in 1428. Donatello reputedly carved the right-hand angel drawing back the curtain, the shallow relief Assumption, and the cardinal's head.

🔒 San Domenico Maggiore

Piazza San Domenico Maggiore.

📞 081 45 91 88. ⭕ daily. ♿

This Gothic church (1289–1324) contains some of the finest Renaissance monuments and sculpture in Naples. The tomb slab of John of Durazzo (died 1335), by Tino da Camaino, is in the south transept. In the sacristy are the 18th-century *Apotheosis of Faith* ceiling frescoes by Solimena. The choir features a paschal candlestick (1585) supported by figures by da Camaino. The Cappellone del Crocifisso contains a medieval painting of the *Crucifixion*, which supposedly spoke to St Thomas Aquinas. The grand Brancaccio tomb by Jacopo della Pila (1492) is in the Chiesa Antica. Also of interest is the Cappella Saluzzo.

🔒 Santa Chiara

Via Benedetto Croce. ⭕ daily. ⬤ Sun pm. **Church** 📞 081 552 62 09.

🖼 ♿ **Cloister** 📞 081 797 12 56.

This 14th-century church was bombed in World War II, but a reconstruction uncovered the original Provençal-Gothic structure. The tombs of the Angevin monarchs are housed here. The tomb of Robert the Wise (died 1343) is by Giovanni and Pacio Bertini; that of Robert's son, Charles of Calabria (died 1328), is by Tino da Camaino, and the tomb of Charles' wife, Mary of Valois (died 1331) is by da Camaino and his followers. Adjacent is a convent with an Angevin cloister designed by Vaccaro (1742) and adorned with fine majolica tiles. There is also a museum of medieval art and a Roman bath house (AD 1).

🔒 Gesù Nuovo

Piazza del Gesù Nuovo 2.

📞 081 551 86 13. ⭕ daily.

The 16th-century Jesuit church was constructed by Valeriano (and later Fanzago and Fuga) from the Severini palace (15th century), of which only an embossed façade survives. The ebullient decoration of the interior (17th century) is fully in accordance with the needs of the Jesuits, who attracted the faithful through drama and direct appeal to the emotions. It is resplendent with coloured marble and paintings, including works by Ribera and Solimena. In 1688 an earthquake destroyed Lanfranco's dome – the present one is 18th-century.

Detail of the embossed façade of Gesù Nuovo

🔒 Sant'Anna e San Bartolomeo dei Lombardi

Via Monteoliveto. 📞 081 551 33 33.

⭕ Tue–Sat (due to restoration, only the Sacristy and the Pietà are open).

Also known as Santa Maria di Monteoliveto, this church was

Mazzoni's *Pietà* (1492) in Sant'Anna e San Bartolomeo dei Lombardi

built in 1411 and restored after World War II. It is a repository of Renaissance art. Entering, past the tomb (1627) of Domenico Fontana (who completed the dome of St Peter's in Rome after Michelangelo's death), the richness of the interior unfolds.

The Cappella Mastrogiudice contains an *Annunciation* panel by Florentine sculptor Benedetto da Maiano (1489) and the Cappella Piccolomini contains Antonio Rossellino's monument (c.1475) to Maria d'Aragona (completed by da Maiano). The Cappella del Santo Sepolcro houses a *Pietà* by Guido Mazzoni (1492). Its eight terracotta figures are considered life-size portraits of the artist's contemporaries. The old Sacristy, frescoed by Vasari (1544), has inlaid stalls by Giovanni da Verona (1510).

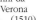

Majolica tiles decorated with scenes of rural life in the cloisters of Santa Chiara

Naples: Museo Archeologico Nazionale

THIS BUILDING, housing one of the world's most important archaeological museums, started life in the late 1500s as the home of the royal cavalry and was rebuilt in the early 17th century as the seat of Naples university. In 1777, when Ferdinand IV transferred the university to the former monastery of Gesù Vecchio, the building was again adapted to house the Real Museo Borbonico and library. In 1860 it became public property. The 1980 earthquake caused much damage to the collections. Major restoration and reorganization of exhibits continue but most areas of the museum are open on Sundays.

Spring Fresco
The fresco removed from the Villa Stabia in the Varano plain is a masterpiece of grace and elegance; the female figure rendered with soft, delicate colours.

Villa of the Papyri

Bust of "Seneca"
Found in the Villa dei Papiri in Herculaneum, this 1st-century BC bronze head was long thought to represent the philosopher Seneca the Elder (c.55 BC–AD 39). Today, however, its identity is less certain.

★ **The Battle of Alexander**
The splendid mosaic from the House of the Faun in Pompeii (see p478) depicts Alexander the Great's victory over Persian emperor Darius III (333 BC).

KEY

☐	Epigraphs
☐	Egyptian collection
☐	Engraved gems
☐	Sculptures
☐	Mosaics
☐	Numismatics
☐	Didactics
☐	Herculaneum & Pompeii
☐	Hall of the Sundial
☐	Prehistoric, Greek and Etruscan collections
☐	Non-exhibition space

The Secret Cabinet
The erotic works from Pompeii and Herculaneum housed here caused embarrassment at the time of the Bourbons. Today, however, they are available for public viewing. (Book ahead).

Blue Vase

This wine vessel found in a Pompeii tomb was made with the so-called glass-cameo technique: a layer of opaque white paste was placed over coloured glass and then engraved with decorative motifs.

VISITORS' CHECKLIST

P. Museo Nazionale 19. 081 564 89 41. M Piazza Cavour-Museo. C64, C83, E1, R1, R4, 24, 47, 110, 135. 9am–8pm Wed–Mon. 1 Jan, 25 Dec. W www.marketplace.it/museo.nazionale

Temple of Isis

Sacrifice of Iphigenia

In this Pompeiian fresco, Iphigenia, daughter of Agamemnon, is about to be sacrificed to Artemis, who saves her by taking a deer instead.

Stairs down to Egyptian Collection

★ Farnese Bull

Excavated in the Baths of Caracalla in Rome (see p427), this is the largest sculptural group (c.200 BC) to have survived from antiquity. The best-known piece in the Farnese Collection, it shows the punishment of Dirce who, having ill-treated Antiope, was tied to an enraged bull by the latter's sons.

Entrance

★ Farnese Hercules

Made by Glykon of Athens, this statue is an enlarged copy of a sculpture by the Greek master Lysippus. Napoleon is said to have regretted leaving it behind when he removed his booty from Italy in 1797.

STAR FEATURES

- ★ The Battle of Alexander
- ★ Farnese Hercules
- ★ Farnese Bull

Exploring Southeast Naples

THE AREA SOUTH of Via A Diaz is home to Naples' castles and royal palace as well as the densely populated Spanish Quarter. On the outskirts of the old town are a number of museums in historic buildings.

♟ Castel Nuovo

Piazza Municipio. 🄲 *081 420 12 41.*
🄾 *9am–7pm Mon–Sat (to 2pm Sun). Last adm: 6pm.* ● *some public hols.*
⚐ **Museo Civico** 🄾 *Mon–Sat.* 🄫

Also known as the Maschio Angioino, this Angevin fortress was built for Charles of Anjou in 1279–82. However, apart from the squat towers and the Cappella Palatina (with Francesco Laurana's *Madonna* of 1474 above the portal), most of the structure is Aragonese.

The castle was the main royal residence. In the Sala dei Baroni, Ferdinand I of Aragon brutally suppressed the ringleaders of the Baron's revolt of 1486. The Aragonese were capable of violence, but they were also patrons of the arts.

The triumphal arch of the castle's entrance (begun 1454) is theirs. Commemorating Alfonso of Aragon's entry to Naples in 1443, this ingenious application of the ancient triumphal arch design was worked on, at least in part, by Laurana. The original bronze doors by Guillaume le Moine (1468) are kept in the Palazzo Reale. Part of the building houses the **Museo Civico**.

The colourful and compact Quartieri Spagnoli

♞ Quartieri Spagnoli

Via Toledo (Roma) to Via Chiaia.
The Spanish Quarter – the neighbourhood west of Via Toledo, sloping up to San Martino and Vomero – is one of the city's most densely populated areas. It was named after the Spanish troops who laid out its grid of narrow streets in the 17th century. This is where the archetypal Neapolitan scene comes to life, in which laundry hung above the streets crowds out the sun. This area is lively by day, sinister by night.

🏛 Museo Nazionale di San Martino

Largo di San Martino 5.
🄲 *081 578 84 18.* 🄾 *8:30am–7:30pm Tue–Sun.* 🈴 🄫 ⚐ **Castel Sant'Elmo** 🄾 *8:30am–7:30pm daily.*
High above Santa Lucia, the Baroque Certosa di San Martino, founded in the 14th century as a Carthusian monastery, has great views of the Bay of Naples. It houses a museum that features a variety of *presepi*, Christmas cribs of Neapolitan tradition. The cloister was completed in 1623–9 by Cosimo Fanzago (the creator of Neapolitan Baroque) to the 16th-century designs of Dosio. The church and choir are other remarkable examples of his virtuosity.

Next to the Certosa, **Castel Sant'Elmo**, built from 1329–43 and rebuilt in the 1500s, offers stunning views over the bay.

🏛 Museo Principe di Aragona Pignatelli Cortes

Riviera di Chiaia 200. 🄲 *081 761 23 56.* 🄾 *9am–2pm Tue–Sun.* ● *1 Jan, 1 May, 15 Aug.* 🄫
The Neo-Classical Villa Pignatelli, once home to the Rothschilds, houses this museum and its interesting collection of porcelain, period furniture, paintings and sculpture.

The bold Castel Nuovo, with the triumphal arch entrance

🏛 Galleria Umberto I

Via Toledo. 🔘 *daily.*
Teatro San Carlo 🎭 *081 797 23 31*
(performance details); Tours: 10am–
3pm Tue–Sun (book in theatre shop).
🌐 *www.teatrosancarlo.it*

Once a focus for fashionable
Neapolitans, the handsome arcades of the Galleria Umberto I
were built in 1887 and rebuilt
after World War II. They face
Italy's largest and oldest opera
house: the **Teatro San Carlo**.
Built for Charles of Bourbon in
1737, and later rebuilt, its fine
auditorium once aroused
envy in the courts of Europe.

Painting of *Lavinia Vecellio* **(c.1540) by Titian in the Museo di Capodimonte**

**Magnificent glass-roofed interior
of the Galleria Umberto I**

🏛 Palazzo Reale

Piazza Plebiscito. **Museo** 🎭 *081 580*
81 11. 🔘 *9am–8pm daily (last adm: 1*
hr before closing). ⬛ *1 Jan, 1 May, 25*
Dec. 🖼 **Biblioteca** 🎭 *as above.*
🔘 *Tue & Thu.* ⬛ *public hols.*

Begun by Domenico Fontana
for the Spanish Viceroys in
1600, and expanded and
embellished by subsequent
residents, Naples' royal palace
is a handsome edifice with
great halls filled with furniture,
tapestries, paintings and porcelain. The small private Teatro
di Corte (1768) was built by
Ferdinando Fuga. The building

houses the Biblioteca Nazionale. The exterior of the palace
has been partly restored –
note the 19th-century statues
rep-resenting the dynasties of
Naples. The huge Piazza del
Plebiscito facing it has been
cleaned up and cleared of
traffic. The great colonnades
sweep towards 19th-century
San Francesco di Paola,
modelled on Rome's Pantheon.

🏛 Villa Floridiana

Via Cimarosa 77. 🎭 *081 229 21 10.*
🔘 *9am–2pm Tue–Sun.* **Park** 🔘 *daily.*
⬛ *1 Jan, 1 May, 15 Aug, 25 Dec.* 🖼

Set in handsome gardens,
this Neo-Classical villa houses
the **Museo Nazionale della
Ceramica Duca di Martina**
which is famous for its collection of ceramics, including
porcelain and majolica.

🏛 Museo di Capodimonte

Parco di Capodimonte. 🎭 *081 749*
91 11. 🔘 *8:30am–7:30pm Tue–*
Sun. 🖼

Begun in 1738 by the Bourbon
king Charles III as a hunting
lodge, the **Palazzo Reale di
Capodimonte** houses this
museum and its magnificent
collections of Italian paintings.

Included are works by Titian,
Botticelli, Raphael and Perugino, much of it originating
in the Farnese family
collections. There is also a
gallery of 19th-century art,
largely from southern Italy.

⛪ Catacombs of San Gennaro

Via di Capodimonte 16. 🎭 *081 741*
10 71. 🔘 *daily.* 🎫 *compulsory.* 🖼

These catacombs – the original
burial place of San Gennaro –
are located near the church of
San Gennaro in Moenia. The
small church was founded in
the 8th century, and is adjoined
by a 17th-century workhouse.
Two tiers of catacombs dating
from the 2nd century penetrate
the tufa, and there are mosaics
and early Christian frescoes.
Further along the street, the
Catacombs of San Gaudioso
commemorate the 5th-century
saint who founded a monastery on the spot. Above is the
17th-century church of Santa
Maria della Sanità.

♣ Castel dell'Ovo

Borgo Marinari. 🎭 *081 246 43 34.*
🔘 *9am–6pm Mon–Sat (to 2pm Sun).*

Away from the centre, this
castle, begun in 1154, occupies
a small island facing, and joining, the Santa Lucia district –
once the site of Naples'
shellfish market. Under the
Normans and Hohenstaufen
it was a royal residence, but
today it belongs to the army.

Beneath its ramparts, tiny
Porta Santa Lucia is filled with
seafood restaurants, and the
Via Partenope running past it
is a lovely promenade that
leads west to Mergellina.

The façade of the Palazzo Reale, Naples' royal palace

Pompeii ❷

A<small>N EARTHQUAKE IN</small> AD 62, which shook Pompeii and damaged many buildings, was merely a prelude to the tragic day in AD 79 when Mount Vesuvius erupted, burying the town in 6 m (20 ft) of pumice and ash. Although it was discovered in the 16th century, serious excavation began only in 1748, revealing a city petrified in time. In some buildings paintings and sculpture have survived, and graffiti is still visible on street walls.

Villa of the Mysteries

★ House of the Vettii
This partly reconstructed patrician villa of the wealthy merchants Aulus Vettius Conviva and Aulus Vettius Restitutus contains frescoes (see pp44–5).

Forum Baths

★ House of the Faun
This famous villa of the wealthy patrician Casii is named after its bronze statuette. The mosaic Battle of Alexander, in the Museo Archeologico Nazionale in Naples, originated here.

0 metres   100
0 yards   100

Forum

In the bakery
of Modesto, carbonized loaves of bread were found.

Sacrarium of the Lares
Close to the Temple of Vespasian, this building housed the statues of Pompeii's guardian deities, the Lares Publici.

STAR SIGHTS
★ House of the Vettii
★ House of the Faun

Macellum
Pompeii's market place was fronted by a portico with two money-changers' kiosks.

PLAN OF POMPEII

VIA DI NOLA

VIA DELL'ABBONDANZA

WESTERN
POMPEII

**Porta Marina
entrance**

**Piazza Anfiteatro
entrance**

☐ Area illustrated below

WESTERN POMPEII

This detailed illustration is of the western area, where the most impressive and intact Roman ruins are located. There are several large patrician villas in the eastern section, as wealthy residents built their homes outside the town centre.

However, much of eastern Pompeii awaits excavation.

Amphitheatre and sports ground

Teatro Grande

Via dell'Abbondanza

This was one of the original and most important roads through ancient Pompeii. Many inns lined the route.

VESUVIUS AND THE CAMPANIAN TOWNS

Nearly 2,000 years after the eruption of Mount Vesuvius, the Roman towns in its shadow are still being released from the petrification that engulfed them. Both Pompeii and Stabiae (Castellammare di Stabia), to the southeast of Naples and the volcano, were smothered by hot ash and pumicestone blown there by the wind. The roofs of the buildings collapsed under the weight of the volcanic debris. To the west, Herculaneum (Ercolano) vanished under a sea of mud. A large number of its buildings have survived, their roofs intact, and many domestic items were preserved by the mud. In all, about 2,000 Pompeiians perished but few, if any, of the residents of Herculaneum died.

In AD 79 Pliny the Elder, the Roman soldier, writer and naturalist, was the commander of a fleet stationed off Misenum (present-day Miseno, west of Naples) and with his nephew Pliny the Younger observed the impending eruption from afar. Eager to see this natural catastrophe closer to hand, Pliny the Elder proceeded to Stabiae, but was overcome by fumes and died. Based on

Pompeiian vase in Museo Nazionale Archeologico

reports by survivors, Pliny the Younger related the first hours of the eruption and his uncle's death in detail in two letters to the Roman historian Tacitus.

Much of our knowledge of the daily lives of the ancient Romans derives from the excavations of Pompeii and Herculaneum. Most of the artifacts from them as well as Stabiae are now in Naples' Museo Archeologico Nazionale *(see pp474–5)*, creating an outstanding collection.

Mount Vesuvius has not erupted since 1944, but occasional rumbles have caused minor earthquakes. Visitors can reach it by train to Castellammare di Stabia, or car. Useful websites include www. guidevesuvio.it and www.laportadelvesuvio.it

**Casts of a dyi[ng]
child in the m[...]**

Santa Maria Capua Vetere ❸

Caserta. 🏛 34,000. FS 🚌 ℹ
Piazza Reale, Caserta (0823 32 22 33).
🚊 *Thu & Sun.*

THIS TOWN boasts a 1st-century AD Roman **amphitheatre**, once Italy's largest after the Colosseum, with well-preserved tunnels beneath it. The town occupies the site of ancient Capua, an Etruscan city and then a flourishing centre during the Roman Empire. It was the scene of the revolt of the gladiators, led by Spartacus in 73 BC. A museum on site recreates the history of the gladiators. Nearby is a **Mithraeum** (2nd–3rd century) with well-preserved frescoes. Finds from the sites are shown in the **Museo Archeologico dell' Antica Capua** in Capua.

🏛 **Amphitheatre**
Piazza 1 Ottobre. 📞 0823 84 42 06.
🕐 *9am–1 hr before sunset Tue–Sun.*
🎫 *valid for* **Mithraeum** 🕐 *Tue–Sun.*
🏛 **Museo Archeologico dell' Antica Capua**
Via Roberto d'Angio 48, Capua. 📞 *0823 84 42 06.* 🕐 *9am–6pm Tue–Sun.* ⬤ *1 Jan, 1 May, 25 Dec.* 🎫

Tunnels under the amphitheatre in Santa Maria Capua Vetere

Caserta ❹

🏛 66,000. FS 🚌 ℹ *Piazza Reale (0823 32 22 33).* 🚊 *Wed & Sat.*

MAGNIFICENTLY OPULENT, the colossal **Palazzo Reale** dominates Caserta. Built for the Bourbon King Charles III, Italy's largest royal palace has over 1,000 rooms, grand apartments and several richly

A fountain in the gardens of the Palazzo Reale at Caserta

adorned royal apartments. It was designed by Luigi Vanvitelli and construction started in 1752. The vast surrounding park boasts fountains, ornamental waterworks, statuary and a lovely English Garden.

ENVIRONS: The little medieval town of **Caserta Vecchia** lies 10 km (6 miles) to the northeast. Its 12th-century cathedral is a fine example of southern Norman architecture. **San Leucio**, 3 km (2 miles) northwest of Caserta, is a model town built by Ferdinand IV. Its thriving silk industry was also founded by the king.

🏛 **Palazzo Reale**
Piazza Carlo III. 📞 *0823 44 80 84.* 🕐 *8:30am–7pm Tue–Sun.* ⬤ *1 Jan, 25 Dec.* 🎫 ♿ **Park** 🕐 *8:30am–1 hr before sunset daily.*

Benevento ❺

🏛 62,000. FS 🚌 ℹ *Piazza Roma 11 (0824 31 99 38).* 🚊 *Fri & Sat.*
🌐 *www.eptbenevento.it*

BENEVENTO, set in a lonely, mountainous province, is home to one of southern Italy's most interesting ancient Roman monuments: the **Arch of Trajan** on Via Traiano. The Roman city, Beneventum, was an important centre. It stood at the end of the first extension of the Via Appia from Capua, and the Arch was erected across the old road in honour of Trajan. Built from AD 114–166 of marble, it is extremely well preserved. The relief sculpture adorning it – scenes from the life of Trajan and mythological subjects – is in excellent condition.

Elsewhere, evidence of the Romans is to be found in the ruined **Roman theatre**, built during Hadrian's reign, and in the **Museo del Sannio**, which contains artifacts from the region, from ancient Greek finds to modern art.

During World War II, the city stood directly in the way of the Allied advance from the south. It was heavily bombed, hence its largely modern appearance today. The Duomo, a 13th-century building reconstructed after the war, has a sculpted façade that, though badly damaged, has since been restored. The remains of its Byzantine bronze doors are within. The town has centuries-old associations

The ornate 2nd-century Roman arch in Benevento, built to honour Trajan

with pagan worship, and a liqueur called Strega (witch) is made here.

⋔ Roman Theatre

Piazza Caio Ponzio Telesino. **▐** 0824 299 70. *Large groups should book in advance.* ◯ *9am–1 hr before sunset daily.* ● *public hols.* ▨ ♿

🏛 Museo del Sannio

Piazza Matteotti. **▐** 0824 218 18. ◯ *9am–1pm Tue–Sun.* ● *1 Jan, 25 Dec.* ▨ ♿

Costiera Amalfitana ❻

Salerno. ▭ ⛴ *Amalfi.* ℹ *Via Roma 19/21, Amalfi (089 87 11 07).* Ⓦ *www.amalfitouristoffice.it*

The small town of Atrani on the Costiera Amalfitana

THE MOST enchanting and most visited route in Campania is that skirting the southern flank of Sorrento's peninsula: the Costiera Amalfitana (Amalfi Coast). Popular pleasures here include dining on grilled fish and sipping Lacrima Christi from the vineyards on the slopes of Vesuvius, beach-hopping and trips to coastal summits to admire the breathtaking views.

From **Sorrento**, a well developed holiday resort, the road winds down to **Positano**, a village clambering down a vertiginous slope to the sea. A top spot for the jet set, it is

nonetheless a good place to swim, or to catch the hydrofoil or ferry to Capri. Further on, **Praiano** is just as fashionable.

Amalfi is the coast's largest town. It was a maritime power before being subdued in 1131 by King Roger of Naples. The world's oldest maritime code, the *Tavole Amalfitane*, originated here. The 13th-century Chiostro del Paradiso flanks the Duomo, a magnificent 9th-century structure fronted by a rich, coloured façade (13th century), and facing the town from the top of a long flight of steps. The style is Lombard-Norman, though the cloisters have a Saracenic-inspired appearance. Amalfi is a tremendously popular resort.

Ravello has the best views on this coast, the prime vantage points being the gardens of Villa Cimbrone and Villa Rufolo. Views from the latter provided inspiration for Wagner's *Parsifal*. The 11th-century Duomo has entrance doors by Barisano da Trani (1179) and an ornate 13th-century ambo (pulpit) held aloft by six spiral columns. The chapel of San Pantaleone contains the blood of its 4th-century namesake, which liquefies annually in May and August.

Beyond **Atrani**, the ruins of a Roman villa at **Minori** show that this coastline has always been a popular holiday spot.

A breathtaking view of the steep village of Positano on the Costiera Amalfitana

Salerno ⓿

Salerno. **FS** 🚌 ⛴ *Salerno.*
ℹ️ *Piazza Ferrovia (089 23 14 32).*

S ALERNO IS A BIG, busy port.
Here the Allies landed in
1943, leaving in their wake a
much bombed, ruinous city.
Once famous for its School of
Medicine (12th century), it is
visited today for its **Duomo**,
an 11th-century structure built
on a 10th-century foundation.
Its best feature is the Atrium,
whose columns came from
nearby Paestum. In the crypt is
the Tomb of St Matthew, which
was brought here in 954.

The **Museo Diocesano** is
home to most of the cathedral
treasures, including an 11th-
century ivory altar-front called
the Paliotto. Before wandering
off down the bustling Corso
Vittorio Emanuele, visit the
Museo Provinciale for local
archaeological finds.

ENVIRONS: The **Cilento** is a
mountainous region south of
Salerno with a remote interior
and a lovely, quiet coastline
that is only slightly more
populous. Among the towns
along the coast, **Agropoli** is a
busy little seaside resort 42 km
(25 miles) south of Salerno.
Outside Castellammare di Velia,
a further 28 km (17 miles) to
the southeast, are the ruins
of the Greek town of **Elea**
(founded 6th century BC),
once famous for its school
of philosophy. It was much
visited by the Romans –
Cicero was here and Horace
came on his doctor's orders
to undergo a treatment of sea

bathing. Excavations have
revealed a magnificent 4th-
century Roman gateway: the
Porta Rosa, Roman baths, the
foundations of a temple and
the remains of the acropolis.

🏛 **Museo Diocesano**
Largo Plebiscito. **(** 089 23 91 26.
⬤ for restoration. 🎫 call for details.
🏛 **Museo Provinciale**
Via San Benedetto.
(089 23 11 35. 🕐 9am–6:30pm
Mon–Sat (to 1pm Sun).

The Temple of Hera I (left) and the Temple of Neptune at Paestum

Paestum ❽

Zona Archeologica. ℹ️ *Via Magna
Grecia 887.* **(** 0828 81 10 16. 🚌
from Salerno. **FS** Paestum. 🕐 9am–
1 hr before sunset daily. **Museum**
(0828 81 10 23. 🕐 9am–7pm
daily. ⬤ 1st & 3rd Mon of month, 1
Jan, 25 Dec. 🎫 ♿

T HIS IS THE MOST important
ancient Greek site south
of Naples in Campania. The
Greeks founded this city on

Capri ❾

Napoli. ⛴ Capri. ℹ️ Piazza Umberto I,
Capri (081 837 06 86). **Grotta Azzurra**
⛴ from Marina Grande. 🕐 in calm
sea. **Certosa** Via Certosa, Capri. **(**
081 837 62 18. 🕐 9am–2pm Tue–Sun.
♿ **Villa Jovis** Via Tiberio. 🕐 daily. 🎫

C APRI'S ENDURING reputation
as a sybaritic paradise is
nearly eclipsed by its notoriety
as a tourist trap. However, the
great views are unmarred by
the throng. The home of
emperors, seat of
monasteries,
place of

exile, former haunt of goats
and fishermen, its fortunes
changed during the 19th
century when English and
German expatriates discovered
its charms. Today it barely has
a "low season"; farmers run
little hotels, and fishermen
rent pleasure boats. Capri has
constant sunshine and enjoys
its well-deserved reputation
as a Garden of
Eden.

The busy port of Salerno

The Grotta Azzurra,
or the Blue Grotto,
is a cave bathed in
iridescent blue light
which can be reached
by tour boat from
Marina Grande.

Anacapri is Capri's
second town.

0 kilometres   1

0 miles   0.5

the edge of the Piana del Sele in the 6th century BC and called it Poseidonia, the City of Poseidon. The Romans renamed it in 273 BC. It fell into decline and was abandoned in the 9th century due to malaria and a Saracen assault and rediscovered in the 18th century.

Paestum has three massive Doric temples in an excellent state of repair: the **Basilica** or **Temple of Hera I** (mid-6th century BC); the **Temple of Neptune** (5th century BC), the largest and most complete at Paestum; and the **Temple of Ceres**, thought to date between its two neighbours.

Excavations have revealed the remains of the ancient city, its public and religious buildings, roads and protective walls. A **museum** contains the extensive finds from the site, including tomb paintings, tomb treasures, some terracotta votive offerings, architectural fragments and sculpture.

A view from the highest point of Procida, called Terra Murata

Ischia and Procida ❿

Napoli. 🚢 Ischia Porto & Procida Porto.
ℹ️ Via Sogliuzzo 72, Ischia (081 507 42 11). Via Roma, Procida (081 810 19 68).
La Mortella ☎ 081 98 62 20.
🕐 9am–7pm Tue, Thu, Sat–Sun.

ISCHIA IS THE BIGGEST island in the Bay of Naples and, with its beach resorts, thermal

springs and therapeutic mud baths, it is nearly as popular as its neighbour, Capri. Ferries dock at **Ischia Porto**, the harbour and modern part of the main town, **Ischia. Ischia Ponte**, the older part, is a short walk away. The northern and western shores are developed; the southern flank of the island is the quietest. Here, the village of **Sant'Angelo** is dominated by a long-extinct volcano, **Monte Epomeo**, whose summit of 788 m (2,585 ft) offers terrific views across the bay. Also worth a visit are the gardens of **La Mortella** in Forie.

The picturesque island of Procida – only 3.5 km (2 miles) long – is less visited by tourists and very tranquil. The swimming is good at **Chiaiolella** and, as at Ischia, there are inexpensive places to stay. The main town, also called **Procida**, is home to the main ferry port – the **Marina Grande**.

There are views towards Vesuvius and the Bay of Naples from the north of the island.

Capri is the main town on the island.

Marina Grande
This is Capri's main port of call for ferries from Naples and other ports on the Tyrrhenian coast. An array of colourful houses overlooks the harbour.

I Faraglioni

Marina Piccola is reached by dramatic Via Krupp.

Villa Jovis
Covering an enormous area, this was the Imperial villa from which Tiberius ruled the Roman Empire during his final years.

Certosa di San Giacomo
Founded in 1371 on the site of one of Tiberius's villas, this Carthusian monastery was suppressed in 1808 and is now in part a school. The distant rocks are I Faraglioni.

ABRUZZO, MOLISE AND PUGLIA

P UGLIA IS THE "HEEL" *of the Italian boot, the Gargano Peninsula is its "spur" and Abruzzo and Molise together form the "ankle". Hugging the southeastern seaboard of Italy and looking towards the Balkans, the mountainous regions of Abruzzo and Molise, united until 1963, differ considerably from Puglia, the richest of the three.*

Abruzzo and Molise are sparsely populated, quiet places where the wild landscape exerts a strong influence. Settled by various Apennine tribes in the Middle Bronze Age, the areas were later subdued by the Romans, united under the Normans in the 12th century and, thereafter, ruled by a succession of dynasties based in Naples. Abruzzo, dominated by the Apennines, is a brooding, introspective land of shepherds. Vertiginous drops preface the ascent to ramshackle hilltowns clinging to the sides of high mountains, semi-abandoned and poor. Molise's landscape is less dramatic. Legends of witches persist in both regions, as do strange fertility rites and rituals celebrating the changing seasons.

Puglia's advantage over its poverty-stricken neighbours is that it is nearly all flat and highly fertile. It produces the largest amounts of olive oil and wine in Italy, and its big cities – Lecce, Bari and Taranto – are lively commercial centres. The region experienced a long-lasting Greek influence, though the golden age of Puglia's past was under the rule of the Normans, followed by Frederick II who, between his return from Germany as emperor in 1220 and his death 30 years later, only spent four years away from here.

Puglia has glorious architecture, particularly in the churches and castles of the north. The curious *trulli* houses in central Puglia, the florid Baroque of Lecce and the Levantine atmosphere of its merchant cities complete the picture of an ancient land subject to more influences from outside the Italian peninsula than from within it.

Traditional dress worn in the town of Scanno in Abruzzo

◁ **The curious *trulli* buildings found in central Puglia, particularly around Alberobello and Locorotondo**

Exploring Abruzzo, Molise and Puglia

DOMINATED BY THE PROLIFIC Apennine mountain range, the hinterland of Abruzzo and Molise forms one of Italy's last wildernesses. At 2,912 m (9,554 ft), the highest peak is the Gran Sasso. Parts of Abruzzo are covered in endless tracts of forest. Molise is characterized by high plains, gentle valleys and lonely peaks. The spectacular Gargano Peninsula in Puglia (Apulia) has a lovely coastline. Reaching south is the fertile Tavoliere plain, and further south a series of upland plateaux (the Murge) descends towards the dry Salentine Peninsula and the Adriatic.

The exotic *trulli* houses in Alberobello in central Puglia

GETTING AROUND

Northern Abruzzo is well served by the A24 and A25–E80, and the S17 traverses the interior of Abruzzo and Molise. The coastal highway (A14–E55) heads south through Abruzzo and Molise into Puglia. Beyond Foggia, it joins the S16 to Taranto. Brindisi, the main port for Greece, is accessible from Bari or Taranto. The roads throughout are good. Train and bus services go to the major centres, with buses only to more remote parts.

0 kilometres   50

0 miles   25

KEY

- Motorway
- Major road
- Minor road
- Scenic route
- River
- Viewpoint

The coast at Vieste on the beautiful Gargano Peninsula in Puglia

Sights at a Glance

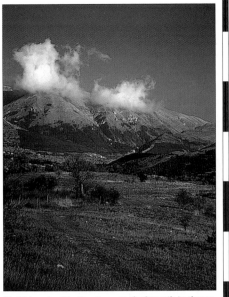

The high peaks of the Gran Sasso, north of L'Aquila in Abruzzo

**Lecce's exuberant Baroque architecture,
epitomized in Santa Croce's rose window**

See Also

The pink and white stone façade of Santa Maria di Collemaggio in L'Aquila

L'Aquila ❶

🏛 *70,000.* 🚆 🚌 🛈 *Via XX Settembre 10 (0862 223 06).* 🚢 *daily.* 🌐 *www.abruzzoturismo.it*

ABRUZZO'S CAPITAL lies at the foot of the **Gran Sasso**, at 2,912 m (9,554 ft) the highest point of the Italian mainland south of the Alps (and good for skiing). Its ancient streets are peppered with churches. The domed **Santa Giusta** (1257), off Via Santa Giusta, has a rose window and a *Martyrdom of St Stephen* (1615) by Cavalier d'Arpino. **Santa Maria di Paganica**, off Via Paganica, has a 14th-century façade and a carved portal. The **Duomo** (1257) in Piazza del Duomo was rebuilt in the 18th century. The massive church of **Santa Maria di Collemaggio**, on Piazza di Collemaggio, has a façade of pink and white stone. It was built in the 13th century by Pietro dal Morrone, who later became Pope Celestine V. In the chapel to the right of the apse is the tomb of the founder who, in 1313, was canonized as St Peter Celestine.

San Bernardino, on Via di San Bernardino, houses the tomb (1505) of San Bernardino of Siena. The church (built 1454–1472), has a façade (1527) by Cola dell'Amatrice and an 18th-century carved ceiling by Ferdinando Mosca.

Detail of Fontanelle delle Novantanove Cannelle in L'Aquila

The second chapel in the south aisle has an altarpiece by Andrea della Robbia, the Renaissance artist.

The medieval **Fontanelle delle Novantanove Cannelle** at the end of Via San Iacopo is a fountain commemorating the 99 villages that Frederick II supposedly united when he founded L'Aquila in 1240.

The **Museo Nazionale d'Abruzzo**, in the 16th-century castle, contains the remains of a prehistoric elephant, Roman artifacts and religious works.

ENVIRONS: North of L'Aquila are the ruins of a **theatre** and **amphitheatre** of ancient **Amiternum**, a Sabine then Roman town, and the birthplace of Sallust (86–c.35 BC), the Roman historian who helped to develop the monograph.

🏛 **Museo Nazionale d'Abruzzo**
Castello Cinquecentesco. 📞 *0862 63 31.* 🕐 *9am–8pm Tue–Sun.* ⬛ *1 May, 25 Dec.* 📷 ♿

Atri ❷

Teramo. 🏛 *11,000.* 🚌 🛈 *Mon.*

THE PRETTIEST in a series of small hilltowns in Abruzzo, Atri is a warren of stepped streets, alleys and passages bound by mostly brick and stone churches and houses. The 13th-century **Duomo**

occupies the site of a Roman bath; the crypt was once a swimming pool, and fragments of the original mosaic floor are visible in the apse. Also in the apse is Andrea Delitio's great 15th-century fresco cycle, in which he combined landscape and architecture in a variety of religious scenes from the Old and New Testaments. The cloister has views of the 15th-century brick campanile.

ENVIRONS: South of Atri is the hilltown of **Penne**. Street by street it is remarkably homogeneous with its buildings of reddish brick, which give the town a warm glow. East of Atri, **Loreto Aprutino** is known for the *Last Judgment* fresco (14th century) in Santa Maria in Piano.

Detail from 15th-century fresco by Andrea Delitio in Atri's Duomo

Sulmona ❸

L'Aquila. 🏛 *26,000.* 🚆 🚌 🛈 *Corso Ovidio 208 (0864 532 76).* 🚢 *Wed & Sat.* 🌐 *www.comune.sulmona.aq.it*

THIS TOWN is famous as the home of both Ovid and *confetti* (sugared almonds). After a wedding ceremony in Abruzzo, the happy couple is pelted with *confetti* as a wish of good fortune. Sulmona is filled with ancient buildings, especially along medieval **Via dell'Ospedale**, imparting a beguiling atmosphere. The palace of the **Annunziata** on

Corso Ovidio, was founded in 1320 and combines Gothic and Renaissance styles. The **Museo Civico** holds a collection of local antiquities, costumes, paintings and the work of goldsmiths formerly housed in the palace. The adjacent church of the **Annunziata**, with a robust Baroque façade, was rebuilt in the 18th century. Behind the church are 1 BC–AD 2 ruins of a Roman house.

At the end of Viale Matteotti is the cathedral of **San Panfilo**, built over a Roman temple. **San Francesco della Scarpa**, in Piazza del Carmine, has a 13th-century portal. Winding past it to the **Fontana del Vecchio** (1474) is an aqueduct that once fuelled local industry.

ENVIRONS: East of Sulmona is the Maiella National Park, a massif of 61 peaks and heavily forested valleys offering walking, bird-watching, climbing and skiing. To the west, Cocullo hosts the May Processione dei Serpari (Festival of Snakes) in which a statue of the patron saint, Domenico Abate, is draped with snakes and carried through the town. In the 11th century he is said to have rid the area of venomous snakes.

🏛 **Museo Civico**
☎ 0864 21 02 16. ☐ 10am–1pm Tue–Sun (also 4–7pm Sun).

OVID, THE LATIN POET

Born in 43 BC, Ovid (Publius Ovidius Naso) was Sulmona's most illustrious son. Not much survives here to remind you of his presence, however, apart from a **Corso Ovidio**, a 20th-century statue of him in Piazza XX Settembre and, just outside the town, a ruin traditionally known as **Ovid's Villa**. Known as one of the greatest poets of Classical Rome, his subjects included love *(Ars Amatoria)* and mythology *(Metamorphoses)*. In AD 8 he was banished into exile on the Black Sea, the far edge of the Roman Empire, after being implicated in a scandal of adultery with Julia, the granddaughter of Emperor Augustus *(see pp44–5)*. Ovid continued to write of his hardships, and died in exile in AD 17.

Scanno ❹

L'Aquila. 🚊 2,400. 🚌 ℹ P. Santa Maria della Valle 12 (0864 743 17). ☐ Tue. 🖥 www.scanno.org

WONDERFULLY well-preserved, this medieval hill-town set in beautiful, wild countryside is one of Abruzzo's most popular attractions. There are alleys and narrow flights of steps, oddly-shaped courtyards into which small churches have been pressed, and ancient mansions in whose windows women can be seen making lace or embroidery.

Traditional costume still worn in Scanno

In the shadow of Apennine peaks and beside lovely **Lago di Scanno**, the town is also a favoured stop on the way to the Parco Nazionale d'Abruzzo *(see pp490–91)*. The summer months are the busiest, with a variety of amusements from riding, boating and camping by the lake, to the August classical music festival. During the January Festa di Sant'Antonio Abate, a large lasagna is cooked outside **Santa Maria della Valle**, built on the remains of a pagan temple. The food is doled out on a first-come, first-served basis.

High Apennine peaks looming above the medieval hill-town of Scanno in Abruzzo

Parco Nazionale d'Abruzzo, Lazio e Molise ❺

THIS VAST PARK, inaugurated in 1922, has a rich landscape of high peaks, rivers, lakes and forests, and is one of Europe's most important nature reserves. Part of a royal hunting reserve until 1877, today it provides refuge for 66 species of mammal, 52 types of reptiles, amphibians and fish, and 230 species of bird, including the golden eagle and white-backed woodpecker, as well as over 2,000 varieties of flora. The park offers an extensive network of paths, and there are opportunities for riding, trekking and climbing.

Iris

Golden eagles may be seen near the Sangro river.

Young Chamois
Dense forests of beech and maple hide the Apennine chamois. There are also red and roe deer in the park.

Forests of beech and black pine provide beautiful scenery.

Pescasseroli
This town is a major centre for information on the area. It has good tourist facilities and a small zoological garden with animals living in the region, such as bears and wolves.

Apennine Wolves
The park guarantees protection for the Apennine wolf, and about 60 wolves survive here. The chances of seeing one, however, are fairly remote.

Marsican Brown Bear
Once hunted almost to extinction, between 80 and 100 brown bears now roam in the park.

VISITORS' CHECKLIST

L'Aquila. FS *Avezzano or Alfedena & then bus to Pescasseroli.*
Pescasseroli. **i** *Via Piave 2, Pescasseroli (0863 91 04 61).*
W *www.parcoabruzzo.it*

Horse Riding

Trekking is an excellent way to explore more remote areas of the park.

The Camosciara
is a spectacular area, home to many wild animals.

Lake Barrea

Created by the artificial damming of the River Sangro, this lake is surrounded by valleys and forests offering walking and pony trekking.

Dense Forests

Beech and maple forests, dotted with black hornbeam, ash, hawthorn, cherry, wild apple and pear, protect the once persecuted bears and wolves.

KEY

▬▬	Major road
▬▬	Minor road
▬ ▬	Walking path
❊	Viewpoint
i	Tourist information

0 kilometres   5

0 miles   5

Lanciano ❻

Chieti. 🏠 35,000. FS ▭
i *Piazza Plebiscito (0872 71 78 10).*
🏛 *Wed & Sat.*

LARGE PARTS of Lanciano's old nucleus remain from the Middle Ages. In the crumbling Civitanova quarter is the 13th-century church of **Santa Maria Maggiore**, with a magnificent 14th-century portal and a silver processional cross (1422). Also in this area is the now disused **San Biagio** (begun c.1059), near the 11th-century **Porta San Biagio** – a rare surviving town gate. The **Duomo** stands on the remains of a Roman bridge dating from the time of Diocletian. An underground passage links the bridge to the **Sanctuary of the Eucharistic Miracle**, where a host and wine that turned into live Flesh and Blood in the 8th century are kept. The Ripa Sacca (Jewish ghetto) was a busy commercial centre in the Middle Ages – the period of Lanciano's greatest prosperity. The hefty walls of the **Torri Montanara** were built then by the Aragonese as a bulwark against attack.

Isole Tremiti ❼

Foggia. ⛴ *San Nicola.* **i** *Via Perrone 17, Foggia (0881 72 36 50).*
W *http://tremiti.planetek.it*

OFF THE GARGANO coast, the Tremiti are the Italian islands least visited by foreigners. **San Domino** is the largest, with a sandy beach and coves. Here in AD 8, Julia, granddaughter of Augustus, was exiled for adultery and died in AD 28. The poet Ovid was allegedly involved (*see p489*). **Santa Maria a Mare**, in **San Nicola**, the administrative centre of the islands, is an abbey-fortress founded in the 8th century. It was turned into a prison in the late 1700s and ultimately became a detention centre for political prisoners, a role it maintained until 1945. Both islands are popular with Italians. The swimming is good, though the coastline of San Nicola is rocky.

The coast near Peschici on the Gargano Peninsula

Gargano Peninsula **8**

Foggia. **FS** **▭** **ℹ** *Piazza del Popolo 10, Manfredonia (0884 58 19 98).* **W** *www.parcogargano.it*

A HIGH, ROCKY SPUR jutting into the Adriatic Sea, the Gargano is a dramatic wilderness dotted with coves and cliffs. Its coastal towns of **Rodi Garganico**, **Peschici**, **Vieste** and **Manfredonia** are popular with holidaymakers. To the east lies the **Foresta Umbra**, a vast woodland of beech, oak, yew and pine, and to the north the salt lakes of **Lesina** and

Typical street scene in the town of Vieste on the Gargano Peninsula

Varano, havens for waterfowl. Plunging through the Gargano is an old pilgrim route (S272) from **San Severo** in the west to the shrine at **Monte Sant' Angelo** in the east. The first stop is **San Marco in Lamis**, which is dominated by a huge 16th-century convent. Further along, **San Giovanni Rotondo** is a focus for pilgrims in search of a cure from Padre Pio (1887–1968), a miracle-worker who is buried here. The last stop is **Monte Sant'Angelo** with its grotto where in 493, according to tradition, the Archangel Michael appeared to the Bishop of Sipontum.

To the south of Manfredonia, beside the ruins of the ancient town of Siponto, is the oriental-inspired 12th-century church of **Santa Maria di Siponto**.

Lucera **9**

Foggia. **👥** *35,000.* **▭** **ℹ** *Via Zuppetta 7 (0881 52 27 62).* **🛒** *Wed.*

THIS WAS ONCE a prosperous Roman colony and, on the northeast edge of town, the ruins of a Roman **amphitheatre** survive. Lucera was rebuilt in the 13th century by Frederick II, who peopled it with 20,000 Sicilian Muslims. It became one of the strongest fortresses in southern Italy, and its **castle** is one of Puglia's most magnificent. Built in 1233 by Frederick II, and enlarged

after 1269, its fortified wall of 900 m (2,953 ft) is interspersed with 24 towers. Of Frederick's original palace, only the base and some vaulting remains.

In 1300 Charles II, who massacred most of Lucera's Muslim population, began the **Duomo** on the site of their main mosque. The high, soaring nave is filled with 15th- and 16th-century frescoes and carvings.

The **Museo Civico Fiorelli** has displays of episodes from throughout Lucera's history.

🏛 Museo Civico Fiorelli
Via de Nicastri 44. **☎** *0881 54 70 41.* **⬤** *for restoration (call 0881 54 86 26).*

The remains of Lucera castle

Troia **10**

Foggia. **👥** *33,000.* **▭** **⬤** *1st & 3rd Sat of month.* **W** *www.pugliaturismo.com*

FOUNDED IN 1017 as a Byzantine fortress against the Lombards, Troia fell to the Normans in 1066. Until Frederick II destroyed it in 1229, the town had been ruled by a succession of powerful bishops who were responsible for producing many remarkable buildings, including Troia's **Duomo** *(see pp462–3).*

Begun in 1093 and constructed over the following 30 years, it exhibits an extraordinary diversity of styles. It successfully blends elements of Lombard, Saracenic and Byzantine style with that of the Pisan-Romanesque.

Elegant blind arcading distinguishes the Duomo's lower storey. The upper sections are characterized by powerfully carved sculpture – projecting lions and bulls. The upper façade displays a rose window with Saracenic-style detailing.

The main entrance, with bronze doors by Oderisio da Beneventano (1119), is dominated by carved capitals and an architrave, both Byzantine in style. Within the Duomo is a Romanesque pulpit (1169).

Trani ⓫

Bari. 🚗 55,000. 🚆 🚌
ℹ️ Palazzo Palmieri, Piazza Trieste 10 (0883 58 88 30). 🅿️ Tue.
🌐 www.pugliaturismo.com

DURING THE MIDDLE AGES this small, lively whitewashed port of Jewish origin bustled with mercantile activity and was filled with merchants and traders from Genoa, Amalfi and Pisa. It reached its peak of prosperity under Frederick II.

Today it is visited for its Norman **Duomo** in Piazza

The façade of Trani's Duomo

Duomo, built mainly from 1159 to 1186 over an earlier church whose predecessor, the Ipogei di San Leucio, dates from the 7th century. It is dedicated to St Nicholas the Pilgrim, a little-remembered miracle worker (died 1094) who was canonized as an act of rivalry against the town of Bari, which possessed the

bones of another, more memorable St Nicholas. The Duomo's most notable external features are its sculptures, particularly surrounding the rose window and the arched window below it, and the entrance portal with bronze doors (1175–9) by Barisano da Trani. The vigour of the interior has recently been revealed following restoration.

Next to the Duomo is the **castle** (1233–49) founded by Frederick II. Rebuilt in the 14th and 15th centuries, it is a well-preserved edifice with one wall dropping sheer into the sea.

The 15th-century Gothic-Renaissance **Palazzo Caccetta**, in Piazza Trieste, is a rare survival. Nearby, on Via Ognissanti, the 12th-century Romanesque church of the **Ognissanti**, the chapel of the Knights Templar erected in the courtyard of their hospital, is notable for its original portico. Other churches worth a visit are Santa Teresa and the monastery of La Colonna.

Castel del Monte ⓬

Località Andria, Bari. ℹ️ Beni Culturali (0883 56 99 97). 🕐 10:15am–7:15pm daily (to 6:15pm in winter). 🚫 1 Jan, 25 Dec. 🎫
🌐 www.pugliaturismo.com

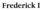

Frederick II

REMOTE IN THE endless plains near Ruvo di Puglia, Castel del Monte, built in the mid-13th century, outclasses every other castle associated with Frederick II. It is also one of the most sophisticated secular buildings of the Middle Ages. The emperor had broad

intellectual interests, and he used his castles as hunting lodges where he could retire from court life with his falcons and books. Inside there are two floors, each with eight rib-vaulted rooms, some still lined with marble. This, and the marble mouldings on the entrance and the upper floor, as well as sophisticated lavatory arrangements, mark the castle as a palace.

Octagonal satellite tower

Graceful, arched windows

Thick and impenetrable walls

Octagonal courtyard

The main entrance portal is in the style of a Roman triumphal arch.

FLOORPLAN OF THE CASTLE
The building is a harmonious geometrical study with two storeys of eight rooms each. The reasons for such precise planning of this giant octagon remain a mystery to this day.

The castle standing alone on the summit of a low hill

Ruvo di Puglia ⑬

Bari. 🏛 24,000. FS 🚌 🛈 *Via Vittorio Veneto 48 (080 361 54 19).* 🅿 *Sat.* 🆆 *www.pugliaturismo.com*

Once celebrated for its vases, Ruvo di Puglia's ceramics industry, producing "Apulian" ware, flourished until the 2nd century BC. The style was inspired by the striking red and black colours of Attic and Corinthian models. The **Museo Archeologico Nazionale Jatta** has a good overview.

The 13th-century **Cattedrale** is a bold example of the Apulian-Romanesque style with a portal that blends Byzantine, Saracenic and Classical motifs.

🏛 Museo Archeologico Nazionale Jatta

Piazza Bovio 35. 📞 080 361 28 48. 🕗 8:30am–1:30pm Mon–Thu (to 7:30pm Fri–Sun). 🔴 1 Jan, 1 May, 25 Dec. 🚫

Bari ⑭

🏛 400,000. ✈ FS 🚌 🚢 🛈 *Piazza Aldo Moro 33a (080 524 23 61).* 🅿 *daily.* 🆆 *www.puglia turismo.com*

Roman Barium was simply a commercial centre, but the city became the regional capital under the Saracens in 847, and was later the seat of the *catapan*, the Byzantine governor of southern Italy. Under the Normans, to whom it fell in 1071, Bari became a centre of maritime significance. Today it is Puglia's lively capital and an important port with ferries to and from Croatia and Greece.

The **Basilica di San Nicola**, one of Puglia's first great Norman churches (begun 1087), has a plain exterior with a tall gabled section flanked by towers. The Apulian-Romanesque portal has carving on the door jambs and arch in Arabic, Byzantine and Classical styles. Beyond the choir screen is a fine 12th-century altar canopy and an episcopal throne (c.11th century). The relics of St Nicholas – patron saint of the city – are buried in the crypt.

The late 12th-century Apulian-Romanesque **Cattedrale** is based on San Nicola, with a dome and one surviving tower (the other one collapsed during an earthquake in 1613). The Baroque portals on the entrance façade incorporate 12th-century

Portal detail of Ruvo di Puglia's Duomo

Sculpture at Bari castle

doorways. The interior has been restored to its medieval simplicity. The canopy over the high altar, the pulpit and the episcopal throne are reconstructions from fragments of the originals. The sacristy, built as a baptistry, is known as the *Trulla*. The crypt houses the remains of San Sabino, Bari's original patron saint.

The city's **castle**, founded by Roger II, was adapted by Frederick II in 1233–9. In the vaulted hall is a collection of plaster casts of sculpture and architectural fragments from various Romanesque monuments in the region.

Bari castle, in the old district known as the Città Vecchia, where most of the town's sights are clustered

Alberobello

Bari. **FS** *to Alberobello & Ostuni.* **H**
*Piazza Ferdinando IV, 4 (080 432 51
71); Via Brigata Regina 29 (080 432 60
30).* **i** *in English, French and German
offered by Trulli e Natura (080 432 38
29).* **W** *www.alberobellonline.net*

I N THE PARCHED landscape of
the **Murge dei Trulli**, there
is a profusion of olive groves,
orchards, vineyards and *trulli*.
Strange circular buildings with
conical roofs and domed within, *trulli* are built from local
limestone stacked without
using mortar. The walls and
openings are generally whitewashed, while the stone
roof tiles often have religious,
pagan or magical symbols
painted on to them. Their
origins are obscure, though the
name is traditionally applied
to ancient round tombs found
in the Roman countryside.
Most *trulli* are souvenir shops.
  Alberobello is a UNESCO
World Heritage site and the
trulli capital. Here the strange
white buildings crowd the
narrow streets, and there are
trulli restaurants, shops and
even a *trulli* cathedral.

Whitewashed and sun-baked *trulli* in Alberobello

ENVIRONS: The white-
washed hilltown of
Locorotondo is
one of the region's
prettiest places and
an important wine
centre. The elegant
streets of **Martina
Franca** are enlivened
by Rococo balconies.
The spectacular **Grotte
di Castellana** are caves
estimated to be 50
million years old.

*Aphrodite in
museum in
Taranto*

Taranto

A *220,000.* **FS** **i** *Corso Umberto I (099 453 23 92).* **a** *Wed, Fri & Sat.*

L ITTLE REMAINS OF the ancient
city of Taras, founded by
Spartans in 708 BC and at its
most prosperous in the mid-
4th century BC. The **Museo
Archeologico Nazionale** has
artifacts that shed light on the
region's early history. During
the museum's restoration, the
highlights of the collection are
on display in Palazzo Pantaleo.

Taranto was heavily bombed
in World War II and is
garlanded by factories. The
picturesque **Città Vecchia**,
an island dividing the Mare
Grande from the Mare
Piccolo, was the site
of the Roman citadel
of Tarentum. A lively
fish market offering
the shellfish for which
the city is famous, is
housed in an Art Nouveau
building. Here, too, is the
Duomo. Founded in 1071,
it has been the subject of
subsequent rebuilding.
The most interesting
features include the
catacomb-like crypt,
with its sarcophagi and
fragmented frescoes, and the
antique marble columns of
the nave. Behind it is the
11th-century **San Domenico
Maggiore**, which later gained
a high double-approach
Baroque staircase. The huge
castle built by Frederick of
Aragon (15th century) covers
the eastern corner of the Città
Vecchia. Now a military area,
the castle is strictly off limits.

**⟐ Museo Archeologico
Nazionale**
Palazzo Pantaleo, Corso Vittorio
Emanuele II. **C** *099 458 17 15.*
O *8:30am–7:30pm daily.*

THE TARANTELLA

Italy's lively and
graceful folk
dance, the
Tarantella,
grew out of
tarantism – the
hysteria that
appeared in 15th-to 17th-
century Italy, and was
prevalent in Galatina (*see
p497*). Alleged victims of
the tarantula spider's bite
could supposedly cure
themselves through
frenzied dancing which
sweated out the poison.
The dance is characterized
by light, quick steps and a
"teasing" flirt. The strange,
private ritual takes place
annually on 29 June at
6am at the celebrations for
the Feast of Saints Peter
and Paul in Galatina,
the only place on the
Salentine Peninsula where
tarantism has survived.

Street-by-Street: Lecce ⑰

L ECCE was the site of the Greek Messapi settlement. It became an important centre of the Roman Empire, and in the Middle Ages developed a strong tradition of scholarship.

Façade detail, Santa Croce

Much of the architecture is in the highly decorative Lecce Baroque style, which flourished in the 1600s and earned the city the name of Florence of the South. This style was possible due to the *pietra di Lecce*, an easily carved stone. Giuseppe Zimbalo (lo Zingarello) was its greatest master. Lecce is also famed for its papier-mâché workshops.

★ Palazzo Vescovile and Duomo
The bishop's palace (rebuilt in 1632), the adjoining Duomo by lo Zingarello (after 1659) and a seminary (1709) enclose the Piazza Duomo.

Tourist information

Chiesa del Rosario
Said to be the finest work by lo Zingarello (begun 1691), the exterior is ornate and idiosyncratic in its detail.

The Seminary once supplied the Vatican with *castrato* singers – eunuchs noted for their high voices.

Porta Rudiae
This 18th-century city gate leads to the suburbs and to the ruins of Roman Rudiae.

Famous papier mâché (carta pasta) workshops

Chiesa del Carmine

STAR SIGHTS
★ **Santa Croce**
★ **Palazzo Vescovile and Duomo**

KEY

– – – Suggested route

0 metres   100

0 yards   100

VISITORS' CHECKLIST

🏛 105,000. 🚊 Viale Oronzo Quarta. 🚌 Via Boito & Via Adua.
ℹ Via Vittorio Emanuele 23 (0832 33 24 63). 🔄 Mon & Fri.
📅 24–26 Aug: Sant'Oronzo; 13–24 Dec: Fiera dei Pupi e Pastori.

The 16th-century Castello lies between ancient city and modern suburbs. A 12th-century construction is enclosed by a wall built later by Charles V. Only one floor is open to the public.

★ **Santa Croce**
Built from 1549 to 1679, Gabriele Riccardi began the façade and interior and lo Zingarello designed the imaginative rose window and pediment.

VIALE XXV LUGLIO

VIA A GRANDI

Church of San Matteo

VIA D'ARAGONA

VIA LECCE

Railway station

A Roman theatre was excavated virtually intact with its orchestra and seats.

Colonna di Sant'Oronzo
St Oronzo was appointed Bishop of Lecce by St Paul in AD 57, and later martyred by the Roman emperor Nero. This bronze statue dates from 1739.

Roman Amphitheatre
Excavated in 1938, only part of this 1st-century BC amphitheatre is visible. Due to restoration, it is closed to the public.

Detail of a 15th-century fresco in Santa Caterina d'Alessandria

Galatina ⑱

Lecce. 🏛 28,000. 🚊 🚌 ⛴ Thu. 📅 29 Jun: Feast of Saints Peter & Paul.

An important Greek colony in the Middle Ages, this town retains its Greek flavour. It is the centre of one of Puglia's chief wine-producing regions, although it is more famous for the St Peter and Paul street festival and for the ritual of tarantism (see p495).

The Gothic church of **Santa Caterina d'Alessandria** on Piazza Orsini was built by Raimondello del Balzo Orsini (begun 1384). It contains early 15th-century frescoes with scenes from the Old and New Testaments that glorify the Orsini, who were feudal lords. Orsini's tomb is in the chancel.

Otranto ⑲

Lecce. 🏛 5,500. 🚊 🚌 ⛴ ℹ Piazza Castello (0836 80 14 36). 📅 Wed.

Today otranto is a shadow of its former self. It was one of Republican Rome's leading ports for trade with Asia Minor and Greece, and under the Byzantines was an important toehold of the Eastern Empire in Italy. In 1070 it fell to the Normans. Turks attacked in 1480 and slaughtered its inhabitants. The 800 survivors were promised their lives if they renounced Christianity: all refused.

The Norman **Duomo** (founded 1080) on Via Duomo houses the bones of the martyrs. There is a 12th-century mosaic floor and a fine crypt. A **castle** (1485–98) built by the Aragonese at the centre of town adds to Otranto's charm and there are some fine beaches close by.

BASILICATA AND CALABRA

*R*EMOTE AND WILD, *Basilicata is one of the poorest regions in Italy. It is underdeveloped and undervisited, and so remains unspoilt. Neighbouring Calabria has been immortalized in the drawings of Edward Lear who, travelling through on a donkey in 1847, was transfixed by the "horror and magnificence" of its savage landscape.*

Today these regions are distinctly separate, but they share a common history and, along with Sicily and Puglia, were part of Magna Graecia. Ancient Metaponto in Basilicata was an important centre, as were Crotone and Locri Epizephiri in Calabria. Their ruins evoke an illustrious past.

After the Greeks came the Romans, followed by Basilian monks. These were members of the Greek-Byzantine church who were fleeing their territories which had been invaded by Muslims. Their religious establishments make up a core of interesting monuments, such as the Cattolica at Stilo or Matera, where the monks took refuge in caves.

Many of the historic remains are Norman, but sporadic evidence of Swabian, Angevin, Aragonese and Spanish occupation also exists.

Centuries of rule by Naples led to the marginalization of Basilicata and Calabria. Nowadays Calabria has a terrifying reputation due to the *'ndrangheta*, the ferocious first cousin to the Mafia, whose activities are a constant menace. Banditry does still exist, but the sensible traveller should have little to fear.

Owing to emigration, Basilicata and Calabria are sparsely populated and have as much to offer in unspoilt countryside as in historic centres. The vast coastline boasts fine beaches, while the interior features the rugged Aspromonte and Sila mountain ranges.

The remote landscape has kept change at bay. Isolated Pentedattilo, for example, preserves customs of Byzantine origin while around San Giorgio Albanese there live close-knit communities of Albanians, descended from 15th-century refugees.

Sparsely populated, rugged countryside surrounding Stilo in southern Calabria

◁ The silent Sassi district in Matera, where dwellings are scooped out of the rock

Exploring Basilicata and Calabria

MOSTLY UPLAND COUNTRY, Basilicata is scattered with Greek ruins (like those at Metaponto), medieval abbeys, Norman castles (such as Melfi's) and isolated hill-towns. Matera, its most interesting city, stands amid an arid lunar landscape of denuded valleys. Calabria is often described as the mountains between the seas. The lovely beaches and virgin landscape around Tropea and Maratea attract many visitors. The Ionian coast's chief attractions are its Greek ruins, such as Caulonia and Locri Epizephiri, and the hill-towns, like Stilo and Gerace, which eventually replaced them.

SIGHTS AT A GLANCE

Repairing nets in the town of Pizzo, northeast of Tropea

The picturesque hill-town of Rivello, north of Maratea in Basilicata

KEY

▦	Motorway
▦	Major road
▦	Minor road
▦	Scenic route
≈	River
✳	Viewpoint

MELFI **1**

2 VENOSA

BOSCO DI MONTICCHIO

S168

3

Bradano

S658

LAGOPESOLE

POTENZA

Salerno

S95

S92

S598

Salerno

RIVELLO

MARATEA

GOLFO DI POLICASTRO

6

S18

PARCO NAZION. DEL POLLIN.

S105

MAR TIRRENO

GOLFO DI SANT'EUFEM

8

TROPEA

GOLFO DI GIOIA

PALMI

STRETTO DI MESSINA

A2-E45

ASPROMONTE

REGGIO DI CALABRIA

11

0 kilometres   50

0 miles   25

PENTEDA\TILO

S106-E90

The port of Maratea on the Tyrrhenian coast of Basilicata

GETTING AROUND

Calabria's Tyrrhenian coast is well served by the A3–E45, a spur of which extends to Potenza in Basilicata. To reach the Ionian coast, it is best to skirt the Aspromonte via the S106–E90 from Reggio to Basilicata. Although the mountains can be crossed, namely on the S280–E848 to Catanzaro, the roads are narrow and pass through isolated countryside. Much of Basilicata is even less accessible, and Matera is more easily reached from Puglia. There are airports at Reggio di Calabria, Lamezia (west of Catanzaro), Bari and Brindisi (Puglia). Trains connect the bigger centres and country buses serve the small towns.

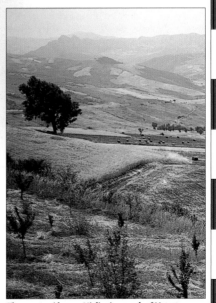

The countryside near Miglionico, south of Matera

SEE ALSO

The impressive castle at Melfi, showing evidence of both Angevin and later construction

Melfi ❶

Potenza. 🏛 15,000. **FS** 🚌 **ℹ** *Via del Gallitello 89 (0971 50 76 11).* 🛒 *Wed & Sat.* **W** *www.aptbasilicata.it*

A BROODING and now almost deserted medieval town, Melfi is crowned by the formidable **castle** where Pope Nicholas II conducted Robert Guiscard's investiture in 1059, thus legitimizing the Normans in the south. Melfi later became the Norman capital. Here Frederick II proclaimed his *Constitutiones Augustales* (1231) which unified his kingdom as a state. In the castle is the **Museo Nazionale del Melfese**, with its collection of Byzantine jewellery.

The **Duomo**, off Via Vittorio Emanuele, was begun in 1155 by William the Bad but rebuilt in the 18th century. Only the campanile survives.

🏛 **Museo Nazionale del Melfese**
Castello di Melfi, Via Normanna. **C** *0972 23 87 26.* 🕐 *daily.* 🌑 *Mon am, 1 Jan, 25 Dec.* 🎫 🚹 🗒 *(Sat & Sun).*

Venosa ❷

Potenza. 🏛 12,000. **FS** 🚌 **ℹ** *Via Garibaldi 42 (open occasionally).* 🛒 *1st Sat & 3rd Thu of month.*

V ENOSA WAS ONE of the most important Roman colonies around 290 BC, and remains of **baths** and an **amphitheatre** survive in the archaeological

zone along Via Vittorio Emanuele. It was also the birthplace of the Latin poet, Horace (65–8 BC), and the site where the Roman general Marcellus died at the hands of Hannibal in 208 BC. Marcellus' reputed **tomb** is in Via Melfi.

The **Duomo**, also on Via Vittorio Emanuele, and the huge **castle** in Piazza Umberto I date from the 16th century.

Occupying the site of a Roman temple is **La Trinità**, a partially ruined abbey complex formed by an older church, possibly early Christian (5th– 6th century). It is backed by an unfinished 11th-century construction, in which Robert Guiscard (died 1085) was buried with his half-brothers and Alberada, his first wife. Only her tomb has survived.

Lagopesole ❸

Potenza. **C** *0971 860 83.* **FS** *to Lagopesole Scalo then bus to town.* 🕐 *9:30am–1pm, 3–5pm daily.* 🚹 **W** *www.aptbasilicata.it*

R ISING DRAMATICALLY on a hill with a village huddled at its feet, Lagopesole's **castle** is the most striking in Basilicata. Dating from 1242–50, it was the last castle Frederick II built. Used as a hunting lodge, it has interesting decoration, particularly the carved heads above the portal of the keep. One is said to be Frederick Barbarossa (the grandfather of Frederick II), and the other is reputedly

Barbarossa's wife, Beatrice. Inside, the royal apartments and chapel can be visited.

Matera ❹

🏛 56,000. **FS** 🚌 **ℹ** *Via de Viti de Marco 9 (0835 33 19 83).* 🎫 *0835 33 67 26 (tours of town & caves).* 🛒 *Sat.*

The Sassi district of Matera

P ERCHED ON THE EDGE of a deep ravine, this town consists of the bustling upper district and the silent lower **Sassi** (caves) district, divided into the Sasso Barisano and the more picturesque Sasso Caveoso. The people of Matera once lived here in dwellings scooped out of the rock. The two parts are odd neighbours, making Matera one of the most fascinating cities in southern Italy.

For the best overview, walk along the **Strada Panoramica dei Sassi** and look down into the caves. From the 8th to the

13th centuries, such caves probably provided refuge for monks from the Byzantine empire. Many chapels, gouged out of the rock, were taken over in the 15th century by peasants. Later, a cave-dwelling Matera evolved and by the 18th century some buildings fronting the caves had become fairly grand mansions and convents. By the 1950s and '60s the Sassi were overtaken by squalor and poverty, and the inhabitants forcibly rehoused. Carlo Levi (1912–75) drew attention to their living conditions in his book *Christ Stopped at Eboli*, comparing the Sassi to Dante's *Inferno*. The area was made a UNESCO World Heritage site in 1993.

Of the 120 *chiese rupestri* (rock-cut churches) in the Sassi and the Agri district outside the town, **Santa Maria di Idris** in the Monte Errone area and **Santa Lucia alle Malve** in the Albanian quarter both contain 13th-century frescoes.

The **Museo della Tortura** (torture), in Via San Biagio, has exhibits dating back to the time of the Inquisition, while the **Museo Nazionale Ridola** provides a background to Matera and the Sassi. The artifacts from many Neolithic trench villages, necropoli and other ancient sites are displayed here.

The Apulian-Romanesque **Duomo** (13th century) in Piazza Duomo has interesting sculpture and an anonymous 12th-century painting of the *Madonna della Bruna*, the patroness of Matera. Via Duomo leads toward **San Francesco d'Assisi** (13th century with Baroque overlay), which commemorates St Francis's visit to Matera in 1218. Other churches to visit are **San Domenico** and **San Giovanni Battista** on Via San Biagio (both 13th century), and the **Purgatorio** (1770) on Via Ridola.

🏛 **Museo Nazionale Ridola**
Via Ridola 24. 📞 0835 31 00 58. 🅾
9am–8pm daily (except Mon am). 🈺

The Tavole Palatine in Metaponto

Metaponto ❺

Zona Archeologica, Matera. 📞 0835 74 53 27. 🚌 FS to Metaponto. 🅾 9am–1 hr before sunset daily. ● 1 Jan, Easter, 25 Dec. 🈺 ♿ W www.aptbasilicata.it

F OUNDED IN THE 7th century BC, ancient Metapontum was once the centre of a wealthy city-state with a philosophical tradition expounded by Pythagoras, who settled here after his expulsion from Croton. Its ruins include the **Tavole Palatine** (6th century BC) at the Bradano River bridge, 15 columns that are part of a Doric temple, probably dedicated to Hera. The **Museo Nazionale di Metaponto** displays artifacts from the site. The ruins of a theatre and the Doric **Temple of Apollo**

Lycius (6th century BC) are in the **Archaeological Zone**. Further south, modern **Policoro** occupies the site of ancient Heracleia (founded 7th–5th century BC). Its **Museo Nazionale della Siritide** has finds from this and other sites.

🏛 **Museo Nazionale di Metaponto**
Metaponto Borgo. 📞 0835 74 53 27. 🅾 daily. ● Mon am & public hols. 🈺 includes Archaeological Zone. ♿

🏛 **Museo Nazionale della Siritide**
Via Colombo 8, Policoro. 📞 0835 97 21 54. 🅾 daily. ● Tue am, 1 Jan, 1 May, 25 Dec. 🈺 ♿

Maratea ❻

Potenza. 🏘 5,000. FS 🚌 🛈 Piazza del Gesù 32 (0973 87 69 08). 🗓 1st & 3rd Sat of month.

A TINY STRETCH of Basilicata meets the Tyrrhenian Sea in the Gulf of Policastro. This unblemished coast is home to Maratea. Its small port (Maratea Inferiore) is beneath the old centre (Maratea Superiore), which straddles the flank of a hill. From here the road climbs Monte Biagio to a summit with breathtaking views where a huge statue of the **Redeemer** stands.

ENVIRONS: Dramatically sited **Rivello**, 23 km (14 miles) to the north, once had a largely Greek population. Byzantine influences can be seen in the churches of **Santa Maria del Poggio** and **Santa Barbara**.

Church of San Francesco in Matera

The small port of Marina di Maratea with fishing boats

A page from the precious *Codex Purpureus Rossanensis*

Rossano ❼

Cosenza. 🚶 *32,000.* 🚆 🚌
🚢 *2nd & 4th Fri of month.*

THIS HANDSOME hill-town was one of the main centres of Byzantine civilization in Calabria. It assumed power when Reggio di Calabria fell to the Saracens in the 9th, 10th and 11th centuries. The **Museo Diocesano** houses the *Codex Purpureus Rossanensis*, a rare 6th-century Greek Gospel with silver lettering and splendidly detailed miniatures.

The Baroque **cathedral** contains the *Madonna Acheropita* fresco, a much venerated Byzantine relic of the 8th or 9th century.

ENVIRONS: On a hilltop to the southeast is the five-domed Greek church of **San Marco** (10th century). The 12th-century **Panaghia**, another Greek church, lies off Via Archivescovado. Both contain fragments of early frescoes. **Santa Maria del Patirion**, on a hilltop 18 km (11 miles) to the west, is magnificently adorned with coloured brickwork, tile and stone. It offers great views over the Piana di Sibari (Plain of Sibari), the alleged location of the fabled city of Sybaris, destroyed in 510 BC. The church has remained virtually unaltered since it was built around 1095.

🏛 **Museo Diocesano**
Palazzo Arcivescovile, Via Arcivescovile.
📞 *0983 52 02 82.* ⬜ *Tue–Sun (Jul–Sep: Mon also).* ⬤ *public hols.*

Tropea ❽

Vibo Valentia. 🚶 *7,000.* 🚆 🚌
ℹ *Piazza Ercole (0963 614 75).*
🚢 *Sat.* Ⓦ *www.tropea.biz*

ONE OF THE MOST picturesque towns on Calabria's largely built-up Tyrrhenian coast, Tropea offers superb views of the sea and beaches. The old town hangs on to a cliffside facing a large rock, formerly an island. The rock is topped by **Santa Maria dell'Isola**, a former medieval Benedictine sanctuary. The **cathedral** at the end of Via Roma is of Norman origin, although it has been rebuilt several times. Inside is a 14th-century painting, the *Madonna di Romania*, by an unknown artist.

Casa Trampo (14th century) and **Palazzo Cesareo** (early 20th century) in Vicolo Manco are the most interesting of the small palaces in Tropea. The latter has a splendid balcony adorned with carvings.

Below the town are pretty beaches and a good choice of places to eat. Other seaside towns to visit are **Palmi** to the south, and **Pizzo** to the north.

Stilo ❾

Reggio di Calabria. 🚶 *3,000.* 🚆 🚌
ℹ *0964 34 26 89 (Siderno).* 🚢 *Tue.*

A SHORT DISTANCE from the coast, Stilo is a ramshackle and earthquake-damaged town clamped to the side of

Monte Consolino. Standing on a ledge looking out over the olive trees is the **Cattolica**, which has made Stilo a focus of dedicated pilgrimage for lovers of Byzantine architecture. Built in the 10th century by Basilian monks, the brick building with its terracotta-tiled roof is based on a Greek cross-in-a-square plan. Four antique, mismatched marble columns divide the interior into nine quadrants. The capitals are placed at the base of the columns, instead of on top, to indicate the triumph of Christianity over paganism. The frescoes within, discovered and restored in 1927, date from the 11th century.

The Cattolica dominates the town, but on Via Tommaso Campanella there is a medieval **Duomo** as well as the 17th-century ruins of the **Convent of San Domenico**, where the philosopher and Dominican friar Tommaso Campanella (1568–1639) lived. The church of **San Francesco**, built around 1400, has an ornate carved wooden altar and a lovely 16th-century painting of the *Madonna del Borgo* (unknown origin). Bivongi, northwest of Stilo, has two churches dedicated to St John: the Byzantine-Norman **San Giovanni Theresti**, and the Norman **San Giovanni Vecchio**.

🔒 **Cattolica**
2 km (1 mile) above Stilo on Via Cattolica. ⬜ *daily.* ♿

The beautiful and unspoilt coastline at Tropea

The distinctive five-domed Cattolica in Stilo

Gerace ⑩

Reggio di Calabria. 🏛 3,000. 🚌
ℹ Pro Loco, Locri (0964 23 27 60).

OCCUPYING an impregnable crag on the northeastern flank of the Aspromonte, this ancient place was founded by refugees from **Locri Epizephiri** who fled in the 9th century to escape Saracen attack. Its defensive character is reinforced by the medieval town walls and the remains of the once impregnable castle.

Apart from the slow pace of life here – where you are as likely to meet a flock of sheep in an alley as a Fiat 500 – the main attraction is Calabria's grandest **Duomo**. This large structure indicates the significance of Gerace at least up to the time of the Normans. Constructed around the early 12th century, rebuilt in the 13th century and restored in the 18th century, the crypt is its chief treasure. Both crypt and church are simple, adorned by a series of antique coloured marble and granite columns probably stolen from the site of

ancient Locri Epizephiri. At the end of Via Cavour is 12th-century **San Giovanello**, part Byzantine and part Norman. Nearby is the Gothic church of **San Francesco d'Assisi** which contains a Baroque marble altar (1615) and the Pisan-style tomb of Niccolò Ruffo (died 1372), a member of a prominent Calabrian family.

ENVIRONS: The vast site of **Locri Epizephiri**, the first Greek city to have a written code of law (660 BC), was a well-known centre of the cult of Persephone. There are remains of **temples**, a **theatre** and Greek and Roman **tombs**. The **Museo** displays a ground plan of the site as well as Greek and Roman votive statues, coins, inscriptions and sculptural fragments.

🏛 Locri Epizephiri

Southwest of Locri on the S106, Contrada Marasà. ◯ 9am–7pm daily.
Museo Nazionale, Contrada Marasà, SS 106. 🕻 0964 39 00 23. ◯ daily.
● 1st and 3rd Mon of the month, 1 May, 25 Dec.

Reggio di Calabria ⑪

🏛 183,000. ✈ FS 🚌 ⛴ ℹ Via Roma 3 (0965 211 71). 🛒 Fri.

THIS IS A TATTY CITY, heavily rebuilt after a major earthquake in 1908. One reason to visit it is the awesome **Museo Nazionale della Magna Grecia**. It houses a fine collection of artifacts from ancient Rhegion – a Greek city on the site of the present town – and from other Greek sites.

Chief among its treasures are the Greek bronzes, larger-than-life statues of warriors dredged from the sea off Riace Marina in 1972. Statue A (460 BC) is thought to be by Phidias, the Athenian sculptor and chief exponent of the idealizing, Classical style. If true, it is a rare survivor because his works, praised in the highest terms by ancient writers, were hitherto only known to us from Roman copies. Statue B (430 BC) has been attributed to Polyclitus. It is possible that the statues originated from the Temple of Delphi, the Athenians' monument to the victory of Marathon.

🏛 Museo Nazionale della Magna Grecia

P. de Nava 26. 🕻 0965 81 22 55 (info); 0965 81 03 81 (to book). ◯ 9am–8pm daily (mid-Jun–mid-Sep: to 11pm Sat–Sun). ● 1st & 3rd Mon of month. 🎟 📷 ♿

Riace Bronzes (6th and 5th century BC) in Reggio's Museo Nazionale

SICILY

ON A CROSSROADS *in the Mediterranean, part of Europe and Africa, yet belonging to neither, Sicily was tramped across by half the ancient civilized world. As conquerors came and went, they left behind a rich and varied cultural deposit. This has resulted in a quirky mixture in almost every aspect of the local vernacular from language, customs and cooking to art and, most notably, the diverse architecture of the island.*

During the 6th and 5th centuries BC, there cannot have been much difference between Athens and the Greek cities of Sicily. Their ruins are among the most spectacular of the ancient Greek world. The Romans took over in the 3rd century BC, followed by the Vandals, Ostrogoths and Byzantines. Not much that is tangible has survived from the days of the Arabs, who ruled from the 9th to 11th centuries, though Palermo's Vucciria is more souk than market. The Norman era, beginning in 1061, spawned brilliant artistic achievements, such as the cathedrals of Monreale and Cefalù, while the eclecticism of that period's architecture is best seen at Santi Pietro e Paolo outside Taormina.

The Sicilian Baroque of the 17th and 18th centuries is just as individual. The palaces and churches of Palermo, reflecting the elaborate ritual of the Spanish Viceregal court, tend towards extravagant display. At Noto, Ragusa, Modica, Siracusa and Catania the buildings are a useful vehicle for the Sicilians' love of ornamentation, itself a remnant from the island's early fling with the Arab world. The style is an expression of the nature of Sicilians, whose sense of pomp and pageantry is both magnificent and extreme.

Sicily is a curiosity, and the legacy of the past is redolent everywhere. The fact that it is an island has intensified the cultural impact of each successive occupier. They say that today there's less Italian blood in Sicilian veins than there is Phoenician, Greek, Arabic, Norman, Spanish or French. The resulting mixture – exotic, spicy and highly inflammable – has created a separate nation at the foot of Italy.

Detail of a 12th-century mosaic from the Palazzo dei Normanni in Palermo

◁ **The beautifully preserved doric Temple of Concord (c.430 BC) in the Valley of the Temples at Agrigento**

Exploring Sicily

Fishermen at work in their boats at Siracusa

THE VAST COASTLINE of Sicily (Sicilia) provides many magnificent beaches, particularly at Taormina and the Golfo di Castellammare by Capo San Vito – part of a huge nature reserve. Sicily's varied interior is characterized by remote hilltowns and plains punctuated by mountain ranges known for spring flowers and wildlife. Among the most spectacular sights is Mount Etna, an active volcano whose lava flows over the centuries have left the land immensely fertile, supporting an abundance of walnut trees, citrus groves and vineyards.

SIGHTS AT A GLANCE

The magnificent temple at Segesta

0 kilometres 50
0 miles 25

KEY

Motorway
Major road
Minor road
Scenic route
River
Viewpoint

SEE ALSO

- *Where to Stay* pp573–5
- *Where to Eat* pp607–8

The Norman Duomo in Palermo

ISOLE EOLIE
(LIPARI)

MAR TIRRENO

MESSINA

TINDARI

A20-E90

A20-E90

STRETTA DI
MESSINA

NEBRODI

S113

TAORMINA

TROINA

S120

NICOSIA

MOUNT ETNA

A19-E932

ENNA

S117b

CATANIA

PIAZZA ARMERINA

GOLFO DI
CATANIA

CALTAGIRONE

PANTALICA

GOLFO DI
AUGUSTA

MAR IONIO

GELA

VITTORIA

PALAZZOLO
ACREIDE

SIRACUSA

COMISO

GOLFO DI GELA

RAGUSA

NOTO

GOLFO DI
NOTO

GETTING AROUND

The A19–E932 links
Palermo and Catania, the
A18–E45 Catania and Messina. The
A20–E90 (Palermo to Messina) is under
construction. The west is accessible from
Palermo on the A29–E90. Ferry routes run
from Messina to Reggio di Calabria, and from
Palermo to Genoa or Naples. Between the
larger towns, train services are efficient, but
for smaller towns the buses are better. Catania and Palermo have international airports.

The scenic town of Cefalù, dominated by a huge rock

Palermo ❶

N ESTLING ON THE protective flank of Monte Pellegrino with Monte Alfano to the east, Palermo lies in a natural amphitheatre called the Conca d'Oro (Golden Shell). Against La Cala harbour, the setting is beautiful and the city, a mix of oriental and European, is without equal despite reduced circumstances. The architecture, ranging in style from Arabic to Norman, Baroque and Art Nouveau, is without comparison in Sicily, making this exotic city an exciting place to explore.

Mosaic detail from Cappella Palatina

Ruined cloister with the red domes of San Giovanni degli Eremiti behind

🏛 San Giovanni degli Eremiti

Via dei Benedettini. 🕻 091 651 50 19. ○ daily (only am on Sun). 🔲
Reflecting Islamic architectural tradition with bulbous domes, corner arches and filigreed windows, this deconsecrated Norman church (1132–48) was built in the grounds of a mosque. Beyond church and mosque, a ruined cloister from a 13th-century monastery encloses a pretty garden.

🏛 Palazzo Reale

Piazza Indipendenza. 🕻 091 705 43 17. **Palazzo Reale** 🕻 091 705 60 01.
○ 9am–noon, 3–5pm Mon–Fri.
Cappella Palatina ○ 9am–noon, 3–5pm Mon–Fri; 9–10am, 11am–1pm Sat; 9–10am, noon–1pm Sun. ●
Easter, 25 Apr, 1 May, 26 Dec.
Also called the Palazzo dei Normanni, this site has been the focus of power since the days of Byzantine rule and is now home to Sicily's regional government. The nucleus of the present building was constructed by the Arabs, but after the Norman conquest of the

city in 1072, it was enlarged and embellished for the Norman court. See the luxurious royal apartments, especially the Sala di Ruggero, and the splendid Cappella Palatina. Built by Roger II (1132–40), this dazzling chapel blends Byzantine, Islamic and Norman styles of craftsmanship. It is lavishly adorned with fine mosaics and marble inlaid with gold. Next to the palace is the eccentrically decorated Porta Nuova (1535).

🔒 Gesù

Piazza Casa Professa. ○ 7–11:30am, 5–6:30pm daily (closed during mass).
In the poor, bomb-devastated Albergheria quarter, near the colourful market of Piazza Ballarò, lies this important Baroque church (1564–1633). Also known as the church of the Casa Professa, the interior is an excellent example of the virtuosity of Sicilian craftsmen in the treatment of marble carving and inlay. The oldest Jesuit church in Sicily, it was heavily restored after suffering extensive damage in World War II.

Sumptuous interior of the Cappella Palatina, Palazzo Reale

Duomo's exterior displaying a mixture of styles

VISITORS' CHECKLIST

800,000. ✈ Punta Raisi 32 km
(20 miles) W. 🚆 Stazione Centra-
le, Piazza Giulio Cesare. 🚌 Via
Balsamo. ⚓ Stazione Marittima,
Molo Vittorio Veneto. ℹ P. Ca-
stelnuovo 35 (091 605 83 51). 🏛
Mon–Sat. 🎉 10–15 Jul: U Festinu
for the city's patron saint, Santa
Rosalia; 4 Sep: Pilgrimage to Santa
Rosalia's grotto; Easter: Byzantine
Catholic celebrations in La Martora-
na. 🌐 www.palermotourism.com

🏛 Duomo

Via Vittorio Emanuele. ☎ 091 33 43
76. 🕐 8am–6:30pm daily (closed
during mass). ♿ 📷 for Treasury.

Founded in 1184 by the
Archbishop of Palermo,
the Duomo displays
many architectural
styles. The
exterior shows
the develop-
ment of the
Gothic style from
the 13th–14th
centuries. The south porch
(1453) is a masterpiece of the
Catalan style, and at the apse
end, sturdy Norman work can
be seen through a decorative
Islamic-inspired overlay. The
dome is 18th century.

Within the much-altered
interior are the tombs of Sicily's
kings. Squeezed into an enclosure by the south porch are
the remains of Emperor Frederick II; his wife, Constance of
Aragon; his mother, Constance,
daughter of Roger II (also
entombed here); and his father,
Henry VI. The Treasury houses
the 12th-century Imperial Diadem of Constance of Aragon,
which was removed from her
tomb in the 18th century.

**Fontana Pretoria with Santa
Caterina in the background**

🏛 Santa Caterina

P. Bellini. 🕐 Sun mass, 29 Apr & Easter.
Although begun in 1566, most
of the internal decoration of
this unique church dates from
the 17th and 18th centuries.
A powerful example of the
Palermitan Baroque, it over-
whelms with colours, textures,
sculpture and marble inlay.
There are illusionistic ceiling
frescoes (18th century) by
Filippo Randazzo in the nave
and Vito d'Anna in the dome.

The church is flanked by
Piazza Pretorio, which is dominated by the huge Mannerist
Fontana Pretorio (1544), now
beautifully restored.

SIGHTS AT A GLANCE

KEY

🅿	Parking
🏛	Church

0 metres   250

0 yards   250

Exploring Palermo

EAST OF THE Quattro Canti, where Via Maqueda and Corso Vittorio Emanuele meet, the city is sprinkled with ornate palaces and more churches. Squeezed behind them are labyrinthine medieval quarters where ancient buildings with crumbling fabric still survive.

🔒 La Martorana
Piazza Bellini. 【 *091 616 16 92.* 〇 *daily (only am on Sun).*

Also called Santa Maria dell' Ammiraglio, this church was built around 1140 by George of Antioch, Roger II's admiral and also an orthodox Greek Christian. The design derives from Norman and Islamic traditions with mosaics possibly by Greek artisans. In the right aisle, King Roger receives the Imperial Diadem from Christ; in the left aisle, George of Antioch is portrayed.

A nearby convent, founded by Eloisa Martorana in 1193, was the site where the Sicilian Parliament met in 1295 and decided, in the wake of the Sicilian Vespers, to hand the crown of Sicily to Frederick of Aragon. The church was presented to the convent in 1433.

Mosaic of Christ with Four Angels in the dome of La Martorana

🔲 Vucciria
Via Roma. 〇 *daily.*

Nowhere is Palermo's Arabic past more apparent than in this medieval casbah-style market which burrows through the ruinous Loggia district below Via Roma. Merchants, hawkers, shoppers and pickpockets crowd an area once the haunt of artisans. The alleys all around are named after their professions, such as silversmiths, dyers and keymakers. This busy market, the largest in Palermo, offers the usual market ware from daily objects to junk, as well as a wide selection of fresh fruit, vegetables, fish and meat.

Stuccoed interior of the Oratorio del Rosario di San Domenico

🔒 Oratorio del Rosario di San Domenico
Via Bambinai 2. 【 *091 32 05 59.* 〇 *daily am.*

The interior of this tiny 16th-century chapel displays elegant Baroque decoration by the master of stucco, Giacomo Serpotta. Created around 1720–30, this was his latest and possibly his finest work. Serpotta's technical virtuosity, not to mention the sensory indulgence and whimsical fantasy in evidence here, is remarkable. The altarpiece is the famous *Madonna of the Rosary* (1624–8) by Anthony Van Dyck, and there are wall paintings by Luca Giordano and Pietro Novelli.

🔒 San Domenico
Piazza San Domenico. 【 *091 32 95 88.* 〇 *daily (only am Mon–Fri).* **Museo del Risorgimento** 【 *091 58 27 74.* 〇 *am only Mon, Wed, Fri.* 🔶 *Aug.* **Cloister** 〇 *by appointment.*

Although the present building was begun in 1640, there has been a Dominican church on the site since the 14th century. Tommaso Maria Napoli, one of the masters of Sicilian Baroque, created the exuberant church façade (1726) and square in front (1724).

Within, the most interesting feature is Antonello Gagini's bas-relief of *Santa Caterina* (1528) in the third chapel on the left. Next to the church is the 14th-century cloister, part of the original monastery which gives access to the Museo del Risorgimento.

🏛 Museo Archeologico Regionale
Piazza Olivella 24. 【 *091 611 68 05.* 〇 *8:30am–6:45pm Tue–Sat (to 1:45pm Mon, Sun, hols).* 🔲

Housed in a former monastery of the Filippini, Sicily's most important museum contains sculpture, architectural fragments and ceramics, bronzes, glassware, jewellery, weapons and terracottas. The collection is taken from the island's Phoenician, Greek and Roman sites of antiquity – Tindari, Termini Imerese, Agrigento, Siracusa, Selinunte and Mozia. The highlights are sculptures from the friezes of the ancient Greek temples at Selinunte.

Palermo's noisy, bustling Vucciria market east of Via Roma

🔒 Oratorio del Rosario di Santa Cita

Via Valverde 3. 📞 091 33 27 79. ⊙ daily am.

This small chapel is dedicated to the Virgin of the Rosary after her miraculous intervention at the Battle of Lepanto (see pp54–5). The stucco relief decoration, again, is the work of Giacomo Serpotta (after 1688): the panel on the rear wall depicts the battle, and other reliefs show scenes from the New Testament, all portrayed with extravagant realism. The neighbouring 16th-century church of Santa Zita, from which the oratory takes its name, is filled with sculptures (1517–27) by Antonello Gagini.

Ornate interior of the Oratorio di Santa Cita

🔒 Oratorio di San Lorenzo

Via Immacolatella 5. ⬤ for restoration.

Lining the walls of this tiny oratory are incredible stucco scenes from the lives of St Francis and St Lawrence, and allegorical figures and putti by Giacomo Serpotta (1699–1706). These remarkable, expressive works exhibit the virtuosity of their creator in the handling of his medium. Caravaggio's *Nativity with St Francis and St Lawrence* (1609) graced the space above the altar until it was stolen in 1969. The oratory lies hidden next to the medieval church of San Francesco d'Assisi (13th century), which is brimming with excellent sculpture. The undoubted highlight of the church is the triumphal arch (1468) by Pietro da Bonitate and Francesco Laurana in the Cappella Mastrantonio.

The Palazzina Cinese (c.1799) set in the Parco della Favorita

🏛 Palazzo Abatellis and Galleria Regionale di Sicilia

Via Alloro 4. 📞 091 623 00 11. ⊙ 9am–2pm, 2:30–7:30pm Mon–Sat (to 1:30pm Sun, hols). 🎫

Matteo Carnelivari built this palace combining Spanish late-Gothic and Italian Renaissance styles in the 15th century. It is home to the Galleria Regionale di Sicilia, which houses Antonello da Messina's *Vergine Annunziate* (1476), Francesco Laurana's marble head of Eleanor of Aragon (15th century), and sculptures by the Gagini. Nearby, the 15th-century church of Santa Maria degli Angeli (or La Gancia) contains works by Antonello Gagini and Giacomo Serpotta.

Vergine Annunziate (1476) by da Messina in the Galleria Regionale

🔒 La Magione

Via Magione 44. 📞 091 617 05 96. ⊙ 8:30am–noon, 3–6.30pm Mon–Sat and for services on Sun. ⬆ 🔓

Restorations have revealed the ancient structure of this church which was damaged in World War II. Founded in 1191 by Matteo d'Aiello, Roger II's chancellor, its simple nave, flanked by fine Gothic columns, makes it a major feature of any tour of Norman Sicily.

🌿 Villa Giulia

Via Abramo Lincoln. ⊙ daily. 🔓 **Orto Botanico** 📞 091 623 82 41. ⊙ daily (Sat, Sun am only). ⬤ pub hols. 🎫 🔓

The formal gardens of the villa were established in the 18th century. Once, with their statues and fountains, they exotically evoked the antique world. Nowadays, the tropical flora and faded grandeur make them a delightful setting for walks. In the adjacent Orto Botanico (botanical gardens) there are magnificent tropical plants. In Léon Dufourny's Neo-Classical Gymnasium (1789), plant specimens can be examined. Villa Giulia is the city's only central park and has good childrens' facilities.

🌿 Parco della Favorita

Entrance on Piazza Leoni & Piazza Generale Cascino. ⊙ daily. 🔓 **Museo Etnografico Siciliano Pitré**, Via Duca degli Abruzzi 1. 📞 091 740 48 90. ⊙ Mon–Fri. ⬤ pub hols. 🎫

This park, laid out as a hunting ground in 1799 by the Bourbon Ferdinand IV, was surrounded by summer villas of the aristocracy. One of these, the Palazzina Cinese (c.1799), was built in a Chinese style for Ferdinand III and Maria Carolina, the sister of Marie Antoinette.

The Museo Etnografico Siciliano Pitré, in the stables of the Palazzina Cinese (under restoration), has a fine collection of objects from Sicilian life.

Monreale ❷

Capital from cloister column

Magnificently adorned, and with a splendid view of the Conca d'Oro, the Duomo at Monreale is one of the great sights of Norman Sicily. Founded in 1172 by the Norman King William II, it flanks a monastery of the Benedictine Order. The interior of the cathedral glitters with mosaics carried out by Sicilian and Byzantine artists – the inspiration of a king who wanted to rival the power of the Archbishop of Palermo. Like Cefalù, and later Palermo, it was to serve as a royal sepulchre.

★ **Christ Pantocrator**
The cathedral's Latin-cross plan focuses on the imposing mosaic of the all-powerful Christ (12th–13th century).

Nave and aisles separated by Roman columns

Magnificent gilded wood ceiling

Apse Exterior
With their rich multi-coloured ornamentation in tufa and marble, the three apses represent the apogee of Norman decoration.

Entrance to Cappella del Crocifisso and Treasury

Original Cosmati floor in choir

The royal tomb of William II, in white marble, flanks the porphyry tomb of William I in the corner of the transept.

Barisano da Trani's bronze door (1179) on the north side is shielded by a portico designed by Gian Domenico and Fazio Gagini (1547–69).

★ **Mosaic Cycle**
Completed in 1182, the rich mosaics show scenes from the Old Testament (nave), Teachings of Christ (aisles, choir and transepts), and the Gospels (side apses). The story of Noah's Ark is depicted here.

★ Cloisters
A masterpiece of Norman artistic expression from the time of William II, the columns – plain, carved or inlaid with richly lustred tiles – support elaborate capitals from which spring Saracenic-style arches.

VISITORS' CHECKLIST

Piazza Duomo.
🚌 809, 8/9 and many others going west.
Church ☎ 091 640 44 13.
🕐 8am–6pm daily. 🕈 📷
Cloister ☎ 091 640 44 03.
🕐 9am–6:30pm Mon–Sat (to 1:30 pm Sun, hols). 📷
Treasury 🕐 8am–12:30pm, 3:30–6pm daily. 📷

The south wall and cloisters survive as elements from the Benedictine monastery.

Small Oriental-inspired fountain

Column Detail
Craftsmen from Campania, Puglia, Lombardy and Sicily worked on the cloister columns. The detail here shows Adam and Eve.

The 18th-century porch is surrounded by two squat towers.

Bronze Door Panel
Bonanno da Pisa's fine bronze door (1185), signed by him, depicts 42 scenes from the Bible set within elaborate borders. The lion and griffin are symbols of the Norman kingdom.

STAR FEATURES

★ Cloisters

★ Mosaic Cycle

★ Christ Pantocrator

Bagheria ❸

Palermo. 🏛 40,000. 🚫 🚌
ℹ Pro Loco, Corso Umberto (091
90 90 20). 🚢 Wed.

TODAY BAGHERIA is almost a
suburb of Palermo, though
open countryside with olive
and orange groves once
separated them. In the 17th
century Giuseppe Branciforte,
Prince of Butera, built a
summer retreat here, starting
a fashion that was quickly
followed by other Palermitan
aristocrats. The town's core is
sprinkled with their Baroque
and Neo-Classical villas.

The **Villa Palagonia** was
designed in 1705 by the
architect Tommaso Maria
Napoli for Ferdinando
Gravina, the Prince
of Palagonia. It has
remarkable architectural
qualities: a complex
open-air staircase leads
to the first floor, and
the principal rooms,
all with unusual shapes,
are arranged around a
curved axis. A later prince
adorned the perimeter wall
with the grotesque stone
monsters which amused the
18th-century traveller Patrick

**Stone figure on
Villa Palagonia**

Brydone, and horrified Goethe,
who also travelled here and
called this the "Palagonian
madhouse". Across
the piazza are **Villa
Valguarnera** (begun
in 1713 by Napoli), set
in its own park, and
Villa Trabia (mid-18th
century), but neither is
open to the public.
Villa Cattolica (18th
century) houses a
modern art gallery.

🏛 **Villa Palagonia**
Piazza Garibaldi 3. 📞 091 93 20 88.
🔵 daily (exept during functions). 🎫
🏛 **Villa Cattolica**
Via Consolare. 📞 091 94 39 02.
🔵 daily. 🎫

Open-air staircase of the eccentric Villa Palagonia in Bagheria

Fishing and pleasure boats moored in the harbour of Trapani

Trapani ❹

🏛 120,000. 🚫 🚌 🚢 ℹ Piazza
Saturno (0923 290 00). 🚢 daily.
🌐 www.apt.trapani.it

OLD TRAPANI occupies a
narrow peninsula. The
best buildings in this lively
quarter are the churches, especially the **Cathedral of San
Lorenzo** (1635) and **Chiesa
del Collegio dei Gesuiti**
(c.1614–40). The façades of
both, and that of the **Palazzo
d'Ali** (17th century) on Via
Garibaldi, display magnificently
the curious ebullience of west
Sicilian Baroque architecture.

The 17th-century **Purgatorio**
on Via San Francesco d'Assisi
contains 18th-century *Misteri* –
realistic, life-sized wooden
statues used annually in the
Good Friday procession. **Santa
Maria del Gesù** on Via Sant'
Agostino should be visited for
the *Madonna degli Angeli* by
Andrea della Robbia (1435–
1525) and Antonello Gagini's
canopy (1521). In the Jewish
quarter, west of Via XXX
Gennaio, the **Palazzo della
Giudecca** (16th century) has a
strangely textured façade.

The **Museo Pepoli** has a
collection of local antiquities.
Of interest are the coral objects
and the Christmas crib figures
(*presepi*), modern versions of
which are made here. Next to
the museum, the **Santuario di
Maria Santissima Annunziata**
contains the *Madonna di
Trapani*, a statue revered by
fishermen and sailors for its
legendary miraculous powers.

🏛 **Museo Pepoli**
Via Conte Agostino Pepoli.
📞 0923 55 32 69. 🔵 9am–1:30pm
Tue–Sun. 🎫

Erice ❺

Trapani. 🏠 29,000. 🚌 ℹ️ *Via Guarrasi 1 (0923 86 93 88).* ⛴️ *Mon.*

Poised on a crag overlooking Trapani, the medieval town of Erice was once the seat of the cult of the fertility goddess Venus Erycina. Her temple stood on the present site of the Norman castle (**Castello di Venere**), beyond the **Villa Balio** public gardens. On a clear day, you can see all the way to Tunisia from the castle. The ancient town of Eryx was renamed Gebel-Hamed by the Arabs, Monte San Giuliano by the Normans and finally Erice in 1934 by Mussolini.

The **Duomo** (14th century) has a 15th-century porch and an earlier battlemented campanile. Inside is a *Madonna` and Child* (c.1469), attributed to either Francesco Laurana or Domenico Gagini. The deconsecrated 13th-century **San Giovanni Battista** on Viale Nunzio Nasi (now a hotel) contains Antonello Gagini's *St John the Evangelist* (1531) and Antonino Gagini's *St John the Baptist* (1539). **San Cataldo**, a plain 14th-century building on Via San Cataldo, houses a holy water stoup (c.1474) from Domenico Gagini's workshop. In the **Museo Cordici** are Antonello Gagini's *Annunciation* (1525), an interesting variety of Classical remains and an old library.

🏛️ **Museo Cordici**
Piazza Umberto I. 📞 *0923 86 91 72.* ⏰ *8:30am–1:30pm Mon–Fri, (9am–2pm Sun), also 2:30–5:30pm Mon, Thu.*

A typical medieval street in the small hill-town of Erice

SICILIAN ISLANDS

Surrounding Sicily are several island groups. The Isole Eolie or Lipari (Aeolian Islands), to which Panaria, Lipari, Vulcano and Stromboli belong, are a mass of extinct, or nearly extinct, volcanoes poking out of the sea off the coast of Milazzo. The Isole Egadi (Egadi Islands), off the coast of Trapani, have a distinctly Arabic flavour. They include Favignana, Levanzo (which has Palaeolithic and Neolithic paintings and drawings), and Marettimo – the smallest and most unspoilt. Ustica, renowned for its marine life and popular among divers, lies north of Palermo. To the south are the remarkably tourist-free Isole Pelagie (Pelagic Islands) – Lampedusa and Linosa, which are North African in character. Remote Pantelleria lies closer to Tunisia than to Sicily.

The biggest and most popular of the Isole Eolie is Lipari, which has a pretty port and a good range of bars, restaurants and hotels. Nearby sulphur-scented Vulcano offers hot mudbaths and black beaches.

Favignana, the largest and most populous of the Isole Egadi, is the scene of the traditional tuna slaughter – la mattanza. This takes place, as it has for centuries, in May. These fishermen are bringing in the nets following the slaughter.

Part of the Isole Pelagie, Lampedusa was once owned by the family of Giuseppe Tomasi di Lampedusa, author of The Leopard, *Sicily's most famous novel. The island is nearer to Malta than Sicily and has clean water and great beaches.*

Marsala ❻

Trapani. 🚶 85,000. FS 🚌 ⛴ ℹ
Via XI Maggio 100 (0923 71 40 97).
⛴ *Tue.* Ⓦ *www.comune.marsala.tp.it*

T HE PORT OF MARSALA is the
home of a thick,
strong, sweet wine
that has been in
production here since
the 18th century. In
1798 Admiral Nelson
ordered vast quantities of
it following the Battle of
the Nile. Its early manu-
facture was presided
over by three British
families living in Sicily.
One of the old ware-
houses where the
wine was produced
is now the **Museo
Archeologico di
Baglio Anselmi**,
housing important
Phoenician artifacts.

**Statue of a
Greek youth in
Museo di Mozia**

The ruins of **Lily-
baeum** are another
attraction. Founded in 397 BC,
this outpost of the Phoenician
Empire was peopled by the
survivors of the massacre by
Dionysius I of Siracusa at
Mozia (ancient Motya) – the
island used by the Phoenicians
as a commercial centre. Best
of all are the reconstructed
remains of a Punic ship
thought to have been active in
the First Punic War (263–241
BC). The **Museo di Mozia** in
the Whitaker villa contains a
remarkable early 5th-century
BC statue of a Greek youth.

The excavations here are
important; what we know of
the Phoenicians today comes
mostly from the Bible, and
from Mozia. The **Duomo**,
begun in the 17th century, was
built on the site of an earlier
church; both were dedicated to
Marsala's patron saint, Thomas
Becket of Canterbury. Its
interior is full of sculptural
works by members of the
Gagini family. The
small **Museo degli
Arazzi**, behind the
Duomo, contains several
magnificent 16th-century
Brussels tapestries.

🏛 **Museo
Archeologico
di Baglio Anselmi**
Via Lungomare. 📞 0923 95
25 35. 🕐 *am daily (Wed &
Fri–Sun also pm).* ♿
🏛 **Museo degli Arazzi**
Via Garappa. 📞 0923 21 62
95. 🕐 *Tue–Sun.* 📷
🏛 **Museo di Mozia**
Isola di Mozia. 📞 0923 71
25 98. 🕐 *daily.* 📷 ♿

Segesta ❼

Trapani. 🚌 *from Trapani & Palermo.*
📞 0924 95 23 56. 🕐 *9am–1 hr
before sunset.*

A CCORDING TO LEGEND, the
ancient town of Segesta –
still largely unexcavated – was
founded by Trojan followers of
Aeneas. It presents one of the
most spectacular sights on the
island: a massive unfinished
temple stranded on a remote
hillside. Its construction was
started between 426 and 416
BC, and it was left incomplete
following the devastation of
Selinunte by the Carthaginians
in 409 BC. Archaeologists

regard the temple as a good
example of "work in progress".
Nearby, close to the summit of
Monte Barbaro, the ruins of an
ancient theatre (3rd century
BC) can be visited. Summer
concerts are now held here.

Selinunte ❽

Trapani. 📞 0924 462 77.
FS *Castelvetrano then bus.*
🕐 *9am–2 hr before sunset.* 📷

F OUNDED IN 651 BC, Selinunte
became one of the great
cities of Magna Graecia – the
part of southern Italy that
was colonized by ancient
Greece – and its toppled ruins
are among Sicily's most
important historic sites. Its
ancient name, Selinus, derives
from the wild celery that still
grows here. The city was an
important port, and its wall
defences can still be seen
around the Acropolis. The
Carthaginians, under Hannibal,
completely destroyed the city
in 409 BC in a battle famous
for its epic and spectacularly
savage proportions.

While the city itself has
virtually disappeared, eight of
its temples are distinguishable,
particularly the so-called
Eastern Temples (E, F and
G). Of these, the columns of
huge Doric **Temple E** (490–
480 BC) have been partially
re-erected. **Temple F** (c.560–
540 BC) is in ruins. **Temple G**
(late 6th century BC), which
had 17 massive side columns,
was one of the greatest Greek
temples ever built.

Higher on the Acropolis lie
the remains of **Temples A**, **B**,
C, **D** and **O**. Metope sculpture
from **Temple C** (early 6th
century), originally located
on the frieze between the
triglyphs, can be seen in the
Museo Archeologico Regionale
in Palermo (*see p512*), along
with ceramics, jewellery and
other artifacts excavated here.
A small **museum** on site
houses less important finds,
as does one in Castelvetrano,
14 km (8.5 miles) north of
Selinunte. The ancient city is
still being excavated; its
North Gate entrance is well
preserved and further north
there is also a **necropolis**.

The spectacularly situated, unfinished Doric temple at Segesta

Cefalù

Palermo. 👥 *14,000.* 🚉 🚌 ℹ️ *Corso Ruggero 77 (0921 42 10 50).* 🚌 *Sat* 🌐 *www.cefalu-tour.pa.it*

THIS PRETTY, unspoilt seaside town, with good beaches and many restaurants and hotels, is dominated by a huge rock known as **La Rocca** – once the site of a Temple of Diana – and by one of the finest Norman cathedrals in Sicily. Begun in 1131 by Roger II, the **Duomo** was intended as the principal religious seat in Sicily. Though it failed to fulfil this function, the building's magnificence has never been eclipsed. Its splendid mosaics (1148), which feature an image of Christ Pantocrator in the apse, are remarkable and often celebrated as purely Byzantine works of art on Sicilian soil.

The **Museo Mandralisca** houses a fine *Portrait of a Man* (c.1465) by Antonello da Messina and an interesting collection of coins, ceramics, vases, minerals and shells.

🏛️ Museo Mandralisca

Via Mandralisca. 📞 *0921 42 15 47.* ⬜ *daily.* 🔲

The twin-towered façade of the Norman Duomo in Cefalù

The lavish apse of Cefalù's Duomo

Agrigento ❿

👥 *57,000.* 🚉 🚌 ⛴️ ℹ️ *Via Empedocle 73 (0922 203 91); Piazza Aldo Moro (0922 204 54).* 🚌 *Fri.*

MODERN AGRIGENTO occupies the site of Akragas, an important city of the ancient Greek world. Founded by Daedalus, according to legend, it was famed for the luxurious lifestyle of its inhabitants, and

was a great power and rival to Siracusa. In 406 BC it fell to the Carthaginians, who sacked and burned it following the flight of its citizens and soldiers.

The historic core of the city, with its medieval streets, focuses on the Via Atenea. **Santo Spirito** (13th century) houses stuccoes by Giacomo Serpotta (1695). **Santa Maria dei Greci** was built on the remains of a 5th-century BC temple – see the flattened columns in the nave. The **Duomo**, founded in the 14th century and altered in the 16th and 17th centuries, exhibits a unique mixture of Arab, Norman and Catalan detailing.

ENVIRONS: The chief reason to visit Agrigento is to see the archaeological zone known as the Valley of the Temples (*see p520*). The **Museo Regionale Archeologico** houses an interesting display of artifacts from the temples and the city, including a collection of vases, coins and Greek and Roman sculpture.

🏛️ Museo Regionale Archeologico

Contrada San Nicola, Viale Panoramica. 📞 *0922 40 15 65.* ⬜ *9am–7pm daily (Sun & Mon am only).* 🔲

THE MAFIA

An international organization founded in Sicily, the Mafia (meaning hostility to law) developed against a background of a cruel State, exploitative nobility and severe poverty. By the late 19th century it had become a criminal organization thriving on property speculation and drug trafficking. Since the "singing" of Tommaso Buscetta and the capture of Toto Riina, the Mafia has been on the defensive against a State that has doubled its efforts against it. Although violence is common, it is not aimed at tourists. Indeed, Sicilians on the whole are known for their hospitality.

Mafia assassination depicted in this scene from the film The Godfather Part III (1990)

Valley of the Temples

STRADDLING A LOW RIDGE to the south of Agrigento, the Valley of the Temples (Valle dei Templi) ranks among the most impressive complexes of ancient Greek buildings outside Greece. Its Doric temples, dating from the 5th century BC, were destroyed in part by the Carthaginians in 406 BC, in part by Christians, who believed the temples to be pagan, in the 6th century. Later, earthquakes wreaked further havoc on them. Today, nine of the original ten temples are still visible and the whole area can be covered in a day. To avoid crowds, visit early in the morning or in the evening.

Telamone from the Temple of Olympian Zeus

Temple of Hephaistos ①
Apart from a couple of incomplete columns still standing, very little remains of this temple, built c.430 BC. It is also called the Temple of Vulcan.

Sanctuary of the Chthonic Divinities ②
At this group of shrines, the forces of nature were worshipped.

San Biagio

Rock Sanctuary of Demeter →

(see p519)

Museo Regionale Archeologico

Via dei Templi

Hellenistic and Roman Quarter

Strada panoramica

San Nicola

Via dei Templi

Catacombs

S115

P

Via Sacra

Temple of Asklepios

S115

Temple of Olympian Zeus ④
Begun c.480 BC, this was the biggest Doric temple ever built. Unfinished at the time of the Carthaginian attack, it is now a toppled ruin. Giant figures known as telamones were used in its construction.

Temple of Herakles ⑥
This is the oldest temple in the valley (late 6th century BC).

Temple of Juno ⑧
Built around 450 BC, this temple still has many intact columns.

Tomb of Theron ⑤
Here are the ruins of a Roman tomb (1st century AD).

Temple of Castor and Pollux ③
This is a controversial assemblage of pieces from other buildings, erected in the 19th century. Modern Agrigento (see p519) is in the background.

KEY

- – – Suggested route
- P   Parking
- —— Ancient walls

0 metres   500

0 yards   500

Temple of Concord ⑦
This beautifully preserved temple (c.430 BC) was converted into a Christian church in the 4th century AD, thus saved from destruction.

Piazza Armerina ⓫

Enna. 🏘 *22,000.* 🚌 🖦 *Via Genera-le Muscara (0935 68 02 01).* 🚢 *Thu.*

Tᴴɪѕ ᴀᴄᴛɪᴠᴇ, ebullient provincial town is half medieval and half Baroque. The 17th-century **Duomo**, at its highest point, is the most interesting of the Baroque buildings.

In August, the lively *Palio dei Normanni* festival attracts many visitors, but the real draw are the mosaics in the **Villa Romana del Casale**, 5 km (3 miles) southwest of the town. The mosaics were only excavated in the 20th century.

It is thought that this huge, once sumptuous villa with its public halls, private quarters, baths and courtyards, belonged to Maximianus Herculeus, Diocletian's co-emperor, from AD 286 to 305. His son and successor, Maxentius, probably continued its decoration, with Constantine taking over on Maxentius's death in 312.

Although little remains of the building fabric, the floors are decorated with some of the finest surviving mosaics from Roman antiquity. The hunting, mythological and domestic scenes, and exotic landscapes, all exhibit astonishingly realistic attention to detail.

🏛 **Villa Romana del Casale**
Contrada Paratore. 📞 *0935 68 00 36.* ⬜ *daily.* 🚫

Roman *Girls in Bikinis* mosaic from the Villa Romana del Casale

Enna ⓬

🏘 *28,000.* 🚉 🚌 🖦 *Piazza Colaianni 6 (0935 50 08 75).* 🚢 *Tue.* 🅦 *www.apt-enna.com*

Iᴍᴘʀᴇɢɴᴀʙʟᴇ on a crag above a fertile landscape where Persephone, mythological daughter of Demeter, once played, Sicily's highest town (942 m/3,090 ft) has been coveted by successive invaders since its earliest days. The venerated seat of the Cult of Demeter (Patroness of Fertility) was at Enna. Her temple stood on the **Rocca Cerere**, not far from the huge **Castello di Lombardia** (13th century) built by Frederick II.

Most of Enna's sights are clustered in the old town, among the ancient streets that open out of the Via Roma. The church of **San Francesco** has a 16th-century tower. **Piazza Crispi**, with its fine views to nearby Calascibetta, is dominated by a copy of Bernini's *Rape of Persephone*. The 14th-century **Duomo**, altered in later centuries, contains parts of Demeter's temple.

The **Museo Alessi** houses the Cathedral Treasury and an interesting coin collection. The **Museo Varisano** has exhibits on the area's history, from Neolithic to Roman. Away from the centre, the octagonal **Torre di Federico II** (13th century) is a former watchtower.

Environs: The ancient hill-town of **Nicosia**, northeast of Enna, was damaged in the 1967 earthquake, but still contains a smattering of churches. San Nicola, built in the 14th century, has a magnificent, carved entrance portal. Inside there is a much venerated wooden crucifix (17th century) by Fra Umile di Petralia. Santa Maria Maggiore houses a 16th-century marble poly-ptych by Antonello Gagini and a throne reputedly used by Charles V in 1535. Further east is **Troina**. It was captured in 1062 by the Normans, whose work survives in the Chiesa Matrice. Southeast of Enna, **Vizzini** commands fine views of the countryside.

🏛 **Museo Alessi**
Via Roma 326. 📞 *0935 50 31 65.* ⬜ *daily.*
🏛 **Museo Varisano**
Piazza Mazzini. 📞 *0935 50 04 18.* ⬜ *daily.* 🚫

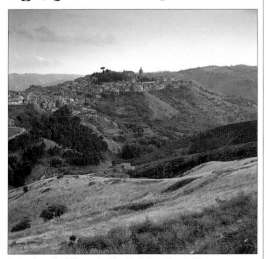
A view from the hills overlooking Vizzini, southeast of Enna

Taormina's magnificently situated Greek theatre, with Mount Etna in the distance

Tindari ⑬

Messina. 📞 0941 36 90 23. 🚉
Patti or Oliveri, then bus. 🕐 9am–1
hr before sunset daily. ♿ 📷

POISED ON THE EDGE of a cliff
overlooking the Golfo di
Patti are the ruins of **Tyndaris**,
almost the last Greek city to
have been founded in Sicily
(395 BC). Apart from the city
walls, the ruins are mostly
Roman, including the **basilica**
and **theatre**. An **antiquarium**
houses artifacts from the site.
A combined ticket allows entry
at the massive 2nd-century
Villa Romana in Patti Marina.
Tindari is better known
for its shrine to a Byzantine
icon, the **Black Madonna**
on Piazzale Belvedere.

Messina ⑭

🏃 275,000. 🚉 🚌 ⛴ 🛈 Piazza
Cairoli 45 (090 293 52 92). 🛳 daily.
🌐 www.azienturismomessina.it

MESSINA HAS BEEN the victim
of earthquakes and
World War II bombing. The
Museo Regionale houses
treasures that include works
by Antonello da Messina and
Caravaggio. **Santissima
Annunziata dei Catalani** in
Piazza Catalani displays the

eclecticism of 12th-century
Norman architecture, with rich
decoration. To visit the the
church, ask at the tourist office.
Outside, GA Montorsoli's
Fontana d'Orione (1547) is
the finest fountain of its kind
from 16th-century Sicily. His
Fontana di Nettuno (1557)
celebrates Messina's foundation
and position in the world as a
principal commercial port.

🏛 Museo Regionale
Via della Libertà 465. 📞 090 36 12
92. 🕐 daily am (Tue, Thu & Sat
also pm). 📷

**Antonello da Messina's *Madonna
and Child* (1473), Museo Regionale**

Taormina ⑮

Messina. 🏃 10,000. 🚉 🚌
🛈 Palazzo Corvaja, Piazza Santa
Caterina (0942 232 43). 🛳 Wed.
🌐 www.gate2taormina.com

SPLENDIDLY SITUATED, Taormina
is Sicily's best-known resort.
It retains an air of exclusivity
while being on the tourist trail,
with sandy beaches and a wide
range of restaurants and hotels.
The most illustrious relic of
the past is the **theatre**. Begun
in the 3rd century BC by the
Greeks, it was subsequently
rebuilt by the Romans. Among
other Classical remains are
the ruins of the **odeon** (for
musical performances) and
the **naumachia** (an artificial
lake for mock-battles). On
Piazza Vittorio Emanuele (site
of the Roman Forum), **Palazzo
Corvaia** (14th century) was
built using stone from a temple
that once stood here. The 13th-
century **Duomo** (renovated in
1636) is a fortress-like building.

ENVIRONS: Taormina's main
beach, **Mazzarò**, boasts clear
waters and is easily reached
from the town. South of Taormina at **Capo Schisò** are the
ruins of ancient **Naxos**. To the
west is **Gole dell'Alcantara**, a
20-m (66-ft) deep gorge of basalt rock, a river and waterfalls.

Mount Etna ⓰

Catania. 🚋 to Linguaglossa or Randazzo; Circumetnea railway from Catania to Riposto. 🚌 to Nicolosi. 🅸 Via G. Garibaldi 63, Nicolosi (095 91 15 05). To hire a guide: 095 791 47 55. 🆆 www.apt.catania.it/etna/index.html

EUROPE'S HIGHEST (3,370 m/ 11,050 ft) and most active volcano, Mount Etna was thought by the Romans to have been the forge of Vulcan (god of fire). A cable car used to go to the top but was destroyed in the 2001 eruption. The climb to the summit should be made only with a guide. The Circumetnea railway runs around the base, offering good views.

Catania ⓱

🚶 365,000. ✈ 🚌 🚆 🅸 Via Cimarosa 10 (095 73 06 211). 🅰 Mon–Sat (general); Sun (antique & bric-a-brac). 🆆 www.apt.catania.it

HAVING BEEN DECIMATED by the earthquake of 1693, Catania was comprehensively

The façade of Catania's Duomo

rebuilt. While it is not a beautiful city, it contains some of the most imaginative lava-built Baroque buildings in Sicily. **Piazza del Duomo**, featuring a lava elephant (Catania's symbol) carrying an Egyptian obelisk, offers a dramatic vista to Mount Etna. In 1736 the Norman **Duomo** was given a new façade by Vaccarini, who also worked on the **Municipio** (finished 1741), on the façade of **Sant'Agata** (1748), on the designs of **Collegio**

Cutelli, probably built by a pupil around 1779, and on **Palazzo Valle** (c.1740–50).

Carrying on the Vaccarini tradition is Stefano Ittar's **San Placido** (around 1768). The frenzied stone carving on the **Palazzo Biscari** (early 18th century) is exceeded by Antonino Amato's unrestrained decoration of the vast Benedictine **convent** (1704) and the adjacent huge church of **San Niccolò** (1730).

On Via Vittorio Emanuele is the **Museo Belliniano**, birthplace of composer Vincenzo Bellini (1801–35). The lava ruins of the **Teatro Romano** (21 BC) are at Piazza Stesicono. **Verga's House**, home of the great Sicilian novelist Giovanni Verga (1840–1922), is on Via Sant' Anna. Via Crociferi is home to 18th-century churches **San Francesco Borgia**, **San Benedetto** and **San Giuliano**, whose interior is Vaccarini's masterpiece (1760). Further along Via Crociferi, the church of **Santo Carcere** contains the prison of St Agatha, who was martyred in AD 253.

INFLUENCES ON TRADITIONAL SICILIAN CUISINE

Sicily has one of Italy's most varied cuisines. The island's unique location – marooned between North Africa, Europe and the eastern Mediterranean – and the invaders it attracted, are responsible for this. The earliest Western cookbook, the now lost *Art of Cooking* (5th century BC), was written by Mithaecus, a Siracusan Greek. Sicily's fertility attracted Greek colonists, who exported oil, wheat, honey, cheese, fruit and vegetables to their homeland. The Arabs introduced oranges, lemons, aubergines and sugar cane. Their love of sweet confections inspired *granita*, a form of flavoured ice, and

An impressive selection of olives displayed in a Palermo market stall

cassata, an elaborate sponge cake with ricotta and candied fruit. The Sicilians love to claim an Arabic origin for their ice cream, but the Greeks and Romans had created an earlier version by chilling their wine with snow from Mount Etna. Traditionally, the peasants existed on a subsistence diet while

the aristocracy enjoyed extravagant fare, and one of the peculiarities of Sicilian food today is that it can be both frugal and handsomely ornate. All of the usual Italian dishes are available, but more interesting are the variations using local ingredients like swordfish, sardines, ricotta cheese, red chillies, aubergines, capers, olives and almond paste.

Marzipan fruits made from almond paste

Shorefront in Siracusa, one of the most beautiful cities of the ancient Greek world

Pantalica ⑱

Siracusa. 🚌 from Siracusa to Sortino then 5-km (3-mile) walk to entrance, or bus from Siracusa to Ferla then 10-km (6-mile) walk to entrance. **Necropolis** ℹ Via San Giovanni alle Catacombe 7, Siracusa. 📞 0931 46 27 11. ⏰ 9am–12:30pm, 2–4:30pm (to 5:30pm summer) Tue–Sun. ♿

REMOTE IN THE desolate Monti Iblei and overlooking the River Anapo is the prehistoric **necropolis** of Pantalica – a pleasant place to walk and picnic. The dead of a large, unexcavated village (occupied from 13th–8th century BC) were buried here in cave-like tombs cut into the rock. More than 5,000 of these tombs were arranged in tiers with a single flat stone sealing each opening.

The inhabitants of Pantalica are thought to have come from coastal **Thapsos**, which was abandoned after raids by warlike tribes from mainland Italy. The site was re-inhabited in the Byzantine period when some tombs were made into

Rock-cut tombs in the prehistoric necropolis of Pantalica

cave dwellings and chapels. Artifacts from the necropolis are displayed in Siracusa's Museo Archeologico Regionale.

Siracusa ⑲

🏛 118,000. 🚆 FS 🚌 ⛴ ℹ Via Maestranza (0931 46 42 55). 🛒 Wed.

Interior of Duomo in Siracusa

SIRACUSA (SYRACUSE) was the most important and powerful Greek city from the 5th to the 3rd centuries BC, and, according to the Roman consul Cicero, the most beautiful. The peninsula **Ortigia** is the hub of the old city. On the mainland, **Achradina**, **Tyche** and **Neapolis** have been occupied almost without a break since the expansion of the city in 480 BC. These were the years of Gelon, tyrant of Gela, when Siracusa was enriched with new temples, theatres and dockyards. The city was a powerful force until 211 BC, when it fell to the Romans in

a battle that also killed the mathematician Archimedes, its most famous inhabitant.

The highlight of Ortigia is the extraordinary **Duomo**, begun in 1728 by architect Andrea Palma. Its Baroque façade masks the **Temple of Athena** (5th century BC), which has been absorbed into the Duomo. Facing the Ponte Nuovo are the ruins of Sicily's earliest Doric temple, the **Temple of Apollo**, which had monolithic columns.

Across from the Duomo is the **Palazzo Beneventano del Bosco** (1778–88), a bold example of Siracusan Baroque, as is **Santa Lucia alla Badia** (1695–1703). In the Municipio a small museum records the history of Ionic temples, and the coin collection of the Galleria Numismatica records Siracusa's past wealth. The delightful **Fonte Aretusa** is frequently referred to by Classical writers as the point where Aretusa emerged from the ground, having been changed into a spring by Artemis to help her escape her lover Alpheus.

At Ortigia's furthest point is the **Castello Maniace**, built by Frederick II around 1239. Here too is the **Gallerie Regionale di Palazzo Bellomo**, with sculpture and paintings including the *Burial of St Lucy* (1608) by Caravaggio.

The painting comes from the church of **Santa Lucia** in the Achradina quarter. This area was flattened during World War II, but the church survived.

It is mostly 17th century with a Norman campanile, and occupies the site where St Lucy, patron saint of Siracusa, was martyred in AD 304. Achradina is now the centre of modern Siracusa.

To the north, in Tyche, is the **Museo Archeologico Regionale Paolo Orsi**, with its important collection of artifacts from the Palaeolithic to the Byzantine era, taken from southeastern sites in Sicily. Included are vases, coins, bronzes, votive objects, busts, sculpture and fragments from Siracusan temples.

The Neapolis quarter and its **Parco Archeologico** feature the Teatro Romano, the Altar of Hieron II and the spectacular Teatro Greco, carved from the hillside. Beyond the Nymphaeum is the 2nd-century AD Roman amphitheatre and the stone quarries, the Latomia del Paradiso featuring the **Ear of Dionysius**. It is thought that 7,000 Athenians were incarcerated here and left to die after their calamitous defeat in 413 BC, in a battle described by Thucydides as "the greatest action in Hellenic history".

ENVIRONS: At **Epipolae**, 8 km (5 miles) north of Neapolis is the **Castle of Euryalus** – the most important ancient Greek fortification to have survived.

🏛 **Gallerie Regionale di Palazzo Bellomo**
Palazzo Bellomo, Via Capodieci 14.
📞 0931 695 11. ⭕ 9am–7pm
Tue–Sat (to 2pm Sun).
🏛 **Museo Archeologico Regionale Paolo Orsi**
Viale Teocrito 66. 📞 0931 46 40 22.
⭕ 9am–1pm, 3–5pm Tue–Sat
(to 1pm Sun). 📷 ♿

Noto ⓴

Siracusa. 🚶 24,000. FS ☷ ℹ
Piazza XVI Maggio (0931 83 67 44).
📅 Mon & 1st & 3rd Tue of the
month. 🌐 www.comune.noto.sr.it

NOTO WAS BUILT from scratch in the early 18th century to replace Noto Antica, which was devastated by an earthquake in 1693. The town was comprehensively designed in Baroque style, using the local white tufa, a limestone that

The façade of the Duomo in Noto rises above a huge staircase

has turned a honey-brown colour from the sun. It is now one of the most enchanting towns in Sicily and a UNESCO World Heritage site.

The twin-towered **Duomo** (completed 1770s) that dominates Noto is by architect Rosario Gagliardi, who also designed the eccentric tower façade of the seminary of **San Salvatore** (18th century) in Piazza Municipio, the convex façade of **San Domenico** (1730s) in Piazza XVI Maggio, and the oval interior of **Santa Chiara** (1730) on Corso

Vittorio Emanuele. The magnificent **Palazzo Trigona** (1781) stands on Via Cavour behind the Duomo. On Via Nicolaci, the **Palazzo Villadorata** (1730s) features a splendid façade adorned with elaborate stone carvings. At the north end of Via Nicolaci, the **Monastery of Montevergine** has a striking curved façade. In mid-May, Via Nicolaci is the site of the Infiorata flower festival. Gagliardi's church of the **Crocifisso** (1728) stands on the town's summit. It contains a sculpture of the Madonna by Francesco Laurana (1471). The **Municipio** (1740s), facing the Duomo, has a fine "billowing" ground floor design.

ENVIRONS: The earthquake of 1693 also devastated the towns of **Modica**, around 30 km (19 miles) to the west, and **Ragusa**, a short distance further. Like Noto, they were rebuilt in the region's rich Baroque style. Gagliardi worked on Modica's **San Giorgio** (early 18th century), on Ragusa's **San Giorgio** (begun around 1746, and one of his masterpieces) and **San Giuseppe** (mid-18th century).

Boisterous carving on the façade of the Palazzo Villadorata in Noto

SARDINIA

I N HIS TRAVELOGUE, Sea and Sardinia, *DH Lawrence wrote that Sardinia was "left outside of time and history". Indeed, the march of time has been slow here, and traditions from ancient Europe have survived – the legacy of invasion by Phoenicians, Carthaginians, Romans, Arabs, Byzantines, Spaniards and Savoyards.*

These traditions are displayed in Sardinia's many festivals – some soberly Christian, others with pagan roots. Several different dialects and languages are spoken in Sardinia. Catalan can be heard in Alghero, and on the island of San Pietro, there is a Ligurian dialect. Even remnants of Phoenician survive. In the south, the traditional influences are Spanish, while pure native strains of people and language survive in the Gennargentu mountains. Peopled by shepherds in isolated communities, this region is so impenetrable that invaders have never bothered it.

Of particular interest are the prehistoric *nuraghe* castles, villages, temples and tombs which litter the countryside – most notably around Barumini, north of Cagliari, and in the Valle dei Nuraghe, south of Sassari. The *nuraghe* were built by a people whose origins constitute one of the Mediterranean's great mysteries. In Cagliari, the capital of Sardinia, there is a museum with an excellent archaeological collection that offers insight into this enigmatic people.

Sassari, Oristano, Alghero and Olbia are all centres of areas marked by their individuality. Some remarkable Pisan-Romanesque churches are located around Sassari and here too dialects reveal close links with the languages of Tuscany. Olbia is a boom town made rich by tourism and the proximity of the jet-setting Costa Smeralda. Sober Nuoro with its province in the shadow of the Gennargentu mountains, by contrast, has little in common with the Sardinia of tourist brochures.

Relaxing during the day in the tiny resort of Carloforte on the Isola di San Pietro, next to Sant'Antioco

◁ **The Bay of Simius east of Cagliari in the southeast corner of Sardinia**

Exploring Sardinia

T HIS ISLAND, called Sardegna in Italian, is characterized by an interior of dramatic, rolling uplands covered in *macchia* – grassland mingled with myrtle, wild thyme, prickly pears and dwarf oaks – and a coastline of beguiling, translucent sea, isolated coves, long sandy beaches and caves. The Gennargentu mountains, with the highest peak at 1,834 m (6,017 ft), shield a nearly impenetrable area of rural villages. In the northeast, mountains fall away dramatically to the Costa Smeralda, Sardinia's most exclusive coastal area. Further south, the shoreline around the Golfo di Orosei is completely unspoilt. Around Oristano in the west the land is flat, leading to the plain of Campidano where the island's corn, fruit and vegetables grow.

Prehistoric nuraghic remains at Su Nuraxi near Barumini

SIGHTS AT A GLANCE

Alghero ❸
Bosa ❹
Cagliari ❾
Cala Gonone ❻
Costa Smeralda ❶
Nuoro ❺
Oristano ❼
Sant'Antioco ❽
Sassari ❷

A typical scene of clothes hanging out to dry in Alghero

SEE ALSO

- **Where to Stay** p575
- **Where to Eat** p609

0 kilometres   50

0 miles   25

GOLFO DELL'ASINARA

PORTO TORRES

SASSARI ❷

GROTTA DI NETTUNO

❸ ALGHERO

TORRALBA

SANTU ANTIN
VALLE
NURAG

❹ MACOME
BOSA

NURAGHE LOSA

ORISTANO
❼

THARROS
GOLFO DI
ORISTANO
ARBOREA

SANTA GIUSTA

CAMPID

MAR DI SARDEGNA

IGLESIAS

ISOLA DI
SAN PIETRO

❽ SANT'ANTIOCO

GOLFO DI
PALMAS

Waves lapping at the rocks on Isola di San Pietro, northwest of Sant'Antioco

KEY

▬▬	Major road
▭▭	Minor road
▭	Scenic route
≈	River
✲	Viewpoint

Southernmost reach of the Gennargentu mountains

GETTING AROUND

Ferries from a wide range of ports on the Italian mainland dock at Cagliari, Olbia and Porto Torres. International and domestic flights use the airports at Cagliari, Olbia and Alghero. The island is neatly cut by the S131. It skirts the Gennargentu mountains, which are accessible only by tortuously winding passes. Branches of the S131 reach Olbia and Nuoro. Express bus and excellent, fast train services connect the major cities, while slower, daily bus services and narrow-gauge trains operate between the smaller towns.

The extravagantly beautiful, *macchia*-scented Costa Smeralda

Costa Smeralda ❶

Sassari. **FS** 🚢 *Olbia.* 🚌 *Porto Cervo.* 🛈 *AAST Olbia, Via Catello Piro 1 (0789 214 53); AAST Arzachena, Via Paolo Dettori 4 (0789 810 90).*

THE FORMERLY WILD Costa Smeralda, stretching from the Golfo di Cugnana to the Golfo di Arzachena, was developed in the late 1950s by a consortium of magnates into one of the world's most opulent holiday resorts. Strict controls keep the area immaculate.

In **Porto Cervo**, the main town, boutiques jostle with nightclubs, fine restaurants and luxury hotels. It caters for the seriously rich – billionaires, crowned heads and pop stars.

ENVIRONS: Head north to rural **Baia Sardinia** and **Cannigione**. From **Palau** ferries leave for **La Maddalena** and **Isola Caprera**, the home of Garibaldi and the **Museo Nazionale Garibaldino**.

🏛 **Museo Nazionale Garibaldino**
Frazione Caprera, Maddalena. 📞 *0789 72 71 62.* 🕐 *9am–1:30pm, 2–6:30pm Tue–Sat (to 1:30pm Sun).* ● *1 Jan, 1 May, 25 Dec.* 📷 ♿

Sassari ❷

🏙 *130,000.* ✈ **FS** 🚌 🛈 *Viale Caprera 36 (079 29 95 44; 079 29 94 15).* 🛍 *Mon.*

FOUNDED BY GENOESE and Pisan merchants early in the 13th century, Sassari is known for its spectacular *Cavalcata*

Sarda festival on Ascension Day, and for being the site of Sardinia's first university. There is a raucous, tight, church-filled medieval quarter around the **Duomo** (11th century with later, mostly Baroque, additions), and to the north is the huge **Fonte Rosello**, a late-Renaissance fountain. The **Museo Archeologico Nazionale "GA Sanna"** is a good starting point for an investigation into the region's nuraghic history.

ENVIRONS: To the southeast along the S131 is the Pisan-Romanesque church of **Santissima Trinità di Saccargia** (1116), with the only extant 13th-century fresco cycle in Sardinia. Further on is the 12th-century church of **San Michele di Salvenero**, and at **Ardara** the basalt-built Romanesque **Santa Maria del Regno**, or "Black Cathedral".

Façade of Santissima Trinità di Saccargia

🏛 **Museo Archeologico Nazionale "GA Sanna"**
Via Roma 64. 📞 *079 27 22 03.* 🕐 *Tue–Sun.* 📷 📹 ♿

Alghero ❸

🏙 *41,000.* ✈ **FS** 🚌 🚢 🛈 *Piazza Porta Terra 9 (079 97 90 54).* 🛍 *Wed.* Ⓦ *www.infoalghero.it*

FOUNDED ON A PENINSULA facing the Bay of Alghero early in the 12th century, and taken from the Genoese Dorias by the Aragonese in 1353, Alghero was peopled by settlers from Barcelona and Valencia. Its original occupants – Ligurians and Sardinians – were expelled with such thoroughness that today the Catalan language and culture is enjoying a revival and the look of old Alghero is consistently Spanish.

Filled with labyrinthine alleys and cobbled streets, the lively port of old Alghero is flanked by battlemented walls and defensive towers on all but the landward section. Facing the Giardino Pubblico is the massive 16th-century **Torre di Porta Terra**, also known as the Jewish Tower after its builders. Around the periphery of the old town are more towers, including **Torre dell'Espero Reial** and **Torre San Giacomo** on Lungomare Colombo, and **Torre della Maddalena** on Piazza Porta Terra. The 16th-century **Duomo** at the bottom of Via Umberto is predominantly Catalan-Gothic with an Aragonese portal. Off Via Carlo Alberto, **San Francesco** (14th century)

A typical house in Alghero

The waterfront at Bosa

has a pretty cloister and octagonal campanile towering over Alghero, and Baroque **San Michele** has a bright tiled dome. In Via Principe Umberto is the **Casa Doria**, the house where the pre-Hispanic rulers of Alghero lived. It has a beautiful Renaissance portal and Gothic-arched window.

ENVIRONS: Take a boat or car trip (the latter involves much climbing down) to the spectacular **Grotta di Nettuno**, a deep natural cave round the point of Capo Caccia, or the nearby **Grotta Verde**.

Bosa ❹

Nuoro. 🚶 8,500. 🚉 🚌 ℹ Pro Loco, Via Azuni 5 (0785 37 61 07). 🛒 Tue.

BOSA IS A SMALL, picturesque seaside town at the mouth of Sardinia's only navigable river, the Temo. The historic **Sa Costa** district struggles up the side of a low hill capped by the **Castello di Serravalle**, built in 1122 by the Malaspina family. The narrow passages and alleys here have changed little since the Middle Ages. By the Temo are **Sas Conzas** – the former dyers' houses and workshops.

Languishing on the riverside, the cosmopolitan **Sa Piatta** district houses the Aragonese-Gothic **Duomo** (15th century) and Romanesque **San Pietro Extramuros** (11th century), with a Gothic façade added by Cistercian monks in the 13th century.

NURAGHE IN SARDINIA

The dominant feature of Sardinia is the 7,000 or so *nuraghe* dotted around the island. Dating from 1800 to 300 BC, these strange, truncated cone structures were built without any bonding from huge basalt blocks taken from extinct volcanoes. To this day, little is known about the identity of the nuraghic people. They must have been well organized and possessed remarkable engineering skills, judging by their buildings, but appear to have left no written word. The mystery of these enigmatic people has intrigued Sardinians for years.

The individual **nuraghe** *are fairly small. A few were fortresses, equipped with wells and other defensive features.*

Su Nuraxi at Barumini (above), Serra Orrios, near Dorgali, and Santu Antine at Torralba are among the most important nuraghe *complexes. Houses, temples, tombs, and even a theatre have been identified.*

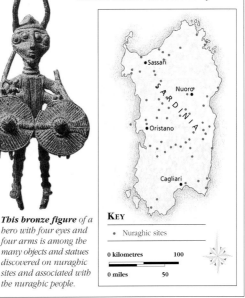

This bronze figure of a hero with four eyes and four arms is among the many objects and statues discovered on nuraghic sites and associated with the nuraghic people.

KEY

• Nuraghic sites

| 0 kilometres | 100 |
| 0 miles | 50 |

Nobel Prize-winning novelist Grazia Deledda from Nuoro

Nuoro ❺

🚶 38,000. 🚈 🚌 ℹ️ *Piazza d'Italia 19 (0784 300 83).* 🚆 *Fri & Sat.*
🌐 *www.enteturismo.nuoro.it*
📅 *29 Aug: Sagra del Redentore.*

THIS TOWN, in a spectacular setting beneath Monte Ortobene and the dramatic Supramonte, was the home of Grazia Deledda, who won the Nobel Prize for Literature in 1926 for her portrayal of the power and passions in the primitive communities around her. A comprehensive collection of ethnic items, such as traditional Sardinian costumes and jewellery, can be seen in the excellent **Museo della Vita e delle Tradizioni Popolari Sarde**. Attending the *Sagra del Redentore* festival is the best way to witness the region's dancing and dialects.

ENVIRONS: Nuoro is on the edge of the Barbagia region,

which has isolated villages of shepherds who have never experienced the hand of any overlord, so impenetrable are the **Gennargentu** mountains. This region was known to the Romans as Barbaria, an area they were never able to subdue. Traces of the traditional lawlessness of the Barbagia can be seen in **Orgosolo**, with its wall murals calling for Sardinia's independence. Rival clans were locked in bloody vendetta for almost 50 years, and the deeds of native bandits form part of local folklore.

In **Mamoiada**'s *Feast of the Mamuthones*, men in sinister masks and traditional costume perform a ritual dance ending with a symbolic "killing" of a scapegoat. The fervour of the event is indicative of the fierce folkloric tradition and deep resistance to change.

🏛 **Museo della Vita e delle Tradizioni Popolari Sarde**
Via Mereu 56. 📞 *0784 24 29 00.*
🕐 *9am–1pm, 3–7pm daily (Jun–Sep: 9am–8pm).* 📷

Cala Gonone ❻

Nuoro. 🚶 800. 🚌 ℹ️ *Pro Loco, via Lamormara 108, Dorgali (0784 962 43).* 🚆 *daily.* 🚤 *to grottoes (Apr–mid-Oct).* 📞 *0784 933 05.*

EAST OF NUORO, between the sea and the mountains, is the hamlet of Cala Gonone – a bustling seaside resort and fishing port, with magnificent beaches. Along the unspoilt coast are the isolated coves of **Cala Luna**, linked with Cala

Gonone by a well-marked two-hour trail, and **Cala Sisine**. The famous **Grotta del Bue Marino**, adorned with weird rock formations, can only be reached by boat.

ENVIRONS: To the south, the villages of **Urzulei**, **Baunei** and **Santa Maria Navarrese**, along the spectacular SS125 road to Tortolì, feature breathtaking landscapes.

Oristano ❼

Cagliari. 🚶 32,000. 🚈 🚌 ℹ️ *EPT, Eleonora 1 (0783 368 31); Pro Loco, Via Vittorio Emanuele 8 (0783 706 21).* 🚆 *Tue & Fri.*

Ruins of Tharros near Oristano

THE PROVINCE of Oristano corresponds roughly with historical Arborea, over which Eleonora ruled *(see opposite)*. She is commemorated by an 18th-century statue in **Piazza Eleonora**. On Corso Vittorio Emanuele is the 16th-century **Casa di Eleonora**, and nearby the **Antiquarium Arborense**, which has Neolithic, nuraghic, Punic and Roman artifacts. The **Torre di San Cristoforo** (1291) in Piazza Roma once formed part of Oristano's fortifications. The **Duomo** (13th century) was later rebuilt in the Baroque style. More interesting are the churches of **Santa Chiara** (1343) on Via Garibaldi and 14th-century **San Martino** on Via Cagliari.

ENVIRONS: The 12th-century Pisan-Romanesque **Cathedral** at Santa Giusta has columns probably taken from Tharros,

Entrance to the Grotta del Bue Marino, south of Cala Gonone

The tiny resort of Carloforte, the capital of Isola di San Pietro

an 8th-century BC Punic settlement whose extensive ruins lie 20 km (12 miles) west of Oristano on the Sinis peninsula.

🏛 Antiquarium Arborense
Palazzo Parpaglia, Via Parpaglia 37. 📞 0783 79 12 62. ⏷ daily. ⬚ ⬚ ⬚

Sant'Antioco ❽

Cagliari. 🚆 🚌 ℹ Pro Loco Piazza Repubblica 31a (0781 84 05 92).

THE MAIN TOWN on this unspoilt island off Sardinia's southern coast is **Sant'Antioco**, once a Phoenician port and an important Roman base. Proof of almost continuous occupation is clear at the **catacombs**, a Phoenician burial place later used by Christians, under the 12th-century basilica of **Sant' Antioco Martire**. The **Antiquarium** contains Phoenician artifacts. The Punic **Tophet** (sanctuary of the goddess Tanit) and the **necropolis** are nearby. The small **Isola di San Pietro** can be reached by ferry from Calasetta.

🎭 Catacombs
Piazza Parrocchia.
📞 0781 830 44.
⏷ daily. ⬚ only. ⬚
🏛 Antiquarium
Via Regina Margherita
113. 📞 0781 835 90. ⏷ daily. ⬤ 1 Jan, Easter, 8, 25 & 26 Dec. ⬚ ⬚
(also allows entry to Tophet and necropolis.)

Cagliari ❾

🏙 250,000. ✈ 🚆 🚌 ⛴
ℹ Piazza Matteotti 9 (070 66 92 55). ⬤ daily; also Sun (flea) and 2nd Sun of month (antiques).
🌐 www.comune.cagliari.it

THE CAPITAL of Sardinia, this site was occupied by the Phoenicians, Carthaginians and Romans, and extensive ruins of the Phoenician city of Nora lie to the southwest of Cagliari. A 2nd-century **amphitheatre** survives from the Roman era, cut from rock.
Discover the town's earlier history in the **Cittadella dei Musei**, the former royal arsenal. It houses several museums, including the **Museo Nazionale Archeologico**. The nuraghic items are the most interesting in the collection, especially the bronze votive statuettes. Also in the Cittadella dei Musei is the **Pinacoteca**, an art gallery.

The 6th-century church of San Saturnino in Cagliari, built on a Greek-cross plan

The old core of Cagliari has an appealing North African character. In the high **Castello** district, the Romans and, later, Pisans built defences. The gracious **Bastione San Remy** on Piazza Costituzione offers magnificent views over the city and surrounding countryside. The **Duomo** is a 20th-century rehash of a Romanesque building. Flanking the entrance are two 12th-century pulpits originally destined for the cathedral in Pisa.
Nearby is the Pisan tower **Torre San Pancrazio** (14th century). From the partially-ruined **Torre dell'Elefante** on Via dell'Università to the port lies the **Marina** quarter, which expanded from the old town in the 16th to 17th centuries. In Piazza San Cosimo, the 6th-century church of **San Saturnino** is a rare monument to Byzantine occupation.

🎭 Amphitheatre
Viale Sant'Ignazio. 📞 070 68 40 00.
⏷ 9am–8pm Tue–Sun.
🏛 Cittadella dei Musei
Piazza Arsenale. 📞 070 68 40 00.
Museo Nazionale Archeologico
⏷ 9am–8pm Tue–Sun. ⬚ ⬚
Pinacoteca ⏷ 9am–8pm Tue–Sun.
⬤ 1 Jan, 1 May, 25 Dec. ⬚ ⬚

ELEONORA OF ARBOREA

A champion against rule from abroad, Eleonora was governing *giudicessa* (judge) of Arborea, one of four administrative divisions of Sardinia, from 1383–1404. Her marriage to Brancaleone Doria consolidated Genoese interests in Sardinia. She rallied the island to keep out Spanish invaders who tried to claim land that had been given to the Aragonese King James II. Her greatest legacy was the completion of the codifying of laws begun by her father. Written in Sardinian, they called for community of property in marriage and the right of women to seek redress from rape.

TRAVELLERS' NEEDS

WHERE TO STAY

PEOPLE COME FROM all over the world to visit Italy and most Italians spend their holidays here as well, particularly in the mountains or by the sea. This means that there is a dazzling range of accommodation options, from splendid hotels in old palazzi and historic residences, to simple family-run *pensioni* and hostels. Most major cities also offer up-market B&Bs. Those who want self-catering accommodation are also well served with everything from stately villas in Tuscany to purpose-built holiday flats in, or near, seaside resorts. Italian hotels are notorious for being expensive and short of services but you can still find excellent value in all price ranges. The hotels listed on pages 542–75 have been selected from every price category as among the best value in each area for style, comfort or location.

Sign for a 3-star hotel

The Gritti Palace, one of Venice's historic palazzi *(see p544)*

GRADINGS

HOTELS IN ITALY are graded with one to five stars. Grading depends on facilities offered rather than atmosphere and each region awards stars according to slightly different criteria.

Sometimes a hotel has a lower rating than it deserves. This may be because the local tourist office has not upgraded it yet or the hotel itself has opted to stay in a lower category to avoid higher taxes.

ALBERGHI

ALBERGO IS ITALIAN for hotel but the term tends to refer to the upper categories. Room sizes vary considerably: in city centres even expensive hotels can have far smaller rooms than their counterparts in other countries, whereas outside the city your room may be more like a small suite. In general, *alberghi* will have private showers in all rooms and the more luxurious have baths. In city centres you may come across the sign *albergo diurno*. This is a day hotel without accommodation but with bathroom, showers, hairdressing, drying and other cleaning facilities you may need when travelling. Day hotels are usually situated at or near the main railway station.

PENSIONI

ALTHOUGH THE TERM *pensione* is no longer in official use, it still describes one- and two-star hotels, most of which are small and family run. On the whole you will meet immaculate standards of cleanliness and friendly, helpful service with basic, although perfectly functional, rooms. However, as *pensioni* are often in old buildings, historic charm may be paid for with noisy, erratic plumbing and dark rooms. Many do not have public rooms other than a sparsely furnished breakfast room. Most will offer at least some rooms with a private shower although rarely a bath. If you intend being out late, check that you'll be able to get back into the *pensione*. Not all of them have night porters after midnight or 1am, but most will at least be able to provide a key to the main door.

If you are planning to stay in a *pensione* in winter, check that it has central heating. Not all of them do and, even in the south, temperatures are low from November to February.

A *locanda* was traditionally an inn, offering cheap food and a place to sleep for the traveller. The word is still in use, particularly in central and northern Italy, but is now synonymous with *pensione* and may be more of an affectation for the benefit of the tourist.

CHAIN HOTELS

THERE ARE VARIOUS Italian chain hotels at the upper end of the market, as well as the usual big internationals. **Jolly** hotels appeal to the business traveller and there

Street sign showing the direction and location of hotels

◁ **Popular café in Piazza Navona, Rome**

Romantic Hotel Villa Pagoda in Nervi, Genoa *(see p555)*

are one or two in most large cities; **Starwood Westin** and **Best Western** are more akin to international luxury chains, while **Notturno Italiano** cater for the more modest budget. **Relais et Châteaux** run charming hotels in historic castles, villas and monasteries with facilities to match.

MEALS AND FACILITIES

ITALIAN HOTELS TEND to offer fewer special facilities than those in many other countries. In spite of the warm summers, for example, air-conditioning is rare in all but five-star hotels, as is 24-hour room service.

Some hotels may insist on full board *(pensione completa)* or half board *(mezza pensione)* in peak season. Avoid this if you can: unless the hotel is very isolated, there will almost certainly be a good range of places to eat nearby. Most hotel rates include breakfast, which in four- and five-star hotels will consist of a large buffet; the *pensioni* breakfast will probably consist of coffee and biscuits or brioches with butter and jam. Once again, try to avoid this as breakfast at a local bar is an enjoyable Italian institution.

For a double room, state if you want twin beds *(letti singoli)* or a double bed *(matrimoniale)*. Bathrooms in all but the most expensive hotels will have showers rather than baths.

CHILDREN

ITALIANS ACCEPT CHILDREN as an ordinary part of life and, although there may not be many special facilities, they are always welcome. Some of the cheaper hotels may not be able to provide cots. However, virtually all hotels, from the simplest to the most grand, will be happy to put a small bed or two into a double room for families travelling together. The price of this is usually an extra 30–40 per cent of the double room rate per bed. Most of the large hotels will also offer a babysitting service.

PRICES

AS A RULE hotels in Italy are not cheap, although prices vary considerably between places and seasons.

Prices, which include tax and service and are quoted per room, start from around €50 for a double room without a bathroom, and can rise to at least €65 with a bath, even for a very basic hotel. A single room will cost about two thirds of a double. Around €100 will get you something comfortable and often picturesque, although not particularly luxurious. For €210 and upwards you can expect a good range of facilities, a pleasant or central location and often a lot of local or historic charm.

Hotel Sant'Anselmo's garden, Rome *(see p565)*

Hotels in the major cities and resorts are likely to be more expensive.

By law hotels have to display their rates in every bedroom. Variation between high and low season can be as much as 100 per cent or more in resorts.

Also, beware of extras: the mini-bar can be extortionate as can charges for parking, laundry or for making telephone calls directly from your hotel bedroom.

BOOKING

BOOK AS SOON AS possible, particularly if you have special requests such as a room with a view, off the street or with a bath. Two months should be ample, but be aware that, during the high season, popular hotels can be fully booked as early as six months in advance.

August tends to be very busy at beach resorts and February at mountain resorts. The same goes for cities and towns depending on their particular cultural calendars *(see pp62–5)*.

You will be asked for a deposit when you book; this can usually be paid for by credit card (even in hotels that do not accept credit cards for final payment); otherwise by international money order.

Under Italian law the hotel must issue you with a receipt *(ricevuta fiscale)* for final payment which you must keep until you leave Italy.

Florence's Hotel Tornabuoni Beacci *(see p559)*

Vaulted central entrance of Hotel Porta Rossa in Florence *(see p558)*

CHECKING IN AND OUT

O N ARRIVAL the management will take your passport to register you with the police. This is a mere formality and it should be returned within an hour or two. You will also have to authorize the hotel to transfer calls to your room.

Checking-out time is usually before noon and may be earlier in small hotels. The room must be vacated but most hotels will allow you to leave luggage in a safe place to be collected later in the day.

SELF-CATERING AND AGRITURISMO

I F YOU INTEND to be based in one area, self-catering accommodation often enjoys a marvellous location and is generally of a high standard.

Across rural Italy there are more than 2,000 farms, villas and mountain chalets offering reasonably priced self-catering or hotel-style accommodation as part of the **Agriturismo** scheme. Facilities range from those of a first-class hotel in

Albergo al Sole, Venice *(see p544)*

beautifully kept villas or ancient castles to basic rooms with the family on a working farm. Some have excellent restaurants which serve farm and local produce, others can arrange riding, fishing or other activity holidays *(see p624)*. There may be a minimum stay requirement, especially in peak season. The booklet *Guida dell'Ospitalità Rurale* can be found in the central office in Rome or the regional offices. Other self-catering options can be arranged through specialized agencies such as **Tailor-Made Tours**, **Vacanze in Italia** and **Magic of Italy** before you leave for Italy, but again, make sure you book in advance; they can be booked up for months.

There are also so-called *residence*, found in the **ENIT** accommodation lists. These are halfway between a hotel and self-catering flats and often offer cooking facilities and some sort of restaurant service.

For stays of several months or more, accommodation agencies for apartments in the city centre as well as the

nearby countryside can be found under *Immobiliari* in the *Pagine Gialle* (Yellow Pages).

BUDGET ACCOMMODATION

A S WELL AS THE International Youth Hostels Association (**AIG** in Italy), tourist offices in the major cities have lists of privately-run hostels. Prices, at around €12 per person per night, are considerably less than even the cheapest *pensioni* but accommodation is in single-sex dormitories and washing facilities may be over-stretched. A room in a private house is another cheap option, offering often small but clean rooms. Bed-and-breakfast accommodation is increasing rapidly but is of variable quality, so only rely on trust-worthy recommendation.

The **Centro Turistico Studentesco** can help students find rooms in university accommodation across Italy. This is not limited to students taking courses, particularly in the summer when resident students are on holiday.

A peaceful alternative is to stay in a convent or monastery with guest accommodation. The rooms are clean, if a little spartan, and they are usually in a secluded area or behind cloister walls. However, strict rules may be a price to pay: most have early curfews and many will not admit members of the opposite sex even when with their spouses. There is no central agency dealing with these but they are included in the **ENIT** accommodation lists for each region.

A boat carrying visitors' luggage to a hotel in Venice

MOUNTAIN REFUGES AND CAMPSITES

Basic ACCOMMODATION in huts and refuges is available in mountainous areas where there is hill-walking and hiking. Most of these huts are owned and run by the **Club Alpino Italiano** whose offices are in Milan.

Campsites abound in the mountains and around the coastal regions. Many of them offer basic accommodation in family-sized cabins (*bungalow*) as well as spaces for tents,

Villa San Michele, a former monastery in Fiesole, Tuscany *(see p560)*

The highest refuge in the Valsesia alps, Rifugio Francesco Pastore

caravans and trailers, with basic facilities such as water, electricity and washing. There is usually a restaurant and, especially in campsites by the sea, there may also be sports facilities such as swimming pools, boat and water sports equipment hire and tennis courts. The **Touring Club Italiano** publishes a full list in *Campeggi e Villaggi Turistici in Italia*, as does **Federcampeggio**.

DISABLED TRAVELLERS

Few HOTELS IN ITALY have special facilities for disabled travellers. Those that do are indicated with the appropriate

symbol in the hotels listings on pages 542–75. In many cases, however, hotels without special facilities will do all they can to accommodate people in wheelchairs by giving them downstairs rooms (when available) and help with lifts or stairs.

FURTHER INFORMATION

The ITALIAN STATE TOURIST office (**ENIT**) has accommodation lists for every region. They are reprinted annually but may not be updated and prices may have changed. Rooms can also be booked at the local **APT** (Azienda Provinciale per il Turismo).

Choosing a Hotel

T HE HOTELS in this guide have been selected from a wide price range for their good value or exceptional location, comfort and style. The chart highlights some of the factors which may influence your choice and gives a brief description of each hotel. Entries are listed by price category within the towns, with colour-coded thumb tabs to indicate the regions covered on each page.

	NUMBER OF ROOMS	RESTAURANT	SWIMMING POOL	GARDEN OR TERRACE
VENICE				
CANNAREGIO: *Giorgione* €€€€ Calle Proverbi, 4587. **Map** 3 B5. ☎ *041 522 58 10.* FAX *041 523 90 92.* @ giorgione@hotelgiorgione.com Well-situated for the Rialto area. This is a recently refurbished hotel in a delightful colour-washed building with a spacious reception area. ▦ TV ▤ ☕	71			▦
CANNAREGIO: *Abbazia* €€€€€ Calle Priuli di Cavalletti, 66–68. **Map** 1 C4. ☎ *041 71 73 33.* FAX *041 71 79 49.* @ info@abbaziahotel.com Quietly situated just off the lively Lista di Spagna area. The rooms are comfortable, if small, and drinks are served in the delightful garden. ▦ TV ▤ ☕	50			▦
CANNAREGIO: *Continental* €€€€€ Lista di Spagna, 166. **Map** 2 D4. ☎ *041 71 51 22.* FAX *041 524 24 32.* @ info@loc A large, well-equipped, modern hotel. Some rooms overlook the Grand Canal, while others are quieter, with views of a tree-shaded square. ▦ TV ▤ ☕	93	▦		▦
CASTELLO: *Locanda La Corte* €€€ Calle Bressana 63/7. **Map** 3 C5. ☎ *041 241 13 00.* FAX *041 241 59 82.* @ info@locandalacorte.it Tucked away in a quiet alley, this 16th-century palace has a lovely courtyard that doubles as the breakfast room during the summer. All mod-cons. ▦ TV ▤ ♿ ☕	18			▦
CASTELLO: *Paganelli* €€€€ Riva degli Schiavoni, 4687. **Map** 8 D2. ☎ *041 522 43 24.* FAX *041 523 92 67.* @ hotelpag@tin.it Excellent views of St Mark's Basin from cosy old-fashioned rooms; those situated in the *dipendenza* (annexe) are less attractive but quieter. ▦ ☕ ▤ TV	22			▦
CASTELLO: *Pensione Wildner* €€€€ Riva degli Schiavoni, 4161. **Map** 8 D2. ☎ *041 522 74 63.* FAX *041 241 46 40.* @ wildner@veneziahotels.com A family-run hotel with simple yet immaculate rooms offering stunning views across to San Giorgio Maggiore. There is also a small bar. ▦ TV ▤ ☕	16	▦		▦
CASTELLO: *Danieli* €€€€€€ Riva degli Schiavoni, 4196. **Map** 7 C2. ☎ *041 522 64 80.* FAX *041 520 02 08.* @ danieli@luxurycollection.com This luxurious hotel was the palace of the Dandolo family and has strong literary and musical connections. Service is impeccable. ▦ TV ▤ ☕	253	▦		▦
CASTELLO: *Londra Palace* €€€€€€ Riva degli Schiavoni, 4171. **Map** 8 D2. ☎ *041 520 05 33.* FAX *041 522 50 32.* @ info@hotellondra.it A lovely stone-faced hotel: the bedrooms feature antique furniture and the best ones are on the lagoon. Tchaikovsky composed his Fourth Symphony here. ▦ TV ▤ ☕	53	▦		▦
DORSODURO: *Montin* €€€ Fondamenta Eremite, 1147. **Map** 6 D3. ☎ *041 522 71 51.* FAX *041 520 02 55.* @ locandamontin@libero.it These rooms are full of charm and character. Book well ahead of your visit. ▤ ☕	11	▦		
DORSODURO: *Pausania* €€€ Fondamenta Gherardini, 2824. **Map** 6 D3. ☎ *041 522 20 83.* FAX *041 522 29 89.* Reasonable prices and friendly staff make this a pleasant place to stay. ▦ TV ▤ ☕	24			▦
DORSODURO: *Agli Alboretti* €€€€ Rio Terrà Antonio Foscarini, 884. **Map** 6 E4. ☎ *041 523 00 58.* FAX *041 521 01 58.* @ alborett@gpnet.it Popular with English and US visitors, this hotel has a cosy reception area and a warm atmosphere. The best rooms look on to the interior gardens. ▦ TV ▤ ☕ **Closed** *Jan.*	23	▦		▦
DORSODURO: *American* €€€€€ Fondamenta Bragadin San Vio 628. **Map** 6 E4. ☎ *041 520 47 33.* FAX *041 520 40 48.* @ reception@hotelamerican.com The rooms in this hotel, near the Accademia, are well-appointed. ▦ TV ▤ ☕	30			▦

	Price categories / Descriptions	NUMBER OF ROOMS	RESTAURANT	SWIMMING POOL	GARDEN OR TERRACE

Price categories for a standard double room for one night, including tax and service charges but not including breakfast:
€ under €52
€€ €52–€100
€€€ €100–€155
€€€€ €155–€205
€€€€€ over €205.

RESTAURANT
A restaurant within the hotel sometimes reserved for residents.
SWIMMING POOL
Hotel swimming pools are usually quite small and are outdoors unless otherwise stated.
GARDEN OR TERRACE
A garden, courtyard or terrace belonging to the hotel, often providing tables for eating outside.
CREDIT CARDS
The major credit cards Visa, MasterCard (Access) and American Express are accepted in hotels with the credit card symbol.

Hotel	Price	Rooms	Restaurant	Pool	Garden
LIDO DI VENEZIA: *Excelsior Palace* — Lungomare Marconi 41. 041 526 02 01. FAX 041 526 72 76. reso77.excelsior@westin.com — A flamboyantly Moorish exterior (even the beach huts are styled like Arabian tents); the comfort of the interior is equally splendid. **Closed** mid-Nov–mid-Mar.	€€€€€	197	■	●	■
LIDO DI VENEZIA: *Hotel des Bains* — Lungomare Marconi 17. 041 526 59 21. FAX 041 526 01 13. desbains@sheraton.com — Thomas Mann wrote his novel *Death in Venice* here. Reception rooms are in Art Deco style, bedrooms are spacious and service superb. **Closed** mid-Nov–mid-Mar.	€€€€€	191	■	●	■
LIDO DI VENEZIA: *Villa Mabapa* — Riviera San Nicolo 16. 041 526 05 90. FAX 041 526 94 41. info@villamabapa.com — Originally built as a private residence in the 1930s, this lovely villa on the promenade by the lagoon retains its original style and atmosphere.	€€€€€	73	■		■
RIALTO: *Rialto* — San Marco 5149. Map 7 A1. 041 520 91 66. FAX 041 523 89 58. info@rialtohotel.com — From its spectacular position by the Rialto bridge, the hotel looks out on to the bustle of the city centre and graceful gondolas. **Hotel restaurant** Apr–Nov.	€€€€	89	■		■
SAN MARCO: *Al Gambero* — Calle dei Fabbri, 4687. Map 7 B2. 041 522 43 84. FAX 041 520 04 31. hotelgambero@tin.it — Situated on one of Venice's main shopping streets, close to the piazza, the Gambero has simple rooms, several with views over the canal.	€€€€	26	■		
SAN MARCO: *Concordia* — Calle Larga San Marco 367. Map 7 B2. 041 520 68 66. FAX 041 520 67 75. info@hotelconcordia.it — Stay at this hotel for its view over St Mark's Square. Book in advance.	€€€€	56	■		
SAN MARCO: *Metropole* — Riva Schiavoni 4149. Map 8 D2. 041 520 50 44. FAX 041 522 36 79. venice@hotelmetropole.com — This hotel is furnished throughout with antique pieces. The restaurant is famous for only offering buffet service, but with a wide choice of specialities.	€€€€	70	■		■
SAN MARCO: *Santo Stefano* — Campo Santo Stefano, 2957. Map 6 F3. 041 520 01 66. FAX 041 522 44 60. info@hotelsantostefanovenezia.com — This tall narrow hotel has good views over the Santo Stefano quarter. Traditional furnishings, but some rooms are cramped.	€€€€	11			
SAN MARCO: *Saturnia & International* — Via XXII Marzo 2398. Map 7 A3. 041 520 83 77. FAX 041 520 71 31. info@hotelsaturnia.it — Set in an ancient palace, this luxury hotel is decorated throughout with antique furniture. There is a charming courtyard with restaurant.	€€€€	91	■		■
SAN MARCO: *La Fenice et des Artistes* — Campiello Fenice, 1936. Map 7 A2. 041 523 23 33. FAX 041 520 37 21. fenice@fenicehotels.it — This pretty hotel is made up of two houses joined together by a small patio. Rooms are comfortable and furnished with antiques.	€€€€€	68	■		■
SAN MARCO: *Flora* — C/ Larga XXII Marzo, 2283a. Map 7 A3. 041 520 58 44. FAX 041 522 82 17. info@hotelflora.it — A charming hotel on a secluded alley near Piazza San Marco. All rooms have their own bathroom. In the summer breakfast is served in the garden.	€€€€€	44			■
SAN MARCO: *Bauer* — Campo San Moisè, 1459. Map 7 A3. 041 520 70 22. FAX 041 520 75 57. booking@bauervenezia.it — A luxury hotel in the heart of Venice, it has been recently refurbished, and can offer unique accommodation overlooking the Grand Canal.	€€€€€	191	■		■

Price categories for a standard double room for one night, including tax and service charges but not including breakfast:
€ under €52
€€ €52–€100
€€€ €100–€155
€€€€ €155–€205
€€€€€ over €205.

RESTAURANT
A restaurant within the hotel sometimes reserved for residents.

SWIMMING POOL
Hotel swimming pools are usually quite small and are outdoors unless otherwise stated.

GARDEN OR TERRACE
A garden, courtyard or terrace belonging to the hotel, often providing tables for eating outside.

CREDIT CARDS
The major credit cards Visa, MasterCard (Access) and American Express are accepted in hotels with the credit card symbol.

	NUMBER OF ROOMS	RESTAURANT	SWIMMING POOL	GARDEN OR TERRACE
SAN MARCO: *Europa & Regina* €€€€€	185	▦		▦
San Marco 2159. **Map** 7 A3. ☎ 041 520 04 77. FAX 041 523 15 33. @ europaregina@westin.com — This splendid hotel was the residence of the 18th-century painter Tiepolo. The terrace on the Grand Canal houses a flamboyant bar and restaurant. � TV ▤ 🖉				
SAN MARCO: *Gritti Palace* €€€€€	91	▦		▦
Santa Maria del Giglio, 2467. **Map** 6 F3. ☎ 041 79 46 11. FAX 041 520 09 42. @ grittipalace@luxurycollection.com — An elegant, sumptuous hotel in a 15th-century palazzo. Rooms are superb and it is charmingly old-fashioned. Ernest Hemingway stayed here while in Venice. 🚪 TV ▤ 🖉				
SAN MARCO: *Monaco and Grand Canal* €€€€€	104	▦		▦
Calle Vallaresso, 1325. **Map** 7 B3. ☎ 041 520 02 11. FAX 041 520 05 01. @ mailbox@hotelmonaco.it — An elegant hotel in an 18th-century palazzo overlooking the Grand Canal. Public rooms are intimate and bedrooms are beautifully decorated. The restaurant is one of the best in Venice. 🚪 TV ▤ 🖉				
SAN MARCO: *Panada* €€€€€	48			
San Marco, 646. **Map** 7 A2. ☎ 041 520 90 88. FAX 041 520 96 19. @ info@hotelpanada.com — Set in a quiet location, this recently renovated 17th-century mansion has an intimate bar lined with antique mirrors. 🚪 TV ▤ 🖉				
SAN POLO: *Alex* €€	11			▦
Rio Terrà Frari, 2606. **Map** 6 E1. ☎ 041 523 13 41. FAX 041 523 13 41. @ mariofiorentini@libero.it — A family-run hotel that makes up for its limited facilities with a friendly welcome and excellent value for money. Ideally located near the Frari.				
SAN POLO: *Hotel Marconi* €€€	26			▦
San Polo, 729. **Map** 7 A1. ☎ 041 522 20 68. FAX 041 522 97 00. @ info@hotelmarconi.it — A refurbished 16th-century palazzo with opulently Venetian reception rooms. Bedrooms are plainer, but some have views of the Grand Canal. 🚪 TV ▤ 🖉				
SANTA CROCE: *Al Sole* €€€	64			▦
Fondamenta Minotta, 136. **Map** 5 C1. ☎ 041 71 08 44. FAX 041 72 22 87. @ info@albergoalsolevenice.com — This 14th-century building is conveniently situated in a quiet corner near the station. It has pleasant rooms and a marble-floored reception area. 🚪 ▤ ♿ 🖉				
SANTA CROCE: *Falier* €€€€	19			▦
Salizzada San Pantalon, 130. **Map** 5 C1. ☎ 041 710 882. FAX 041 520 65 54. @ falier@tin.it — On the edge of the student district, the reasonably priced Falier is away from the main hotel area of Venice. It has recently been restored. 🚪 TV ▤ 🖉				
TORCELLO: *Locanda Cipriani* €€€€€	6	▦		▦
Piazza Santa Fosca 29. ☎ 041 73 01 50. FAX 041 73 54 33. @ info@locandacipriani.com — Book in advance for this hotel, off the beaten tourist track. 🚪 ▤ **Closed** *Jan.*				

THE VENETO AND FRIULI

	NUMBER OF ROOMS	RESTAURANT	SWIMMING POOL	GARDEN OR TERRACE
ASOLO: *Villa Cipriani* €€€€€	31	▦		▦
Via Canova 298, Asolo. ☎ 0423 52 34 11. FAX 0423 95 20 95. w www.sheraton.com/villacipriani — This superbly comfortable hotel is set in a 16th-century villa where Robert Browning once lived. A popular feature is its beautiful garden which has a lovely view. A good base for exploring a wider area. 🚪 TV ▤ 🖉 P				
BARDOLINO: *Kriss International* €€	33	▦		▦
Lungolago Cipriani 3, 37011. ☎ 045 621 24 33. FAX 045 721 02 42. @ kriss@kriss.it — A modern hotel on a promontory jutting into the lake with views from every room. Guests can use the private beach. 🚪 TV ▤ 🖉 P **Closed** *Dec–Jan.*				
BASSANO DEL GRAPPA: *Bonotto Hotel Belvedere* €€	87	▦		
Piazzale G Giardino 14, 36061. ☎ 0424 52 98 45. FAX 0424 52 98 49. @ belvederehotel@bonotto.it — Set on one of Bassano's main squares, this busy hotel is the best equipped in the area. Rooms are comfortable and service is good. 🚪 TV ▤ 🖉 P				

BASSANO DEL GRAPPA: *Victoria* €€ 23
Viale Diaz 33, 36061. 📞 *0424 50 36 20.* FAX *0424 50 31 30.* @ info@hotelvictoria-bassano.com
Just outside the city walls, this pleasant hotel has comfortable rooms. It is a busy hotel that can be noisy but is well placed for sightseeing.

BELLUNO: *Astor* €€ 38
Piazza dei Martiri 26e, 32100. 📞 *0437 94 20 94.* FAX *0437 94 24 93.* @ astorhotel@libero.it
Centrally situated, this hotel is popular with skiers in winter. The rooms are well-designed and comfortable, offering good value for money.

CHIOGGIA: *Grande Italia* €€€ 57
Rione S. Andrea 597, 30015. 📞 *041 40 05 15.* FAX *041 40 01 85.* @ hgi@hotelgrandeitalia.com
This unpretentious old-fashioned hotel, at the head of the main street, has comfortable rooms and is well-situated for boats running to Venice.

CIVIDALE DEL FRIULI: *Locanda al Castello* €€€ 17
Via del Castello 20, 33043. 📞 *0432 73 32 42.* FAX *0432 70 09 01.* @ castello@ud.nettuno.it
An attractive historic building, this was once a castle and a Jesuit monastery before its most recent incarnation as a welcoming friendly hotel with wonderful views. Closed *20 Jan–10 Feb.*

CONEGLIANO: *Il Faè* €€ 8
Via Faè 1, San Pietro di Feletto, 31020. 📞 *0438 78 71 17.* FAX *0438 78 78 15.* @ mail@ilfae.com
This comfortable B&B is housed in a converted farmhouse amongst hills and vineyards. Good views over the foothills of the Alps. Ten minutes drive from Conegliano.

CORTINA D'AMPEZZO: *Montana* €€ 31
Corso Italia 94, 32043. 📞 *0436 860 48.* FAX *0436 86 82 11.* @ montana@cortina-hotel.com
This hotel is conveniently situated in the town centre, close to the main shopping area. The area is traffic free making the hotel quiet and a popular choice. Closed *Jun & Nov.*

CORTINA D'AMPEZZO: *Menardi* €€€ 51
Via Majon 110, 32043. 📞 *0436 24 00.* FAX *0436 86 21 83.* @ info@hotelmenardi.it
Family-run since 1900, this hotel is tastefully furnished with antiques and has a welcoming atmosphere. Closed *Apr–mid-May, mid-Sep–mid-Dec.*

GARDA: *Bisesti* €€ 90
Corso Italia 34, 37016. 📞 *045 725 57 66.* FAX *045 725 59 27.* @ info@hotelbisesti.it
Located near the town centre and the lake. Many rooms in this modern holiday hotel have their own balcony and there is a garden. Closed *Nov–Mar.*

GARDA: *Locanda San Vigilio* €€€€€ 7
San Vigilio, 37016. 📞 *045 725 66 88.* FAX *045 725 65 51.* @ info@punta-sanvigilio.it
One of the loveliest, most exclusive hotels on Lake Garda. Comfort and service live up to all expectations and there is a private beach. Closed *mid-Nov–mid-Mar.*

MALCESINE: *Sailing Center Hotel* €€€ 32
Località Molini Campagnola 3, 37018. 📞 *045 740 00 55.* FAX *045 740 03 92.*
@ info@hotelsailing.com
A modern hotel just outside town, away from the crowds. Rooms are cool and pleasant, and there is a tennis court and private beach. Closed *Oct–Apr.*

PADUA: *Augustus Terme* €€€ 120
Viale Stazione 150, Montegrotto Terme 35036. 📞 *049 79 32 00.* FAX *049 79 35 18.*
@ info@hotelaugustus.com
A big, comfortable hotel with tennis courts and hot thermal springs.

PADUA: *Donatello* €€€€ 44
Via del Santo 104, 35123. 📞 *049 875 06 34.* FAX *049 875 08 29.* @ info@hoteldonatello.net
A modern hotel in an old building with comfortable rooms. Named after the sculptor of the equestrian statue of Gattamelata in the square. Closed *25 Dec.*

PADUA: *Grande Italia* €€€€ 60
Corso del Popolo 81, 35131. 📞 *049 876 11 11.* FAX *049 875 08 50.* @ info@hotelgrandeitalia.it
Situated close to many of the city's main sights, this hotel is very good value for money. The rooms are slightly basic, but comfortable.

PADUA: *Plaza* €€€€ 142
Corso Milano 40, 35139. 📞 *049 65 68 22.* FAX *049 66 11 17.* @ plaza@plazapadova.it
An established and efficiently run hotel with a deserved good reputation. It provides a full range of services and a warm welcome.

	NUMBER OF ROOMS	RESTAURANT	SWIMMING POOL	GARDEN OR TERRACE

Price categories for a standard double room for one night, including tax and service charges but not including breakfast:
€ under €52
€€ €52–€100
€€€ €100–€155
€€€€ €155–€205
€€€€€ over €205.

RESTAURANT
A restaurant within the hotel sometimes reserved for residents.
SWIMMING POOL
Hotel swimming pools are usually quite small and are outdoors unless otherwise stated.
GARDEN OR TERRACE
A garden, courtyard or terrace belonging to the hotel, often providing tables for eating outside.
CREDIT CARDS
The major credit cards Visa, MasterCard (Access) and American Express are accepted in hotels with the credit card symbol.

		Rooms	Rest.	Pool	Garden
PESCHIERA DEL GARDA: *Peschiera* €€	Via Parini 4, 37010. **☎** 045 755 05 26. **FAX** 045 755 04 44. **@** info@hotel-peschiera.com. This hotel is set in its own grounds, with lofty, cool bedrooms. There are fine lake views and a private swimming pool. ⚏ 🅿 **Closed** *Jan–Feb.*	30	▦	●	▦
PORDENONE: *Palace Hotel Moderno* €€€	Viale Martelli 1, 33170. **☎** 0434 282 15. **FAX** 0434 52 03 15. **@** info@palacehotelmoderno.it. A comfortable, recently refurbished traditional hotel with a good range of facilities in all bedrooms. It is centrally located close to the station. The restaurant specializes in traditional cuisine, particularly fish dishes. ⚏ 📺 ▤ 🍽 🅿	94	▦		
SAN FLORIANO DEL COLLIO: *Golf Hotel Castello Formentini* €€€€	Via Oslavia 2, 34070. **☎** 0481 88 40 51. **FAX** 0481 88 40 52. **@** isabellaformentini@tiscalinet.it. A lovely 18th-century building furnished with antiques and set in its own well-kept grounds with a nine-hole golf course and tennis courts. ⚏ 📺 🍽 **Closed** *mid-Dec–Jan.*	14		●	▦
TORRI DEL BENACO: *Hotel Gardesana* €€€	Piazza Calderini 20, 37010. **☎** 045 722 54 11. **FAX** 045 722 57 71. **@** info@hotel-gardesana.com. The 15th-century harbourmaster's house overlooking Lake Garda has been converted into a friendly, comfortable hotel. Ask for a room on the third floor; they are quieter and have wonderful views of the lake. ⚏ 📺 ▤ 🍽 🅿 **Closed** *Nov–mid-Mar.*	34	▦		▦
TREVISO: *Campeol* €€	Piazza Ancillotto 4, 31100. **☎** & **FAX** 0422 56 601. **@** info@albergocampeol.it. One of Treviso's best budget hotels, Campeol is clean and welcoming, and situated in the heart of the historic centre. There is an excellent restaurant opposite. ⚏ 📺 🍽	14			
TREVISO: *Ca' del Galletto* €€€	Via Santa Bona Vecchia 30, 31100. **☎** 0422 43 25 50. **FAX** 0422 43 25 10. **@** info@hotelcadelgalletto.it. Set in its own grounds and only ten minutes' walk from the city walls, this efficiently-run hotel has good-sized modern bedrooms. ⚏ 📺 ▤ 🍽 🅿	67	▦		
TRIESTE: *Jolly* €€€€	Corso Cavour 7, 34132. **☎** 040 760 00 55. **FAX** 040 36 26 99. **@** trieste@jollyhotels.it. A modern hotel aiming at business as well as holiday clientele. The well-equipped rooms are spacious if slightly impersonally decorated. ⚏ 📺 ▤ ♿ 🍽	174	▦		
TRIESTE: *Grand Hotel Duchi d'Aosta* €€€€€	Piazza Unità d'Italia 2, 34121. **☎** 040 760 00 11. **FAX** 040 36 60 92. **@** info@magesta.com. A palace from a bygone era, this hotel has enormous rooms fitted with modern conveniences. It is set in the old part of town, near the fort. ⚏ 📺 ▤ ♿ 🍽 🅿	55	▦		
UDINE: *Quo Vadis* €€	Piazzale Cella 28, 33100. **☎** 0432 210 91. **FAX** 0432 210 92. **@** hotelquovadis@libero.it. A comfortable hotel on a tranquil tree-lined street. The decor is mixed (some rooms have rather fussy wallpaper) but there are plenty of plants. ⚏ 📺 🍽 🅿	26			▦
VERONA: *Il Torcolo* €€€	Vicolo Listone 3, 37121. **☎** 045 800 75 12. **FAX** 045 800 40 58. **@** hoteltorcolo@virgilio.it. This friendly hotel close to the Arena is popular during the opera season. It has a breakfast terrace, and some pretty and traditional rooms. ⚏ 📺 ▤ 🍽 🅿 **Closed** *mid-end Jan.*	19			▦
VERONA: *Accademia* €€€€	Via Scala 12, 37121. **☎** 045 596 222. **FAX** 045 800 84 40. **@** accademia@accademiavr.it. Blending modern and ancient architecture, this ornate 17th-century building has a central location. The well-known restaurant offers regional cuisine. ⚏ 📺 ▤ 🍽 🅿	95	▦		
VERONA: *Giulietta e Romeo* €€€€	Vicolo Tre Marchetti 3, 37121. **☎** 045 800 35 54. **FAX** 045 801 08 62. **@** info@giuliettaeromeo.com. Situated in a quiet street just behind the Arena, the bedrooms are spacious and comfortable with modern furnishings. Breakfast is served in the bar. ⚏ 📺 ▤ 🍽 🅿	31			

VERONA: *Due Torri Hotel Baglioni*   €€€€€ | 91
Piazza Sant'Anastasia 4, 37121. **℃** *045 59 50 44.* **FAX** *045 800 41 30.*
@ duetorri.verona@baglionihotels.com
In the heart of medieval Verona, this is one of Italy's most eccentric hotels. Each
bedroom is decorated and furnished in the style of a different era. 🖼 📺 🗎 🗢 🅿

VICENZA: *Casa San Raffaele*   €€€ | 29
Viale X Giugno 10, 36100. **℃** *0444 54 57 67.* **FAX** *0444 54 22 59.* **@** albergosanraffaele@tin.it
A tranquil hotel with excellent views set on the slopes of Monte Berico. The
comfortable rooms make this one of the best budget choices in the area. 🖼 🗢 🅿

VICENZA: *Campo Marzio*   €€€€ | 35
Via Roma 21, 36100. **℃** *0444 54 57 00.* **FAX** *0444 32 04 95.* **@** info@hotelcampomarzio.com
A stylish hotel with good facilities near the city centre. Bedrooms are
large, light and well furnished, and the location is peaceful. 🖼 📺 🗎 🗢 🅿

TRENTINO-ALTO ADIGE

BOLZANO (BOZEN): *Asterix*   €€ | 25
Piazza Mazzini 35, 39100. **℃** *0471 27 33 01.* **FAX** *0471 26 00 21.* **@** info@hotelasterix.it
Set in the newer part of central Bolzano, the Asterix is a simple but quite
comfortable town hotel which is excellent value for money. 🖼 📺 🗢 🅿

BOLZANO (BOZEN): *Engel*   €€ | 60
Via San Valentino, Nova Levante 39056. **℃** *0471 61 31 31.* **FAX** *0471 61 34 04.*
@ resort@hotel-engel.com
In a small town near Bolzano, the Engel is a good choice for families and
the sporty, with hiking and skiing nearby. 🖼 🗢 🅿 **Closed** *mid-Apr–mid-May.*

BOLZANO (BOZEN): *Luna-Mondschein*   €€€ | 75
Via Piave 15, 39100. **℃** *0471 97 56 42.* **FAX** *0471 97 55 77.* **@** info@hotel-luna.it
The Luna-Mondschein dates from 1798, although the buildings have been much
added to since then. A pleasant garden allows for summer dining. 🖼 📺 🗢 🅿

BRESSANONE (BRIXEN): *Dominik*   €€€ | 36
Via Terzo di Sotto 13, 39042. **℃** *0472 83 01 44.* **FAX** *0472 83 65 54.* **W** www.hoteldominik.com
The Dominik is furnished with antiques, although the buildings themselves date
from the 1970s. It is set near the River Rienza and the Rapp gardens. 🖼 📺 🗢 🅿

BRESSANONE (BRIXEN): *Elephant*   €€€€ | 44
Via Rio Bianco 4, 39042. **℃** *0472 83 27 50.* **FAX** *0472 83 65 79.* **@** info@hotelelephant.com
A smart hotel that dates from the 16th century. While offering all modern comforts
(including sauna), it has retained a strong historical atmosphere. 🖼 📺 🗢 🅿
Closed *mid-end Nov; Jan–Feb.*

BRUNICO (BRUNECK): *Andreas Hofer*   €€ | 54
Via Campo Tures 1, 39031. **℃** *0474 55 14 69.* **FAX** *0474 55 12 83.* **@** hotel@andreashofer.it
A family-run chalet with wooden Alpine-style furniture. The hotel is set in its own
garden and some of the rooms have balconies. 🖼 📺 🗢 🅿 **Closed** *3 wks May; 10 days Dec.*

CALDARO (KALTERN): *Leuchtenburg*   €€ | 19
Campi al Lago 100, 39052. **℃** *0471 96 00 93.* **FAX** *0471 96 01 55.* **@** pensionleuchtenburg@iol.it
Set in a beautiful 16th-century farmhouse surrounded by vineyards, some of the
simple bedrooms are furnished with traditional painted furniture. 🖼 📺 🗢 🅿 **Closed** *Nov–Mar.*

CANAZEI: *Park Hotel Faloria*   €€ | 36
Strada de Pareda 103, 38032. **℃** *0462 60 11 18.* **FAX** *0462 60 27 15.* **@** faloriahotel@tiscali.it
Surrounded by its own well-kept gardens, this friendly hotel is managed by
its owners. Some bedrooms have balconies. 🖼 📺 🗢 🅿 **Closed** *Apr–Jun, Oct–Dec.*

CASTELROTTO (KASTELRUTH): *Cavallino d'Oro*   €€ | 23
Piazza Kraus 1, 39040. **℃** *0471 70 63 37.* **FAX** *0471 70 71 72.* **@** cavallino@cavallino.it
This charming hotel is set in a pretty village 26 km (16 miles) from Bolzano, where
traditional costume is still worn. The rooms are well-kept. 🖼 📺 🗢 🅿 **Closed** *Nov.*

CAVALESE: *Fiemme*   €€ | 10
Via Cavazzal 27, 38033. **℃** *0462 34 17 20.* **FAX** *0462 23 11 51.*
A modern hotel in a peaceful setting with good views, conveniently
close to both the town centre and the bus station. It also has a sauna.
🖼 📺 🗢 🅿 **Closed** *mid-Apr–mid-Jun.*

COLFOSCO: *Cappella*   €€€€ | 63
Strada Pecei 17, 39030. **℃** *0471 83 61 83.* **FAX** *0471 83 65 61.* **@** info@hotelcappella.com
A recently restored chalet in the Dolomites, opened by the present owner's grandfather.
The hotel has also opened an art gallery. 🖼 📺 🗢 🅿 **Closed** *Apr–Jun; Oct–Dec.*

Price categories for a standard double room for one night, including tax and service charges but not including breakfast: € under €52 €€ €52–€100 €€€ €100–€155 €€€€ €155–€205 €€€€€ over €205.	**RESTAURANT** A restaurant within the hotel sometimes reserved for residents. **SWIMMING POOL** Hotel swimming pools are usually quite small and are outdoors unless otherwise stated. **GARDEN OR TERRACE** A garden, courtyard or terrace belonging to the hotel, often providing tables for eating outside. **CREDIT CARDS** The major credit cards Visa, MasterCard (Access) and American Express are accepted in hotels with the credit card symbol.	NUMBER OF ROOMS / RESTAURANT / SWIMMING POOL / GARDEN OR TERRACE	

FIE ALLO SCILIAR: *Romantik Hotel Turm* €€€€ 40
Piazza della Chiesa 9, 39050. **C** 0471 72 50 14. **FAX** 0471 72 54 74. **@** info@hotelturm.it
The art collection displayed on the walls and the restaurant, one of Italy's best, are the main attractions at this friendly hotel. 🛏 TV 🍽 P **Closed** Nov–mid-Dec.

MADONNA DI CAMPIGLIO: *Grifone* €€€ 38
Via Vallesinella 7, 38084. **C** 0465 44 20 02. **FAX** 0465 44 05 40. **@** info@hotelgrifone.it
Although this modern wooden chalet near a lake is rather ordinarily decorated and furnished, it offers a great range of facilities for winter sports holidays.
🛏 TV 🍽 P **Closed** Apr–Jun, mid-Sep–early Dec.

MALLES VENOSTA (MALS IM VINSCHGAU): *Garberhof* €€€ 29
Via Nazionale 25, 39024. **C** 0473 83 13 99. **FAX** 0473 83 19 50. **@** info@garberhof.com
This modern chalet-style hotel with extensive panoramic terraces has a good range of sports and leisure facilities. 🛏 TV 🍽 P **Closed** Nov.

MERANO (MERAN): *Der Pünthof* €€€ 12
Via Steinach 25, Lagundo, 39022. **C** 0473 44 85 53. **FAX** 0473 44 99 19. **@** info@puenthof.com
Set in peaceful and attractive gardens, this farmhouse dates back to the Middle Ages. Inside, wooden floors and ceilings match the Alpine furniture. 🛏 TV 🍽 P **Closed** mid-Nov–2 wks before Easter.

MERANO (MERAN): *Castello Labers* €€€€ 35
Via Labers 25, 39012. **C** 0473 23 44 84. **FAX** 0473 23 41 46. **W** www.castellolabers.it
A romantic castle is the setting for this high-class country hotel. There are wonderful views over the surrounding vineyards and woods. 🛏 TV 🍽 P **Closed** 10 Nov–Mar.

MERANO (MERAN): *Castel Rundegg* €€€€ 30
Via Scena 2, 39012. **C** 0473 23 41 00. **FAX** 0473 23 72 00. **@** info@rundegg.com
Parts of this fairy-tale castle date from the 12th century. Inside, the atmosphere continues with traditional wood furniture, beamed ceilings and parquet floors. 🛏 TV 🍽 P

ORTISEI (SANKT ULRICH): *Hell* €€€ 25
Via Promenade 3, 39046. **C** 0471 79 67 85. **FAX** 0471 79 81 96. **@** info@hotelhell.it
A pleasant hotel that is open for the skiing season and during the summer. It has a sauna and a gym, and is set in a peaceful part of town. 🛏 TV 🍽 P **Closed** Apr–Jun, mid-Oct–20 Dec.

PERGINE VALSUGANA: *Castel Pergine* €€ 21
Via al Castello 10, 38057. **C** 0461 53 11 58. **FAX** 0461 53 13 29. **@** verena@castelpergine.it
Set in a 13th-century castle with exquisite views over the countryside. The interior is simply decorated and has traditional wooden furnishings. 🍽 P **Closed** Nov–Mar.

RASUN ANTERSELVA (RASEN ANTHOLZ): *Ansitz Heufler* €€€ 9
Rasun di Sopra 37, 39030. **C** 0474 49 85 82. **FAX** 0474 49 80 46. **@** info@heufler.com
In the historic centre of town, this beautifully decorated 16th-century castle has large rooms and a pleasant garden. 🛏 🍽 P **Closed** mid-Mar–mid-Apr.

RIVA DEL GARDA: *Hotel Centrale* €€ 70
Piazza 3 Novembre 27, 38066. **C** 0464 55 23 44. **FAX** 0464 55 21 38.
@ centrale@welcometogardalake.com
A centrally located hotel with good views of Lake Garda. 🛏 TV 🍽

RIVA DEL GARDA: *Europa* €€€ 63
Piazza Catena 9, 38066. **C** 0464 55 54 33. **FAX** 0464 52 17 77. **@** info@hoteleuropariva.com
A colour-washed building next to the lake and near the bustling town centre. Many of the simply furnished bedrooms have views over the lake. 🛏 🍽 TV 🍽 P **Closed** Dec–Feb.

SAN PAOLO (ST PAULS): *Schloss Korb* €€€€ 55
Via Castel d'Appiano 5, Missiano 39050. **C** 0471 63 60 00. **FAX** 0471 63 60 33.
@ hotel-schloss-korb@dnet.it
Partly set in a 13th-century castle, this prettily furnished hotel also has a more modern annexe, and tennis courts for residents. 🛏 TV P **Closed** Nov–Mar.

TIRES (TIERS): *Stefaner* €€ 16
San Cipriano 88d, 39050. **C** *0471 64 21 75.* **FAX** *0471 64 23 02.* **@** info@stefaner.com
A friendly chalet on the edge of the western Dolomites. Bedrooms are light and
spacious. Balconies are decked with flowers. **TV** **P** **Closed** *Nov–Dec.*

TRENTO: *Accademia* €€€ 42
Vicolo Colico 4–6, 38100. **C** *0461 23 36 00.* **FAX** *0461 23 01 74.* **@** info@accademiahotel.it
Set in a well-restored medieval building right in the historic centre of Trento. The
interior of this relaxing hotel, although essentially modern, retains many original
features. The restaurant is also very good. **TV** **Closed** *Christmas period.*

VIPITENO (STERZING): *Hotel Schwarzer Adler* €€€ 35
Piazza Città 1, 39049. **C** *0472 76 40 64.* **FAX** *0472 76 65 22.* **@** schwarzeradler@rolmail.net
A comfortable hotel for winter sports or summer walking holidays. Leisure facilities
include a sauna, gym and good restaurant. **TV** **P** **Closed** *5 Nov–5 Dec; last 10 days in Jun.*

LOMBARDY

BELLAGIO: *La Pergola* €€ 11
Piazza del Porto 4, 22021. **C** *031 95 02 63.* **FAX** *031 95 02 53.* **W** www.lapergolabellagio.it
An attractive hotel tucked away to the south of Lake Como, charmingly
furnished in an old-fashioned style with a rustic and friendly atmosphere. **TV**

BELLAGIO: *Florence* €€€ 32
Piazza Mazzini 46, 22021. **C** *031 95 03 42.* **FAX** *031 95 17 22.*
This friendly hotel has a bar, and its rooms overlook the lively port of Lake
Como. The hotel has plenty of charm, and tastefully furnished rooms. **TV**

BORMIO: *Palace* €€€€ 80
Via Milano 54, 23032. **C** *0342 90 31 31.* **FAX** *0342 90 33 66.* **W** www.palacebormio.it
A recently built hotel with a wide range of business and leisure facilities
that include a gym, sunbeds, a discotheque and a piano bar. **TV** **P**

BRATTO DELLA PRESOLANA (BERGAMO): *Hotel Milano* €€€ 69
Via Silvio Pellico 3, 24020. **C** *034 631 211.* **FAX** *034 636 236.* **@** info@hotelmilano.com
In the foothills of the Alps, this hotel offers a large array of sports to its guests. The
less energetic are pampered with eight styles of pillow and a cigar menu. **TV** **P**

BRESCIA: *Park Hotel Ca' Noa* €€€ 79
Via Triumplina 66, 25127. **C** *030 39 87 62.* **FAX** *030 39 87 64.* **@** info@hotelcanoa.it
A beautiful modern hotel set in its own grounds with tasteful and bright
decor, large, spacious public rooms and excellent service. **TV** **P**

CERVESINA: *Castello di San Gaudenzio* €€€ 45
Via Mulino 1, Frazione San Gaudenzio 27050. **C** *0383 33 31.* **FAX** *0383 33 34 09.*
W www.castellosangaudenzio.com
A wonderful hotel in a building partly dating from the 1400s. Furnishings are from
various periods, from 18th-century French to 16th-century baronial. **TV** **P**

COLOGNE FRANCIACORTA: *Cappuccini* €€€€ 8
Via Cappuccini 54, 25033. **C** *030 715 72 54.* **FAX** *030 715 72 57.* **@** info@cappuccini.it
A converted convent (built in 1569). Long hallways and white rooms create
a pleasant monastic atmosphere. Good leisure facilities. **TV** **P**

COMO: *Metropole & Suisse au Lac* €€€ 71
Piazza Cavour 19, 22100. **C** *031 26 94 44.* **FAX** *031 30 08 08.* **W** www.hotelmetropolesuisse.com
Hotel established in 1892 by the lake and recently renovated. Excellent location for
strolling or shopping. Facilities include a restaurant with outside terrace. **TV** **P**

CREMONA: *Duomo* €€ 18
Via Gonfalonieri 13, 26100. **C** *0372 352 42.* **FAX** *0372 45 83 92.*
Unsurprisingly, given its name, this hotel is right next to the cathedral in
Cremona's historic centre. Some of the rooms have good views. **TV** **P**

CREMONA: *Continental* €€€ 62
Piazza della Libertà 26, 26100. **C** *0372 43 41 41.* **FAX** *0372 45 48 73.*
W www.hotelcontinentalcremona.it
This central, luxurious hotel has been owned and run by the Ghiraldi family since 1920.
Rooms are comfortable and the restaurant is one of the best in the city. **TV** **P**

DESENZANO DEL GARDA: *Piroscafo* €€ 32
Via Porto Vecchio 11, 25015. **C** *030 914 11 28.* **FAX** *030 991 25 86.* **@** piroscaf@tin.it
An attractive old hotel, well placed for all the town's amenities. Bedrooms
at the front have balconies overlooking the busy old port. **TV**

		Price categories for a standard double room for one night, including tax and service charges but not including breakfast: € under €52 €€ €52–€100 €€€ €100–€155 €€€€ €155–€205 €€€€€ over €205.	NUMBER OF ROOMS	RESTAURANT	SWIMMING POOL	GARDEN OR TERRACE

RESTAURANT
A restaurant within the hotel sometimes reserved for residents.

SWIMMING POOL
Hotel swimming pools are usually quite small and are outdoors unless otherwise stated.

GARDEN OR TERRACE
A garden, courtyard or terrace belonging to the hotel, often providing tables for eating outside.

CREDIT CARDS
The major credit cards Visa, MasterCard (Access) and American Express are accepted in hotels with the credit card symbol.

Hotel	Rooms	Restaurant	Swimming Pool	Garden or Terrace
GARDONE RIVIERA: *Villa del Sogno* €€€€€ Via Zanardelli 107, 25083. **[** 0365 29 01 81. **FAX** 0365 29 02 30. **@** info@villadelsogno.it A turn-of-the-century villa set in beautiful gardens and furnished with antiques of various periods. All rooms are spacious and light; this is a good choice for those seeking luxurious tranquillity.	31	■	●	■
GARDONE RIVIERA: *Villa Fiordaliso* €€€€€ Corso Zanardelli 150, 25083. **[** 0365 201 58. **FAX** 0365 29 00 11. **[w]** www.villafiordaliso.it This beautiful, eclectic villa overlooking Lake Garda has comfortable rooms. It was once the private residence of Clara Petacci, Mussolini's lover.	7	■		
LIMONE SUL GARDA: *Capo Reamol* €€ Via IV Novembre 92, 25010. **[** 0365 95 40 40. **FAX** 0365 95 42 62. **@** caporeamol@gardaresort.it A stunning location on the edge of the lake below the main road. Rooms are spacious and all have their own terrace. Sports and leisure facilities are excellent for families and include private beach, gym and jacuzzi.	60	■	●	■
LIVIGNO: *Camana Veglia* €€€ Via Ostaria 583, 23030. **[** 0342 99 63 10. **FAX** 0342 99 69 04. **@** camana@mottini.com Set in a typical chalet that dates from the beginning of the last century. The interior is wood-panelled and furnished in Alpine style.	12	■		■
MANTOVA: *Broletto* €€€ Via Accademia 1, 46100. **[** 0376 32 67 84. **FAX** 0376 22 12 97. **@** hotel.broletto@libero.it A small, immaculate hotel in a renovated 16th-century town house. Rooms are bright with attractive modern furnishings and polished marble floors.	16			
MANTOVA: *Rechigi* €€€€ Via Calvi 30, 46100. **[** 0376 32 07 81. **FAX** 0376 22 02 91. **[w]** www.rechigi.com Although located in the historical city centre, the hotel is innovatively modern. Decorated with contemporary art, it regularly houses exhibitions.	60			■
MANTOVA: *Villa dei Tigli* €€€€€ Via Cantarana 20, 46040. **[** 0376 65 06 91. **FAX** 0376 65 06 49. **@** info@hotelvilladeitigli.it A charming villa set in a quiet park in the country. The hotel has a gym with swimming pools and sauna, and runs a shuttle service to the city.	31	■	●	■
MILAN: *Antica Locanda Solferino* €€€€ Via Castelfidardo 2, 20121. **[** 02 657 01 29. **FAX** 02 657 13 61. **@** info@anticalocandasolferino.it Excellent value at this surprisingly rustic old inn. Bedrooms are small but nicely decorated with old furniture, paintings and flowery wallpaper. There is also an informal bistro next door to the hotel. Book in advance.	11			
MILAN: *Zurigo* €€€€ Corso Italia 11a, 20122. **[** 02 72 02 22 60. **FAX** 02 72 00 00 13. **@** zurigo@brerahotels.it A newly restored hotel whose central location appeals to both business and holiday travellers. Guests can borrow bicycles for sightseeing.	40			
MILAN: *Capitol Millennium* €€€€€ Via Cimarosa 6. **[** 02 43 85 91. **FAX** 02 469 47 24. **@** booking@capitolmillennium.com After major restructuring this hotel now boasts excellent facilities. The rooms are wood-panelled and the marble bathrooms have a jacuzzi shower or tub. The public spaces are tastefully decorated and there is a gym, restaurant and bar.	66	■		
MILAN: *Cavour* €€€€€ Via Fatebenefratelli 21, 20121. **[** 02 657 20 51. **FAX** 02 659 22 63. **[w]** www.hotelcavour.it Very well placed for Milan's main sights, this recently restored city hotel has good-sized, comfortable rooms and a pleasant bar.	113			
MILAN: *Pierre Milano* €€€€€ Via de Amicis 32, 20123. **[** 02 72 00 05 81. **FAX** 02 805 21 57. **[w]** www.hotelpierremilano.it A luxurious hotel that blends traditional and modern styles in its interior design and furnishings. The restaurant is one of the best in Milan.	51	■		

PAVIA: *Moderno* €€€ 53
Viale Vittorio Emanuele 41, 27100. 📞 0382 30 34 01. 𝐅𝐀𝐗 0382 252 25. 🆆 www.hotelmoderno.it
Set in a restored palazzo, the Moderno is a calm, well-run establishment
with a welcoming atmosphere and comfortable rooms. 🛏 📺 🍽 💳 🅿

RANCO: *Sole* €€€€€ 15
Piazza Venezia 5, 21020. 📞 0331 97 65 07. 𝐅𝐀𝐗 0331 97 66 20. @ ivanett@tin.it
The restaurant is the highlight of the Sole which has been in the same family
for five generations. The few rooms are in newly built suites and some have
lovely views over Lake Maggiore (these do cost slightly more). 🛏 📺 🍽 💳 🅿

RIVA DEL GARDA: *Luise* €€€€ 76
Viale Rovereto 9, 38066. 📞 0464 55 27 96. 𝐅𝐀𝐗 0464 55 42 50. @ info@hotelluise.com
A few minutes away from the lake this hotel has a well-tended garden and tennis
courts. The hotel also offers facilities for mountain-biking enthusiasts. 🛏 📺 🍽 💳 🅿

RIVA DI SOLTO: *Miranda da Oreste* €€ 25
Via Cornello 8, 24060. 📞 035 98 60 21. 𝐅𝐀𝐗 035 98 00 55. 🆆 www.albergomiranda.it
A simple, family-run, recently renovated pensione. The restaurant serves
good local cuisine on a terrace with views of Lake Iseo. 🛏 📺 💳 🅿

SABBIONETA: *Al Duca* €€ 10
Via della Stamperia 18, 46018. 📞 0375 524 74. 𝐅𝐀𝐗 0375 220 021. @ al.duca@tin.it
A plain but comfortable family-run pensione in a much-converted Renaissance
palazzo, located in the historic centre. Prices are very reasonable. 🛏 📺 🍽 💳

SALÒ: *Romantik Hotel Laurin* €€€€ 30
Viale Landi 9, 25087. 📞 0365 220 22. 𝐅𝐀𝐗 0365 223 82. @ laurinbs@tin.it
A family hotel in a pretty lakeside villa on a sheltered bay. Spacious bedrooms
and a happy atmosphere, as well as a beach and tennis courts. 🛏 📺 💳 🅿

SIRMIONE SUL GARDA: *Villa Cortine Palace Hotel* €€€€€ 54
Via Grotte 6, 25019. 📞 030 990 58 90. 𝐅𝐀𝐗 030 91 63 90. 🆆 www.hotelvillacortine.com
Huge, frescoed rooms furnished with antiques in this luxurious and tranquil
hotel set in a Classical villa. Excellent service and comfort. 🛏 📺 🍽 💳 🅿

TREMEZZO: *San Giorgio* €€€ 26
Via Regina 81, Località Lenno 22016. 📞 0344 404 15. 𝐅𝐀𝐗 0344 415 91. @ sangiorgiohotel@libero.it
Set in its own large garden, the San Giorgio is a traditional hotel with elegant
terraces and public rooms. Ask for a room with a view of Lake Como. 🛏 💳 🅿

VALSOLDA: *Stella d'Italia* €€€ 34
Piazza Roma 1, San Mamete 22010. 📞 0344 681 39. 𝐅𝐀𝐗 0344 687 29. @ info@stelladitalia.com
An exquisite setting with a shady terrace right on the edge of Lake Lugano.
Rooms have lake views and are prettily decorated with floral prints and bright
bedspreads. Guests can use the lakeside lido and the hotel library. 🛏 📺 💳 🅿

VARENNA: *Hotel du Lac* €€€€ 17
Via del Prestino 4, 23829. 📞 0341 83 02 38. 𝐅𝐀𝐗 0341 83 10 81. 🆆 www.albergodulac.com
There are wonderful views from this delightfully peaceful hotel overlooking
Lake Como. Furnishings are simple but comfortable and modern. 🛏 📺 🍽 💳 🅿

VALLE D'AOSTA AND PIEDMONT

ALESSANDRIA: *Domus* €€€ 26
Via Castellani 12, 15100. 📞 0131 433 05. 𝐅𝐀𝐗 0131 23 20 19. @ efuganti@tin.it
Very centrally located and close to the station, the Domus is however quiet
and peaceful inside. All the rooms have double beds. 🛏 📺 🍽 💳 🅿

AOSTA: *Europe* €€€ 63
Piazza Narbonne 8, 11100. 📞 0165 23 63 63. 𝐅𝐀𝐗 0165 40 566. 🆆 www.ethotels.com
In the historical city centre, this modern hotel offers excellent hospitality,
a renowned restaurant, and a fitness centre. 🛏 📺 🍽 💳 🅿

AOSTA: *Milleluci* €€€€ 31
Località Porossan Roppoz 15, 11100. 📞 0165 23 52 78. 𝐅𝐀𝐗 0165 23 52 84.
🆆 www.hotelmilleluci.com
An old farmhouse, attractively restored, is the setting for this pleasant hotel. The
lounge has a wonderful fireplace. Sauna and gym also available. 🛏 📺 💳 🅿

ARONA: *Giardino* €€ 56
Corso Repubblica 1, 28041. 📞 0322 459 94. 𝐅𝐀𝐗 0322 24 94 01. 🆆 www.giardinoarona.com
A friendly, comfortable lakeside hotel. A large terrace offers spectacular views
over Lake Maggiore and bedrooms are tastefully furnished. 🛏 📺 🍽 💳

Price categories for a standard double room for one night, including tax and service charges but not including breakfast:
€ under €52
€€ €52–€100
€€€ €100–€155
€€€€ €155–€205
€€€€€ over €205.

RESTAURANT
A restaurant within the hotel sometimes reserved for residents.

SWIMMING POOL
Hotel swimming pools are usually quite small and are outdoors unless otherwise stated.

GARDEN OR TERRACE
A garden, courtyard or terrace belonging to the hotel, often providing tables for eating outside.

CREDIT CARDS
The major credit cards Visa, MasterCard (Access) and American Express are accepted in hotels with the credit card symbol.

	NUMBER OF ROOMS	RESTAURANT	SWIMMING POOL	GARDEN OR TERRACE
ASTI: *Lis* €€ Viale Fratelli Rosselli 10, 14100. ☎ 0141 59 50 51. FAX 0141 35 38 45. @ hotellis@tin.it Centrally but peacefully located opposite the town's public gardens and close to the historic centre. Rooms are modern and well-equipped. 🛏 TV ▤ ✉ P	29			
ASTI: *Aleramo* €€€ Via Emanuele Filiberto 13, 14100. ☎ 0141 59 56 61. FAX 0141 300 39. W www.hotel.aleramo.it A slick, modern hotel in the centre of town and close to the station. Rooms have a good range of facilities, including hairdriers and safes. 🛏 TV ▤ ✉ P	42			
ASTI: *Salera* €€€ Via Monsignor Marello 19, 14100. ☎ 0141 41 01 69. FAX 0141 41 03 72. W www.salera-lis.com A modern, comfortable hotel well placed for the motorway. Rooms are simply but attractively furnished and all are equipped with mini-bar. 🛏 TV ▤ ✉ ♿ P	50	▦		
BREUIL-CERVINIA: *Hermitage* €€€€€ Via Piolet 1, 11021. ☎ 0166 94 89 98. FAX 0166 94 90 32. @ info@hotelhermitage.com Those looking for luxury and charm will find it here. This well-equipped modern hotel has bright and flower-filled rooms. 🛏 TV ✉ ♿ P	36	▦	●	
BREUIL-CERVINIA: *Les Neiges d'Antan* €€€€€ Frazione Cret-Perrères, 11021. ☎ 0166 94 87 75. FAX 0166 94 88 52. W www.lesneigesdantan.it A delightful mountain chalet hotel attached to one of the best restaurants in the area. Inside it is all clean white walls and original wooden beams. 🛏 TV ✉ P	24	▦		▦
CANNERO RIVIERA: *Cannero* €€€ Lungo Lago 2, 28821. ☎ 0323 78 80 46 (Nov–Mar: 0323 78 81 13). FAX 0323 78 80 48. @ info@hotelcannero.com Although modernized, the Cannero, set in a former monastery, has retained the atmosphere of other times. It also has tennis courts and a restaurant. 🛏 TV ▤ ✉ ♿ P	55	▦	●	▦
CANNOBIO: *Pironi* €€€ Via Marconi 35, 28822. ☎ 0323 706 24. FAX 0323 721 84. @ info@pironihotel.it Housed in a 15th-century palazzo, the hotel retains many original features, such as the inner courtyard. Bedrooms have views over the lake or old town. 🛏 TV ✉ P **Closed** Nov–Mar.	12			
CHAMPOLUC: *Villa Anna Maria* €€€ Via Croues 5, 11020. ☎ 0125 30 71 28. FAX 0125 30 79 84. W www.hotelvillaannamaria.com A simple country hotel in a 1920s chalet-style house with lots of wood panelling. The restaurant offers simple but excellent food. 🛏 TV ✉ P	21	▦		▦
COGNE: *Bellevue* €€€€ Rue Grand Paradis 22, 11012. ☎ 0165 748 25. FAX 0165 74 91 92. @ info@hotelbellevue.it This is a beautifully situated hotel surrounded by meadows and with excellent views of the Gran Paradiso. Guests are expected to take half-board. 🛏 TV ✉ ♿ P	38	▦	●	▦
COURMAYEUR: *La Grange* €€ Strada la Brenva 1, Entreves 11013. ☎ 0165 86 97 33. FAX 0165 86 97 44. @ lagrange@mbtlc.it A restructured barn, which has been in the same family since the 14th century, is the setting for this clean, bright Alpine hotel. Furnishings are new but based on traditional designs, and the atmosphere is cosy and homely. 🛏 TV ✉ P	23			▦
COURMAYEUR: *Gallia Gran Baita* €€€€ Strada Larzey Courmayeur, 11013. ☎ 0165 84 40 40. FAX 0165 84 48 05. @ granbaita@sogliahotels.com A modern, luxury hotel catering to the upmarket skier; it has saunas, a fitness centre, beauty parlour and free transport to the slopes. 🛏 TV ✉ ♿ P	53	▦	●	▦
COURMAYEUR: *Palace Bron* €€€€ Via Plan Gorret 41, 11013. ☎ 0165 84 67 42. FAX 0165 84 40 15. @ hotelpb@tin.it An elegant family-run hotel that is furnished in the style of a smart home. Most of the rooms have balconies with wonderful views. 🛏 TV ✉ P	27	▦		▦

CUNEO: *Smeraldo* €€ 19
Corso Nizza 27, 12100. **[** 0171 69 63 67. **FAX** 0171 69 80 76. **W** www.italiaabc.it/hsmeraldo
A reasonably priced hotel located on one of the main roads of central Cuneo;
the historic centre is easily reached by bus or on foot. 🛏 TV 🖥 P

DOMODOSSOLA: *Corona* €€€ 32
Via Marconi 8, 28845. **[** 0324 24 21 14. **FAX** 0324 24 28 42. **@** htcorona@tin.it
Set in the centre of town, the Corona combines tradition with modern
convenience. The restaurant offers a range of local cuisine. 🛏 TV 🍽 🖥 P

IVREA: *Castello San Giuseppe* €€€ 23
Località Castello San Giuseppe, Chiaverano 10010. **[** 0125 42 43 70. **FAX** 0125 64 12 78.
W www.castellosangiuseppe.it
The rooms in this peaceful former convent are traditionally furnished. 🛏 TV 🖥 P

LAKE MAGGIORE: *Verbano* €€€ 12
Via Ugo Ara 2, Isola dei Pescatori 28049. **[** 0323 304 08. **FAX** 0323 331 29. **W** www.hotelverbano.it
A rambling villa is the setting for this friendly hotel with views over the lake.
All of the prettily decorated bedrooms have their own balcony. 🛏 🖥

NOVARA: *Bussola* €€€ 94
Via Boggiani 54, 28100. **[** 0321 45 08 10. **FAX** 0321 45 27 86. **W** www.labussolanovara.it
The modern Bussola hotel is pleasantly and comfortably decorated. The
popular restaurant holds dinner dances on Saturday nights. 🛏 TV 🍽 🖥 P

NOVARA: *Italia* €€€ 63
Via Paolo Solaroli 8, 28100. **[** 0321 39 93 16. **FAX** 0321 39 93 10. **W** www.panciolihotels.it
Located in the centre of Novara next to the cathedral, the Italia is comfortable
and well-run. The hotel's restaurant is also very good. 🛏 TV 🍽 🖥 P

ORTA SAN GIULIO: *Leon d'Oro* €€ 35
Piazza Motta 42, 28016. **[** 0322 911 991. **FAX** 0322 903 03. **@** albergoleondoro@tiscalinet.it
Beautifully located on the shores of Lake Orta, the bedrooms have functional,
if rather bland, decor and some have balconies with views. 🛏 TV 🖥

ORTA SAN GIULIO: *Bussola* €€€ 24
Strada Panoramica 24, 28016. **[** 0322 91 19 13. **FAX** 0322 91 19 34. **@** hotelbussola@yahoo.it
The hotel is a traditional villa set in a pretty flower-filled garden with views
over the lake. Guests are expected to take half-board in summer. 🛏 TV 🖥 P

ORTA SAN GIULIO: *Orta* €€€ 35
Piazza Motta 1, 28016. **[** 0322 902 53. **FAX** 0322 90 56 46. **W** www.hotelorta.it
Set on the main piazza of Orta San Giulio, the hotel terrace overlooks the lake.
It has a pleasant old-fashioned atmosphere and spacious rooms. 🛏 TV 🖥 ♿

PONT-SAINT-MARTIN: *Ponte Romano* €€ 13
Piazza IV Novembre 14, 11026. **[** 0125 80 43 29. **FAX** 0125 80 71 08.
@ hotel.ponteromano@libero.it
Attractively located next to an ancient Roman bridge, this small, comfortable
family-run hotel is conveniently close to the centre of town. 🛏 TV 🖥 P

SAN GIORGIO MONFERRATO: *Castello San Giorgio* €€€ 11
Via Cavalli d'Olivola 3, 15020. **[** 0142 80 62 03. **FAX** 0142 80 65 05. **W** www.castellodisangiorgio.it
An elegant, refined hotel with an excellent restaurant in a pretty castle set
in its own grounds 6 km (4 miles) from Casale Monferrato. 🛏 TV 🍽 🖥 P

SAUZE D'OULX: *Il Capricorno* €€€ 7
Case Sparse 21, Le Clotes 10050. **[** 0122 85 02 73. **FAX** 0122 85 00 55. **W** www.chaletilcapricorno.it
Set on the wooded hills above the village, this is a delightfully traditional
chalet hotel with traditional wooden beams and furniture. 🛏 TV 🖥

SESTRIERE: *Principe di Piemonte* €€€€€ 100
Via Sauze 3b, 10058. **[** 0122 79 41. **FAX** 0122 75 54 11. **@** reservation.ptp@framon-hotels.it
This was once the grand hotel of Sestriere and it is still plush and extremely
comfortable. It has everything you will need from sauna to shops. 🛏 TV 🖥 P

SUSA: *Napoleon* €€€€ 62
Via Mazzini 44, 10059. **[** 0122 62 28 55. **FAX** 0122 319 00. **W** www.hotelnapoleon.it
The Napoleon is a modern, clean hotel in the town centre. 🛏 TV 🍽 🖥 ♿ P

TURIN: *Conte Biancamano* €€€ 24
Corso Vittorio Emanuele II 73, 10128. **[** 011 562 32 81. **FAX** 011 562 37 89. **@** cbhtl.to@iol.it
A centrally placed family-run hotel whose public rooms are decorated with
paintings and chandeliers. Bedrooms are light and spacious. 🛏 TV 🖥

For key to symbols see back flap

Price categories for a standard double room for one night, including tax and service charges but not including breakfast:
€ under €52
€€ €52–€100
€€€ €100–€155
€€€€ €155–€205
€€€€€ over €205.

RESTAURANT
A restaurant within the hotel sometimes reserved for residents.
SWIMMING POOL
Hotel swimming pools are usually quite small and are outdoors unless otherwise stated.
GARDEN OR TERRACE
A garden, courtyard or terrace belonging to the hotel, often providing tables for eating outside.
CREDIT CARDS
The major credit cards Visa, MasterCard (Access) and American Express are accepted in hotels with the credit card symbol.

	NUMBER OF ROOMS	RESTAURANT	SWIMMING POOL	GARDEN OR TERRACE
TURIN: *Victoria* €€€ Via Nino Costa 4, 10123. 011 561 19 09. FAX 011 561 18 06. www.hotelvictoria-torino.com The comfortable, pretty rooms in this modern hotel combine function with innovative decor; choose the Egyptian or New Orleans rooms.	106			
TURIN: *Genova e Stazione* €€€€ Via Sacchi 14b, 10128. 011 562 94 00. FAX 011 562 98 96. @ info@albergogenova.it Well placed in the city centre, close to the station. Bedrooms are decorated in a mixture of styles including Art Deco and 18th century.	78			
TURIN: *Grand Hotel Sitea* €€€€€ Via Carlo Alberto 35, 10123. 011 51 70 171. FAX 011 54 80 90. @ sitea@thi.it This elegant, traditional hotel located in the heart of the city offers excellent standards of service and a renowned restaurant.	114	■		■
TURIN: *Turin Palace* €€€€€ Via Sacchi 8, 10128. 011 562 55 11. FAX 011 561 21 87. @ palace@thi.it Dating from 1872, Turin's smartest hotel has an impressive array of modern facilities. The sumptuous rooms are furnished with antiques.	121	■		
TURIN: *Villa Sassi-El Toulà* €€€€€ Strada al Traforo del Pino 47, 10132. 011 898 05 56. FAX 011 898 00 95. www.villasassi.com Set in a beautiful 17th-century villa, this luxurious hotel just outside Turin still has many original features such as marble floors and candelabra.	16	■		■
VARALLO SESIA: *Vecchio Albergo Sacro Monte* €€ Regione Sacro Monte 14, 13019. 0163 542 54. FAX 0163 511 89. www.laproxima.it/albergo-smonte A peaceful hotel in a restored 16th-century building at the entrance to the Sacro Monte. Many of the original features have been retained.	24	■		■

LIGURIA

	NUMBER OF ROOMS	RESTAURANT	SWIMMING POOL	GARDEN OR TERRACE
CAMOGLI: *Casmona* €€€ Salita Pineto 13. 0185 770015. FAX 0185 775030. This simple and friendly hotel enjoys a good location overlooking the sea. Spacious rooms and a restaurant specialising in fish dishes add to its charm.	19	■		■
CAMOGLI: *Cenobio dei Dogi* €€€€ Via Cuneo 34, 16032. 0185 72 41 00. FAX 0185 77 27 96. www.cenobio.it A vast luxurious hotel that offers everything you would expect for the price. It has tennis courts, panoramic terraces and its own beach.	107	■	●	■
FINALE LIGURE: *Punta Est* €€€€ Via Aurelia 1, 17024. 019 60 06 11. FAX 019 60 06 11. www.puntaest.com An 18th-century villa overlooking the sea is the setting for this elegant hotel. The interior is spacious and furnished with antiques while the terraces and gardens offer some wonderful views. Half-board is normally offered.	40	■	●	■
GARLENDA: *La Meridiana* €€€€€ Via ai Castelli, 17033. 0182 58 02 71. FAX 0182 58 01 50. @ meridiana@relaischateaux.com Guests come to this elegant country villa hotel to play golf at the course next door. The hotel offers tennis and sauna. Mini-apartments are also available.	28	■	●	■
GENOA: *Best Western Hotel Metropoli* €€€ Vico dei Migliorini 8, 16123. 010 246 88 88. FAX 010 246 86 86. @ metropoli.ge@bestwestern.it Conveniently placed for both business and sightseeing, the hotel offers tastefully decorated rooms equipped with mini-bars and hairdriers.	48			
GENOA: *Nuovo Astoria* €€€ Piazza Brignole 4, 16122. 010 87 33 16. FAX 010 831 73 26. @ astorige@tin.it A simple, no frills, modern hotel in the centre of Genoa, very close to the station and a short walk from the city's main sights.	69			

GENOA: *Ramada Hotel e Suite* €€€€ 97
Via Balbi 38, 16126. **(** *010 269 91.* **FAX** *010 246 29 42.* **@** info.genova@advancehotel.com
Centrally situated this hotel has an excellent range of facilities including valet
service, a sauna and a gym fitted with the latest equipment. 🛏 TV ▤ 🗐 P

MONTEROSSO AL MARE: *Porto Roca* €€€€€ 43
Localitá Corone 1, 19016. **(** *0187 81 75 02.* **FAX** *0187 81 76 92.*
@ portoroca@portoroca.it
Set on a cliff overlooking the sea in a charming village in the Cinque Terre, the
decor in this hotel is a congenial combination of different styles. 🛏 TV ▤ 🗐

NERVI: *Villa Pagoda* €€€€ 17
Via Capolungo 15, 16167. **(** *010 372 61 61.* **FAX** *010 32 12 18.* **W** www.villapagoda.it
A splendidly romantic early 19th-century villa set in spectacular gardens.
Rooms are large and the decor is bright and clean. 🛏 TV ▤ 🗐 P

PORTOFINO: *Eden* €€€€ 9
Via Dritto 18, 16034. **(** *0185 26 90 91.* **FAX** *0185 26 90 47.* **@** edenportofino@libero.it
Conveniently located just behind the piazza of the pretty harbour, the Eden
is, as its name suggests, set in an attractive garden. Bedrooms are simple
but well-equipped. 🛏 TV ▤ 🗐

PORTOVENERE: *Genio* €€ 7
Piazza Bastreri 8, 19025. **(** *0187 79 06 11.* **FAX** *0187 79 06 11.*
A delightful hotel built into the walls of the medieval castle in 1924.
Rooms are simple, but it is one of the best value hotels in the area. 🛏 TV

RAPALLO: *Stella* €€ 27
Via Aurelia Ponente 6, 16035. **(** *0185 503 67.* **FAX** *0185 27 28 37.* **@** posta@hotelstella-riviera.com
A tall, thin, pink villa with good panoramic views of the sea from
the roof terrace. The decor is a little stark but the owners are particularly
friendly and welcoming. 🛏 TV ▤ 🗐 P

SAN REMO: *Nyala Suite* €€€€ 81
Via Strada Solaro 134, 18038. **(** *0184 667 668.* **FAX** *0184 666 059.* **W** www.nyalahotel.com
Located in a quiet residential area and surrounded by a tropical garden,
the hotel offers a swimming pool and very spacious rooms. The restaurant
has a special vegetarian menu. 🛏 TV ▤ 🗐 P

SAN REMO: *Royal* €€€€€ 136
Corso Imperatrice 80, 18038. **(** *0184 53 91.* **FAX** *0184 66 14 45.*
W www.royalhotelsanremo.com **@** royal@royalhotelsanremo.com
A traditional deluxe seaside hotel. The comfortable bedrooms are decorated with
delicate floral patterns. There is a range of sports and leisure facilities. 🛏 TV ▤ 🗐 P

SESTRI LEVANTE: *Grand Hotel dei Castelli* €€€€ 30
Via Penisola 26, 16039. **(** *0185 48 72 20.* **FAX** *0185 447 67.* **@** info@hoteldeicastelli.com
Set in spectacular gardens rising from the sea, this converted castle is decorated
with mosaics and Moorish columns. The service is very cordial. 🛏 TV ▤ 🗐 P

EMILIA-ROMAGNA

BOLOGNA: *Commercianti* €€€€ 34
Via de Pignattari 11, 40124. **(** *051 23 30 52.* **FAX** *051 22 47 33.* **@** commercianti@inbo.it
This was Bologna's first town hall in the 12th century and sympathetic
refurbishment has retained some of its medieval features; some bedrooms
are in the tower. 🛏 TV ▤ 🗐 P

BOLOGNA: *Orologio* €€€€ 29
Via IV Novembre 10, 40123. **(** *051 23 12 53.* **FAX** *051 26 05 52.* **@** orologio@inbo.it
Set in the medieval historic centre, nearly all of the rooms in this quiet town
hotel have exceptional views over Piazza Maggiore. 🛏 TV ▤ 🗐 P

BOLOGNA: *Corona d'Oro 1890* €€€€€ 35
Via Oberdan 12, 40126. **(** *051 23 64 56.* **FAX** *051 26 26 79.* **@** corona@inbo.it
Parts of the building date back to the 14th century and there has been
a hotel here for more than 100 years. Today it has an old-fashioned elegance,
with Art Nouveau friezes combined with all mod cons. 🛏 TV ▤ 🗐 P

BUSSETO: *I Due Foscari* €€ 20
Piazza Carlo Rossi 15, 43011. **(** *0524 93 00 39.* **FAX** *0524 916 25.*
Kitschly decorated and furnished in Hollywood medieval style with mock
Gothic windows and wood beams, this hotel is popular with film stars who
come here especially for the annual opera season in June and July. 🛏 TV ▤ 🗐 P

For key to symbols see back flap

Price categories for a standard double room for one night, including tax and service charges but not including breakfast:
€ under €52
€€ €52–€100
€€€ €100–€155
€€€€ €155–€205
€€€€€ over €205.

RESTAURANT
A restaurant within the hotel sometimes reserved for residents.
SWIMMING POOL
Hotel swimming pools are usually quite small and are outdoors unless otherwise stated.
GARDEN OR TERRACE
A garden, courtyard or terrace belonging to the hotel, often providing tables for eating outside.
CREDIT CARDS
The major credit cards Visa, MasterCard (Access) and American Express are accepted in hotels with the credit card symbol.

	NUMBER OF ROOMS	RESTAURANT	SWIMMING POOL	GARDEN OR TERRACE

CASTELFRANCO EMILIA: *Villa Gaidello Club* €€
Via Gaidello 18, 41013. (059 92 68 06. FAX 059 92 66 20. @ gaidello@tin.it
There are only three suites, so the atmosphere at the "club" is exclusive. This is a lovely 18th-century farmhouse set amid peaceful grounds with a lake.
Rooms: 6 | Restaurant ■ | | Garden or Terrace ■

CESENATICO: *Miramare* €€€
Viale Carducci 2, 47042. (0547 800 06. FAX 0547 847 85. W www.hrmiramare.it
Excellently placed for both beach fans and for those who want to explore the surrounding countryside, the Miramare has a good range of sports and leisure facilities and hosts an important local tennis training ground.
Rooms: 30 | Restaurant ■ | Swimming Pool ● |

FAENZA: *Vittoria* €€
Corso Garibaldi 23, 48018. (0546 215 08. FAX 0546 291 36. @ info@hotel-vittoria.com
The hotel, in the historic centre and close to the station, is Art Nouveau in style and has frescoes in the hall and some of the bedrooms.
Rooms: 49 | Restaurant ■ | | Garden or Terrace ■

FERRARA: *Carlton* €€
Via Garibaldi, 93. (0532 211 130. FAX 0532 205 766. @ info@hotelcarlton.net
Close to the monuments of the city, this modern and efficient hotel is well-run and well-equipped. Service is always attentive and courteous.
Rooms: 66 | Restaurant ■ | | Garden or Terrace ■

FERRARA: *Ripagrande* €€€
Via Ripagrande 21, 44100. (0532 76 52 50. FAX 0532 76 43 77. @ ripahotel@mbox.4net.it
A very attractively restored Renaissance palace is the setting for this smart, well-run hotel. Rooms are light and many are furnished with antiques; those with balconies have lovely views over Ferrara.
Rooms: 40 | Restaurant ■ | | Garden or Terrace ■

FERRARA: *Duchessa Isabella* €€€€€
Via Palestro 70, 44100. (0532 20 21 21. FAX 0532 20 26 38. @ info@duchessaisabella.it
A splendid hotel set in a 15th-century palazzo in the centre of Ferrara, named after Isabella d'Este who was famous for her parties. Impeccable service and luxurious bedrooms that look out onto a garden full of birds.
Rooms: 27 | Restaurant ■ | | Garden or Terrace ■

MARINA DI RAVENNA: *Bermuda* €€
Viale della Pace 363, 48023. (0544 53 05 60. FAX 0544 53 16 43. @ hotelbermuda@libero.it
Set in the pine woods near the beach 10 km (6 miles) from Ravenna, this modern family-run hotel is basic but clean and welcoming.
Rooms: 23 | Restaurant ■ | |

MODENA: *Canalgrande* €€€€
Corso Canalgrande N 6, 41100. (059 21 71 60. FAX 059 221 674. @ info@canalgrandehotel.it
Located in the city centre, this former monastery is an outstanding piece of Neo-Classical architecture, richly decorated and featuring original paintings.
Rooms: 68 | | | Garden or Terrace ■

PARMA: *Torino* €€€
Via Angelo Mazza 7, 43100. (0521 28 10 46. FAX 0521 23 07 25. @ info@hotel-torino.it
A restuctured former convent, the Torino has been in the same family for three generations and offers peaceful accommodation in the heart of Parma. Bedrooms and public rooms are furnished with Art Nouveau artifacts.
Rooms: 33 | | | Garden or Terrace ■

PARMA: *Star Hotel du Parc* €€€€
Viale Piacenza 12c, 43100. (0521 29 29 29. FAX 0521 29 28 28. @ duparc.pr@starhotels.it
A modern hotel in the centre of Parma, this example of industrial architecture dating from 1921 has a full range of facilities on offer.
Rooms: 169 | Restaurant ■ | |

PIACENZA: *Eurohotel* €€
Via Cristoforo Colombo 29, 29100. (0523 60 60 11. FAX 0523 60 60 13. @ eurohotel@libero.it
A reasonably priced pensione located just outside the historic centre and within easy reach of the train station.
Rooms: 65 | | |

PORTICO DI ROMAGNA: *Al Vecchio Convento* €€
Via Roma 7, 47010. (0543 96 70 53. FAX 0543 96 71 57. @ info@vecchioconvento.it
An exquisite hotel, tastefully furnished with simple antiques and white linen, all combining to create an impression of space and tranquillity.
Rooms: 15 | Restaurant ■ | | Garden or Terrace ■

RAVENNA: *Argentario* €€ | 28
Via di Roma 45, 48100. ☎ 0544 355 55. ℻ 0544 351 47. @ hotelargentario@tin.it
Well situated in the heart of Ravenna, close to its main monuments and the
public gardens, this is a well-equipped hotel with attractive rooms. 🛏 📺 📖 🍽

RAVENNA: *Bisanzio* €€€ | 38
Via Salara 30, 48100. ☎ 0544 21 71 11. ℻ 0544 325 39. @ info@bisanziohotel.com
A faded façade hides a welcoming, modern interior overlooking a pretty
garden, conveniently located in the centre of Ravenna. 🛏 📺 📖 🍽

REGGIO NELL'EMILIA: *Hotel Posta* €€€€ | 43
Piazza del Monte 2, 42100. ☎ 0522 43 29 44. ℻ 0522 45 26 02. @ booking@hotelposta.re.it
Located in the historic centre, this comfortable hotel has very original decor. An
austere medieval façade hides an embellished Rococo interior. 🛏 📺 📖 🍽 P

RICCIONE: *Hotel des Nations* €€€€€ | 32
Lungomare Costituzione 2, 47838. ☎ 0541 647 878. ℻ 0541 645 154. @ info@desnations.it
New Age hotel on the seafront, decorated in soft colours to harmonize
body and spirit. Various treatments available on request to relax the body,
soul and mind. Private yacht available for excursions. 🛏 📺 📖 🍽 P

RIMINI: *Rosabianca* €€ | 50
Viale Tripoli 195. ☎ 0541 390 666. ℻ 0541 390 666. @ info@rosabianca.com
A modern, recently renovated hotel close to both the beach and the historic
centre of Rimini. Guests can make use of the private beach huts. 🛏 📺 📖 🍽 P

RIMINI: *Ambasciatori* €€€€ | 64
Viale Vespucci 22, 47037. ☎ 0541 555 61. ℻ 0541 237 90. @ info@hotelambasciatori.it
This elegant and modern hotel is well situated and most rooms have a sea view. The
roof-garden offers views of the coast and there is a wellness centre. 🛏 📺 📖 🍽 P

RIMINI: *Grand Hotel* €€€€€ | 117
Via Ramuscio 1, 47900. ☎ 0541 560 00. ℻ 0541 568 66. @ info@grandhotelrimini.com
Conveniently situated near the seafront, the port and the station, this large, well-
equipped, smart hotel has tennis courts and its own beach. 🛏 📺 📖 🍽 P

SANTARCANGELO DI ROMAGNA: *Hotel della Porta* €€ | 22
Via Andrea Costa 85, 47822. ☎ 0541 62 21 52. ℻ 0541 62 21 68. @ info@hoteldellaporta.com
This hotel is in a region steeped in references to Dante's *Divine Comedy* (see
pp30–31). Frescoes and antiques decorate some of the rooms. 🛏 📺 📖 🍽 & P

FLORENCE

FLORENCE: *Rovezzano Bed & Breakfast* €€ | 6
Via Aretina 417, 50136. **Map** 3 B4. ☎ 055 69 00 23. ℻ 055 69 10 02. @ rovezzano@virgilio.it
Located within a Renaissance villa 1 km (0.6 mile) east of Florence,
this is a quiet B&B immersed in the countryside. 🛏 P

FLORENCE: *Ariele* €€€ | 39
2 km (1 mile) W, Via Magenta 11, 50123. **Map** 1 A4. ☎ 055 21 15 09. ℻ 055 26 85 21.
@ hotel.ariele@libero.it
This is a quiet, homely hotel with spacious rooms and antique furniture. 🛏 📺 📖 🍽 P

FLORENCE: *Hotel Villa Belvedere* €€€ | 26
Via Benedetto Castelli 3, 50124. **Map** 3 A5. ☎ 055 22 25 01. ℻ 055 22 31 63.
@ reception@villa-belvedere.com
A spacious 1930s villa set in landscaped grounds near the Boboli Gardens.
The first-floor terraces have good views of the garden. 🛏 📺 📖 🍽 P

FLORENCE: *Pensione Annalena* €€€ | 20
Via Romana 34, 50125. **Map** 3 A3. ☎ 055 22 24 02. ℻ 055 22 24 03. @ info@hotelannalena.it
A 15th-century hotel with spacious, simply but attractively decorated
bedrooms. The public areas are all contained in one great hall. 🛏 📺 🍽

FLORENCE: *Piccolo Hotel* €€€ | 10
Via San Gallo 51, 50123. **Map** 2 D4. ☎ 055 47 55 19. ℻ 055 47 45 15.
@ info@piccolohotelfirenze.com
The rooms in this charming hotel close to the city centre are simply decorated,
with a few refined touches. It also offers free bikes for sightseeing tours. 🛏 📺 📖 & P

FLORENCE: *Hotel Cellai* €€€€ | 47
Via XXVII Aprile 14, 50129. **Map** 2 D4. ☎ 055 48 92 91. ℻ 055 47 03 87. @ info@hotelcellai.it
A beautifully restored 18th-century building houses this family-run hotel in
the heart of Florence. Beautiful views and helpful staff. 🛏 📺 📖 🍽 P

Price categories for a standard double room for one night, including tax and service charges but not including breakfast: € under €52 €€ €52–€100 €€€ €100–€155 €€€€ €155–€205 €€€€€ over €205.	**RESTAURANT** A restaurant within the hotel sometimes reserved for residents. **SWIMMING POOL** Hotel swimming pools are usually quite small and are outdoors unless otherwise stated. **GARDEN OR TERRACE** A garden, courtyard or terrace belonging to the hotel, often providing tables for eating outside. **CREDIT CARDS** The major credit cards Visa, MasterCard (Access) and American Express are accepted in hotels with the credit card symbol.	NUMBER OF ROOMS	RESTAURANT	SWIMMING POOL	GARDEN OR TERRACE
FLORENCE: *Hotel Loggiato dei Serviti* €€€€€ Piazza della SS Annunziata 3, 50122. **Map** 2 D4. **(** 055 28 95 92. **FAX** 055 28 95 95. @ info@loggiatodeiservitihotel.it Built in 1527, the reception areas in this hotel near the Spedale degli Innocenti have vaulted ceilings and a bar area flanked by stone columns. ☎ TV ☷	29			
FLORENCE: *Hotel Monna Lisa* €€€€€ Borgo Pinti 27, 50121. **Map** 2 E5. **(** 055 247 97 51. **FAX** 055 247 97 55. @ hotel@monnalisa.it A stone courtyard leads into this Renaissance palazzo. Some bedrooms are huge, with old furniture and high ceilings; the new wing has contemporary decor. ☎ TV ☷ ☷ P ☷	45			▓
FLORENCE: *Hotel Porta Rossa* €€€€€ Via Porta Rossa 19, 50123. **Map** 3 C1 (5 C3). **(** 055 28 75 51. **FAX** 055 28 21 79. Italy's second-oldest hotel dates from 1386 and has a welcoming atmosphere and huge bedrooms. All rooms have antique furnishings. ☎ TV ☷ ☷ ☷	78			
FLORENCE: *Hotel Silla* €€€€€ Via dei Renai 5, 50125. **Map** 4 D2 (6 E5). **(** 055 234 28 88. **FAX** 055 234 14 37. @ hotelsilla@tin.it This 16th-century hotel is approached through an elegant courtyard with a grand staircase. There is a pretty terrace giving views of the Arno. ☎ TV ☷ ☷ P	36			▓
FLORENCE: *Morandi alla Crocetta* €€€€€ Via Laura 50, 50121. **Map** 2 E4. **(** 055 234 47 47. **FAX** 055 248 09 54. @ welcome@hotelmorandi.it A lovely former convent decorated with antique rugs and plants. ☎ TV ☷ ☷ P	10			
FLORENCE: *Orto de' Medici* €€€€€ Via San Gallo 30, 50129. **Map** 2 D4. **(** 055 48 34 27. **FAX** 055 46 12 76. @ hotel@ortodeimedici.it A recently renovated family hotel with dark red decor and frescoed, stuccoed ceilings that give it the impression of a grand mansion. ☎ TV ☷ ☷	31			▓
FLORENCE: *Grand Hotel Villa Cora* €€€€€ Viale Machiavelli 18, 50125. **Map** 3 A3. **(** 055 229 84 51. **FAX** 055 22 90 86. @ reservations@villacora.it A stunning Renaissance building with balustraded terraces. The reception rooms are decorated with frescoed ceilings and varnished wooden floors. ☎ TV ☷ ☷ P	48	▓	●	▓
FLORENCE: *Hotel Brunelleschi* €€€€€ Piazza Santa Elisabetta 3, 50122. **Map** 6 D2. **(** 055 273 70. **FAX** 055 21 96 53. @ info@hotelbrunelleschi.it This unique hotel was built inside a Byzantine tower. It is therefore wonderfully atmospheric with stunning views over Florence from the roof terrace. ☎ TV ☷ ☷ P	89	▓		
FLORENCE: *Hotel Continentale* €€€€€ Vicolo dell'Oro 6r, 50123. **Map** 3 C1 (5 C4). **(** 055 272 62. **FAX** 055 28 31 39. @ continental@lungarnohotels.com In a prime location near the Ponte Vecchio, the hotel's bar and top-floor suites overlook the river. The Continentale was fully renovated in 2002. ☎ TV ☷ ☷	43			▓
FLORENCE: *Hotel Excelsior* €€€€€ Piazza d'Ognissanti 3, 50123. **Map** 1 B5 (5 A2). **(** 055 27 151. **FAX** 055 21 02 78. @ excelsiorflorence@westin.com Occupying two houses rebuilt in 1815, the hotel is decorated with gracious marble floors and stained glass with lovely views over the Arno. ☎ TV ☷ ☷ P ☷	168	▓		
FLORENCE: *Hotel Helvetia e Bristol* €€€€€ Via de' Pescioni 2, 50123. **Map** 1 C5 (5 C2). **(** 055 28 78 14. **FAX** 055 28 83 53. A luxurious 18th-century hotel a few steps from the Duomo, with antiques, a domed, stained glass ceiling and a splendid wood and marble bar. ☎ TV ☷ ☷ P	67	▓		
FLORENCE: *Hotel Hermitage* €€€€€ Vicolo Marzio 1, 50122. **Map** 6 D4. **(** 055 28 72 16. **FAX** 055 21 22 08. @ florence@hermitagehotel.com Set in a medieval building with great views from the upper-storey rooms. ☎ TV ☷ ☷	28			▓

FLORENCE: *Hotel J and J* €€€€€ | 18 | | | ▦
Via di Mezzo 20, 50121. **Map** 2 E5. **(** 055 26 31 21. **FAX** 055 24 02 82. **@** jandj@dada.it
This pretty, peaceful hotel is set in a former 16th-century monastery and
has windows set between old stone arches and frescoed ceilings. **☎** **TV** **▤** **✍**

FLORENCE: *Hotel Montebello Splendid* €€€€€ | 48 | ▦ | | ▦
Via Montebello 60. **Map** 1 A5 (5 A2). **(** 055 239 80 51. **FAX** 055 21 18 67.
@ info@montebellosplendid.it
A 19th-century villa elegantly transformed into an intimate hotel near the city
centre. Lovely garden and restaurant with outdoor seating. **☎** **TV** **▤** **✍** **P**

FLORENCE: *Hotel Regency* €€€€€ | 34 | ▦ | | ▦
Piazza Massimo d'Azeglio 3, 50121. **Map** 2 F5. **(** 055 24 52 47. **FAX** 055 234 67 35.
@ info@regency-hotel.com
Behind the modest exterior of a Florentine town house lies a grand, Classical-
style reception area and bar with wood-panelling decor. **☎** **TV** **✍** **P**

FLORENCE: *Hotel Tornabuoni Beacci* €€€€€ | 40 | ▦ | | ▦
Via de' Tornabuoni 3, 50123. **Map** 1 C5 (5 C2). **(** 055 21 26 45. **FAX** 055 28 35 94.
@ info@tornabuonihotels.com
This former palazzo on a busy central street has wide carpeted hallways and lounge
areas furnished with antiques and tapestries. Bedrooms are luxurious. **☎** **TV** **▤** **✍** **P**

FLORENCE: *Londra* €€€€€ | 158 | ▦ | | ▦
Via Jacopo da Diacceto, 16-18, 50123. **Map** 1 B4. **(** 055 238 27 91. **FAX** 055 21 06 82.
@ info@hotellondra.com
Located near the railway station, this hotel offers a gym and sauna and special services
for children. Some rooms have PC, fax and modem. Bikes can be hired. **☎** **TV** **▤** **✍** **P**

FLORENCE: *Rivoli* €€€€€ | 60 | ● | | ▦
Via della Scala 33, 50123. **Map** 1 A4 (5 A1). **(** 055 278 61. **FAX** 055 29 40 41. **@** info@hotelrivoli.it
A spacious, 15th-century hotel decorated to a high standard. **☎** **TV** **▤** **✍** **P**

FLORENCE: *Torre di Bellosguardo* €€€€€ | 16 | ● | | ▦
Via Roti Michelozzi 2, 50124. **Map** 5 B5 **(** 055 229 81 45. **FAX** 055 22 90 08.
@ info@torrebellosguardo.com
This 16th-century villa is situated on a hill outside the historic city centre to the
southwest, in an area called Bellosguardo. Inside, huge rooms are filled with
antiques and Persian rugs. There are spectacular views over Florence. **☎** **▤** **✍** **P**

FLORENCE: *Villa La Massa* €€€€€ | 37 | ▦ | ● | ▦
Via la Massa 24, Candeli 50012. **(** 055 626 11. **FAX** 055 63 31 02. **@** info@villalamassa.com
On a riverside setting 6 km (4 miles) northeast of Florence, this luxurious 17th-century
hotel has elegant rooms with antique furniture. **☎** **TV** **▤** **✍** **P** **⅃**

TUSCANY

AREZZO: *Castello di Gargonza* €€€ | 46 | ▦ | ● | ▦
Gargonza, Monte San Savino, 52048. **(** 0575 84 70 21. **FAX** 0575 84 70 54. **W** www.gargonza.it
A sweeping tree-lined driveway curves around the walls of this castle guest-house,
which also has other rooms and apartments in the grounds. The views are magnificent
and weekly services are held in the pretty frescoed chapel. **☎** **✍** **P**

CORTONA: *Hotel San Luca* €€€ | 57 | ▦ | | ▦
Piazzale Garibaldi 2, 52044. **(** 0575 63 04 60. **FAX** 0575 63 01 05. **W** www.sanlucacortona.com
This hillside hotel has simple bedrooms, but the comfortable reception
rooms offer good panoramas over the surrounding valleys. **☎** **TV** **▤** **✍** **P**

CORTONA: *Hotel San Michele* €€€ | 43 | | | ▦
Via Guelfa 15, 52044. **(** 0575 60 43 48. **FAX** 0575 63 01 47. **@** info@sanmichele.net
A beautifully restored Renaissance palazzo on a narrow street. A maze of
corridors leads to comfortable bedrooms and a superb attic suite. **☎** **TV** **▤** **✍** **P**

CASTELLINA IN CHIANTI: *Tenuta di Ricavo* €€€€€ | 23 | ▦ | ● | ▦
Località Ricavo, 53011. **(** 0577 74 02 21. **FAX** 0577 74 10 14. **@** ricavo@ricavo.com
A charming hotel occupying the entire hamlet and furnished with a mixture of
antiques and rustic furniture. Many rooms are in old country houses. **☎** **✍** **P**

ELBA: *Airone del Parco e delle Terme* €€€ | 85 | ▦ | ● | ▦
Località San Giovanni, 57037. **(** 0565 92 91 11. **FAX** 0565 91 74 84.
@ info@hotelairone.com
This hotel provides a complete range of facilities: park, a beach, two swimming
pools, spa, beauty centre, and a private boat for excursions. **☎** **TV** **▤** **✍** **P**

	NUMBER OF ROOMS	RESTAURANT	SWIMMING POOL	GARDEN OR TERRACE

Price categories for a standard double room for one night, including tax and service charges but not including breakfast:
€ under €52
€€ €52–€100
€€€ €100–€155
€€€€ €155–€205
€€€€€ over €205.

RESTAURANT
A restaurant within the hotel sometimes reserved for residents.
SWIMMING POOL
Hotel swimming pools are usually quite small and are outdoors unless otherwise stated.
GARDEN OR TERRACE
A garden, courtyard or terrace belonging to the hotel, often providing tables for eating outside.
CREDIT CARDS
The major credit cards Visa, MasterCard (Access) and American Express are accepted in hotels with the credit card symbol.

ELBA: *Capo Sud* €€€ Località Lacona, 57037. **C** *0565 96 40 21.* **FAX** *0565 96 42 63.* **@** info@hotelcaposud.it A village-like resort with excellent bay views. The rooms are housed in a complex of villas and the restaurant serves produce from its orchard. ⌂ TV ▤ P	40	■	●	■
FIESOLE: *Hotel Villa Bonelli* €€€ Via F Poeti 1, 50014. **C** *055 595 13.* **FAX** *055 59 89 42.* **@** info@hotelvillabonelli.com This simple, friendly hotel is pleasantly furnished and has excellent views of the surrounding countryside. ⌂ TV ▤ ⊘ P	20			■
FIESOLE: *Villa San Michele* €€€€€ Via Doccia 4, 50014. **C** *055 567 82 00.* **FAX** *055 59 87 34.* **@** reservations@villasanmichele.net Allegedly designed by Michelangelo, the beautiful monastery has extensive grounds and beautiful panoramas over the city from the loggia. ⌂ TV ▤ ⊘ P	42	■	●	■
GAIOLE IN CHIANTI: *Castello di Spaltenna* €€€€€ Pieve di Spaltenna, 53013. **C** *0577 74 94 83.* **FAX** *0577 74 92 69.* **W** www.spaltenna.it A beautiful, fortified former monastery with spacious rooms overlooking a courtyard; some rooms have jacuzzis. The restaurant is excellent. ⌂ TV ▤ ⊘ P	39	■	●	■
GIGLIO PORTO: *Castello Monticello* €€ Via Provinciale, 58013. **C** *0564 80 92 52.* **FAX** *0564 80 94 73.* **@** info@hotelcastellomonticello.com A castle hotel, it was originally built on this pretty island as a private house. It sits on a hill, and there are superb views from the bedrooms. ⌂ TV ▤ ⊘ P	27	■		■
LUCCA: *Piccolo Hotel Puccini* €€ Via di Poggio 9, 55100. **C** *0583 554 21.* **FAX** *0583 534 87.* **@** info@hotelpuccini.com Housed in a lovely old stone building, this smart, small hotel has an attractive bar that overlooks the pretty narrow street outside. ⌂ TV ⊘	14			
LUCCA: *Hotel Universo* €€€ Piazza del Giglio 1, 55100. **C** *0583 49 36 78.* **FAX** *0583 95 48 54.* **@** info@hoteluniversolucca.com This slightly worn hotel has large and comfortable bedrooms, some with views of the square. The big luxurious bathrooms are an added attraction. ⌂ TV ▤ ⊘	55	■		■
LUCCA: *Locanda L'Elisa* €€€€€ Via Nuova per Pisa 1952, 55050. **C** *0583 37 97 37.* **FAX** *0583 37 90 19.* **@** locanda.elisa@lunet.it This Parisian-style stately home has a peaceful and luxurious atmosphere. Bedrooms are decorated with antiques, and there are two elegant drawing rooms. ⌂ TV ⊘	10	■	●	■
MONTERIGGIONI: *Albergo Casalta* € Località Strove, 53035. **C** *0577 30 10 02.* **FAX** *0577 30 10 02.* Housed in a 1,000-year-old building, a central hearth in the reception adds to the warm and welcoming atmosphere. The restaurant is also very elegant. ⌂ ⊘	10	■	●	
PISA: *Duomo* €€€ Via S Maria 94. **C** *050 56 18 94.* **FAX** *050 56 04 18.* **@** info@grandhotelduomo.it This very comfortable hotel has a spectacular view of the Tower and the other monuments of the city from its roof garden. ⌂ TV ▤ ⊘ P	93	■		■
PISA: *Royal Victoria Hotel* €€€ Lungarno Pacinotti 12, 56126. **C** *050 94 01 11.* **FAX** *050 94 01 80.* **@** mail@royalvictoria.it A dignified hotel built in the 19th century. It retains several original features, including exquisite *trompe l'oeil* drapery and wood-panelled doors. ⌂ TV ⊘ P	48			
PISTOIA: *Albergo Patria* €€ Via Crispi 8, 51100. **C** *0573 251 87.* **FAX** *0573 36 81 68.* **@** info@patriahotel.com An ancient hotel with a dark, modern interior and 1970s bedrooms. It is well placed for sightseeing, and upper bedrooms have excellent views of the Duomo. ⌂ TV ⊘	28			
PISTOIA: *Hotel Piccolo Ritz* €€ Via Vannucci 67, 51100. **C** *0573 267 75 16.* **FAX** *0573 277 98.* This small hotel lives up to its name and has a pleasant, frescoed café-style bar. ⌂ TV ⊘	21			

PORTO ERCOLE: *Il Pellicano* €€€€€ | 41
Località Sbarcatello, 58018. **[** *0564 85 81 11.* **FAX** *0564 83 34 18.* **@** info@pellicanohotel.com
Luxurious and exclusive with its own rocky beach, this old-style Tuscan villa has
wonderful views. Rooms are elegantly furnished with antiques. ▦ TV ▤ 📷 P

RADDA IN CHIANTI: *Villa Miranda* €€ | 40
Siena 53017. **[** *0577 73 80 21.* **FAX** *0577 73 86 68.* **W** www.hotelvillamiranda.it
Run by the same family since the original building (the Post House) was built
in 1842. Bedrooms have beamed ceilings and brass bedsteads. ▦ ▤ 📷 P

SAN GIMIGNANO: *Albergo Leon Bianco* €€€ | 25
Piazza della Cisterna 13, 53037. **[** *0577 94 12 94.* **FAX** *0577 94 21 23.* **@** info@leonbianco.com
Airy rooms with pleasant views and terracotta floors typify this former
palazzo. Parts of the original stone wall can still be seen. ▦ TV ▤ 📷

SAN GIMIGNANO: *Hotel Villa Belvedere* €€€ | 12
Via Dante 14, 53037. **[** *0577 94 05 39.* **FAX** *0577 94 03 27.* **@** hotel.villa.belvedere@tin.it
A pretty terracotta villa set in a cypress-filled garden with hammocks. Light, modern
bedrooms are painted in soothing pastel shades. TV ▤ 📷 P

SAN GIMIGNANO: *Villa San Paolo* €€€€ | 18
Strada per Certaldo, 53037. **[** *0577 95 51 00.* **FAX** *0577 95 51 13.* **@** info@hotelvillasanpaolo.com
An attractive hillside villa set in terraced gardens with tennis courts. Inside
there are pretty bedrooms and intimate lounges. ▦ TV ▤ 📷 P **Closed** *Jan–Mar.*

SIENA: *Hotel Chiusarelli* €€€ | 49
Viale Curtatone 15, 53100. **[** *0577 28 05 62.* **FAX** *0577 27 11 77.* **@** info@chiusarelli.com
A pretty villa that still looks slightly the worse for wear in spite of its recent
restoration. The pleasant garden is filled with palm trees. ▦ TV ▤ 📷 P

SIENA: *Santa Caterina* €€€ | 19
Via Enea Silvio Piccolomini 7, 53100. **[** *0577 22 11 05.* **FAX** *0577 27 10 87.* **@** info@hscsiena.it
The comfortable rooms overlook the marvellous flower garden which has
charming views of the red roofs of Siena. The Santa Caterina, situated near
the Porta Romana, was once a privately owned villa. ▦ TV ▤ 📷 P

SIENA: *Villa Patrizia* €€€€ | 33
Via Fiorentina 58, 53100. **[** *0577 504 31.* **FAX** *0577 504 42.* **@** info@villapatrizia.it
A rambling old villa on the city's northern outskirts. The bedrooms,
all of which look out onto the gardens, are simply furnished but
comfortable and quiet. ▦ TV ▤ 📷 P

SIENA: *Villa Scacciapensieri* €€€€ | 31
Via di Scacciapensieri 10, 53100. **[** *0577 41 44 1.* **FAX** *0577 27 08 54.* **@** villasca@tin.it
Set in attractive grounds, this villa features an old-fashioned lounge with a huge
stone fireplace. The spacious bedrooms have views of Siena. ▦ TV ▤ 📷 P

SIENA: *Hotel Certosa di Maggiano* €€€€€ | 17
Strada di Certosa 82, 53100. **[** *0577 28 81 80.* **FAX** *0577 28 81 89.* **@** certosa@relaischateaux.fr
A former Carthusian monastery built in 1314 and turned into an exclusive,
peaceful retreat. The rooms are adorned with antique paintings. ▦ TV ▤ 📷 P

SINALUNGA: *Locanda L'Amorosa* €€€€€ | 20
L'Amorosa, 53048. **[** *0577 67 94 97.* **FAX** *0577 63 20 01.* **@** locanda@amorosa.it
An enchanting stone and pink terracotta building is the setting for this beautiful
inn. The luxurious bedrooms are quiet and comfortable. ▦ TV ▤ 📷 P

VIAREGGIO: *Hotel President* €€€€€ | 37
Viale Carducci 5, 55049. **[** *0584 96 27 12.* **FAX** *0584 96 36 58.* **@** info@hotelpresident.it
A smart seaside hotel with attractively refurbished and comfortable bedrooms.
There are excellent sea views from the roof-top restaurant. ▦ TV 📷

VOLTERRA: *Albergo Villa Nencini* €€ | 35
Borgo Santo Stefano 55, 56048. **[** *0588 863 86.* **FAX** *0588 806 01.* **W** www.villanencini.it
A stone country hotel set in a park a few minutes from the town. Cool, light
bedrooms, a smart breakfast room, basement trattoria and terrace. ▦ TV 📷 P

UMBRIA

ASSISI: *Country House* €€ | 15
Via di Valecchie 41, Località Valecchie, 06081. **[** *075 81 63 63.*
FAX *075 81 61 55.* **W** www.countryhousetreesse.com
A convenient 700 m (half a mile) from the centre of Assisi, this
1920s villa is set amid peaceful countryside. ▦ TV ▤ 📷 P

For key to symbols see back flap

Price categories for a standard double room for one night, including tax and service charges but not including breakfast:
€ under €52
€€ €52–€100
€€€ €100–€155
€€€€ €155–€205
€€€€€ over €205.

RESTAURANT
A restaurant within the hotel sometimes reserved for residents.
SWIMMING POOL
Hotel swimming pools are usually quite small and are outdoors unless otherwise stated.
GARDEN OR TERRACE
A garden, courtyard or terrace belonging to the hotel, often providing tables for eating outside.
CREDIT CARDS
The major credit cards Visa, MasterCard (Access) and American Express are accepted in hotels with the credit card symbol.

	NUMBER OF ROOMS	RESTAURANT	SWIMMING POOL	GARDEN OR TERRACE
ASSISI: *Umbra* €€ Via degli Archi 6, 06081. 075 81 22 40. FAX 075 81 36 53. info@hotelumbra.it A friendly hotel located in an atmospheric back street in the historic centre. Comfortable rooms and charming terrace.	25	▦		▦
ASSISI: *Dei Priori* €€€ Corso Mazzini 15, 06081. 075 81 22 37. FAX 075 81 68 04. hpriori@tiscalinet.it Set in a 17th-century building in the historic centre, the bedrooms are pretty and fresh and there is a lovely vaulted dining room.	34	▦		
ASSISI: *Romantik Hotel Le Silve* €€€€ Località Armenzano di Assisi, 06081. 075 801 90 00. FAX 075 801 90 05. hotellesilve@tin.it Located about 12 km (7 miles) from Assisi, this hotel has wonderful views of the Tuscan hills as well as an excellent range of sports and leisure facilities.	15	▦	●	▦
CAMPELLO SUL CLITUNNO: *Il Vecchio Molino* €€ Via del Tempio 34, Località Pissignano 06042. 0743 52 11 22. FAX 0743 27 50 97. vecchiomolino@perugiaonline.com Set in a converted mill on an island in the river, the bedrooms are spacious and comfortable. A Roman temple can be seen from the garden. **Closed** Nov–Mar.	13			▦
CASTIGLIONE DEL LAGO: *Miralago* €€ Piazza Mazzini 6, 06061. 075 95 11 57. FAX 075 95 19 24. hotelmiralago@tin.it Set in the centre of this town on the shores of Lake Trasimeno, the Miralago is a small, family-run hotel. Fresh fish from the lake is served in the restaurant.	19	▦		▦
CITTÀ DI CASTELLO: *Tiferno* €€€ Piazza Raffaello Sanzio 13, 06012 (near Perugia). 0758 55 03 31. FAX 0758 52 11 96. info@hoteltiferno.it A 17th-century palace that was turned into a monastery; it has been a hotel since 1895. The restructuring has respected the original architecture.	38	▦		▦
FONTIGNANO: *Villa di Monte Solare* €€€ Via Montali 7, Colle San Paolo 06007. 075 83 23 76. FAX 075 835 54 62. info@villamontesolare.it A beautiful 18th-century villa with terracotta floors, period furniture and frescoes. Colle San Paolo is 25 km (15 miles) from Perugia.	28	▦	●	▦
GUBBIO: *Bosone Palace* €€ Via XX Settembre 22, 06024. 075 922 06 88. FAX 075 922 05 52. bosone@mencarelligroup.com Set in the Palazzo Raffaelli, one of the oldest palazzi in the historic centre, the Bosone has a mixture of bedrooms from the spectacular to the ordinary. All of them, however, have a wonderfully historic atmosphere.	30			
GUBBIO: *Oderisi-Balestrieri* €€ Via Mazzatinti 2/12, 06024. 075 922 06 62. FAX 075 922 06 63. www.rosatihotels.com A hotel in the medieval town centre; the rooms are pleasantly furnished with modern, wooden beams, bedsteads and tables.	35			
GUBBIO: *Villa Montegranelli* €€€ Località Monteluiano, 06024. 075 922 01 85. FAX 075 927 33 72. villa.montegranelli@tin.it An elegant country villa about 4 km (2 miles) from Gubbio with attractive bedrooms and a highly recommended restaurant *(see p596)*.	21	▦		▦
LAKE TRASIMENO: *Hotel da Sauro* €€ Isola Maggiore, 06060. 075 82 61 68. FAX 075 82 51 30. hotelsauro@libero.it A basic hotel with friendly staff in an exceptional location. Isola Maggiore remains fairly isolated making this a quiet and simple retreat.	12			▦
MONTEFALCO: *Ringhiera Umbra* € Via G Mameli 20, 06036. 0742 37 91 66. FAX 0742 37 91 66. A simple yet immaculately kept hotel in a historic building in the centre of Montefalco. The reasonably priced restaurant is in a vaulted room.	20	▦		

MONTEFALCO: *Villa Pambuffetti* €€€€ | 15
Via della Vittoria 20, 06036. ☎ *0742 37 94 17.* FAX *0742 37 92 45.* Ⓦ *www.villapambuffetti.com*
The spacious and comfortable bedrooms in this hotel are all different. The tower room has wonderful views of the surrounding country. 🛏 TV 🍽 🌃 P

NORCIA: *Garden* € | 50
Viale XX Settembre 2b, 06046. ☎ *0743 81 66 87.* FAX *0743 81 66 87.* @ *hotelgarden@libero.it*
Close to the centre of Norcia, this hotel has basic but comfortable rooms. 🛏 TV 🌃 P

ORVIETO: *Virgilio* € | 15
Piazza Duomo 5–6, 05018. ☎ *0763 34 18 82.* FAX *0763 34 37 97.* @ *info@hotelvirgilio.com*
Located in central Orvieto, this simple hotel was converted by the owner from what was once his home. Some rooms have views of the cathedral. 🛏 TV 🌃

ORVIETO: *La Badia* €€€€ | 28
Località la Badia 8, 05019. ☎ *0763 30 19 59.* FAX *0763 30 53 96.* @ *labadia.hotel@tin.it*
Housed in a spectacular former monastery, parts of which date back to the 12th century, modern comfort is combined with medieval splendour. 🛏 TV 🍽 🌃 P

ORVIETO: *Villa Ciconia* €€€€ | 12
Via dei Tigli 69, 05019. ☎ *0763 30 55 82.* FAX *0763 30 20 77.* @ *villaciconia@libero.it*
Set in lovely grounds a short distance out of Orvieto, this 16th-century country house makes a peaceful base from which to explore Umbria. 🛏 TV 🍽 🌃 P

PERUGIA: *Lo Spedalicchio* €€ | 25
Piazza Bruno Buozzi 3, Ospedalicchio 06080. ☎ *075 801 03 23.* FAX *075 801 03 23.*
@ *info@lospedalicchio.it*
Built within the walls of a 14th-century fortress, the rooms are simply but comfortably decorated in keeping with the style of the building. 🛏 🍽 TV 🌃 P

PERUGIA: *Sant'Ercolano* €€ | 15
Via del Bovaro 9, 06100. ☎ *075 572 46 50.* FAX *075 572 46 32.* @ *s_ercolano@yahoo.it*
Well-located in the historic centre of Perugia. Rooms are basic but clean. 🛏 TV 🌃

PERUGIA: *Locanda della Posta* €€€€ | 40
Corso Vannucci 97, 06100. ☎ *075 572 89 25.* FAX *075 573 25 62.* @ *novelber@tin.it*
This elegant 200-year-old hotel is housed in a charming old palazzo on the pedestrianized main street of the historic centre. 🛏 TV 🍽 🌃

PERUGIA: *Brufani* €€€€€ | 94
Piazza Italia 12, 06100. ☎ *075 573 25 41.* FAX *075 572 02 10.* @ *brufani@tin.it*
Opened in 1884, the public rooms of this exclusive hotel were painted by Lillis, the German interior designer. The views are spectacular. 🛏 TV 🍽 🌃 P

SPELLO: *La Bastiglia* €€ | 33
Piazza Vallegloria 7, 06038. ☎ *0742 65 12 77.* FAX *0742 30 11 59.* @ *fancelli@labastiglia.com*
An adapted old mill is the setting for this airy, homely hotel whose extensive terraces give excellent views over the surrounding countryside. 🛏 TV 🍽 🌃 P

SPELLO: *Palazzo Bocci* €€€ | 23
Via Cavour 17, 06038. ☎ *0742 30 10 21.* FAX *0742 30 14 64.* @ *bocci@bcsnet.it*
Set in a much restored 14th-century palazzo in the centre of Spello, this hotel combines modern convenience with traditional charm. 🛏 TV 🍽 🌃 P

SPOLETO: *Charleston* € | 21
Piazza Collicola 10, 06049. ☎ *0743 22 00 52.* FAX *0743 22 12 44.* @ *info@hotelcharleston.it*
A 17th-century building in the centre of Spoleto. The modern and traditional furnishings in this hotel create an uncluttered yet homely feel. 🛏 TV 🍽 🌃 P

SPOLETO: *Aurora* €€ | 23
Via Apollinare 3, 06049. ☎ *0743 22 03 15.* FAX *0743 22 18 85.* @ *info@hotelauroraspoleto.it*
A good value hotel in the historic centre. It is connected to the Apollinare restaurant and (unusually for this price) all rooms have mini-bars. 🛏 TV 🌃 P ♿

SPOLETO: *Gattapone* €€€ | 15
Via del Ponte 6, 06049. ☎ *0743 22 34 47.* FAX *0743 22 34 48.* @ *info@hotelgattapone.it*
A smart bed and breakfast built on the highest point of the town, five minutes' walk from the centre with excellent views of the Ponte delle Torri. 🛏 TV 🍽 🌃 P

TODI: *Bramante* €€€ | 57
Via Orvietana 48, 06059. ☎ *075 894 83 81.* FAX *075 894 80 74.*
@ *bramante@hotelbramante.it*
Although rebuilt, parts of the 13th-century convent remain and the simple furnishings add to the peaceful atmosphere. A tennis court is also available. 🛏 TV 🍽 🌃 P

Price categories for a standard double room for one night, including tax and service charges but not including breakfast:
€ under €52
€€ €52–€100
€€€ €100–€155
€€€€ €155–€205
€€€€€ over €205.

RESTAURANT
A restaurant within the hotel sometimes reserved for residents.
SWIMMING POOL
Hotel swimming pools are usually quite small and are outdoors unless otherwise stated.
GARDEN OR TERRACE
A garden, courtyard or terrace belonging to the hotel, often providing tables for eating outside.
CREDIT CARDS
The major credit cards Visa, MasterCard (Access) and American Express are accepted in hotels with the credit card symbol.

	NUMBER OF ROOMS	RESTAURANT	SWIMMING POOL	GARDEN OR TERRACE
TODI: *Hotel Fonte Cesia* €€€ Via Lorenzo Leonj 3, 06059. 📞 075 894 37 37. 📠 075 894 46 77. @ fontecesia@fontecesia.it A beautiful 17th-century palazzo is the setting for this elegant and intimate hotel that combines traditional charm with all modern comforts.	36	■		■
TORGIANO: *Le Tre Vaselle* €€€€ Via G Garibaldi 48, 06089. 📞 075 988 04 47. 📠 075 988 02 14. @ 3vaselle@3vaselle.it Set in a 17th-century country house, the hotel has retained its terracotta floor tiles and beamed ceilings and is furnished with rural antiques.	61	■	●	■
LE MARCHE				
ACQUAVIVA PICENA: *Hotel O'Viv* €€ Via Marziale 43, 63030. 📞 0735 76 46 49. 📠 0735 76 50 54. Set in an attractive palazzo in the medieval town centre, the bedrooms in this traditional hotel are spacious with wonderful views from the terrace.	12	■		■
ANCONA: *Grand Hotel Palace* €€€ Lungomare Vanvitelli 24. 📞 071 20 18 13. 📠 071 207 48 32. @ palace.ancona@libero.it Once the private palace of a noble family, this stylish hotel is located near the harbour. There is a beautiful panorama from the roof terrace.	40	■		■
ANCONA: *Emilia* €€€€ Poggio di Portonovo, 60020. 📞 071 80 11 45. 📠 071 80 13 30. @ info@hotelemilia.com A refined hotel with bright and pretty interior decorations. As well as hosting concerts for the Ancona Jazz festival in its elegant garden, the Emilia organizes an annual art prize and has a collection of contemporary art.	29	■	●	■
FOLIGNANO: *Villa Pigna* €€ Viale Assisi 33, 63040. 📞 0736 49 18 68. 📠 0736 49 21 79. @ info@hotelvillapigna.it A modern, efficiently-run hotel in the centre of town. The public rooms are attractive and the bedrooms, if unexceptional, are satisfactory.	50	■		■
JESI: *Federico II* €€€ Via Ancona 100, 60035. 📞 0731 21 10 79. 📠 0731 572 21. @ info@hotelfederico2.it A slick post-modern hotel offering a massive range of facilities: indoor pool, gym, and a conference centre. A little impersonal, but comfortable.	130	■	●	■
MONTECASSIANO: *Villa Quiete* €€ Località Vallecascia, 62010. 📞 & 📠 0733 59 95 59. ⊞ www.gestire2000.com A country villa hotel set in its own beautiful gardens. Some of the pretty rooms have antique furnishings. There are also two suites.	38	■		■
PESARO: *Villa Serena* €€€ Via San Nicola 6–3, 61100. 📞 0721 552 11. 📠 0721 559 27. @ info@villa-serena.it This 17th-century mansion, set in its own well-kept grounds, is a very comfortable, friendly hotel where no two rooms are alike.	9	■	●	■
PESARO: *Vittoria* €€€ Via A Vespucci 2, Piazzale Libertà 2, 61100. 📞 0721 343 43. 📠 0721 652 04. @ info@viphotels.it The Vittoria is a perfect combination of old-fashioned charm and modern convenience. It has a good range of facilities and is close to the sea.	27	■	●	■
PORTONOVO: *Fortino Napoleonico* €€€€ Via Poggio 166, 60020. 📞 071 80 14 50. 📠 071 80 14 54. @ info@hotelfortino.it Built to protect the coast from the marauding English during the Napoleonic wars, the fortress has been comfortably restored with tasteful decor and antiques, and has its own beach. Now even the English are welcome.	33	■		■
SAN BENEDETTO DEL TRONTO: *Sabbia d'Oro* €€ Viale Marconi 46, 63039. 📞 0735 849 11. 📠 0735 819 67. @ info@hotelsabbiadoro.net A modern beach hotel in this busy, fashionable resort. Rooms are well-designed and comfortable, and each has a mini-bar and safe.	63		●	

SAN LEO: *Castello* €€ 14
Piazza Dante Alighieri 12, 61018. 0541 91 62 14. **FAX** 0541 92 69 26. albergo-castello@libero.it
Housed in a restored 16th-century town building in the town centre, the white
tiles and light colours in the interior create an airy atmosphere. 🛏 TV 🖉

SAN MARINO: *Panoramic* €€ 27
Via Voltone 89, 47890. 0549 99 23 59. **FAX** 0549 99 03 56. cenci@omniway.sm
A family-run hotel in a tranquil part of this independent republic in the middle
of Italy. The Panoramic is particularly proud of its restaurant. 🛏 TV 🖉 P

SIROLO: *Monte Conero* €€ 60
Via Monteconero 26, 60020. 071 933 05 92. **FAX** 071 933 03 65. info@hotelmonteconero.it
Splendid sea views from this hotel in an 11th-century monastery. Rooms are bright
and have their own balconies. Half or full board during July and August. 🛏 TV 🖉 P

URBINO: *Locanda la Brombolona* € 12
Località Sant'Andrea in Primicilio 22, 61029. & **FAX** 0722 535 01.
A peaceful base from which to explore the area, this hotel has beautiful views. 🛏 P

URBINO: *Bonconte* €€ 23
Via delle Mura 28, 61029. 0722 24 63. **FAX** 0722 47 82. bonconte@viphotels.it
A recently refurbished old villa; furnishings include some antiques among
the more modern suites. The bright rooms are well-equipped. 🛏 TV ▤ 🖉

ROME

AVENTINE: *Sant'Anselmo* €€ 45
Piazza Sant'Anselmo 2, 00153. **Map** 6 E3. 06 574 51 74. **FAX** 06 578 36 04.
W www.aventinohotels.com
A pretty villa on the peaceful Aventine within walking distance of the
Colosseum. It has a secluded garden and and hand-painted furniture. 🛏 TV 🖉 P

AVENTINE: *Domus Aventina* €€€€€ 26
Via di Santa Prisca 11b, 00153. **Map** 6 E3. 06 574 61 35. **FAX** 06 57 30 00 44.
W www.domus-aventina.com
Situated in a 14th-century convent at the foot of the Aventine Hill, the hotel
offers large, simply decorated rooms, most of them with balconies. 🛏 TV ▤ 🖉

CAMPO DE' FIORI: *In Parione* €€€ 16
Via dei Chiavari 32, 00186. **Map** 2 F4. 06 68 80 25 60. **FAX** 06 683 40 94. W www.inparione.com
A small, centrally located hotel with great views over Rome's rooftops. 🛏 TV ▤ 🖉 &

CAMPO DE' FIORI: *Teatro di Pompeo* €€€ 13
Largo del Pallaro 8, 00186. **Map** 2 F4. 06 68 30 01 70. **FAX** 06 68 80 55 31.
W www.hotelteatrodipompeo.it
A small courteously run hotel whose basement breakfast room is in the ruins
of Pompey the Great's theatre. Bedrooms have beamed ceilings. 🛏 TV 🖉 P

FORUM: *Lancelot* €€€ 60
Via Capo d'Africa 47. **Map** 7 B1. 06 70 45 06 15. **FAX** 06 70 45 06 40. W www.lancelothotel.com
Family-run hotel near the Colosseum, with tastefully furnished rooms. 🛏 TV 🖉 P

FORUM: *Forum* €€€€€ 78
Via Tor de' Conti 25, 00184. **Map** 3 C5. 06 679 24 46. **FAX** 06 678 64 79.
W www.hotelforumrome.com
An old-fashioned hotel with wood-panelled public rooms and a sunny
roof-terrace restaurant with views over the archaeological zone. 🛏 TV ▤ 🖉 P

NAZIONALE: *Artemide* €€€€€ 84
Via Nazionale 22, 00184. **Map** 3 C4. 06 48 99 11. **FAX** 06 489 917 00.
W www.venere.it/roma/artemide
Stylish hotel harmonizing early 20th-century architecture and Art Nouveau motifs.
The adjoining Caffetteria Nazionale is a popular cofee shop/restaurant. 🛏 TV ▤ 🖉

NAZIONALE: *St Regis Grand* €€€€€ 161
Via V. E. Orlando 3, 00185. **Map** 5 C3. 06 470 91. **FAX** 06 474 73 07. W www.stregis.com/grandrome
A world of Cherubs and rich pastel rugs awaits you at this fine hotel. Good standard
rooms, some with antique furniture. Excellent restaurant. 🛏 TV ▤ 🖉 P &

PANTHEON: *Abruzzi* €€€€€ 25
Piazza della Rotonda 69, 00186. **Map** 2 F4. 06 679 20 21. **FAX** 06 69 78 80 76.
W www.hotelabruzzi.it
Terracotta-tiled floors in an ochre-coloured palazzo overlooking the Pantheon.
The Abruzzi provides clean, simple but pleasant rooms without breakfast.

For key to symbols see back flap

Price categories for a standard double room for one night, including tax and service charges but not including breakfast:
€ under €52
€€ €52–€100
€€€ €100–€155
€€€€ €155–€205
€€€€€ over €205.

RESTAURANT
A restaurant within the hotel sometimes reserved for residents.

SWIMMING POOL
Hotel swimming pools are usually quite small and are outdoors unless otherwise stated.

GARDEN OR TERRACE
A garden, courtyard or terrace belonging to the hotel, often providing tables for eating outside.

CREDIT CARDS
The major credit cards Visa, MasterCard (Access) and American Express are accepted in hotels with the credit card symbol.

	NUMBER OF ROOMS	RESTAURANT	SWIMMING POOL	GARDEN OR TERRACE
PANTHEON: *Santa Chiara* €€€€ Via di Santa Chiara 21, 00186. **Map** 2 F4. 06 687 29 79. FAX 06 687 31 44. W www.albergosantachiara.com A conveniently located hotel with cool, marble reception area and well-furnished bedrooms. Rooms facing the street can be noisy. 🛏 TV 📖 🌿	96			
PANTHEON: *Grand Hotel de la Minerve* €€€€€ Piazza della Minerva 69, 00186. **Map** 3 A4. 06 69 52 01. FAX 06 679 41 65. W www.hotel-invest.com The interior features semi-translucent Venetian glass and marble, and the bedrooms are spacious and bright. The roof terrace commands magnificent views. 🛏 TV 📖 🌿 ♒	134	▦		▦
PANTHEON: *Nazionale* €€€€€ Piazza di Montecitorio 131, 00186. **Map** 3 A3. 06 69 50 01. FAX 06 678 66 77. W www.nazionaleroma.it This hotel's comfortable and mostly large rooms are furnished with British and Italian antiques. The hotel is popular with business travellers and well-heeled tourists. 🛏 TV 🌿	80	▦		
PANTHEON: *Sole al Pantheon* €€€€€ Piazza della Rotonda 63, 00186. **Map** 2 F4. 06 678 04 41. FAX 06 69 94 06 89. W www.hotelsolealpantheon.com A historic hotel dating from 1467. Some of its beautiful modernized rooms have painted panelled ceilings and magical views of the Pantheon. 🛏 TV 📖 🌿	25			
PIAZZA NAVONA: *Navona* €€€ Via dei Sediari 8, 00186. **Map** 2 F4. 06 686 42 03. FAX 06 68 80 38 02. W www.hotelnavona.com Book well ahead for this superbly located hotel. Comfortable rooms. 🛏 📖 ♒	21			
PIAZZA NAVONA: *Due Torri* €€€€ Vicolo del Leonetto 23–25, 00186. **Map** 2 F3. 06 687 69 83. FAX 06 686 54 42. W www.hotelduetorriroma.com An amiable hotel tucked into an alleyway in the artisans' district. 🛏 TV 📖 🌿	26			▦
PIAZZA NAVONA: *Raphael* €€€€€ Largo Febo 2, 00186. **Map** 2 F3. 06 68 28 31. FAX 06 687 89 93. W www.raphaelhotel.com An ivy-clad luxury hotel whose reception is full of antique statues and modern sculpture. It has a restaurant and elegantly furnished bedrooms. 🛏 TV 📖 🌿	59	▦		
PIAZZA DI SPAGNA: *Jonella* €€ Via della Croce 41, 00187. **Map** 3 A2. 06 679 79 66. FAX 06 446 23 68. The relatively low prices and location on one of the main shopping streets of the Piazza di Spagna area make this simple B&B well worth considering. **Closed** Feb–Mar, Dec.	4			
PIAZZA DI SPAGNA: *Condotti* €€€ Via Mario de' Fiori 37, 00187. **Map** 3 A2. 06 679 46 61. FAX 06 679 04 57. W www.hotelcondotti.com A friendly hotel with well-decorated rooms in the designer shopping district. 🛏 TV 📖 🌿	16			▦
PIAZZA DI SPAGNA: *Gregoriana* €€€ Via Gregoriana 18, 00187. **Map** 3 B2. 06 679 42 69. FAX 06 678 42 58. This stylish hotel has an interesting variety of decoration, including some unusual leopard-spotted wallpaper. Bedrooms, however, are flowery and fresh. 🛏 TV 📖	20			
PIAZZA DI SPAGNA: *Margutta* €€€ Via Laurina 34, 00187. **Map** 3 A1. 06 322 36 74. FAX 06 320 03 95. Pretty rooms on a quiet street. Book in advance if you want one of the three attic rooms that share a roof terrace. Public rooms are airy and bright. 🛏 🌿	24			
PIAZZA DI SPAGNA: *Scalinata di Spagna* €€€€ Piazza Trinità dei Monti 17, 00187. **Map** 3 B2. 06 679 30 06. FAX 06 69 94 05 98. W www.hotelscalinata.com A convivial hotel in a small 18th-century villa at the top of the Spanish Steps. The rooms that open on to the terrace have exquisite views. 🛏 TV 📖 🌿 P	16			▦

PIAZZA DI SPAGNA: *Hassler* €€€€€ | 102
Piazza Trinità dei Monti 6, 00187. **Map** 3 B2. 06 69 93 40. FAX 06 678 99 91.
www.hotelhasslerroma.com
Venetian glass chandeliers and wood-panelled bathrooms retain the air of a
more extravagant era. Magnificent views from the roof-terrace.

TERMINI: *Katty* € | 17
Via Palestro 35, 00185. **Map** 4 E1. & FAX 06 444 12 16.
The Katty has clean, basic rooms. It is extremely popular, so book early.

TERMINI: *Cervia* €€ | 28
Via Palestro 55, 00185. **Map** 4 F2. 06 49 10 57. FAX 06 49 10 56. www.hotelcervia.com
Some of the rooms have been refurbished with sponge-painted walls and private
bathrooms; the rest are a bit more basic. The public areas are immaculate.

TERMINI: *Hotel Giuliana* €€ | 11
Via Agostini Depretis 70, 00185. **Map** 4 F4. 06 488 07 95. www.hotelgiuliana.com
A husband-and-wife team runs this small, welcoming hotel close to Santa Maria
Maggiore. Rooms are simple but fairly spacious, with en-suite bathrooms.

TERMINI: *Restivo* €€ | 6
Via Palestro 55, 00185. **Map** 4 F2. 06 446 21 72. FAX 06 445 26 29.
This small hotel is beautifully maintained. Guests return again and again.

TERMINI: *Canada* €€€ | 70
Via Vicenza 58, 00185. **Map** 4 F2. 06 445 77 70. FAX 06 445 07 49. www.hotelcanadaroma.com
A good, mid-range hotel behind Termini station, which has a pleasant lounge-bar
with attractive cane seats and squashy sofas. Courteous service.

TERMINI: *Diana* €€€ | 171
Via Principe Amedeo 4. **Map** 4 E3. 06 482 75 41. FAX 06 48 69 98. www.hoteldianaroma.com
This pleasant hotel offers tastefully furnished rooms.

TRASTEVERE: *San Francesco* €€€ | 24
Via Jacopa de' Settesoli 7, 00153. **Map** 6 2D. 06 58 30 00 51. FAX 06 58 33 34 13.
www.hotelsanfrancesco.net
This hotel stands near the site where San Francis of Assisi lodged on his trip to Rome.
Rooms are traditionally furnished and there are lovely rooftop views.

VATICAN: *Alimandi* €€€ | 35
Via Tunisi 8, 00192. **Map** 3 D1. 06 39 72 63 00. FAX 06 39 72 39 43. www.alimandi.org
A simple pensione near the entrance to the Vatican museums.

VATICAN: *Columbus* €€€€ | 92
Via della Conciliazione 33, 00193. **Map** 1 C3. 06 686 54 35. FAX 06 686 48 74.
www.hotelcolumbus.net
Occupying a former monastery near St Peter's Square, the hotel's function room
is in the old refectory and has retained its original frescoes.

VATICAN: *Visconti Palace* €€€€ | 247
Via Federico Cesi 37, 00193. **Map** 2 E2. 06 36 84. FAX 06 32 00 551. www.viscontipalace.com
This modern and efficient hotel is in an ideal location and provides large common
spaces and well-decorated rooms. There is a piano bar nightly.

VATICAN: *Hotel dei Mellini* €€€€€ | 80
Via Muzio Clementi 81. **Map** 2 F2. 06 32 47 71. FAX 06 32 47 78 01. www.hotelmellini.com
The cool style of this chic hotel attracts international travellers.
Contemporary works of art adorn the interior public spaces.

VIA VENETO: *La Residenza* €€€€ | 26
Via Emilia 22–24, 00187. **Map** 3 C1. 06 488 07 89. FAX 06 48 57 21.
www.thegianettihotelsgroup.com
An elegant, courteously run hotel in a quiet villa, with stylish public rooms,
comfortable bedrooms and a delightful canopied terrace.

VIA VENETO: *Alexandra* €€€€€ | 45
Via Veneto 18, 00187. **Map** 3 C1. 06 488 19 43. FAX 06 487 18 04. alexandra@venere.it
A good value hotel on this expensive street, the Alexandra has a pleasant
breakfast room and each bedroom has been decorated differently.

VIA VENETO: *Ambasciatori Palace* €€€€€ | 148
Via Vittorio Veneto 62, 00187. **Map** 3 C1. 06 474 93. FAX 06 474 36 01.
www.hotelambasciatoripalace.com
Set in a historical building, the plush furnishings add to the air of luxury.

<table>
<tr><td colspan="2">

Price categories for a standard double room for one night, including tax and service charges but not including breakfast:
€ under €52
€€ €52–€100
€€€ €100–€155
€€€€ €155–€205
€€€€€ over €205.

</td><td>

RESTAURANT
A restaurant within the hotel sometimes reserved for residents.
SWIMMING POOL
Hotel swimming pools are usually quite small and are outdoors unless otherwise stated.
GARDEN OR TERRACE
A garden, courtyard or terrace belonging to the hotel, often providing tables for eating outside.
CREDIT CARDS
The major credit cards Visa, MasterCard (Access) and American Express are accepted in hotels with the credit card symbol.

</td></tr>
</table>

	NUMBER OF ROOMS	RESTAURANT	SWIMMING POOL	GARDEN OR TERRACE
VIA VENETO: *Excelsior* €€€€€ Via Veneto 125, 00187. **Map** 3 C1. (06 47 081. FAX 06 482 62 05. w www.westin.com/excelsiorrome This extravagant hotel has sumptuous public rooms with marble floors and brocade furnishings. Bedrooms are elegant and spacious. 🛗 TV 🍽 🅿	327	▦		
VILLA BORGHESE: *Villa Borghese* €€€€ Via Pinciana 31, 00198. (06 854 96 48. FAX 06 841 41 00. w www.hotelvillaborghese.it This pleasant hotel has the atmosphere of a private home rather than a hotel. Rooms are small but comfortable and are tastefully decorated. 🛗 TV 🅿	32			▦
VILLA BORGHESE: *Lord Byron* €€€€€ Via Notaris 5, 00197. (06 322 04 04. FAX 06 322 04 05. w www.lordbyronhotel.com A small, refined hotel housed in a former stately home in the Parioli district, the Lord Byron has lavishly decorated public rooms. 🛗 TV 🍽	34	▦		▦

LAZIO				
ANAGNI: *Villa La Floridiana* €€€ Via Casilina, km 63,700, 03012. (0775 76 99 60. FAX 0775 77 45 27. w www.villalafloridiana.it A beautiful medieval village is the setting for this charming villa with a traditional faded pink façade, green shutters and large, comfortable rooms. 🛗 TV 🍽 🅿	9	▦		▦
BAGNI DI TIVOLI: *Grand Hotel Duca d'Este* €€€€ Via Tiburtina Valeria 330, 00011. (0774 38 83. FAX 0774 38 81 01. w www.ducadeste.com A modern well-equipped hotel near Tivoli and Villa Adriana and within easy reach of Rome by road or rail. Suites have satellite TV and jacuzzis. 🛗 TV 🍽 🅿	184	▦	●	▦
FORMIA: *Castello Miramare* €€€€ Via Balze di Pagnano, 04023. (0771 70 01 38. FAX 0771 70 01 39. w www.hotelcastellomiramare.it The castle was built in 1910 on a hill in the centre of Formia with fine views over the sea. Spacious bedrooms are decorated in Spanish style. 🛗 TV 🍽 🅿	10	▦		▦
GROTTAFERRATA: *Villa Fiorio* €€€€€ Viale Dusmet 25, 00046. (06 945 48 007. FAX 06 945 48 009. w www.villafiorio.it Built as a summer residence at the turn of the century, this pretty villa, which retains some original frescoes, has large, cool and quiet rooms. 🛗 TV 🍽 🅿	24	▦	●	▦
ISOLA DI PONZA: *Grand Hotel Santa Domitilla* €€€€€ Via Panoramica, 04027. (0771 80 99 51. FAX 0771 809 99 55. w www.santadomitilla.com A beautiful setting for this modern but stylish four-star hotel with a dense garden. Wicker furniture and rocking chairs create a friendly atmosphere. 🛗 TV 🍽 🅿	50	▦	●	▦
LADISPOLI: *La Posta Vecchia* €€€€€ Località Palo Laziale, 00055. (06 994 95 01. FAX 06 994 95 07. w www.lapostavecchia.com A magnificent 17th-century villa on the sea, this is one of Italy's most luxurious hotels. All rooms are exquisitely and individually decorated with antiques. 🛗 TV 🍽 🅿	19	▦	●	▦
PALESTRINA: *Stella* € Piazzale della Liberazione 3, 00036. (06 953 81 72. FAX 06 957 33 60. w www.hotelstella.it A friendly, peaceful hotel in the historic centre of Palestrina close to the town's sights and with an excellent restaurant. 🛗 TV 🍽 🅿	30	▦		
SABAUDIA: *Oasi di Kufra* €€€€ Via Lungomare Km 29,800, 04016. (0773 51 91. FAX 0773 51 988. w www.oasidikufra.it Luminous hotel amid sandy dunes. With its private beach and fitness centre, it offers balconies in most rooms and suites overlooking the sea. 🛗 TV 🍽 🅿	120	▦		▦
SAN FELICE CIRCEO: *Punta Rossa* €€€€€ Via delle Batterie 37, 04017. (0773 54 80 85. FAX 0773 54 80 75. w www.puntarossa.it A charming hotel set in a garden that leads down to the sea. Rooms are in various buildings, all have terraces and sea views. 🛗 TV 🍽 🅿	33	▦	●	▦

SUBIACO: *Livata* €€ 84
Via dei Boschi 28, Località Monte Livata, 00028. (0774 82 60 31. FAX 0774 82 60 33.
A good choice if you're visiting the monastery of San Benedetto, the Livata
is a friendly country hotel with tennis courts and attractive gardens. 🛏 🍴 P

TARQUINIA LIDO: *La Torraccia* €€ 18
Viale Mediterraneo 45, 01010. (0766 86 43 75. FAX 0766 86 42 96. W www.torraccia.it
A modern, comfortable hotel set in pinewoods 200 m (656 ft) from the
sea. All rooms have a terrace and there is a private beach. 🛏 TV 🍴 P

VITERBO: *Balletti Palace* €€ 105
Via Molini 8, 01100. (0761 34 47 77. FAX 0761 34 50 60. W www.balletti.com
A modern hotel set in Viterbo's historic centre with elegant bedrooms and
suites. There is no restaurant but the Grenier Café serves light meals. 🛏 TV 🍴 P

VITERBO: *Balletti Park* €€ 136
Via Umbria 2, San Martino al Cimino 01030. (0761 37 71. FAX 0761 37 94 96. W www.balletti.com
A modern hotel set in its own extensive gardens. There are sports facilities
and a health centre as well as some independent apartments. 🛏 TV 🍴 P

NAPLES AND CAMPANIA

AMALFI: *Marina Riviera* €€€€ 22
Via P Comite 19, 84011. (089 87 11 04. FAX 089 87 10 24. W www.marinariviera.it
This Mediterranean-style seaside hotel offers simple, tasteful rooms, and an
attractive patio overlooking the beach for leisurely breakfasts. 🛏 TV 🍴 P

AMALFI: *Luna Convento* €€€€ 44
Via Comite 33, 84011. (089 87 10 02. FAX 089 87 13 33. W www.lunahotel.it
This tastefully furnished 13th-century monastery overlooking the sea makes a
luxurious, peaceful base from which to explore the countryside. 🛏 TV 🍴 P

AMALFI: *Santa Caterina* €€€€€ 66
Via SS Amalfitana 9, 84011. (089 87 10 12. FAX 089 87 13 51. W www.hotelsantacaterina.it
This is a luxurious property set amid lemon groves. Two elevators can whisk
you from the spectacular suites to the private beach in seconds. Enjoy the
sea view from the hotel terraces or the high tech gym. 🛏 TV 🍴 P

BAIA DOMIZIA: *Hotel della Baia* €€€€ 50
Via dell'Erica, 81030. (0823 72 13 44. FAX 0823 72 15 56. W www.hoteldellabaia.it
A charming, friendly hotel run by three sisters with its own private beach.
The pretty bedrooms are comfortable and all have sea views. 🛏 TV 🍴 P

BENEVENTO: *Grand Hotel Italiano* €€ 71
Viale Principe di Napoli 137, 82100. (0824 241 11. FAX 0824 217 58. W www.hotel-italiano.it
The Italiano family are justly proud of the hotel's reputation for courtesy
and good service. Public areas are spacious and elegant. 🛏 TV 🍴 P

CAPRI: *Villa Sarah* €€€€ 20
Via Tiberio 3a, 80073. (081 837 78 17. FAX 081 837 72 15. W www.villasarah.it
A peaceful family-run villa hotel set among the island's vineyards. Rooms
are clean and pretty and home produce is served for breakfast. 🛏 TV 🍴

CAPRI: *Punta Tragara* €€€€€ 43
Via Tragara 57, 80073. (081 837 08 44. FAX 081 837 77 90. W www.hoteltragara.com
A sumptuous hotel built into a cliff over the sea, designed by Le Corbusier,
with all the comforts of a luxury residence. No children under 12. 🛏 TV 🍴

CASERTA: *Europa* €€€ 60
Via Roma 19, 81100. (0823 32 54 00. FAX 0823 32 54 00. W www.hoteleuropacaserta.it
A smart modern hotel conveniently placed in central Caserta. The Europa also has
several mini-apartments with cooking facilities for longer stays. 🛏 TV 🍴 P

ISCHIA: *La Villarosa* €€ 37
Via Giacinto Gigante 5, Porto d'Ischia 80070. (081 99 13 16. FAX 081 99 24 25.
W www.lavillarosa.it
An enchanting hotel set in a beautiful tropical garden. Many of the charming
rooms have balconies filled with bougainvilleas. Sauna and massage are on offer.
🛏 TV 🍴 P Closed Nov–Mar.

ISCHIA: *Pensione Il Monastero* €€€ 22
Castello Aragonese 3, Ischia Ponte 80070. (081 99 24 35. FAX 081 99 24 35.
W www.castelloaragonese.it
A charming, simple pensione set in a converted monastery. 🛏 🍴

For key to symbols see back flap

<table>
<tr><td colspan="2">

Price categories for a standard double room for one night, including tax and service charges but not including breakfast:

€ under €52
€€ €52–€100
€€€ €100–€155
€€€€ €155–€205
€€€€€ over €205.

</td><td colspan="2">

RESTAURANT
A restaurant within the hotel sometimes reserved for residents.
SWIMMING POOL
Hotel swimming pools are usually quite small and are outdoors unless otherwise stated.
GARDEN OR TERRACE
A garden, courtyard or terrace belonging to the hotel, often providing tables for eating outside.
CREDIT CARDS
The major credit cards Visa, MasterCard (Access) and American Express are accepted in hotels with the credit card symbol.

</td></tr>
</table>

		NUMBER OF ROOMS	RESTAURANT	SWIMMING POOL	GARDEN OR TERRACE
NAPLES: *Rex* €€€ Via Palepoli 12, 80132. **[** 081 764 93 89. **FAX** 081 764 92 27. **W** www.hotel-rex.it A friendly, family hotel on the seafront of Naples and well placed for theatres. Public rooms are elegantly furnished with wicker chairs. ⊟ TV ▤ ☑ **P**		37			
NAPLES: *Britannique* €€€€ Corso Vittorio Emanuele 133, 80121. **[** 081 761 41 45. **FAX** 081 66 97 60. **W** www.hotelbritannique.it A smart, modern hotel above the centre of Naples. Bedrooms are attractively decorated and there are spectacular views from the roof terrace. ⊟ TV ▤ ☑ **P**		86	▦		▦
NAPLES: *San Francesco* €€€€ Corso Vittorio Emanuele 328, 80135. **[** 081 423 91 11. **FAX** 081 251 24 85. **W** www.hotelsanfrancesco.it Housed in a beautifully converted 15th-century convent below the Castel del Elmo. Luxurious rooms, a roof terrace and splendid views over the bay. ⊟ TV ▤ & ☑ **P**		50	▦	●	▦
NAPLES: *Grande Albergo Vesuvio* €€€€€ Via Partenope 45, 80121. **[** 081 764 00 44. **FAX** 081 764 44 83. **W** www.vesuvio.it Founded in 1882, the Grande overlooks the marina in central Naples. It has marble bathrooms and antiques, and a "baby" room with toys. ⊟ TV ▤ & ☑ **P**		163	▦		
PAESTUM: *Le Palme* €€ Via Poseidonia 123, 84063. **[** 0828 85 10 25. **FAX** 0828 85 15 07. **W** www.lepalme.it A pleasant, peaceful seaside hotel with tennis courts and its own beach. Rooms are comfortable and the hotel is set in attractive grounds. ⊟ TV ▤ ☑ **P**		84	▦	●	▦
POSITANO: *L'Ancora* €€€€ Via Colombo 36, 84017. **[** 089 87 53 18. **FAX** 089 81 17 84. **W** www.htlancora.it Excellent value in expensive Positano from this modern, central hotel with sea views. The good-sized bedrooms are comfortable. ⊟ TV ▤ ☑ **P** Closed *Jan–Feb.*		25			▦
POSITANO: *Palazzo Murat* €€€€€ Via dei Mulini 23, 84017. **[** 089 87 51 77. **FAX** 089 81 14 19. **W** www.palazzomurat.it A pretty 18th-century palazzo in central Positano, near the cathedral. Rooms have traditional wooden furniture, and some have balconies. ⊟ TV ▤ ☑		30	▦		▦
RAVELLO: *Graal* €€€ Via della Repubblica 8, 84010. **[** 089 85 72 22. **FAX** 089 85 75 51. **W** www.hotelgraal.it The hotel has a wonderful swimming pool with attractive views over Ravello. The restaurant serves good local specialities. ⊟ TV ▤ ☑ **P**		35	▦	●	▦
RAVELLO: *Palumbo* €€€€€ Via San Giovanni del Toro 16, 84010. **[** 089 85 72 44. **FAX** 089 85 81 33. **W** www.hotelpalumbo.it This 12th-century palazzo has been run as a hotel by the same family for more than 100 years. Furnishings are elegant and there are antiques in some bedrooms. Rooms in the modern annexe are cheaper. Use of a swimming pool. ⊟ TV ▤ ☑ **P**		18	▦		▦
SALERNO: *Olimpico* €€€ Litoranea di Pontecagno, Salerno. **[** 089 20 30 04. **FAX** 089 20 34 58. **W** www.hotelolimpico.it Situated just outside Salerno, this is a good-value family hotel with a private beach. Modern rooms, most with balconies and sea views. ⊟ TV ▤ ☑ **P**		38	▦		▦
SAPRI: *Mediterraneo* €€ Via Verdi, 84073. **[** 0973 39 17 74. **FAX** 0973 39 20 33 (summer); 0973 60 48 04 (winter). **W** www.hotelmed.it Excellent value at this comfortable, no frills hotel built right next to the rocky beach with garden and terrace overlooking the sea. All rooms have balconies. ⊟ TV ▤ ☑ **P**		20	▦		▦
SAPRI: *Tirreno* €€ Lungomare Italia 73, 84073. **[** 0973 39 10 06. **FAX** 0973 39 11 57. **W** www.hoteltirrenosapri.it A good-value pensione facing the sea. Inside it is airy and light and some bedrooms have their own balconies. The restaurant serves local specialities. ⊟ ▤ TV ☑ **P**		44	▦		▦

SORRENTO: *Bellevue Syrene* €€€€€ | 76
Piazza della Vittoria 5, 80067. **℡** *081 878 10 24.* **FAX** *081 878 39 63.* **W** *www.bellevue.it*
A typical grand beach hotel, now slightly faded. It is perched on the cliffs with a lift
to take guests down to the private beach. Sumptuous bedrooms. **⊟ TV 目 ⊘ P**

SORRENTO: *Grand Hotel Cocumella* €€€€€ | 53
Via Cocumella 7, 80065. **℡** *081 878 29 33.* **FAX** *081 878 37 12.* **W** *www.cocumella.com*
Opulent elegance from another era characterizes this peaceful hotel on the Amalfi
coast set in fragrant and peaceful gardens. The sea is nearby and the hotel sailing boat
will take guests to Capri for the day. Gym and sauna are available. **⊟ TV 目 ⊘ P**

ABRUZZO, MOLISE AND PUGLIA

ALBEROBELLO: *Colle del Sole* €€ | 37
Via Indipendenza 63, 70011. **℡** *080 432 18 14.* **FAX** *080 432 13 70.* **W** *www.trulliland.it*
A comfortable, modern hotel with a balcony for every bedroom. Art and
photo exhibitions are sometimes arranged in the restaurant. **⊟ TV 目 ⊘ P**

ALBEROBELLO: *Dei Trulli* €€€€ | 28
Via Cadore 32, 70011. **℡** *080 432 35 55.* **FAX** *080 432 35 60.* **W** *www.hoteldeitrulli.it*
The hotel is set in a mini-village of *trulli (see p495).* Furnishings are simple,
even stark, but the grounds are pleasant. Half board in summer. **⊟ TV 目 ⊘ P**

BARI: *Boston* €€€ | 70
Via Piccinni 155, 70122. **℡** *080 521 66 33.* **FAX** *080 524 68 02.* **W** *www.bostonbari.it*
A modern hotel near the historic centre of Bari. Furnishings are stylish and functional
and there is much dark wood panelling. Half board optional. **⊟ TV 目 ⊘ P**

BARI: *Palace Hotel* €€€€€ | 200
Via Lombardi 13, 70122. **℡** *080 521 65 51.* **FAX** *080 521 14 99.* **W** *www.palacehotelbari.it*
This hotel provides excellent service, a panoramic roof terrace and a
delicious buffet breakfast with something for everyone. **⊟ TV 目 ⊘ P**

GARGANO PENINSULA: *Seggio* €€€ | 30
Via Veste 7, Vieste 71019. **℡** *0884 70 81 23.* **FAX** *0884 70 87 27.* **W** *www.vieste.net/seggio*
Perched on a small cliff over its own private bay, this restored 17th-century
building was the original town hall. Half board obligatory in August.
⊟ TV 目 ⊘ P Closed *Nov–Mar.*

ISOLE TREMITI: *Kyrie* €€€€ | 70
San Domino, 71040. **℡** *0882 46 32 41.* **FAX** *0882 46 34 15.* **@** *koltreno@hotmail.com*
The largest and best-equipped of the Tremiti hotels. It is located in the pinewoods
next to the sea. Apartments available. **⊟ TV 目 ⊘ Closed** *Sep–Mar.*

L'AQUILA: *Hotel San Michele* €€ | 32
Via dei Giardini 6, 67100. **℡** *0862 42 02 60.* **FAX** *0862 270 60.* **W** *www.stmichelehotel.it*
In the heart of the city, this is a modern, attractive and friendly hotel. **⊟ TV 目 ⊘ P**

L'AQUILA: *Grand Hotel e del Parco* €€€ | 36
Corso Federico II 74, 67100. **℡** *0862 41 32 40.* **FAX** *0862 659 38.* **W** *www.grandhotel.it*
A comfortable, modern hotel in the centre of L'Aquila within easy reach
of the ski-slopes and hiking trails of the Gran Sasso. The hotel also has a
health centre, complete with saunas and Turkish baths. **⊟ TV 目 ⊘ P**

LECCE: *B&B Centro Storico* €€ | 8
Via A Vignes 12, 73100. **℡** *0832 24 28 28.* **FAX** *0832 24 27 27.* **W** *www.bedandbreakfast.lecce.it*
This friendly B&B in a 16th-century palazzo has beautifully decorated rooms
and a panoramic roof terrace looking over Lecce's historic centre. **TV 目 ⊘ P**

LECCE: *Hotel President* €€€ | 150
Via Salandra No 6. **℡** *0832 45 61 11.* **FAX** *0832 45 66 32.* **W** *www.hotelpresidentlecce.it*
Large and modern hotel with a good reputation and good service.
The excellent restaurant has a well-stocked wine cellar. **⊟ TV 目 ⊘ P**

MARINA DI LESINA: *Maddalena Hotel* €€€ | 74
Via Saturno 82, 71010. **℡** *0882 99 50 76.* **FAX** *0882 99 54 34.* **@** *koltreno@hotmail.com*
A modern beach hotel with a range of sports and leisure facilities, including a private
beach. The restaurant serves a variety of local fish dishes. **⊟ TV 目 ⊘ P Closed** *Dec–Feb.*

MONOPOLI: *Il Melograno* €€€€ | 37
Contrada Torricella 345, 70043. **℡** *080 690 90 30.* **FAX** *080 74 79 08.* **W** *www.melograno.com*
An oasis of tranquillity, this 16th-century building is furnished with antiques. There
are tennis courts and a private beach. The hotel also runs cookery classes and
owns a sailing boat for excursions. Full board obligatory in August. **⊟ TV 目 ⊘ P**

For key to symbols see back flap

Price categories for a standard double room for one night, including tax and service charges but not including breakfast: € under €52 €€ €52–€100 €€€ €100–€155 €€€€ €155–€205 €€€€€ over €205.	**RESTAURANT** A restaurant within the hotel sometimes reserved for residents. **SWIMMING POOL** Hotel swimming pools are usually quite small and are outdoors unless otherwise stated. **GARDEN OR TERRACE** A garden, courtyard or terrace belonging to the hotel, often providing tables for eating outside. **CREDIT CARDS** The major credit cards Visa, MasterCard (Access) and American Express are accepted in hotels with the credit card symbol.	**NUMBER OF ROOMS** / **RESTAURANT** / **SWIMMING POOL** / **GARDEN OR TERRACE**	

Hotel	Number of Rooms	Restaurant	Swimming Pool	Garden or Terrace
RUVO DI PUGLIA: *Talos* €€ Via Rodolfo Morandi 12, 70037. **☎** 080 361 16 45. **FAX** 080 360 26 40. **W** www.hoteltalos.it A simple, modern hotel that is good value for travellers on a budget. It is well placed for exploring the surrounding countryside. 🛏 TV 🍴 🇮 P	20	▪		▪
SCANNO: *Mille Pini* €€ Via Pescara 2, 67038. **☎** 0864 74 72 64; 0864 743 87. **FAX** 0864 74 98 18. **W** www.millepiniscanno.it A friendly, good-value chalet hotel at the foot of Monte Rotondo chairlift. Facilities are simple and rustic but comfortable and there is a restaurant. 🛏 TV 🇮 P	25	▪		
SULMONA: *Italia* €€ Piazza Salvatore Tommasi 3, 67039. **☎** & **FAX** 0864 523 08. A charming ivy-covered town house in a quiet square. Furnishings vary from modern utility to antique, giving a lived-in feeling to this friendly hotel. 🛏 P	25			
TARANTO: *Plaza* €€ Via d'Aquino 46, 74100. **☎** 099 459 07 75. **FAX** 099 459 06 75. **W** www.hotelplazataranto.com A big, city hotel that is very well placed in the newer part of Taranto near the major sights. Both business and holiday guests are catered for. Good value. 🛏 TV 🍴 🇮 P	105	▪		

BASILICATA AND CALABRIA

Hotel	Number of Rooms	Restaurant	Swimming Pool	Garden or Terrace
COSENZA: *Royal* €€ Via Molinella 24e, 87100. **☎** 0984 41 21 65. **FAX** 0984 41 17 77. **W** www.hotelroyalsas.com One of the best modern hotels in Cosenza, though the decor is somewhat dated. Conveniently located in the centre of town, not far from the station. 🛏 TV 🍴 🇮 P	44	▪		▪
MATERA: *De Nicola* €€ Via Nazionale 158, 75100. **☎** 0835 38 51 11. **FAX** 0835 38 51 13. **W** www.hoteldenicola.it A large modern hotel in central Matera close to the station and easily accessible from the motorway. Bedrooms are functional. 🛏 TV 🍴 *(some)* 🇮 P	105	▪		▪
MARATEA: *Romantik Hotel, Villa Cheta Elite* €€€€ Via Timpone 46, Acquafredda 85041. **☎** 0973 87 81 34. **FAX** 0973 87 81 35. **W** www.villacheta.it An elegant, Liberty-style villa with stunning views over a picturesque bay. The comfortable rooms are attractively furnished in traditional southern Italian style and staff and service are friendly and polite. 🛏 🍴 🇮 P **Closed** *Dec–mid-Mar.*	23	▪		▪
METAPONTO LIDO: *Turismo* €€ Viale delle Ninfe 5, 75010. **☎** 0835 74 19 18. **FAX** 0835 74 19 17. **W** www.hoteldenicola.it/turismo A functional, if unexceptional, seaside hotel with its own beach and bar. The restaurant has outside tables for summer dining. 🛏 🍴 🇮 **Closed** *Oct–May.*	62	▪		▪
PARGHELIA: *Baia Paraelios* €€€€€ Località Fornace, 83861 (nr Tropea). **☎** 0963 60 03 00. **FAX** 0963 60 00 74. **W** www.clubvacanze.com A village of 72 bungalows, each with terrace and sitting room, with views over the sea. The restaurant is on a beach terrace. 🛏 🍴 🇮 P **Closed** *mid-Sep–May.*	87	▪	●	▪
REGGIO DI CALABRIA: *Altafiumura* €€€€€ Santa Trada di Cannitello, 89010 Villa San Giovanni. **☎** 0965 75 98 04. **FAX** 0965 75 95 66. **W** www.altafiumurahotel.it This hotel is housed in a beautifully restored, 18th-century Bourbon castle. It boasts a spectacular cliff-top setting, lush gardens, sumptuous suites and a spa. 🛏 TV 🍴 ♿ 🇮 P	128	▪	●	▪
ROSSANO SCALO: *Giardino d'Iti* €€ C. da Amica, 87068. **☎** & **FAX** 0983 645 08. **W** www.giardinoiti.it A beautiful, 17th-century farmhouse offering cool and quiet accommodation amongst olive groves and orange trees. Excellent food. Cookery courses available. 🛏 ♿ 🇮 P	14	▪		▪
STILO: *San Giorgio* €€ Via R Citarelli 1, 89049. **☎** & **FAX** 0964 77 50 47. **W** www.hotelsangiorgiostilo.it This comfortable hotel is located in a restored 17th-century palazzo and furnished with some 18th-century antiques. 🛏 TV 🍴 🇮 P **Closed** *Nov–Mar.*	15	▪	●	▪

TROPEA: *Umberto* €€ — 27
c/ da Vipisco snc, 89865, S Domenica di Ricadi. & FAX 0963 66 90 68. www.hotel-umberto.it
Friendly, family-run hotel set in lush, extensive gardens, with stunning views over the Aeolian Islands and Stromboli and a large sun terrace.

VENOSA: *Il Guiscardo* €€ — 36
Via Accademia dei Rinascenti 106, 85029. 0972 32 362. FAX 0972 32 916.
@ hotelguiscardo@mail.trinus.it
Modern hotel with wonderful views from the terrace over the red roofs of Venosa's historic centre. Bedrooms are elegant and public rooms spacious.

SICILY

ACIREALE: *Excelsior Palace* €€€ — 229
Via delle Terme 103, 95024. 095 604 444. FAX 095 605 441. www.shr.it
Well placed for visiting the sights of east Sicily and close to the Santa Venera Spa, this hotel set in a 19th-century building offers all modern comforts.

AGRIGENTO: *Colleverde Park Hotel* €€€€ — 48
Via dei Templi, 92100. 0922 295 55. FAX 0922 290 12. @ mail@colleverde-hotel.it
A peaceful modern hotel in the Valley of the Temples, with stunning views. The facilities include safes in the bedrooms and a gym.

AGRIGENTO: *Grand Hotel dei Templi* €€€€ — 146
Viale L Sciascia, Villaggio Mose 92100. 0922 61 01 75. FAX 0922 60 66 85.
www.grandhoteldeitempli.com
Set in an extensive park with a swimming pool, this large, well-equipped hotel lies just outside Agrigento. Rooms are comfortably furnished. Sun terrace.

AGRIGENTO: *Villa Athena* €€€€€ — 40
Via Panoramica dei Templi 53, 92100. 0922 59 62 88. FAX 0922 40 21 80.
www.hotelvillaathena.com
Set in an 18th-century villa just outside Agrigento. The decor is modern but the gardens are exquisite, with views of the Temple of Concord.

CATANIA: *Nettuno* €€€€ — 101
Viale Ruggero di Lauria 121, 95126. 095 712 52 52. FAX 095 49 80 66. www.hotel-nettuno.it
A well-equipped, modern hotel overlooking the sea. Outdoor pool.

CEFALÙ: *Riva del Sole* €€€ — 28
Viale Lungomare Cefalù 25, 90015. 0921 42 12 30. FAX 0921 42 19 84. www.rivadelsole.com
A hotel on the seafront with good views. Rooms are rather basic, but there is a sun terrace and a shadier internal courtyard with tables. **Closed** Nov.

ISOLE EGADI: *Egadi Favignana* €€€ — 10
Via Colombo 17, Favignana 91023. 0923 92 12 32. FAX 0923 92 16 36.
www.egadi.com/albergoegadi
A friendly pensione attached to one of the best restaurants on the island. Favignana is famous for its tuna, which comes from the local fisheries.

ISOLE EOLIE: *Pensione Villa Diana* €€ — 12
Via Diana Tufo, Lipari 98055. & FAX 090 981 14 03. www.villadiana.com
A comfortable family hotel with antiques in some rooms, and spacious terraces. **Closed** Nov–Mar.

ISOLE EOLIE: *La Sciara Residence* €€€ — 60
Via Soldato Cincotta, Isola Stromboli 98050. 090 98 61 21. FAX 090 98 62 84. www.lasciara.it
A splendid garden is the setting for this spacious and comfortable hotel. Mini-apartments are also available. Half board obligatory in August. **Closed** Oct–Apr.

ISOLE EOLIE: *Raya* €€€€ — 36
Via San Pietro, Isola Panarea 98050. 090 98 30 13. FAX 090 98 31 03. www.hotelraya.it
This modern, fashionable hotel consists of pink and white houses on terraces descending to the sea. The restaurant and bar overlook the port. **Closed** Nov–Feb.

ERICE: *Moderno* €€€ — 40
Via Vittorio Emanuele 67, 91016. 0923 86 93 00. FAX 0923 86 91 39. www.pippocatalano.it
A family-run hotel that has some attractively old-fashioned bedrooms as well as some more modern ones. Excellent views from the terrace.

ERICE: *Elimo* €€€€ — 21
Via Vittorio Emanuele 75, 91016. 0923 86 93 77. FAX 0923 86 92 52. www.charmerelax.com
An 18th-century villa with traditional Sicilian wall, ceiling and floor tiles. Centrally located, the hotel has spectacular views as far as the Egadi Islands.

For key to symbols see back flap

Price categories for a standard double room for one night, including tax and service charges but not including breakfast:
€ under €52
€€ €52–€100
€€€ €100–€155
€€€€ €155–€205
€€€€€ over €205.

RESTAURANT
A restaurant within the hotel sometimes reserved for residents.

SWIMMING POOL
Hotel swimming pools are usually quite small and are outdoors unless otherwise stated.

GARDEN OR TERRACE
A garden, courtyard or terrace belonging to the hotel, often providing tables for eating outside.

CREDIT CARDS
The major credit cards Visa, MasterCard (Access) and American Express are accepted in hotels with the credit card symbol.

	NUMBER OF ROOMS	RESTAURANT	SWIMMING POOL	GARDEN OR TERRACE
GIARDINI-NAXOS: *Arathena Rocks* €€€ Via Calcide Eubea 55, 98035. ☎ 0942 513 49. FAX 0942 516 90. W www.hotelarathena.com A friendly hotel near the beach and slightly out of this busy resort. Rooms are bright and airy with sea or garden views. Closed *Oct–Easter.*	50	■	●	■
MARSALA: *President* €€€ Via Nino Bixio 1, 91025. ☎ 0923 99 93 33. FAX 0923 99 91 15. W www.presidentmarsala.it About 1 km (half a mile) from the centre of town this modern, comfortable hotel serves Sicilian and international cuisine in the restaurant.	128	■	●	■
MESSINA: *Paradis* €€ Via Consolare Pompea 441, 98168. ☎ 090 31 06 82. FAX 090 31 20 43. W www.hotelparadis.it About 3 km (2 miles) out of central Messina, the Paradis has good sea views and an excellent restaurant. Rooms are basic but satisfactory. All have balconies.	88	■		■
PALERMO: *San Paolo Palace* €€€ Via Messina Marine 91. ☎ 091 621 11 12. FAX 091 621 53 00. W www.sanpaolopalace.it This large, modern building overlooking the bay offers a complete range of services: roof terrace with swimming pool, panoramic restaurant, piano bar, spacious gym, and sauna.	290	■	●	■
PALERMO: *Splendid Hotel La Torre* €€€ Via Piano Gallo 11, Mondello 90151. ☎ 091 45 02 22. FAX 091 45 00 33. W www.latorre.com A big, traditional seaside hotel, set on a promontory with its own private beach. Some bedrooms have their own balcony with sea views.	168	■	●	■
PALERMO: *Grand Hotel Villa Igiea* €€€€ Salita Belmonte 43, 90142. ☎ 091 631 21 11. FAX 091 54 76 54. W www.acquamarchia.it An exquisite hotel dating from the beginning of the last century with Art Nouveau stained glass and wall paintings. It is set by the sea in gardens with their own ancient ruins. An elegant cocktail bar opens onto the terrace.	114	■	●	■
SCIACCA: *Grand Hotel delle Terme* €€€ Viale delle Terme 1, 92019. ☎ 0925 231 33. FAX 0925 870 02. W www.grandhoteldelleterme.com A spa hotel with access (for an extra charge) to the local mineral springs that were used by the Phoenicians more than 2,000 years ago.	77	■	●	■
SIRACUSA: *Gran Bretagna* €€ Via Savoia 21, 96100. ☎ 0931 687 65. FAX 0931 44 90 78. W www.hotelgranbretagna.it A small, friendly, family-run hotel with comfortable rooms.	16			■
SIRACUSA: *Villa Lucia* €€ Trav. Mondello 1, 1 Contrada Isola, 96100. ☎ 0931 697 56. FAX 0931 72 10 07. W www.villaluciasiracusa.it This beautiful villa, situated in the middle of a Mediterranean park close to the sea, offers a relaxing stay in pretty surroundings.	15	■	●	■
SIRACUSA: *Grand Hotel Villa Politi* €€€€ Via Maria Politi Laudien 2, 96100. ☎ 0931 41 21 21. FAX 0931 360 61. W www.villapoliti.com An old-fashioned hotel whose vast reception rooms belong to another era. The hotel dates from the early 20th century.	100	■	●	■
TAORMINA: *Villa Belvedere* €€€ Via Bagnoli Croci 79, 98039. ☎ 0942 237 91. FAX 0942 62 58 30. W www.villabelvedere.it A very comfortable, family hotel in the centre of Taormina. Some rooms have sea views and balconies. Closed *mid-Jan–mid-Mar; mid-Nov–mid-Dec.*	46		●	
TAORMINA: *Romantik Villa Ducale* €€€€ Via Leonardo da Vinci 60, 98039. ☎ 0942 281 53. FAX 0942 287 10. W www.villaducale.com This elegant villa is now a comfortable hotel. The rooms are all different, furnished with antiques and with excellent views of Mount Etna and the sea.	13			■

TAORMINA: *Grand Hotel Timeo & Villa Flora* €€€€€ | 59
Via Teatro Greco 59, 98039. **[** 094 22 38 01. **FAX** 094 262 85 01. **[W]** www.framon-hotels.com
Since 1884 this exclusive villa has attracted such guests as Marconi, Gide and de
Maupassant. All guests can enjoy a complimentary afternoon tea.

TAORMINA: *San Domenico Palace* €€€€€ | 108
Piazza San Domenico 5, 98039. **[** 0942 61 31 11. **FAX** 0942 62 55 06. **[W]** www.sandomenico.thi.it
A peaceful, 15th-century monastery restored and furnished with genuine antiques.
This is one of the most luxurious hotels in Europe and it has a beautiful formal
garden as well as an elegant swimming pool.

TRAPANI: *Vittoria* €€ | 65
Piazza Vittorio Emanuele, 91100. **[** 0923 87 30 44. **FAX** 0923 298 70. **[W]** www.hotelvittoriatrapani.it
Very conveniently placed in the centre of Trapani, this modern
functional hotel has very simple, well-designed furnishings.

TRAPANI: *Baia dei Mulini* €€€ | 94
Lungomare Dante Alighieri, 91100. **[** 0923 58 41 11. **FAX** 0923 56 74 22. **[W]** www.baiadeimulini.it
A modern hotel on the seafront with all you need for a beach holiday (tennis,
discotheque). A good base from which to explore the region.

SARDINIA

ALGHERO: *Villa las Tronas* €€€€ | 25
Lungomare Valencia 1, 07041. **[** 079 98 18 18. **FAX** 079 98 10 44. **[W]** www.hotelvillalastronas.it
A mustard-coloured villa on a promontory is the setting for this comfortable,
elegantly decorated hotel. Public rooms are full of gilt and 18th-century
French-style furniture; bedrooms are simpler but pretty.

CAGLIARI: *Italia* €€€ | 113
Via Sardegna 31, 09124. **[** 070 66 04 10. **FAX** 070 65 02 40. **[W]** www.sardegnasud.com
Housed in two much-restored palazzi in central Cagliari, this slightly shabby
hotel is a convenient base from which to explore the countryside.

CAGLIARI: *Sardegna* €€€ | 90
Via Lunigiana 50, 09122. **[** 070 28 62 45. **FAX** 070 29 04 69. **[W]** www.shg.it
A modern hotel close to the town centre and about 2 km (1 mile) from the
airport. The rooms are comfortably but simply decorated.

ISOLA DI SAN PIETRO: *Hotel Paola e Primo Maggio* €€ | 21
Tacca Rossa, Carloforte 09014. **[** 0781 85 00 98. **FAX** 0781 85 01 04. **[W]** www.carloforte.net/hotelpaola
A modern pensione overlooking the sea with lovely views and charging very
reasonable prices. There is a shady terrace for outside dining.

NUORO: *Hotel Sacchi* €€ | 24
Monte Ortobene, Nuoro. **[** 0784 312 00. **FAX** 0784 340 30. **[W]** www.hotelsacchi.it
A charming, rustic pensione in a hamlet high above Nuoro. The home-cooking is
excellent and the views over the Barbagia mountains spectacular.

OLIENA: *Su Gologone* €€€ | 68
Località Su Gologone, 08025. **[** 0784 28 75 12. **FAX** 0784 28 76 68. **[W]** www.sugologone.it
A rambling villa in the mountainous Barbagia region is the setting for this delightfully
peaceful hotel. Good range of sports. **Closed** *Nov–mid-Dec, Jan–mid-Mar.*

PORTO CERVO: *Balocco* €€€ | 34
Località Liscia di Vacca, 07020. **[** 0789 915 55. **FAX** 0789 915 10. **[W]** www.hotelbalocco.it
An attractive, airy hotel surrounded by palm-filled grounds and terraces for every room.
It offers comparatively good value for the fashionable Costa Smeralda, but beware:
prices double for the summer season. **Closed** *Nov–Mar.*

PORTO CERVO: *Capriccioli* €€€€ | 46
Località Capriccioli, 07020. **[** 0789 960 04. **FAX** 0789 964 22. **[W]** www.hotelcapriccioli.it
One of the best value hotels on the expensive Costa Smeralda. This family-run hotel is
close to the beach and has an excellent restaurant. **Closed** *Oct–mid-Apr.*

PORTO ROTONDO: *Sporting* €€€€€ | 27
Porto Rotondo, 07026. **[** 0789 340 05. **FAX** 0789 343 83. **[W]** www.sportingportorotondo.it
An oasis of comfort on the Costa Smeralda with its own beach. Rooms have flower-filled
terraces. There is a golf course nearby. Half board. **Closed** *Oct–Mar.*

SASSARI: *Leonardo da Vinci* €€ | 118
Via Roma 79, 07100. **[** 079 28 07 44. **FAX** 079 285 72 33. **[W]** www.leonardodavincihotel.it
A large, comfortable hotel a few minutes' walk from the city centre. Furnishings
are functional, but there is a sense of space and tranquillity.

WHERE TO EAT

FOOD IS A serious subject in Italy. The Italians are justly proud of their fine cuisine and wines and many sociable hours are spent around the table. One of the great pleasures of travelling in Italy is exploring regional variations in pasta, breads and cheeses. Whether it is spinach-filled *tortelloni* from the north or stuffed sweet red peppers from the south, restaurants will rarely serve anything other than

Waiter at Alberto Ciarla *(see p601)*

Italian specialities. You don't have to head to the most expensive places for good food; a simple *trattoria*, which has to answer to the local clientele, will often serve much better fare than the nearby international restaurant. However, whether it is a crowded *osteria* or a terrace with sea views, this introduction gives a few practical tips on types of restaurants, ordering and service to help you enjoy eating out in Italy.

TYPES OF RESTAURANTS AND SNACK BARS

TRADITIONALLY a *trattoria* and an *osteria* were cheaper and more popular alternatives to the smarter *ristorante*. These days, however, the terms are interchangeable and high cost is not always indicative of memorably delicious food.

A *pizzeria* is usually a cheap place to eat (as little as €10 with beer) and many serve pasta, meat and fish dishes as well as pizzas. *Pizzerie* are often open in the evening only, especially those with wood-fired ovens (*forno a legna*).

A *birreria* is another cheap option, serving pasta and snacks such as sausages and hamburgers. An *enoteca*, or *vineria*, is in fact a place to taste wine; however, as Italians will rarely drink without eating, there will normally be a range of light dishes on offer as well as a superb selection of wines. Prices vary and tend not to be cheap for the quantities served.

El Gato restaurant, Chioggia, famous for its fish *(see p580)*

At lunch time and in the early evening *rosticcerie* sell roast chicken, slices of pizza (*pizza al taglio*) and other snacks to take away. Pizza al taglio, with various different toppings, can also be bought straight from the baker. Bars have filled rolls (*panini*) and sandwiches (*tramezzini*) and some have a *tavola calda* counter with hot dishes for under €6.

Stop at a *gelateria* for ice cream, with a sometimes mesmerizing choice of different flavours, or a *pasticceria* for one of a dazzling variety of sweet and savoury pastries, cakes and biscuits.

EATING HOURS

LUNCH IS generally served between 1pm and 2:30pm and, particularly in the south, all other activity stops between these hours. Dinner is at about 8pm and goes on until 11pm or later (in the south eating hours tend to be later). It is not unusual to see tables still full from lunch at 4pm or diners sipping *digestivi* well after midnight.

RESERVATIONS

GOOD RESTAURANTS in Italy are likely to be popular, so reserve a table if you can. Otherwise, get there early to avoid having to queue. Many restaurants close for a few weeks in either winter or the summer holiday season so phone first if in doubt.

THE MENU

ITALIAN MEALS consist of at least three or four courses and restaurants generally expect you to eat at least two. The *antipasto* (starter), is followed by the *primo*, of pasta, rice or soup. The *secondo* is the main meat or fish course with vegetables or salad (as *contorni*). Fruit, cheese or dessert follow, with coffee and a *digestivo* such as *grappa* or a bitter *amaro* to finish the meal.

Menus usually change with the season to make use of the best and freshest local produce and the day's specials may be recited to you by the waiter rather than written down.

Villa Crespi in Piedmont, inspired by the Arabian Nights *(see p587)*

Persevere, if you don't immediately understand, using the menu information at the beginning of each section (see p672).

VEGETARIANS

WHILE FEW PLACES advertise specifically vegetarian meals, you are unlikely to have much trouble choosing from an Italian menu. Many pasta and *antipasto* dishes use no meat at all and for a main course you can ask for a selection of vegetables from the *contorni*. Vegetarians eat particularly well in spring when the first new vegetables come into the markets, and in autumn when wild mushrooms abound.

WINE AND DRINKS

MANY REGIONS have their own *aperitivo* for before the meal and a *digestivo* for afterwards. Universal alternatives are *prosecco* (dry fizzy white wine) or an *analcolico* (non-alcoholic) aperitif and *grappa* as a digestive. House wine (red or white) will be a simple local wine served by the litre or fraction thereof and will generally be perfectly palatable. In addition, all but the cheapest places have a range of other local and regional wines specially selected to accompany the food on the menu. For this reason, it is unusual to come across many non-Italian wines.

Tap water (*acqua del rubinetto*) is always drinkable and often very good, but Italy has a massive range of mineral waters. Fizzy ones (*frizzante*) may contain carbon dioxide

The 11th-century Badia a Coltibuono in Gaiole in Chianti (see p593)

while *naturale* can mean still or naturally sparkling. The popular *Ferrarelle* lies somewhere between the two. If you particularly want a still water ask for *non gassata*.

PAYING

TAX AND SERVICE are usually included in the menu prices but it is normal to leave a small tip (from €1 to €5). Take note of the cover charge (*coperto*): an unavoidable extra that basically covers bread (whether you eat it or not) and is charged per person.

Credit cards are not always accepted in Italy, particularly in smaller towns, and it is wise to check before you eat.

DRESS

ITALIANS GENERALLY tend to look smart but don't necessarily expect visitors to do the same. In most places you will not be expected to dress particularly smartly; however, very scruffy or dirty clothes are unlikely to get you good or particularly friendly service.

CHILDREN

CHILDREN ARE welcome in all but the smartest establishments and throughout Italy restaurants are likely to be filled with extensive Italian families for Sunday lunch. Facilities such as high-chairs or special menus are rare, but most places will provide cushions and small portions.

Roman trattoria, Sora Lella, on Tiber Island (see p599)

SMOKING

SMOKING IS STILL a popular pastime in Italy. However, new smoking laws, due to come into effect in early 2005, will make all restaurants in the country non-smoking establishments. You should be prepared to step outside if you want to light up.

WHEELCHAIR ACCESS

FEW RESTAURANTS have special facilities for people in wheelchairs, but let them know you are coming in advance so they can reserve a suitable table and be ready to help if necessary when you arrive.

La Marinella restaurant overlooking the Amalfi coast (see p603)

Choosing a Restaurant

THE RESTAURANTS in this guide have been selected across a wide range of price categories for their good value, exceptional food and interesting location. This chart lists the restaurants by region, starting with Venice. The thumb tabs on the side of the page use the same colour-coding as the corresponding regional chapter in the main section of the guide.

	FIXED PRICE MENU	GOOD WINE LIST	FORMAL DRESS	OUTDOOR TABLES

VENICE

BURANO: *Ai Pescatori* €€€€
Piazza Galuppi 371, 30012. ☎ *041 73 06 50.*
A welcoming restaurant whose menu includes lobster and *tagliolini* (flat pasta) with cuttlefish. In winter the menu includes excellent game. The extensive wine list offers foreign as well as Italian wines. ● *Wed; 1–15 Jan.* 🔲 ▤

●	▦		▦

BURANO: *Da Romano* €€€€
Via Galuppi 221, 30012. ☎ *041 73 00 30.*
A pretty restaurant founded in the 1800s, now run by a descendant of the original owner. The cooking is traditional and the fish is excellent. ● *Tue; mid-Dec–Jan.* 🔲 ▤

●			▦

CANNAREGIO: *Osteria al Bacco* €€€
Fondamenta delle Cappuccine 3054, 30121. **Map** 2 D2. ☎ *041 71 74 93.*
A rustic restaurant with a pretty shaded courtyard. The menu serves mainly fish, and includes *spaghetti* with black cuttlefish-ink sauce. ● *Mon; 2 wks Jan, 2 wks Aug.* 🔲

			▦

CANNAREGIO: *Vini Da Gigio* €€€
Fondamenta San Felice 3628a, 30131. **Map** 3 A4. ☎ *041 528 51 40.*
A cosy restaurant serving traditional Venetian cuisine with a difference. Try the *risotto* of prawns and grilled cuttlefish. Book in advance. ● *Mon; mid-Jan–Feb, late Aug.* 🔲 ▤

	▦		

CANNAREGIO: *Fiaschetteria Toscana* €€€€
Salizzada San Giovanni Crisostomo 5719, 30131. **Map** 3 B5. ☎ *041 528 52 81.*
The Busatto family offer many Venetian dishes such as warm salad of lagoon fish and turbot with black butter and capers. ● *Mon lunch, Tue; late-Jul–late-Aug.* 🔲 ▤

	▦		▦

CASTELLO: *Arcimboldo* €€€€
Calle dei Furlani 3219, 30122. **Map** 8 D1. ☎ *041 528 65 69.*
Named after the 16th-century painter who used vegetables and fruit to create portraits of people. The food is similarly innovative today; try sea bass with tomatoes or marinated salmon with citrus fruit. ● *Tue; 10 days in Aug.* 🔲 ▤

●	▦		▦

CASTELLO: *La Corte Sconta* €€€€
Calle del Pestrin 3886, 30122. **Map** 7 A3. ☎ *041 522 70 24.*
This simple eating house has become one of the city's top restaurants. The fish and the home-made pasta are both superb. ● *Sun, Mon; 7 Jan–7 Feb, 21 Jul–16 Aug.* 🔲 ▤

	▦		▦

CASTELLO: *Da Remigio* €€€€
Salizzada dei Greci 3416, 30122. **Map** 8 D2. ☎ *041 523 00 89.*
A lively local fish restaurant with a robust and straightforward menu. Booking is advisable. ● *Mon eve, Tue; Christmas–20 Jan, last wk Jul.* 🔲 ▤

	▦		

DORSODURO: *Taverna San Trovaso* €€
Fondamenta Priuli 1016, 30123. **Map** 6 E3. ☎ *041 520 37 03.*
A cheerful, bustling restaurant between the Accademia and the Zattere. The cooking is straightforward and includes pizzas. ● *Mon.* 🔲 ▤

●			

DORSODURO: *La Bitta* €€€
Calle Lunga S. Barnaba 2753/a. **Map** 5 C3. ☎ *041 523 05 31.*
This cosy restaurant is one of the few in Venice that does not serve fish. The meats, however, are superb and the desserts divine. ● *lunch; Sun; 3 wks Jul.* 🔲

	▦		▦

DORSODURO: *Trattoria alla Madonna* €€€
Calle della Madonna 594, 30123. **Map** 7 A1. ☎ *041 522 38 24.*
This is a bustling, well-known fish restaurant. There are often queues for tables here so arrive early. ● *Wed; 25 Dec–31 Jan, 5–20 Aug.* 🔲 ▤

DORSODURO: *Ai Gondolieri* €€€€€
San Vio 366, 30123. **Map** 6 F4. ☎ *041 528 63 96.*
Housed in a sympathetically restored old inn. Good regional specialities including *sformati* (soufflé) with wild herbs and mushroom soups. ● *lunch; Tue; Jun–Aug.* 🔲 ▤

	▦		

		FIXED PRICE MENU	GOOD WINE LIST	FORMAL DRESS	OUTDOOR TABLES
Average prices for a three-course meal for one, including a half-bottle of house wine, tax and service: € under €18 €€ €18–€30 €€€ €30–€40 €€€€ €40–€52 €€€€€ over €52.	**FIXED-PRICE MENU** A fixed-price menu on offer, usually with three courses. **GOOD WINE LIST** Denotes a wide range of good quality wines. **FORMAL DRESS** Some restaurants require men to wear a jacket and tie. **OUTDOOR TABLES** Tables for eating outdoors, often with a good view. **CREDIT CARDS** The symbol shows that major credit cards are accepted.				
DORSODURO: *Locanda Montin* €€€€€ Fondamenta Eremite 1147, 30123. **Map** 6 D3. (041 522 71 51. A famous restaurant with artistic and literary connections. Food and service can vary in quality but there is a lively atmosphere. ● *Wed.*			■		■
GIUDECCA: *Cipriani* €€€€€ Giudecca 10, 30122. (041 520 77 44. One of Venice's most exclusive restaurants, the *Cipriani* offers impeccable food and service in elegant surroundings. Panoramic terrace. ● *Nov–Mar.*		●	■	●	■
GIUDECCA: *Harry's Dolci* €€€€€ Fondamenta San Biagio 773, 30133. **Map** 6 D5. (041 522 48 44. Originally a bar and tea-room, this is now a restaurant serving similar food to Harry's Bar in San Marco. Try *carpaccio* (marinated, sliced raw beef), the pasta and beans, and the house chocolate cake. ● *Tue; Mon–Wed (mid-Oct–Easter).*			■		
MAZZORBO: *Antica Trattoria alla Maddalena* €€ Mazzorbo 7b, Burano 30012. (041 73 01 51. This modest restaurant, popular with the locals, acts as a local bar as well as an eating house. It has a tranquil atmosphere, however, and the wild duck served with *polenta* is famous throughout the area. ● *Thu; Christmas–mid-Jan.*			■		■
SAN MARCO: *Al Conte Pescaor* €€€€ Piscina San Zulian 544b, 30124. **Map** 7 B1. (041 522 14 83. A little restaurant with a superb fish menu. The clientele is mainly local people, which guarantees the high quality of the food. ● *Sun.*			■		
SAN MARCO: *Antico Martini* €€€€€ Campo San Fantin 1983, 30124. **Map** 7 A2. (041 522 41 21. This smart restaurant overlooks the Fenice theatre. The cooking is creative: try the lamb with caper sauce. ● *Tue, Wed lunch.*		●	■	■	
SAN MARCO: *Da Raffaele* €€€€€ Ponte delle Ostreghe 2347, 30124. **Map** 7 A3. (041 523 23 17. A romantic setting in which to eat regional dishes. Try the *granseola* (spider crab), *risotto* with scampi and *rombo alla Raffaele* (turbot). ● *Thu; Dec–early Feb.*			■		
SAN MARCO: *La Caravella* €€€€€ Calle Larga XXII Marzo 2397, 30124. **Map** 7 A3. (041 520 89 01. Now the only restaurant in the Hotel Saturnia, *La Caravella* has a beautiful setting with a waterside terrace by the Grand Canal. The food is outstanding, with speciality dishes including fish soup.			■		
SAN MARCO: *Harry's Bar* €€€€€ Calle Vallaresso 1323, 30124. **Map** 7 B3. (041 528 57 77. People come here because it is so famous. The wine list and cocktails are good but the food is not particularly exciting for the price.		●	■		
SAN POLO: *Antica Trattoria Poste Vecie* €€€€ Rialto Pescheria 1608, 30123. **Map** 3 A5. (041 72 18 22. This stylish restaurant near the fish market claims to be the oldest in Venice. Dishes include home-made pasta as well as lovely desserts. ● *Tue.*			■		
SAN POLO: *Da Fiore* €€€€€ Calle del Scaleter 2202a. **Map** 2 E5. (041 72 13 08. Fish specialities include a wonderful seafood *antipasto*, grilled fish and *fritto misto* (mixed fried fish). Try the house white wine. ● *Sun, Mon; 3 wks Aug, 2 wks Dec.*			■		
TORCELLO: *Locanda Cipriani* €€€€€ Piazza Santa Fosca 29, 30121. (041 73 01 50. Transformed from a fishermen's inn in the 1930s, dishes include *fritto misto* and a *risotto* with vegetables from the kitchen garden. ● *Tue; Jan.*			■		■

Average prices for a three-course meal for one, including a half-bottle of house wine, tax and service:
€ under €18
€€ €18–€30
€€€ €30–€40
€€€€ €40–€52
€€€€€ over €52.

FIXED-PRICE MENU
A fixed-price menu on offer, usually with three courses.
GOOD WINE LIST
Denotes a wide range of good quality wines.
FORMAL DRESS
Some restaurants require men to wear a jacket and tie.
OUTDOOR TABLES
Tables for eating outdoors, often with a good view.
CREDIT CARDS
The symbol shows that major credit cards are accepted.

	FIXED PRICE MENU	GOOD WINE LIST	FORMAL DRESS	OUTDOOR TABLES
THE VENETO AND FRIULI				
ASOLO: *Villa Cipriani* €€€€€ Via Canova 298, 31011. 0423 95 21 66. Set in one of the grand hotels of the Veneto. Local ingredients are used in the creative cuisine with dishes such as *gnocchi* of ricotta with rosemary.		■	●	■
BELLUNO: *Terracotta* €€ Via Garibaldi 61. 0437 94 26 44. Regional specialities include *pappardelle* (wide ribbon pasta) with smoked ricotta, *radicchio* and speck, or chickpea and prawn soup. ● *Tue eve, Wed; last 2 wks Jun.*		■		■
BREGANZE: *Al Toresan* €€ Via Zabarella 1, 36042. 0445 87 32 60. In the autumn the locals flock here for the wild mushroom dishes. The cooking is hearty and is complemented by local wines. ● *Thu; 1–25 Aug.*		■		
CAORLE: *Duilio* €€ Via Strada Nuova 19, 30021. 0421 810 87. A spacious restaurant where the fish-based regional cuisine is given a creative slant. Try the dried cod with *polenta.* ● *Mon (winter); 2 wks Jan.*		■		■
CASTELFRANCO: *Barbesin* €€ Via Montebelluna 41, 31033. 0423 49 04 46. A restaurant serving regional specialities, including *risotto* with fish, or vegetables, or porcini mushrooms. ● *Wed eve, Thu; 1 wk Jan, 2 wks Aug.*	●	■		■
CHIOGGIA: *El Gato* €€€€ Campo Sant'Andrea 653, 30015. 041 40 18 06. Classic cooking based on seafood in an elegant, slightly restrained setting. The delicious desserts are highly recommended. ● *Mon, Tue lunch; 2 wks Jan.*	●	■		■
CIVIDALE DEL FRIULI: *Zorutti* €€ Borgo di Ponte 9, 33043. 0432 73 11 00. A family-run restaurant with a well-deserved reputation for good, regional cuisine served in generous portions. The house speciality is *buzara,* a local speciality of *spaghetti* with seafood, giant prawns or lobster. ● *Mon; mid-end Jan.*	●	■		
CONEGLIANO: *Al Salisà* €€ Via XX Settembre 2, 31015. 0438 242 88. An elegant restaurant set in a medieval house with a pretty veranda for eating outdoors. The traditional menu includes *lumache* (snails) and home-made pastas served with a range of vegetarian sauces. ● *Wed.*		■		
CORTINA D'AMPEZZO: *Baita Fraina* €€€ Località Fraina 1, 32043. 0436 36 34. An elegant alpine restaurant, with wood fittings and a panoramic terrace. The food is robust and extremely good value. ● *Mon (Jan–Feb); Easter–Jun, Oct–Nov.*		■		
DOLO: *Alla Posta* €€€€ Via Ca' Tron 33, 30031. 041 41 07 40. This superb restaurant in an old Venetian posthouse prepares regional specialities with fresh ingredients and well-blended flavours. ● *Mon; 2 wks Jan, 2 wks Jun–Jul.*	●	■		■
GORIZIA: *Nanut* €€ Via Trieste 118, 34170. 0481 205 95. A long-established trattoria in the industrial zone. It serves good local food; *gnocchi,* market vegetables, meats, and fish on Friday. ● *Sat, Sun; Aug, 2 wks Christmas.*				■
GRADO: *Trattoria de Toni* €€€€ Piazza Duca d'Aosta 37, 34073. 0431 801 04. A traditional trattoria in the historic centre, the house speciality is *boreto alla Gradese,* a fish stew cooked in oil and vinegar. ● *Wed; Jan–Dec.*		■		■

GRANCONA: *Isetta* €€
Via Pederiva 96, 36040. 0444 88 99 92.
Regional food, with the emphasis on grilled meats and good puddings, in the Berici hills. Ten rooms are also available. ● Tue eve, Wed.

LAKE GARDA: *Antica Locanda Mincio* €€€
Via Buonarroti 12, Località Borghetto, Valeggio sul Mincio 37067. 045 795 00 59.
Once a staging post, this is now a delightful restaurant with frescoed walls and open fireplaces serving good regional food. ● Wed, Thu; 2 wks Feb, 2 wks Nov.

LAKE GARDA: *Locanda San Vigilio* €€€€€
Località San Vigilio, Garda 37016. 045 725 66 88.
This excellent restaurant overlooking Lake Garda has an *antipasto* buffet and an astounding range of freshwater fish and seafood dishes. ● Nov–Mar (Tue until mid-Apr).

MONTECCHIA DI CROSARA: *Baba-jaga* €€€€
Via Cabalao 11, 37030. 045 745 02 22.
Black-truffle *risotto* and prawns with courgettes, tomatoes and leeks are a good choice in the Soave wine-producing area. ● Sun eve, Mon; 3 wks Jan, 3 wks Aug.

NOVENTA PADOVANA: *Boccadoro* €€€
Via della Resistenza 49, 35027. 049 62 50 29.
Good Paduan food is served in this family-run restaurant. The goose is well worth sampling. ● Tue eve, Wed; 2 wks Jan, 2 wks Aug.

ODERZO: *Dussin* €€
Via Maggiore 60, Località Piavon, 31046. 0422 75 21 30.
Good-value, traditional cuisine is served here. Fish is a speciality, with such dishes as seafood *risotto* and grilled tuna. ● Mon eve, Tue; 10 days Jan, 2 wks Aug–Sep.

PADUA: *La Braseria* €€
Via Tommaseo 48, 35100. 049 876 09 07.
A friendly restaurant with straightforward cooking. *Penne* with porcini mushrooms and smoked bacon are recommended. ● Sat lunch, Sun; eves Aug.

PADUA: *Osteria L'Anfora* €€
Via dei Soncin 13, 35122. 049 65 66 29.
Traditional Veneto cuisine, with elements originally brought by Renaissance merchants from far afield, is served in a lively atmosphere. ● Sun; 1–6 Jan, 2 wks Aug.

PADUA: *San Pietro* €€€
Via San Pietro 95, 35149. 049 876 03 30.
Perfect for regional dishes, cooked with fresh, local ingredients. Friendly, attentive service and informal atmosphere. ● Sat (Jun–10 Sep), Sun; Jul, 2 wks Christmas.

PADUA: *Antico Brolo* €€€€
Corso Milano 22, 35100. 049 66 45 55.
This quietly elegant restaurant delivers appropriately elegant food such as ravioli stuffed with courgette flowers. ● Mon; 1 wk Aug.

PORDENONE: *Vecia Osteria del Moro* €€€
Via Castello 2, 33170. 0434 286 58.
A refined restaurant set in a beautifully restored 13th-century convent. Daily specials include rabbit with *polenta*. ● Sun (summer); 2 wks Jan, 2 wks Aug.

ROVIGO: *Trattoria al Sole* €€
Via Bedendo Nino 6, 45100. 0425 22 917.
An old-fashioned trattoria, serving unpretentious, traditional local cuisine. Try the tripe or *baccalà alla vicentina* (salt cod). ● Sun; 8 days Aug.

TREVISO: *Toni del Spin* €€
Via Inferiore 7, 31100. 0422 54 38 29.
A homely restaurant serving regional fare. House specialities include pasta and *fagioli* (beans), baked tripe and tiramisù. ● Sun, Mon lunch; Aug.

TREVISO: *Ristorante Beccherie* €€€
Piazza Ancillotto 10, 31100. 0422 54 08 71.
Housed in a lovely building reminiscent of Venetian splendour. The guinea fowl in pepper sauce is a particular delicacy. ● Sun eve, Mon; 15–30 Jul.

TREVISO: *Osteria all'Antica Torre* €€€€
Via Inferiore 55, 31100. 0422 58 36 94.
Exemplary wines accompany superb local cuisine. In season, *radicchio* (endive) is used in many ways, including in the digestive *grappa*. ● Sun; Aug.

Average prices for a three-course meal for one, including a half-bottle of house wine, tax and service:
€ under €18
€€ €18–€30
€€€ €30–€40
€€€€ €40–€52
€€€€€ over €52.

FIXED-PRICE MENU
A fixed-price menu on offer, usually with three courses.
GOOD WINE LIST
Denotes a wide range of good quality wines.
FORMAL DRESS
Some restaurants require men to wear a jacket and tie.
OUTDOOR TABLES
Tables for eating outdoors, often with a good view.
CREDIT CARDS
The symbol shows that major credit cards are accepted.

	FIXED PRICE MENU	GOOD WINE LIST	FORMAL DRESS	OUTDOOR TABLES
TRIESTE: *Al Bragozzo* €€ Riva Sauro 22, 34124. 040 30 30 01. The menu changes from week to week, depending on the local produce available. This lively restaurant is popular with locals. ● Sun, Mon; 2 wks Jan, 2 wks Jul.		■		■
TRIESTE: *Harry's Grill* €€€€ Piazza Unità d'Italia 2, 34121. 040 66 06 06. This restaurant is distinguished by its central position and high-class cuisine. Try *ravioli* with *melanzane* (eggplant) filling and *astice* (crayfish) sauce. ● Sun.		■		■
UDINE: *Agli Amici* €€€€ Via Liguria 250, Località Godia, 33100. 0432 56 54 11. Friulian dishes, such as *cappe sante all'aglio orsino* (scallops with wild garlic) are cooked with flair here. ● Sun eve, Mon; Jan, Jul.	●	■		■
VERONA: *Al Bersagliere* €€ Via dietro Pallone 1, 37121. 045 800 48 24. Traditional Veronese food in a friendly atmosphere. Dishes include *pastisada* (meat stew) and *bigoli con l'anatra* (pasta with duck). ● Sun; Easter, Christmas.		■		■
VERONA: *Arche* €€€€€ Via Arche Scaligere 6, 37121. 045 800 74 15. A long-established fish restaurant serving spaghetti with clams in *cartoccio* and rock lobster in *serenissima saor* marinade. ● Sun, Mon lunch; 6–28 Jan.	●	■		
VERONA: *Il Desco* €€€€€ Via dietro San Sebastiano 5–7, 37121. 045 59 53 58. One of Italy's best restaurants, set in a 16th-century palazzo. Dishes include *risotto con zucca* (pumpkin) *e amarone* (wine). ● Sun, Mon (exc Jul–Aug); 2 wks Jan, 2 wks Jun.		■	●	
VICENZA: *Taverna Aeolia* €€ Piazza Conte da Schio 1, Costozza di Longare 36023. 0444 55 50 36. This restaurant is housed in an elegant villa with a beautiful frescoed ceiling. The menu specializes in creative meat dishes. ● Tue; 1–15 Nov.	●	■		■
VICENZA: *Antica Trattoria Tre Visi* €€€ Corso Palladio 25, 36100. 0444 32 48 68. The building, in the historic centre, dates from 1483. Diners can see into the kitchen where the excellent local dishes are prepared. ● Sun eve, Mon; Jul.	●	■		■
VICENZA: *Cinzia e Valerio* €€€€ Piazzetta Porta Padova 65–67, 36100. 0444 50 52 13. A stylish restaurant within the city walls, serving nothing but fish. Dishes include a mixed plate of scampi and squid. ● Sun eve, Mon; 25 Dec–5 Jan, 3 wks Aug.	●	■		
TRENTINO-ALTO ADIGE				
ARCO: *Alla Lega* €€ Via Vergolano 8, 38062. 0464 51 62 05. A lively, family-run restaurant housed in a rustically elegant 18th-century building with a beautiful courtyard. The food is traditional, including such dishes as wild mushroom *risotto*, cured meats and trout with *polenta*. ● Wed; Feb–mid-Mar.		■		■
BOLZANO (BOZEN): *L'Aquila Rossa* €€ Via Goethe 3, 39100. 0471 97 39 38. This restaurant is housed in one of the oldest buildings in Bolzano's historic centre. Try the *gnocchi tirolesi* and roast venison, and choose from over 200 international wines. ● Sun; 3 wks Jul.		■		■
BOLZANO (BOZEN): *Domino* €€ Piazza Walther 1, 39100. 0471 32 41 05. This town-centre wine bar is a good stop for a delicious lunchtime snack with a glass of wine. New menu daily. ● eve; Sun.		■		■

BOLZANO (BOZEN): *Rastbichler* €€€
Via Cadorna 1, 39100. ☎ *0471 26 11 31.*
This restaurant is known for its excellent fish and generously served grilled
meats. Typical South Tyrol decor. ● *Sat lunch, Sun; 2 wks Jan, 2 wks Aug.* ▤

BRESSANONE (BRIXEN): *Fink* €€€
Via Portici Minori 4, 39042. ☎ *0472 83 48 83.*
Popular with locals who come to sample the immaculately prepared dishes such
as black *polenta* or *knödel* (a kind of dumpling). ● *Tue eve, Wed; Feb.* ▤ ⚡ ♿

BRESSANONE (BRIXEN): *Oste Scuro-Finsterwirt* €€€
Vicolo Duomo 3, 39042. ☎ *0472 83 53 43.*
One of the oldest buildings in the historic centre, it specializes in imaginative
regional cuisine using local produce. ● *Sun eve, Mon; 3 wks Jan, 2 wks Jun–Jul.* ▤ ♿ ▦

BRUNICO (BRUNECK): *Oberraut* €€
Via Ameto 1, Località Amaten, 39031. ☎ *0474 55 99 77.*
Set in woods, this Tyrolean-style restaurant specializes in local game and seasonal
dishes. There is a tantalizing dessert list. ● *Thu (exc Aug); 2 wks Jan.* ▤ ♿

CARZANO: *Le Rose* €€
Via XVIII Settembre 35, 38050. ☎ *0461 76 61 77.*
This popular Valsugana restaurant concentrates on fish and seasonal
produce. Try the *tortelli* of fish with *porcini* mushrooms. ● *Mon.* ▤ ♿

CAVALESE: *Costa Salici* €€€
Via Costa dei Salici 10, 38033. ☎ *0462 34 01 40.*
A popular restaurant with dishes such as home-made pasta with mushrooms,
marinated venison and pear *strudel*. Book ahead. ● *Mon, Tue lunch; Oct.* ▤ ♿ ⚡

CIVEZZANO: *Maso Cantanghel* €€€
Via della Madonnina 33, 38045. ☎ *0461 85 87 14.*
An excellent restaurant just outside Trento. Food is simple yet delicious; garden
vegetables, roasted meats and home-made pasta. ● *Sat, Sun; 2 wks Aug.* ▤ ♿

LEVICO TERME: *Boivin* €€
Via Garibaldi 9, 38056. ☎ *0461 70 16 70.*
This excellent trattoria is one of the best places to taste authentic, local cuisine;
booking is recommended. Only open evenings and for Sunday lunch. ● *Mon.* ▤

MADONNA DI CAMPIGLIO: *Hermitage* €€€€
Via Castelletto Inferiore 63, 38084. ☎ *0465 44 15 58.*
Set in a private park at the foot of the Dolomites, serving imaginative regional cuisine,
with fresh-flavoured, tasty dishes. Open evenings only. ● *May–Jun, Oct–Nov.* ▤ ⚡

MALLES VENOSTA (MALS IM VINSCHGAU): *Greif* €€
Via Generale Verdross 40a, 39024. ☎ *0473 83 14 29.*
Here the chef creates Tyrolean dishes using organic produce. The restaurant
also serves a vegetarian menu. ● *Sun; 2 wks Jun, 2 wks Nov.* ▤ ⚡ ♿

MALLES VENOSTA (MALS IM VINSCHGAU): *Weisses Kreuz* €€
Località Burgusio 82, 39024. ☎ *0473 83 13 07.*
This great-value restaurant serves traditional fare such as *knödel* (dumplings), roasted
meats and strudels. ● *Thu; 1 month before Christmas, 1 month after Easter.* ▤ ♿

MERANO (MERAN): *Artemis* €€
Via Giuseppe Verdi 72, 39012. ☎ *0473 44 62 82.*
Good Italian and international cuisine is served here. Live classical music
(Thursdays only) and vegetarian buffet. ● *Sun, Mon; Jan–Feb.* ▤

MERANO (MERAN): *Sissi* €€€€
Via Galilei 44, 39012. ☎ *0473 23 10 62.*
A 19th-century building close to the town centre, the Sissi offers a refined, seasonal
menu combining traditional and modern dishes. ● *Mon; mid-Jan–Feb.* ▤ ▦

MOENA: *Malga Panna* €€€€
Via Costalunga 26, 38035. ☎ *0462 57 34 89.*
Mushrooms and game are served at this romantic restaurant in a rustic setting about
1 km (half a mile) from the town centre. ● *Mon (winter); May–Jun, Oct–Nov.* ▤ ♿ ⚡

ROVERETO: *Novecento* €€€
Corso Rosmini 82d, 38068. ☎ *0464 43 54 54.*
A refined restaurant, part of a hotel in the middle of Rovereto, serving some
carefully prepared local dishes. ● *Sun; 3 wks Jan, 3 wks Aug.* ▤ ▦ ⚡

	FIXED PRICE MENU	GOOD WINE LIST	FORMAL DRESS	OUTDOOR TABLES

ROVERETO: *Al Borgo*   €€€€€ | ● | ▦ | |
Via Garibaldi 13, 38068. **(** *0464 43 63 00.*
Centrally situated, Al Borgo is one of the best restaurants in the Trentino region. It uses local produce and offers dishes such as *strangolapreti*, tiny dumplings with potato and spinach or seasonal vegetables. ● *Sun eve, Mon; 20–30 Jan, 3 wks Jul.* ▤

TRENTO: *Birreria Pedavena Pizzeria*   €€ | | | | ▦
Via S Croce 15. **(** *0461 98 62 55.*
Lively beer hall-cum-eatery in the town centre, serving traditional fare.
● *Tue; mid-Jul–mid-Aug.* ▤ ▨

TRENTO: *Al Tino*   €€ | | ▦ | |
Via Santissima Trinità 10, 38100. **(** *0461 98 41 09.*
Situated in an historic building in the centre of Trento, this traditional trattoria is lively and popular as well as good value. Booking is advisable. ● *Sun; 1 wk mid-Aug.* ▤ ▤

TRENTO: *Osteria A le Due Spade*   €€€€ | | ▦ | ▦
Via Don Rizzi 11, 38100. **(** *0461 23 43 43.*
A welcoming cellar restaurant near the Duomo, serving traditional cuisine, including game and freshwater fish. ● *Sun, Mon lunch; end-Jun–beg Jul.* ▤ ▤ ▨

VAL DI VIZZE (PFITSCH): *Pretzhof*   €€€ | | ▦ | ▦
Località Tulve 259, 39040. **(** *0472 76 44 55.*
Karl and Ulli Mair run this peaceful country inn, using fresh produce from their own farm to concoct Tyrolean specialities. ● *Mon, Tue (exc Aug).* ▤

VIPITENO: *Kleine Flamme*   €€€ | ● | ▦ | ▦
Città Nuova 31, 39049. **(** *0472 76 60 65.*
A high standard of creative cuisine is matched by attentive service and attention to detail at this small, chic restaurant in a 16th-century building. ● *Sun, Mon.* ▤ ▤

LOMBARDY

BELLAGIO: *Silvio*   €€€ | | | | ▦
Via Carcano 12, 22021. **(** *031 95 03 22.* **W** www.bellagiosilvio.com
Silvio and his son Cristian catch much of the lake fish which is used for patés, pasta sauces, *ravioli* and *risottos*. There is a relaxed atmosphere in this lovely restaurant and hotel with beautiful lakeside views. ● *Jan, Feb.*

BERGAMO: *Vineria Cozzi*   €€€ | ● | ▦ | ▦
Via Colleoni 22, 24129. **(** *035 23 88 36.*
An attractive, old wine shop in 19th-century style. Dishes and pies are accompanied by a good wine list. Try *polenta* with truffled cheese. ● *Wed; 1 wk Jan, 2 wks Jul.* ▤

BERGAMO: *Taverna del Colleoni dell'Angelo*   €€€€€ | ● | ▦ | ● | ▦
Piazza Vecchia 7, 24129. **(** *035 23 25 96.* **W** www.colleonidellangelo.com
An elegant taverna. Specialities include pasta with squid, prawns with light *polenta* and delicious desserts. ● *Mon; 2 wks Aug.* ▤ ▨ ▤

BORMIO: *Al Filò*   €€€ | ● | ▦ | |
Via Dante 6, 23032. **(** *0342 90 17 32.*
A restaurant in a 17th-century barn. It serves local cuisine with specialities based on game, mushrooms and cured meats. ● *Mon, Tue lunch; May–Jun.* ▤

BRESCIA: *Trattoria Mezzeria*   €€ | | | |
Via Trieste 66, 25121. **(** *030 403 06.*
A busy trattoria serving home-made pasta or squash *gnocchi*, with main dishes such as stewed rabbit *alle Bresciana*. ● *Sun; Aug.* ▤

CASTELVECCANA: *Sant'Antonio*   €€ | ● | | | ▦
Località Sant'Antonio, 21010. **(** *0332 52 11 66.*
This restaurant is set in a delightful 10th-century village with views of Lake Maggiore. The menu includes an excellent *polenta* with boiled meats. ● *Mon.*

COMO: *Sant'Anna 1907* €€€
Via Turati 3, 22100. **(** *031 50 52 66.* **W** www.santanna1907.com
This restaurant has been run by the Fontana family for three generations.
The traditional dishes include fish *risotto* and veal in an olive crust.
● *Sat lunch, Sun; Aug; 1 wk Dec.*

CREMONA: *Mellini* €€€
Via Bissolati 105, 26100. **(** *0372 305 35.*
A cosy, family-run restaurant with a good choice of dishes prepared with great flair,
using exclusively fresh and local ingredients and seafish of the highest quality. Try the
pumpkin *tortelli, risotto* with mushrooms or bass with potatoes. ● *Sun eve, Mon; Aug.*

CREMONA: *Osteria Porta Mosa* €€€
Via Santa Maria in Betlem 11, 26100. **(** *0372 41 18 03.*
A refined trattoria with excellent wines and simple dishes, such as *ravioli*, smoked
sword fish and *polenta* with seasonal sauces. Wine shop. ● *Sun; Aug, 26 Dec–6 Jan.*

GARGNANO DEL GARDA: *La Tortuga* €€€€€
Via XXIV Maggio 5, Porticciolo di Gargnano, 25084. **(** *0365 712 51.*
A charming lakeside location for light imaginative cuisine.
Try the *coregone* with tomatoes and capers. ● *lunch; Tue; Jan, Feb.*

LAKE COMO: *Locanda dell'Isola Comacina* €€€€€
Isola Comacina, 22010. **(** *0344 567 55.*
Set by the water's edge on an otherwise uninhabited island. A wonderful
five-course set menu of fish dishes is served. ● *Tue (16 Sep–14 Jun); Nov–Mar.*

LECCO: *Casa di Lucia* €€
Via Lucia 27, Località Acquate 23900. **(** *0341 49 45 94.*
In a 17th-century house, traditional fare such as salami, *bresaola* (cured beef),
rabbit and *pasta e fagioli* is served with good national wines. ● *Sat lunch, Sun; Aug.*

MANERBA DEL GARDA: *Capriccio* €€€€€
Piazza San Bernardo 6, Località Montinelle, 25080. **(** *0365 55 11 24.*
W www.ristorantecapriccio.it
Local fish and olive oil are used in the cuisine at Capriccio. Desserts include a muscat-
grape jelly with peach sauce. Excellent views are a bonus. ● *lunch, Tue; Jan–Feb.*

MANTOVA: *Ai Ranari* €€
Via Trieste 11, 46100. **(** *0376 32 84 31.*
A simple trattoria. Dishes are Mantuan and include pumpkin *tortelli*
with butter sauce and meat *polenta*. ● *Mon; 2 wks Jul, 1 wk Aug.*

MANTOVA: *L'Ochina Bianca* €€
Via Finzi 2, 46100. **(** *0376 32 37 00.*
A simple restaurant serving some of the less well-known local specialities
such as meat parcels with sausage and cheese. ● *Mon; 3 wks Aug.*

MANTOVA: *Il Cigno Trattoria dei Martini* €€€€
Piazza Carlo d'Arco 1, 46100. **(** *0376 32 71 01.*
Fine Mantuan cuisine is accompanied by excellent wines. Try *bottarga*
(tuna roe) and *tortelli di zucce* (pumpkin). ● *Mon, Tue; Aug, 1st wk Jan.*

MILAN: *Geppo* €€
Via Morgagni 37, 20124. **(** *02 29 51 48 62.*
A fun atmosphere and wide range of pizzas are on offer here. Try the
valdostane (spinach, tomato, mozzarella and taleggio cheese). ● *Sun.*

MILAN: *Premiata Pizzeria* €€
Alzaia Naviglio Grande 2, 20144. **(** *02 89 40 06 48.*
This lively, informal restaurant is always busy but the service is efficient and friendly.
The dining room is spacious and fitted with antiques; in the summer the tables
are laid outside in the beautiful courtyard. ● *Tue lunch.*

MILAN: *Ba Ba Reeba* €€
Via Corridoni 1, 20122. **(** *02 55 01 12 67.*
This is different, in that its cuisine is exclusively Spanish. Specialities include
baccalà (dried salt cod) and fillet in red wine sauce. ● *Sat lunch; Sun; 3 wks Aug.*

MILAN: *La Capanna* €€€
Via Donatello 9, 20131. **(** *02 29 40 08 84.*
Do not be put off by the plain appearance, since the food, based
on traditional Tuscan cuisine, is exceptional; fresh pasta and
home-made puddings. ● *Wed, Sat lunch; Aug.*

Average prices for a three-course meal for one, including a half-bottle of house wine, tax and service:
€ under €18
€€ €18–€30
€€€ €30–€40
€€€€ €40–€52
€€€€€ over €52.

FIXED-PRICE MENU
A fixed-price menu on offer, usually with three courses.

GOOD WINE LIST
Denotes a wide range of good quality wines.

FORMAL DRESS
Some restaurants require men to wear a jacket and tie.

OUTDOOR TABLES
Tables for eating outdoors, often with a good view.

CREDIT CARDS
The symbol shows that major credit cards are accepted.

	FIXED PRICE MENU	GOOD WINE LIST	FORMAL DRESS	OUTDOOR TABLES

MILAN: *Lucca*   €€€ | | ▓ | |
Via Castaldi 33, 20100. 📞 02 29 52 66 68.
Great for business lunches and popular for dinner, the cuisine is Tuscan and Mediterranean in style. 🗂 ≣ ⬤ *Aug.*

MILAN: *Aimo e Nadia*   €€€€€ | ● | ▓ | ● |
Via Montecuccoli 6, 20147. 📞 02 41 68 86. 🌐 www.aimoenadia.com
A small, chic restaurant which is famed for its delicious, imaginative dishes, prepared with select, seasonal ingredients. ⬤ *Sat lunch, Sun; 1 wk Jan, Aug.* 🗂 ≣

MONTE ISOLA: *La Foresta*   €€€€ | | ▓ | ▓ |
Località Peschiera Maraglio 174, 25050. 📞 030 988 62 10.
Lake fish form the basis of the menu, making this popular with lovers of all sorts of local freshwater fish. ⬤ *Wed; 2 wks Oct, 20 Dec–end-Feb.* 🗂 ≣

PAVIA: *Locanda Vecchia Pavia al Mulino*   €€€€€ | ● | ▓ | ▓ |
Via al Monumento 5, Località Certosa, 27012. 📞 0382 92 58 94.
Frothy desserts follow creative dishes that bring a light touch to local specialities. The service is cordial and attentive. ⬤ *Mon, Wed lunch; 3 wks Jan, 2 wks Aug.* 🗂 ≣ ♿

SALÒ: *Alla Campagnola*   €€€ | | ▓ | ▓ |
Via Brunati 11, 25087. 📞 0365 221 53.
A mother and sons team offers interesting traditional recipes including pasta stuffed with pumpkin or aubergine. ⬤ *Mon, Tue lunch; Jan.* 🗂

VALLE D'AOSTA AND PIEDMONT

ACQUI TERME: *La Schiavia*   €€€ | ● | ▓ | |
Vicolo della Schiavia, 15011. 📞 0144 559 39.
An elegant, family-run restaurant on the ground floor of a 17th-century palazzo. Cuisine is regional including a mix of vegetables and fish. ⬤ *Sun; 2 wks Aug.* 🗂

ALBA: *Porta San Martino*   €€€ | ● | ▓ | |
Via Einaudi 5, 12051. 📞 0173 36 23 35.
Excellent value at this refined restaurant with good service and a menu of local specialities: *vitello tonnato* (veal with a sauce of tuna and capers) and *brasato* (meat) in Barbaresco wine sauce. ⬤ *Mon; 2 wks Jul, 2 wks Aug.* 🗂

ALESSANDRIA: *Il Grappolo*   €€€ | ● | ▓ | ▓ |
Via Casale 28, 15100. 📞 0131 25 32 17. 🌐 www.ristoranteilgrappolo.it
Piedmontese cuisine with a few borrowed touches. Try the *agnolotti* (stuffed pasta) *all'Alessandrina*. ⬤ *Mon eve, Tue; 1 wk Jan, 2 wks Aug.* 🗂 ♿

AOSTA: *Grotta Azzurra*   €€ | | ▓ | ▓ |
Via Croix de Ville 97, 11100. 📞 0165 26 24 74.
This good pizzeria also serves excellent fish, pasta and *risotto*. Try the seafood salad, *risotto* or fish soup as a first course. ⬤ *Wed; Jul.* 🗂

AOSTA: *Vecchia Aosta*   €€ | ● | ▓ | ▓ |
Piazza Porta Pretoria 4c, 11100. 📞 0165 36 11 86.
Set into the old Roman wall, the Vecchia Aosta offers typical regional dishes such as vegetable terrines and *ravioli*. ⬤ *Wed; 2 wks Feb, 2 wks Oct.* 🗂

AOSTA: *Trattoria degli Artisti*   €€€ | | | | ▓ |
Via Maillet 5/78, 11100. 📞 0165 409 60.
A small, cosy restaurant set in one of Aosta's oldest buildings. Specialities include *polenta* with game or *au gratin*, and vegetable mousse. Good pear tart. ⬤ *Sun, Mon; Jun.* 🗂

ASTI: *Gener Neuv*   €€€€€ | ● | ▓ | ▓ |
Lungotanaro 4, 14100. 📞 0141 55 72 70. 🌐 www.generneuv.it
This peacefully rustic restaurant about 1 km (half a mile) from the town centre serves carefully prepared local dishes, and the family who runs it offers attentive service. ⬤ *Sun eve & Mon (Jan–Jul); Aug.* 🗂

BRA: *Osteria Boccondivino*　　　€€
Via Mendicità Istruita 14, 12042. [0172 42 56 74.
An informal restaurant with Piedmontese cuisine. Try stuffed veal, rabbit
in white wine sauce and *panna cotta* (crème brûlée). ● Sun, Mon.

BREUIL-CERVINIA: *Les Neiges d'Antan*　　　€€€€
Frazione Cret de Perrères 10, 11021. [0166 94 87 75. W www.lesneigesdantan.it
Elegantly rustic, this restaurant has beautiful mountain views and serves
carefully prepared rich mountain fare. ● May–Jun, Oct–Nov.

CANNOBIO: *Del Lago*　　　€€€€€
Via Nazionale 2, Località Carmine Inferiore 28822. [0323 705 95. W www.enotecalago.com
A lovely lakeside restaurant where the imaginative cuisine combines
sometimes surprising flavours to great effect. ● Tue, Wed lunch; Nov–Feb.

CASALE MONFERRATO: *La Torre*　　　€€€€
Via Garoglio 3, 15033. [0142 702 95. W www.ristorante-latorre.it
An elegant restaurant with panoramic views near the town centre. The creative cuisine
uses seasonal ingredients. ● Tue eve, Wed; 1 wk Jan, 3 wks Aug, 1 wk Dec.

COGNE: *Lou Ressignon*　　　€€
Rue Mines de Cogne 22, 11012. [0165 740 34.
A 17th-century inn with an open fireplace. Rustic cuisine with salamis,
polenta and grilled meats. ● Mon eve, Tue; 2 wks Jun, 2 wks Sep, Nov.

COSTIGLIOLE D'ASTI: *Collavini*　　　€€€
Strada Traniera 24, 14055. [0141 96 64 40. W www.ristorantecollavini.it
Good service and carefully prepared simple food combine to make the Collavini
popular. Five rooms are available to rent. ● Tue pm, Wed; 3 wks Jan, 3 wks Aug.

COURMAYEUR: *Pierre Alexis 1877*　　　€€€
Via Marconi 54, 11013. [0165 84 35 17.
A converted barn in the historic centre with dishes based on local traditions; beef in
four sauces and *ravioli di cacciagione* (game). ● Mon (spring & autumn); May.

CUNEO: *Osteria della Chiocciola*　　　€€
Via Fossano 1, 12100. [0171 662 77.
An excellent restaurant where seasonal fare is combined with the appropriate
wines. Winter has full-bodied reds. ● Sun; 1 wk Jan, 1 wk Aug.

DOMODOSSOLA: *Piemonte da Sciolla*　　　€€
Piazza della Convenzione 4, 28845. [0324 24 26 33.
Immaculately prepared regional specialities such as *gnocchi* with rye and
chestnuts, set in a historic building. ● Wed; 2 wks Jan, 2 wks Aug, 1 wk Sep.

FEISOGLIO: *Piemonte da Renato*　　　€€
Via Firenze 19, 12050. [0173 83 11 16.
A family atmosphere at this trattoria serving seasonal specialities, especially
dishes with white and black truffles. Booking is advisable. ● Dec–Easter.

IVREA: *La Trattoria il Boccon di Vino*　　　€€
Via Aosta 47, 10015. [0125 489 98.
A bright restaurant where the food is simple and based on regional cuisine.
Try the smoked fish in vegetable sauce. ● Thu; 2 wks Aug.

NOVARA: *La Famiglia*　　　€€€€
Via Solaroli 10, 28100. [0321 39 95 29. W www.panciolihotels.it
A small, peaceful restaurant, its walls painted with frescoes of
Lake Maggiore. The cuisine specializes in fresh fish and *risottos*.

NOVARA: *Osteria del Laghetto*　　　€€€€€
Case Sparse 11, Località Veveri, 28100. [0321 62 15 79.
Set in a park, the flower-filled Laghetto specializes in dishes using fresh fish, truffles
and mushrooms. Booking is advisable. ● Sat lunch, Sun; 1 wk Aug, Dec–Jan.

ORTA SAN GIULIO: *Villa Crespi*　　　€€€€€
Via Generale Fava 18, 28016. [0322 91 19 02.
The decor is based on the Arabian Nights. The imaginative cuisine uses seasonal
truffles and *foie gras* (liver pâté). ● Tue (Sep–Jun); Jan, 2 wks Feb.

SAINT VINCENT: *Nuovo Batezar*　　　€€€€€
Via Marconi 1, 11027. [0166 51 31 64.
An excellent restaurant serving classic cuisine with special touches (*ravioli* with
lobster sauce, pheasant in *polenta* crust). ● Wed, Mon–Fri lunch; 3 wks Jun, 2 wks Nov.

For key to symbols see back flap

	FIXED-PRICE MENU	GOOD WINE LIST	FORMAL DRESS	OUTDOOR TABLES

Average prices for a three-course meal for one, including a half-bottle of house wine, tax and service:
€ under €18
€€ €18–€30
€€€ €30–€40
€€€€ €40–€52
€€€€€ over €52.

FIXED-PRICE MENU
A fixed-price menu on offer, usually with three courses.

GOOD WINE LIST
Denotes a wide range of good quality wines.

FORMAL DRESS
Some restaurants require men to wear a jacket and tie.

OUTDOOR TABLES
Tables for eating outdoors, often with a good view.

CREDIT CARDS
The symbol shows that major credit cards are accepted.

SAN SECONDO DI PINEROLO: *La Ciau* €€€
Via Castello di Miradolo 2, 10060. 📞 0121 50 06 11.
Care and innovation go into the preparation of regional dishes. Try the *agnolotti* (pasta) stuffed with meat and the home-baked bread. ● *Wed; Jan.* ▨
FIXED-PRICE MENU ● · GOOD WINE LIST ▦ · OUTDOOR TABLES ▦

SESTRIERE: *Braciere del Possetto* €€€
Piazza Agnélli 2, 10058. 📞 0122 761 29.
This is one of the best places to taste Piedmontese dishes, exquisitely prepared, as well as a range of Italian and French cheeses. ● *Wed; May, Oct.* ▨
GOOD WINE LIST ▦

SORISO: *Al Sorriso* €€€€€
Via Roma 18, 28016. 📞 0322 98 32 28. W www.alsorriso.com
One of the most acclaimed restaurants in Italy. The cuisine makes use of what's in season locally and draws on a wide range of traditions from Italy and abroad. ● *Mon, Tue; 2 wks Jan, 3 wks Aug.* ▨ ▤
FIXED-PRICE MENU ● · GOOD WINE LIST ▦ · FORMAL DRESS ●

STRESA: *La Piemontese* €€€€
Via Mazzini 25, 28049. 📞 0323 302 35.
An elegant but unstuffy restaurant with impeccable service. The cuisine is creative, and prices are very fair. ● *Mon; Sun eve (Oct–Mar); Dec–Jan.*
FIXED-PRICE MENU ● · GOOD WINE LIST ▦ · OUTDOOR TABLES ▦

TURIN: *Birilli* €€€
Strada Val San Martino 6, 10131. 📞 011 819 05 67. W www.birilli.com
A friendly, cheerful restaurant opened in 1991 as part of a family-run chain whose first branch opened in Los Angeles in 1929. Simple dishes include meats and the house pasta *Birilli* (with tomato and bacon). ● *Sun (winter).* ▨
FIXED-PRICE MENU ● · OUTDOOR TABLES ▦

TURIN: *Porto di Savona* €€€
Piazza Vittorio Veneto 2, 10100. 📞 011 817 35 00. W www.portodisavona.com
A friendly restaurant set in an 18th-century building in central Turin. The regional cuisine includes such dishes as *gnocchi* with gorgonzola and meats braised in Barolo wine. ● *Mon, Tue lunch; 2 wks Jan, 2 wks Aug.* ▨ ▤
GOOD WINE LIST ▦ · OUTDOOR TABLES ▦

TURIN: *Saletta* €€€
Via Belfiore 37, 10126. 📞 011 668 78 67.
A warm, friendly atmosphere in central Turin. House specialities include meat braised in Barolo wine, and a fluffy *zabaglione*. ● *Sun; Aug.* ▨ ▤
GOOD WINE LIST ▦

TURIN: *Spada Reale* €€€
Via Principe Amedeo 53, 10123. 📞 011 817 13 63.
This newly restored restaurant provides a rustic setting in which to try regional dishes. Family-run, it is lively and informal, serving good-value food. ● *Sun, Sat lunch; Aug.* ▨
FIXED-PRICE MENU ● · GOOD WINE LIST ▦

TURIN: *Neuv Caval 'd Brôns* €€€€
Piazza San Carlo 151, 10123. 📞 011 562 74 83. W www.newcaval.com
An elegant, spacious restaurant offering excellent food from a range of cuisine including vegetarian dishes. Specialities include the renowned mint and chocolate pudding *Santa Vittoria*. ● *Sat lunch, Sun; Aug.* ▨ ◩ ▤
FIXED-PRICE MENU ● · GOOD WINE LIST ▦ · FORMAL DRESS ●

VERBANIA PALLANZA: *Milano* €€€€€
Corso Zanitello 2, 28048. 📞 0323 55 68 16.
Close to the town centre, the Milano has lake views and a romantic interior. Dishes include *tagliolini* with lake fish. ● *Mon dinner, Tue; mid-Nov–Feb; 1 wk Jun.* ▨
GOOD WINE LIST ▦ · OUTDOOR TABLES ▦

VERCELLI: *Il Paiolo* €€€
Viale Garibaldi 72, 13100. 📞 0161 25 05 77.
A country trattoria in the historic centre, it specializes in local cuisine. The Vercellese *risotto* is particularly recommended. ● *Thu; mid-Jul–mid-Aug.* ▨ ▤
GOOD WINE LIST ▦

VERCELLI: *Il Giardinetto* €€€€
Via Sereno 3, 13100. 📞 0161 25 72 30.
The restaurant of an elegant villa hotel, it specializes in cuisine with truffles and mushrooms. Try the *foie gras* with apple and wine sauce. ● *Mon; 3 wks Aug.* ▨ ▤
GOOD WINE LIST ▦ · OUTDOOR TABLES ▦

VILLARFOCCHIARDO: *La Giaconera* €€€€
Via Antica di Francia 1, 10050. 011 964 50 00.
This elegant staging inn makes good use of seasonal ingredients such as truffles, game and choice vegetables. *Tue; 2 wks Aug.*

LIGURIA

CAMOGLI: *La Cucina di Nonna Nina* €€€
Via Molfino 126, San Rocco di Camogli 16032. 0185 77 38 35.
"If you're in a hurry" says the menu, "relax; our food is prepared according to traditional methods." The atmosphere is friendly and there are wonderful views of the Golfo Paradiso. *Wed; 2 wks Jan, 3 wks Nov.*

CAMOGLI: *Rosa* €€€€
Largo Casabona 11, 16032. 0185 77 34 11.
Set in a pretty villa on the Golfo Paradiso, the menu offers exquisitely prepared fish such as pasta with fresh anchovies. *Tue; mid-Jan–mid-Feb, 2 wks Nov.*

CERVO: *Giorgio* €€€€€
Via Volta 19, 18010. 0183 40 01 75.
Booking is absolutely essential at this popular spot for regional cuisine with a different twist. The dishes are mainly fresh fish and seafood; the *branzino* (sea bass) with rosemary and beans is exceptional. *Tue; last 2 wks Jan, Nov.*

DOLCEACQUA: *Il Castello Ex Gastone* €€€
Piazza Garibaldi 2, 18035. 0184 20 65 77.
Home-made pasta and regional meat dishes are two of the attractions at this elegant restaurant in the historic centre. *Mon, Tue; 3 wks Nov.*

GENOA: *Da Genio* €€
Salita San Leonardo 61r, 16128. 010 58 84 63.
Popular with locals, this restaurant has an animated atmosphere. The food is delicious, and includes grilled swordfish and anchovies stuffed with capers. *Sun; Aug.*

GENOA: *Do' Colla* €€
Via alla Chiesa di Murta 10, Località Bolzaneto, 16162. 010 740 85 79.
It is worth heading the few kilometres out of Genoa to taste the exquisite home-style Ligurian cooking of this simple *trattoria*. *Sun eve, Mon; 2 wks Jan, Aug.*

LEVANTO: *Tumelin* €€€€
Via Grillo 32, 19015. 0187 80 83 79.
The restaurant is 100m from the sea and the menu includes a selection of wonderful seafood appetisers. Friendly service. *Thu; Jan.*

MANAROLA: *Marina Piccola* €€€
Via Lo Scalo 16, 19010. 0187 92 01 03.
There are wonderful sea views from this restaurant whose menu of regional specialities includes seafood *antipasti*, pesto and grilled fish. *Tue; Nov.*

NERVI: *Astor* €€€
Viale delle Palme 16–18, 16167. 010 32 90 11. www.astorhotel.it
This hotel restaurant offers a good selection of dishes including pesto, fish and the local pasta dish *(pansotti)* with wild herbs and nut sauce.

PORTOFINO: *Puny* €€€€€
Piazza Martiri Olivetta 5, 16034. 0185 26 90 37.
A spectacular view of the bay of Portofino accompanies the well-prepared regional dishes and crisp Ligurian wines. *Thu; Jan, Feb, 2 wks Dec.*

PORTOVENERE: *Le Bocche* €€€€€
Calata Doria 102, 19025. 0187 79 06 22.
Reinterpreted regional recipes form the basis of the exclusively fish menu. Set on the tip of the Portovenere peninsula with views over the sea. *Tue; Nov–Dec.*

RAPALLO: *Roccabruna* €€€
Via Sotto la Croce 6, Località Savagna 16035. 0185 26 14 00.
Set on a pretty terrace away from the crowds on the seafront, this restaurant simply serves the menu of the day, from the *antipasti* to the wines. *Mon; Jan.*

SAN REMO: *Paolo e Barbara* €€€€€
Via Roma 47, 18038. 0184 53 16 53. www.paolobarbara.it
In one of the most renowned restaurants in Liguria, the cuisine is based on local and Mediterranean specialities, especially fish and seafood.
Wed, Thu; last week Jun–first week Jul, 2 wks Dec.

| | FIXED PRICE MENU | GOOD WINE LIST | FORMAL DRESS | OUTDOOR TABLES |

Average prices for a three-course meal for one, including a half-bottle of house wine, tax and service:
€ under €18
€€ €18–€30
€€€ €30–€40
€€€€ €40–€52
€€€€€ over €52.

FIXED-PRICE MENU
A fixed-price menu on offer, usually with three courses.
GOOD WINE LIST
Denotes a wide range of good quality wines.
FORMAL DRESS
Some restaurants require men to wear a jacket and tie.
OUTDOOR TABLES
Tables for eating outdoors, often with a good view.
CREDIT CARDS
The symbol shows that major credit cards are accepted.

Restaurant		FIXED PRICE MENU	GOOD WINE LIST	FORMAL DRESS	OUTDOOR TABLES
VERNAZZA: *Gambero Rosso* Piazza Marconi 7, 19018. 0187 81 22 65. Rice with lemon and prawns, *gamberoni in pigiama* (deep-fried prawns) and *pansotti (see p174)* with cocoa and thyme are only some of the imaginatively interpreted Ligurian dishes in this newly refurbished restaurant. Mon; Dec–Feb.	€€€	●			■

EMILIA-ROMAGNA

Restaurant		FIXED PRICE MENU	GOOD WINE LIST	FORMAL DRESS	OUTDOOR TABLES
BOLOGNA: *Antica Trattoria Spiga* Via Broccaindosso 21a, 40125. 051 23 00 63. A homely, authentic trattoria, with immaculately prepared traditional cuisine. Specialities include lasagne, *tortellini* and *gnocchi*. Mon eve, Sun; Aug.	€€	●			
BOLOGNA: *Antica Trattoria del Cacciatore* Via Caduti di Casteldebole 25, 40132. 051 56 42 03. This country inn in a park near the airport offers local and international dishes. It is also known for game. Sun eve, Mon; 1 wk Jan, 2 wks Aug.	€€€€		■		
BOLOGNA: *Pappagallo* Piazza Mercanzia 3c, 40125. 051 23 28 07. Housed in a 14th-century palazzo in the historic centre, this elegant restaurant serves Bolognese dishes, *tortellini* and lasagna. Sun; Aug.	€€€€€		■		
CASTELL'ARQUATO: *Da Faccini* Località Sant' Antonio 10, 29014. 0523 89 63 40. Pasta and game are the highlights. Try *gnocchi* with carrots, duck and truffle *ravioli* and rabbit with mustard. Wed; 1 wk Jul, 1 wk Jan.	€€€		■		■
CASTELL'ARQUATO: *Maps* Piazza Europa 3, 29014. 0523 80 44 11. In a restructured medieval mill in the historic centre, fish is the mainstay of a menu that changes according to the market. Tue; 1 wk Jan, 2 wks Aug, 1 wk Dec.	€€€€		■		■
FAENZA: *Le Volte* Corso Mazzini 54, 48018. 0546 66 16 00. Housed in an atmospheric building in the historic centre. The food is delicious with a strong Pugliese influence. Try green *gnocchi* with tomato and basil, and chicken with olives. Sun; 2 wks Jul, 2 wks Aug.	€€	●	■		■
FERRARA: *Quel Fantastico Giovedì* Via Castelnuovo 9, 44100. 0532 76 05 70. A bright restaurant whose varied and creative menu includes Japanese-style sushi of salmon. Book in advance. Wed; last week Jan, last week Jul–15 Aug.	€€	●	■		
FERRARA: *La Sgarbata* Via Sgarbata 84, 44100. 0532 71 21 10. A country trattoria on the outskirts of Ferrara which serves speciality fish dishes as well as rich and tasty pizzas. Mon, Tue.	€€€	●			■
FIDENZA: *Del Duomo* Via Micheli 27, 43036. 0524 52 42 68. Near the cathedral, the menu includes home-made *spaghetti* with mushrooms and tripe *alla parmigiana*. Mon; 1 wk Jul, 3 wks Aug.	€€		■		
GORO: *Ferrari* Via Antonio Brugnoli 240–4, 44020. 0533 99 64 48. Next to the fish market, the menu changes every day to make use of the best of the day's catch; the menu is almost entirely fish, but also includes pizza. Wed.	€€€	●	■		■
MODENA: *Al Boschetto da Loris* Via Due Canali Nord 198, 41100. 059 25 17 59. A rustic restaurant set in a vast park. Specialities include *tortellini* in chicken broth, *ragù* sauce and spit-roasted meats. Wed; 2 wks Aug.	€€	●	■		■

MODENA: *Fini* €€€€€
Piazzetta San Francesco, 41100. 059 22 33 14.
A mainstay of local cuisine with exquisite dishes: *tortellini*, lasagna di *maccheroni* and delicious desserts. Mon, Tue; late Jul–late Aug, last week Dec.

PARMA: *Aldo* €€
Piazzale Inzani 15, 43100. 0521 20 60 01.
A trattoria serving classics with interesting touches: smoked roast beef, and guinea fowl with orange sauce. Sun eve, Mon; mid-Jul–mid-Aug.

PARMA: *Le Viole* €€
Strada Nuova 60a, Località Castelnuovo Golese, 43031. 0521 60 10 00.
A delightful place to eat offering a successful mix of modern ideas and tradition. Try the *fagottini* (parcels) of turkey with vegetables, and the home-made desserts.
Wed, Thu lunch; 2 wks Jan, 1 wk Feb, 1 wk Aug.

PIACENZA: *Don Carlos* €€€
Strada Aguzzafame 85, 29100. 0523 49 98 00.
The cuisine in this elegant fish restaurant uses fresh seasonal ingredients. Try the seafood and bean salad, and pickled salmon. lunch, Mon.

PIACENZA: *Antica Osteria del Teatro* €€€€€
Via Verdi 16, 29100. 0523 32 37 77.
An excellent wine list accompanies a menu of imaginative dishes prepared with immense flair from the best of local produce. Set in a 15th-century palazzo. Sun, Mon; Aug.

RAVENNA: *Villa Antica* €
Via Faentina 136, 48100. 0544 50 05 22.
Set in a 19th-century villa, the menu here changes seasonally. Mainstays include home-made pastas, grilled or roasted meats and fish. Game only in season. Tue.

RIMINI: *Europa* €€€€
Via Roma 51, 47037. 0541 287 61.
Fish forms the basis of the menu here, with dishes including salad of warm fish with *radicchio* and seafood *spaghetti*. Sun; 1 wk Aug.

RIMINI: *Acero Rosso* €€€€€
Viale Tiberio 11, 47037. 0541 535 77.
Tasteful decor and exquisite food. The menu includes *carpaccio di scampi* with basil sauce, and *tagliolini* with zucchini flowers and shrimp.
lunch, Sun eve, Mon; 1 wk Aug.

FLORENCE

FLORENCE: *Palle D'Oro* €
Via Sant'Antonino 43r, 50123. Map 1 C5 (5 C1). 055 28 83 83.
Sparse, simple, spotlessly clean trattoria. The food is basic but cooked well and there is a very good take-away sandwich bar at the front. Sun; Aug.

FLORENCE: *Trattoria Mario* €
Via Rosina 2r, 50123. Map 1 C4. 055 21 85 50.
A popular lunchtime trattoria. Specials change daily; on Thursday there is *gnocchi* and on Friday, fish. eves; Sun; Aug.

FLORENCE: *Acquacotta* €€
Via de' Pilastri 51r, 50124. Map 2 E5. 055 24 29 07.
A cheap, three-roomed restaurant named after a Florentine vegetable soup. Grilled meats and other Tuscan specialities are also featured. Tue pm, Wed; Aug.

FLORENCE: *Cafaggi* €€
Via Guelfa 35r, 50123. Map 1 C4. 055 29 49 89.
This classic Tuscan trattoria has been in business for 80 years. It uses oil and wines from the family farm. *Crostini* (toasts), *zuppa di certosina* and *involtini* (roulade) are particularly good dishes on the varied menu. Sun; 2 wks Jul, 2 wks Aug.

FLORENCE: *Da Pennello* €€
Via Dante Alighieri 4r, 50100. Map 4 D1. 055 29 48 48.
Book well ahead or risk a long wait for a table. This popular restaurant is famous for its extensive *antipasti*, a meal in themselves. Sun, Mon; Aug; 1 wk Dec.

FLORENCE: *Enoteca Fuori Porta* €€
Via Monte alle Croci 10r, 50122. Map 4 3E. 055 234 2483.
This wine bar is popular with locals and visitors alike for its excellent *crostoni* with assorted toppings and of course, the wide-ranging wine list. Sun.

Average prices for a three-course meal for one, including a half-bottle of house wine, tax and service: € under €18 €€ €18–€30 €€€ €30–€40 €€€€ €40–€52 €€€€€ over €52.	**FIXED-PRICE MENU** A fixed-price menu on offer, usually with three courses. **GOOD WINE LIST** Denotes a wide range of good quality wines. **FORMAL DRESS** Some restaurants require men to wear a jacket and tie. **OUTDOOR TABLES** Tables for eating outdoors, often with a good view. **CREDIT CARDS** The symbol shows that major credit cards are accepted.		

	FIXED PRICE MENU	GOOD WINE LIST	FORMAL DRESS	OUTDOOR TABLES
FLORENCE: *I' Francescano* €€ Largo Bargellini 16, 50120. **Map** 4 E1. ⟨ 055 24 16 05. A smartly fitted restaurant of wood, marble and *objets d'art*. The menu is based on seasonal ingredients and changes weekly. ● *Tue (Oct–Apr).* ▣ ▤ ♿		▦		
FLORENCE: *Le Mossacce* €€ Via del Pronconsolo 55r, 50122. **Map** 2 D5 (6 E2). ⟨ 055 29 43 61. Do not be put off by the multilingual menus, the paper tablecloths and the chaos; the 100-year-old Mossacce serves robust Tuscan food. ● *Sat, Sun.* ▣	●			
FLORENCE: *San Zanobi* €€ Via San Zanobi 33r, 50100. **Map** 1 C4. ⟨ 055 47 52 86. Delicate, inventive food served in a sedate, refined dining room. The dishes, based on a Florentine theme, are light and well presented. ● *Sun.* ▣ ▤ ♿				
FLORENCE: *Il Santo Bevitore* €€ Via di Santo Spirito 64/r. **Map** 3 B1. ⟨ 055 21 12 64. This friendly *enoteca* offers delicately flavoured, innovative dishes made with high-quality traditional ingredients. ● *Sun.* ▣ ▤ ⚡ ♿		▦		
FLORENCE: *Trattoria Angiolino* €€ Via di Santo Spirito 36r, 50125. **Map** 3 B1. ⟨ 055 239 89 76. An attractive restaurant with a typically Florentine, bustling atmosphere. The food is traditional Tuscan style, from vegetable soups to grilled meats. In winter an iron stove in the middle of the restaurant is lit. ● *Mon (Nov–Mar).* ▣		▦		
FLORENCE: *Trattoria Zà Zà* €€ Piazza del Mercato Centrale 26r, 50123. **Map** 1 C4. ⟨ 055 21 54 11. A canteen-like restaurant that is always packed. The food is Tuscan. Excellent soups include *ribollita* (vegetables), and *passata di fagioli* (bean purée). ● *Sun.* ▣	●			▦
FLORENCE: *Buca dell'Orafo* €€€ Volta de' Girolami 28r, 50122. **Map** 6 D4. ⟨ 055 21 36 19. A friendly hole-in-the-wall that is a long-time favourite with Florentines. The homely cooking is based on home-made pasta, and daily specials include the typically Tuscan *ribollita* (vegetable soup), pasta and *fagioli* (beans). ● *Sun, Mon lunch; Aug.* ▤				
FLORENCE: *Da Ganino* €€€ Piazza dei Cimatori 4r, 50122. **Map** 6 D3. ⟨ 055 21 41 25. This small, friendly restaurant, popular with locals, offers all the basics of local fare, including *ravioli* with butter and sage, and *fritto di carne* (fried meats) ● *Sun.* ▣ ▤		▦		▦
FLORENCE: *Dino* €€€ Via Ghibellina 51r, 50122. **Map** 4 D1 (6 E3). ⟨ 055 24 14 52. This well-regarded restaurant in a beautiful 14th-century palazzo has one of the best wine lists in Florence and a menu of local dishes. ● *Sun eve, Mon.* ▣ ▤		▦		
FLORENCE: *Paoli* €€€ Via dei Tavolini 12r, 50100. **Map** 6 D3 (4 D1). ⟨ 055 21 62 15. A spectacular setting: the dining room is a vaulted hall smothered in medieval frescoes. The restaurant specializes in typically Tuscan dishes. ● *Tue; Aug.* ▣ ▤	●	▦		
FLORENCE: *Alle Murate* €€€€ Via Ghibellina 52r, 50122. **Map** 4 E1. ⟨ 055 24 06 18. Popular with locals, this refined restaurant offers a great range of creative, Tuscan dishes. The food combines Italian staples with more far-flung Mediterranean cuisines, and there are light and interesting desserts. ● *lunch, Mon; 2 wks Dec.* ▣ ▤	●	▦		
FLORENCE: *Buca Mario* €€€€ Piazza degli Ottaviani 16r, 50100. **Map** 1 B5. ⟨ 055 21 41 79. A crowded restaurant where it is normal to book or queue for a table. Enjoy the home-made pasta and grilled meats at good prices. ● *Wed, Thu lunch; Aug.* ▣ ▤ ♿		▦		

FLORENCE: *LOBS* €€€€
Via Faenza 75r, 50100. **Map** 1 C4. 055 21 24 78.
A fish restaurant offering pasta dishes for lunch (*gnocchi* with shrimp, *spaghetti* with clams) and assorted platters at dinner. Oysters and shellfish are a speciality.

FLORENCE: *Sabatini* €€€€
Via Panzani 9a, 50123. **Map** 1 C5 (5 C1). 055 28 28 02.
Once Florence's best restaurant, the cuisine (Italian and international) is sometimes excellent and the ambience and service are good. *Mon.*

FLORENCE: *La Taverna del Bronzino* €€€€
Via delle Ruote 27r, 50129. **Map** 2 D3. 055 49 52 20.
Named after the Florentine painter who had connections with the 15th-century palazzo which houses this restaurant. Highest-quality cooking. *Sun; Aug.*

FLORENCE: *Cibreo* €€€€€
Via Andrea del Verrocchio 8r, 50122. **Map** 4 E1. 055 234 11 00.
Superbly prepared Tuscan food in an informal atmosphere. There is no pasta, but specialities include tripe and kidneys. For the squeamish there are many non-offal alternatives such as duck stuffed with sultanas. *Sun, Mon; 1 wk Jan, Aug.*

FLORENCE: *Enoteca Pinchiorri* €€€€€
Via Ghibellina 87, 50122. **Map** 1 A4 (5 A1). 055 24 27 77.
Often described as Italy's best restaurant with the finest wine cellar in Europe, the Pinchiorri is on the ground floor of a 15th-century palazzo. The Tuscan- and French-inspired cuisine includes a wonderful mix of dishes. *Sun, Mon, Wed lunch; Aug.*

TUSCANY

AREZZO: *Buca di San Francesco* €€€
Via San Francesco 1, 52100. 0575 232 71.
The medieval atmosphere and position alongside the church of Piero della Francesca's fresco cycle make this an obvious choice. *Mon eve, Tue.*

ARTIMINO: *Da Delfina* €€€€
Via della Chiesa, 50041. 055 871 80 74.
A lovely restaurant outside a walled medieval village. Game is a speciality, as is pork with fennel and black Tuscan cabbage. *Sun eve, Mon.*

CAPALBIO: *Da Maria* €€€
Piazza Giordano, 58011. 0564 89 60 14.
Holidaying politicians from Rome sit down with locals to enjoy soundly cooked Maremma specialities like wild boar and pasta with truffles. *Tue (Oct–Apr).*

CASTELNUOVO BERARDENGA: *La Bottega del Trenta* €€€€€
Via Santa Caterina 2, Villa a Sesta 53019. 0577 35 92 26.
A tasteful restaurant serving adventurous cooking including duck breast with wild fennel and delicious desserts. *Tue, Wed, Mon–Sat lunch; 2 wks Jan, 2 wks Feb.*

COLLE DI VAL D'ELSA: *L'Antica Trattoria* €€€€
Piazza Arnolfo 23, 53034. 0577 92 37 47.
A homely, family-run restaurant dedicated to traditional regional cuisine. The setting is medieval and the service lively and attentive. *Tue; 1 wk Jan, 1 wk Dec.*

CORTONA: *Locanda nel Loggiato* €€
Piazza Pescheria 3, 54044. 0575 63 05 75.
Set in a quaint medieval loggia, the atmosphere is cool and sedate and the home-made *ravioli* stuffed with fondue, delicious. *Wed (Oct–May); Nov–Dec.*

ELBA: *Publius* €€€€
Piazza XX Settembre, Poggio di Marciana 57030. 0565 992 08.
A pleasant trattoria with one of the best wine cellars on Elba. In addition to fish, you can eat wild mushrooms, game and wild boar. *Nov–Mar.*

GAIOLE IN CHIANTI: *Badia a Coltibuono* €€€
Badia a Coltibuono, 53013. 0577 74 94 24.
Set in front of an 11th-century abbey, at the heart of a vineyard whose oils and wines are used in the restaurant. The menu includes spit-roasted meats and delicious desserts. Tours of the estate are on offer for wine tasters. *Mon; Jan, Feb.*

LIVORNO: *La Chiave* €€€
Scali delle Cantine 52, 57100. 0586 88 86 09.
Refined and elegant dining from a menu that chef and owner Carla Novelli changes every fortnight. *lunch, Wed; Aug.*

For key to symbols see back flap

Average prices for a three-course meal for one, including a half-bottle of house wine, tax and service: © under €18 ©© €18–€30 ©©© €30–€40 ©©©© €40–€52 ©©©©© over €52.	**FIXED-PRICE MENU** A fixed-price menu on offer, usually with three courses. **GOOD WINE LIST** Denotes a wide range of good quality wines. **FORMAL DRESS** Some restaurants require men to wear a jacket and tie. **OUTDOOR TABLES** Tables for eating outdoors, often with a good view. **CREDIT CARDS** The symbol shows that major credit cards are accepted.	FIXED PRICE MENU	GOOD WINE LIST	FORMAL DRESS	OUTDOOR TABLES

LUCCA: *Buca di Sant'Antonio* €€€
Via della Cervia 3, 55100. 0583 558 81.
This is Lucca's most famous restaurant of traditional rustic cooking. It serves a range of local dishes, such as *fettuccine sul piccione* (pasta and pigeon). ● *Sun eve, Mon; Jul.*

MASSA MARITTIMA: *Bracali* €€€€€
Frazione Ghirlanda 2, 58024. 0566 90 23 18.
Mouth-watering Maremma cooking in a family restaurant; thinly sliced wild boar, pigeon with honey and guinea fowl with white grapes. ● *Mon, Tue; Jan, Nov.*

MONTALCINO: *Taverna dei Barbi* €€€
Località Podernovi, 53024. 0577 84 12 00.
Superb country cooking, served with Brunello wines, in a renowned restaurant that also has wonderful views over the surrounding hills. ● *Tue eve, Wed; Jan.*

MONTECATINI TERME: *Gourmet* €€€€€
Via Amendola 6, 51016. 0572 77 10 12.
This is an elegant restaurant in a wonderful 19th-century building. The atmosphere is relaxing, the fish dishes are sublime. ● *Tue; 2 wks Jan, 3 wks Aug.*

MONTEPULCIANO: *Il Cantuccio* €€€
Via delle Cantine 1/2, 53045. 0578 75 78 70.
Located in a 13th-century palace, Il Cantuccio combines great atmosphere and traditional food. The speciality is *pici alla nana* (pasta with a duck sauce). ● *Mon.*

MONTERIGGIONI: *Il Pozzo* €€€
Piazza Roma 2, 53035. 0577 30 41 27.
A stone-walled restaurant in the charming medieval village of Monteriggioni. The Sienese food is simple and enthusiastically prepared, and the home-made desserts are well-known in the surrounding region. ● *Sun eve, Mon; 3 wks Jan, 1 wk Feb.*

ORBETELLO: *Osteria del Lupacante* €€€
Corso Italia 103, 58015. 0564 86 76 18.
The cooking concentrates on fish and seafood specialities with some touches of adventure; look out for mussels in Marsala sauce, grilled prawns and courgette flowers with squid. ● *Tue (Oct–May).*

PESCIA: *Cecco* €€€
Via Francesca Forti 96, 51017. 0572 47 79 55.
A friendly local restaurant where the food is often outstanding. Try the local Pescia asparagus, and *cioncia* (the house main course). ● *Mon; Jan, Jul.*

PIENZA: *Da Falco* €€€
Piazza Dante Alighieri 3, 53026. 0578 74 85 51.
A friendly local restaurant with excellent *antipasti* and a magnificent choice of *primi* and *secondi* from a menu of local specialities. ● *Fri.*

PISA: *Al Ristoro dei Vecchi Macelli* €€€€
Via Volturno 49, 56126. 050 204 24.
Innovative dishes in a pleasant, intimate restaurant that serves light Tuscan food with an adventurous twist. Fish, seafood and game specialities are delicately prepared and the desserts are a delight. ● *Wed, Sun lunch; 2 wks Aug.*

PISTOIA: *La Bottegaia* €€
Via del Lastrone 4. 0573 36 56 02.
Close to Piazza del Duomo, this restaurant offers locally produced cold meats and traditional dishes such as *pappa al pomodoro* and stewed veal. ● *Mon; Aug.*

POPPI: *Il Cedro* €€€
Via di Camaldoli 20, Località Moggiona, 52010. 0575 55 60 80.
Venison, wild boar and guinea fowl in Marsala wine are among some of the excellent specialities of Il Cedro. This good-value restaurant stands in a wonderful setting that overlooks forests and mountains. Book ahead. ● *Mon (winter).*

Restaurant	FIXED PRICE MENU	GOOD WINE LIST	FORMAL DRESS	OUTDOOR TABLES
Lucca: Buca di Sant'Antonio				
Massa Marittima: Bracali	●			
Montalcino: Taverna dei Barbi		■		■
Montecatini Terme: Gourmet		■	●	
Montepulciano: Il Cantuccio		■		
Monteriggioni: Il Pozzo		■		
Orbetello: Osteria del Lupacante	●	■		■
Pescia: Cecco		■		■
Pienza: Da Falco	●	■		
Pisa: Al Ristoro dei Vecchi Macelli	●	■		
Pistoia: La Bottegaia		■		■
Poppi: Il Cedro		■		

PORTO SANTO STEFANO: *La Bussola* €€
Viale Marconi, 58019. 0564 81 42 25.
The menu includes some excellent seafood pastas as well as simpler grilled
fish. From the terrace there are fine views of the sea. *Mon; Nov.*

PRATO: *Il Piraña* €€€€€
Via Valentini 110, 50047. 0574 257 46.
Rated as one of the best fish and seafood restaurants in Tuscany; do not be put off
by its setting or over-precious modern interior. *Sat lunch, Sun; Aug.*

SAN GIMIGNANO: *Le Terrazze* €€€€
Albergo la Cisterna, Piazza della Cisterna 24, 53037. 0577 94 03 28.
Set within the medieval walls, with views over the rolling hills of southern Tuscany,
one of the dining rooms forms part of a 13th-century palazzo. Good for regional
specialities with some novelties. *Tue, Wed lunch; Jan–Mar.*

SANSEPOLCRO: *Paola e Marco Mercati* €€€
Via Palmiro Togliatti 68, 52037. 0575 73 48 75.
A restaurant whose dishes include Tuscan black cabbage cooked with white truffles,
vegetable *ravioli*, roast pigeon and *gnocchi*. *lunch, Sun; 2 wks Jun, 2 wks Jul.*

SATURNIA: *Bacco e Cerere* €€€
Via Mazzini 4, 58050. & FAX 0564 60 12 35.
The wide range of *antipasti* available at this small, friendly restaurant is an excellent
introduction to Maremman cuisine. This is the only place in town that serves *zuppa di
ricotta* (soup of ricotta cheese). Over 800 wines. *lunch; Wed; 10 Jan–1 Mar.*

SATURNIA: *I Due Cippi da Michele* €€€
Piazza Vittorio Veneto 26a, 58050. 0564 60 10 74.
One of the region's most popular restaurants, it is a touchstone for Maremma cuisine
and its traditional offerings are good value. *Tue (Oct–Jun); 2 wks Jan, 1 wk Dec.*

SIENA: *Guidoriccio* €€
Via G Duprè 2, 53100. & FAX 0577 443 50.
Housed in Siena's 14th-century Palazzo Berlinguori, this quiet restaurant offers traditional
Sienese cuisine with a modern twist. Homemade pasta and seasonal dishes.

SIENA: *Al Marsili* €€€
Via del Castoro 3, 53100. 0577 471 54.
Set in an 11th-century building, Al Marsili, long regarded as one of the best
restaurants in Siena, offers good regional specialities. *Mon.*

SIENA: *Enzo* €€€
Via Camolia 49, 53100. 0577 28 12 77. FAX 0577 497 60.
Highly rated by both locals and tourists, Enzo blends traditional and innovative
cooking, using high-quality, mainly local ingredients. *Sun; 2 wks Jul.*

SIENA: *Osteria le Logge* €€€€
Via del Porrione 33, 53100. 0577 480 13.
Siena's prettiest restaurant, with dark wood and marble interior. Home-
produced oils and Montalcino wines accompany dishes that include
guinea fowl, duck and fennel, and rabbit with capers. *Sun; Jan.*

SOVANA: *Taverna Etrusca* €€
Piazza del Pretorio 16, 58010. 0564 61 61 83.
A small restaurant with a medieval dining area. The carefully produced cuisine
is Tuscan with sophisticated touches. *Mon; 3 wks Jan, 1 wk Feb.*

VIAREGGIO: *Romano* €€€€€
Via Mazzini 120, 55049. 0584 313 82.
This is one of Tuscany's best fish and seafood restaurants. The service is
courteous and friendly and the wines are well-priced. *Mon, Tue lunch; Jan.*

UMBRIA

AMELIA: *Anita* €
Via Roma 31, 05022. 0744 98 21 46.
This simple restaurant offers no-frills local food, such as *crostini* (toasted bread with
toppings), roasted meats, pasta with porcini mushrooms and wild boar. *Mon.*

ASSISI: *Medioevo* €€€
Via Arco dei Priori 4b, 06081. 075 81 30 68.
An elegant restaurant in old Assisi. Try the home-made pastas (with black truffles in
season). Meat is cooked to traditional recipes. Great desserts. *Wed, Sun eve; Jan.*

Average prices for a three-course meal for one, including a half-bottle of house wine, tax and service:
€ under €18
€€ €18–€30
€€€ €30–€40
€€€€ €40–€52
€€€€€ over €52.

FIXED-PRICE MENU
A fixed-price menu on offer, usually with three courses.
GOOD WINE LIST
Denotes a wide range of good quality wines.
FORMAL DRESS
Some restaurants require men to wear a jacket and tie.
OUTDOOR TABLES
Tables for eating outdoors, often with a good view.
CREDIT CARDS
The symbol shows that major credit cards are accepted.

	FIXED PRICE MENU	GOOD WINE LIST	FORMAL DRESS	OUTDOOR TABLES
ASSISI: *San Francesco* €€€		■		
BASCHI: *Vissani* €€€€€	●	■	●	
CAMPELLO SUL CLITUNNO: *Trattoria Pettino* €€		■		■
CITTÀ DI CASTELLO: *Amici Miei* €	●	■		
CITTÀ DI CASTELLO: *Il Bersaglio* €€€	●	■		■
FOLIGNO: *Villa Roncalli* €€€€	●	■	●	■
GUBBIO: *Alcatraz* €€€	●			■
GUBBIO: *Villa Montegranelli* €€€	●	■		■
MAGIONE: *La Fattoria di Montemelino* €		■		■
NARNI: *Monte del Grano 1696* €€€	●	■		■
NORCIA: *Dal Francese* €€€				
ORVIETO: *La Volpe e l'Uva* €€		■		

ASSISI: *San Francesco* €€€
Via San Francesco 52, 06081. ☎ 075 81 23 29.
A carefully chosen seasonal menu might include *carpaccio* of porcini mushrooms (raw, thinly sliced), home-made pâté and steak with truffles. ● *Wed; 2 wks Jul.*

BASCHI: *Vissani* €€€€€
Strada Statale 448, Todi-Baschi, 05023. ☎ 0744 95 02 06.
Gianfranco Vissani is famous throughout Italy for his haute cuisine, served in elegant surroundings. Choose your own music. ● *Wed, Thu lunch, Sun eve; mid-Jul–mid-Aug.*

CAMPELLO SUL CLITUNNO: *Trattoria Pettino* €€
Frazione Pettino 31, 06042. ☎ 0743 27 60 21.
Set in the middle of the mountains in an old restored house. The *bruschetta* and, in season, the plethora of dishes with truffles are delicious. ● *Tue.*

CITTÀ DI CASTELLO: *Amici Miei* €
Via del Monte 2, 06012. ☎ 075 855 99 04.
Set in the storerooms of a 16th-century palazzo in the historic centre, the menu is based on regional cuisine. The tasting menu changes daily. ● *Wed; Jan, Dec.*

CITTÀ DI CASTELLO: *Il Bersaglio* €€€
Via Vittorio Emanuele Orlando 14, 06012. ☎ 075 855 55 34.
A traditional Umbrian restaurant with specialities including *gnocchetti* (little *gnocchi*) with truffles. ● *Wed; Jan, 2 wks Jun–Jul.*

FOLIGNO: *Villa Roncalli* €€€€
Via Roma 25, 06034. ☎ 0742 39 10 91.
A charming country inn set in its own garden 1 km (half a mile) from Foligno. Regional specialities are well prepared using fresh ingredients. ● *lunch, Mon; 10 days Jan, 15–30 Aug.*

GUBBIO: *Alcatraz* €€€
Località Santa Cristina 53, 06020. ☎ 075 922 99 38.
At this Agriturist centre about 25 km (15 miles) southwest of Gubbio, the simple but tasty food benefits from the organic products they use. Reservations recommended.

GUBBIO: *Villa Montegranelli* €€€
Località Monteluiano, 06024. ☎ 075 922 01 85.
Set in an 18th-century villa with an elegantly rural atmosphere. Exquisitely made specialities include *crostini* (toasts) with *porcini* mushroom terrine and chestnut flour pancakes with melted cheese and ricotta.

MAGIONE: *La Fattoria di Montemelino* €
Via dei Montemelini 22, Località Montemelino, 06063. ☎ 075 84 36 06.
Another of the simple, reliable Agriturist restaurants. This one serves traditional Umbrian fare, grilled meats and, in season, *ravioli* of *porcini* mushrooms. ● *Tue.*

NARNI: *Monte del Grano 1696* €€€
Strada Guadamello 128, Località San Vito 05030. ☎ 0744 74 91 43.
Much care goes into creating a pleasant atmosphere in which to sample the excellent regional dishes. In season, try the truffles and *porcini* mushrooms. ● *Mon, Tue–Fri lunch; Nov.*

NORCIA: *Dal Francese* €€€
Via Riguardati 16, 06046. ☎ 0743 81 62 90.
A country-style trattoria in the centre of Norcia. It offers regional specialities such as a truffle-based menu-degustazione in season. ● *Fri (Nov–Jul).*

ORVIETO: *La Volpe e l'Uva* €€
Via Ripa Corsica 1, 05018. ☎ 0763 34 16 12.
A popular trattoria in the centre of Orvieto offering a variety of regional dishes that change with the season at reasonable prices. ● *Mon–Tue; Jan.*

ORVIETO: *I Sette Consoli* €€€€
Piazza Sant'Angelo 1a, 05018. ☎ 0763 34 39 11.
A comfortable, friendly restaurant with a garden for summer dining. Try *baccalà* (salt cod) marinated in apple vinegar with potato salad, stuffed rabbit, bean soup with fennel, and fish *ravioli*. ● *Wed, Sun pm (winter); 15–28 Feb, mid-Jun–mid-Jul.* ⧉ ▤

PASSIGNANO SUL TRASIMENO: *Cacciatori da Luciano* €€€€
Lungolago Pompei 11, 06065. ☎ 075 82 72 10.
The menu is based on sea fish, including scampi salad, fish *carpaccio* (raw, thinly sliced fish), *risotto* of different types of prawn and shrimp and grilled sole. Some of the desserts are made with forest fruits. ● *Wed.* ⧉ ▤

PERUGIA: *Giò Arte e Vini* €€
Via Ruggero d'Andreotto 19, 06124. ☎ 075 573 11 00.
Famous for its spectacular selection of wines and well-chosen regional dishes with special touches. The pumpkin *ravioli* and the *trecciola di agnello* (lamb) are particularly good. ● *Sun eve, Mon lunch.* ⧉ ▤ ⧗

PERUGIA: *Osteria del Gambero* €€€
Via Baldeschi 17, 06122. ☎ 075 573 54 61.
Advanced booking is recommended for this highly-regarded restaurant where chef Angelo Zarbo innovates on traditional Umbrian dishes. ● *Mon; 2 wks Jan, 2 wks Aug.* ⧉ ⧗

PERUGIA: *Osteria del Bartolo* €€€€
Via Bartolo 30, 06122. ☎ 075 573 15 61.
An elegant restaurant that is one of the mainstays of the Perugian eating tradition. Many items are home-made. ● *Wed lunch, Sun.* ⧉ ▤

SPOLETO: *Il Tartufo* €€€€
Piazza Garibaldi 24, 06049. ☎ 0743 402 36.
The floor of one of the dining rooms is ancient Roman. Well-tried regional specialities, including, not surprisingly, truffles, as well as other delights such as barley soup and duck in Sagrantino wine sauce. ● *Sun eve, Mon; last 2 wks Jan & Jul.* ⧉ ▤

SPOLETO: *Le Casaline* €€€
Località Poreta di Spoleto, Frazione Casaline, 06042. ☎ 0743 52 11 13.
An oasis of calm in a restored 18th-century mill. Try the *gnocchi* stuffed with mushrooms or wild boar *alla cacciatora* (in wine and tomato sauce). ● *Mon.* ⧉ ⧗

TERNI: *Da Carlino* €€
Via Piemonte 1, 05100. ☎ 0744 42 01 63.
Robust rustic food, such as *crostini* with local salami, *tagliatelle* with truffles or duck sauce, lamb, and some fish dishes. ● *Mon; 2 wks Aug.* ⧉

TODI: *Lucaroni* €€
Via Cortesi 7, 06059. ☎ 075 894 26 94.
Regional fish, meat and game (including hare, duck and lamb with truffles). Puddings, such as *crema* with warm chocolate, are also good. ● *eves; Tue.* ⧉

TODI: *La Mulinella* €€
Località Pontenaia 29, Località Vasciano, 06059. ☎ 075 894 47 79.
In the countryside about 2 km (1 mile) from Todi serving simple, reliable dishes. The home-made pastas and roasted meats are recommended. ● *Mon.* ⧗ ▤

TREVI: *La Taverna del Pescatore* €€€
Via della Chiesa Tonda 50, Località Pigge, 06039. ☎ 0742 78 09 20.
The freshest of local produce is combined and cooked in simple yet exquisite recipes and the atmosphere is relaxed with attentive service. ● *Wed; 2 wks Jan.* ⧉

MARCHE

ANCONA: *La Moretta* €€€
Piazza Plebiscito 52, 60124. ☎ 071 20 23 17.
A lovely traditional restaurant serving excellent local dishes; *polenta* with *calamari* and truffles, and *brodetto anconetano*, a rich fish soup. ● *Sun; 1 wk Jan.* ⧉ ⧗ ▤

ANCONA: *Passetto* €€€€
Piazza IV Novembre 1, 60124. ☎ 071 332 14.
Outside eating with sea views. Good fish and meat dishes. ● *Sun eve, Mon; 2 wks Aug.* ⧉

ASCOLI PICENO: *C'era una Volta* €
Via Piagge 336, Località Piagge, 63100. ☎ 0736 26 17 80.
This restaurant offers simple but tasty dishes, such as stuffed *gnocchi*, in a homely atmosphere. There are beautiful views from the farmhouse garden. ● *Tue.* ⧉

Average prices for a three-course meal for one, including a half-bottle of house wine, tax and service:
€ under €18
€€ €18–€30
€€€ €30–€40
€€€€ €40–€52
€€€€€ over €52.

FIXED-PRICE MENU
A fixed-price menu on offer, usually with three courses.
GOOD WINE LIST
Denotes a wide range of good quality wines.
FORMAL DRESS
Some restaurants require men to wear a jacket and tie.
OUTDOOR TABLES
Tables for eating outdoors, often with a good view.
CREDIT CARDS
The symbol shows that major credit cards are accepted.

	FIXED PRICE MENU	GOOD WINE LIST	FORMAL DRESS	OUTDOOR TABLES
FABRIANO: *Villa Marchese del Grillo* €€€ Via Rocchetta 73, Frazione Rocchetta. 0732 62 56 90. Set in a restored 18th-century villa, this restaurant combines attentive service with relaxed informality. Try the lamb with *taleggio* and peas. ● Sun eve, Mon; Jan.	●	■		■
FANO: *Ristorantino da Giulio* €€€ Viale Adriatico 100, 61032. 0721 80 56 80. A calm restaurant situated just opposite the beach. The cuisine is basically regional, with the chef's personal touches. Fish *antipasti* are recommended, as is the fish soup which you need to reserve. In the summer, it occasionally hosts opera recitals. ● Tue; Nov.	●			■
JESI: *Tana Libera Tutti* €€€ Piazza Pontelli 1, 60035. 0731 592 37. A dignified restaurant where Mediterranean dishes are prepared with care. Try the fish *risotto*, or the baked fish. ● Sun; 1 wk Jan, 1 wk Aug.				■
LORETO: *Andreina* €€ Via Buffolareccia 14, 60025. 071 97 01 24. A grandmother-and-grandson team prepares traditional cuisine with home-made pasta, chicken, rabbit and game, followed by tempting desserts. ● Tue.	●	■		■
MACERATA: *Da Secondo* €€ Via Pescheria Vecchia 26–28, 62100. 0733 26 09 12. The regional cuisine, such as *vincisgrassi alla Macerata* (local lasagna) and *frittura mista* (batter-fried fish or meat and vegetables), is recommended at this restaurant. Enjoy the elegant atmosphere. ● Mon; 2 wks Aug.		■		
NUMANA: *La Costarella* €€€€ Via IV Novembre 35, 60026. 071 736 02 97. Booking is advisable in this specialist fish restaurant; pasta with black cuttlefish ink and fried fish with courgette flowers. ● Tue; Nov–Easter.		■		
PESARO: *Da Teresa* €€€ Viale Trieste 180, 61100. 0721 300 96. A gracious restaurant offering imaginatively prepared dishes based on local cuisine. As well as exquisite fish and seafood there are a few meat dishes and delightful desserts to follow. ● Sun, Mon; Dec–Mar.	●	■		
PESARO: *Da Alceo* €€€€€ Via Panoramica Ardizio 121, 61100. 0721 39 03 18. A famous fish restaurant with a spectacular panoramic terrace serving *gnocchi* with shellfish, and *risotto*. Desserts are home-made and tasty. ● Sun eve, Mon.		■		■
SENIGALLIA: *Uliassi* €€€€€ Via Banchina di Levante 6, 60019. 071 654 63. Run by a brother and sister, this is a friendly restaurant offering a high standard of cuisine. Try the speciality pasta with prawns and asparagus. ● Mon; Jan–Feb.	●	■		■
SIROLO: *Rocco* €€€€ Via Torrione 1, 60020. 071 933 05 58. Open during the spring and summer evenings only, Rocco serves delicious (mainly fish) dishes such as *gnocchi* with clams, fried mixed fish and vegetables and sea bass with a sauce of lettuce and balsamic vinegar. ● Tue (except summer); Nov–Mar.	●	■		■
URBANIA: *Big Ben* €€ Corso Vittorio Emanuele 61, 61049. 0722 31 97 95. In the historic centre of town, Big Ben's specialities include *tagliolini* (pasta) with truffles, grilled lamb, good cheeses and home-made desserts. ● lunch; Wed.		■		■
URBINO: *Vecchia Urbino* €€ Via del Vasari 3–5, 61029. 0722 44 47. A restaurant serving simply prepared traditional dishes, including *vincisgrassi* (the local lasagna), rabbit, and *polenta* with mushrooms. ● Tue.	●	■		

ROME

AVENTINE: *Perilli a Testaccio*   €€
Via Marmorata 39, 00153. **Map** 6 E3. **06 574 63 18.**
An archetypal noisy Roman trattoria serving a regular clientele with robust, Roman
fare that includes artichokes and *rigatoni alla pajata*. ● *Wed; Aug.*

AVENTINE: *Checchino dal 1887*   €€€€€
Via di Monte Testaccio 30, 00153. **Map** 6 D4. **06 574 63 18.**
Roman cuisine is served at old tables under vaulted ceilings with an open fire
in winter. ● *Mon (Oct – May), Sun eve; Mon eve, Sun (Jun – Sep); Aug; 1 wk Dec.*

CAMPO DE' FIORI: *Dal Pompiere*   €€€
Via Santa Maria dei Calderari 38, 00186. **Map** 2 F5. **06 686 83 77.**
In the heart of the Jewish ghetto, on the first floor of the Palazzo Cenci
Bolognetti with frescoed, beamed ceilings. The food is classical, including
fried courgette flowers and *rigatoni alla pajata*. ● *Sun; Aug.*

CAMPO DE' FIORI: *Il Drappo*   €€€
Vicolo del Malpasso 9, 00186. **Map** 2 E4. **06 687 73 65.**
An intimate restaurant, serving Sardinian cuisine; *seadas* (sweet cheese-filled
ravioli) and *mirto* liqueur. ● *Sun; 3 wks Aug.*

CAMPO DE' FIORI: *Monserrato*   €€€
Via Monserrato 96, 00186. **Map** 2 E4. **06 687 33 86.**
This restaurant serves reliably good food. The *gnocchi alle vongole veraci*
(*gnocchi* with clams) are very good for starters and the *rombo al forno con
patate* (oven-cooked turbot with potatoes) is always a treat. ● *Mon, 2 wks Aug.*

CAMPO DE' FIORI: *Camponeschi*   €€€€€
Piazza Farnese 50, 00186. **Map** 2 E5. **06 687 49 27.**
Modern and regional Italian cooking, and French specialities, served in a lush interior
on one of the most beautiful piazzas in Rome. ● *lunch, Sun; 2 wks Aug.*

CAMPO DE' FIORI: *Sora Lella*   €€€€€
Via di Ponte Quattro Capi 16, 00186. **Map** 6 D1. **06 686 16 01.**
Situated on the picturesque Tiber Island, this restaurant is popular with visitors.
Traditional Roman dishes are served in elegant surroundings. ● *Sun; Aug.*

ESQUILINE: *Trattoria Monti*   €€€
Via di San Vito 19, 00185. **Map** 4 E4. **06 446 65 73.**
Dishes from the Marches are prepared by Franca Camerucci. Specialities
include *ravioli di ricotta*. ● *Sun pm, Mon; Aug, 2 wks Dec–Jan.*

ESQUILINE: *Agata e Romeo*   €€€€€
Via Carlo Alberto 45, 00185. **Map** 4 E4. **06 446 61 15.**
Agata cooks predominantly Roman and southern Italian fare while Romeo serves.
Tranquil atmosphere and well-spaced tables. ● *2 wks Jan, 2 wks Aug.*

JANICULUM: *Antico Arco*   €€€€€
Via San Pancrazio 1, 00152. **Map** 5 A1. **06 581 52 74.**
This restaurant in elegant surroundings offers creative seasonal fare, including
guinea fowl with apples and *foie gras*. ● *lunch Mon–Sat, Sun; Aug.*

LATERAN: *Alfredo a Via Gabi*   €€
Via Gabi 36–38, 00183. **Map** 8 E3. **06 77 20 67 92.**
A spacious trattoria with ample portions. Try the *spaghetti* with swordfish sauce,
coniglio con tartufo (rabbit with truffles) and *panna cotta*. ● *Tue; Aug.*

PANTHEON: *Da Gino*   €€
Vicolo Rosini 4, 00186. **Map** 3 A3. **06 687 34 34.**
An ancient, traditional Roman trattoria full of journalists, politicians
and the initiated. Daily dishes include *gnocchi*, *ossobuco* and *baccalà*
as well as some classic sturdy soups. ● *Sun; Aug.*

PANTHEON: *Myosotis*   €€€
Vicolo della Vaccarella 3/5, 00186. **Map** 2 F3. **06 686 55 54.**
A foodie temple for those who want to keep an eye on their pocket. An imaginative
approach and the freshest ingredients. ● *lunch Mon, Sun; 2 wks Aug.*

PANTHEON: *Sangallo*   €€€
Vicolo della Vaccarella 11a, 00186. **Map** 2 F3. **06 686 55 49.**
Small bistro specializing in regional fish dishes and a huge array of *antipasti*,
including many types of vegetables and seafood. ● *lunch, Sun; Aug.*

For key to symbols see back flap

	FIXED PRICE MENU	GOOD WINE LIST	FORMAL DRESS	OUTDOOR TABLES

Average prices for a three-course meal for one, including a half-bottle of house wine, tax and service:
€ under €18
€€ €18–€30
€€€ €30–€40
€€€€ €40–€52
€€€€€ over €52.

FIXED-PRICE MENU
A fixed-price menu on offer, usually with three courses.

GOOD WINE LIST
Denotes a wide range of good quality wines.

FORMAL DRESS
Some restaurants require men to wear a jacket and tie.

OUTDOOR TABLES
Tables for eating outdoors, often with a good view.

CREDIT CARDS
The symbol shows that major credit cards are accepted.

PANTHEON: *El Toulà* €€€€€
Via della Lupa 29b, 00186. **Map** 2 F3. 06 687 34 98.
One of Rome's most exclusive and traditional restaurants. The cuisine is mainly Venetian, the service and the wines are superb. ● *Sat lunch, Sun; Aug.*
(Fixed Price Menu ● | Good Wine List ■ | Formal Dress ●)

PIAZZA NAVONA: *La Taverna da Giovanni* €€
Via del Banco di Santo Spirito 58, 00186. **Map** 2 D3. 06 686 41 16.
A crowded trattoria with a family atmosphere. The *rigatoni all'amatriciana* (pasta with spicy bacon and tomato) is a speciality, as are the traditional *gnocchi*, *baccalà* (salt cod) and tripe on Thursday, Friday and Saturday respectively. ● *Mon.*
(Fixed Price Menu ● | Good Wine List ■ | Outdoor Tables ■)

PIAZZA NAVONA: *Il Passetto* €€€€
Via Zanardelli 14, 00186. **Map** 2 F3. 06 68 80 36 96. www.ristorantepassetto.com
This restaurant seems to belong to another age: the decor is retro and the menu traditional. The home-made desserts, such as *mousse al cioccolato bianco e nero* (white-and-dark-chocolate mousse), deserve special mention.
(Good Wine List ■ | Outdoor Tables ■)

PIAZZA DI SPAGNA: *Al 34* €€
Via Mario de' Fiori 34, 00187. **Map** 3 A2. 06 679 50 91.
The perfect setting for a comfortable chat or a romantic tête-à-tête. The extensive menu offers mostly southern Italian cuisine. ● *Mon; 3 wks Aug.*
(Fixed Price Menu ● | Outdoor Tables ■)

PIAZZA DI SPAGNA: *Birreria Viennese* €€
Via della Croce 21, 00187. **Map** 3 A2. 06 679 55 69.
Traditional beers and Austrian specialities have been served here for more than 60 years. Try the sausages, goulash, sauerkraut or the Wienerschnitzel.
(Fixed Price Menu ●)

PIAZZA DI SPAGNA: *Mario alla Vite* €€€
Via della Vite 55, 00187. **Map** 3 A2. 06 678 38 18.
Simple, honest Tuscan fare. The service can be haphazard but the *ribollita*, *fagioli al fiasco* (beans), steaks and desserts make up for it. ● *Sun; Aug.*
(Good Wine List ■ | Outdoor Tables ■)

PIAZZA DI SPAGNA: *Porto di Ripetta* €€€€
Via di Ripetta 250, 00187. **Map** 2 F2. 06 361 23 76.
A friendly restaurant serving wonderful dishes with fish and seafood brought in daily. Try the swordfish or the fish soup. ● *Sun, Mon lunch; 2 wks Aug.*
(Fixed Price Menu ● | Good Wine List ■ | Formal Dress ●)

QUIRINAL: *Colline Emiliane* €€€
Via degli Avignonesi 22, 00187. **Map** 3 C3. 06 481 75 38.
A small, family trattoria serving specialities from Emilia-Romagna; home-made pasta, salami, boiled meats and *salsa verde* (parsley, onion and anchovy sauce) and Emilian wines. ● *Fri; Aug.*
(Good Wine List ■)

QUIRINAL: *Il Posto Accanto* €€€
Via del Boschetto 36a, 00184. **Map** 3 C4. 06 474 30 02.
This elegant family-run restaurant owes its success to a carefully chosen menu based on home-made pasta, fish and meat. ● *Sat lunch; Sun; Aug.*
(Good Wine List ■)

QUIRINAL: *Al Moro* €€€€€
Vicolo delle Bollette 13, 00185. **Map** 3 B3. 06 678 34 95.
A reliable choice for traditional Roman cooking in this typical, and crowded, trattoria. Fresh local ingredients are used to make dishes such as *bucatini all'amatriciana* and *spaghetti alla Moro* (a version of *carbonara*). ● *Sun; Aug.*
(Formal Dress ● | Outdoor Tables ■)

TERMINI: *Coriolano* €€€€
Via Ancona 14. **Map** 4 E1. 06 44 24 98 63.
The menu at this restaurant changes with the seasons. Only the freshest ingredients are used for dishes such as home-made *ravioli* and *capretto* (kid). ● *3 wks Aug.*
(Good Wine List ■)

TRASTEVERE: *Da Lucia* €€
Vicolo del Mattonato 2b, 00153. **Map** 5 C1. 06 580 36 01.
A popular, crowded trattoria serving basic Roman cuisine. Try the *pasta e ceci* and the *spaghetti alla gricia* (pecorino, pancetta and pepper). ● *Mon; 2 wks Aug.*
(Outdoor Tables ■)

TRASTEVERE: *Asinocotto* €€€
Via dei Vascellari 48. **Map** 8 D1. 06 589 89 85.
This casually elegant restaurant offers imaginative cooking with dishes such as aubergine, rocket and nettle ravioli and sea bass with truffle. *lunch Mon–Sat; 3 wks Jan.*

TRASTEVERE: *La Cornucopia* €€€
Piazza in Piscinula 18. **Map** 6 D1. 06 580 03 80.
Come here for excellent *antipasti* and simply cooked fish dishes such as *spigola al vapore* (steamed sea bass). Candlelight adds to the ambience. *Tue.*

TRASTEVERE: *Romolo nel Giardino della Fornarina* €€€
Via Porta Settimiana 8, 00153. **Map** 2 E5. 06 581 82 84.
La Fornarina was Raphael's mistress and this is said to have been her home. In summer the Roman food is served in the courtyard. *Mon; Aug.*

TRASTEVERE: *Da Paris* €€€€
Piazza San Calisto 7a, 00153. **Map** 5 C1. 06 581 53 78.
A Roman-Jewish restaurant popular with locals. Home-made pasta and traditional dishes include *minestra di arzilla* (ray), tripe and exquisite *fritto misto* (batter-fried fish) with vegetables. *Sun eve, Mon; 2 wks Aug.*

TRASTEVERE: *Alberto Ciarla* €€€€€
Piazza San Cosimato 40, 00153. **Map** 5 C1. 06 581 86 68.
This is the place to enjoy fish and seafood. From oysters to scampi, the menu is based on the day's catch. Elegant and dramatic decor. *lunch; Sun; 1 wk Jan, 1 wk Aug.*

VATICAN: *Romolo* €€
Via Fosse di Castello 19, 00193. **Map** 4 D3. 06 686 16 03.
This unpretentious trattoria serves a full range of classic Italian dishes from *spaghetti alla carbonara* to *cotolette alla milanese* (breaded veal escalopes). Roman specialities include *coda alla vaccinara* (oxtail stew) and chick pea soup. *Mon; 2 wks Aug.*

VATICAN: *Les Etoiles* €€€€€
Via dei Bastioni 1, 00193. **Map** 2 D2. 06 687 32 33.
This rooftop restaurant sits atop the Atlante Star hotel. Speciality dishes include *tagliolini* (pasta) with clams and, in season, game and truffles.

VIA VENETO: *Cantina Cantarini* €€€
Piazza Sallustio 12, 00187. **Map** 4 D1. 06 48 55 28.
A popular local trattoria with friendly service. Meat is served from Monday to Thursday lunchtime, fish for the rest of the week. *Sun; 2 wks Aug, 2 wks Dec.*

VIA VENETO: *Giovanni* €€€€
Via Marche 64, 00187. **Map** 3 C1. 06 482 18 34.
A crowded restaurant popular with locals. Traditional food from the Marches, including fresh fish, pasta and *ossobuco*. *Fri eve, Sat; Aug.*

VIA VENETO: *George's* €€€€€
Via Marche 7, 00187. **Map** 3 C1. 06 42 08 45 75.
A survivor from the Dolce Vita era with a nostalgic air of luxurious elegance. Service is impeccable and there is a tempting selection of international dishes. *Sun; Aug.*

VIA VENETO: *Tullio* €€€€€
Via San Nicola da Tolentino 26, 00187. **Map** 3 C2. 06 474 55 60.
A genuine Tuscan restaurant frequented by an enthusiastic crowd. Typical dishes include porcini mushrooms in numerous ways. *Sun; Aug.*

VILLA BORGHESE: *Al Ceppo* €€€€€
Via Panama 2, 00198. 06 841 96 96.
Run by two sisters who serve a strictly seasonal menu of traditional dishes with flashes of inspiration in a hospitable atmosphere. *Mon; 2 wks Aug.*

VILLA BORGHESE: *Relais la Piscine* €€€€€
Via G Mangili 6. 06 321 61 26.
The restaurant of the Aldrovandi Palace Hotel is especially beautiful in summer, when tables are set outside on the terrace by the pool. The chef produces excellent, typically Mediterranean dishes using prime meat, fish and vegetables.

LAZIO

ALATRI: *La Rosetta* €€
Via del Duomo 35, 03011. 0775 43 45 68.
A quiet restaurant near the 6th-century BC acropolis. Try the *maccheroni alla ciociara* (wine, herb, bacon and meat sauce). *Tue (Oct–May); 1 wk Jan, 2 wks Jul.*

For key to symbols see back flap

	FIXED PRICE MENU	GOOD WINE LIST	FORMAL DRESS	OUTDOOR TABLES

Average prices for a three-course meal for one, including a half-bottle of house wine, tax and service:
€ under €18
€€ €18–€30
€€€ €30–€40
€€€€ €40–€52
€€€€€ over €52.

FIXED-PRICE MENU
A fixed-price menu on offer, usually with three courses.
GOOD WINE LIST
Denotes a wide range of good quality wines.
FORMAL DRESS
Some restaurants require men to wear a jacket and tie.
OUTDOOR TABLES
Tables for eating outdoors, often with a good view.
CREDIT CARDS
The symbol shows that major credit cards are accepted.

CASPERIA: *Geco 107*   €€   ■ Good Wine List   ■ Outdoor Tables
Piazza Municipio 10, 02041. 32 83 39 84 79.
An original wine bar displaying works of art in this pretty north Lazio village. A good place to taste local wines, cheeses, hams and olive oils. ● *Tue–Thu; 3 wks Nov.*

CERVETERI: *Da Fiore*   €€   ■ Outdoor Tables
Via San Paolo 4, Località Procoio 00052. 06 99 20 42 50.
A simple country trattoria: specialities include home-cooked pastas with *ragù*, rabbit and grilled meats. The *bruschette* and pizzas are also good. ● *Tue; 2 wks Sep.*

FRASCATI: *Enoteca Frascati*   €€€   ■ Good Wine List
Via Diaz 42, 00044. 06 941 74 49.
More than 400 wines accompany a good range of light dishes. Try the soups and the fresh pasta with mushrooms and truffles. ● *Mon–Sat lunch, Sun; Aug.*

GAETA: *La Cianciola*   €€   ● Fixed Price Menu   ■ Outdoor Tables
Vico 2 Buonomo 16, 04024. 0771 46 61 90.
A charming trattoria hidden up a little alley into which tables are tightly packed. Try the pasta with aubergines and shellfish. ● *Mon; Nov.*

NETTUNO: *Cacciatori dal 1896*   €€€€   ■ Good Wine List
Via Matteotti 27–29, 00048. 06 988 03 30.
A large, rustically furnished restaurant with a veranda overlooking the sea. Fish is caught daily, and the dishes are inspired by regional recipes. ● *Wed.*

OSTIA ANTICA: *Il Monumento*   €€€   ■ Outdoor Tables
Piazza Umberto I 8, 00119. 06 565 00 21.
A fish-based menu; the house speciality, *spaghetti al Monumento*, is served with seafood sauce. ● *Mon; 1 wk Jan, 2 wks Aug.*

SPERLONGA: *La Bisaccia*   €€€€   ■ Outdoor Tables
Via Romita 25, 04029. 0771 54 85 76.
Linguine with wild asparagus and prawns is a highlight of this restaurant that also makes use of local fish for soups and grills. ● *Tue; Nov.*

TIVOLI: *Villa Esedra*   €€€   ■ Outdoor Tables
Via di Villa Adriana 51, Località Villa Adriana 00010. 0774 53 47 16.
Typical menu with fresh *antipasti* such as seafood salad and grilled fish to follow. In the evening there are also pizzas. ● *Mon.*

TREVIGNANO: *Ristorante Il Palazzetto*   €€€   ■ Formal Dress   ■ Outdoor Tables
Piazza Vittorio Emanuele III 15, 00069. 06 999 92 54.
A little restaurant with views over Lake Bracciano. The excellent menu makes good use of sea and lake fish, including *ravioli al persico* (perch) and delicious scampi soups. Desserts are home-made. ● *Mon, Tue.*

TUSCANIA: *Al Gallo*   €€€€   ■ Good Wine List
Via del Gallo 22, 01017. 0761 44 33 88.
An unusual interpretation of regional dishes has created an exceptionally good menu. Warm atmosphere and charming service. ● *Mon; 4 wks Jan–Feb.*

VITERBO: *Porta Romana*   €€   ● Fixed Price Menu
Via della Bontà 12, 01100. 0761 30 71 18.
A simple trattoria where a wide range of classic dishes is immaculately prepared. In the winter, try *pignataccia*, a Viterbo speciality of mixed veal, beef and pork cooked on a slow fire with celery, carrots and potatoes. ● *Sun; 2 wks Aug.*

NAPLES AND CAMPANIA

AGROPOLI: *Il Ceppo*   €€€€   ■ Good Wine List   ■ Outdoor Tables
Via Madonna Del Carmine 31, 84043. 0974 84 30 36. W www.hotelristoranteilceppo.com
A wonderful range of local fish and home-made pastas and pizzas; try the *spaghetti* with seafood, prawns in lemon sauce or the fish soups. ● *Mon eve; Nov.*

AMALFI: *La Marinella*　€€
Via Lungomare dei Cavalieri di San Giovanni di Gerusalemme 1, 84011. 📞 089 87 10 43.
A lively, friendly restaurant overlooking the the Amalfi coast. Much fish is
served as well as the traditional local specialities. ● *Fri (winter); Nov–Mar.* 🅿 ⛐

AMALFI: *Eolo*　€€€€
Via Comite 3, 84011. 📞 089 87 12 41.
Situated in the historic centre of Amalfi, this restaurant's menu changes every fortnight to
make use of seasonal ingredients. Quality food. ● *Tue (winter); Nov–Mar.* 🅿 ▤

BENEVENTO: *Gino e Pina*　€€
Viale dell'Università, 82100. 📞 0824 249 47. 🅆 www.ginoepina.it
In the heart of the historic centre; try *cardone* (a type of thistle) and the *pampanelle
alla Gino e Pina* (asparagus and shellfish pasta). ● *Sun; Aug, Christmas.* 🅿 ▤ ⛐

CAPRI: *La Pergola*　€€€
Traversa Lo Palazzo 2, 80073. 📞 081 837 74 14.
A pleasant family atmosphere, large garden and delicious food bring many regular
customers here. Excellent home-made lemon tart. ● *Sun (exc Jun–Sep); Nov–Dec.* 🅿 ▤

CAPRI: *La Savardina da Eduardo*　€€€
Via Lo Capo 8, 80073. 📞 081 837 63 00.
This is one of the most traditional restaurants in Capri, with orange trees, sea views
and tasty regional specialities. ● *dinner (Mar, Apr); Tue; Nov–Feb (exc Christmas).* 🅿

CAPRI: *Quisi del Grand Hotel Quisisana*　€€€€€
Via Camerelle 2, 80073. 📞 081 837 07 88. 🅆 www.quisi.com
The atmosphere is elegant and the food is delightful. Try the succulent roast duck
with peaches and hot apple pie with Calvados. ● *lunch; Sun (May–Oct); Nov–Mar.* 🅿 ▤

ISCHIA: *Da Peppina di Renato*　€€€
Via Bocca 23, Località Forio 80075. 📞 081 99 83 12.
Basic fare served in this simple trattoria; *pasta e fagioli*, soups, grilled
meats and pizzas cooked in a wood oven. ● *Wed; Nov–Mar.* 🅿 ▤ ⛐

ISCHIA: *La Tavernetta Pirata Sant'Angelo*　€€€€
Via Sant'Angelo 77, Località Serrara Fontana 80070. 📞 081 99 92 51.
You can relax in this peaceful corner, where you find a good choice of
pasta with Mediterranean sauces, salads, or fried fish. ● *Wed; Nov–Feb.* 🅿 ⛐

FAICCHIO: *La Campagnola*　€€
Via San Nicola 22, Località Massa 82030. 📞 0824 81 40 81.
Set in a village 38 km (23 miles) northwest of Benevento, serving simple tasty cuisine.
Try *torciglioni ai funghi porcini* (pasta with porcini mushrooms). ● *Wed; Sep.* 🅿

NAPLES: *Da Ettore*　€€
Via Santa Lucia 56. 📞 081 764 04 98.
This is a popular pizzeria and trattoria serving typical Neapolitan cuisine. Good pizzas
and excellent seafood pasta (with mussels or clams). ● *Sun & Mon eve; Aug.* 🅿 ⛐

NAPLES: *Vadinchenia*　€€
Via Pontano 21. 📞 081 66 02 65.
Delicate dishes often based on fish abound on the innovative, seasonal
menu at this restaurant. The desserts are delicious. ● *Sun; Aug.* 🅿

NAPLES: *Amici Miei*　€€€
Via Monte di Dio 78. 📞 081 764 60 63.
A classic menu with mainly meat dishes. Excellent main courses, especially
pasta with vegetables and pulses. Cosy atmosphere. ● *Mon, Sun eve; Aug.* ▤

NAPLES: *La Cantinella*　€€€€€
Via Nazario Sauro 23, 80132. 📞 081 764 86 84. 🅆 www.lacantinella.it
One of Naples' most famous restaurants, with a reputation for its carefully
and successfully prepared regional cuisine. ● *Sun (May–Sep); 3 wks Aug.* 🅿 ▤

NAPLES: *La Sacrestia*　€€€€€
Via Orazio 116, 80122. 📞 081 66 41 86. 🅆 www.lasacrestia.it
An attractive setting with views of the Gulf of Naples. The food is excellent,
and the atmosphere elegant but informal. ● *Sun eve, Mon; Aug.* 🅿 ▤ ⛐ ⛐

NERANO: *Taverna del Capitano*　€€€€€
Piazza delle Sirene 10, Località Marina del Cantone 80068. 📞 081 808 10 28.
A refined restaurant on the beach serving regional specialities with some creative
touches; try the fish in breadcrumbs and herbs. ● *Mon; Jan, Feb.* 🅿 ▤ ⛐ ⛐

	FIXED PRICE MENU	GOOD WINE LIST	FORMAL DRESS	OUTDOOR TABLES

Average prices for a three-course meal for one, including a half-bottle of house wine, tax and service:
€ under €18
€€ €18–€30
€€€ €30–€40
€€€€ €40–€52
€€€€€ over €52.

FIXED-PRICE MENU
A fixed-price menu on offer, usually with three courses.
GOOD WINE LIST
Denotes a wide range of good quality wines.
FORMAL DRESS
Some restaurants require men to wear a jacket and tie.
OUTDOOR TABLES
Tables for eating outdoors, often with a good view.
CREDIT CARDS
The symbol shows that major credit cards are accepted.

Restaurant		FIXED PRICE MENU	GOOD WINE LIST	FORMAL DRESS	OUTDOOR TABLES
PAESTUM: *La Pergola* — Via Nazionale 1, Capaccio Scalo 84040. 0828 72 33 77. Innovative regional cuisine that makes use of seasonal produce in a rustic restaurant 3 km (2 miles) from the ruins of Paestum. Mon (exc Jul–Sep).	€€€		■		■
POMPEII: *Il Principe* — Piazza B Longo 8, 80045. 081 850 55 66. www.ilprincipe.com This airy, refined restaurant is close to the excavations. Its cuisine is based on fish and includes fish-filled *ravioli* and turbot with vegetables. Mon, Sun eve (exc Apr–Jun, Sep–Oct); 1–20 Aug, Christmas.	€€€€€		■	●	
POSITANO: *Da Adolfo* — Località Laurito 40, 84017. 089 87 50 22. A free boat leaves Positano harbour every half hour for this charming beach trattoria serving *spaghetti* with clams or courgettes with grilled mozzarella. eve; Oct–Mar.	€€€	●			
POSITANO: *La Sponda* — Via Colombo 30, 84017. 089 87 50 66. www.sirenuse.it A sumptuous restaurant where guests are treated like family friends. A tempting range of modern and traditional dishes based on fresh fish is on offer.	€€€€€	●	■		■
SALERNO: *Pizzeria Vicolo della Neve* — Vicolo della Neve 24, 84100. 089 22 57 05. A pizzeria in the historic centre also serving a range of dishes such as *pasta e fagioli, baccalà* casserole and sausages with broccoli. lunch; Wed; Dec–Mar.	€				
SALERNO: *Al Cenacolo* — Piazza Alfano I 4, 84100. 089 23 88 18. Dedicated cuisine with a menu that changes daily to make good use of local ingredients. Pasta and bread are home-made. Sun eve, Mon; Aug; Christmas.	€€€€€		■		
SANT'AGATA SUI DUE GOLFI: *Don Alfonso 1890* — Piazza Sant'Agata 11, 80064. 081 878 00 26. www.donalfonso1890.com Set in elegant gardens, dishes include seafood and fish specialities and delicious traditional desserts. Mon, Tue (exc eve Jul–Aug); Jan–Mar.	€€€€€	●	■		■
SICIGNANO DEGLI ALBURNI: *La Taverna* — Via Nazionale 139, Frazione Scorzo 84020. 0828 97 80 50. An 18th-century country inn, near Salerno. The regional cuisine includes salamis, bean and chickpea soups and grilled meats. Wed; Jul.	€€				
SORRENTO: *Antico Frantoio* — Via Casarlano 8, Località Casarlano 80067. 081 878 58 45. www.ristoranteanticofrantoio.it A great variety of dishes for all courses, made from local ingredients. Try the pizzas, the corn bread and the beer brewed at the next-door *birreria*.	€€€		■		■

ABRUZZO, MOLISE AND PUGLIA

Restaurant		FIXED PRICE MENU	GOOD WINE LIST	FORMAL DRESS	OUTDOOR TABLES
ALBEROBELLO: *La Chiusa di Chietri* — Km 29,800, SS 172 dei Trulli, 70011. 080 432 54 81, 080 432 35 58. www.lachiusadichietri.it The location for this large restaurant, a park, provides beautiful views and makes it ideal for children. Traditional, regional fare is on offer.	€€€		■		■
ALBEROBELLO: *Il Poeta Contadino* — Via Indipendenza 21, 70011. 080 432 19 17. An elegant restaurant where the excellent service matches the high standard of both food and wine. The cuisine makes imaginative use of fresh local ingredients, offering both fish and meat dishes. Mon (exc Jul–Sep); Jan.	€€€€€	●	■		■
BARI: *Kilimangiaro* — Lungomare Starita 64, 70123. 080 534 76 10. A homely trattoria and pizzeria on the seafront. Specialities include *orecchiette* (ear-shaped pasta) with *rucola* (rocket), fish and meat kebabs. Wed; 15 Dec–15 Jan.	€€		■		■

BARI: *Terranima* €€
Via Putignani 213, 70123. 📞 *080 521 97 25.*
Popular trattoria serving a menu of typical Puglia fare, such as *orecchiette* (ear-shaped pasta) with monkfish. Friendly staff and pleasant setting ● *Sun eve; Aug.*

GALLIPOLI: *Il Capriccio* €€€
Viale Bovio 14/16. 📞 *0833 26 15 45.*
This restaurant serves up classical regional cuisine, including plenty of fresh fish. ● *Mon (winter); Nov.*

ISOLE TREMITI: *Al Gabbiano* €€
San Domino, 71040. 📞 *0882 46 34 10.* 🌐 www.hotel-gabbiano.com
The food here is based on the best fish from the sea. Try the traditional fish soup and fresh fish roasted in a case of salt. Eels are a speciality. Rooms are available.

L'AQUILA: *Ernesto* €€
Piazza Palazzo 22, 67100. 📞 *0862 210 94.*
A peaceful, sophisticated place to eat. The menu is a tasty, creative mix inspired by different sources and there is a wine bar attached. ● *Sun, Mon.*

LOCOROTONDO: *Al Casale* €€
Via Gorizia 39, 70010. 📞 *080 431 13 77.*
This restaurant/hotel in the heart of the *trulli* region specializes in local seafood dishes. Children are welcome. ● *Wed.*

OTRANTO: *Vecchia Otranto* €€€
Corso Garibaldi 96, 73028. 📞 *0836 80 15 75.*
Good marine and other regional specialities in this traditional trattoria include pasta with sea urchin and pepper sauce. ● *Thu; Nov, 1 wk Jan.*

OVINDOLI: *Il Pozzo* €€
Via Monumento dell'Alpino, 67046. 📞 *0863 71 01 91.*
Wonderful mountain setting for this atmospheric restaurant in the historic centre of town. The food is traditional and robust. ● *Wed; end Sep.*

PORTO CESAREO: *L'Angolo di Beppe* €€
Via Zanella 24, Località Torre Lapillo, 73050. 📞 *0833 56 53 05.*
A cosy atmosphere and elegant decor with a large open fire in winter. The cuisine is based on fish, and mixes local and international traditions. ● *Mon.*

ROCCA DI MEZZO: *La Fiorita* €
Piazza Principe di Piemonte 3, 67048. 📞 *0862 91 74 67.*
Efficient, friendly service in this family-run trattoria where the food is based on local products from the Abruzzi mountains. ● *Tue; 2 wks Sep.*

SULMONA: *Rigoletto* €€
Via Stazione Introacqua 46, 67039. 📞 *0864 555 29.*
A short walk from the centre of town. Home-made pastas are served with beans, *scamorza* (soft cheese), rabbit and truffles. ● *Mon, Sun; 2 wks Jan.*

TARANTO: *Le Vecchie Cantine* €€€
Via Girasoli 23, Frazione Lama 74020. 📞 *099 777 25 89.* 🌐 www.levecchiecantine.it
Set in restored storerooms just outside Taranto. A tasty fish and seafood menu, such as *carpaccio* of swordfish and *fusilli* with sardines. ● *lunch (exc Sun); Wed; Jan.*

TARANTO: *Al Faro* €€€€
Via Galeso 126, 74100. 📞 *099 471 44 44.*
The menu is exclusively marine, using locally caught fish and seafood for *antipasti*, soups, *risotto* and grills. Rooms available. ● *Sun; Dec–Jan.*

TERMOLI: *Z' Bass* €€€
Via Oberdan 8, 86039. 📞 *0875 70 67 03.*
This friendly, welcoming trattoria offers a high level of cuisine using fresh, seasonal ingredients. There is also an extensive wine list available. ● *Mon.*

TRANI: *Torrente Antico* €€€€€
Via Fusco 3, 70059. 📞 *0883 48 79 11.*
Exquisite, lightly prepared dishes based on traditional regional cuisine with modern touches. The wine list is also extensive. ● *Sun eve, Mon; 2nd wk Jan, last 2 wks Jul.*

VIESTE: *Il Trabucco dell'Hotel Pizzomunno* €€€€
Lungomare di Pizzomunno km 1, 71019. 📞 *0884 70 87 41.*
Surrounded by gardens and very close to the sea. The cuisine has some creative touches and the dishes are light and tasty. ● *mid-Oct–Easter.*

For key to symbols see back flap

	FIXED PRICE MENU	GOOD WINE LIST	FORMAL DRESS	OUTDOOR TABLES

Average prices for a three-course meal for one, including a half-bottle of house wine, tax and service:
€ under €18
€€ €18–€30
€€€ €30–€40
€€€€ €40–€52
€€€€€ over €52.

FIXED-PRICE MENU
A fixed-price menu on offer, usually with three courses.
GOOD WINE LIST
Denotes a wide range of good quality wines.
FORMAL DRESS
Some restaurants require men to wear a jacket and tie.
OUTDOOR TABLES
Tables for eating outdoors, often with a good view.
CREDIT CARDS
The symbol shows that major credit cards are accepted.

VILLETTA BARREA: *Trattoria del Pescatore* €€ Via B Virgilio 175, 67030. [0864 891 52. A simple, family-run riverside trattoria in the Abruzzo National Park. Regional dishes include trout and home-made *chitarrini* (pasta cut like guitar strings). ● Tue. ⬛				

BASILICATA AND CALABRIA

BIVONGI: *Vecchia Miniera* €€ Contrada Perrocalli, 89040. [0964 73 18 69. Regional cuisine such as pasta with *sugo di capra* (goat sauce), a favourite ancient Roman dish, in this village just outside Stilo. ● Mon. ▦ ⚡ ♿		▦		▦
MARATEA: *Taverna Rovita* €€€€ Via Rovita 13, 85046. [0973 87 65 88. An elegant country restaurant with white walls and tiled floors serving regional cuisine. Try the *risotto* of asparagus and venison. ● Tue; Nov–mid-Dec. ⬛ ⚡		▦		
MATERA: *Al Casino del Diavolo* €€ Via La Martella, 75100. [0835 26 19 86. ⬜ www.casinodeldiavolo.com Excellent Matera fare at this elegant, traditional restaurant set in an olive grove just outside the town. Try *orecchiette* (ear-shaped pasta) with broccoli. ● Mon. ▦ ♿		▦		▦
MATERA: *Il Terrazzino Sui Sassi* €€ Vicolo San Giuseppe 7, 75100. [0835 33 25 03. In the Sassi district *(see p502)*, the restaurant has a panoramic terrace. Try soups of grains and chickpeas, or grilled lamb *involtini* (lamb parcels). ● Tue; part of Jun. ⬛	●	▦		▦
MATERA: *Venusio* €€€€ Via Lussemburgo 2, Borgo Venusio 75100. [0835 25 90 81. An elegant restaurant 6 km (4 miles) south of Matera. Specialities include fish baked in a bread case, fish *tortelli*, mushrooms and various *antipasti*. ● Mon; Jan, Aug. ⬛ ▦ ⚡ ♿	●	▦		▦
MELFI: *Vaddone* €€ Contrada Abruzzese, 85025. [0972 243 23. A well-known trattoria serving delicious soups of pulses and grilled meats. Very good value. ● Mon. ⬛ ♿	●	▦		▦
POTENZA: *Z' Mingo* €€ Contrada Botte 2, 85100. [0971 44 59 29. This simple trattoria is the perfect place to join the locals eating regional fare. On the menu: fresh pasta, roasted meats and local cheeses and salamis. ● Mon; Aug. ⬛				
REGGIO DI CALABRIA: *Villeggiante* €€ Via Eremo-Condera 31, Località Mariannazzo 89125. [0965 250 21. A Reggio Calabrian institution where good simple fare is well prepared and served informally. Try *spaghetti* with broccoli or rich, spicy sausages. ⬛ ▦	●	▦		
ROSSANO: *I Tre Moschettieri* €€ Loc. Santa Caterina, 87067. [0983 51 58 38. This is a simple, traditional trattoria serving fresh pasta and fish specialities. Try the sardines in spiced vinegar or the cuttlefish specials. Great ice cream. ● Sep. ⬛ ▦				
SCILLA: *La Grotta Azzurra* €€€ Via Cristoforo Colombo, 89058. [0965 75 48 89. A wonderful setting on the beach where, according to legend, Ulysses came ashore. This basic trattoria serves mainly fish. ● Mon lunch; Dec–Jan. ⬛ ▦ ♿		▦		▦
TROPEA: *Pimm's* €€€€€ Corso Vittorio Emanuele 60, 88038. [0963 66 61 05. A beautiful setting with a sea view in the historic centre. Simple, local fare, well prepared and pleasantly served. Start with seafood *crostini* or smoked swordfish, then try pasta with sea urchins and stuffed, grilled squid. ● Mon; Mar, Nov.	●	▦		

VENOSA: *Il Guiscardo*   €€
Via Accademia dei Rinascenti 106, 85029. 0972 323 62.
This restaurant specializes in seafood and traditional Basilicata and
Puglia cuisine. The atmosphere is simple and children are welcome.
Panoramic views. ● *Sun.*

SICILY

AGRIGENTO: *Kalos*   €€€
Piazzetta San Calogero 1, 92100. 0922 263 89.
A bright restaurant with original and well-prepared cuisine. Try pasta with pistachio
and gorgonzola, grilled fish and *cassata* of ricotta. ● *Sun; 2 wks Jan, 2 wks Nov.*

AGRIGENTO: *Kókalos*   €€€
Via Cavaleri Magazzeni, 92100. 0922 60 64 27. www.ristorante-kokalos.com
A friendly rustic trattoria with an extensive terrace facing the Temple of Juno.
Try the *fettucine* in orange sauce, fresh grilled fish and almond parfait.

AGRIGENTO: *Trattoria del Pescatore*   €€€
Lungomare Falcone e Borsellino 20, Località Lido di San Leone 92100. 0922 41 43 42.
The chef chooses the fish daily and uses it, sometimes raw, in simple but
delicious dishes with oil and lemon juice. The pasta speciality is *spaghetti*
with swordfish, aubergine and basil. ● *Mon; Oct–Apr.*

BAGHERIA: *Don Ciccio*   €€
Via del Cavaliere 87, 90011. 091 93 24 42.
This town-centre trattoria concentrates on regional specialities. Look out for
pasta with sardines, broccoli, tuna and other sauces. ● *Sun, Wed; Aug.*

CATANIA: *I Vicere*   €€
Via Grotte Bianche 97, 95129. 095 32 01 88.
Outside dining on a terrace with spectacular views. Good food, particularly
the succulent pork fillet in mandarin sauce. ● *Tue (winter).*

CEFALÙ: *L'Antica Corte*   €€
Corso Ruggero 193, 90015. 0921 42 32 28.
A trattoria-pizzeria in an old courtyard in the historic centre, the cuisine
is local with influences from almost-forgotten old Sicilian recipes.
● *Thu (exc Jun–Sep), Sat & Sun (Feb); Nov.*

ENNA: *Ariston*   €€€
Via Roma 353, 94100. 0935 260 38.
In the heart of Enna, with a selection of fish dishes as well as meat specialities, such
as stuffed lamb, or bean and pea soup and *frittata* (omelette). ● *Sun; Aug.*

ERICE: *Monte San Giuliano*   €€€
Via San Rocco 7, 91016. 0923 86 95 95.
Located in the centre of town, the menu is based on Sicilian traditions and includes
fresh pasta with sardines, and couscous with fish. ● *Mon; 2 wks Jan, 2 wks Nov.*

ERICE: *Osteria di Venere*   €€€
Via Roma 6, 91016. 0923 86 93 62.
A delightful restaurant in an attractive 17th-century building. The menu
is basically Sicilian and Mediterranean. ● *Wed (winter).*

ISOLE EOLIE: *Filippino*   €€€€
Piazza del Municipio, Lipari 98055. 090 981 10 02. www.filippino.it
An essentially Sicilian, sea-based menu includes swordfish, home-made *maccheroni*
and some excellent *cassata Siciliana.* ● *Mon (Oct– Apr); 15 Nov–25 Dec.*

MARSALA: *Delfino*   €€
Via Lungomare Mediterraneo 672, 91025. 0923 96 95 65.
Three lovely rooms all with views over either the sea or the garden. Try
the sunflower *spaghetti* or sword fish *alla Messinese.* ● *Tue.*

MARSALA: *Mothia*   €€
Contrada Ettore Infersa 13, 91016. 0923 74 52 55.
Simple, delicious cooking with home-made bread, pasta, desserts and cakes. The
tagliatelle with lobster sauce is particularly good. ● *Tue (winter).*

PALERMO: *Temptation*   €€
Via Torretta 94, Località Sferracavallo 90148. 091 691 11 04.
This trattoria offers an all-inclusive menu of seafood *antipasti*, and the pasta
with aubergines and fried fish is particularly recommended. ● *Thu.*

	FIXED-PRICE MENU	GOOD WINE LIST	FORMAL DRESS	OUTDOOR TABLES

Average prices for a three-course meal for one, including a half-bottle of house wine, tax and service:
€ under €18
€€ €18–€30
€€€ €30–€40
€€€€ €40–€52
€€€€€ over €52.

FIXED-PRICE MENU
A fixed-price menu on offer, usually with three courses.

GOOD WINE LIST
Denotes a wide range of good quality wines.

FORMAL DRESS
Some restaurants require men to wear a jacket and tie.

OUTDOOR TABLES
Tables for eating outdoors, often with a good view.

CREDIT CARDS
The symbol shows that major credit cards are accepted.

	FP	GW	FD	OT
PALERMO: *Sympaty* €€€ Via Piano Gallo 18, Località Mondello 90151. ☎ 091 45 44 70. The dining room has good views over the bay of Mondello and the menu is almost exclusively fish. Try *ricci* (little sea urchins), octopus and squid. ● *Mon; Nov.*	●	▦		▦
PALERMO: *La Scuderia* €€€€ Viale del Fante 9, 90146. ☎ 091 52 03 23. w www.lascuderiasnc.it Set in the Parco della Favorita, this elegant restaurant sticks to traditional Sicilian cuisine, carefully and deliciously prepared. ● *Sun; 2 wks Aug.*		▦		
RAGUSA: *La Ciotola* €€€ Via Archimede 23, 9710. ☎ 0932 22 89 44. This elegant, modern restaurant in the city centre serves well-prepared specialities like *maccheroncini* with aubergine, and much fish. ● *Mon; Aug.*		▦		
SCIACCA: *Hostaria del Vicolo* €€€ Vicolo Sammaritano 10, 92019. ☎ 0925 230 71. The menu is Sicilian with dishes such as *tagliatelle* with prawns, aubergine and *bottarga* (tuna eggs), and tasty desserts. ● *Mon eve; 2 wks Oct.*		▦		
SELINUNTE: *Lido Azzurro* €€ Via Marco Polo 51, Località Marinella 91022. ☎ 0924 462 11. A bustling trattoria with views of the top of the acropolis from the terrace. There's a wide range of buffet-style *antipasti*. ● *Nov–Feb.*				▦
SIRACUSA: *Minerva* € Piazza Duomo 20, 96100. ☎ 0931 694 04. A pizzeria right in the historic centre, with a wide and imaginative range of pizzas on offer. Tables are outside in the cathedral square. ● *Mon (winter).*		▦		▦
SIRACUSA: *La Foglia* €€ Via Capodieci 29, 96100. ☎ 0931 662 33. Vegetables and pulses are the mainstays at this restaurant in the historic centre. Try fresh pasta with vegetables or fish and the soups. ● *Tue (winter).*	●	▦		
SIRACUSA: *Jonico 'a Rutta 'e Ciauli* €€€ Riviera Dionisio il Grande 194, 96100. ☎ 0931 655 40. This restaurant has a bright dining room with walls covered with Sicilian ceramics and agricultural artifacts. The cuisine is regional and traditional. ● *Tue; Easter, Christmas.*		▦		▦
TAORMINA: *Pizzeria Vecchia Taormina* € Vico Ebrei 3, 98039. ☎ 0942 62 55 89. A traditional pizzeria in the old Jewish quarter of Taormina. There is a massive range of Sicilian-style pizzas and delicious *antipasti*. ● *Wed eve; Jul.*				▦
TAORMINA: *Al Duomo* €€€€€ Vico Ebrei 11, 98039. ☎ 0942 62 56 56. w www.ristorantealduomo.it A typical Sicilian trattoria, dishes include tuna and swordfish. ● *Wed (winter); Feb.*		▦		▦
TAORMINA: *La Giara* €€€€€ Vicolo La Floresta 1, 98039. ☎ 0942 233 60. A pretty restaurant and piano bar with beautiful views over the bay. Try *ravioli* with aubergine and wild fennel *involtini* (parcels). ● *Mon–Fri (Nov–Mar).*		▦		▦
TRAPANI: *Da Peppe* €€€ Via Spalti 50, 91100. ☎ 0923 282 46. Trapani specialities served as well as house dishes established over the years. The mainstay is fish, including locally caught tuna. ● *Sun eve (winter), Mon; Dec–Jan.*	●	▦		▦
TRAPANI: *P&G* €€€ Via Spalti 1, 91100. ☎ 0923 54 77 01. This restaurant has become an institution in Trapani. During the annual tuna *mattanza*, fresh tuna is served in a huge variety of ways. ● *Sun; Aug–mid-Sep.*		▦		

SARDINIA

ALGHERO: *Al Tuguri*   €€€
Via Maiorca 113, 07041. [079 97 67 72. [W] www.altuguri.it
A pretty restaurant in a 15th-century building in the historic centre, with an interesting
menu of Catalan and other Mediterranean specialities. ● Sun; Dec–Jan. ▣ ▤ ⚡

ALGHERO: *La Lepanto*   €€€
Via Carlo Alberto 135, 07041. [079 97 91 16.
Regional dishes, such as *bottarga* (tuna roe) and lobster and other creative
dishes: warm octopus, and scampi with pecorino. ● Mon (winter). ▣ ▤

BOSA: *Mannu da Giancarlo e Rita*   €€
Viale Alghero 28, 08013. [0785 37 53 06. [W] www.mannuhotel.it
A smart, modern restaurant offering extremely good local fish specialities;
Bosa is famous for fresh lobster, which is served here in a celery sauce. ▣ ▤ ⚡

CAGLIARI: *Nuovo Saint Pierre*   €€
Via Coghinas 15, 09122. [070 27 15 78.
Traditional dishes include wild boar with lentils, wild asparagus *risotto*, roasted
lamb and stuffed beef. Fish is served in summer. ● Sun; Sep. ▣ ▤ ⚡ ♿

CAGLIARI: *Dal Corsaro*   €€€€€
Viale Regina Margherita 28, 09124. [070 66 43 18.
Good service and a pleasant atmosphere in which to enjoy regional dishes
(fish *ravioli*), original creations (*tagliatelle* with courgettes and clams) and some
Cagliari classics. Vegetarian dishes also available. ● Sun; Aug. ▣ ▤ ⚡

CALASETTA: *Da Pasqualino*   €€€
Via Regina Margherita, 09011. [0781 884 73.
Delicious local fish-based specialities are served in this simple and relaxed trattoria,
including fish soups, *bottarga* (tuna roe) and lobster. ● Tue (winter); Feb. ▣ ▤ ⚡ ♿

NUORO: *Canne al Vento*   €€€
Viale Repubblica 66, 08100. [0784 20 17 62.
This restaurant offers roast meats, excellent cheeses, octopus salad and a hot *seadas*
(honey dessert). Vegetarians are also catered for. ● Sun; Easter, Christmas. ▣ ▤ ♿

OLBIA: *Gallura*   €€€€
Corso Umberto 145. [0789 246 48.
This is considered to be one of the finest seafood restaurants in Sardinia. Serves all kinds
of fish, shellfish and crustaceans. Mouthwatering antipasti. ● Mon; end-Dec–beg Jan. ▣ ▤

OLIENA: *CK*   €€€
Corso ML King 2/4, 08025. [0784 28 80 24.
Typical local specialities in this family-run restaurant include game and herbs, fresh
cheese *ravioli* and honey desserts. ● lunch; Mon (winter), Sun (Jun–Sep). ▣ ▤ ⚡

ORISTANO: *Il Faro*   €€€€
Via Bellini 25, 09170. [0783 700 02.
One of Sardinia's best restaurants, serving regional dishes based on what is fresh in
the market that day, particularly fish and seafood. ● Sun; Jul, Christmas. ▣ ▤ ⚡ ♿

PORTO CERVO: *Gianni Pedrinelli*   €€€€€
Località Piccolo Pevero, 07020. [0789 924 36.
The menu is regional serving much fish. Try the house speciality, a typically
Sardinian dish, *porcettu allo spiedo* (pork on the spit). ● Oct–Feb. ▣

PORTO ROTONDO: *Da Giovannino*   €€€€€
Piazza Quadra, 07026. [0789 352 80.
Popular with Italian politicos and media types, who dine on expensive but
delicious (and attentively served) Mediterranean specialities, which are
accompanied by superb wines. ● Sun eve, Mon (winter). ▣ ▤ ♿

PORTOSCUSO: *La Ghinghetta*   €€€€€
Via Cavour 26, Località Sa Caletta, 09010. [0781 50 81 43. [@] la.ghinghetta@tiscalinet.it
Set in a charming fishing village, the almost exclusively fish-based menu adds a
different twist to local specialities. Rooms available. ● Sun; Nov–Mar. ▣ ▤

SASSARI: *Cenacolo*   €€€
Via Ozieri 2, 07100. [079 23 62 51.
The menu here offers the very best of sea and land regional specialities according
to the season: there are mushrooms in autumn, seafood in summer and appropriate
vegetables all year round. ● Sun; Aug, 2 wks Christmas. ▣ ▤ ⚡ ♿

SURVIVAL
GUIDE

PRACTICAL INFORMATION

ENTE NAZIONALE
ITALIANO PER IL TURISMO
Tourist board logo

Ask any Italian and they will almost certainly tell you that Italy is the most beautiful country in the world. They may not be far wrong. However, the charm and allure of Italy may help to veil some of her numerous practical problems. Getting information is rarely straightforward; public

offices and banks are nearly always crippled by long queues and bureaucracy, and the postal service is renowned for its inefficiency. This section, together with some forward planning and a little patience, should help you cope with some of Italy's idiosyncrasies.

Tourists crossing the Ponte della Paglia in Venice (see p105)

VISAS AND PERMESSO DI SOGGIORNO

European Union nationals and citizens of the US, Canada, Australia and New Zealand do not need visas for stays of up to three months. Most European Union (EU) visitors need only a valid identity document, but visitors from UK, Ireland, Denmark and Sweden do need a passport. All visitors should check requirements with the Italian embassy before travelling and, officially, declare themselves to the Italian police within eight days of arrival.

If you are staying in a hotel or campsite, this will be done for you, otherwise contact the local *Questura* (police station).

Anyone wishing to stay in Italy for more than three months (eight days for non-EU citizens) will have to obtain a *permesso di soggiorno* (permit to stay). You can apply for a permit at any main police station, *Questura di Provincia*. You must apply for the correct permit, either a permit to work (*lavoro*) or a permit to study (*studio*). For each permit you will need to submit a written

application (*domanda*), passport-style photographs and photocopies of your passport. If you are looking for work, these items need to be accompanied by proof of your future employment in Italy or other means of financial support.

To apply for a study permit, it is necessary to get a letter from the relevant school or university giving details of your course. This then has to be sent to the Italian consulate in your country of origin to obtain an official covering letter, or declaration. You will also need some form of guarantee that your medical bills will be paid should you become ill or have an accident. A comprehensive insurance policy (*see p617*) would be sufficient.

WHEN TO VISIT

Italy's towns and historic sites are extremely popular attractions and it is worth considering this when planning your trip. Rome, Florence and Venice are all crowded from spring to October and it is advisable to book a hotel well in advance. In August the cities are generally slightly

less busy, abandoned by their inhabitants for the summer holidays. At Easter, Rome is overrun by pilgrims and tourists, and in February, Venice triples its population during Carnevale (*see p65*). Seaside resorts fill up during July and August, whereas June and September can be equally hot but less crowded. The seas and beaches are notably cleaner at the beginning of summer. December to March is the time of year for skiing, although the first snow often falls as early as November. Most sights are open all year, except on some public holidays (*see p65*) and often two or more Mondays each month (*see p614*).

Rome's renowned Tazza d'Oro café, an ideal rest stop after sightseeing

SEASONAL DIFFERENCES

The northern part of Italy is generally more temperate than the south, which has a Mediterranean climate. June to September is hot and in peak summer, also humid. Summer storms can be quite dramatic, but often only last a few hours. Spring and autumn are ideal for visiting cities; temperatures are mild. Winter can be bitterly cold, especially in the north. *The Climate of Italy* on pages 68–9 takes a detailed look at the country's regional weather.

◁ **The beautiful Piazza del Campo in Siena, meeting place for visitors and locals**

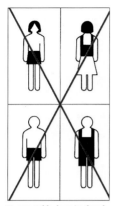

Unacceptable dress in church: both sexes are required to cover torsos and upper arms

ETIQUETTE AND TIPPING

PEOPLE IN ITALY ARE friendly towards foreign visitors. On entering a shop or bar it is customary to greet people with a general *buon giorno* (good morning) or *buona sera* (good evening), and the same applies when leaving. They will also try to be helpful when asked directions in the street. If your Italian is slight, *scusi* followed by the name of the place you wish to go to will often suffice. *Grazie* (thank you) is replied to with *prego* (you're welcome).

Tipping in restaurants is expected when the 15 per cent service is not included. However, as much as 10 per cent would be considered generous and a tip is often not expected at all in family-run restaurants. Taxi drivers and hotel porters expect a few euros if they have been helpful. You could simply round the bill up to the nearest €2.

Italians are very dress-conscious and unusual clothes do get noticed. In places of worship, cover your torso and upper arms; shorts and skirts must reach below the knee.

While smoking in public places is commonplace, drunkenness is not tolerated.

CUSTOMS

ON 30 JUNE 1999, the intra-EU Duty and Tax Free Allowances, better known as Duty-free and mainly affecting such high-tax items as alcohol, perfumes and tobacco, were abolished. However, for EU residents the amount of these goods that can be imported for personal use has increased.

Consulates can generally provide up-to-date information on particular customs regulations. To find out what you can take back from Italy to non-EU countries, contact that particular country's customs department, who will be able to advise you.

TAX EXEMPTION

VALUE ADDED TAX (IVA in Italy) ranges from 12–35 per cent, depending on the item. Non-European Union citizens making purchases in Italy can claim an IVA rebate, provided the total expenditure is over €155. It is a long process, and it is easier to get a refund if you shop where you see the "Euro Free Tax" sign, rather than from a market stall, for example. Show your passport to the shop assistant, complete a form, and the IVA will be deducted from your bill. Alternatively present a customs officer with your purchases and their receipts upon departure. He or she will stamp the receipts, which you then send to the vendor. A refund should eventually be sent to you.

The clock of San Giacomo di Rialto in Venice *(see p93)*

ITALIAN TIME

ITALY IS ONE HOUR ahead of Greenwich Mean Time (GMT). The clocks are put forward one hour in March and back in October. For example: London is one hour behind Italy; Sydney is nine hours ahead; while Ottawa is six hours behind.

ELECTRICAL ADAPTORS

THE VOLTAGE IN ITALY is 220 volts, with two-pin round-pronged plugs. For European appliances, the plug can simply be changed over, whereas US equipment will need an adaptor. Italian plugs come in many different sizes, without any apparent special purpose, and you can buy adaptors or even just swap plugs. It is worth buying travel plugs before you leave as they are difficult to find in Italy. Most hotels with three or more stars have hairdriers and shaving points in all bedrooms, but check the voltage first, to be safe.

Standard Italian plug

BOOKING TICKETS

THEATRES IN ITALY do not always take bookings over the telephone – you have to visit the box office in person. However, there are agencies, such as **Box Office**, **Virtours** and **Amitonline**, that will book tickets for you (for a fee). Opera tickets are sold months in advance, with just a few held back until two days prior to the performance. Tickets for rock and jazz concerts are also sold at some record shops whose names appear on the publicity posters.

Tourist Information

The NATIONAL tourist board, **ENIT**, has branches in capital cities worldwide and offers general information on Italy. For more specific requests, contact the local tourist offices. The addresses and telephone numbers are listed under each town or city, directly under the title, and they are plotted on the town and city maps. An EPT *(Ente Provinciale di Turismo)* has information on its town and surrounding province, whereas an APT *(Azienda di Promozione Turistica)* deals exclusively with individual towns. Both offices help with practical information such as hotel bookings and tours. They also provide free maps and guidebooks in various languages. The EPT and APT can refer you to local tour guides and advise on trips and excursions.

Small towns will have a *Pro Loco*, a tourist office run by the local administration, which is sometimes open only during the tourist season. It is usually located in the town hall *(comune)*.

Sign for tourist information

Tours

Many tour companies organize coach trips, with English-speaking guides, that include all the main tourist attractions in Italy. American Express offices in Rome, Florence, Venice and

A guided group tour through the streets of Florence

A student relaxing in the sun in Gaiole in Chianti

Milan organize local trips and **CIT** offers coach tours that go all over the country. If you are looking for something a little more personal and off the beaten track, check the local pages of national newspapers for tour groups or organizations. Local tourist boards will also be able to advise you. Always employ official guides and be sure to establish the fee in advance. For information on various specialist holidays, turn to pages 624–5.

Sightseeing Permits

To visit certain sites in Rome, such as those which are not normally open to tourists, you need a written permit, which can be obtained from:

Comune di Roma
Soprintendenze Comunale
Piazza Lovatelli 35, Rome. **Map** 3 A5.
C *06 67 10 32 38.* **FAX** *06 696 81 17.*

Sightseeing Opening Hours

Italian museums are gradually conforming to new regulations, particularly in the north and centre, opening from 9am–7pm daily, except for Mondays. In winter, however, many revert to slightly earlier closing times, particularly on Sundays, but it is best to check. Privately run and smaller museums have their own times, so it is advisable to phone in advance. Archaeological sites are generally open from 9am to one hour

before sunset, Tuesday to Sunday. Churches are usually open from about 7am–12:30pm and 4–7pm. However, they often prefer not to let tourists in during services, so Sunday is not the best day to visit.

Daytime sightseeing on a tranquil canal in Venice

Admission Charges

Sightseeing fees range from €2 to €8. Churches are usually free, but some expect a donation, and you will need coins to illuminate works of art. Reductions for students are not always offered but many state-run museums and archaeological sites allow free entry for EU residents under 18 and over 60 years of age. Large groups are often entitled to a discount as well. If reductions are available, you will need to show a valid form of identification.

Student Information

The NATIONAL student travel organization, **CTS** (Centro Turistico Studentesco), has branches throughout Italy and

Europe. They issue the International Student Identity Card (ISIC) and the Youth International Educational Exchange Card (YIEE). Both can be used, along with a passport, for discounts at museums and other tourist attractions. The ISIC card also gives access to a 24-hour telephone helpline that provides general advice and information. As well as issuing youth cards, CTS

ISIC card

offers cut-price car hire and will organize holidays and courses. For details about youth hostels, contact the **Associazione Italiana Alberghi per la Gioventù** (the Italian YHA), provided that you are a current member.

TRAVELLING WITH CHILDREN

ON THE WHOLE, Italians love children, to an extent that sometimes seems over-indulgent. Most trattorias and pizzerias welcome them and there are no rules excluding children from bars. Hotels also welcome children, but smaller establishments usually have limited facilities. Some of the more up-market hotels may offer a babysitting service. It is a common sight to see children playing outside fairly late at night, especially in summer. Most towns have playgrounds and many have summer fun-fairs. For young swimmers, the calm Mediterranean is ideal.

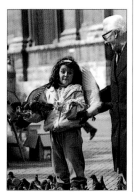

Fascinated child feeding pigeons at Piazza Navona, Rome

DISABLED TRAVELLERS

AWARENESS of the needs of the disabled is low, but improving, with ramps and lifts being added to museums and some churches. Trains and buses are also becoming more disabled-friendly. In Milan **AIAS** (Associazione Italiana Assistenza Spastici) and in Rome **CO.INN** provide information and general assistance.

A mechanically operated wheelchair ramp across a bridge

RELIGIOUS SERVICES

ALMOST 85 PER CENT of the population is Catholic. Sunday mass is celebrated throughout the country, while in the principal churches services are also held during the week. In major cities some churches, such as the church of San Silvestro (Piazza San Silvestro) in Rome, offer services and confession in English. For some visitors, a trip to Rome will include an audience with the pope (*p409*).

Although Italy is predominantly Catholic, all the main religious beliefs are represented. For details contact the main centres in Rome.

CONVERSION CHART

Imperial to Metric
1 inch = 2.54 centimetres
1 foot = 30 centimetres
1 mile = 1.6 kilometres
1 ounce = 28 grams
1 pound = 454 grams
1 pint = 0.57 litre
1 gallon = 4.6 litres

Metric to Imperial
1 centimetre = 0.4 inch
1 metre = 3 feet 3 inches
1 kilometre = 0.6 mile
1 gram = 0.04 ounce
1 kilogram = 2.2 pounds
1 litre = 1.8 pints

Personal Security and Health

Aᴌᴛʜᴏᴜɢʜ ɪᴛᴀʟʏ ɪs ɢᴇɴᴇʀᴀʟʟʏ a safe place for visitors, it is wise to keep a watchful eye on your personal belongings, especially in the larger towns and cities. There is a conspicuous police presence throughout the country, and in the event of an emergency or crime, any of the police officers described in this section will be able to assist you and tell you where to go to report an incident. If you fall ill, pharmacies are a good first stop where medically trained staff can give advice or tell you where to find further help. In an emergency, the Casualty Department *(Pronto Soccorso)* of any hospital will treat you.

Commissariato di Polizia – a police station

Police car

Green Cross ambulance in Venice

Roman fire engine

Pᴇʀsᴏɴᴀʟ Pʀᴏᴘᴇʀᴛʏ

Pᴇᴛᴛʏ ᴛʜᴇғᴛ such as pick-pocketing, bag snatching and car theft is rife. In the event of a theft you must report it within 24 hours to the nearest *questura* or *commissariato* (police station).

Avoid leaving anything visible in an unattended car, including a car radio. If you have to leave luggage in a car, find a hotel that has private parking. When making a purchase, always check your change and do not keep wallets in back pockets, especially on buses or in other crowded places. "Bum bags" and money belts are a favourite target for pickpockets, so try to keep them hidden. When walking, hold bags and cameras on the

inside of the pavement so as not to tempt motorized snatchers and do not show expensive cameras and video equipment in areas off tourist routes. The safest way to carry large sums of money is to use travellers' cheques.

Try to keep your travellers' cheques and receipts separate, together with a photocopy of vital documents, in case of loss or theft. It is also advisable to get comprehensive travel insurance that covers theft of personal possessions in addition to covering cancellation/delay of flights, loss/damage of luggage, money and other valuables, as well as personal liability and accidents. If you do need to make an insurance claim for stolen or lost property, you must get a copy of the report *(denuncia)* from the police station when you report the incident. In case of lost passports, go to your embassy or consulate; for lost travellers' cheques, contact the issuing company's nearest office.

Lᴇɢᴀʟ Assɪsᴛᴀɴᴄᴇ

A ᴄᴏᴍᴘʀᴇʜᴇɴsɪᴠᴇ insurance package should include cover for legal assistance and advice. If you do not have insurance cover, contact your embassy as soon as possible after an incident, such as an accident, occurs. The embassy can offer advice and should

provide you with a list of English- and Italian-speaking lawyers who are knowledgeable about both the Italian and English legal systems.

Pᴇʀsᴏɴᴀʟ Sᴇᴄᴜʀɪᴛʏ

Aᴌᴛʜᴏᴜɢʜ ᴘᴇᴛᴛʏ ᴄʀɪᴍᴇ in the cities is frequent, violent crime in Italy is rare. However, it is common for people to raise their voices aggressively during an argument. Usually, remaining calm and being polite will help to defuse the situation. Always be wary of unofficial tour guides, taxi drivers or strangers who wish to assist you or advise you on accommodation, restaurants or shops as they may expect something in return.

Wᴏᴍᴇɴ Tʀᴀᴠᴇʟʟᴇʀs

Wᴏᴍᴇɴ ᴛʀᴀᴠᴇʟʟɪɴɢ on their own in Italy are likely to meet with a lot of attention. Although this is often more of an irritation than a danger, it is best to keep away from lonely, unlit streets and areas

A team of *carabinieri* in traffic police uniform

near railway stations at night. Walking quickly and purposefully is a good way to avoid any unwanted attention. The staff at hotels and restaurants generally treat their single female guests and customers with extra care and attention.

THE POLICE

THERE ARE SEVERAL different police forces in Italy and each one fulfils a particular role. The state police, *la polizia*, wear blue uniforms and drive blue cars. They deal with most crimes. The *carabinieri* are militarily trained and wear dark blue and black uniforms with red striped trousers. These officers deal with a variety of offences from organized crime to speeding and can also conduct random security checks. The *guardia di finanza* are the financial police force (the fraud squad), and wear grey uniforms with yellow striped trousers. The *vigili urbani*, or the municipal traffic police, wear blue and white uniforms in winter and white during the summer. Even though they are not official police officers, the *vigili urbani* can issue heavy fines for traffic and parking offences. They can usually be spotted patrolling the streets, enforcing laws or directing traffic. Officers from any of the forces will be able to help.

Municipal policeman

INTERPRETERS

INDEPENDENT INTERPRETERS and translators often advertise their services in newspapers and foreign-language bookshops. You will find agencies listed in the Yellow Pages *(Pagine Gialle)* and the AITI *(Associazione Italiana di Traduttori e Interpreti)* has a list of qualified translators and interpreters. In an emergency, your embassy will be able to provide an interpreter.

Outside a Florentine pharmacy with a green cross sign

MEDICAL TREATMENT

EMERGENCY MEDICAL care in Italy is free for all EU citizens. The E111 form, which is available from main post offices throughout the UK, covers emergencies only; private medical insurance is needed for all other types of treatment. The E111 comes with a booklet that contains general health advice and information about how to claim free medical treatment when travelling abroad. In order for the form to be valid, it has to be completed in full and stamped at a post office in the UK before your journey.

Non-EU citizens should try to arrive in Italy with comprehensive private medical insurance to cover all eventualities. If you do need emergency treatment, go to the *Pronto Soccorso* (Casualty Department) of the nearest hospital.

No inoculations are needed for Italy, but mosquito repellent is advisable in summer. Repelling creams and sprays can be found in pharmacies, and electrical devices can be bought which burn tablets.

EMERGENCY SUPPLIES

VARIOUS MEDICAL products, including homeopathic medicines, are available in any pharmacy *(farmacia)*, but a prescription is often required. Thanks to a night rota *(servizio notturno)*, there is always a pharmacy open in all cities and most towns.

Those that are open at night are listed in the local pages of daily newspapers and on all pharmacy doors.

Tabacchi (tobacco) shops are a good source of many useful supplies and are easily recognized by their "T" signs (see below). Apart from tobacco, cigarettes and matches, you can buy razors and batteries, bus and metro tickets, telephone cards and parking cards. At some, you can also purchase postage stamps and get parcels weighed and costed.

A Tabacchi shop, with its characteristic white "T" sign

Banking and Local Currency

VIRTUALLY ALL ITALIAN HOTELS, many shops, large restaurants and petrol stations now accept major credit cards. Only in the more off-the-beaten-track locations will you have difficulties without euros. When you pay with a credit card, you might be asked to show identification, such as your passport. Foreign currency can be changed in banks, although these are often crowded and service tends to be slow. All banks will cash travellers' cheques and cashpoint machines *(bancomat)* will accept cards with a PIN number. Most machines also accept MasterCard (Access), VISA and American Express cards. Although banks often have the best exchange rates, bureaux de change and foreign exchange machines can be more convenient.

Electronic exchange machine

Cash dispenser which also accepts VISA and MasterCard (Access)

Changing Money

BANKING HOURS are somewhat restrictive and can also be slightly erratic so it is safest to acquire some local currency before you arrive in Italy. Exchange rates will vary from place to place.

Once you arrive, the most convenient way to change money is to use the electronic exchange machines, which are located at all major airports, train stations and banks. The machines have multilingual instructions and the exchange rate is clearly displayed on the screen. You simply feed in notes of the same foreign currency and you will receive euros in return.

Bureaux de change can be found in all main towns. Although they are easier to use, they tend to have higher exchange rates and charge more commission than banks.

Travellers'Cheques

TRAVELLERS' CHEQUES are the safest way to carry large sums of money. Choose a well-known name such as Thomas Cook or American Express. There is a minimum commission charge, which makes changing small sums of money uneconomical. Check the exchange rates before you travel and decide whether sterling, dollar or euro travellers' cheques are more appropriate. Euro travellers' cheques may be difficult to cash because it is not very profitable for the exchanger.

Regional Differences in Cost of Living

THE NORTH is generally more expensive than the south, but there are many exceptions. Restaurants and hotels off the beaten track are usually better value, and buying locally made produce is cost effective if you avoid obvious tourist traps.

Metal-detecting security doors found at most banks

Banking Hours

BANKS ARE USUALLY open between 8:30am and 1:30pm, Monday to Friday. Most also open for an hour in the afternoon, from about 2:15pm to 3pm or 2:30pm until 3:30pm, depending on the bank. All banks close at weekends and for public holidays, and they also close early the day before a major holiday. Bureaux de change however, are often open all day, and in some places, also late at night.

Using Banks

FOR SECURITY PURPOSES, most banks have electronic double doors with metal detectors, allowing one person in at a time. Metal objects and bags should first be deposited in lockers situated in the foyer. Press the button to open the outer door, then wait for it to close behind you. The inner door then opens automatically. Do not be alarmed by the heavily armed guards that patrol most banks in Italy.

Changing money at a bank can be a frustrating process involving endless form-filling and queuing. First you have to go to the window that displays the *cambio* sign and then to the *cassa* to obtain your money. If in doubt, ask someone in order to avoid waiting in the wrong queue.

If you need to have money sent to you in Italy, banks at home can telex money to an Italian bank, but it takes about a week. American Express, Thomas Cook and Western Union all provide swifter money transfer services, with a charge to the sender.

THE EURO

TWELVE COUNTRIES have replaced their traditional currencies with a single European currency, the euro. Austria, Belgium, Finland, France, Germany, Greece, Ireland, Italy, Luxembourg, Netherlands, Portugal and Spain chose to join the new currency; the UK, Denmark and Sweden stayed out, with an option to review their situation. The euro was introduced on 1 January 1999, but only for banking purposes. Notes and coins came into circulation on 1 January 2002. A transition period allowed euros and lire to be used simultaneously, with lire phased out by March 2002. All euro notes and coins can be used anywhere inside the participating member states.

Bank Notes

Euro bank notes have seven denominations. The €5 note (grey in colour) is the smallest, followed by the €10 note (pink), €20 note (blue), €50 note (orange), €100 note (green), €200 note (yellow) and €500 note (purple). All notes show the 12 stars of the European Union.

5 euros

10 euros

20 euros

50 euros

100 euros

200 euros

500 euros

2 euros

1 euro

50 cents

20 cents

10 cents

Coins

The euro has eight coin denominations: €1 and €2; 50 cents, 20 cents, 10 cents, 5 cents, 2 cents and 1 cent. The €2 and €1 coins are both silver and gold in colour. The 50-, 20- and 10-cent coins are gold. The 5-, 2- and 1-cent coins are bronze.

5 cents

2 cents

1 cent

Communications

Although the Italian postal service is known for being very slow, Italy's other forms of communication, at least in the cities, are more efficient. Fax machines, courier services and telephones are all widespread, and Internet points are available throughout Italy. Foreign-language newspapers and magazines are on sale in all cities and most large towns. Both state-run and privately owned television stations exist, but only satellite television and radio stations broadcast foreign-language programmes.

Telephone company logo

Public Telephones

The Italian national telephone company is Telecom Italia. Coin-operated telephones are being phased out and replaced by new, card-operated machines. The latest public telephones have instructions in five languages (Italian, English, French, Spanish and German). To select a language, push the top right-hand button. Although some telephones will take both cards and coins, most only accept a Telecom credit card.

Telephone sign

Phone cards (*carta* or *scheda telefonica*) can be purchased from bars, newspaper kiosks, post offices and *tabacchi* displaying the black-and-white T sign. When making long-distance or international calls from a coin-operated phone, make sure you have plenty of change at hand. If you don't put enough coins in to start with, you will be disconnected and the phone will retain your money. An alternative is to look for a *telefono a scatti*, or metered phone. These can be found in some bars and restaurants, as well as in specially designated phone centres. You will be assigned a metered phone and pay at the end of your call. Although no premium is charged, it is wise to check the rate before making a call. Prices tend to be fairly reasonable.

International phone cards, on sale at *tabacchi* and newsstands, are still the cheapest way to call abroad. Some cards offer as many as 3 hours of calls for about €10, depending on the country being called. Dial the toll-free number on the card and then enter the secret code found by scratching off the silver strip on the back of the card. You will be told the amount of credit available and then asked to dial the number you wish to call.

E-mail

E-mail is a convenient way to keep in touch with friends and family when travelling through Italy. Telecom Italia, the Italian national phone company, is setting up Internet services in the country's major train stations and public phone centres. Time is purchased using a regular phone card.

Some major chains of Internet points sell magnetic cards with credit that can be used in any of their stores throughout Italy. **Internet Train**, with branches in 25 cities, is the most visible. Visit its website for a full list of stores.

In addition, small Internet points abound (usually clustered around train stations and university areas) and users can buy computer time in blocks as short as 15 minutes. There are usually student discounts available, and cost per minute decreases as the amount of time purchased increases.

Internet Train
W www.internettrain.it

Using a Telecom Italia Card Telephone

1 Lift the receiver and wait for the dialling tone.

2 Insert a phone card in the slot.

3 The display shows how much credit is left.

4 Dial the number and wait to be connected.

5 If you still have credit and want to make a second call, press the "follow-on call" button.

To use a card, break off the marked corner and insert, arrow first.

DIRECTORY

Remember to always use the full area code (including the first zero), even when phoning within a city.

USEFUL NUMBERS

Directory Enquiries
📞 *12.*

International Directory Enquiries
📞 *4176.*

Operator Services
📞 *170* (also for reverse charge and calling card calls).

British Operator
📞 *4124.*

American Operators
📞 *800 17 24 44* (AT&T).
📞 *800 17 24 01* (MCI Worldphone).
📞 *800 17 24 05* (Sprint).

Australian Operators
📞 *800 17 26 10* (Telstra).
📞 *800 17 26 11* (Optus).

COUNTRY CODES

To call Italy from these countries dial the code and then the full area code (including the 0) and the number.

📞 *00 39 – UK*
📞 *0 1139 – US & Canada*
📞 *00 39 – Ireland*
📞 *00 1139 – Australia*

TV AND RADIO

TELEVISION CHANNELS in Italy include the state-owned RAI (Uno, Due and Tre) and Mediaset (Retequattro, Canale Cinque and Italia Uno). There are also many local channels. Most foreign programmes are dubbed into Italian, although satellite channels, such as Sky, CNN and RTL, show news and sports programmes in a variety of languages. There are three national radio stations and hundreds of local stations. The BBC World Service is on 17640 and 15485 kHz (short wave) during the day and 648 kHz (medium wave) day and night.

NEWSPAPERS

THE MAIN NATIONAL daily newspapers are *La Stampa*, *Il Corriere della Sera* and *La Repubblica*. Papers with the most detailed news of Italy's major cities include *Il Mattino* for Naples, *Il Messaggero* for Rome, *La Nazione* for Florence and *Il Giornale* for Milan.

All newspapers have local pages and listings for cinemas, theatres, main concerts and other cultural events. In Rome and Milan, *La Repubblica* also publishes regular "what's on and where to go" supplements called *TrovaRoma* and *Vivi-Milano*. Florence's *Firenze Spettacolo* and Rome's *Roma C'è* are weekly entertainment listings magazines. *Time Out Rome* offers the same type of information at regular intervals.

British and American papers, such as the *International Herald Tribune*, *International Guardian*, and *USA Today*, are readily available and tend to arrive in the main cities at around midday on the day of issue.

POST OFFICE

POST OFFICES AND also some tobacconists weigh and price letters and sell stamps. Local post offices open from 8:25am–1:50pm weekdays, and from 8:25am–12 noon on Saturday. Main post offices are open from 8:25am–7pm non-stop.

The Vatican City and the state of San Marino have their own postal system and stamps. Bear in mind that letters bearing San Marino or Vatican stamps can only be posted in San Marino and Vatican post boxes.

Letters and postcards destined for Europe cost the same as post within Italy.

City letters   Other destinations

Italian post box

Post Office sign

The red post boxes (blue in the Vatican) usually have two slots labelled *per la città* (for the city only) and *tutte le altre destinazioni* (for all other destinations).

Italian post is notorious for its unreliability and letters can take between four days and two weeks to arrive. The postal service is particularly slow in August, when delivery can take up to a month.

For a faster service, send letters express *(posta priori-taria)*. More reliable are recorded delivery *(raccoman-data)* and recorded delivery with an arrival receipt *(raccomandata con ricevuta di ritorno)*. However, anything of value should be sent by insured post *(assicurata)*.

For urgent communications, try state couriers *Posta celere* and *Cai post*, which are based at all main post offices. They guarantee delivery within 24–72 hours and are far cheaper than private couriers. Main post offices also provide telegram and fax services. The fax service, however, is not available for certain countries.

Post offices also provide a *fermo posta* service (poste restante) for a small collection fee. Send letters to the central post office, c/o Fermo Posta. You will need to show some identification (such as your passport) when collecting your mail.

REGIONS OF ITALY

ITALY CONSISTS OF 20 regions that are divided into provinces. Each province has a *capoluogo* (an administrative capital) and a *sigla*, the initials of the capital. For example, FI stands for the *capoluogo* of Florence *(Firenze)*. The *sigla* appears on car licence plates registered before 1994 and denotes the origins of the vehicle owner. The code can also be used to address mail, appearing after the town name.

Shopping

ITALY IS KNOWN FOR ITS QUALITY designer goods, ranging from chic clothing and sleek cars to stylish household items. There is a strong tradition of craftsmanship, often from family-run businesses, and there are numerous markets selling regional specialities. Apart from the town markets, it is not a country for bargains, but the joys of window shopping will offer plenty of compensation.

Fresh vegetables on display at a Florentine market stall

OPENING HOURS

OPENING TIMES for shops are usually 9:30am–1pm and around 3:30–8pm, Tuesday to Saturday and Monday afternoons. However, shopkeepers are increasingly working to more flexible hours. There are not that many large department stores, but most large towns will have a Standa, Upim and perhaps a Coin or Rinascente. These stores are often open non-stop (*orario continuato*) from 9am–8pm, Monday to Saturday. Boutiques generally open later; music and bookshops sometimes stay open after 8pm and on Sundays.

FOOD SHOPS

EVEN THOUGH there are supermarkets throughout Italy, the specialist shops, although more expensive, are still the most interesting way to shop. A *forno* has the best bread and a *macellaio* has the finest meat (go to a *norcineria* for pork products). Vegetables are freshest from market stalls or the *fruttivendolo*. You can buy cakes at the *pasticceria*, milk at the *latteria*, and pasta, ham, cheese and general foods at the often impressively stocked *alimentari*. Here you can also buy wine, but for a wider choice, head for the *enoteca*, *vineria* or *vinaio*, where you can sometimes taste the wine before purchasing.

MARKETS

ALL TOWNS HAVE regional markets that take place each week. Large towns will have several small daily markets followed by a weekly flea market, usually held on a Sunday. In this guide the main market days are listed under each town. Traders set up at 5am and start to clear away at about 1:30pm.

Food is sold by the *etto* (100 grams) and the *chilo* (kilo) (*see p615*), or in numbers (two onions, etc). Food stalls selling seasonal products generally have fresher and less expensive produce than the shops. Bargaining is not usually done when buying food, but it is worth asking for a discount (*sconto*) for clothes and other items.

SEASONAL PRODUCE

TO MAKE THE MOST of Italian food, try to buy and eat what is in season. Grapes and mushrooms are best in autumn, whereas spring is the season for asparagus, strawberries and Roman artichokes. In winter, vegetables such as cauliflower and broccoli are at their best, as are lemons from Amalfi and Sicilian blood oranges. Summer is the time for plums, pears and cherries, as well as courgettes, aubergines, tomatoes and melon.

CLOTHES AND DESIGNER SHOPS

ITALY IS RENOWNED worldwide for its fashion industry. Milan is the fashion capital and Via Monte Napoleone, in the city centre, is lined with designer boutiques. All large towns will have a selection of designer shops, usually situated near each other. Less expensive clothes are available in markets and many high-street shops, where the styles tend to be more conventional.

Protective bag with designer label

Souvenir shop in Ostuni, near Brindisi, Puglia

Italy is also famous for leather shoes and bags, the prices of which tend to be reasonable.

Sales *(saldi)* are held in summer and winter. Second-hand shops can be expensive, but the quality and condition of the clothes are usually very good. Larger markets have stalls piled high with used clothes. Rummage through and you will often find bargains. Many markets sell fake Ray Ban sunglasses, Lacoste T-shirts and Levi's jeans. Some shops have signs that read *ingresso libero* (browsers welcome), but do not be surprised if a sales assistant approaches you as soon as you walk in.

An elegant designer clothes boutique in Treviso

Colourful shop display of leather handbags in Florence

JEWELLERY AND ANTIQUE SHOPS

G LITZY GOLD JEWELLERY is very popular in Italy and every *gioielleria* (jewellery shop) will have a wide selection. For more unusual items, try the *bigiotteria* or artisan shops *(oreficeria).* Antique stores like *Antichità* and *Antiquariato* sell furniture and ornaments of varying quality and prices. You will rarely find bargains in Italy, except perhaps at the *Fiere dell'Antiquariato* (antique fairs), held throughout the year all over the country.

INTERIOR DESIGN AND HOUSEHOLD WARES

I NTERIOR DESIGN is another Italian sector where top names demand extravagant prices, with many shops concentrating on modern, high-tech styles.

There are household shops in cities and towns throughout the country. Italian kitchen-ware is particularly striking, with its stainless steel and copper pots, pans and utensils. For the lowest prices, avoid the tourist shops and, if possible, buy directly from the manufacturer. Less expensive items include the characteristic brown espresso and cappuccino cups sold in all markets.

REGIONAL SPECIALITIES

M ANY OF ITALY'S regional specialities are world famous: Parma ham, Chianti wine, olive oil and *grappa*. Regional sweets, including the Sienese *panforte* and Sicilian marzipan, are also well-known, as are cheeses such as Gorgonzola from Lombardy and Parmesan from Emilia-Romagna. Traditional crafts are still practised in Italy and range from delicate lacework and glassware in the Veneto to leatherwork, jewellery and marbled paper in Florence. Italian ceramics include elaborate Tuscan pottery, hand-painted dishes around Amalfi and De Simone's stylized designer plates from Sicily.

Display of decorative glazed pottery from Tuscany

SIZE CHART

For Australian sizes follow the British and American conversions.

Women's dresses, coats and skirts

Italian	38	40	42	44	46	48	50
British	8	10	12	14	16	18	20
American	6	8	10	12	14	16	18

Women's shoes

Italian	36	37	38	39	40	41
British	3	4	5	6	7	8
American	5	6	7	8	9	10

Men's suits

Italian	44	46	48	50	52	54	56	58 (size)
British	34	36	38	40	42	44	46	48 (inches)
American	34	36	38	40	42	44	46	48 (inches)

Men's shirts (collar size)

Italian	36	38	39	41	42	43	44	45 (cm)
British	14	15	15½	16	16½	17	17½	18 (inches)
American	14	15	15½	16	16½	17	17½	18 (inches)

Men's shoes

Italian	39	40	41	42	43	44	45	46
British	6	7	7½	8	9	10	11	12
American	7	7½	8	8½	9½	10½	11	11½

Specialist Holidays and Outdoor Activities

Exploring the countryside on horseback

ITALY OFFERS AN AMAZING variety of cultural, sporting and leisure activities. However, many schools and groups require annual membership and short-term activities are often expensive and difficult to find. Information on current leisure and sporting events in a specific region is available from the tourist office listed for each town in this guide. For details on annual festivals, see *Italy Through the Year* on pages 62–5. The following suggestions include some of the most popular as well as some more unusual pursuits.

Cycling on the tree-lined flatlands of the Po Delta

WALKING, CYCLING AND HORSERIDING

SOME ITALIAN BRANCHES of the **World Wide Fund for Nature (WWF)** organize walks and treks. **Club Alpino Italiano (CAI)** runs trekking and climbing excursions and the **Italian Birds Protection League (LIPU)** arranges nature walks and bird-watching trips. The military *IGM* maps are the most detailed but unfortunately are only available from specialist map shops.

Cycling is popular despite Italy's mountainous landscape. Travel bookshops stock publications with suggested routes, such as the Po Delta, which has miles of scenic flatlands.

Many riding schools organize trips and outings, which are also advertised in the local press. For general information, contact the **Federazione Italiana di Sport Equestre**.

MOUNTAIN SPORTS

THE MOST WELL-EQUIPPED and famous ski resorts are in the Dolomites, in the Italian Alps and around Turin, the city which will host the 2006 Winter Olympics. There are also smaller and less expensive resorts in the Apennines and in Sicily. Package ski holidays, arranged from outside Italy, offer the best deals. The **Federazione Arrampicata Sportiva Italiana** has a list of mountain climbing schools that arrange climbs for all levels.

Ski lift near the desolate Falzarego Pass, in the heart of the Dolomites

ARCHAEOLOGICAL DIGS

THE BRITISH MONTHLY magazine *Archaeology Abroad*, available in the UK, gives a comprehensive list of archaeology groups and digs worldwide. In Italy, the **Gruppo Archeologico Romano** runs two-week digs in various regions. There are summer and winter digs, for both adults and children. The group has contacts with local archaeological organizations as well.

ITALIAN LANGUAGE AND CULTURE

FOR A WIDE SELECTION of material on courses and schools in Italy, contact the Italian consulate in your home country. The **Società Dante Alighieri** provides courses in the Italian language, history of art, literature and culture. There are both full- and part-time courses available, for every level. Language schools abound in Italy's main cities and are advertised in the Yellow Pages *(Pagine Gialle)* or foreign language bookshops and newspapers. For young students, **Intercultura** will organize weekly, monthly and year-long exchanges including language courses, accommodation with Italian families and enrolment in Italian schools.

Group hiking tour in the Dolomites of Trentino-Alto Adige *(see p78)*

A lesson in Italian cookery in Sicily

In recent years, cooking holidays run by English-speaking experts in Italian cooking have become very popular. **Tasting Places**, for example, does wine tours and week-long courses in Italian cuisine, and provides beautiful private accommodation. The course locations include the Veneto, Sicily, Tuscany and Umbria. Wine-tasting tours are organized by local tourist boards. The Università per Stranieri in Perugia runs courses on Italian culture, history and cooking.

WATER SPORTS

Most lakes and many seaside resorts rent out sailing boats, canoes and windsurfing equipment. Lessons and courses are organized by clubs, which usually require membership. For a list of authorized associations contact the **Federazione Italiana di Canoa e Kayak** and the **Federazione Italiana di Vela**. Weekend and weekly sailing holidays and courses are featured in the magazine *Avventure nel Mondo* and most travel agents have a selection of sailing holidays.

Swimming pools are expensive in Italy and many do not accept people on a daily basis. You often have to pay a membership fee and a monthly tariff. Some of the luxurious hotels open their pools to the public in summer, but at pricy rates. Water parks are popular and provide pools, slides, wave machines and games. Before diving into any lakes or rivers (and even the sea near main towns) it is best to check that the water is not polluted. The **Federazione Italiana di**

Attività Subacquee runs underwater diving courses, and can give information on all local centres.

AIR SPORTS

There are schools nationwide that offer hang-gliding and flying courses, but the minimum duration of each course is one month. For information and a list of schools contact the **AeroClub Italia**. You must be licensed before you can fly and all crafts must be registered with AeroClub.

OTHER SPORTS

Golf is a popular sport in Italy and there are plenty of courses to choose from. Home membership and handicap are often required for daily access to a club.

Italian tennis clubs usually operate on a membership basis, unless you are invited as a member's guest. The national **Federazione Italiana di Tennis** has a list of all the tennis clubs in Italy. The opportunity to watch a professional football game should not be missed. Seats can be scarce, so book tickets in advance from the stadium. Most Serie A matches are played on Sundays, with international games taking place on Tuesdays and Wednesdays.

Sailing in Italy, a popular leisure activity and competitive sport

TRAVEL INFORMATION

ITALY HAS TRANSPORT SYSTEMS of varying efficiency, from the modern road, bus and rail networks of the north to the slower and more antiquated systems of the south. Numerous airlines operate flights to several of the country's major airports, while within Italy itself the national carrier Alitalia, and several smaller companies, provide an extensive network of internal flights.

Alitalia aircraft

Connections by road to the rest of Europe are good, though Alpine roads can be adversely affected by the weather. Motorways and other roads within the country are generally good, but can be busy at weekends and peak periods. Italy also has an efficient system of ferries connecting Sicily, Sardinia and many of the smaller off-shore islands. Many of these are car ferries, and are busy in summer.

Arriving by Air

ROME'S LEONARDO DA VINCI (Fiumicino) and Milan's Malpensa are the key airports for long-haul flights into Italy. Milan's Linate airport handles some European flights, and most European airlines also fly to Venice, Turin, Naples and Pisa (for Florence). Many airlines are now flying regularly to smaller cities such as Florence, Genoa, Bologna, Verona and Bergamo, while charter flights serve summer destinations in peak season such as Catania, Olbia and Rimini.

Part of the extension to Fiumicino airport, Rome

LONG-HAUL FLIGHTS

IF YOU ARE FLYING from the United States, Continental, Delta and United Airlines operate regular direct scheduled flights to Rome and Milan, with services from New York, Washington, Los Angeles, Boston and Chicago. Canadian Airlines flies from Montreal and Toronto, and Qantas flies from Sydney and Melbourne.

A regular service between Rome and Milan and New York, San Francisco, Los Angeles, Boston, Chicago, Montreal, Toronto and Sydney is also offered by the Italian state airline, Alitalia.

It may, however, be more convenient and cheaper for long-haul passengers to take a budget flight to London,

Frankfurt, Paris, Athens or Amsterdam and then continue with their journey to Italy (by aeroplane or train) from there.

EUROPEAN FLIGHTS

IT HAS NEVER been so easy to get to Italy by air. **British Airways** and **Alitalia** and its partners fly to Rome and Milan from most major European cities and other, often low-cost, "no-frills" airlines now offer flights to all parts of Italy from London and other UK cities. (For Sicily's two major cities, Palermo and Catania, a change of flight at one of the mainland airports may be necessary.) **BMI british midland** flies to Milan from Heathrow;

Meridiana serves Florence and Cagliari from Gatwick; **Ryanair** flies to seven airports (including Genoa, Rome-Ciampino, Turin and Venice-Treviso) from Stansted; and **easyJet**, also from Stansted, serves Rome-Ciampino, Milan, Bologna, Venice and Naples, and also Rome from Bristol.

TICKETS AND FARES

FARES VARY enormously according to season and supply and demand. You can usually get the best deals by booking well in advance, especially if you are planning to travel around Christmas time or in the summer.

Consult a good travel agent or check availability on the Internet. If you are based in the UK, it may be worthwhile to scour the small ads of newspapers for charter and discounted scheduled flights on major routes.

AIRPORT
Rome (Fiumicino)
Rome (Ciampino)
Milan (Linate)
Milan (Malpensa)
Pisa (Galileo Galilei)
Venice (Marco Polo)
Venice (Treviso)

The entrance hall at Pisa airport

Most charters leave from Gatwick or Luton, and may land at a city's second (and often less convenient) airport. Fares tend to vary greatly during the year, but the most expensive periods are during the summer months and over the Christmas and Easter holidays. Where possible ask for available student discounts.

Shuttle bus to car hire lots at Fiumicino

PACKAGE HOLIDAYS

PACKAGE HOLIDAYS to Italy are usually cheaper than travelling independently, unless you are travelling on a tight budget and are prepared to make use of youth hostels and campsites. Rome, Florence and Venice are often offered as separate or linked package deals, and many operators have packages to the Tuscan and Umbrian countryside, Sicily, the Italian Lakes, the Italian Riviera, Naples and the Amalfi coast. In winter, ski packages are available to many Alpine resorts. Specialist packages, such as cooking, walking and art tours, are becoming increasingly common. In cities, different tour operators may use different hotels, so it is worth shopping around for the most pleasant (and centrally located) hotels. Many operators include transfers from the airport to your hotel. Some will include a tour guide.

FLY-DRIVE DEALS

MANY TRAVEL AGENTS and car-hire firms will organize special fly-drive packages that enable you to book a flight and have a hire car waiting for you at your destination. This is usually cheaper and involves fewer formalities than renting a car on arrival. Most major car hire firms such as Hertz, Avis and Budget (and many minor ones as well) have offices located at the major Italian airports.

The quayside at Venice's Marco Polo airport

INFORMATION	DISTANCE TO CITY CENTRE	TAXI FARE TO CITY CENTRE	PUBLIC TRANSPORT TO CITY CENTRE
📞 06 65 95 1	35 km (22 miles)	€45	🚆 30 mins
📞 06 65 95 1	15 km (9 miles)	€40	🚌 Ⓜ 60 mins
📞 02 7485 2200	10 km (6 miles)	€15–€18	🚌 20 mins
📞 02 7485 2200	40 km (25 miles)	€55–€65	🚌 1 hr
📞 050 84 93 00	2 km (1 mile)	€10	🚆 to Pisa: 5 mins / 🚆 to Florence: 1 hr
📞 041 260 92 60	13 km (8 miles)	€75 by Water Taxi	🚤 90 mins / 🚌 20 mins
📞 0422 31 51 11	30 km (18 miles)	€50 to Venice	🚌 to Treviso: 20 mins / 🚌 to Venice: 30 mins

Arriving by Sea, Rail and Road

Orient-Express logo

I**TALY IS SERVED BY AN EXTENSIVE** network of roads, railways and international ferry lines. Road and rail links cross into the country from France, Switzerland, Austria and Slovenia, and there are through train services from as far afield as Moscow, London and Barcelona. Road connections into the country are generally of motorway standard, though delays can occur at some of the many Alpine passes and tunnels during bad weather or peak summer holiday periods.

Do-it-yourself help points with train information on screens

Ticket windows at Florence's Santa Maria Novella station

European cities to Milan, Turin, Venice and Verona. There are also direct services from Vienna, Spain and the south of France. Motorail connections exist from several centres in northern Europe and the Channel ports.

The increased popularity of low-fares airlines has made international train travel a less convenient option. Special discount fares, however, are often available for senior travellers and for people under 26. Trains can be extremely busy during peak periods, particularly on Friday and Sunday evenings, and during the Christmas and Easter holiday periods. July and August can also be frantically busy, especially on routes from Germany and ports connecting with Greek ferries in the south. Reservations on most services are inexpensive and advisable.

ARRIVING BY CAR

M**OST ROADS** into Italy from the rest of Europe involve Alpine crossings by tunnel or mountain passes. The notable exceptions are the approach from Slovenia in the northeast (on the A4 motorway) and the route along the French Riviera that enters Italy as the A10 motorway at Ventimiglia.

The most popular route from Geneva and southeast France is via the Mont Blanc tunnel and A5 motorway, entering Italy close to Aosta and Turin. Another busy approach (from Switzerland) uses the St Bernard Pass and tunnel.

Further east, the main route from Austria and southern Germany crosses the Brenner Pass and goes down to Verona on the A22 motorway via Trento and the Adige valley. Weather conditions rarely close the passes, but snow and fog can make progress slow on the winding roads through the mountains. Most motorways are toll-roads; you pay as you exit the motorway.

ARRIVING BY TRAIN

A**FTER AIR TRAVEL**, arriving by train is the least painful way to reach Italy. Countless through services (including many sleepers) link Italian towns and cities with places as far afield as Brussels, Moscow and Barcelona. Connections from Paris (and London, via Eurostar) run to Turin, Milan, Venice, Bologna, Florence or along Italy's west coast, via Genoa and Pisa, to Rome and Naples. Services also operate from German, Swiss and other northern

BINARIO 17

Platform sign

← **uscita**

Exit sign

The sleeping car on an international Eurocity train

ARRIVING BY BOAT

M**OST PEOPLE** arriving in Italy by boat do so from Greece, which is linked by services from Corfu and Patras to Brindisi and other ports in southeast Italy. Services are particularly crowded in the summer months, as are the connecting train services from Brindisi to the rest of Italy.

Other international ferry connections include boats from Malta, Tunisia and other North African ports to Palermo, Naples and various southern Italian ports. Boats also run from towns in the south of France to Genoa, Livorno and ports on the Italian Riviera.

ARRIVING BY COACH

COACH TRAVEL to Italy is relatively cheap (though often not much cheaper than trains), but long journey times make it one of the least comfortable ways to travel. Some coach companies have now introduced plane-coach deals, whereby you can travel by coach on one leg of your trip and by air on the other. At the moment there are thrice-weekly services in summer from the UK to Turin, Milan, Bologna and Rome. The journey time from London to Milan is about 27 hours, and about 36 hours to Rome. A night on the road is thus unavoidable. **National Express Eurolines** runs weekly coaches from London's Victoria Coach Station to all of Italy's major cities as far as Rome. Buses travel via Dover, Calais, Paris and Lyon and it

SITA coach arriving at the station in Florence

is useful to take some euros with you for the probable stops en route.

Travelling Around by Ferry

ITALY'S LARGE NUMBER of off-shore islands mean that it has a large and well-developed network of ferries, as well as services to the rest of Europe and North Africa.

One of the Moby Lines car ferries that sail the Mediterranean

FERRIES

CAR FERRIES are a convenient link with the beautiful islands scattered off the Italian mainland. Boats for Sardinia leave from Civitavecchia (north of Rome), Livorno and Genoa, and depart for Sicily from Naples and Reggio di Calabria. Ferries run from the major Sicilian ports to the Egadi and the Aeolian archipelagoes, as well as to countless other small islands around Sicily (although ferries to the smaller islands do not always carry cars).

Boats also ply between Elba and Piombino, as well as the smaller islands of the Tuscan archipelago such as Capraia. Ferries run from ports close to Rome to Ponza and its surrounding islands, and from Naples to Capri and Ischia. On the east coast the Tremiti islands are linked to ports on the Gargano peninsula.

Hydrofoils are increasingly complementing conventional ferries, particularly on the busy routes to Capri and Ischia.

Queues are common in summer, and you should book well ahead if you wish to travel to Sardinia in July or August, especially if taking a vehicle. Bookings can be made online, through travel agents or at a ferry line's agents in your own country.

For current schedules and fares, visit the relevant website.

ROUTE	FERRY COMPANY	TELEPHONE INFORMATION
Piombino – Elba	Moby Lines W www.mobylines.it	C 0565 22 12 12 (Piombino) C 0565 91 41 33 (Portoferraio)
Civitavecchia – Cagliari	Sardinia Ferries W www.sardiniaferries.com	C 0766 50 07 14 (Civitavecchia)
Genoa – Sardinia	Tirrenia W www.tirrenia.it	C 070 66 60 65 (Cagliari) C 0789 20 71 06 (Olbia) C 010 269 81 (Genoa)
Livorno – Sardinia	Moby Lines Sardinia Ferries	C 0789 279 27 (Olbia) C 199 40 05 00 (bookings)
Genoa/Livorno – Palermo	Grandi Navi Veloci W www.gnv.it	C 091 58 74 04 (Palermo)
Naples – Palermo	Tirrenia	C 091 602 11 11 (Palermo)
Naples – Cagliari	Tirrenia	C 081 251 47 63 (Naples)

Travelling Around by Train

FS Logo

TRAIN TRAVEL is one of the best ways to explore Italy. Tickets are inexpensive, services frequent, and rolling stock some of the most modern in Europe. Services can be busy, but the days of rampant overcrowding are mostly over. Lines often run through lovely countryside, from mountain lakes to rolling plateaux, and they provide more convenient links between cities than roads or air travel. Only in the south, or deeply rural areas, are services slow and infrequent.

A Eurostar– Italy's fastest train

The concourse at Stazione Termini, Rome

THE NETWORK

THE BULK OF ITALY'S rail network is an integrated state-run system operated by the Ferrovie dello Stato (FS). A few privately run lines fill crucial gaps left by the FS, but through tickets are generally available where travel involves both networks. FS and private lines often (but not always) share the same main station *(stazione)*, and also charge similar fares.

TRAINS

THE FS IS in the process of changing the categories of trains, but in practice the same broad divisions will continue to apply. The fast Eurostar and a handful of other special high-speed trains almost always require pre-booking of seats. Intercity (IC) trains and Eurocity (EC) trains only stop at major stations and require the payment of a first- or second-class supplement *(un supplemento)* on top of the standard ticket (supplements can be bought on the train, but are more expensive). *Espresso* (Espr) and *Diretto* (Dir) trains make more stops and require no supplement (you may also find

these trains called *Regionali* and *Interregionali*). *Locali* stop at all stations.

Rolling stock has improved in recent years, especially on Intercity trains, which are now usually modern and air-conditioned. Branch line carriages can still be ancient. Facilities for the disabled exist on many Intercity trains.

FS train in Verona station

TICKETS AND FARES

TICKETS (BIGLIETTI) are available as single *(andata)* or return *(andata e ritorno)* in first *(prima)* or second class *(seconda classe)*. They can be bought at some travel agents or at any station ticket office *(biglietteria)*. Automatic ticket machines are being introduced, and you can also

buy tickets for journeys of up to 250 km (155 miles) from newsstands or station tobacconists (such a ticket is called *biglietto a fascia chilometrica*). Be sure to validate all tickets on both outbound and return journeys, or you will be fined. A ticket's validity usually starts on the day of purchase, so be sure to specify the day of travel when buying tickets in advance.

Fares are calculated on a kilometric basis and are among the cheapest in western Europe. Return fares offer a 15 per cent discount on trips of up to 250 km (155 miles), while special family tickets allow one child under 12 to travel free with two fare-paying adults.

Refunds involve a complicated process and are very difficult to obtain. It is important, therefore, to buy the correct ticket before travelling.

PASSES

THE FS PROVIDES two basic passes: the *Biglietto Chilometrico*, valid for two months, allowing 3,000 km (1,865 miles) of travel for up to five people for a maximum of 20 journeys; and the Italy Flexi Rail Card, permitting unlimited travel for four, eight or 12 days within any month, with special rates for students. The Italy Flexi Rail Card is only available to non-residents.

TIMETABLES

IF YOU PLAN to use trains often, pick up a timetable *(un orario)*. The official FS timetable is comprehensive but heavy. A better buy is the small *Pozzorario*, issued twice yearly and available from station kiosks and newsstands. Or visit www.fs-on-line.it for an online timetable.

VALIDITY AND RESERVATIONS

SINGLE OR RETURN TICKETS are valid for up to two months from the date of purchase. If a seat reservation is made with the ticket, however, the date you wish to travel will be stamped automatically on the ticket. Undated tickets for up to 250 km (155 miles) can also be purchased at newsstands, and must be validated on the day of travel. Reservations are a good idea on and around public holidays and can be made at most main stations for the high-speed trains. Larger stations generally have separate windows for making reservations (*prenotazioni*).

REDUCTIONS

DISCOUNTS of 20 per cent are available with a *Carta Verde*, for travellers aged between 12 and 26; and with a *Carta d'Argento*, for travellers over 60. Passes are not valid during Christmas and at certain periods in high summer. They can be bought from main line stations and are valid for a year.

LEFT LUGGAGE

MAIN CITY STATIONS usually have left luggage facilities. Most are manned (but the smaller stations have self-service lockers), and you may need to present a passport or other form of identification when depositing or collecting bags. Fees are calculated per bag.

Left luggage logo

MACHINES FOR FS RAIL TICKETS

These machines are easy to use, and most have instructions in six languages on screen. They accept coins, notes and credit cards.

1 Select your destination.

2 The price is shown on the display.

3 Insert coins, notes, or an American Express, Visa or Diners Club card.

4 Take your ticket and change.

5 You must insert your ticket here to validate it for your journey.

ITALY'S PRINCIPAL FS NETWORK

The Italian state rail network operates various different types of service. Check what is on offer before buying your ticket.

KEY

● Main stations
○ Other stations
— Principal rail route
- - Route over water

Travelling Around by Car

The classic Fiat 500

AMOTORING TOUR OF ITALY is the most practical way of exploring the country, though you should take into account high petrol prices, the difficulty of parking in many medieval towns and the Italians' occasionally erratic approach to driving. A car is invaluable in the countryside and for extensive touring, but less useful if you are only visiting a few major towns and cities, as the traffic congestion makes driving slow.

Blue signs showing main roads and green signs showing motorways

Automatic tollbooths on the motorway outside Florence

WHAT TO TAKE

DRIVERS FROM OUTSIDE Italy bringing their own foreign-registered cars into the country must be at least 18 years old and carry a Green Card (for insurance purposes), all the vehicle's registration documents, and a full, valid driving licence (*patente* in Italian). Any UK or other EU nationals who do not have the standard EU "pink" licence and are planning to stay for more than six months will need an Italian translation of their licence, obtainable from most motoring organizations or from the Italian state tourist office in your home country. A red warning triangle must also be carried at all times, for use in the event of a breakdown.

PETROL

PETROL (*benzina*) in Italy is some of the most expensive in Europe (diesel, or *gasolio*, is a little cheaper). Although many petrol stations are now self-service, it is still common to be served by an attendant. Most petrol stations follow normal shop hours so make sure you have a full tank before lunchtime or public

holidays. On motorways petrol stations tend to be open 24 hours a day. Credit cards are usually accepted.

ROADS

ITALY HAS A GOOD network of motorways, though many have a total of only four lanes, often leading to congestion.

Rules and Regulations

Italy uses standard European road signs. Drive on the right and give way to traffic from the right. Seat belts (la cintura) are compulsory in the front and the back, and children should be properly restrained. The speed limit in urban areas is 50 km/h (30 mph); outside urban areas it is 110 km/h (70 mph) on dual carriageways and 90 km/h on all other secondary roads. On motorways (autostrade) the limit is 130 km/h (80 mph) for vehicles over 1100cc and 110 km/h (70 mph) for all vehicles under 1100cc. All documentation must be carried with you.

One-way street

Busy routes include the A1 from Bologna to Florence and between Bologna, Parma and Milan. Tolls are payable on all but a handful of motorways, again leading to congestion at tollbooths (*Alt Stazione*) at weekends and busy holiday periods. Payment is made at the end of the journey in cash or pre-paid magnetic cards called VIAcards, available from tobacconists and the ACI.

Secondary roads are known as Nazionali (N) or as Strade Statali (SS), and vary enormously in quality, the worst being in the south. Mountain roads are usually good, but distances can be deceptive on winding roads and in winter snow chains are obligatory on many higher routes. Some back roads (known as *strade bianche*, or "white roads") have only a gravel surface, but are still marked on motoring maps. These are slow, but usually passable to cars, if you drive carefully.

No stopping   **End of speed restriction**

Pedestrianized street – no traffic   **Give way to oncoming traffic**

No parking   **Danger (often with description)**

A car rental office at Fiumicino airport, Rome

CAR HIRE

Car HIRE *(autonoleggio)* is expensive in Italy, and should be organized beforehand through fly-drive deals *(see p627)* or pre-booked with firms who have branches in Italy. For on the spot hire Italian firms may be cheaper than big international names. Agencies are listed in Yellow Pages *(Pagine Gialle)* under Autonoleggio. Most airports have car hire offices on site.

To rent a car in Italy you must be over 21 and have held a valid driver's licence for at least a year. Visitors from outside the EU require an international licence, though in practice not all hire firms insist on this. Check the small print of the agreement for insurance cover.

CAR HIRE NUMBERS

Avis
📞 199 10 01 33 (toll-free).

Europcar
📞 800 01 44 10 (toll-free).

Hertz
📞 199 11 22 11 (toll-free).

Maggiore (Rome)
📞 06 854 86 98.

Sixt (Rome)
📞 06 65 96 51.

ACCIDENTS AND BREAKDOWNS

If YOU HAVE AN ACCIDENT or a breakdown, switch on your hazard warning lights and place a warning triangle 50 m (164 ft) behind your car. Then (for breakdowns) call the ACI emergency number (116) or the emergency services (112 or 113). The ACI will tow any foreign-registered car free to

the nearest ACI-affiliated garage. They also do free repairs for members of affiliated associations, such as the AA and RAC in Britain.

If you have an accident keep calm, and do not admit liability or make any statements that might incriminate you later. Simply swap car and insurance details, names and addresses.

PARKING

Parking IN MOST Italian cities and large towns is a problem. Many historic centres have restricted daytime access and baffling one-way systems. Other areas may be reserved for residents' parking (marked *riservato ai residenti*). Most towns have metered parking areas that charge an hourly fee paid with coins, cards or coupons bought from *tabacchi*.

Parking disc

Cars can be towed away or clamped, especially in areas marked *zona rimozione* (particularly on street-cleaning days). Call the Municipal Police *(Vigili)* to retrieve your car.

SAFETY

Car THEFT IS RIFE in Italy. Never leave anything in your car, and (if possible) always remove radio-cassette players. Leave your car in a guarded car park whenever you can. Be especially careful driving at night, when Italian driving is more cavalier than usual, and when many traffic lights switch to flashing amber. Hitching *(autostop)* is not a good idea (and is not common), certainly never for women on their own.

Official parking area patrolled by attendant

DISTANCE CHART

ROME								**10** Distance in kilometres			
								10 Distance in miles			
286 / 178	**ANCONA**										
748 / 465	617 / 383	**AOSTA**									
383 / 238	219 / 136	401 / 249	**BOLOGNA**								
645 / 401	494 / 307	449 / 279	280 / 174	**BOLZANO**							
278 / 173	262 / 163	470 / 292	106 / 66	367 / 228	**FLORENCE**						
510 / 317	506 / 315	245 / 152	291 / 181	422 / 262	225 / 140	**GENOA**					
601 / 373	614 / 382	1220 / 758	822 / 511	1097 / 682	871 / 541	1103 / 685	**LECCE**				
575 / 357	426 / 265	181 / 113	210 / 130	295 / 183	299 / 186	145 / 90	1029 / 639	**MILAN**			
219 / 136	409 / 254	959 / 596	594 / 369	856 / 532	489 / 304	714 / 444	393 / 244	786 / 488	**NAPLES**		
673 / 418	547 / 340	110 / 68	332 / 206	410 / 255	395 / 245	170 / 106	1150 / 715	138 / 86	884 / 549	**TURIN**	
530 / 329	364 / 226	442 / 275	154 / 96	214 / 133	255 / 158	397 / 247	967 / 601	273 / 170	741 / 460	402 / 250	**VENICE**

Travelling within Cities

Pedestrian zone sign

The BEST WAYS of getting around Italian cities differ from place to place. In Rome buses are most useful, in Milan the metro is more efficient, and in Venice you will need to take a boat to get about. Trams still run in some cities, such as Milan and Rome. Cars are a liability almost everywhere, unlike walking, which in many cases is the easiest way to negotiate the tight historic cores of Italian towns and cities. Florence has a large limited-traffic zone, and most towns now have a pedestrian area in the centre.

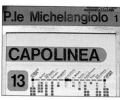

Bus stop displaying the route

A Roman bus in the red and grey livery of ATAC

One of the distinctive orange city buses, central Verona

BUSES AND TRAMS

VIRTUALLY EVERY ITALIAN city and large town has a bus system. Most are cheap, comprehensive and as efficient as traffic and narrow streets will allow and vary only slightly from city to city. Bus stops are known as *fermate*, and increasingly (notably in Rome) list full details of the routes they serve. Buses (*autobus*) usually run from about 6am to midnight, and there are night buses (*servizio notturno*) in larger cities. If you arrive in a town by train, stations are invariably linked to the centre by shuttle buses from the station forecourt (tickets are usually available from the station bar or tobacconist).

TICKETS

TICKETS (*biglietti*) must be bought before boarding the bus from kiosks belonging to the bus company (ATAF in Florence, ATAC in Rome), bars, newsstands or tobacconists displaying the bus company's sticker. A few cities also have on-street vending machines around the main transport hubs. It is worth buying more than one ticket at a time, as outlets often close in the afternoon or early evening. Discounted tickets (*un blocchetto*), or day- or week-long visitors' tickets and passes (*una tessera* or *tesserino*) are also available. In some cities tickets are valid for any number of journeys within a given time. The ATAC website has more details on buses in Rome.

ATAC
Ⓦ www.atac.roma.it

USING BUSES AND TRAMS

BOARD BUSES via the front and rear doors, and exit via the central doors. Buses usually only have a driver and no conductor (though night buses may have a conductor from whom tickets can be bought). Tickets must be validated by punching them in machines at the front or rear of the bus. There are large on-the-spot fines if you are caught without a properly validated ticket. The front, low seats on buses are for people with children, the elderly and the disabled.

Most larger cities have transport information offices at the main train station or piazza which provide free maps, timetables and tickets.

The majority of city buses are painted bright orange and display the final destination (*capolinea*) on the front.

METROPOLITANA

UNDERGROUND systems, known as *metropolitana* (*la metro* for short), are found in Rome and Milan. Rome's network amounts to just two lines, A and B, which converge at Stazione Termini, the city's central railway station. Several stations are useful for key sights, and at peak times the lines provide the best way of

Metro sign

crossing the city quickly. Stations are fairly dingy – though rarely dangerous – and train carriages can be stiflingly hot in summer. In Milan the network is more extensive, with three principal lines – MM1 (the red line), MM2 (green) and MM3 (yellow) – that meet at the hub stations of Stazione Centrale, Duomo, Cadorna and Lima. These three lines give easy access to the

Termini Metro station, Rome

Waiting for a fare at an official rank in Florence

majority of the city's main sights.

Metro tickets in both cities are available from the same sources as bus and tram tickets, and from machines and ticket offices in underground stations. Tickets in Rome are valid for one journey only, though the special *BIG* ticket offers a day's travel on bus, tram and metro. In Milan, by contrast, ordinary metro tickets are valid for 75 minutes for any number of journeys and can also be used on the buses and trams.

It is unwise to buy tickets from people outside stations, as they are invariably already used or otherwise invalid.

WALKING

WALKING can be a wonderful way to explore Italy's historic towns and cities, most of whose historic centres are smaller than you might expect. Traffic can be a curse, however, especially in narrow streets (Rome is worst in this respect), but many cities are introducing pedestrianized areas or cutting down on car access around key tourist sights. On certain Sundays *(Domenica a Piedi)*, entire town centres may be designated traffic-free zones.

Italian towns have plenty of shady squares and cafés to escape the heat of the summer sun, and churches and cathedrals also provide cool retreats from the rigours of sightseeing. Most sights are well signposted (churches,

Stay on the pavement at all costs

Marginally less dangerous to cross

museums and other places of interest are often indicated by yellow signs). Always carry your valuables well out of sight. The best times to walk are in the cool of the morning, or in the early evening, when you can join in the pre-dinner stroll known as the *passeggiata*.

TAXIS

ONLY ACCEPT RIDES in official taxis. These may be of different colours in the different cities, but all will have a "Taxi" sign on the roof. Most drivers are honest (if not terribly friendly), but there are many supplements that can be legitimately levied. Generally an extra charge is made for each piece of luggage placed in the boot, for rides between 10pm and 7am, on Sundays and public holidays, and for journeys to and from airports. It is worth fixing a price before you set off to or from airports, especially in Rome or Naples.

In theory, taxis cannot be hailed. Take one at an official taxi stand (usually found at the station, main piazza or close to key tourist sights) or reserve one by phone. When you order a taxi by phone, take the driver's code name, eg Napoli 18. If you call a cab, the meter will run from your call. In the event of any dispute, note the cab's number and ask the nearest policeman to arbitrate.

CYCLE HIRE

MANY TOWNS and cities, especially those popular with visitors, have stands and shops offering bikes and scooters for rent. You can usually rent hourly or by the day, and you may have to leave your passport with the shop as a deposit. Be very careful, however, if riding a bike in the busy traffic of the larger towns and cities.

INTER-CITY TRANSPORT: COACHES

Long-haul buses *(pullman* or *corriere)* between towns operate in a similar way to local buses, though you can usually buy tickets on board, and services are often run by different companies in different-coloured buses (blue is the most common colour for *pullman*, orange for city buses). Coaches in some

Rome – Gubbio bus

areas may be run by several companies (notably around Florence and in Tuscany), and not all operate from the same termini. Services often depart from outside railway stations, or from a town's main piazza. If in doubt, ask at local tourist offices. A reduced service may operate at weekends, when offices are shut.

Rome
COTRAL
800 15 00 08.
Lazzi
06 884 08 40.
Appian
06 48 78 61.

Tuscany
Lazzi
055 35 10 61.
Sita
800 37 37 60.
Tra-In
0577 20 42 45.

National & International
Sita
055 29 49 55.
www. sita-on-line.it

Travelling Around Venice

F OR VISITORS TO VENICE, the *vaporetti* or waterbuses *(see pp130–31)* provide an entertaining form of public transport, although most journeys within the city can usually be covered more quickly on foot. The main route through the city for the *vaporetti* is the Grand Canal. Waterbuses also supply a useful service connecting outlying points on the periphery of Venice, and linking the city to the islands in the lagoon. The most important service from a visitor's point of view is the No. 1. This operates from one end of the Grand Canal to the other and travels slowly enough for you to admire the parade of palaces at the waterside *(see pp84–9)*.

Vaporetto stop at the Giardini Pubblici, Venice

A *vaporetto* pulling into San Marco

The smaller, sleeker *motoscafo*

THE BOATS

T HE ORIGINAL *vaporetti* were steam-powered (*vaporetto* means little steamer); today they are mostly diesel-run motor boats, with a handful of electric, battery-powered prototypes. Although all the boats tend to be called *vaporetti*, the word only really applies to the large wide boats used on slow routes, such as No. 1. These boats provide the best views. *Motoscafi* are the slimmer, smaller boats that look old but go at a fair pace, while *motonavi* are two-tier boats that run to the islands.

TYPES OF TICKET

I F BOOTHS AT landing stages are closed, single tickets can be purchased on board at no extra charge.

A good way to save money, however, is by buying a 24-hour or 72-hour ticket. These tickets entitle the holder to unlimited travel on most lines.

Visitors who are planning to stay more than just a few days can also save money

by buying a monthly season ticket (*abbonamento*), which is available from ticket offices. Holders of Rolling Venice cards (offering information packs and discounts to 14- to 30-year-olds) can buy a three-day youth pass.

The "Laguna Nord" ticket enables you to travel on the LN line, visiting the islands of Murano, Mazzorbo, Burano, Torcello and on to the Lido, for up to 12 hours. The LN departs from San Zaccaria and Fondamente Nuove.

On some boats you may have to buy a ticket for each piece of large luggage you are carrying, and you must remember to date-stamp tickets if purchased in advance.

HOURS OF SERVICE

T HE MAIN ROUTES run every 10 to 20 minutes until the early evening. Services are reduced after 11pm, but they run all night. From June to September the services are more frequent and certain routes are extended. Timetables are on sale at main landing stages. Be warned: from May to September the main routes and island boats are very crowded.

VAPORETTO INFORMATION

ACTV (Information Office)
Piazzale Roma, Venice. **Map** 5 B1.
(041 2424. **W** www.actv.it

TRAGHETTI

T RAGHETTI are gondola ferries that cross the Grand Canal at seven different points, providing a useful service for pedestrians. Few tourists make use of this cheap (about 50 cents per trip), constant service. Points where *traghetti* cross the Grand Canal are marked on the Street Finder maps *(see pp120–29)*. A gondola on yellow street signs points to *traghetti* stops.

A two-tier *motonave* on its way to Torcello

GONDOLAS

GONDOLAS are a luxury form of transport used only by visitors and Venetians at weddings. Before boarding, check the official tariffs and agree a price with the gondolier. Official costs are around €50 for 45 minutes, rising to €80 after 8pm. During the low season, you may also be able to negotiate a lower fee, and a journey shorter than the usual 50 minutes.

WATER TAXIS

FOR THOSE with little time and sufficient funds, the fastest and most practical means of getting from A to B is by water taxi. The craft are sleek, white or polished wood motorboats, all equipped with a cabin. They zip to and from the airport in only 20 minutes. There are 16 water taxi ranks, including one at the airport and the Lido.

A water taxi

Beware of extra charges for luggage, waiting, night service and for calling out a taxi. When the *vaporetti* go on strike, taxis are scarce.

WATER TAXI STANDS

**Radio Taxi
(all of Venice)**
[041 522 23 03.

Piazzale Roma
Map 5 B1.
[041 71 69 22.

Crossing the Grand Canal by *tragbetto*

THE MAIN ROUTES

① Confusingly called the *Accelerato*, this is the slow boat down the Grand Canal, stopping at every landing stage. The route starts at Piazzale Roma, travels the length of the Grand Canal, then from San Marco it heads east to the Lido.

⑧② The 82 is the faster route down the Grand Canal, making only six stops. The route is circular, starting at San Zaccaria, continuing westwards along the Giudecca Canal to Tronchetto and Piazzale Roma, then down the Grand Canal back to San Zaccaria.

⑤① ⑤② These lines skirt the periphery of Venice and have been extended to the Lido. The circular *Giracittà* route provides a scenic tour of Venice, though to do the whole circuit you have to change boats at Fondamente Nuove.

Ⓝ This line departs from the Fondamente Nuove and runs to the main islands in the northern lagoon: Murano, Mazzorbo, Burano and Torcello, then loops via Punta Sabbioni and the Lido, before concluding at San Zaccaria.

USING THE VAPORETTI

1 Tickets are available at most landing stages, some bars, shops and tobacconists displaying the ACTV sign. It is also possible to buy them on board. The price of a ticket remains the same whether you are going one stop or travelling the whole line.

2 Signs on the landing stage tell you the direction of the boats stopping there.

3 Tickets should be punched at the automatic machines on the landing stages before each journey. Inspectors rarely board the boats and this makes it surprisingly easy for tourists (and Venetians) to hop on and off the boats without a validated ticket. However, there are steep fines for any passengers caught without tickets.

4 An indicator board at the front of each boat gives the line number and main stops. (Ignore the black numbers on the boat's side.)

5 Each landing stage has its name clearly marked on a board. Most stops have two landing stages and it is quite easy, particularly if it is crowded and you can't see which way the boat is facing, to board a boat travelling in the wrong direction. It is helpful to watch which direction the boat is approaching from; if in doubt, check with the boatman.

General Index

Acknowledgments

DORLING KINDERSLEY would like to thank the following people whose contributions and assistance have made the preparation of this book possible.

CONTRIBUTORS
Paul Duncan is an expert on art and architectural history and has published a guide to Sicily as well as one on Italy's hill-towns.
Tim Jepson, formerly Rome correspondent for the *Sunday Telegraph*, has written guides to Tuscany, Umbria, Rome and Venice, a complete guide to Italy, *Italy by Train* and *Wild Italy*, a guide to Italy's nature reserves.
Andrew Gumbel, former Reuters correspondent in Rome, has written a number of guide books and is the correspondent for the *Independent* in Rome.
Christopher Catling has written guides to Florence and Tuscany, the Veneto and the Italian Lakes and is particularly interested in archaeology.
Sam Cole works for Reuters in Rome, where he has lived for some years, and contributes regularly to guidebooks on Rome and the Lazio region.

ADDITIONAL CONTRIBUTORS
Dominic Robertson, Mick Hamer, Richard Langham Smith.

ADDITIONAL PHOTOGRAPHY
Giuseppe Carfagna & Associati, Peter Chadwick, Andy Crawford, Philip Dowell, Mike Dunning, Philip Enticknap, Steve Gorton, Dave King, Neil Mersh, Roger Moss, Poppy, Kim Sayer, James Stevenson, Clive Streeter, David Ward, Matthew Ward.

ADDITIONAL ILLUSTRATIONS
Andrea Corbella, Richard Draper, Kevin Jones Associates, Chris Orr and Associates, Robbie Polley, Simon Roulstone, Martin Woodward.

CARTOGRAPHIC RESEARCH
Jane Hugill, Samantha James, Jennifer Skelley.

DESIGN AND EDITORIAL ASSISTANCE
Gillian Allan, Gaye Allen, Douglas Amrine, Emily Anderson, Tessa Bindloss, Hilary Bird, Sally-Ann Bloomfield, Samantha Borland, Isabel Boucher, Hugo Bowles, Caroline Brooke, Paola Cacucciola, Stefano Cavedoni, Margaret Chang, Elspeth Collier, Sherry Collins, Lucinda Cooke, Cooling Brown, Michelle Crane, Gary Cross, Felicity Crowe, Peter Douglas, Mandy Dredge, Stephanie Driver, Michael Ellis, Adele Evans, Danny Farnham, Jackie Gordon, Angela-Marie Graham, Caroline Greene, Vanessa Hamilton, Sally-Ann Hibbard, Tim Hollis, Gail Jones, Steve Knowlden, Leonie Loudon, Siri Lowe, Sarah Martin, Georgina Matthews, Ferdie McDonald, Ian Midson, Rebecca Milner, Adam Moore, Jennifer Mussett, Alice Peebles, Tamsin Pender, Marianne Petrou, Gillian Price, David Pugh, Jake Reimann, David Roberts, Evelyn Robertson, Carolyn Ryden, Simon Ryder, Giuseppina Russo, Alison Stace, Hugh Thompson, Jo-Ann Titmarsh, Elaine Verweymeren, Ingrid Vienings, Karen Villabona, Stewart J Wild, Veronica Wood.

DORLING KINDERSLEY would also like to thank the following for their assistance: Azienda Autonoma di Soggiorno Cura e Turismo, Napoli; Azienda Promozione Turistica del Trentino, Trento; Osservatorio Geofisico dell'Università di Modena; Bell'Italia; Enotria Winecellars.

PHOTOGRAPHY PERMISSION
DORLING KINDERSLEY would like to thank the following for their assistance and kind permission to photograph at their establishments: Assessorato Beni Culturali Comune di Padova. Le Soprintendenze Archeologiche di Agrigento, di Enna, di Etruria Meridionale, per il Lazio, di Napoli, di Pompei, di Reggio Calabria e di Roma. Le Soprintendenze per i Beni Ambientali e Architettonici di Bolzano, di Napoli, di Potenza, della Provincia di Firenze e Pistoia, di Ravenna, di Roma, di Siena e di Urbino. Le Soprintendenze per i Beni Ambientali, Architettonici, Artistici e Storici di Caserta, di Cosenza, di Palermo, di Pisa, di Salerno e di Venezia. Le Soprintendenze per i Beni Artistici e Storici della Provincia di Firenze e Pistoia, di Milano e di Roma. Also all the other churches, museums, hotels, shops, restaurants, galleries and sights too numerous to thank individually.

PICTURE CREDITS
t = top; tl = top left; tc = top centre; tr = top right; cla = centre left above; ca = centre above; cra = centre right above; cl = centre left; c = centre; cr = centre right; clb = centre left below; cb = centre below; crb = centre right below; bl = bottom left; b = bottom; bc = bottom centre; br = bottom right.

Works of art have been reproduced with the permission of the following copyright holders:
© ADAGP, Paris and DACS, London 1996 *Bird in Space* by Constantin Brancusi 101cl; © DACS, 1996 *Mother and Son* by Carlo Carrà 190t.

DORLING KINDERSLEY would like to thank the following for their assistance: Eric Crighton: 79cra, FIAT: 212c, Gucci Ltd: 35cr, Prada, Milan: 35c, National Archaeological Museum, Naples: 479b, National Maritime Museum 36c, Royal Botanic Gardens, Kew: 79ca, Science Museum: 36cla, Telecom Italia: 620tc.

The publisher would like to thank the following individuals, companies and picture libraries for permission to reproduce their photographs:
ACCADEMIA ITALIANA: Sue Bond 479c; AFE, Rome:

34clb, 34cb, 35tl; Giuseppe Carfagna 188b, 194b, 210tl, 210b, 214tl, 216b, 217t, 227t; Claudio Cerquetti 64t, 65bl, 65t; Enrico Martino 54cl, 62tr; Roberto Merlo 228b, 231t, 231b; Piero Servo 259t, 261b; Gustavo Tomsich 219b; Archivio APT Monregalese 221t; Action Plus: Mike Hewitt 66ca; Glyn Kirk 67tr; Alitalia: 626t, 626b; Allsport: Mark Thompson: 67cl; Simon Bruty: 67tl; Ancient Art and Architecture: 39t, 465br; Archiv für Kunst und Geschichte, London: 24bl, 30b, *Rossini* (1820), Camuccini, Museo Teatrale alla Scala, Milan 32br, 33bl, 37br, *Pope Sixtus IV Naming Platina Prefect of the Library*, Melozzo da Forlì (1477), Pinacoteca Vaticana, Rome 38, 40tl, *Statue of Augustus from Prima Porta* (1st century AD) 45tl, *The Gift of Constantine* (1246), Oratorio di San Silvestro, Rome 46cl, *Frederick I Barbarossa as a Crusader* (1188), Biblioteca Apostolica Vaticana, Rome 49bl, 52tl, *Giving the Keys to St Peter*, Perugino (1482), Sistine Chapel, Vatican, Rome 52cla, 52bl, *Machiavelli*, Santi di Tito, Palazzo Vecchio, Florence 53br, *Andrea Palladio*, Meyer 54cb, *Goethe in the Campagna*, Tischbein (1787), Stadelsches Kunstinstitut, Frankfurt 56cl, *Venetian Carnival in the Eighteenth Century*, Anon (19th century) 56clb, *Bonaparte Crossing the Alps*, David, Schloss Charlottenburg, Berlin 57cr, 57bl, 102t, 102b, 191b, 346–7, 450b, *Archimedes*, Museo Capitolino, Rome 465bl, 489t, 493c; Stefan Diller *St Francis Appearing to the Brothers at Arles* (1295–1300), San Francesco, Assisi 49tl; Erich Lessing *Margrave Gualtieri of Saluzzo Chooses the Poor Farmer's Daughter, Griseldis, for his Wife*, di Stefano, Galleria dell'Accademia Carrara, Bergamo 30crb, *The Vision of St Augustine* (1502), Carpaccio, Chiesa di San Giorgio degli Schiavoni, Venice 53cr, 214b, 260b, 475b; Archivio IGDA, Milan: 196t, 196c, 197b, 505bl, 505br; Emporio Armani: 20cl, 35tc; Artemide, GB Ltd: 35clb.

Mario Bettella 519c, 526c; Frank Blackburn: 259c; Osvaldo Böhm, Venice: 85t, 90c, 107t; Bridgeman Art Library, London/New York: 42c, Ambrosiana, Milan 189t; Bargello, Florence 271b, 275c; Bibliothèque Nationale, Paris: *Marco Polo with Elephants and Camels Arriving at Hormuz, Gulf of Persia, from India*, Livre des Merveilles Fr 2810 f.14v 37t; British Museum, London *Etruscan Vase Showing Boxers Fighting* 41tl, *Flask Decorated with Christian Symbols* 46tl, *Greek Attic Red-Figure Vase depicting Odysseus with the Sirens*, Stamnos 465cb; Galleria dell'Accademia Carrara, Bergamo 193t; Galleria Borghese, Rome 429cl; Galleria degli Uffizi, Florence 22tl, 25tl, 25br, *Self-Portrait*, Raphael Sanzio of Urbino 53bl, 279b, 281b: K & B News Photo, Florence 268tl; Santa Maria Novella, Florence 289b; Museo Civico, Prato 318b; Louvre, Paris *Statuette of Herakles Brandishing his Club*, Classical Greek, Argive period 464t; Mausoleo di

Galla Placidia, Ravenna 260tr; Museo di San Marco, Florence 289b; Musée d'Orsay, Paris - Giraudon *Les Romains de la Decadence*, Thomas Couture 385t; Museo delle Sinopie, Camposanto, Pisa 23clb; Palazzo dei Normanni, Palermo *Scene with Centaurs from the Room of King Ruggero* 507b; Pinacoteca di Brera, Milan 190c, 190b, 191t, Private Collection *Theodoric I* (455–526 AD) *Ostrogothic King of Italy* 46b; San Francesco, Arezzo 23tr; San Francesco, Assisi 345c; San Sebastiano, Venice 25crb; San Zaccaria, Venice 29c, 29tr, 95c; Santa Croce, Florence 276bl, 277cb; Santa Maria Gloriosa dei Frari, Venice 24tr; Santa Maria Novella, Florence 23cla; Scrovegni (Arena) Chapel, Padua 22tr; Scuola di San Giorgio degli Schiavoni, Venice 116b; Staatliche Museen, Berlin *Septimius Severus and Family* 45b; Vatican Museums and Galleries, Rome 411b; Walker Art Gallery, Liverpool *Aeschylus and Hygieia* 464b; British Museum, London: 42cl.

Capitoline Museum, Rome: 377cr; Demetrio Carrasco: 98br, 636tr; Cephas Picture Library Mick Rock: 2–3, 19t, 20t, 176tr, 177b, 177tr, 234–5, 243tl, 243tr, 456–7, 610–1; JL Charmet, Paris: 343br, 479t; Ciga Hotels: 87cb; Foto Elio e Stefano Ciol: 73cra, 158bl, 158br, 159bl, 159bc, 159br; Comune di Asti: 64cl; Stephani Colasanti: 72bl; Joe Cornish: 18t, 78tr, 132, 154t, 236–7, 304, 354, 445b, 521b; Giancarlo Costa: 9c, 30t, 31cr, 31tr, 31tl, 71c, 171c, 176tl, 457c, 537c, 611c.

Il Dagherrotipo: 630cl; Archivio Arte 199t; Archivio Storico 31b, 198b, 253b; Salvatore Barba 490t; Alberto Berni 217bl; Riccardo Catani 485b; Marco Cerruti 172t, 205b, 207b, 208b; Antonio Cittadini 182b, 186b, 194t ; Gianni Dolfini 534b; Riccardo d'Errico 66tr, 239t, 260c; Maurizio Fraschetti 480; Diane Haines 167br, 625br; Maurizio Leoni 63c; Marco Melodia 491b, 531t, 624tl, 624cl; Stefano Occhibelli 65c, 246, 386, 391bl; Giorgio Oddi 239cr, 244t, 497tr; Bruno Pantaloni 67bl; Donato Fierro Perez 517cb; Marco Ravasini 164t, 533c; Giovanni Rinaldi 21t, 62bl, 63tl, 173bl, 223b, 388c, 357t, 363t, 450c, 466, 483t, 490bl, 490br, 491c, 517cr, 535t, 535c; Lorenzo Scaramella 452c; Stefania Servili 166t; James Darell: 338; CM Dixon: 411cb; Chris Donaghue The Oxford Photo Library: 113t.

Electa: 150c, 151c, 151t; Empics: 66cra, 66cbl; John Marsh 66b; ET Archive: 32bc, 41c, 42tl, 45cr, 48cr–49cl, 53tl, 55tl, 59b, 465t, 515b; Mary Evans Picture Library: 30clb, 31cl, 37ca, 58b, 58crb, 59cr, 60cb, 76tr, 237c, 310t, 316t, 381ca, 383bl, 399b, 432c, 495cr, 534t.

Archivio Storico Fiat, Turin: 60tr; Ferrari: 34b; APT Folignate e Nocera Umbra: 351t; Werner

FORMAN ARCHIVE: 41br, 47tr, 425br; CONSORZIO FRASASSI: 362b.

STUDIO GAVIRATI, Gubbio: 342c; APT GENOVA: Roberto Merlo 230bl; GIRAUDON, Paris: *Aphrodite Persuading Helen to Follow Paris to Troy,* Museo Nazionale di Villa Giulia, Rome 41clb, *Pharmacy,* Museo della Civiltà Romana 44cb, *Grandes Chroniques de France; Coronation of Charlemagne in St Peter's by Leon III,* Musée Goya, Castres 47tl, *Taking of Constantinople,* Basilica of St John the Evangelist, Ravenna 49cr, *Dante's Hell with Commentary of Guiniforte delli Bargigi* (Ms2017 fol 245), Bibliothèque Nationale, Paris 50cb, *Portrait of St Ignatius of Loyola,* Rubens, Musée Brukenthal, Sibiu 55ca, *Charles III's Fleet at Naples 6th October 1759,* Joli de Dipi, Museo del Prado, Madrid 56tr, *Inauguration of the Naples-Portici Railway,* Fergola (1839), Museo Nazionale di San Martino, Naples 58clb, *Piedmontese and French at the Battle of San Martino in 1859* Anon, Museo Centrale del Risorgimento, Rome 59tl, 102c, 103t, 191c, 260tl; ALINARI-GIRAUDON: *St Mark Appearing to the Venetians Looking for His Body,* Tintoretto (1568), Brera Art Gallery, Milan 25tr, *Shrine,* House of the Vettii, Pompeii 45cb, *St Gregory in his Study* (Inv 285), Pinacoteca Nazionale, Bologna 47bl, *Portrait of Victor Emmanuel II,* Dugoni (1866), Galleria d'Arte Moderna, Palazzo Pitti, Florence 58tl, 103b, 190t, *Louis II of Gonzaga and his Court,* Andrea Mantegna (1466–74), Museo di Palazzo Ducale, Mantova 200–201, 279tl-tr, *History of Pope Alexander III: Building of the City of Alexandria,* Aretino Spinello (1407), Palazzo Pubblico, Siena 51cr; ALINARI-SEAT-GIRAUDON: 219c; FLAMMARION-GIRAUDON: *Poem by Donizo in Honour of Queen Matilda,* Biblioteca Apostolica, Vatican 48ca; LAUROS-GIRAUDON: *Portrait of Francis Petrarch* 50b, *Liber notabilium Philippi Septimi, francorum regis a libris Galieni extractus* (Ms 334 569 fig17), Guy of Pavia (1345), Musée Condé, Chantilly 51b, *Gallery of Views of Ancient Rome,* Pannini (1758), Musée du Louvre, Paris 56cr, 57cl, *Portrait of the Artist,* Bernini, Private Collection 54tl, *Four Angels and Symbols of the Evangelists,* 28tr–29tcr; ORSI-BATTAGLINI-GIRAUDON: *Madonna of the Shadow,* Museum of San Marco, Florence 28c, *Supplice de Savonarola* Anon 52cl; JACKIE GORDON: 631; THE RONALD GRANT ARCHIVE: 61b; Paramount *The Godfather Part III* (1990) 519b; Riama *La Dolce Vita* (1960) 61tl; TCF *Boccaccio '70* (1962) 19cl, *The Name of the Rose* (1986) 30cla; PALAZZO VENIER DEI LEONI, PEGGY GUGGENHEIM COLLECTION, VENICE: 87cla.

PHOTO HALUPKA: 116t; ROBERT HARDING PICTURE LIBRARY: 1c, 66tl, 185b, 262, 380cl, 404, 409b, 615b, 624b; Dumrath 261c; HP Merton 160, 624tr;

Roy Rainford 483cr; JOHN HESELTINE: 451t; MICHAEL HOLFORD: 43ca, 374b; HOTEL PORTA ROSSA: 540t; HOTEL VILLA PAGODA: 539t; THE HULTON DEUTSCH COLLECTION: 60br, 85cla, 86cla, 86br, 151br, 365c; Keystone 60ca.

THE IMAGE BANK, London: 324b; Marcella Pedone 181b; Andrea Pistolesi 247b; Guido Rossi 10b, 43cb; IMPACT: 305b; INDEX, Florence: 274c, 317t, 317cr; ISTITUTO E MUSEO DI STORIA DELLA SCIENZA DI FIRENZE: Franca Principe 36b, 277c.

TIM JEPSON: 341t.

FRANK LANE PICTURE AGENCY: 208t, 209t, 209c, 209b; M Melodia/Panda 490ca.

MAGNUM, London: Abbas 61clb; THE MANSELL COLLECTION: 48cl, 383tl; MARCONI LTD 36t; MARKA: L Barbazza 93tr; E Cerretelli 117b; M Motta 617t; Piranha 189br; MASTERSTUDIO, Pescara: 488c; su concessione del MINISTERO PER I BENI CULTURALI E AMBIENTALI: *The Last Supper,* da Vinci, Leonardo 192b; MIRROR SYNDICATION INTERNATIONAL: 36clb; MOBY LINES: 629b; FOTO MODENA: 258t, 361c; TONY MOTT: 449b, 454t; MUSEO DIOCESANO DI ROSSANO 504t.

NHPA: Laurie Campbell 79crb; Gerard Lacz 79br; Silvestris Fotoservice 79cr; BY COURTESY OF THE NATIONAL PORTRAIT GALLERY, London: (detail) *Percy Bysshe Shelley,* Amelia Curran (1819) 56tl; GRAZIA NERI: 48tl; Roberta Krasnig 620bl; Marco Bruzzo 64br; Cameraphoto 104bl; Marcello Mencarini 84br; NIPPON TELEVISION NETWORK: 414c–415c, 414t, 414b–415bl, 415t, 415br, 416b; PETER NOBLE: 308t, 326–7, 331b, 616b.

L'OCCHIO DI CRISTALLO/STUDIO FOTOGRAFICO DI GIORGIO OLIVERO: 221b; APT ORVIETO: Massimo Roncella 348t; OXFORD SCIENTIFIC FILMS: Stan Osolinski 337c.

PADOVA - MUSEI CIVICI - CAPPELLA SCROVEGNI: 73cr, 150t, 150cla, 150clb, 151cra, 151crb, 151bl; PADOVA - MUSEI CIVICI AGLI EREMITANI: 152t, 152c; LUCIANO PEDICINI - ARCHIVIO dell'ARTE: 352b, 394t, 459t, 470tl, 474t, 474ca, 474cb, 474b, 475t, 475ca, 475cr, 477t, 514b; APT PESARO - LE MARCHE: 358c; PICTURES COLOUR LIBRARY: 530b, 532l; ANDREA PISTOLESI: 16; PNALM ARCHIVE: in association with www.abruzzonatura.com 490bc; POPPERFOTO: 60tl, 61ca, 61cb.

SARAH QUILL, Venice: 86t, 90b, 96tl.

RETROGRAPH ARCHIVE: 33c; REX FEATURES: 33t; Steve Wood 35tr, 189bl.

SCALA GROUP SPA: 22b, 23b, 24br, 25ca, 25bl, 32tl, 388cla, *Portrait of Claudio Monteverdi,* Domenico

Feti, Accademia, Venice 32bl, *Portolan of Italy* (16th century), Loggia dei Lanzi, Firenze 283bl, Museo Correr, Venice 39b, *Etruscan Bronze Liver*, Museo Civico, Piacenza 40cl, *Earrings*, Museo Etrusco Guarnacci, Volterra 40br, 40cr–41cl, *Crater from Pescia Romana*, Museo Archeologico, Grosseto 41bc, *Terracotta Vase in the Shape of an Elephant*, Museo Nazionale, Naples 42cr, *Cicero denounces Catiline*, Palazzo Madama, Rome 43tl, 43bl, *Circus Scene Mosaic - Gladiator Fight*, Galleria Borghese, Rome 44t, 44br, *Theodolinda Melts the Gold for the New Church* (15th century), Famiglia Zavattari, Duomo, Monza 46clb, 46cr–47cl, 47b, *Tomb Relief depicting a School*, Matteo Gandoni, Museo Civico, Bologna 48b, *Detail from an Ambo of Frederick II* (13th century), Cattedrale, Bitonto 49cb, *Guidoriccio da Fogliano at the Siege of Note Massi*, Simone Martini, Palazzo Pubblico, Siena 50cl, 51tl, *Return of Gregory XI from Avignon* Giorgio Vasari, Sala Regia, Vatican 51cb, 52br, 52cr–53cl, 53crb, *Clement VII in Conversation with Charles V*, Giorgio Vasari, Palazzo Vecchio, Florence 54cla, *Portrait of Pierluigi da Palestrina*, Istituto dei Padri dell'Oratorio, Rome 54br, *Revolt at Masaniello*, Domenico Gargiulo, Museo di San Martino, Naples 55crb, 56br, 57tl, 57crb, 58cla, 58cr–59cl, 59crb, 91c, 96c, 114br, 140c, 214tr, 218b, 252t, 255t, 257t, 261t, 266c, 266b, 267t, 268c, 268b, 269t, 269b, 272, 274tr, 275tr, 275b, 278t, 278c, 278b, 279ca, 279cb, 280t, 280b, 281t, 282c, 283bl, 284t, 284b, 285t, 285b, 286t, 286c, 287t, 288bl, 290t, 290cl, 290cra, 290crb, 290b, 291t, 291cla, 291clb, 291cr, 291bl, 291br, 293bl, 294tr, 294tl, 294c, 295t, 295cl, 295b, 315c, 315b, 320t, 320cla, 320c, 320ca, 320cr–321cl, 320cb, 320b, 321cr, 321cb, 321cra, 321t, 321b, 322t, 322b, 328b, 330t, 331cl, 334cla, 335b, 344t, 344c, 345b, 348b, 349c, 360t, 360b, 361t, 361bl, 367br, 374c, 390bl, 392t, 394c, 401c, 406tl, 406c, 406b, 407t, 408b, 409t, 410t, 410cb, 411c, 413t, 413c, 413b, 417t, 417b, 495c, 497tl, 513b, 514tr, 520t, 521t, 522b, 533b; SCIENCE PHOTO LIBRARY: 11t; Argonne National Laboratory 37cr; JOHN FERRO SIMS: 20b, 21b, 80, 170–171, 355b, 364–365, 444, 526b; AGENZIA SINTESI, ROME: 616tl; MARIO SOSTER DI

ALAGNA: 541c; FRANK SPOONER PICTURES: Diffidenti 532b; Gamma 61cr, 61tc; SPORTING PICTURES: 66crb, 67cb, 67cra; TONY STONE IMAGES: 79cla; Stephen Studd 27tr, 179cr; AGENZIA FOTOGRAFICA STRADELLA, Milan: Bersanetti 185c; Lamberto Caenazzo 530t; Francesco Gavazzini 208c; F Giaccone 510c; Mozzati 360clb; Massimo Pacifico 491t; Ettore Re 483crb; Ghigo Roli 483b; Giulio Vegi 517t; Amedeo Vergani 202, 206b, 226t, 249t; SYGMA: 63tr.

TASTING ITALY: Martin Brigdale 625t; TATE GALLERY PUBLICATIONS: 60bl; APT DELL'ALTA VALLE DEL TEVERE: Museo del Duomo 50tl; TOURING CLUB OF ITALY: 196b, Cresci 518t; ARCHIVIO CITTÀ DI TORINO Settore Turismo: 213t, 213b; Davide Bogliacino 205t; FOTOTECA APT del TRENTINO: Foto di Banal 168t; Foto di Faganello 167t, 169c.

VENICE SIMPLON-ORIENT-EXPRESS: 628tl; VILLA CRESPI: 576b.

CHARLIE WAITE: 17b; EDIZIONE WHITE STAR: Marcello Bertinetti 81b; Giulio Veggi 8–9, 70–71, 133b; FIONA WILD: 524–5; PETER WILSON: 5t, 88–89; WORLD PICTURES: 536–7.

Front Endpaper:
JOE CORNISH: Lcrb, Rc, Rtcr; IL DAGHERROTIPO: Marco Melodia Lbl; Stefano Occhibelli Rtl; Giovanni Rinaldi Rbl; JAMES DARELL: Rcl; ROBERT HARDING PICTURE LIBRARY: Lc, H.P. Merton Rtcl; JOHN FERRO SIMS: Ltr, Rbc; AGENZIA FOTOGRAFICA STRADELLA, Milan: Amadeo Vergani Ltl.

Back Endpaper:
IL DAGHERROTIPO: Stefano Occhibelli cl; ROBERT HARDING PICTURE LIBRARY: Rolf Richardson tl.

JACKET
FRONT – DK PICTURE LIBRARY: cr; John Heseltine cbl; Clive Streeter bc; GETTY IMAGES, Ulf Sjostedt main image. BACK – DK PICTURE LIBRARY: John Heseltine t; KIM SAYER B. Spine – GETTY IMAGES: Ulf Sjostedt.

All other images copyright © DORLING KINDERSLEY. For further information: www.dkimages.com

Phrase Book

In Emergency

Help!	**Aiuto!**	eye-**yoo**-toh
Stop!	**Fermate!**	fair-**mah**-teh
Call a doctor.	**Chiama un medico**	kee-**ah**-mah oon **meh**-dee-koh
Call an ambulance.	**Chiama un' ambulanza**	kee-**ah**-mah oon am-boo-**lan**-tsa
Call the police.	**Chiama la polizia**	kee-**ah**-mah ee pol-ee-**tsee**-ah
Call the fire brigade.	**Chiama i pompieri**	kee-**ah**-mah ee pom-pee-**air**-ee
Where is the telephone?	**Dov'è il telefono?**	dov-**eh** eel teh-**leh**-foh-noh?
The nearest hospital?	**L'ospedale più vicino?**	loss-peh-**dah**-leh pee-**oo** vee-**chee**-noh?

Communication Essentials

Yes/No	**Sì/No**	**see**/ noh
Please	**Per favore**	pair fah-**vor**-eh
Thank you	**Grazie**	**grah**-tsee-eh
Excuse me	**Mi scusi**	mee **skoo**-zee
Hello	**Buon giorno**	bwon **jor**-noh
Goodbye	**Arrivederci**	ah-ree-veh-**dair**-chee
Good evening	**Buona sera**	**bwon**-ah **sair**-ah
morning	**la mattina**	lah mah-**tee**-nah
afternoon	**il pomeriggio**	eel poh-meh-**ree**-joh
evening	**la sera**	lah **sair**-ah
yesterday	**ieri**	ee-**air**-ee
today	**oggi**	**oh**-jee
tomorrow	**domani**	doh-**mah**-nee
here	**qui**	kwee
there	**la**	lah
What?	**Quale?**	**kwah**-leh?
When?	**Quando?**	**kwan**-doh?
Why?	**Perchè?**	pair-**keh**?
Where?	**Dove?**	**doh**-veh?

Useful Phrases

How are you?	**Come sta?**	**koh**-meh stah?
Very well, thank you.	**Molto bene, grazie.**	**moll**-toh **beh**-neh **grah**-tsee-eh
Pleased to meet you.	**Piacere di conoscerla.**	pee-ah-**chair**-eh dee coh-**noh**-shair-lah
See you later.	**A più tardi.**	ah pee-oo **tar**-dee
That's fine.	**Va bene.**	va **beh**-neh
Where is/are ...?	**Dov'è/Dove sono ...?**	dov-**eh**/doveh **soh**noh?
How long does it take to get to ...?	**Quanto tempo ci vuole per andare a ...?**	**kwan**-toh **tem**-poh chee voo-**oh**-leh pair an-**dar**-eh ah ...?
How do I get to ...?	**Come faccio per arrivare a ...?**	koh-meh **fah**-choh pair arri-**var**-eh ah..?
Do you speak English?	**Parla inglese?**	**par**-lah een-**gleh**-zeh?
I don't understand.	**Non capisco.**	non ka-**pee**-skoh
Could you speak more slowly, please?	**Può parlare più lentamente, per favore?**	pwoh par-**lah**-reh pee-**oo** len-ta-**men**-teh pair fah-**vor**-eh?
I'm sorry.	**Mi dispiace.**	mee dee-spee-**ah**-cheh

Useful Words

big	**grande**	**gran**-deh
small	**piccolo**	**pee**-koh-loh
hot	**caldo**	**kal**-doh
cold	**freddo**	**fred**-doh
good	**buono**	**bwoh**-noh
bad	**cattivo**	kat-**tee**-voh
enough	**basta**	**bas**-tah
well	**bene**	**beh**-neh
open	**aperto**	ah-**pair**-toh
closed	**chiuso**	kee-**oo**-zoh
left	**a sinistra**	ah see-**nee**-strah
right	**a destra**	ah **dess**-trah
straight on	**sempre dritto**	**sem**-preh **dree**-toh
near	**vicino**	vee-**chee**-noh
far	**lontano**	lon-**tah**-noh
up	**su**	soo
down	**giù**	joo
early	**presto**	**press**-toh
late	**tardi**	**tar**-dee
entrance	**entrata**	en-**trah**-tah
exit	**uscita**	oo-**shee**-ta
toilet	**il gabinetto**	eel gah-bee-**net**-toh
free, unoccupied	**libero**	**lee**-bair-oh
free, no charge	**gratuito**	grah-**too**-ee-toh

Making a Telephone Call

I'd like to place a long-distance call.	**Vorrei fare una interurbana.**	vor-**ray far**-eh oona in-tair-oor-**bah**-nah
I'd like to make a reverse-charge call.	**Vorrei fare una telefonata a carico del destinatario.**	vor-**ray far**-eh oona teh-leh-fon-**ah**-tah ah **kar**-ee-koh dell dess-tee-nah-**tar**-ree-oh
I'll try again later.	**Ritelefono più tardi.**	ree-teh-**leh**-foh-noh pee-oo **tar**-dee
Can I leave a message?	**Posso lasciare un messaggio?**	**poss**-oh lash-**ah**-reh oon mess-**sah**-joh?
Hold on.	**Un attimo, per favore**	oon **ah**-tee-moh, pair fah-**vor**-eh
Could you speak up a little please?	**Può parlare più forte, per favore?**	pwoh par-**lah**-reh pee-**oo for**-teh, pair fah-**vor**-eh?
local call	**telefonata locale**	te-leh-fon-**ah**-tah loh-cah-leh

Shopping

How much does this cost?	**Quant'è, per favore?**	kwan-**teh** pair fah-**vor**-eh?
I would like ...	**Vorrei ...**	vor-**ray**
Do you have ...?	**Avete ...?**	ah-**veh**-teh.. ?
I'm just looking.	**Sto soltanto guardando.**	stoh sol-**tan**-toh gwar-**dan**-doh
Do you take credit cards?	**Accettate carte di credito?**	ah-chet-**tah**-teh **kar**-teh dee **creh**-dee-toh?
What time do you open/close?	**A che ora apre/ chiude?**	ah keh or-ah **ah**-preh/kee-**oo**-deh?
this one	**questo**	**kweh**-stoh
that one	**quello**	**kwell**-oh
expensive	**caro**	**kar**-oh
cheap	**a buon prezzo**	ah bwon **pret**-soh
size, clothes	**la taglia**	lah **tah**-lee-ah
size, shoes	**il numero**	eel **noo**-mair-oh
white	**bianco**	bee-**ang**-koh
black	**nero**	**neh**-roh
red	**rosso**	**ross**-oh
yellow	**giallo**	**jal**-loh
green	**verde**	**vair**-deh
blue	**blu**	bloo

Types of Shop

antique dealer	**l'antiquario**	lan-tee-**kwah**-ree-oh
bakery	**il forno /il panificio**	eel **for**-no /eel pan-ee-**fee**-choh
bank	**la banca**	lah **bang**-kah
bookshop	**la libreria**	lah lee-breh-**ree**-ah
butcher	**la macelleria**	lah mah-chell-eh-**ree**-ah
cake shop	**la pasticceria**	lah pas-tee-chair-**ee**-ah
chemist	**la farmacia**	lah far-mah-**chee**-ah
delicatessen	**la salumeria**	lah sah-loo-meh-**ree**-ah
department store	**il grande magazzino**	eel **gran**-deh mag-gad-**zee**-noh
fishmonger	**il pescivendolo**	eel pesh-ee-**ven**-doh-loh
florist	**il fioraio**	eel fee-or-**eye**-oh
greengrocer	**il fruttivendolo**	eel froo-tee-**ven**-doh-loh
grocery	**alimentari**	ah-lee-men-**tah**-ree
hairdresser	**il parrucchiere**	eel par-oo-kee-**air**-eh
ice cream parlour	**la gelateria**	lah jel-lah-tair-**ree**-ah
market	**il mercato**	eel mair-**kah**-toh
newsstand	**l'edicola**	leh-**dee**-koh-lah
post office	**l'ufficio postale**	loo-**fee**-choh pos-**tah**-leh
shoe shop	**il negozio di scarpe**	eel neh-**goh**-tsioh dee **skar**-peh
supermarket	**il supermercato**	eel su-pair-mair-**kah**-toh
tobacconist	**il tabaccaio**	eel tah-bak-**eye**-oh
travel agency	**l'agenzia di viaggi**	lah-jen-**tsee**-ah dee vee-**ad**-jee

Sightseeing

art gallery	**la pinacoteca**	lah peena-koh-**teh**-kah
bus stop	**la fermata dell'autobus**	lah fair-**mah**-tah dell **ow**-toh-booss
church	**la chiesa**	lah kee-**eh**-zah
	la basilica	lah bah-**seel**-i-kah
closed for holidays	**chiuso per le ferie**	kee-**oo**-zoh pair leh **fair**-ee-eh
garden	**il giardino**	eel jar-**dee**-no
library	**la biblioteca**	lah beeb-lee-oh-**teh**-kah
museum	**il museo**	eel moo-**zeh**-oh
railway station	**la stazione**	lah stah-tsee-**oh**-neh
tourist information	**l'ufficio di turismo**	loo-**fee**-choh dee too-**ree**-smoh

STAYING IN A HOTEL

Do you have any vacant rooms?	**Avete camere libere?**	ah-**veh**-teh **kah**-mair-eh **lee**-bair-eh?
double room	**una camera doppia**	oona **kah**-mair-ah **doh**-pee-ah
with double bed	**con letto matrimoniale**	kon **let**-toh mah-tree-moh-nee-**ah**-leh
twin room	**una camera con due letti**	oona **kah**-mair-ah kon **doo**-eh **let**-tee
single room	**una camera singola**	oona **kah**-mair-ah **sing**-goh-lah
room with a bath, shower	**una camera con bagno, con doccia**	oona **kah**-mair-ah kon **ban**-yoh, kon **dot**-chah
porter	**il facchino**	eel fah-**kee**-noh
key	**la chiave**	lah kee-**ah**-veh
I have a reservation.	**Ho fatto una prenotazione.**	oh **fat**-toh oona preh-noh-tah-tsee-**oh**-neh

EATING OUT

Have you got a table for ...?	**Avete una tavola per ... ?**	ah-**veh**-teh oona **tah**-voh-lah pair ...?
I'd like to reserve a table.	**Vorrei riservare una tavola.**	vor-**ray** ree-sair-**vah**-reh oona **tah**-voh-lah
breakfast	**colazione**	koh-lah-tsee-**oh**-neh
lunch	**pranzo**	**pran**-tsoh
dinner	**cena**	**cheh**-nah
The bill, please.	**Il conto, per favore.**	eel **kon**-toh pair fah-**vor**-eh
I am a vegetarian.	**Sono vegetariano/a.**	**soh**-noh **veh**-jeh-tar-ee-**ah**-noh/nah
waitress	**cameriera**	kah-mair-ee-**air**-ah
waiter	**cameriere**	kah-mair-ee-**air**-eh
fixed price menu	**il menù a prezzo fisso**	eel meh-**noo** ah **pret**-soh **fee**-soh
dish of the day	**piatto del giorno**	pee-**ah**-toh dell **jor**-no
starter	**antipasto**	an-tee-**pass**-toh
first course	**il primo**	eel **pree**-moh
main course	**il secondo**	eel seh-**kon**-doh
vegetables	**il contorno**	eel kon-**tor**-noh
dessert	**il dolce**	eel **doll**-cheh
cover charge	**il coperto**	eel koh-**pair**-toh
wine list	**la lista dei vini**	lah **lee**-stah day **vee**-nee
rare	**al sangue**	al **sang**-gweh
medium	**al puntino**	al poon-**tee**-noh
well done	**ben cotto**	ben **kot**-toh
glass	**il bicchiere**	eel bee-kee-**air**-eh
bottle	**la bottiglia**	lah bot-**teel**-yah
knife	**il coltello**	eel kol-**tell**-oh
fork	**la forchetta**	lah for-**ket**-tah
spoon	**il cucchiaio**	eel koo-kee-**eye**-oh

MENU DECODER

l'acqua minerale gassata/naturale	**lah**-kwah mee-nair-**ah**-leh gah-**zah**-tah/ nah-too-rah-leh	mineral water fizzy/still
agnello	ah-**niell**-oh	lamb
aceto	ah-**cheh**-toh	vinegar
aglio	**al**-ee-oh	garlic
al forno	al **for**-noh	baked
alla griglia	ah-lah **greel**-yah	grilled
l'aragosta	lah-rah-**goss**-tah	lobster
arrosto	ar-**ross**-toh	roast
la birra	lah **beer**-rah	beer
la bistecca	lah bee-**stek**-kah	steak
il brodo	eel **broh**-doh	broth
il burro	eel **boor**-oh	butter
il caffè	eel kah-**feh**	coffee
i calamari	ee kah-lah-**mah**-ree	squid
i carciofi	ee kar-**choff**-ee	artichokes
la carne	la **kar**-neh	meat
carne di maiale	**kar**-neh dee mah-**yah**-leh	pork
la cipolla	la chip-**oh**-lah	onion
i contorni	ee kon-**tor**-nee	vegetables
i fagioli	ee fah-**joh**-lee	beans
il fegato	eel **fay**-gah-toh	liver
il finocchio	eel fee-**nok**-ee-oh	fennel
il formaggio	eel for-**mad**-joh	cheese
le fragole	leh **frah**-goh-leh	strawberries
il fritto misto	eel free-toh **mees**-toh	mixed fried dish
la frutta	la **froot**-tah	fruit
frutti di mare	froo-tee dee mah-**reh**	seafood
i funghi	ee **foon**-ghee	mushrooms
i gamberi	ee **gam**-bair-ee	prawns
il gelato	eel jel-**lah**-toh	ice cream
l'insalata	leen-sah-lah-tah	salad

il latte	eel **laht**-teh	milk
lesso	**less**-oh	boiled
il manzo	eel **man**-tsoh	beef
la melanzana	lah meh-lan-**tsah**-nah	aubergine
la minestra	lah mee-**ness**-trah	soup
l'olio	loh-lee-oh	oil
il pane	eel **pah**-neh	bread
le patate	leh pah-**tah**-teh	potatoes
le patatine fritte	leh pah-tah-**teen**-eh **free**-teh	chips
il pepe	eel **peh**-peh	pepper
la pesca	lah **pess**-kah	peach
il pesce	eel **pesh**-eh	fish
il pollo	eel **poll**-oh	chicken
il pomodoro	eel poh-moh-**dor**-oh	tomato
il prosciutto cotto/crudo	eel pro-**shoo**-toh **kot**-toh/**kroo**-doh	ham cooked/cured
il riso	eel **ree**-zoh	rice
il sale	eel **sah**-leh	salt
la salsiccia	lah sal-**see**-chah	sausage
le seppie	leh **sep**-pee-eh	cuttlefish
secco	**sek**-koh	dry
la sogliola	lah **soll**-yoh-lah	sole
i spinaci	ee spee-**nah**-chee	spinach
succo d'arancia/ di limone	**soo**-koh dah-**ran**-chah/ dee lee-**moh**-neh	orange /lemon juice
il tè	eel **teh**	tea
la tisana	lah tee-**zah**-nah	herbal tea
il tonno	eel **ton**-noh	tuna
la torta	lah **tor**-tah	cake/tart
l'uovo	loo-**oh**-voh	egg
vino bianco	**vee**-noh bee-**ang**-koh	white wine
vino rosso	**vee**-noh **ross**-oh	red wine
il vitello	eel vee-**tell**-oh	veal
le vongole	leh **von**-goh-leh	clams
lo zucchero	loh **zoo**-kair-oh	sugar
gli zucchini	lyee dzu-**kee**-nee	courgettes
la zuppa	lah **tsoo**-pah	soup

NUMBERS

1	**uno**	**oo**-noh
2	**due**	**doo**-eh
3	**tre**	treh
4	**quattro**	**kwat**-roh
5	**cinque**	**ching**-kweh
6	**sei**	**say**-ee
7	**sette**	**set**-teh
8	**otto**	**ot**-toh
9	**nove**	**noh**-veh
10	**dieci**	dee-**eh**-chee
11	**undici**	**oon**-dee-chee
12	**dodici**	**doh**-dee-chee
13	**tredici**	**tray**-dee-chee
14	**quattordici**	kwat-**tor**-dee-chee
15	**quindici**	**kwin**-dee-chee
16	**sedici**	**say**-dee-chee
17	**diciassette**	dee-chah-**set**-teh
18	**diciotto**	dee-**chot**-toh
19	**diciannove**	dee-chah-**noh**-veh
20	**venti**	**ven**-tee
30	**trenta**	**tren**-tah
40	**quaranta**	kwah-**ran**-tah
50	**cinquanta**	ching-**kwan**-tah
60	**sessanta**	sess-**an**-tah
70	**settanta**	set-**tan**-tah
80	**ottanta**	ot-**tan**-tah
90	**novanta**	noh-**van**-tah
100	**cento**	**chen**-toh
1,000	**mille**	**mee**-leh
2,000	**duemila**	**doo**-eh **mee**-lah
5,000	**cinquemila**	**ching**-kweh **mee**-lah
1,000,000	**un milione**	oon meel-**yoh**-neh

TIME

one minute	**un minuto**	oon mee-**noo**-toh
one hour	**un'ora**	oon **or**-ah
half an hour	**mezz'ora**	medz-**or**-ah
a day	**un giorno**	oon **jor**-noh
a week	**una settimana**	oona set-tee-**mah**-nah
Monday	**lunedì**	loo-neh-**dee**
Tuesday	**martedì**	mar-teh-**dee**
Wednesday	**mercoledì**	mair-koh-leh-**dee**
Thursday	**giovedì**	joh-veh-**dee**
Friday	**venerdì**	ven-air-**dee**
Saturday	**sabato**	**sah**-bah-toh
Sunday	**domenica**	doh-**meh**-nee-kah